ROUTLEDGE LIBRARY EDITIONS:
POLITICAL PROTEST

Volume 14

THE MINERS' STRIKE, 1984–5

THE MINERS' STRIKE, 1984–5

Loss Without Limit

MARTIN ADENEY AND JOHN LLOYD

Routledge
Taylor & Francis Group
LONDON AND NEW YORK

First published in 1986 by Routledge & Kegan Paul Ltd

This edition first published in 2022
by Routledge
2 Park Square, Milton Park, Abingdon, Oxon OX14 4RN

and by Routledge
605 Third Avenue, New York, NY 10158

Routledge is an imprint of the Taylor & Francis Group, an informa business

British Library Cataloguing in Publication Data
A catalogue record for this book is available from the British Library

ISBN: 978-1-03-203038-8 (Set)
ISBN: 978-1-00-319086-8 (Set) (ebk)
ISBN: 978-1-03-201482-1 (Volume 14) (hbk)
ISBN: 978-1-03-201488-3 (Volume 14) (pbk)
ISBN: 978-1-00-317883-5 (Volume 14) (ebk)

DOI: 10.4324/9781003178835

Publisher's Note
The publisher has gone to great lengths to ensure the quality of this reprint but points out that some imperfections in the original copies may be apparent.

Disclaimer
The publisher has made every effort to trace copyright holders and would welcome correspondence from those they have been unable to trace.

THE MINERS' STRIKE 1984–5
LOSS WITHOUT LIMIT

Martin Adeney and John Lloyd

Routledge & Kegan Paul
London

For Ann and Marcia

First published in 1986 by
Routledge & Kegan Paul Ltd
11 New Fetter Lane, London EC4P 4EE

Reprinted 1987

First published as a paperback 1988

Set in Plantin
by Columns of Reading
and printed in Great Britain
by Cox & Wyman Ltd
Reading, Berks

British Library Cataloguing in Publication Data
Adeney, Martin
The miners' strike 1984–5: loss without limit
1. Coal Strike, Great Britain, 1984–5
I. Title II. Lloyd, John
331.89'2822334'0941 HD5365.M6152 1984
ISBN 0–7102–0694–1
ISBN 0–7102–1371–9 (pbk)

Contents

Illustrations

Preface

The sub-title of this book comes from a reply made by Arthur Scargill to the House of Commons Select Committee on Energy in November 1982. Pressed for his view on uneconomic pits, he said, 'As far as I am concerned, the loss is without limit because I am more interested in the investment which our men have put into this industry.'

Loss without limit; it is almost a text for the strike. The government's blank cheque to the electricity generating boards; the huge bills for the policing; the damage to the fabric of society from the scenes witnessed during the dispute; the cost to the pits; the limitless antipathy that developed between working and striking miners; above all the bitter financial and personal suffering of miners and their families.

In this book we have attempted to talk to as many people with first-hand involvement in the events as we could. Unless otherwise stated, quotations are from our interviews with them.

Our thanks are due to many people who helped us, in the NUM and the wider trade union movement, at the Coal Board and in industry, among lawyers and police, and in Whitehall and the House of Commons. They are too numerous to mention, and a number, on both sides of the argument, were anxious that their names should not be used. We owe a considerable debt to our colleagues at the BBC and the *Financial Times* – especially, at the BBC, John Fryer, and at the *FT* Geoffrey Owen, Philip Bassett and the *FT* labour staff. Our gratitude goes too to the *Sheffield Star* for the use of the files of day-to-day events in South Yorkshire.

Almost everyone we asked agreed to talk to us. There were two glaring exceptions and they were the most obvious. Arthur Scargill and Ian MacGregor are for once united in insisting on putting out their own authorised versions only.

1
The choice

The job of this book is not to give a chronological account of the mineworkers' strike of March 1984 to March 1985: others have done that.[1] It is rather to understand it.

The strike, constantly dramatic in itself, appeared to fade quickly from view as the waters of British civil society gratefully closed over it. The government sank in the polls – from a September 1984 figure of 42 per cent to a February 1986 figure of 34 per cent: rather the kind of figure which might be expected of a government midway through a second term. The tremors still were felt along the fibres of the TUC and the Labour Party: Arthur Scargill, the most compelling activist-orator of his generation, could still turn in the votes at the TUC and the Labour Party Conference in 1985 for a motion committing the Labour Party to reimburse the union for its fines and reinstate sacked miners, which most of the TUC elders regarded as undesirable. But the greater issues were the unions' attitudes to present employment law, and the shape of employment law to come, and the familiar old chestnut of incomes policy. The daily and nightly news ceased to have one constant focus, and reflected a new round of arms talks between the old US president and a new Soviet leader, the violent dying agonies of apartheid, inner city riots and inner-cabinet feuds. The miners no longer intruded into everyday life through the screen or the printed page, which was how the vast majority of citizens of this and other countries experienced them.

The strike did not produce a clear effect, as the Falklands War produced a clear electoral victory over a Labour Party in shambles. Arthur Scargill was not toppled by a union howling for the blood of the man who had led them to defeat. Peter Walker stayed at the Energy Department through cabinet changes, Ian MacGregor (knighted in June 1986 towards the end of his chairmanship of the National Coal Board) carried on his crablike advance to reconstruction as though merely retreading ground from which a mighty wave had swept him back. It had not grazed society's skin: it had cut deeply instead. It was a measure for almost every element in British public life, and for millions of private citizens. It remains so in its aftermath.

The government was well prepared, in three senses. First, it had had to decline combat with the mineworkers in February 1981, when the NCB's pit closure plan, necessitated by pressure from the government to cut losses, was withdrawn and instead money was pumped into the industry to mask its underlying cash crisis. Arthur Scargill, then a year away from the national presidency which had been his ambition for a decade or more, knew it for what it was: 'the government sidestepped the issue because they realised they could not win,' he commented a few weeks after the event. 'It's got to be recognised that the government merely avoided an actual confrontation.'[2]

It learned from that. After Nigel Lawson replaced David Howell, the sacrificial lamb, at Energy in September of that year, the stocks at the power stations were rapidly and deliberately built up, the contingency planning sharpened, a new and very 'dry' chairman appointed to head the Central Electricity Generating Board with the explicit brief of preparing for the eventuality of a strike (Sir Walter Marshall now Lord Marshall, one of the clutch of 'strike honours'). The government did not lay a deep and complex plot to stimulate a miners' strike in the early spring of 1985 with complete foreknowledge that the National Union of Mineworkers would split, the trade union movement would prove largely impotent in providing support, and the weather would turn out remarkably fine: rather it read Arthur Scargill as a man who meant what he said about the necessity of industrial action both to halt pit closures and to destabilise government, and the NUM as a union capable of and willing to follow such a remarkably strong and clear lead.

Second, and perhaps as important, was a sea-change in government will and philosophy since Edward Heath 'lost' to the mineworkers in 1974. 'By 1972 Heath reckoned he had given the policies a chance, and they did not work . . . when in 1981 and 1982 Margaret Thatcher seemed to face a similar difficulty . . . she held on.'[3]

Holding on, a dominant virtue of the Thatcher governments, meant in political terms conceding very little indeed to the objections of those with whom the government found itself in conflict – as Heath did most vividly in his 'U turn' period, when he rapidly constructed a centralised, social democratic polity which the unions rejected on purely party political grounds. Thatcher accepted sharp division and rode out the consequences because the ideological and philosophical debate which had effected a change in the upper echelons of the Tory Party over the 1974–84 decade prepared her and her colleagues to do so.

The touchstone of their position is *freedom*, defined in this context as freedom of the individual to develop his or her capacities as far as possible under the law. The objections of the left, that such freedom may be a necessary but is certainly an insufficient condition for an advanced democracy in which government policy deliberately widened the distribution of wealth, was hardly heeded. Instead, such arguments were conjured away by concentration on opponents' weaknesses – ambiguity over violence, say, or over the seriousness of the challenge to the state. In sum, it was an ideological weapon forged for conflict, best when tested, most effective when its blade caught the reflection of foes' confusion, equivocation and internal struggles. In that sense, the miners' strike, though not sought, provided a field in which the Thatcher government could deploy its best divisions.

Third, it had 'restored management's right to manage'. Most managers, while increasingly critical of the restrictive economic stance and particularly of the persistently high rates of interest, still conceded to government a large part of the creation of a climate in which being the boss counted for something. It was an explicit point at issue during the strike: the fact that it was won, in the end, strengthened the concept and the practice, especially in the state sector, or in those corporations recently in the state sector. Within six months of the ending of the miners' strike, management in the railways – that other great state monolith – faced down a strike threat by 11,000 guards over the introduction of driver-only-operated trains, and saw the men affected vote against strike action, albeit by a slim margin.

Even before the strike, the common experience of union officials was that their efforts to encourage militancy – leaving aside such protected areas as Labour-controlled town halls, Fleet Street printing rooms or ITV studios – very largely failed. After all, the trade union movement's adumbration of the strategy of 'new realism' (to the disgust of the NUM president) was an all but explicit admission that the old levers were not responding to the old pulls where it mattered – at the base. Though there is some evidence for the general proposition that British management and unions tacitly colluded to take the 'easy' way out of the recession – that is, to declare, and acquiesce in, large-scale redundancies rather than attempt to keep more people in work at lower wages – the result of these big lay-off programmes was to instil a respect among many workers for the fact of retaining a job.

The National Coal Board emerged from the far end of the strike in apparently terrible shape. It had no piece of paper which allowed it to close uneconomic pits by agreement, ostensibly its goal throughout the dispute. Its pits were often in ruins, its workforce surly and internally at war, its markets eaten by imports of coal, its management at top level at each other's throats, its chairman and its political master openly feuding. By October 1985, 11 months before MacGregor was due to retire, Walker appointed Sir Robert Haslam, chairman of the British Steel Corporation, to replace him, effectively reducing his last year to the status of caretaking for the advent of a man for whom the NCB chairman had no great regard. Sales did pick up, and productivity, spurred by the need of striking miners to earn high bonuses to get out of debt, reached unheard-of levels – over 3 tonnes per manshift by the end of 1985, up from a pre-strike average of around 2.4 tms: but NCB executives knew well enough that much of the extra sales were restocking power plants, a one-off boost which appeared unsustainable. By the spring of 1985, with oil prices tumbling, the NCB faced yet another challenge: a new era of relatively cheap oil, which reduced its productivity improvements greatly in importance. *The Economist* (3 May 1986) said that without the productivity rise – of 24 per cent between 1983/84 and the last quarters of 1985/86 – 'the fall in the world oil price would have been an appalling disaster for the industry. As it is, it is merely a disaster.'

But the core issue – the board's right to manage – had been settled, unequivocally in its favour. MacGregor had succeeded in one thing above all others: in burying forever the Morrisonian-socialist ideology which permeated the board, and which encouraged a progressive advance of the unions, especially the NUM, into a position of joint authority over the industry. The greatest of the state monoliths, and the one over which more passion and emotion was spent in bringing it into public ownership than any other, the board retained the marks of its origins most of all in the place accorded to the unions in management's scheme of things. A tacit bargain underlay it: unions were brought progressively deeper into the board's procedures on condition they retained an attachment to the over-all aims of the industry. But in practice that gave officials at every level substantial power of veto and in the 1970s and early 1980s increasingly – so management thought – constrained executive freedom to manoeuvre. MacGregor cleaved through all that. He did not like unions, but he recognised a place for them: it was firmly below that of management, and that is where they now, unmistakably, are.

The NUM is unlikely to recover – not because of the fissures which have opened up all through it during and since the strike; not because it lost so badly; not because of its leadership – though all of these were and are issues with which it, and the labour movement more widely, has had to deal. It is unlikely to recover because it has forfeited national trust in its ability to deliver coal regularly. For all the sentiment and reverence (mawkish, much of it) which surrounds the miners' place in society, at bottom there is the expectation that coal miners dig coal, which produces power. A union which is so constituted and so led as to put that equation in constant doubt except where matters are arranged in its terms cannot hope again to command pride of place in the labour movement. By being treated as a special case under the Heath government of 1970–74, the miners had struck a tacit bargain with the remainder of society: they got a better deal than most men who depend on muscle and nerve, *but they got it for producing*. Arthur Scargill's huge ambition was to extend, infinitely it seemed, that bargain – to ensure that miners were *so* well rewarded, *so* secure in their jobs, in *such* a well planned collectivist-utopian society – that it could never be concluded. There was at times an almost fearful symmetry between the two sides during the strike, and between the two main characters, Scargill and MacGregor. But for MacGregor, for much of the strike at least, a settlement *was* there: for Scargill (not the NUM, for *Scargill*) it would have meant a shameful bargain, a settling for a finite quantity when the demands were really infinite.

The scale of the ambitions of both sides dictated a conflict fought on a large field: it was the police and the law which attempted to hem it in to 'decent' proportions, aided by such forces of law and order as the bishops, the TUC, the media, the political parties – all or most of whom attempted to make it what it was only in part, a conventional industrial dispute. The police were deployed in larger numbers than had ever before been seen, deployed with growing efficiency by the National Reporting Centre in London, camped for weeks on end in Nottinghamshire, Derbyshire and Yorkshire. The riot control techniques which had been in ever more frequent use during riots in inner cities, football grounds and in such industrial conflicts as the 1980 steel strike were employed with skill against pickets who were, though numerous, never properly organised as a fighting force: the contest was unequal. By the later part of 1984, as the struggles on the picket lines during the surges back to work became increasingly bitter, both sides were brutalised: the police banged truncheons on riot shields as if auditioning for *Zulu*; the pickets strewed the roads with bunches of nails welded together to lame the police horses which charged them. Worse: as 'scabs' were identified, some were brutally beaten, their families terrorised; as police gave chase discipline sometimes gave way to brutality.

When Mrs Shirley Williams, addressing the Social Democrats' conference in Torquay early in September 1985, heard of the Handsworth riots, she instinctively blamed the miners' pickets for providing a model for the rioters. The similarity was certainly seductive: in both cases, groups who had come to believe themselves under attack rounded on their most obvious attackers, the police. It could be pressed further: though the urban riots of 1981 and 1985, the football-ground gladiatorials of 1983, 84 and 85, the pitched industrial battles outside steel plants, the *Stockport Messenger*, and most famously outside pits were all discrete, individual, and united most obviously by looking much the same under the lurid glare of the TV lights – still the questions which attended on them all were: would these young men be doing this if the society were more secure for young workers? Had the breaking of the assumption that schooling gave way to working lifted inhibitions, not just from the unemployed – perhaps not mainly the unemployed – but from a whole layer of youth?

It was traditional common, not new employment law, which was used against the NUM and which in the end choked much of the life out of it: and it was its own members, not the state, who were the most active agents. The Coal Board, and the other state industries, were positively forbidden to use the Employment Acts when they wished to: government, having advertised them as mild, balanced, 'step-by-step' affairs, found when the largest test for them came that they would be too inflammatory to be unleashed. The miners who took their own union to court were far from the first union members to do so, but in doing it so publicly, and over such an issue (as it was represented) as internal union democracy, they stood as examplars for millions of workers elsewhere who could as easily resent the union as depend on it, and who took to the government's balloting provisions the more gladly for the sober example afforded them by the ballotless mineworkers.

It was the internal struggles, the working out on the streets and the courts of divisions within the miners themselves, which so confounded the labour movement. Unity was always its favourite word. Neil Kinnock had acceded to the Labour Party leadership quoting Bevan's fading dictum that the movement had a passionate attachment to unity. It was no rhetorical claim: rare among West European union centres, the TUC enfolded all unions which claimed independence from the employers within itself. But this was the division of its vanguard: the public unravelling of a carefully sewn together federation of mineworkers, brought together under a single employer, cossetted and flattered by the labour movement to believe in their own unique fraternity. Kinnock had no choice but to distance himself from it if he and his party were to remain as serious contenders for power. The TUC was less fortunate, more committed, and more deeply wounded. In the months that followed the miners' strike, the unions were embroiled in enervating internal arguments over the authority of the TUC, the future political posture of unions and the nature of democracy – all exposed by the relentless grinding of the miners' strike.

More fundamentally still, the conduct of the miners' strike, and the aims of the union's leadership, posed once more the choice which British labourism hated to make: the choice between revolutionary and revisionist socialism. The first had been put on the agenda, albeit in a confused and contradictory way, by the attempt to create a new model Labour Party under the guidance of Tony Benn in the late 1970s and early 1980s. The mineworkers for the first time provided the troops. Here was the opportunity, if not to overthrow the state, then to destabilise it, to prepare the ground for an overthrow later, once the working class had recovered confidence in its own power after the debilitating years of Thatcher. It was couched in those terms: no one who wished to take the message could mistake it. The British labour movement shuffled with embarrassment; tried to rehabilitate the strike into the ambit of a comprehensible dispute with objectives, tactics and a way out; failed; but at the end knew, for the most part, that it could no longer dabble in being revolutionary. Arthur Scargill, right about many things, was right that the strike would politicise the working class. It forced them to see revolutionary politics in embryo at least, and confirmed their attachment to reformism. It offered them the possibility of joining a machine being forged to overthrow a reactionary government, and pushed them to express the view, in polls and by-elections, that the government should be supported because it was for order, if nothing else. Kinnock hardly needed to be taught the lesson – he had had his turning away from the true faith marked by a shower of silver coins to mark his Judas-status when he voted against Benn for deputy-leader at the 1981 Labour conference – but it rubbed home what he knew. Labour's left claimed the miners' strike as a victory in forging new bonds between city activists and the miners. The split and warring Communist Party saw it for what it was: vanguardism.

As for the miners' themselves? They had fought to preserve jobs – or some of them had – and did no such thing. By mid-1986 some 40,000 miners had left the industry, many grateful for the redundancy money and a chance to get out of a web of bitterness and demoralisation. Many said they would do it all again and many had clearly enjoyed the experience: they had lived at a pitch, physically, intellectually, morally even, which they could not expect to again, and which most who have not undergone war would never emulate. The work stayed much the same: hard, noisy, risky. They had not been able to change the rules.

2
The coal question

'Coal is our prime national asset and it is a wasting asset. It is in the interests of the state that it should be won and used to the best advantage.' So said the Sankey Commission which enquired into the problems of the mining industry at the end of the First World War. The words could serve as a text for any of the controversies and bitter industrial and political confrontations which have swirled around the coal industry in the last hundred years, its basic questions – how coal should be used and to whose advantage – still a matter of fierce and unresolved debate.

Ever since the end of the seventeenth century when coal began to replace the disappearing forests as a prime source of household fuel and then to power the emerging industrial revolution, its seams have run thick and deep under the commerce of industrial, political and cultural life in Britain.

In 1830 as the railway age dawned, 23 million tons were mined in Britain. Twenty years later that had doubled. By 1870 it was past the hundred million tons, and in the peak year of 1913 no less than 287 million tons were produced by a workforce of over a million miners. Almost one in ten of every working men was a miner. Seventy three million tons, not far short of today's annual deep-mined total, was shipped for export in fleets of colliers.

But the story of British coal in the twentieth century is one of rapidly alternating feast and famine. The pre-First World War peak was never regained, and the post-war years saw a drop in demand with proposals for longer hours and smaller wages answered by strikes and lock-outs and labour unrest culminating in the biggest trauma in labour history this century, the 1926 General Strike.

After the Second World War the switchback progress continued. Unable at first to produce enough coal to meet the demand, with Polish workers drafted in to try and dig the coal whose absence had caused power cuts and shut-downs in the bleak winter of 1947, production peaked in 1955 at 225 million tonnes. But then as other forms of energy, particularly cheap oil, made their presence felt and major customers like the railways switched away, the decline was precipitate.

In fifteen years, coal production was almost halved, and the number of miners cut by even more, from 700,000 to less than 300,000. Forecasts of further decline looked unshakable. But by the mid-1970s the roller-coaster was off again. The OPEC oil price had quadrupled, and the coal industry was once more recruiting extra men as it tried, and failed, to meet new urgent production targets. Then, just when the production increases started to come through after new investment in the late 1970s, they coincided with the biggest post-war decline in industrial activity in Britain and the western world. Mountains of unsold coal piled up again, fuelling the demands for fresh pit closures.

By now tonnages were measured in metric tonnes as improved transport meant that British coal was increasingly competing with coal brought from almost anywhere on the globe. Enormous new coal finds had been made in Britain, in places like the east of Yorkshire, Oxfordshire and the Midlands where there were few, if any, mines, and huge new measures were found stretching out under the North Sea. Sixty per cent of coal reserves were to be found in only five countries, the United States (25 per cent), the USSR (16½ per cent), China (14.9 per cent), Britain (7 per cent) and Australia (5 per cent). But it was not a perfect market; in the whole of Western Europe there were only about forty major customers, and a premium was being paid for coal which was judged not liable to interruption of supply.

It was difficult to find an industry where the economic predictions had been so frequently and disastrously wrong; a sharp lesson for those who believed that either the successive post-war Plans for Coal could be written in stone, or that the economic sums of today would necessarily apply tomorrow.

As throughout the century owners and politicians and later a nationalised board grappled with the cruellest and most basic market conditions, so the consequences were borne by men and women employed in what was recognised as one of the cruellest occupations, although one whose strange hellish romance did not go unnoticed. So George Orwell wrote in 1937 in his essay 'Down the Mine':

> All of us really owe the comparative decency of our lives to poor drudges underground, blackened to the eyes with their throats full of coal dust, driving their shovels forward with arms and belly muscles of steel.

By the 1980s conditions had markedly improved with mechanisation, miners now supplied with helmets and working overalls and boots by the

Coal Board, and with subsidised transport and coal available. But it was still possible to find a few pits where coal tubs were filled with picks and shovels and plenty of seams where men had to work at heights of less than three feet and often in water and intense heat too. By the most brutal measure, 30 miners were killed at work in 1983, the year before the strike, and that was an improvement.

Annual accident-at-work figures showed mining and quarrying to be by far the most dangerous occupations employing large numbers. Its record in 1983 of 330 serious accidents per 100,000 employed was worse than ill-regulated construction (200), itself five times worse than manufacturing, and only exceeded by deep-sea fishing (333), where few worked. In the same year there were 824 serious accidents to NCB miners, and over 18,000 cases (roughly 1 in 10) where men were off work for more than three days for injuries caused by their work.

The solidarity and community generated in response to the hardships in mining areas was a national by-word and eagerly tapped by a string of romantic novelists. A recurrent theme was the progress of miner or miner's son away from the pit, often via a hard-won education, to better things. Indeed it was one of the paradoxes of the 1984 miners' strike that it should be to retain as many jobs as possible down the pit particularly for miners' children, while a generation of miners had declared that their dearest wish was that their children should not have to follow them underground.

By the 1980s the communities were changing, although some of them were still among the few single-industry villages remaining in the country. From the stone Victorian terraces of the narrow Welsh valleys to the lines of municipal semi-detached housing marching over the built-up ridges of South Yorkshire, there was more money about. Some Welsh villages had been left high and dry on their hillsides, their mining pensioners with little to do but hire video-cassettes from the local post-offices, while there had been such a huge migration from the north-east (reduced in 25 years from 201 to 20 pits) that many of the union leaders in the Midlands spoke with north-east accents.

But elsewhere a decade close to the top of the manual earnings league after the strike of the 1970s and the new bonus schemes were showing results. Town centre developers were keen on investing in mining areas, as in the 1980s they seemed one of the few places where there was certain to be money to spend. At the same time workers moving out of the industries like engineering, desperately hit by the decline of British industry after 1979, looked for mining jobs as secure and relatively well-paid employment, so diluting some of the traditional mining strongholds. Brass bands and miners' choirs continued, but most of the old miners' welfare libraries where Welsh and other miners' leaders had studied to better themselves were gone, sold off to provide funds for the new welfare halls, effectively large drinking clubs with games rooms, stages for shows, and often sports facilities. As the Coal Board pursued a policy in the 1970s of selling off its tied housing at cheap rates, miners benefitted and took out mortgages and improvement grants. Many, including miners leaders, adduced this as a reason why the NUM consistently rejected industrial action over a series of ballots in the 1980s, although the sums involved in the loans were often relatively small.

The miners' image had changed too. From the rather guiltily forgotten underground workman, his strike victories in the early 1970s brought him a new recognition as a force to be reckoned with in the industrial and political life of the country and altered the public view, particularly among Labour activists. Asked on the eve of his retirement what he thought he had achieved for the miner, NUM president Joe Gormley replied that when he had begun, nobody had wanted to know them. Now, he said, 'Everyone wants to be related to a miner.'

The union too, the most obvious manifestation of the solidarity over the years, shared in the changes. For years it fought for its rights and recognition, campaigning for the nationalisation of the mines. When that came, some of its leaders joined in the management of the industry, others in the new established procedures and privileges which were offered. Union branch secretaries as a matter of course had offices in the pithead complex; miners went automatically on to their books, and the Coal Board deducted their dues for them and paid them direct to the union.

But there remained a persistent strand of recusancy, of union leaders who saw too close an involvement with the board as collaboration, of betrayal of traditional militancy. The NUM did not always sit easy with other unions. The memories of 1926 and what they saw as betrayal lingered on, while many other union leaders regarded the NUM as something of a union apart, interested in its narrow ends, not always in the wider interests of unions with membership in many different industries. They acknowledged the miners' achievements in their victories of 1972 and 1974, but resented the union's tendency always to wish to be a special case.

The trade union movement's 'Brigade of Guards' was one classic description of the NUM but 'a middle-sized union with a lot of history but not much industrial power' was another patronising summation of the NUM by one leading union figure in the early 1980s. He was either wrong or prematurely wise.

Politicians were constantly reminded of the power and the problems of coal. The Labour Party's roots had always been entwined deeply with the miners and their struggles. Keir Hardie himself had been an Ayrshire coal miner, and in 1984 the Labour Party leader was a miner's son, drawn away from the pit community like so many before him by the advantages of education.

In the 1920s the Communist Party too had made the miners one of its key power bases, dominating it in Scotland and for a time in South Wales and Kent so that even in 1984 members of the party or recent ex-members still held key posts in all three areas, and the formulas and vocabulary of the party were part of the common currency of the union.

For the Conservatives, coal and the miners were a recurrent fixation. From 1926 to 1972 and 1974, the miners' challenges had come during periods of Conservative government. When Mrs Thatcher assumed power in 1979, one of the key precepts of her government was to avoid a confrontation with the miners it could not win. Her predecessors like Winston Churchill who, as Home Secretary, had faced the law and order problems of earlier miners' challenges and had been reviled by miners for police actions at Tonypandy, were acutely aware of the way the problems of the mine owners had endlessly been deposited on the government's doorstep.

So it was with an air of inevitability and relief from both sides that under the Labour government the nationalisation of the industry urged by the Labour movement for so long and recommended by the government-appointed Sankey Commission as long ago as 1919 finally became reality on 1 January 1947. It was a symbol of a new consensus, a post-war bargain between organised labour and the establishment which was to continue for over thirty years until it met the ideological challenge of the Conservative government under Mrs Thatcher which saw in it the root of Britain's economic decline.

It was an intensely emotional moment which was to warm Labour movement supporters through the coming difficulties of the Attlee government and the freezing weeks which followed as the newly nationalised industry proved unable to produce enough coal to power industry or warm homes in the face of the coldest winter for years.

On the symbolic vesting day of 1 January miners sang and applauded as they gathered at pitheads to see the flag of the new NCB run up on the flagpoles from which the standards of the old and largely discredited coal owners had fluttered.

From the start this was an industry where things were to be different. The first item set out for the board under the 1946 Coal Industry Nationalisation Act was to secure 'the safety, health and welfare of persons in their employment'. Second came 'the benefit of the practical knowledge and experience of such persons', and only third was the provision 'that the revenues of the Board shall not be less than sufficient for meeting all their outgoings . . . on an average of good and bad years'. Even this was a mild statement of economic priorities, and the good and bad year average was to provide plenty of loopholes for future NCB chairmen until it was changed by a Conservative government in 1980 to an insistence on break-even yearly targets.

The structure of the board mirrored the conception. The first chairman was a former coal owner, Lord Hyndley of Powell Duffryn. But he presided over a central board on a model created by Labour's Herbert Morrison, on which sat symbolically the former TUC general secretary, Walter Citrine, the very man who had negotiated against the coal owners in 1926, and was now establishing the new British Electricity Authority to run the soon-to-be-nationalised electricity supply industry. Alongside him was the former NUM general secretary, Ebby Edwards, who had resigned his post to join the board.

Industrial relations was given a new look. The board was obliged not only to negotiate terms and conditions with the unions, but also to hold formal consultations with them about safety and health and the general running of the industry. Arbitration machinery was established to avoid national disputes, which both sides agreed would be binding. Coupled with a rule of the new NUM – recently formed from the old Miners Federation of Great Britain – which required a two-thirds majority for strike action, it prevented national disputes for years, although local strikes proved much more intractable.

The practice grew up that the board's industrial relations department should be run by former officials of the NUM or other established trade union officers. So much was it in the NUM's gift that there was a fierce row when the NUM objected to jobs going to men from other unions which they believed should be reserved for NUM men. The tradition continued, though with diminished force. In 1984 Ned Smith, who was Director General of Industrial Relations, came from a close-knit mining family, while his deputy Kevan Hunt was a former NUM branch delegate, a contemporary and rival of the NUM general secretary, Peter Heathfield in north Derbyshire. And the Smith job would have gone earlier to one of the members of the NUM executive in 1984, Ken Toon, the anti-Scargill secretary of south Derbyshire, if he had not turned down the post after a problem over arranging pensions.

The insular nature of the board was reinforced by a recommendation from the Fleck committee in 1955 that board members should normally come from within the industry. The board's third chairman was a former president of the Northumberland NUM, Jim, later Sir James, Bowman and he was succeeded by another of the Labour movement's own, Alfred, later Lord, Robens, a Labour front-bencher who had been Minister of Labour at the end of the Attlee government.

But the idea of the Coal Board's operations as socialism at work was a myth. Out in the coal fields many managers and mining engineers remained as tough and uncompromising as ever, wrestling with the problems of awkward geology and sometimes awkward union officials. The cult of macho management might have been born, and indeed lived on, in many coal fields in ways little different from those of the days of private ownership.

Similarly, union distrust of the management did not vanish. A persistent faction in the NUM, highly politicised, argued strongly against 'collaboration' from the start. An early target was the way in which the union rapidly agreed to suspend the historic milestone of the 'five-day week agreement' it had just wrung from the new board. Descendants of the grouping were to dominate the union in the 1980s.

'Collusive, collaborative arrangements' was how one prominent British manager, bloodied in the battles between management and labour in manufacturing industry, typed the style as he watched the change of chairmanship in 1983. But it was a gross over-simplification. More incontestable was the charge that the board had become introspective, cut off from international business changes, dominated by its own home-grown mining engineers. Undeniable was that the Conservative perception as set out by Anthony Sampson in his *Anatomy of Britain* in 1962, was 'Hobart House [the NCB headquarters] has become a favourite Tory symbol of socialist bureaucracy.'[1]

As the board wrestled to cope with the rapid and contradictory switches in the energy market, struggling and failing at first to get production and manpower levels up, then facing a colossal drop in traditional demand, two consistent trends dominated its first thirty years of operation; an enormous reduction in the numbers of pits and miners, and a change in the use of coal so that the market for British coal became dominated by one single customer – the electricity industry.

On vesting day in 1947 the board had inherited 980 pits. Even in 1955 there were still 850 producing 225 million tonnes. But then in fifteen years they were more than halved, reduced to 292 producing 135 million tonnes. These were economic closures with a vengeance.

In human terms, it was devastating. At the end of 1955 the industry had virtually the same number of men as on vesting day, just under 700,000. In 1970–1 the numbers were down to 287,000. But even the statistics could not encompass the changes that took place; a vast programme of transfers and organised industrial mobility which the Wilberforce enquiry in 1972 described as 'a rundown which is without parallel in British industry in terms of the social and economic costs for the mining community'.

Thousands of men and their families were transferred away from areas like Durham and Scotland into the larger and more profitable pits in Yorkshire and the Midlands. The Coal Board, with stocks of tied housing inherited from the old coal companies, was heavily involved in the arranging of accommodation and in some cases large encampments of caravans were set up.

For miners, less accustomed than most of the rest of the country to changing jobs and employers and having to move for work, it was a huge change. It led to Arthur Scargill's persistent declaration twenty years later that the miners would not again become 'industrial gypsies'. But at the time, largely under the cool and communicative chairmanship of Robens, there was markedly little protest. A major factor of course was that these were times of full employment and even labour shortage.

The effect on mining attitudes was mixed. Imported Scottish radicalism was one of the things which helped to change the traditionally middle-of-the-road Yorkshire area of the NUM, but in Nottinghamshire and the Midlands, with particularly large proportions of transferred men, their experience of facing up to change was perhaps one reason why so many worked in 1984–5.

The other shift was in the use of coal. In 1947, when British industry used 150 million tonnes of coal a year, about one-sixth, 27 million tonnes, was used to generate electricity. By 1970–1, of 122 million tonnes going to industry, well over half, 74.7 million tonnes, was headed for the Central Electricity Generating Board and the South of Scotland Generating Board. A vast programme of building had produced a line of huge power stations tethered like anchored battleships along the eastern flank of the Yorkshire coalfield, with another arc along the river Trent farther south in Nottingham. Coal had come to account for 80 per cent of the CEGB's normal output.

The change had two consequences. The first, at the beginning unnoticed, was that it restored enormous industrial power to the miners. When the miners in 1972 spread their picketing away from their pits to the railways and the power stations, hitting supplies of other fuels too to power stations, the nation and the miners themselves suddenly woke up to the strangehold they had obtained.

The other inevitability was that the Coal Board's single biggest customer began to have a much bigger say in the way the coal industry should be run. A series of chairmen complained bitterly about what came to be called the NCB's 'tail of uneconomic pits'. Even in 1986 the Electricity Council Chairman, Philip Jones, was banging the same drum, announcing that coal was accounting for over a third of the cost of electricity: 'Coal prices to the CEGB are now 55 times higher than they were 50 years ago. Over the same period electricity prices have increased nine times, while the cost of living has increased 21 times.'

As the big electricity users in industry complained to the government about their disadvantage in world markets because of the disproportionate cost to them of power supplies, there were plenty of industrialists to point the finger at the coal industry, complaining that its practices and its jobs were being preserved at the cost of workers in other industries.

Government absorbed the lesson of 1972 with a succession of internal papers which pointed out the dangers of being too dependent on a single source of energy supply.

The year 1972 was a watershed, catapulting the industry to a political prominence and sensitivity which was to last for a dozen years, and was grossly unwelcome to many Coal Board managers who found the commercial operation of their enterprises suddenly under the spotlight, subject to political fluctuation and direction, and having to take account of a new rampant union.

For the union too it marked an enormous shift, partly achieved, partly still to come. During the 1960s the whole climate of the unions had been changing. They and the Labour Party had been moving to the left. The election of the first Labour government for 13 years in 1964 was followed by fierce criticism of its performance and emergence of new radical leadership such as the so-called 'terrible twins', Jack Jones and Hugh Scanlon.

In the coal industry, as alternative job opportunities started to shrink in what Harold Wilson euphemistically described as the 'shake-out', attitudes hardened. There was a lively and growing left grouping in the NUM which was pressing for official action, and encouraging unofficial action over wages.

The NUM withdrew from the compulsory arbitration procedures in 1961, was involved in widespread unofficial strikes over wages in 1969 and 1970 (where Yorkshire played a leading part), and in 1971 changed its rules to reduce the majority to allow a strike to 55 per cent.

Cutting their teeth in this radical atmosphere were many of the men who would be prominent in the union a decade later, including Arthur Scargill and the more experienced Mick McGahey who in 1971 was defeated for the NUM presidency by Joe Gormley. Gormley, himself a shrewd judge of current moods, had been elected on what was on paper a radical programme and rode, sometimes unhappily, the tiger of the new militancy.

The 1972 strike was about wages, restoring the miners to the top of the wages league from the seventeenth position to which they had slipped in years of public obscurity. But the way they unexpectedly smashed the government's pay policy in the process and then in 1974 forced the election which brought down the Heath government, brought industrial and political prominence to coal which it had not had for years.

By itself, it might still have been a fading wonder. What completed the turning of the tables was the sudden coherence of OPEC after the Six-day War and the quadrupling of the price of coal's biggest industrial rival, so-called 'cheap' oil. These two factors powered the new drive for coal production which marked the 1970s. Externally it was a time of accommodation with the unions, of social contracts, planning agreements (one signed ceremonially between government, board and union at the NUM's Torquay conference), and the automatic reception of the unions into the committees, if not the corridors, of power.

Inside the industry, the incoming Labour government in 1974 set out to prepare a tripartite 'Plan for Coal', the name echoing earlier optimistic programmes by the board immediately post-nationalisation. It proposed vigorous new investment compensating for the exhaustion of older pits at the rate of 2 million tonnes capacity a year. Coal production was to rise from its current 127 million tonnes to 135 million tonnes a year by 1985. For the board it meant thinking had to be stood on its head. From managing gradual decline engines had to be reversed once again and the vast enterprise pointed towards expansion.

It had a rough start. Although the number of miners was increased in 1974–5 for the first time for many years, production went down. Elaborate discussions and joint visits by union and management teams had little effect. The NCB chairman, Sir Derek (now Lord) Ezra, and Gormley agreed to go for incentive payments, a scheme which was bitterly opposed by the left who saw it as a return to the divisive piecework schemes which they had finally succeeded in replacing with a national powerloading agreement. Defeated at the 1977 annual conference, Gormley outflanked the left by allowing areas to negotiate their own in what became a national framework. It was tricky constitutionally, but the courts rejected an action to stop it brought by left-wing areas.

The effect was rapid. From 1978–9 deep-mined production started to revive. The incentive scheme gave miners more money and diminished the intensity of the left's drive to win big annual increases on basic pay rates.

But once again, the rocks lay ahead. Just at the point that production targets started to be hit and new low-cost investment to come on stream, the bottom was torn from the market.

It was the struggle to resolve this, a choice between relying on rapid, if brutal, adjustment to market forces or the bi-partisan collaborative management which characterised the 1970s, which now became acute and which brought about the 1984–5 miners' strike.

The roots of the conflict lay in the rejection of the collaboration of the 1970s by two of the three parties; by the leadership of the NUM where the anti-collaborationist left, triumphing with the election victory of Arthur Scargill, determined to make a decisive break with the policies of Gormley whom he detested; and by the new-style conservatism of Margaret Thatcher which saw in the Coal Board and its supposedly cosy relationship with the NUM a paradigm of the soft feather-bedding and acceptance of enormous subsidy which it believed had destroyed Britain's economic prospects.

Both sides were heavily influenced by ideology but also by the experience of the board after 1974, the period characterised by the partnership and friendship between the Coal Board chairman, Derek

Ezra, and the NUM president, Joe (later Lord) Gormley.

It was the time of the social contract, and after two victories in three years, the NUM started with the whip hand. New machinery was established, a joint policy advisory committee to encourage the unions to discuss marketing and research as well as wages and conditions. Area review meetings discussed all pits rather than just those in trouble. The chairman annually addressed the NUM conference and the Coal Board customarily arranged a reception in the evening where members of the executive could parade their singing talent and the left could demonstrate their principles by staying away.

But it was not all cosy. The wily Gormley, who had started his union career as the toughest piece-rate negotiator for his gang in a Lancashire pit, drove a hard bargain. Shrewdly manipulating the left's push for militant action, he secured what was usually the best pay rise for any group every year and topped it up with some other sweetener, early retirement provisions, or free working clothing, or extra payments for washing time.

Inside the union, he faced down annual auctions by the left-wing areas to set the highest figure for the coming year's pay demand, defusing commitments to industrial action if they fell short by shrewd use of the ballot vote.

In the Coal Board meanwhile Ezra, typed as a 'French bureaucrat' by one of his senior staff, emphasised the committee structures with a general purposes committee bringing together relevant board members and the powerful directors-general who headed the key departments such as marketing and industrial relations. As Ezra himself put his policy, 'It was a consensual one of seeking to get the maximum areas of agreement. It did not mean we went to the length of always agreeing to what other people wanted. All I did deliberately was to seek the maximum area of agreement. That applied both within the management and with the unions.'

It fitted the national mood, but in retrospect the incoming conservatives believed that the chance to tackle the tail of uneconomic pits was missed. Some pits did go, largely through exhaustion. Five pits closed and 2 were merged in 1977–8, 9 in 1978–9; five in 1979–80 and 10 in 1980–1. But it was well short of even the 2 million tonnes a year capacity which Plan for Coal had envisaged.

At the time it hardly seemed to matter. Some area directors like Philip Weekes in South Wales were upset when their decisions to close pits like Deep Duffryn were overruled from London after Gormley's intervention. But it was a time of maximising production which was at last responding, and even in 1979 the board was so short of production that as one executive put it, 'We were shaking the bushes at the edges of the stocking grounds looking for the last bit of dust.'

Then suddenly the market collapsed. Just as the pits were at last producing more, industrial recession on a scale not seen since the 1930s, and the increasing success of energy conservation in the face of high oil prices, produced a crisis.

Sir Norman Siddall, then deputy chairman, sums up the problem: 'There was a great expectation in the early seventies of great expansion because of the hike in oil prices. A lot of people expected it. I wasn't quite so enthusiastic because it really wasn't there. A lot of the plans were over-enthusiastic.

'There was always this difficulty. You never seem to be able to get the numbers right in this industry. There is either too much or too little.

'As soon as things become more realistic and successful technically, we always seem to hit the rocks in some other direction.

'Technically things were good in the late seventies. A lot of the new capacity was beginning to come on stream. It didn't follow the idea of Plan for Coal because that had got so far behind with new mines that people had to turn to extension of life at existing pits which was far cheaper. It was a windfall.'

It was the incoming Conservative government which was faced with the new crisis. In opposition it had devised a plan to reduce the cost of the board. Its method was to introduce a new Coal Industry Act which rolled up the various complex grants to the industry in a single deficit grant which would make plain the cost. The idea was that it would educate the country about the real position and so set an early deadline – 1983–4 – by which the industry would become self-supporting.

Ezra fought hard against the new system, but the government insisted, stiffened by the continuing rise in unsold coal. Between March 1980 and 1981 the board's stocks almost doubled, from 12 million to nearly 21 million tonnes. Customers' stocks increased too.

Under treasury pressure, the cabinet went for a much bigger target for reducing old capacity. Instead of 2.3 million to 3 million tonnes a year, which the energy minister, David Howell, wanted, they opted for 4 million tonnes.

The débâcle of February 1981 followed. The speeding up of closures had become apparent at local level and the NUM demanded a national meeting. On 10 February, at a rowdy and overcrowded meeting at Hobart House, with the full executives of all three mining unions, Ezra under pressure gave an estimate that 'between 20 and 50 pits' would close over the next five years.

The union reacted furiously. Gormley sought a meeting with the government, threatened a national ballot on strike action, and in South Wales, Kent and other areas, unofficial action began.

It was a major test for the new government, facing a battle with the one group of workers against whom the received wisdom was that they could not hope to win. *The Times* carried a leader page article headed 'Miners v Tories; the supreme test that faces Mrs Thatcher'.

The union met David Howell on the evening of 18 February after a day of guidance to journalists that there was no change in the government's attitude. The meeting told a different story. The government had decided to cut its losses and back down. Howell had been for sticking it out, but Thatcher, advised in particular by her deputy William Whitelaw and Employment Secretary Jim Prior, had decided that they could not fight and win. The deciding factor was the level of coal stocks, and the argument that carried was the one which said it was the wrong time to take the miners on. The ground would have to be picked more carefully.

The miners could scarcely believe it, though Gormley characteristically used the climb-down to press for more money for the industry. Howell found himself signing almost open cheques for costs of stocking the increasing mountains of coal, of underwriting the price for keeping more pits open, compensating for a reduction in imports of coal by customers like the electricity industry, and improving redundancy terms for miners.

It was a demoralising climb-down for the Conservatives and they set out to learn the lessons. For the Coal Board too, the memories of that meeting on 10 February remained as a warning. For Arthur Scargill, a repetition of such a confrontation, where the board would set out in grand terms proposals for cutback and closure for the whole industry, became a target which he believed could once more galvanise the miners into action, and which he finally achieved on 6 March 1984.

Joe Gormley had no doubt that what had brought matters to a head was Ezra's statement giving numbers of pits to be closed. As he put it, 'It was probably the most stupid statement that he ever made. The fact was that he was only talking about a two-year closure programme of 23 pits, 18 of which had been discussed and a few already agreed. And over a five-year period, it probably would have been about 50 pits in the normal course of events.

'But by putting it blatantly as a target figure like that, he gave the militants the perfect platform they needed, "fifty pits" became the issue, along with the projected loss of 30,000 jobs.'[2]

What Ezra had done, as Gormley's account makes clear, was to violate the understanding between the union and board about how things were carried out. The prospects of pits were matters for areas to discuss. That was important not just for the directors of the areas who operate like barons within their own bailiwick, but perhaps even more so for local union leaders who still operated what was in many ways a federal union, and who would have much of their *raison d'être* and importance removed if everything was transferred on to a national plane.

Under the understanding, very detailed information was made available to the unions, often informally and confidentially, about the situation in different pits. At local level matters could often be agreed provided that those who made the deals were not then obliged to defend them on a national platform.

The most obvious example of the process was in Scotland, where, with Mick McGahey as union president and James Cowan as area director, agreement had been reached on a number of closures without any appeal to national level. Similarly in north Derbyshire, which was steadily running out of coal, the area secretary Peter Heathfield had agreed the programme of closure because of exhaustion with area director Ken Moses for a period of years ahead.

There is still speculation about why Ezra gave the numbers. He argues that he had no option. His colleagues talk of the pressures of the meeting with members of the NUM baying for an answer. Some Conservatives still accuse him of setting up a confrontation which would force the government to back down.

The climb-down dismayed many of the area directors and Coal Board members, the men of whom Gormley said, 'I've accused them many times of being so conservative in their outlook that I get frightened for them.'[2] In fact the closures went ahead but more slowly – eleven pits in 1981–2, the most for seven years.

Meanwhile the government was making its own moves to ensure it was never caught again. Under the cover of the new deal for financing coal stocks, it moved extra tonnages into the power stations. From the summer of 1981 the statistics of stocks held by the generating boards were for the first time amongst those supplied to the prime minister for her weekly scan of key indicators. On occasions, the new Energy Minister, Nigel Lawson, who had succeeded Howell, would be asked to explain them.

By the end of October 1982 a record amount of coal had been shifted during the summer, increasing net stocks by 13 million tonnes to 29 millions. This was deliberate policy, reversing the pre-1981 view when ministers resisted stockpiling because of treasury pressure to keep down costs. But it was also due to the problems the Coal Board had in selling what it was producing. As Sir Norman Siddall puts it, 'It was purely fortuitous. The market disappeared and God himself could not have closed pits fast enough to prevent the stock accumulating.'

In 1982, there had been a double change at the top. Gormley, having hung on until retiring age to keep the left out as long as possible, finally had to retire and was succeeded in a landslide victory by Arthur Scargill. Ezra meanwhile chose to depart at the same time, to sighs of relief from government ministers, and after a long period of uncertainty in Whitehall, his deputy, Norman Siddall took over.

Siddall's appointment was the last chance the government gave for the Coal Board to set its own house in order. Although he was Ezra's deputy, he was no automatic choice. A number of names were canvassed, and Siddall himself had other concerns. At the end of 1981, he had a heart by-pass operation, and the wound obstinately refused to heal. Later Siddall was to say that, as 1982 began, he had no interests in whether he was to become chairman, his concern was only whether he would survive.

As he lay recovering, one of the names mooted, though swiftly put on one side, was that of the Scottish American who had been brought in to rescue the British Steel Corporation, Ian MacGregor. But it was rapidly decided that he must complete the job he had started at steel.

Siddall's appointment was greeted with relief by Coal Board managers. Here was a man, a mining engineer to his fingertips who still lived in a mining area in Mansfield, although working in London, and was known to be unhappy about the pace of change under Ezra.

His term was for twelve months only, on doctor's advice. Knowing that time was short, he set himself the target of doing the difficult things he believed the industry needed to prepare the way for a younger man. He said openly that he would not object if that man came from outside the industry.

The pace of closure was stepped up with pits carefully targeted at local level. Siddall was invited to the NUM conference where he was warmly welcomed by Arthur Scargill as a fellow Yorkshireman who knew the industry. His speech, read in his gruff, unemphatic way, spelt out the need to reduce capacity by 8 million tonnes to adjust to market conditions. There was little reaction.

The board paced things shrewdly. Scargill, spoiling for a fight in his first year as president, led the union into a ballot linking pay and closures and lost. Then, in an apparent repeat of 1981, he was pushed against his better judgment into another dispute and ballot over the closure of a Welsh pit, Ty Mawr–Lewis Merthyr. Again he lost.

During the year 17 pits closed and 7 were merged and 23,000 men left the industry, progress which was to encourage the board a year later to map out a programme of the same scale which it believed the miners could accept, the plan which was to become famous as '20 pits and 20,000 jobs'.

Scargill, attempting to repeat the 1981 confrontation, demanded a national showdown about the board's closure plans. Brandishing leaked documents from the board about the economics of pits, he insisted there was a 'hit list' of pits. Siddall denied it absolutely, insisted that matters were dealt with piecemeal by local areas, and, when he met the NUM, pulled in all the area directors so that no one on the union side should claim that he was hearing new information which he had not been given locally.

The question of course is whether this step-by-step approach by the Board could have continued, or was bound to lead to confrontation. Siddall's own view is, 'I think it could have continued. It's very difficult looking back, and I don't know how long they could have done it. But I think by getting involved in this over-all plan, and multiplying the figures up, Arthur was able to encourage his troops.'

The government meanwhile was putting pressure on the Coal Board in other ways. As part of a routine scan of nationalised industries, the Monopolies and Mergers Commission undertook an investigation of the Board, and the Commons Select Committee on Energy embarked on a series of hearings which produced a report at the end of 1982. Both talked of the need to cut back on uneconomic capacity, and the MMC report proposed changes in the management structure of the Coal Board. The Select Committee report called on the board to reduce capacity further to bring it into line with anticipated demand, and said bluntly that the expansion of markets foreseen in Plan for Coal was now 'highly unlikely'. The two documents set out in some detail the argument about uneconomic pits which was to become an endless refrain in 1984–5.

The NCB view was expressed by Siddall at the NUM annual conference in 1982: 'Because we have been so richly blessed by nature, we don't have to go on scratching about in places where, because of the geological conditions, no amount of skill and effort by management and men can ever succeed. While we have such vast resources to go for, it cannot be right that about 12 per cent of our output should lose £250 millions as it did last year.'

The view was strongly endorsed by the MMC report which found seventy collieries with operating losses of more than £10 a tonne, and made it clear that the figure would have been higher if interest charges to the industry were apportioned to individual collieries as it considered realistic. It described the closure of high-cost pits with no real chance of returning to profitability as 'the single most effective measure in reducing costs and improving average efficiency'.

The NUM had refused to co-operate with the commission, but it was summoned to give evidence to the Select Committee, and used the opportunity to set out its view of the economic arguments. It did so in three ways: by questioning the basis of the sums; by widening the arguments to include social costs; and by pointing up its sharply different philosophical approach, which went so far as to suggest that coal should be removed from the considerations of the market altogether.

It queried the figures by declaring that what constituted an 'uneconomic pit' was 'a matter of entirely subjective and arbitrary definition'. It questioned the basis on which the NCB worked out depreciation charges, claimed that it undervalued its stocks, and pointed to the growing costs of subsidence claims. It pointed up the growing burden of interest charges as the industry modernised and suggested that they had been higher because of requirements that borrowing should be done through the government.

It also rehearsed the argument, to be made much of in 1984, that Britain produced the cheapest deep-mined coal in Europe. It was certainly true in Western Europe. Here a number of countries with significantly smaller coal industries were subsidising heavily, reducing energy costs to consumers and also softening the impact of rapid phasing-out of coal altogether. In 1984 NCB figures put subsidies in France at £19.19 a tonne; in West Germany at £12.06 and in Britain at only £4.11. Figures for Eastern Europe, and particularly Poland which was a major factor in 1984, were impossible to come by.

The social cost of pit closures was quantified for the NUM during the strike by Andrew Glyn, of Corpus Christi College, Oxford.[3] His conclusion that 'there are no pits whatsoever whose closure would benefit government revenue' was based on a calculation which set the notional subsidy saved per miner in a closed pit against the redundancy pay for him, plus the dole payment of a man who might have taken his job when he retired. It added in the loss of tax from, and payment of dole to, workers elsewhere in the board and in other industries who would be consequentially affected. The calculation assumed that virtually no redundant miners found other work, and that if they did, they would effectively take work from someone else. According to that calculation, the subsidy saved of £6,875 per man compared with costs that ranged from over £20,000 in the first year to over £10,000 by the sixth year.

But there was an even more basic philosophic difference between the board and, in particular, Arthur Scargill. The board's line in 1984 was that production must be brought into line with what could be sold, particularly with imported Australian and American coal being cheaper at coastal locations. But for the miners, the view was to be heard that coal was a national asset, and should be mined anyway and could even be given away to help pensioners or provide cheap electricity; the exact antithesis of the market argument.

Scargill's own view was set out in his reply to questions from the Select Committee about the criteria for closing pits: 'Where there are resources of coal . . . even if there is a loss on the production of that coal, then that coal should be produced.' Then pressed farther about what level of loss was acceptable, he encapsulated his philosophy in words which might have served as a text for the strike: 'As far as I am concerned, the loss is without limit because I am more interested in the investment our men have put into this industry.'

The union's concerns were meanwhile being heightened by what was happening to manpower in the industry. As the arguments continued about pit economics, the board was moving not just over pits but also on the numbers of miners.

There has been a tradition of high turnover of labour in the mining industry. In times of high employment, men have tended to move in and out of the industry as they have chosen. So as late as 1977, the board was running heavy recruiting campaigns. As a matter of policy it recruited 40 per cent more engineering craftsmen than needed because it saw them poached by other industries after it had trained them.

But then as unemployment rose, things began to change and a sharp brake was applied to recruitment. In important mining areas unemployment went up. In the Barnsley travel-to-work area it rose from 13.9 per cent in March 1982 to 15.9 per cent in March 1984 (both above the national average). In Doncaster it went from 15.9 per cent in March 1982 to 16.7 per cent in March 1984. On Wearside, which includes some major Durham collieries, a rate of 18.8 per cent in March 1982 was up to 21.2 per cent in March 1984.

The Coal Board's problems were compounded by a huge drop in absenteeism which meant that it had the equivalent of 20,000 extra men working in the industry. So discipline was increased, voluntary redundancy encouraged, and recruitment cut back. Recruits fell from 25,800 in 1979–80 to 10,000 the following year and as few as 2,600 in the year before the strike.

Many were juveniles, often miners' children, but these numbers too were dropping. Nationally they went down from 3,800 in 1981–2 to 1,700 two years later. In Yorkshire the numbers were halved. In the north-east coal fields of Northumberland and Durham, where 319 under-18s had been employed in 1982–3, none at all were taken on in 1983–4. Put simply, jobs for their children were disappearing before the miners' eyes just at the time when other work was becoming very difficult to find.

Part of the solution from the board and the government was to do what had been done in the steel industry and the docks: to improve redundancy pay. The board had a perennial demand from the NUM for retirement at 55, and Siddall was only too keenly aware that he had more than enough men over 50 in the industry who would like an opportunity to get out to give him the reductions he wanted. The trick, as he conceded, was how to let them leave without disrupting the pits.

Redundancy pay was increased both in 1981 and then in April 1983. From 8,100 redundancies in 1982–3 the number more than doubled, to 18,100 in the following year. Then the new scheme had come in with terms which the NCB's newspaper estimated could mean that a married man aged 50 with thirty years service who earned £180 a week could receive over £22,000 in lump sums and be paid over £75 a week from a mixture of pensions and benefit.

But most of the men from pits which were closing opted to stay. Between 1973 and 1982 the Select Committee says that of 21,597 affected by the closure of 59 pits, 14,864 were transferred to work at other pits and 5,670 took redundancy. The big numbers – 34,015 – had come from collieries which did not close, some of them giving way to men whose pits had shut. Of the total redundancies – 39,685 – the huge majority – 36,040 – were aged 55 or over.

The union argued before the Select Committee that the redundancies meant jobs lost for good and that it also affected communities by depriving them of work and business. In practice things were more complex. Miners who transferred to other pits usually stayed where they were. There was nothing like the huge shifts of population which occurred in the 1950s and 60s. In many cases miners had little if any greater distance to travel.

Of the seven pits closed in the north east between 1982 and 1984, the majority of the men at three of the pits either had no increase in travel to their new pit or had to go 4 miles at most. Elsewhere travel was increased by up to 10 or 12 miles each way. Men transferred were paid £1,500 transfer grant and were able to use the comprehensive systems of Coal Board buses which provided free or cheap travel to work or, in some cases, had their car journeys subsidised. At the new Selby complex in Yorkshire, specially designed with large car parks, men transferred from pits closed 20 miles away had all costs over £2.30 a week paid by the NCB. Similarly in South Wales few men moved house.

As Siddall prepared to retire in the summer of 1983 his farewell message talked of 'clear progress' to making the industry as efficient as possible. Productivity was the best for many years; output and sales should roughly balance and, he went on, 'Mineworkers have remained for several years at the top of the wages league for industrial workers, a position justified by their jobs. The coal industry has a good reputation for consulting its work people over all matters that concern them directly or indirectly. And even when redundancy has to be resorted to, we have so far maintained the voluntary principle and have been able to offer terms unmatched by any other industry.

'These policies have been followed not out of sentiment but because they make good sense and ensure the possibility of good relations for further generations. Without good people all the clever technologies and capital investment come to nothing.'

It was as good a statement as any about the ethos which pervaded the Coal Board before the arrival of Ian MacGregor.

The government had been delighted with Siddall's performance. Mrs Thatcher invited him to Downing Street to press him to stay on, a request later repeated. On the strongest doctor's orders, he turned it down. His term was extended for three months, and he left in September 1983.

His legacy was an industry getting to grips with its problems, a home-grown management dealing with problems in its own way, but, in spite of optimistic words about supply and demand being in balance, still looking at 60 million tonnes of unused stock in the country, the equivalent of six months' production. At national level it was largely in the hands of old men in their 60s. As Siddall acknowledged, there was room for changes.

His chairmanship had been characterised by a determination to tackle the problems of the industry but to do his best to avoid provoking a national confrontation. That was done by concentrating on the local level and being aware of the Scargill strategy of transferring everything to a national plane, where as Siddall acknowledged, 'any numbers you add up in this industry look awful because there is such a large multiplier.'

The way to deal with Scargill, he would explain to politicians and civil servants, was 'to step to one side and let him fall through the ropes,' and he criticised the received civil service view that they must be ready sooner or later for a showdown with Scargill. 'If you keep talking about it long enough, you will get it,' was his warning. But he knew it had been disregarded when the announcement came that his successor was to be Ian MacGregor. He had acknowledged the case for someone outside the industry but had not expected someone older.

It was a surprise. He had not been consulted. The advice of civil servants in the department of energy had been against MacGregor, but the government had decided that it was time for a shake-up in the board. The MMC report, which MacGregor came to describe as 'my Bible' had criticised the domination of the board by home-grown mining engineers. It was time for the experience of private and international business that was MacGregor's forte to be used to revamp the board.

It was a clear signal of the break from the post-war past, paralleling the triumph in the union of the tendency which rejected co-operation with the board. It was a signal and a challenge to the NUM, and for all the cautious months of wary circling which followed, the clash of strongly held philosophies was inevitable. It might only have been checked by the mechanism of the ballot which brought the less politicised and more matter-of-fact voices of the men in the industry into play.

Siddall, departing, saw it clearly: 'MacGregor was a natural for Arthur to latch on to. He had told me that his chosen three for a new chairman, would be MacGregor, Michael Edwardes, and somebody else, because he knew he could make a great deal of trouble out of any of them. He was looking for something to hang his hat on.'

3
'There's only one Arthur Scargill'

Would the strike have taken place without Arthur Scargill? Many believed it would not: more believed that, while it might have been inevitable (given the scale of job loss required), it would have lasted only a few weeks and been settled with a fudge. It is a common belief in government, in the labour movement and in the NCB that Scargill, by sheer personal force, greatly prolonged the strike and greatly raised the stakes; that he, largely alone, turned the strike from what it might have been – a partial victory – into a complete defeat because *he* had to be beaten. *He* was the embodiment of the enemy within.

For Peter Walker, the strike was 'Scargill's strike'. When, in November 1984, he met the seven TUC elders charged with trying to find a settlement, he told them that the miners could have had a good deal but that Scargill could not be dealt with; he was, he said, a man apart from the normal processes of give and take. It struck a deep chord in the hearts of men battered by hours of the president's rhetoric, for he treated them as he treated everyone outside his inner circle, as at best a doubtful ally who had to be tongue-lashed on to the straight and narrow, and kept there by the same means.

Ian MacGregor grew to loathe him. In April he talked of him (in an interview with *The Times*) as an actor manqué; by September he was unwisely seduced by a BBC radio interviewer into doubting his sanity; by the closing months of the strike he saw him as a ranting tyrant, whose use of terror on his own people meant that he was far beyond the pale of rational discussion.

Those of his own people who turned on him were fascinated by him even as they struggled against him. For Roy Lynk, the Nottinghamshire NUM official who became general secretary of the Union of Democratic Mineworkers, Scargill was at the root of all the ills which beset the NUM, and which had turned it from 'the finest union in the world' to a dictatorship. For Lynk and his colleagues elsewhere in the coal fields who joined the anti-Scargill camp, no other NUM leader – even those in

Nottinghamshire who, in remaining loyal to the NUM executive, had to be disloyal to their own members – could approach the malignity and power of the NUM president.

But for his followers, during the strike at least, the relationship was like a modern equivalent of King Arthur and his knights. 'Arthur Scargill, Arthur Scargill, we'll support you ever more,' they sang (to the tune of *Cwm Rhondda*); and 'Arthur Scargill walks on water' (to the tune of *Deck the Walls*); and 'There's only one Arthur Scargill' (to the tune of *Guantanamera*), and sometimes just 'Arthur, Arthur, Arthur', shouted again and again and again. Did it bother him? one of us asked him early on in the strike. No, he said, it was the action of mineworkers who saw me vilified on the media and were seeking to redress the balance. That was probably right. The heavier the establishment fire upon him, the more he was caricatured and lampooned and thundered against, the more those who threw in their lot with him drew closer to him, hugged him to themselves, almost as a talisman, an idol. For them, he expressed their best: he roused them, to actions in their own and others' defence of which they did not think themselves capable; he expressed and gave point to their feelings of resentment, of insecurity, of class hatred. He never became one of the establishment which most of his members felt, rightly, excluded them, or condescended to them, or sought to buy them off. He never showed himself open to compromise, or to weakening his position, or to simple human weariness, even when they did. Bob McSporran, the leader of the Midlands power group who served briefly on the NUM executive during the second part of the strike, said of his president: 'Whatever you think of his policies, you have to admire him. We all did admire him; that's one reason we remained united.'

His members were often less considered: many of them simply worshipped him. On 30 May Scargill was arrested on the Orgreave picket lines. On his release from the Rotherham court, miners surged about him in the hot sun. He put out his hand to them, shaking theirs. After such an encounter, one young miner in his 20s held up his hand in the air, waving it in the faces of his comrades. 'I'll not wash this!' he cried.

Who *were* they following? What kind of man was able to stir the love and dedication of men as tough and sceptical as any in the country? And why was he able to exercise a control over his close colleagues on the executive, his 'Red Guard' in the country and his reluctant allies in the trade union movement to the point where none found it possible to control him and thus bring the strike to a decent end?

First, he is a terribly political animal. In the thirty years of his active political involvement he has developed a set of political principles which, when added together, produce a kind of communist-syndicalism which it is impossible to believe would work in practice – but the discrete components of this set of principles, and the way in which they are transmitted, have at different times had a great appeal to mineworkers and to the left.

The framework is Marxist. Scargill's period in the Young Communist League was one in which education, especially of the young, was taken seriously by the Communist Party: he attended education classes in London conducted by James Klugmann, long-time editor of *Marxism Today* and – an irony – Frank Chapple, then a member of the Electrical Trades Union's executive. The key text for the British CP is *The British Road to Socialism*, whose first edition – still current during Scargill's period in the YCL – was approved by Stalin. It is a document of great ambiguity which carefully hedges its bets as to whether parliamentary democracy should continue after the triumph of socialism in Britain: the Leninist texts like *The State and Revolution* were unequivocally hostile to such a possibility.

Scargill joined the YCL in 1955, and was elected to its national committee in 1956. It was a period of upheaval in the Communist movement: Krushchev's 'secret speech' exposing the errors of Stalinism had been leaked to largely disbelieving western CPs the year previously: in 1956, the Soviet intervention in Hungary provoked a rash of resignations (Les Cannon and Frank Chapple, future general secretaries of the ETU, among them); the intellectual ferment it stimulated saw the founding of the journal which became the *New Left Review*, and assisted the growth of the tiny shoots of British Trotskyism. The CPGB, never a mass party, was already declining by the mid-1950s from its post-war membership peak of around 100,000. These events accelerated that decline.

They passed Scargill by. Like most industrial militants, he did not join the CP to take a position on international alignments, but to find intellectual and political support for the war of position with the employer. Scargill visited the Soviet Union in 1957, and Hungary in 1959, in Communist delegations: he left the YCL in 1962 or 63, either resigning or being expelled: he has at different times criticised the Soviet Union for being repressive, and the Krushchev regime for attempting to expunge Stalin's memory.

He has maintained since the mid-1960s, a pure 'revolutionary' line on the issue of class struggle, *the* defining tenet of a Communist. Marx's concept was that the development of capitalism had produced antagonistic classes, the working class and the bourgeoisie or middle class, whose economic struggle would dominate the political scene and end in the victory of the working class and the creation of a classless society once communism had been established. It was Lenin's genius which took the concept as the basic task of a communist party, making it the handmaiden to history. The British party devoutly believed in this: its main theorists, R. Palme Dutt and Klugmann (especially the former), were careful to keep close to the Soviet line in all matters of sustance. It is a belief which Scargill has retained, ironically while many Communist parties, including the British, are quietly or noisily disposing of it.

The CPGB reached the apogee of its influence on the working class within the NUM and its predecessor, the Mineworkers Federation of Great Britain. This was especially the case in South Wales and Scotland, though in the 1950s – when Scargill was first growing to maturity – in Yorkshire also. It did not 'bring' either militancy or theoretical perspective to the miners: these already existed, most conspicuously in the South Wales Reform Committee – 'the most developed flowering of native proletarian thought in the British Labour movement'[1] – which produced *The Miners' Next Step*, arguing for workers' control of the pits. But it did represent a centre of organisation and, for a few, of training, education and selection for leadership which no other organisation could consistently rival. Arthur Horner and Will Paynter were the outstanding products of the communist tradition, both from South Wales; Dai Francis continued the tradition: from Scotland came the stern Moffat family (one was still on the national executive for the strike), Lawrence Daly, Bill McClean, presently Mick McGahey and George Bolton; from Yorkshire Peter Tait, Sammy Taylor, Jock Kane; from Derbyshire, Bert Wynn; from Kent, Jack Dunn, presently Jack Collins. Their style was intense, treating political and trade union matters with a high seriousness which most workers, miners or other, found daunting but which a few took to with great eagerness. They were an elite and saw themselves to be so. 'We had an opinion in those days that the Communist Party was the vanguard of the workers. You had to be honest, sober, industrious, good citizen – those were the qualities we were looking for and of course everybody doesn't come into that.'[2] And again: 'We accepted the fact that we were now professional revolutionaries, in the same way that Stalin was, and all the old Bolshevist leaders . . . the psychology that developed in those valleys among the leaders, *not the rank and file* [my italics], was that we were to be forever unemployed and therefore we have to be professional revolutionaries. That only by revolution could we solve the unemployed problem.'[3]

That sense of being men apart, almost of destiny, was transferred from the Communist Party to the union and it became accepted by many within the trade union movement, within political circles and more widely. A little before the 1984–85 strike, Vic Allen wrote that 'during the last decade the National Union of Mineworkers has established itself as the most politically potent union in Britain. . . . The explanation lies partly in the actual industrial power miners wield but also in the determination with which they collectively use their industrial strength and in the solidarity which their actions evoke from other groups of workers.'[4]

Allen, the chronicler of, and participant in, the development of the contemporary NUM left, dates the beginning of the present strength of the left grouping to the crucial meeting of representatives of Derbyshire, Kent, Scotland, South Wales and Yorkshire at the County Hotel in Sheffield on Saturday 5 August 1967. Their purpose was to select a candidate to succeed Will Paynter as general secretary of the union when he retired the following December. Before that period, attempts to get a left front going had been stymied by the distrust of Communists for the non-Communist left. Both Abe and Alex Moffat in Scotland had preferred to stand aloof from such a venture. The Communists in that period accounted for 6 votes in an NEC of 26, while the total left vote was rarely more than 8. The left group did collaborate, in 1964, to produce a pamphlet called *A Plan for the Miners*, which attacked the accelerating pit closure programme and called for better wages and working conditions. Produced by the Derbyshire area, it had the strong backing of Bert Wynn, then Derbyshire area secretary, and Bill Whitehead, the South Wales president – but it was easily enough kicked out of serious discussion by the right-wing leadership of the union.

However the new grouping, crossing the sectarian division between Communist and socialist, drawing on leading officials from a number of areas, benefitting from a rising tide of protest against closures and rising expectations for pay and conditions which a Labour government had helped to encourage, was a formidable one. At the same time, the growing confidence of the left in Yorkshire was signalled by the inauguration of a regular series of meetings open to all miners under the rubric of the Barnsley Miners' Forum, meeting monthly on Friday evenings. Scargill was one of its founders, and its secretary. The rather enclosed politics of the NUM left, all but monopolised by the Communist Party, had come out.

This was to prove a momentous political event. The left succeeded in having Daly elected (he was to disappoint them later), and in June 1971 Mick McGahey lost to Joe Gormley for the post of president by the relatively narrow margin of 117,663 to 92,883 in a 67 per cent poll. (Allen says that McGahey behaved with ultra propriety in not canvassing, while Gormley did not[5] – a point partially confirmed by Gormley, who says in his autobiography[6] that he saw the rules as being 'pretty flexible'.) The success of the 1972 and 1974 strikes gave the left a tremendous boost. While it is quite wrong to say, as Allen does, that Gormley was simply an actor for whom 'the stage was set . . . he simply walked on it and obediently said his lines,'[7] still it is true that McGahey, the vice president, better expressed the aggressive, self-confident mood of the miners in those days. And from 'nowhere', as far as the general public was concerned, came Arthur Scargill, whose organisation of the Saltley Gate picket on 10 February 1972 propelled him into national fame – fame which he both encouraged and built upon. He told one of the authors, then covering the event for *The Guardian*, that the support of the miners' pickets by the Birmingham engineering workers had meant that 'everything I have always believed in and idolised crystallised'.

Scargill believed in the class struggle. The sight of the engineering workers' union banners coming over the hill to the depot – which he describes in interviews in vividly cinematic terms – was a passage in the class war, the arrival of reinforcements to win a victory that, though not of huge importance industrially, was of enormous symbolic weight. Class struggle, the root belief of the Communist leaders of the miners, the theory which they had confirmed from their practice of struggle against the private mine owners, had been preserved for use against a nationalised industry and against a government which refused to concede the miners' demands. Class struggle, downplayed by both Horner and Paynter because they believed nationalisation represented a fundamental shift which had to be supported (and because they were muzzled by the right majority on their executives) came into the NUM leadership, undiluted, with the assumption of Scargill to the presidency in April 1982.

No one could doubt it was coming. By 1982 the consciousness of who Scargill was and what he stood for had travelled so far beyond the alarmed circles of NCB management and the increasingly confident gatherings of the NUM left, as to embrace most of the country. It has always been Scargill's strength that he made public his beliefs that, however much he might manoeuvre and scheme for tactical advantage within the union, he was never to be found to be defensive on political grounds. Though he has never displayed the grasp of Marxist theory shown by Daly or McGahey, he has been incomparably better at putting it, in uncompromising form, across.

His first major rehearsal of this was at the intellectual altar of British Marxism, *New Left Review*. *NLR* has had, especially in recent years, a practice of remaining aloof from much of what constitutes left politics in the UK. It delivers a contemptuous essay from time to time on the hopeless philistinism, or reformism, or mediocrity, of the labour movement, then returns gratefully to its cultivation of European and other foreign Marxist scholars. But after the 1972 and 1974 strikes and his election to the Yorkshire presidency, Scargill appeared to be something new and radical enough to treat seriously: the magazine introduced an interview with him in June 1975 with the comment that 'Scargill's views represent an intransigent pursuit of proletarian class interests that has not been seen for many decades.'

The interview has the element which is usually present in a Scargill appearance, in whatever form, in the media: enormous self-projection.

'Later in this interview,' he says at an early stage, 'I will tell you of the most amazing picketing that ever took place [Saltley] during the 1972 strike, which was handled very similarly to a military operation. I believe in a class war you have to fight with the tools at your disposal. . . . You see, we took the view that we were in a class war, not playing cricket on the village green *like they did in 1926* [my italics]. We were out to defeat Heath and Heath's policies because we were fighting a government. . . . We had to declare *war* [*NLR*'s italics] on them and the only way you could declare war was to attack the vulnerable points. . . . We were fighting a class war and you don't fight a class war with sticks and bladders. You fight a war with weapons that are going to win it.'

As a class warrior, Scargill was and is unimpressed by the loyalty to labour governments which trade union leaderships try to show. 'The one thing that annoys me,' he said, 'is that we've got one set of standards when we've got a Tory government and a completely different set of standards when we've got a Labour government.' Behind Scargill's words was the memory – present in most miners who were in the industry in the 1960s – of the tremendous run-down in pits and manpower under the chairmanship of Lord Robens and the governments of Harold Wilson: as Robens makes clear in his memoirs on his chairmanship, the 1964–70 period was one where both the prime minister and whoever occupied the Ministry of Fuel and Power (it had many occupants) were convinced of the cost advantage of nuclear power, and of oil. Robens writes: 'Between 1965/66 and 1968/69 we closed no fewer than 204 collieries. This rate of a pit closure almost every week for four years was achieved under a Labour Government. In fact under Labour, perhaps because of Harold Wilson's enthusiasm for technological change, we shut pits at a faster rate than when the Conservatives were in office.'[8] This period left a deep resentment from miners who did not in the least share Scargill's ideological opposition to right-wing labour.

In this, as in all of his union work, the NUM president shows a consistent ability to marry his own revolutionary political views with those of a militant wage bargainer, out to get the best for his members. Where Horner and Paynter had actually been *inhibited* by their politics – as Communists, they believed so much in the public ownership of the pits that they were prepared to moderate actions to buttress nationalisation – Scargill simply married wage militancy to a kind of syndicalism. 'What we should really do,' he said to the *Review* interviewers, 'is go in harder into the attack because a Labour government should never, ever find itself in a position of conflict with the trade unions . . . if it does then it has nothing in common with socialism and nothing in common with working-class principles. . . . I'm not prepared to pay for the crisis of capitalism at the expense of the people I represent.'

He was frank about the need to be a good reformist as a prelude to being a good revolutionary, recognising the inhibitions of his predecessors: 'The very fact of being able to achieve all that we have won with Marxist, progressive, left-wing leadership strengthens our movement. If you've got a revolutionary leadership that can't even win wage increases but can go on platforms all over Britain on the Irish question and a thousand and one other things, the workers won't have any faith in that leadership. That's been one of the problems in the past in this union . . . progressive leaders who do not know how to fight properly for their members.'

Towards the end of the interview, Scargill was invited to expand further on his view of society, and of the achievement of socialist power. It was not a precise vision, but in so far as it can be interpreted it was, once again, a revolutionary one. Asked how he would destroy the power of the capitalist class, Scargill replied that he would reform the Labour Party as far as possible by ending the proscriptions which keep out Communists; to get the party to accept conference decisions determined by the union bloc vote: 'the bloc vote could become ours if we [presumably the left] won the leadership in the unions.' Once having won the unions, then the Labour Party under new management could 'take us so far along the road to a socialist Britain, and then the social democratic party will have completely served its purpose. We would then need a totally new socialist party embracing the whole of the left that could complete the job of taking Britain into a new socialist era.'

Never again would Scargill so unambiguously expound his views, but also he would never contradict them: what he told his respectful interlocutors was for real. In an interview in *Marxism Today* in April 1981, for instance, he repeats his call for the removal of the proscriptions on Communists, for the change in the Labour Party to a fully socialist party sustained by left trade unions, repeats too his antipathy to any attempts, through wages policy, to help solve capitalism's crisis. He says of workers' control that 'it's the apologists' alternative to socialism' and talks instead of using collective bargaining – or trade union strength – to force through everything that is desired, from a wage increase to policy decisions on 'unemployment, investment, planning and expansion in industry'. Here, the conception is that mass pressure secures socialism through managements' fear of disruption: 'The only way we can achieve socialism in the first instance is by involving in mass struggle workers for an alternative economic policy now, but one that does not include or involve workers' control, seats on the board of management or worker participation. I am for the trade union movement itself exercising power, exercising authority and compelling management, be it private or nationalised, to do certain things in terms of investment, planning, extension and development in the same way that we've been able to do on wages and conditions for many years. The very fact that miners within 36 hours of 40,000 of them coming out on strike [in February 1981, over a pit closure programme], were able to change a government's course as far as pit closures were concerned is a clear demonstration that it can be done.' (Earlier in the same interview though, Scargill had said, acutely, that, 'The Government sidestepped the issue because they realised they could not win.')

Scargill's political views were a matter of public record and debate for years before he assumed the national presidency, and they did not change before the strike and have not changed because of it. He did not, on assuming the national presidency, do what many on the left have done, that is, keep his Marxism separate from his union practice. On the contrary, he used his expressed convictions as the framework for all his actions, and as the spur for his decisions. Nearly everyone assumed he would mellow. Gormley did so, writing in his autobiography that 'I had to learn my lessons as I went along. Arthur will also have to learn his lessons as he goes along. If he takes these lessons to heart, I see no reason why he should not make an excellent President.'[9]

Len Murray, the TUC general secretary (to September 1984) did grasp that Scargill was different, in part because he was snubbed so often in trying to get to know him as he rose to prominence. He saw from an early stage that one of Scargill's dominant aims when he took control would be, in the first instance, to recreate his union in the image of a new model army, stripped for action, and that this aim would co-exist, and be of a piece with, other objectives. 'I was critical of Scargill for having too many objectives: more than he could handle. He was seeking to put himself at the head of the TUC as the determiner of industrial policy, as the proponent of political change, he had the objective of recreating the NUM, indeed of imposing his will on the NUM; and once MacGregor was appointed, he wanted to beat him into the ground.'

In the immediate run-up to his election, Scargill published, in September 1981, a pamphlet – essentially his manifesto – called *Miners in the Eighties*. In it, he argued for the supremacy of conference decisions – and contrasted the 'democratic' nature of conference with the 'undemocratic' nature of the national executive. There is ample justification for the claim: the rules, first adopted in 1944, were a compromise between centralisation and area autonomy, which built on the latter principle by giving all areas, no matter how small, at least one seat on the national executive and limiting all areas, no matter how big, to at most three. This meant, as Scargill said in his pamphlet, that 'four areas, with a little over 4,000 members, can outvote Yorkshire who have 69,000 members but are restricted to three representatives.' Conference, by contrast, was more representative in the purely numerical sense: each area could send two delegates per 5,000 members (or part thereof) and one more for each additional 2,500 members. There, the Yorkshire vote – often what Scargill meant when he talked of increased democracy in the union – could command, in the late 1970s and early 1980s, around one-third of the votes.

The conference was a true miners' soviet, with decision-making devolved on men who had become, as the left rose to power in the union, almost uniformly radicalised. It underpinned Scargill throughout the strike, helped keep the executive in line, and even in defeat remained largely faithful to him.

It was at his first conference as president that Scargill, in a speech which future events were to make a key political text of the time, fused together his political and industrial strategies. He began by interpreting his huge presidential majority – 70.3 per cent of all votes cast – as 'an emphatic vote in favour of the policies I pursued during the election campaign'. The first priority for the union would be 'to protect the coal industry from the ravages of the market mechanism. . . . If we do not save our pits from closure, then all our struggles become meaningless. . . . We shall never again relive the experiences of the 1960s and it would be suicidal of the government or the board to think otherwise . . . I hope that this conference will endorse my call to make opposition to pit closures its central task.'

True to his comment in *New Left Review* that revolutionaries have to pay attention to wage bargaining, a central section of the speech laid out an impressive list of improvements in pay and conditions – including the wholly justified demand that 'miners must be amongst the highest paid in society. What the system pays doctors, politicians and senior managerial staff should also be paid to miners.'

But the most important part of the speech was its interpretation of how the union's democracy works. It is no simple matter in the NUM: the country's most federal union, made up of areas which are themselves independent unions, with a policy-making conference, a national executive, two co-equal national officers, and the requirement to hold a national ballot vote before strike action, the union has many focuses of power: add to these the network of consultative and advisory committees in which the NUM meets the board and the two other mining unions – the National Association of Colliery Overmen Deputies and Shotfirers and the British Association of Colliery Management – and it is clear that the president's job should be one of some delicacy. Scargill cut through all such considerations: national conference was the supreme body, its decisions 'binding on me, on the National Executive Committee and on the union a a whole'.

This led to the crux of the argument: 'Members have every right to demand total commitment from me as President and to insist that I prosecute resolutions passed at Conference. Loyalty, however, works both ways. I also have every right to demand total support from the members of this union. Leadership is only as strong as the backing it receives from the rank and file – and if, at the end of the day, the union's claims cannot be met through negotiation, we have every right to demand your backing in an individual ballot. Given that support all the demands of the union can become a reality.' This drive to centralise the union was to be one of the president's largest mistakes – though it was an aim shared, with some reservations, by other left-wingers on the executive.

The Inverness conference paved the way for the emergence of a new model army with one leader bent on two goals which were wholly intertwined: the rapid and continuous improvement of miners' wages, conditions and status through the most militant free collective bargaining; and the achievement of a fully socialist society in which all substantial economic activity was in state ownership through the exercise of working-class power with the miners at its head.

Of great importance is the fact that these aims are *intertwined*, and for practical purposes could not be separated. This was both a strength and a weakness for Scargill during the strike: his opponents, the NCB and the government, could and did make much of the strike's revolutionary dimension: for his part, Scargill could and did play down the revolutionary side to the strike in most public statements, while using that dimension in some forums to claim leadership of the working-class resistance to Thatcherism. It was the main contributor to the confusion in the Coal Board: those executives who pushed for a negotiated settlement, as Ned Smith, the NCB's director-general of industrial relations, picked up on the wage bargaining element in Scargill's position. Ian MacGregor and his advisers, with many in the government, increasingly saw only the revolutionary dimension.

Vic Allen, as close to Scargill politically as anyone, provides the neatest summary of him: 'He is highly committed to the cause of his members, which he defines in political terms and believes can only be fulfilled through socialism.'[10] The concept of the NUM as at once wholly separate from, and at the head of, organised workers is fundamental to Scargill's thinking. In the *NLR* interview and in other places, Scargill rounds on his colleagues elsewhere in the labour movement for making deals with labour on wage restraint, counterposing to that the unfettered bargaining by unions maximising their industrial strength. He was, before the 1984–5 strike, the best placed to hold such a position: the miners' leverage on the economy, coupled with their solidarity, gave them a positional power unrivalled by any other. The NUM could get what it wanted, and thus any 'social contract' was merely a hindrance to sectional gains, even where such a 'hindrance' was part of a policy of redistribution. Scargill has always mocked such social-democratic claims, insisting that not until the establishment of socialism can any redistributive policy be on the agenda. It is a shrewd conflation of sectional self-interest with a certain kind of fundamentalist Marxism: most miners could appreciate the first part of the formula and thus appear to be swallowing it all.[11]

In the two years as president before the strike, Scargill acted in a way wholly consistent with his previous statements and with his 1982 conference speech. Within the union executive, he was able to turn a narrow right-wing majority into a solid left majority through the replacement of Gormley supporters by his own, or, more importantly, by the incorporation of the old right into the left camp for most practical purposes. In the first category, Scargill secured, by the election in the period between his assumption of the presidency and the strike, of Billy Etherington to the secretaryship of the Durham Mechanics, of Jim Colgan to the secretaryship of the Midlands area, of Billy Stobbs as the delegate from Durham, and (during the strike itself) the election of Bob McSporran to the secretaryship of the Power Group, supporters who were to turn out to be more Scargillite than the 'old' left. Importantly, none were Communists: indeed, all were Labour Party men who had been part of the party's radicalisation in the 1970s, a movement in which Scargill had played a leading part.

But the collapse of the old right was as vital: the men involved were Sid Vincent, secretary of Lancashire, Ray Chadburn, president of Nottinghamshire, Tommy Callan, secretary of Durham, and Denis Murphy, president of Northumberland. Sid Vincent, the most extrovert of the executive, declared in his customary mixture of shrewdness and naivety from the floor of the 1982 conference that 'If you can't beat them, join them.' The others were less flamboyant but also joined.

'Joining them' meant that the old tradition of a divided executive, where most issues which involved consideration of industrial action were settled on a closely tied vote, was replaced by one which the new president strived to make monolithic. Time and again, in announcing decisions to the press in the customary post-executive briefing, Scargill would declare a decision 'unanimous' (often adding: 'and for the benefit of the *Sun*, that means everybody'). The means of achieving unanimity was often to hold a vote on a motion which resulted in a left majority, then to put back to the executive a substantive motion which would often get the agreement of all since the right knew they had lost the argument. Even where opinions remained divided, the opposing minority were often small, since the core right group was small: Trevor Bell, secretary of the Colliery Officials and Staffs Area, Jack Jones, secretary of Leicestershire, Ken Toon, secretary of South Derbyshire, Ted McKay, secretary of North Wales, Roy Ottey, secretary of the Power Group (until July 1984), and Harry Hanlon, secretary of the Cumberland area.

With the exception of COSA, all of these areas were tiny: Hanlon's 'area' went down, soon after the strike, to no more than 150 men doing development work in his area's remaining pit, Haig.

Why? Why did the right not retain a sense of cohesion and identity, and – once it became clear to most on the executive that the strike could not be won, as it did by the end of 1984 – force a settlement? First, the right was not the automatic voting fodder for Gormley as the left claimed it to be: indeed, Gormley could often fail to deliver the vote on the executive to a policy which he had indicated to the board he would accept – thus fuelling resentment from many of the managers towards Derek (now Lord) Ezra who developed a close alliance with Gormley after 1974. In 1976 Gormley only narrowly convinced the national executive to recommend the miners to vote to accept stage two of the social contract, bringing them a 4.5 per cent rise, or only £3. In 1979, soon after the election of the first Thatcher government, Gormley – with a conference resolution calling for a faceworkers' wage of £140 at his back – managed a 20 per cent pay offer which brought faceworkers to just over £100: his executive unanimously voted it down, much to his disgust. 'You could say that the moderates were only obeying that conference decision.' But the truth went deeper than that. They were fed up with years and years of the 'antis' voting against everything. They had had enough of all the years of mudslinging they had had to endure, and the accusations of being too soft. So now they just said, 'Bugger it! We're sick and tired of these people riding on our backs. We'll join them for once, and recommend non-acceptance, and see what happens.' What happened was a narrow vote in favour of the offer, by 113,160 to 107,656. Gormley comments: 'A turn-about like that can be demoralising for the union. The executive should try to lead, but seek to do it by reading its members' feelings correctly. It can't afford to have that sort of rebuff too often, because then it becomes a delegation of leadership to the members, and that's not what the NEC is elected to do.'[12]

Many moderates did not draw the same lesson. Gormley believes that, as it became clearer that a split right wing offering three weak candidates – Bell, Chadburn and Bernard Donaghy, then president of Lancashire – would be no match for the Scargill juggernaut, they played 'chicken' and voted with the left to avoid being continually outflanked. In the last instance, in December 1981, only 7 voted to accept a wages offer of between 9.5 and 10.5 per cent: the left proposed a special conference which recommended strike action in a ballot vote: that vote was lost by 55 per cent to 45 per cent. (Gormley wrote an article in the *Daily Express* before the ballot, effectively recommending a vote against strike action: he survived the subsequent censure motion by 13 votes to 12. The moderate vote at least – just – supported its leader.)

Second, only the hard core were ideologically to the right. Bell had been close to Gormley as head of the union's industrial relations department and shared his views. Toon and Jones were older men, from the Midlands tradition of right-wing Labourism, who had watched the leftwards drift in both their union and their party with some horror. But the others were facing growing pressures from the layer just below their own: that all-important (especially in the NUM) group of activists and local officials who sit on the area executives and run the branches. In the north-east, Lancashire and even in Nottinghamshire, left-wingers were taking these jobs, most of whom were keen followers of Scargill. Vincent, Callan, Murphy and Chadburn all felt this in the late 1970s and early 1980s, and it helped reform their political positions – which were never dogmatically held in the first place.

The most powerful persuader, however, was the situation in the industry. As the country dived into recession, demand for coal stagnated – a fact disguised for some time by stockpiling of coal, but well known to miners' leaders. The government nagged away at Ezra to get his costs down and to shut uneconomic pits: he stalled for as long as possible then, faced with legislation decreeing that the industry break even, he produced in February 1981 a list of 23 pits that had to close forthwith. The union prepared itself for action and the board and government backed away, but it was clear that the party should have been over. Sir Norman Siddall, Ezra's long-time deputy, took over a little after Scargill did and shut 20 pits, surviving two more failed ballot votes in doing so. Yet, though it appeared in these ballots – in both cases industrial action was rejected by 61 to 39 per cent – that the members were leery of a fight, Scargill managed to hold the moral ascendancy over his executive colleagues by pursuing a high-profile and single-minded campaign on the issue of pit closures. He managed to convince the majority that the board, even before Ian MacGregor became NCB chairman on 1 September 1983, was set on slashing back capacity and jobs. The main reason he did so was because he was (broadly) right.

His main tactic was to insist on the existence of a secret 'hit list' of pits which would be closed. On 24 June 1982 he went to his first formal meeting with Siddall to demand the list: on being refused it, he and most of the executive (Ottey was the exception) walked out. On 2 November, the day he announced that the first ballot under his presidency had come out decisively against a strike, he brandished a 'secret document sent by an NCB mole' which showed that 75 pits were on the hit list (the NCB responded by calling the list a statistical exercise). Many of his colleagues grew sick of the hit list ploy, believing it set up an Aunt Sally which the board could easily knock down. But real pits *were* shutting: real miners *were* leaving the industry, taking the relatively generous terms offered on compulsory redundancies. Siddall was succeeding, in his ponderous, measured, painstaking way, in trimming the industry. Most government ministers thought him first class, especially after Ezra; Scargill and the left were on their mettle to find a *casus belli*.

MacGregor may not have been a necessary condition for the strike, but he was certainly of assistance. He was an outsider not just to the coal industry but to post-war British culture. His period at the British Steel Corporation could be plausibly, if wrongly, represented as one of declaring large-scale manpower cuts (most of that had been effected under the very un-butcher-like Sir Charles Villiers). His customary courtesy to the NUM leaders veiled a belief that the relationship between the board and the unions was incestuous and inhibiting. Bit by bit, especially through management changes, he tried to force his reluctant managers to move away from the consensual stasis in which he believed they were locked. And worst of all, he emphasised two things which most board chairmen had tended to play down: the need to compete in a market for energy which was by then a buyers' one; and the need to lessen dependence on the government. He allied himself, not with the industry, but with the taxpayer. Like the prime minister, with whom he enjoyed a good and trusting relationship, he would as much as say, 'This place is costing you people a lot of money: somebody should do something about it.'

MacGregor's position left the moderates nowhere to go. The board had become used, through the years, to distinguishing between the various shades of the left: it was meat and drink to their industrial relations cadres, many of whom had come up through left politics themselves. They had encouraged the right against the left, on occasion the reverse: chairmen and area directors accepted as part of their job that their area NUM leaders had to be dined and especially wined, cajoled and flattered and at times threatened, offered this in return for that, in order to get changes through. Siddall, when deputy chairman, used to go to areas where a pit was coming up for closure and spend time with the area leaders; in Scotland, he would sit up much of the night drinking whisky with Mick McGahey, to ease the thing through. MacGregor wanted none of that.

Unlike any of the previous chairmen, he had an overriding concept of the world energy picture, into which he fitted the board. Accustomed to operating on a world scale, with a deep fascination for the workings of the market across continents, he could see with great clarity the relative position of the NCB – producing, inefficiently, high-priced coal in a crowded marketplace with an impatient government to answer to. If the miners' leaders would not see the realities of life, too bad: he tended to see them all as undifferentiated socialists, political extremists who did not represent their members. Privately, he believed unions were an abomination, and while he could not and did not betray that in public, neither could he make the personal gestures which had been considered essential for the chairman of the board to make to keep the wheels greased and turning. The right of the NUM executive always needed some counterweight to the left arguments provided by the board or by the government – loyalty to nationalisation, loyalty to a Labour government, the need to keep costs down to avoid redundancies, even the personality of the chairman himself. But none of this was forthcoming: MacGregor's American accent aroused the hostility of the men, and his off-the-cuff comments – as when he told miners in Yorkshire that women miners in the US could work harder than they could – became infamous. Though area and industrial relations managers tried to provide the emollience, the coldness at the top froze out any 'NCB' party on the NUM executive.

MacGregor was, of course, only part of the problem for the right: the second was the prime minister herself. Tommy Callan, the former secretary of the Durham area, commented as he retired in October 1985, after 50 years in the pits and in the union, 'I used to be a moderate: but with Thatcher's hard regime, I have been pushed to the left. I think that's true of a great number of people in our movement.' Actually, people in the labour movement were pushed both to the left and right by Thatcher's 'hard regime': the Labour Party leadership, and many activists, moved quite rapidly to the right after, and in part because of, the miners' strike. But in the NUM, the dynamism and conviction politics of the president pointed the activists and officials in one direction only – for a time.

The final reason is the least noble, but perhaps the most powerful. The 'moderates' just gave up. In October 1983, the executive voted unanimously to impose an overtime ban in protest against the board's pay offer of 5.2 per cent and against its plans to close 70 pits. Roy Ottey writes of this: 'I have to accept the collective responsibility for decisions which were made. I cannot explain the failure of many of us to argue more vociferously against confrontation and in favour of consultation and negotiation. It is true that there was a school of thought, often voiced outside Executive meetings, which went along the lines of "Let Arthur dig the hole big enough and he'll fall in." I suppose we had grown slightly too complacent because we knew about the individual ballot vote contained in rule 43 . . . also there had been the three recent ballot votes which had rejected strike action over pay or pit closures.'[13] This cry was used again and again during the strike – at the end it was not just the moderates who were crying it.

The net result of all of these rationales and calculations was that Scargill, by the time he went into the strike, had an executive which was no longer at odds with the will of conference: he had achieved what he laid out in his inaugural presidential speech. The public policy of the union was his policy. At leadership and activist level, the union was his.

The triumph of politics could not, though, have been complete without a concomitant triumph of the will. Unlike McGahey of his contemporaries on the executive, or Paynter and Horner of the previous generation, Arthur Scargill impresses himself on his colleagues and others less by power of argument – though he is a formidable maker of a case, and had ambitions to be a lawyer – than by force of personality. It is inevitably more difficult to define than the ideological make-up of the man: but it is no less important.

He is personally the least relaxing of men. Where, of the three rational leaders, McGahey would uncoil his intellect and wit over a chain of strong cigarettes and whiskies far into the night, and Heathfield escaped to his family and the golf course when he could, Scargill worked tremendously hard by any standards – and by union leader standards, where work is generally liberally interspersed with hard socialising and drinking, he is a phenomenon. He had cut smoking dead after seeing a cancer warning in a cinema, and he confined drink to a 'social' half pint. He could be tremendously amiable and charming: but the very power of his charm made it difficult to accept as other than a carefully produced front. He did not offer, socially or publicly, any of the usual weaknesses or habits or dependencies which allow others to feel comfortable, or a little superior. It was not just that he did not let people close to him: it is that his personality is one which seeks to establish a relationship with all of his colleagues and others in his public life which is objective, in the sense that it is based upon the other's political or professional position, and not related to the potential of friendliness. He demands and receives either adulation or detestation: more mundane responses appear rarely sought. His public effect is beyond doubt. Most of those who later turned against him had voted for him as president. As David Prendergast, the Notts area financial officer says, 'I thought he had it all.' During his election campaign, an ex-policeman turned miner told one of us the same thing. This spell-binding quality, which some at least felt ashamed of having fallen under afterwards, helped give his mass meetings the name of 'Nuremberg Rallies', not because Scargill was seen as a Nazi figure (though some among his enemies did come so to see him) but because of the focus upon the one personality, the compelling power of the rhetoric.

Vic Allen writes of him that 'he has some qualities writ large. He is in some ways egocentric but then it is a condition of leadership that he should be. *He is an intensely shy person, and tends to project himself as a form of protection* [my italics]. . . . [he] is ambitious but not in the conceited sense. It is unlikely that he will be lured from his position by 30 pieces of silver. His living standard has barely altered since I first met him. He now runs a Jaguar but he has always liked big cars. He lives in the same bungalow, which he and his family periodically vacate due to mining subsidence. . . . He is excessively hard working and goes to great lengths to remain in contact with his members. His work schedule would destroy most people.'[14]

The suggestion of shyness would raise a horse laugh from most: Arthur Scargill *shy*? But it is an intriguing and possibly a shrewd observation: in many ways, most of all perhaps in his forcefulness, Scargill does betray both a shyness and a deeply driven quality. His manner of coping with these qualities has been to impose on others his own sense of urgency of the task that needs to be done.

His egocentricity is, however – with respect to Allen – more than just the normal self-assurance that a public figure needs. Indeed, if Allen is right, it could be the compensation for its *lack*. He habitually refers to himself in the third person, and tells stories largely about himself: a fine, if flattering, portrait of him in the *Observer* magazine on 17 May 1979 related him impressing businessmen at a train lunch table with such sallies as 'If I have more than one lager someone will say: "Look, there's Arthur Scargill getting drunk" ' – betraying a tremendously sensitive, even anxious, regard for his public image (what is the 'Arthur Scargill' that others are looking at *supposed* to do?).

He is deeply engaged with the media – hostile usually, in a hugely overblown way ('filth', 'garbage', 'vermin' are so commonplace as to be now genuinely unremarkable to the press corps whose presence he can still command). Much of this is, of course, a political objection and a great deal of it has objective validation: Scargill became, since assuming the NUM national presidency and especially during the strike, the object of press hostility, especially from the right-wing tabloids, which rarely recognised reasonable boundaries between comment and slander, and even those papers which did recognise such boundaries often loaded the scales of the comment heavily against him.

But it went further than that. Scargill entered into a symbiosis with the media – yet it was one which, for all that he believed himself the dominant partner, ultimately worked more to the media's advantage than to his. There is no doubt that his mastery of the TV medium helped secure him his 70 per cent presidential vote, focussed attention on his propaganda rather than that of the Coal Board at crucial moments, and allowed him to 'win' the media war with MacGregor. No doubt, too, that his public relations sense, his feel for what the papers and the networks wanted, was usually good: his unveiling of the leaked 'hit-list' of 75 pits from a so-called NCB 'mole' was a publicity coup, albeit a bogus one.

During the strike, however, his hectoring style to the press, his disinclination to devolve any effective press relations to anyone other than himself, and in the end his defensiveness and obfuscation alienated most of the middle ground. A well meaning delegation of industrial correspondents who saw Heathfield in the second month of the strike to propose a more 'professional' press set-up (essentially to provide quotes and instant reaction to the events of the day) drew a furious reaction from Scargill when he heard of it. A mild criticism of the press relations in *The Guardian* after the strike drew an equally inflamed response.

He saw the press as undifferentiated hostility. He had little conception of or sympathy for pluralistic opinion in those papers which practised it. His own 'remedy' for the press was nationalisation, without any explicit recognition of the dangers that might arise from such an outcome, not least for the left where the government of the day was Tory. He would privately differentiate between reports and reporters, praising some and condemning others on grounds any news editor would recognise. Publicly, none of that was even hinted at. The force of his dismissal of the press, his manifest desire to dictate its values and agenda, set up a tense relationship on both sides which inevitably fed through into coverage. Increasingly he became caricaturable as mad, a caricature which was grossly unfair to a man whose self-control was so powerful, but one whose roots lay in the ultra-defensive way in which the NUM president dealt with press enquiries.

More damaging than the inability to form an at least apparently easy relationship with the press was his lack of a relationship with other union leaders. David Basnett, the TUC's elder statesman during the strike, and general secretary of the General, Municipal and Boilermakers' Union (to end-1985), says of Scargill, 'I don't know anyone that had a relationship with him . . . he didn't see any need to strike up a relationship with the TUC.' Len Murray says, 'There was a distance between me, and the TUC, and Scargill from the beginning of his appearance on the national scene. I was invited to the Yorkshire miners' gala in 1975. I saw that as an opportunity to establish a relationship with Scargill during the course of the visit – but he very politely but very coldly pushed me right away. I saw it as an opportunity lost.'

Both Basnett and Murray see in Scargill's coldness to them personally a political meaning: it is here, in the mix of personal and ideological purposes, where Scargill was most formidable. His own sensitive, solitary, dogmatic, intense nature chimed in with something in the psychology of the mineworkers, and with the conspiratorial and sectarian politics of the far left. He drew upon all three strands – the personal, the industrial/mass psychological and the ideological – and fused them into the new political construct – Scargillism – which, like its companion construct, Thatcherism, was indivisible from the personality of its progenitor.

Basnett says of Scargill that had he struck up a relationship with a group on the TUC, 'what he did would have been more difficult for him' – an acknowledgment that the ties of personal and industrial obligations, the political groupings and the alliances for advancement which are the stock-in-trade of most TUC leaders, enforce at least a minimum level of collective restraint on the actions of any one leader.

Murray goes further. He says: 'The miners were very conscious of their separate identity from the TUC (though Gormley had fewer illusions about that many others). The view was still held at that time [mid-1970s], to an extent anyway, that the miners were the aristocracy of the working class, the stormtroopers of the movement. That was a view that was highly convenient to both the miners and to the TUC, in terms of its effects on successive governments – and of course that was at the heart of Scargill's view. He saw the TUC as a provider merely of resources and support, on terms determined by the NUM, over which the TUC would have no control – and this view flowed from his view of the miners at the head of the working-class movement.'

Recalling Scargill's period on the general council – he was elected to it in September 1980, and left during his third year on the council after having been refused a seat on the major TUC committees on taking over the presidency – Murray says that, 'If he had been put on, say, the economic committee (which was considered) then it would have provoked a lot of criticism. People would have said: who the hell is Scargill? even – what the hell is the NUM? . . . He could have done what other people do: accept it. But there was no question about being "inter pares" with him: he always had to be "primus".

'I tried more than once to get in touch with him: I tried to get him to come over to talks; I indicated my willingness to go over – but I had no response, none whatever. At the very least I wanted to be able to weigh him up, and for him to weigh me up – but it was not possible. But this was part of his total attitude towards the TUC: he was a million miles away. It was a great pity. I think the 1926 strike was a major factor: he wanted the "crime" [of the TUC] expiated, and he wanted it expiated in the dispute. He saw the only thing the TUC could do would be to expiate its crime in 1926.'

Scargill did have close allies on the TUC left, some of whom – such as Ray Buckton of the train drivers and Jimmy Knapp of the railway workers – became relatively close to him for a time. He was, after all, a dependable ally, always willing to pledge support for struggles, always willing to attempt to deliver it. Rodney Bickerstaffe, the general secretary of the National Union of Public Employees, owed the NUM a considerable debt because of its support for his nurses and ancillary workers during the 1982 health service dispute. Jack Dromey, a national officer in the Transport and General Workers Union at the time of the dispute, spoke on many miners' platforms – with the memory at the back of his mind of Scargill's appearance on the picket lines at the Grunwick film processing laboratory when he was organising demonstrations in

1977. Scargill held markers on many of his colleagues.

The left-wing leaders did come together in a Co-ordinating Committee during the strike, and were able to deliver limited support. Most of their success came on the railways. Buckton and Knapp, at considerable cost to their unions' funds and with considerable strain on their authority with their members, stopped much of the coal traffic on rail – the Midlands was the major, and decisive, exception – and Jim Slater (Seamen) stopped much of the coal carrying in UK-owned ships (it came in in foreign ships, however). But they played no role in the strike itself: when they objected to the increased violence on the picket lines, Scargill simply said nothing or blamed the police.

One of the more practical questions thrown up by the NUM president's enigmatic personality was: How does he keep going? As Allen noted above, his work rate was phenomenal. During the strike, the light in his tenth-floor office in the NUM's headquarters would shine out across Sheffield into the small hours. At times he would sit through the night, writing speeches, preparing negotiating positions. He did show some signs of malaise towards the end of the strike, and was advised by his doctor to change his eating habits and took vitamin pills. But he never perceptibly let up.

Jim Colgan, the Midlands area secretary, told a rally in Birmingham in November that, 'About six weeks ago I was knackered and I said to Arthur Scargill: "How do you keep going?" He said three words to me and it lifted me up. He said, "Jim, we are right." We are right. And I have remembered these words ever since.'

Colgan had pointed to a central fact in his leader's approach. It is at once his most impressive attribute and his greatest source of weakness. It is his attachment to certain principles, an attachment which remains *wholly irrespective of changing circumstances*. It is well exemplified in an interview he gave the *Financial Times* relatively early in the strike. Asked if he was sure his members would continue to support him, he said there were two options on pit closures: 'One, you accept the plan and allow the pit to close. Alternatively you fight it. If you fight and you have lost, at least you fought it.' Later, asked how far he was prepared to compromise if the miners began returning to work, he replied: 'If I am the last person rejecting the closure plan, then that will be my position. That is the important thing. *If I'm right, I'll stick there* [my italics]. I don't know how some people live with themselves if they fudge or compromise on an agreement. You either take a stance on principle and if it is a principle then you don't back down – or you don't take a stance.'

The sense of rightness – defined in moral, or principled, rather than practical, terms – was of tremendous importance to Scargill's dominance of the executive and of the activists. As we saw, the executive was led by people on the left who had seen Scargill come to power, and by those from the left who came to power after he did, while the right had either gone over to his position or were determined to let him take the rap for any mistakes. Gradually, it became clear that the *only* people who could or would act against his leadership was the old left, and they were trapped by precisely the insistence on principle which Scargill made such a feature of his presidency. They too were men of principle. It was how they had distinguished themselves from the right, especially from Gormley, whom they were accustomed to castigating as an unprincipled man who sought to get his way – as over incentive payments – by all kinds of devious ploys. And even though such left leaders as Heathfield (when secretary of North Derbyshire) or McGahey (in his capacity as president of Scotland) quietly acquiesced in closures in their areas, they were transformed on the national stage, as men like Siddall knew. On the NEC, the clash between left and right, especially when left was in the minority as it usually was until Scargill's assumption of power, meant that no retreat from the principled decision, which meant *conference* decisions, was possible. The fact that their president was a man of such 'principle' that he could not find a compromise even when a compromise was the best he could get for his members was a source of great grief to the left-wingers in the latter half of the strike. But politically they were trapped.

And personally they were overwhelmed. Bill Keys, then general secretary of the print union Sogat, a left-winger but one soaked in the win-some, lose-some school of industrial relations, was something of a father confessor for left-wing NUM executive members who arranged to meet him to tell him of their fears and their horror of the way the strike was dragging to a defeat. As it reached its final stages, and the TUC liaison group of general secretaries (of whom Keys was one) produced a final offer from the NCB, Keys knew that a number of left-wingers on the executive were prepared to settle. He left them to go to a meeting in Congress House convinced that they would take the package. 'It was one of the most surprised moments of my life when Arthur comes down about an hour later and says, "They've rejected the document unanimously." I asked myself, How could this happen? How? How can a man have that power over his people? I just don't know.'

An element of his character of great importance to him was his identification of Arthur (A.J.) Cook as his role model. The close similarities between the two men were extraordinary, almost eerie. Cook, campaigning on a left ticket with the support of the Communist Party, was elected secretary of the MFGB in June 1924 – like Scargill, two years before a strike. Like Scargill, he had been in, and then left, the CP. Like Scargill, he could arouse his members to huge displays of enthusiasm and devotion. Arthur Horner writes in his autobiography that, 'He could electrify the meetings . . . he was expressing the thoughts of his audience

. . . he was the burning expression of their anger and the inquities they were suffering.'[15]

Like Scargill, he was more concerned with the political dimension of his role than the industrial one. Like Scargill, he attracted demonological status from politicians and the press, the more adulation because of that from his members. Like Scargill, he distrusted the TUC and refused to accept guidance from its leaders. Like Scargill, he regarded fidelity to a set political line as the overriding necessity, irrespective of the damage wreaked on the labour movement or even on his own union.

Cook, at the painful end of his short life (he died of cancer at the age of 47) appeared to dilute his radicalism, and to accept a role within the 'respectable' labour movement. The Communist Party, which had supported him, turned bitterly against him, calling him a social fascist. Here the similarity with Scargill (to date) ends; indeed, Scargill has since the end of the strike been criticised by the CP for ultra-leftism.

In a pointed tribute to Cook issued in 1986 by the Socialist Workers' Party, Paul Foot, the talented Trotskyist columnist for the *Daily Mirror*, talks of 'great working-class leaders who can lead their class in the heat of the struggle, impervious to the most awful onslaught from the other side. Of such leaders Arthur Cook was undoubtedly one.' It could be, and was meant to be, the kind of 'epitaph' Scargill would write for himself.[16]

Was he a serious revolutionary figure? It is our judgment that he was, though it is not one shared by, for example, Neil Kinnock, who grew to know him, and dislike him almost as much as Ian MacGregor did. He was no Lenin, either in ability or vision: and he always included in his strategy demands for economic improvements which were attractive to miners and which he wished to achieve. But he has no consistent interest in being *simply* a militant bargainer: as Allen has noted, he sees his members' interests, and his own future, as indivisible from the struggle for a socialism which is seen in the same terms as Communists have always prefigured a fully Communist state. It was an irony which he has shown no signs of appreciating that his efforts in the 1984–5 strike achieved neither reforms nor revolution; indeed, made both less likely than they had been before his appearance on the national scene.

Footnote: the 'Troika'

Vic Allen, defending Scargill in the *New Society* of 24 January 1985, says: 'There can be no other union which has such a wealth of intellect and experience among its officials. It is an insult to both Michael McGahey the vice president and to Peter Heathfield the general secretary to imply they are not equal participators in national decision-making. Peter Heathfield argues his case passionately, and in some ways in a less compromising manner than Scargill does. If Scargill steps down, and either Heathfield or McGahey took his place, the course of the strike would remain unchanged in so far as they could influence it.'

The point is a strong one: Heathfield and McGahey, who with Scargill made up what McGahey called the 'Troika', are both independently extraordinary men. Allen is certainly right about Heathfield, who in public and private can switch from an amiable charm into a denunciatory passion which can surpass that of his president. In speeches he made with Scargill and McGahey in the late autumn of 1984, seeking to raise the spirits of their men, he displayed a venom towards the NACODS leadership – which had just settled its dispute without going on strike – which was chilling to hear. Heathfield it was who was the link for most industrial correspondents, spending much of his evenings taking calls at his Chesterfield home, ensuring that some NUM perspective was present in those who cared to use it.

McGahey's role was of tremendous importance in the TUC. He sat on the general council, retaining the one NUM seat after Scargill gave up in disgust. He had the respect of most general council members, even of the right. He had the friendship of many on the left. He began to signal alarm when, by midsummer, the tactic seemed to consist almost wholly of mass picketing, and the débâcle of Orgreave greatly perturbed him and others on the old left. Thereafter, he managed to cajole Scargill into a more accommodating posture *vis-à-vis* the TUC, and was the lynchpin of securing the negotiations between the 'Troika' and Murray, Ray Buckton, then TUC President, and Basnett for the TUC on the eve of the September 1984 Congress, which produced the ultimately useless pledge of TUC support.

But Allen's claim that these two were 'equal participators in national decision making' simply is wrong. Heathfield tried his best to lead a 'normal' life, and when he was not travelling to talks or speaking in the evenings, he went home at six. As Scargill privately reminded reporters, he had scraped in as general secretary in January 1984 in the middle of an overtime vote with 3,516 votes over John Walsh, a little known North Yorkshire agent, and he came from a relatively small area. He was immediately the focus of hopes of the NCB, the government and the TUC centre right to tame Scargill, but he did not have the base either in the old or new left, or with the born-again moderates, ever to make that likely – indeed, these expectations, which were of course reported, made it the less likely that they would be met. Heathfield, whatever his reservations, threw his public lot in with Scargill and never deviated from that posture.

McGahey had been the leader of the left. As Allen records, he and Scargill had in the latter half of the 1970s drifted apart – to the point of not speaking – because of their competition for the left's nomination for leadership. But Gormley ditched McGahey's chances: by remaining as president after 1980, when McGahey was 55 and thus under rule ineligible to stand for national office, he made certain of the nomination for Scargill. McGahey, publicly and typically, threw himself behind the younger man and unified a potentially divided left: Scargill paid him generous public gratitude, as well he might.

McGahey was seen in the press as being Scargill's Svengali; it was simply untrue. First, he had problems enough in Scotland in the early 1980s, where a tough area director – Albert Wheeler – was cracking down hard on loss-making pits. Second, his health was faltering: he suffers from emphysema, a miner's complaint, aggravated by heavy whisky drinking, heavy smoking of strong cigarettes and only sporadic eating.

By the time the strike broke, he was further away from Scargill than the latter's own full-time staff – none of whom were able to influence the president, but who performed his bidding. He was frequently in Scotland, rather than in Sheffield: even when in Sheffield, he spent long hours in his hotel rather than in the NUM office: at other times, he was in London at TUC meetings. His purchase on day-to-day policy was at best periodic, strongest when he was roused into opposition. He came under increasing pressure from colleagues in the Communist Party, of which he was a lifetime member, to change the leadership's tactics. He confessed privately to friends that he was in despair. But he could do nothing: his loyalty to Scargill, which in practice meant a position in policy-making subordinate to his, was – once given – complete.

4

'A hoary old bastard who only wants to win'

The public perception of Ian MacGregor has always been a confused one, a mixture of strong but often contradictory images. It was not helped during the strike by his own infrequent and erratic performances on the national stage.

There was, for example, MacGregor as old man. Queuing for his tea at Glasgow airport in his modest mac like an unassuming family doctor, he was yet the man for whom British governments twice paid millions to run problem industries when he was already well past pensionable age.

Christened 'Mac the knife' by the unions within days of taking over British Steel, he was still the Chairman who established an 'Alamein line' below which he did not allow the business to retreat (even though it meant continuing losses).

Regarded as the great international management expert and motivator of men, he yet came to preside over such a demoralised and divided group at the Coal Board in the middle of the strike that even his natural supporters in British industry suggested it was time for him to go.

The elements of the paradox are all true. MacGregor fostered a deliberate unpretentiousness alongside an enormous self-opinion. His ruthlessness in business and distrust of trade unions was allied with an emotional romanticism about manufacturing and a wish to expand and build. A vast range of experience across the globe did not prevent him finding difficulty in heading a small and united team.

So how did it come about that this man, variously described as 'this elderly American import' and the 'man with the best track record in the world in the metallic industries' was called on in preference to the British managers of his day to run not one but two of Britain's most important and sensitive national industries?

The start was modest enough. He was born on 21 September 1912 in the shadow of the British Aluminium smelter at Kinlochleven in Argyllshire in Scotland, where his father was an accountant at the plant. After school at George Watson's College, Edinburgh and Hillhead High

School in Glasgow there was a first class degree in metallurgy at Glasgow University. Then his first job was in his father's old firm as a trainee manager for British Aluminium. Later he moved to the Glasgow steel firm of William Beardmore. 'Scottish industrial training is a hard school,' he once said. 'I learned the importance of hard work and long hours.'

It was the hungry thirties and Clydeside was one of the worst affected by the slump. MacGregor was shaped by the effect of the depression around him. Fifty years later he was to make an emotional speech to the Glasgow Chamber of Commerce recalling the twenty-seven months when the great hulk of the partly built *Queen Mary* lay rusting on the Clydebank slipway, all work stopped. What struck him was the surge of hope when work restarted. He saw it as a paradigm of the need for business to invest and expand. In contrast to his 'butcher' tag, he has been an advocate of world-wide free trade and great investment projects to boost industry.

Came the war, and MacGregor joined the Ministry of Supply and in 1940 was sent to Washington as a technical advisor on arms and materials purchases, later being seconded to the US Army Ordnance Department. After the war, MacGregor and his Welsh wife Sybil remained in the USA and he made his career there.

After work with a Mid-West engineering company, his key move was made in 1957 when he became a vice-president of the Climax Molybdenum company, which later merged to form the American Metal Company, AMAX.

Molybdenum, a form of nickel, was MacGregor's making. The obscure mineral is alloyed to increase the strength of steel. Demand spiralled as gas and oil exploration, with their requirements for tough steel, grew. AMAX cornered the market. It became the world's largest producer of molybdenum, MacGregor one of the world's greatest experts. As the price soared, so did his fortunes. In 1966 he became president of the company (the number two position) and in 1969 chairman of the board.

They were years of ebullient growth. 'A decade of diversification,' MacGregor called it as he bought up company after company. AMAX became the world's largest producer of tungsten, expanded in a variety of other metals and, turning to his origins, MacGregor took it into aluminium, even discussing merger plans with his old employer, British Aluminium.

He was an insatiable globe-trotter – mines in Botswana, investments in Australian iron-ore. He persuaded the Japanese to take shares in his aluminium business. Spotting trends ahead of competitors, the company invested in oil and gas including the Dutch North Sea.

And then were was coal. In 1969 AMAX bought Ayrshire Collieries, the eleventh biggest US producer. By opening new mines, particularly in the West, production tripled, and the company is now the third biggest US producer with output of about 40 million tonnes annually, getting on for half the NCB's production. It has a single underground mine, at Wabash in Illinois, and depends mainly on vast opencast strip mines worked by huge cranes and bulldozers.

It was at one of these, Belle Ayr in Wyoming, later to become the largest producing coal mine in the USA, that MacGregor was first labelled a union-buster. In 1974, a year after it opened, AMAX refused to renew the contract with the union. The fifty or so miners struck. AMAX threatened them with the sack and gave detailed instructions about how to resign from the union. After two months the company was able to resume production. The union picketed unsuccessfully for two years.

At a special stockholders' meeting that year to approve the sale of 20 per cent of the company to Standard Oil of California, union representatives accused Socal of 'bankrolling AMAX's attempt to break the United Mineworkers of America'. MacGregor, described in the *New York Times* as 'visibly annoyed' by the union's goading, then told one protesting miner, 'My first job was in a foundry, wheeling sand the same as you did.' After the meeting he said, in words similar to those he used a decade later in Britain, 'The union is trying to strongarm us. It's rather a sad reflection of labor relations in the United States today.'

MacGregor reputedly remarked of the strikers, 'All they got was the belle air.' It was a key fight with long-term effects. The UMWA has largely failed to organise the coal mines in the western United States although until recently it maintained a tight grip in the East. All the AMAX mines in the eastern states are unionised.

The one underground mine, Wabash, was opened in 1973 while MacGregor was chairman. Producing about 2½ million tonnes a year, its production exceeds any NCB pit apart from the new Selby complex. The nearest comparison is probably Kellingley in Yorkshire, a much older pit, which produces slightly less than 2 million tonnes with about double the workforce. But its seams are not quite as thick as the American which range between five and nine and a half feet. Like most British coal, Wabash production goes to power stations on long-term contracts. But unlike most British mines, its exhaustion in twenty or thirty years is taken for granted by a workforce which largely does not come from traditional mining families.

This was the coalmining background from which MacGregor came.

His tough stand over Belle Ayr has obvious parallels with Britain later. But even then he wobbled. In the middle of the dispute he looked for a settlement and suggested bringing in a rival union, the Operating Engineers, instead. The suggestion appalled his industrial relations team, who felt they had the battle won. Their tough line prevailed.

It all went to help MacGregor's growing business reputation, based on his success at AMAX and his encyclopaedic range of business contacts and information. The company grew and grew. In 1975 it reached 59th position in *Fortune* magazine's league table of most profitable US companies with sales up 900 per cent in the decade.

The clue was expansion, on the premise that continuing inflation would help repay the large sums borrowed. Profits reached 160 million dollars in 1978, up from the 60 million when MacGregor took over, but in his final year they were down to 69 million dollars.

In 1984 the picture was sharply different. The company was heavily into loss, losing 238 million dollars, although that was better than the 489 million the year before. The molybdenum market had collapsed and recession intervened. The company had begun a major programme of selling its assets.

The question, of course, is was it too rapid expansion under MacGregor or poor management since his guiding hand was removed? The answer, probably both. The company was trying to unload some of the unhappy MacGregor acquisitions such as fertilisers and forest products, but two of its biggest money-makers, coal and aluminium, both bought under MacGregor, were making record profits.

At AMAX MacGregor was very much the boss. Critics noted the way the deliberately diffused nature of the company meant that almost the only man who received all the information for deciding company plans was the chairman. When he wanted a piece of research done, he would often give the same task to a number of people separately. They would only know they were on the same investigation if they bumped into each other in the library. His aides at the time were puzzled by his later apparent dislike of publicity. Their memory is of his enjoyment in public speaking and ready availability for interview afterwards. But they also recall having sometimes to work hard to garner the facts to back up his statements.

A workaholic, MacGregor lived the job seven days a week. He was a shrewd financier, persuading the Japanese to buy into the company and selling 20 per cent to Standard Oil of California at what some analysts estimated was three times the market price. 'Every stunt in the book to raise finance,' was one uncharitable Wall Street summing up.

'You talk stock prices, geological developments, industrial relations, economics and general business through every meal weekday or weekend. There is brilliance there. But the main thing is that he has a most highly developed way of getting people to work together,' said one colleague.

'An incessant traveller, he is at home on every continent and well versed in the art of propitiating politicians of every stripe,' said *Fortune* magazine, noting MacGregor's predilection for jetting round the world helped by a prized technique of sleeping on aircraft which seems to consist of sinking into a comatose state without alcohol or food.

The chairman of a British company recalls dinner with a friend and MacGregor in New York. 'They spent the whole evening competing with each other, comparing how many miles they had flown, how many board meetings they had attended in how many different countries. I was so overwhelmed that the only thing I could do was to challenge the other man to a race back to our hotel.'

MacGregor later told aides at the Coal Board that he had been listed for a job as an assistant secretary of state in the American State Department under Henry Kissinger, handling economic matters. His old AMAX colleagues cannot recall it. In the event, he settled for a year as president of the International Chamber of Commerce. 'His idea of a fun weekend,' said one assistant, 'would be to fly the Atlantic for a big business congress.'

He had always maintained his Scottish links. He owned a house, a modest two-storey pile beside the Crinan canal in his native Argyllshire, and returned for holidays. He was on the board of an Edinburgh investment company, Atlantic Assets, and kept links with London merchant bankers. But he was not involved with mainstream British business until the government put him on the board of the reconstructed British Leyland in 1975.

MacGregor, close to the end of his time at AMAX, had trailed his coat, making clear he would like to do something to help British industry, and the motor industry in particular, in which his acquaintances had always noted his particular interest.

Eric Varley, then Industry Minister, says, 'He had a record of industrial efficiency and overall performance. He was said to be very sad about the demise of British industry, manufacturing in particular. He was saddened by the fact that it was slipping badly and our role in the world was going down. He wanted to contribute and believed he could, based on his US experience. That is how he was encouraged.'

Sir Leslie Murphy, later chairman of the National Enterprise Board which had the responsibility for Leyland, said, 'He wanted to help. He had a feeling of patriotism and there is no doubt that he was motivated by the feeling that one of the things wrong with the UK was that the public sector was badly managed. He wanted to do something. The initiative came from him. One couldn't help but be grateful.'

It was part time, but MacGregor became one of Murphy's two or three closest confidants on the company. Soon, with the sudden death of the chairman, Sir Ronald Edwards, it was MacGregor who was phoning Sir Richard Dobson from Connecticut to offer him the job, a situation which astonished Sir Michael Edwardes, a member of the NEB, who had not even heard of the suggestion until Sir Richard asked his advice.

Eighteen months later, MacGregor was being invited to take over as active chairman, as the continual restructuring failed. By now he had retired from AMAX to work for the New York merchant bank of Lehman Brothers. His great achievement there was to arrange a large and initially highly successful steel merger between Jones and Laughlin and LTV, creating a company about the size of the British Steel Corporation, with whom he was later to compare it favourably. But by 1985, like most of American big steel, it was in deep trouble.

When MacGregor turned down Leyland because it required too much time, the job of chief executive was offered to Michael Edwardes with MacGregor prepared to be the part-time chairman. According to Edwardes's account,[1] he said he would only accept the job if he could be chairman as well. When he met MacGregor at Kennedy Airport, New York, 'he readily saw my point and offered to be deputy chairman'.

The two men have since fallen out and are highly jealous of each other. But MacGregor backed Edwardes over his cuts and plant closures. Insiders, however, describe him as 'not such a hawk as he later became' and discount the suggestions that it was MacGregor rather than Edwardes who initiated the tough sacking decisions and the challenging work-force ballots.

They were impressed with his knowledgeability allied to a surprising ability, apparent later at steel, to get through to the shopfloor on an individual basis. As Geoff Armstrong, then personnel director of BL Cars put it, 'He has always been good at factory visits.'

'Most people do it in the form of a Royal tour. He was able to talk on the same level as a worker. He would ask questions about why a man was using one machine rather than another, why he was milling from a certain angle; technical questions.'

It was his sensational appointment in 1980 as chairman of the British Steel Corporation which brought an almost unknown MacGregor to British public attention. It was an industry shattered by a bitter strike; its traditional customers deserting at a terrifying rate; a national joke for its ability to lose huge sums, at the time £2 million a day.

The idea that a 67-year-old American could turn it round at an age where his counterparts were drawing their pensions seemed an insult to British management. The sensation, though, was the financial arrangement. MacGregor received the official salary, £48,500 a year, but the merchant bank Lazard Freres in New York, where he was now a partner, received a transfer fee which, depending on MacGregor's performance, could reach £1.8 million. (In the event he was reckoned mostly, but not totally, successful and £1.5 millions was paid out.)

The transfer fee caused outrage across the political spectrum. MacGregor at a stiff introductory press conference made a ponderous reference to a current football transfer worked out with the Employment

Minister, Jim Prior, the night before. Unfortunately he got the details wrong. One friendly captain of British industry wrote him a letter saying that he thoroughly disapproved of the arrangement but hoped that he would leave Britain with a steel industry worth the name. MacGregor replied that he would.

It was a rough start. In retrospect some believe that the transfer fee reflected MacGregor's embarrassment at leaving Lazard's so soon. Used mainly as a man to introduce influential people and possible clients, he had not pulled off any more big deals like the LTV steel merger.

He had not been first choice for BSC, but ironically it was probably the transfer fee which made it possible. The salary was too low for the British managers being considered, and government policy and possible knock-on effects prevented it being raised.

The BSC job could have been made for MacGregor. A metallurgist, he knew the industry, prices and markets backwards. He prided himself on his management abilities and salesmanship, an ideal mix for BSC where sales and marketing was probably a greater weakness than the inefficiencies in the plants.

His first year brought an almost miraculous transformation. Losses were halved in 1981–2 from £668 millions to £358 millions. Management morale at rock bottom was picked off the ground, markets fought for, ministers badgered about anything, like energy costs, which affected performance.

More significant still was the change of mood. Llanwern near Newport in South Wales was one of the five big integrated plants. When MacGregor took over it was everybody's favourite candidate for closure with a dismal record for productivity and labour disputes. A year on its workforce was halved, job demarcations largely abolished and shop stewards talking of a new mood as productivity reached European levels.

He was lucky. The unions were drained by the long strike. The previous management team of Sir Charles Villiers and Bob Scholey had arranged most of the slimming down which took place under MacGregor. The government gave him assistance his predecessors had not received over restructuring.

But he still made a remarkable job of it. Reading the mood of the workforce, he sidestepped the embittered national leadership of the largest steel union, the Iron and Steel Trades Confederation, and made local deals which the men welcomed. A push into the export markets his predecessors had abandoned was accompanied by a crusade for quality.

By the end of the year, it was possible to find convenors, competitors and customers all prepared to praise his achievements. He badgered the carmakers to use more British steel. The fussiest, Ford, agreed to step up from 30 to 50 per cent because of improvements in quality. General Motors, making an increasing proportion of its Vauxhall cars on the continent, agreed to take a proportion of British steel for its European manufacture.

The plaudits came from many sides. On the platform at the conference of the National Union of Blastfurnacemen, he was praised by its leaders. Frank Cottam, the national officer for steel of the General and Municipal Workers, who was to be a key anti-Scargill figure in 1984, described MacGregor as the kind of general who would sacrifice a division to save an army. He likened the union officials to stretcher-bearers. MacGregor, he said, had pushed ahead with things which needed doing but for which voluntary agreement would not have been forthcoming.

The odd man out was Bill Sirs of the ISTC. Alienated from management after the strike, he found himself outflanked by MacGregor's insistence on local deals. When MacGregor finally produced his survival plan, which meant more cuts, he got the Electoral Reform Society to supervise a ballot which in spite of a partial ISTC boycott, produced a MacGregor victory.

It was a tactic straight out of the BL textbook, and one which MacGregor would dearly have loved to employ in the coal strike after the NUM had refused a ballot. But in that case he was persuaded out of it by the warnings of his industrial relations team and the refusal of the Electoral Reform Society to carry it out.

Sirs had pressed MacGregor to sack his deputy, Bob Scholey, who had been the union's *bête noire* during the steel strike. But far from doing so, MacGregor, in one of the key successes of his chairmanship, kept him on and remotivated him after the disappointment of being passed over in favour of an elderly outsider.

Scholey, known throughout the industry as 'Black Bob' because of his habit of wearing a black safety helmet, eventually became BSC chairman in 1986. He became MacGregor's closest advisor in the office of chief executive which he had established. By winning the confidence of Scholey, an aggressive tough-talking Yorkshireman, MacGregor became accepted too by 'the Sheffield mafia' in BSC, a group of prominent managers from the old private United Steel company, who held most of the key positions.

This was a striking difference from what was to happen at the Coal Board, where MacGregor became convinced that the top brass were out to undermine him. The chairman of a major British company described MacGregor addressing his company's managers. 'He is not a charismatic man. But as he went on, people were impressed with him. What came over strongly was the pride he took in doing the job with the people he had available.' As one of his team at steel put it, 'We knew this was our last chance. We could see the strengths of the man. Yet he was prepared to say our management was as good as any he had worked with.'

MacGregor knew the technical side inside out and could communicate with both managers and shopfloor technicians, but to BSC's immense relief, they found he could also handle the politics in a way his predecessor, Sir Charles Villiers, could not. One executive says, 'The big contribution he made was to keep the government off our backs, while we got the industry sorted out.' He was of course in an almost fireproof position. He did not need the work and, after the transfer rumpus, to sack him was unthinkable.

It is questionable whether any British businessman would have been secure enough to argue, as MacGregor did, against a further huge cutback. Instead of dropping from capacity of 14.4 million tonnes a year to 10 or even 8 million, MacGregor, establishing what he called his 'Alamein line' beyond which he would retreat no further, brought it down to a notional 14 million, a tiny drop.

During his chairmanship, the workforce was almost halved, from 150,000 to 85,000. Most of that had been agreed before he arrived, but the slim-down continued throughout his time. Trading losses were halved in his first year, but they went sharply back up to £386 millions after sudden unforeseen recession knocked orders back in the second year. In his final year (in which he served six months of the financial year) things improved again, but a loss of £218 million was still short of the elusive break-even target he had set. Ironically it was blamed on the costs of the miners' strike.

MacGregor was helped by the good relations he established with the prime minister. He got a buzz, clearly noted by his associates, out of being so close to political power. Mrs Thatcher, showing a typical prime minister's predilection to latch on to favourite businessmen for expert advice, clearly appreciated MacGregor's world businessman style.

Their political views were very similar, and as one ex-minister put it with the exaggeration necessary from across the political divide, 'Maggie was so besotted with him. He is extremely plausible and can be engaging. It's all a bit like the Gilbert and Sullivan song – the young man who is so very profound. You don't know what he is driving at, but it's all so very profound, it must be you who are a bit bloody stupid.'

So there was success of a kind at BSC, and he must have seemed the ideal man for the next problem industry, coal, as its subsidies and stockpiles mounted. The plan to move MacGregor was first floated eighteen months before he actually moved, when the government wanted a successor to Ezra, but it came to little; there was still too much to do at steel.

A year later he was heavily courted by the Secretary of State for Energy Nigel Lawson, and his coal minister John Moore. It was a flattering challenge and he took little persuading. Not all were so keen, particularly civil servants. Patrick Jenkin, the Secretary of State for Industry, wanted MacGregor to finish at steel. Lawson wanted him straight away. MacGregor suggested a characteristic compromise; he would do both jobs. Whitehall did not take it seriously.

This time there was no transfer fee and bonus. Instead an almost equally large payment of half a million pounds a year was to be made to Lazards. Negotiations were prolonged over the tax position of MacGregor's Eaton Square flat. Curiously, even after the appointment was announced, MacGregor was still counselling the man he was to succeed, Sir Norman Siddall, to stay on, perhaps in a role like president of the board.

And so on 1 September 1983, three weeks short of his seventy-first birthday, Ian MacGregor arrived at Hobart House, the red-brick NCB headquarters next door to the old BSC headquarters which he had just made it his business to sell.

Many, including some civil servants at the Department of Energy, who counselled against the appointment, saw it as a provocation. But for ministers there were some obvious advantages. Apart from his obvious commercial and private sector abilities, he knew about marketing. If anyone could shift the growing stockpiles, this could be the man. Nor was the Energy Department displeased with the obvious links with the prime minister, links which might be used to smooth the way or even relax expenditure restraints if the going got tough.

But for the unions, it was a signal like the hoisting of a battle ensign. 'Mac the knife' was the obvious nickname. Arthur Scargill simply refused to pronounce his name at all, referring to him scornfully as 'Macburger' and other names. Mick McGahey saw it as a 'declaration of war on the British miners'. He says, 'He was prepared to butcher any industry. Having declared his position, the miners had to take action.'

Yet the brief was no different than Siddall's – to cut the drain on the public purse and deal with the mounting stockpiles. The Energy Department also saw him sorting out Coal Board management. Hobart House was, in a favourite word, 'rotten'. Although there was acknowledged to be talent in the areas, a major shake-up was wanted nationally, particularly as many senior men were approaching the age of retirement.

This chimed in with the recommendations of the Monopolies and Mergers Commission which suggested linking performance more to commercial criteria and bringing in more thinking from outside industries by recruiting both on to the main board and to lower levels. It was not radically new. It was simply trying to bring the board into line with what had earlier been attempted by other nationalised industries, such as those where MacGregor had first-hand experience, BL and Steel, or indeed by the assertion of managerial control in some sprawling private conglomerates. MacGregor's commitment to free enterprise was undoubted; advising Mrs Thatcher against changes in the Law of the Sea which would restrict private companies exploiting undersea minerals; pressing the case for a private enterprise solution to the Channel crossing, devising and promoting his own scheme, half-tunnel, half-bridge, which was eventually turned down. He took a global view, prepared to discuss comparative national growth rates at a press conference about personnel changes.

On a personal level, he liked tough language and adopted Americanisms. Phrases like 'pulling our wagons round in a circle' or his own description of himself as 'a hoary old bastard who only wants to win' were delivered with obvious relish. Asked about his future when his successor was appointed long before his official departure, he growled back, 'I'm no quitter.' He would talk of interference 'from the front office', meaning the government, and of 'weals on my back' from government criticism after the strike.

In spite of the image, many who worked with him on both sides of the Atlantic found him indecisive. They found him an ideas man, plucking out all sorts of thoughts but often unable to distinguish between the likely and the loopy. The man who described the ideal steelworks as the place where you could fire a rifle and hit nobody, employed what some styled the 'shotgun technique' in private, discharging a hail of ideas from which others could pick up the pieces.

He worked best when there were others to bounce the ideas off and make sense of them. At BSC there had been Scholey and David Prior, his personal assistant, son of the then Tory cabinet minister, Jim Prior. At coal such people were conspicuously lacking. MacGregor's sudden changes of tack and sudden inspirations in the strike were to dismay his aides and confuse negotiations. Casual talk of concessions was not always followed by firm proposals. On the NUM side, Peter Heathfield, who prided himself on his honesty, was particularly upset by what he saw as MacGregor's untrustworthiness.

As his record at steel or AMAX showed, he was not by nature a closer of factories, or a firer of men. Kevan Hunt, who became head of industrial relations at the NCB said, 'MacGregor wants to turn mediocrity into excellence. That is the drive in the man. But you recognise that there are going to be casualties because everyone can't rise to the occasion. His view is that men in our job have a responsibility to create some sort of Phoenix in terms of new enterprise.'

He flinched from the consequences of his harsh decisions. It was left to others to make the dismissals, at the Coal Board usually to his deputy, Jimmy Cowan. Almost unfailingly courteous to people's faces, he could be astonishingly cold and rough at other times. When the Coal Board's director of public relations throughout most of the strike, Geoff Kirk, took early retirement after a row with MacGregor, the whole business was handled by Cowan. MacGregor, who had consulted Kirk almost every morning of the strike, never spoke to him again or said a word of appreciation or thanks. When Kirk subsequently drowned in a boating accident off Skye, MacGregor's office vetoed a press statement paying tribute to him.

A prominent British company chairman once had an apparently cordial dinner with MacGregor at which he then raised the possibility of buying a small but successful steel plant from BSC which MacGregor wanted to shut down. He was startled by the sharp and immediate response from MacGregor: 'If you try and compete with us, we'll burn your ass off.'

This side of him was often disguised by his reluctance to say 'No' to ideas even when he disapproved of them. It was disconcerting when people got the impression in meetings that he was going along with their suggestions, and only afterwards was an aide such as Prior sent to explain that, in reality, the chairman wanted something quite different.

So the image of MacGregor as a butcher was a simplistic one. By nature he was a man for expansion, but he would take cold hard decisions if he believed the facts demanded it. And there was a strong emotionality in the man which helped power his dealings with the unions. Observing MacGregor at a meeting or in an interview, there comes a time when you can see the emotion starting to break through. He folds his arms tightly, leans back and starts to rock as if holding himself in, as though keeping the lid on a pressure cooker. It was in such circumstances that some of the most heartfelt and awkward MacGregor utterances – the wish to prosecute the miners' leaders for inciting violence, the tough statements about sitting out the strike, the crack about worries over Arthur Scargill's mental and physical health – burst out.

It was also, one suspects, the way his bitter comments about ministerial intervention were delivered after the strike. For all the cracks he made about the 'front office' he bitterly resented having to supply them with information about his management of the board. In previous strikes Ezra or his deputy had always been available to see ministers every day. Although MacGregor often spoke to Energy Minister Peter Walker at breakfast time by telephone, he made it clear that there would not be personal contact at that level this time. Walker had to impose himself on him. Civil servants in the Energy Department found increasing difficulties in getting information from the board, a tendency which if anything increased after the strike when MacGregor appointees in the board started to follow their chairman's policy of keeping information from the government and avoiding the risk of being accused of disloyalty to an increasingly prickly MacGregor.

As we have seen, at AMAX, critics noticed that the flow of information was channelled to MacGregor so that he alone had the full picture. For him, knowledge was power.

He was not at his best in large meetings, whether with mining equipment manufacturers or trade unions, where he tended to freeze and be very stiff. Small gatherings were different. There he would push his ideas and become almost garrulous. But his attention span was short. Aides at both steel and coal remark on the difficulty he would have in keeping his mind from wandering on to other subjects during an hour-long meeting. Some took it, wrongly, for a sign of senility.

This impatience hampered negotiations. Peter McNestry, the NACODS general secretary, was outraged by MacGregor's behaviour at their crucial talks. He described him as sitting with his head down, apparently nodding off, and then, when the talks at first failed, saying, 'Good, now we can all go home.' One reason given for the comparatively early finishes and frequent breaks in the negotiations with the NUM was MacGregor's reluctance to negotiate late at night. In another industry, they would probably have continued into the small hours. But by contrast, others remark on MacGregor's amazing resilience, arriving at his desk in the morning fresh and lively after a punishing schedule with frequent international flights.

His distrust of the press seemed to grow. At BSC, he was almost inaccessible except when he called selected journalists to breakfast meetings. He played a teasing game, agreeing to talk but then referring requests for interviews back to his staff who appeared to block them. Yet he obviously enjoyed being courted by the press. During the early months of the dispute, he began visibly to warm to television appearances, relishing the barbed remark, before things went very wrong.

In spite of his unassuming manner, modesty was not part of his make-up. Conscious of the interest in his views, he recorded his thoughts early in the dispute, and sent the tapes to America, for, as he put it, 'safe-keeping', later for use in a self-justifying autobiography rushed out for the end of his time at the NCB.

Politically his views could best be described as Reaganite. He believed strongly that the major cause of the decline of Britain was the power of the unions, particularly single industry unions. It was the itch to do something about that decline which would inevitably lead to a battle over management's right to manage which had brought him back to Britain. It chimed, of course, precisely with the view of the Thatcher government.

Even so, there was little sign of the approaching confrontation in MacGregor's first weeks at the NCB. The Hobart House management were impressed with his courtly good manners, his air of 'American bonhomie'. As one put it, 'Nobody saw any bared teeth. We only saw a relaxed transatlantic man who beguiled those who had expected sharp teeth and claws.'

They became quickly aware of one of the most powerful MacGregor beliefs – his conviction that the facts, hard commercial statistics, must inevitably convince. It was the conviction that the facts, about sales, costs, and targets must be faced, and once faced would be remorselessly convincing, which powered his first few months at the board, as he pointed to the details of the MMC report as 'my bible'. The attitude led him willingly, even hopefully, into the kind of setpiece confrontation, or facing of facts, which his predecessor had been so anxious to side-step.

Even before Siddall had left, MacGregor had put in the management consultants, McKinseys, to make recommendations. The principal effect, as at steel, was to centralise the lines of communication so that they all ran into the new office of the chief executive, which MacGregor chose to share with one of his two deputies, Jimmy Cowan.

Senior board officials, accustomed to consult among themselves before submitting proposals designed for the board, found themselves instead communicating individually with the chief executive's office. Discussions with their colleagues had to be arranged informally or not at all.

In parallel, MacGregor embarked on a major pruning of the board. As at British Steel, he had insisted, as a condition of appointment, that he should have the *de facto* say on appointments. It could not be absolute. It was by statute the duty of the minister. But it was agreed that the government would use 'its best endeavours' to get MacGregor the men he wanted. In practice, chairmen have a considerable say over who is appointed, but the almost absolute deal struck with MacGregor came close to frustrating the purposes of the Act. Peter Walker, who became Secretary of State for Energy after MacGregor's appointment, however admits to little difference between MacGregor's position and that of other nationalised industry chairmen. He was to clash with him during and after the strike over MacGregor's wish to keep as much from the department as possible, and over the appointment of a new deputy and a successor.

But to begin with, the new chairman wasted no time on reconstituting the board. One deputy chairman, John Mills, his name insultingly mispronounced by MacGregor at an early directors' meeting as 'Miles', was gone by Easter. The long-serving director of the South Wales area, Philip Weekes, ceased to be a member of the full board at about the same time. In their place came a string of non-executive directors; Colin Barker, a former Ford finance director who had been with MacGregor at BSC; Sir Melvyn Rosser, a Welsh chartered accountant; David Newbigging, a former Taipan from Hong Kong who had run the old colonial firm of Jardine Matheson; Tommy MacPherson, a Scottish industrialist and friend of MacGregor, and so on. It was all in line with the MMC recommendations.

MacGregor had picked on Jimmy Cowan as the man to help him run the board from the small chief executive's office. A shrewd tough Scotsman who had impressed the government with his tough wage-bargaining under Siddall, Cowan is a diminutive, taciturn man, and at 64 he had recently had a heart bypass operation. He made his reputation in a ten-year stint as director of the Scottish area, where he had struck up a working arrangement with the Communist president of the area, the national NUM vice president, Mick McGahey.

But he had some crucial drawbacks. He got on badly with many of the area directors, and he was a very poor communicator in public or private, sometimes not even finishing his sentences, concluding with a shrug or a silence. Cowan, who describes himself as 'extremely secretive; I refuse to communicate on almost anything,' was summed up by one colleague like this: 'Jimmy is the worst communicator in the world, and always has been. He is intelligent, shrewd, introvert and suspicious of everyone.' It was scarcely the best choice for a man who would smooth MacGregor's path into the hearts and minds of the industry. If MacGregor had thought he was getting the same link which Scholey at BSC had provided, he was to be disappointed.

So as board members departed, and others came rapidly to retiring age, the South Wales director, Philip Weekes, recorded in his diary, 'The National Board is now effectively two little old Scotsmen with no nether millstone on which to grind their ideas, and no one to challenge them.'

MacGregor's first moves were, however, to give more power to the area directors, the men who actually run operations in the coal fields. (Like mediaeval barons, they look after their own bailiwick but are directed from Hobart House. The National Coal Board itself, with a mixture of full- and part-time members, meets monthly, and at the start of the MacGregor era the day-to-day running was largely in the hands of five directors-general who were not on the board and took instructions from it. They included Ned Smith, for industrial relations, and Malcolm Edwards, for marketing, both crucial men in the strike.)

Meeting the area directors formally in September 1983, after informal dinners with them previously, MacGregor insisted they were the key men. He left it to Ned Smith to spell out the policy for dealing with the NUM. The pitch was that things would continue as under Siddall. The guiding principle, said Smith, was that Scargill must not be allowed to win – ever. But he repeated that there should be no confrontations and that they should continue the softly-softly local approach. MacGregor publicly backed him.

Meanwhile he pleased the area directors by lifting the ceiling for expenditure. They could authorise from half a million pounds to five million, effectively the cost of a new coal face. It was long overdue.

Yet as the weeks went by, and old acquaintances departed, they came to feel that they knew less and less what was going on at Hobart House, and that more and more of the decisions which mattered were being drawn into MacGregor's hands. When it came to setting out their budgets for the coming year, they were to have more interference and more direction than they could remember. It was to lead eventually to Cortonwood.

But as MacGregor got to grips with the details, there was little sign of the explosion to come. At breakfast meetings with industrial correspondents he showed charts of the cost per tonne at various pits but concentrated on the large slice of pits which were only a short way from profit. The big lossmakers were largely ignored.

The industrial relations strategy remained the same, though in retrospect those involved remember the cautionary noises which came from MacGregor. There was typically no outright disagreement but remarks like 'do you reckon?' or 'I find that a bit curious.'

A meeting with the unions and Arthur Scargill was delayed, but when it came the two men posed for a friendly handshake in the front lobby of Hobart House. There was even some meeting of minds. Both men, for different reasons, were anxious to sell more coal, widening the market, and to push ahead with research and technical development.

But relations with the unions began to sour when the NUM instituted an overtime ban over the board's 5.2 per cent pay offer. Although it helped to reduce the build-up of stocks and improved the board's cash-flow, it began to make a sorry mess of the already horrific profit and loss account. As it continued, it began to try MacGregor's patience, never his strongest suit. It also impeded his attempt to get to know the industry in the way he favoured most, by pit visits and personal contact with the men. On 22 February 1984, on a visit to Ellington colliery in Northumberland, he was pushed to the ground and temporarily stunned in a demonstration by miners protesting against cuts at a neighbouring pit. MacGregor, though back in his office the next morning, was badly shaken up and affected by the changing temper of the industry.

Meanwhile he continued to arrange to meet the unions to discuss what to do about the worsening financial and over-supply position. Characteristically he relied on the facts to persuade. The unions wanted a tripartite approach with government to resolve it, which for the NUM effectively meant a new government underwriting of the industry with a redrawing of the Plan for Coal, the settlement made with Labour in 1974.

At a crucial meeting with the unions on 13 December 1983 MacGregor had been pressed again by the NUM about his intentions for the industry and individual pits. To the astonishment of his team ('I nearly fell off my chair,' said one participant) he promised the facts and figures they wanted, the very national setting of the stage which Siddall had so long avoided. MacGregor saw it in the context of getting the unions to face facts; Scargill and the NUM in terms of getting the board to come clean on plans which they believed could then be used to persuade their members to take industrial action to thwart them.

Meanwhile the board, with Cowan in the lead, was pressing area directors for bigger capacity reductions, and a speeding up of the Siddall tempo of shut-downs, while other senior staff were urging MacGregor to delay the formal setting-out of his plans until after the peak winter demand for coal was over.

5
Fear of the abyss

A mystery surrounds the beginning of the miners' strike. Was it a matter of accident? Or was it carefully planned by one side or the other? The most frequent version of the latter option – the conspiracy theory – is that the government and the board jointly planned to 'pull the miners on to the punch'; that the closure of Cortonwood Colliery in South Yorkshire, coupled with the near-simultaneous announcement that twenty pits were to close in 1984–5 over and above the twenty which had closed in the preceding twelve months, was a well timed and well executed strategy, with the specific aim in mind of stimulating a strike which would then be smashed.

That interpretation cannot be sustained: senior government officials and ministers are to be believed when they say, as they do, that no government would deliberately provoke a fight with the National Union of Mineworkers, especially when the option of continuing to cut capacity without necessarily triggering industrial action did appear available.

But strategy there was. The concrete situation facing government and the board was that, after the election of Arthur Scargill, the NUM was led by men determined to use industrial action both to save jobs and to destroy government. Sir John Hoskyns, head of the prime minister's central policy review staff at the time, recalls that 'The moment Scargill was elected it was clear the balloon would go up.' In such a case, the line between preparing for the eventuality of a strike blurs into planning for its inevitability.

The Conservatives had a humiliation to expunge: their defeats at the hands of the mineworkers in 1972 and 1974. In both these instances, the miners had been mobilised to pursue a wages claim. They were opposed by the government because it was operating an incomes policy which it did not wish to see any group break. The first lesson which Mrs Thatcher learned from these engagements, and the most important one, was that a government should not involve itself in wage fixing, even in the public sector. The new Conservatism, developed in the period of opposition from 1974 to 1979, was infused as much by such practical lessons learned from the seats round the cabinet table as it was by the theoretical constructs of Ferdinand von Hayek or Milton Friedman – though their prescriptions naturally appealed to those who had lost faith in the virtues of corporatism. Though the government *did* become involved in the 1984–5 strike, it could plausibly claim to be a bystander for much of the time, and was never physically present in the negotiations – a source of great strength and flexibility for it, a great weakness for an NUM leadership attempting to pin the blame on it.

Mrs Thatcher also saw the great weaknesses in the Wilson and Callaghan governments of 1974–9. They had come into government on the back of union power and the social contract with the unions was at the base of their policy, especially in the first two years. While it is true that many of the objectives of that policy were jettisoned under the pressure of recession, the government always relied on union co-operation for its credibility.

Thus when that co-operation was withdrawn in the 'winter of discontent' of 1979–9, it was fatal. The trade union movement could and did destroy 'its own' government in order to break the then 5 per cent pay limit. Leaders such as Alan Fisher of NUPE and Moss Evans, the newly elected general secretary of the TGWU, put accommodation of the undoubted pressures on them from below before the preservation of Labour. It was a possibly fatal calculation for the party's future as a government. At the end of that period, the man who had been Permanent Secretary at the Department of Employment throughout it wrote that the union movement 'has no institution for self-regulation of [its] activities. It has so far successfully resisted attempts by governments to regulate its main activities by law. For these reasons it presents governments with a unique problem. The difficulties this causes for governments and the country may be too serious for the status quo to be maintained.'[1]

It was so seen: the status quo was dismantled – so far and so fast that by the time the Thatcher government had to face its greatest engagement, its opponent did not have the levers to pull which had been available to it ten years before.

A further consequence of the strikes of the early 1970s was the development of contingency planning at a higher level than had been seen before. The siege of Saltley, which occurred the day (10 February) after a state of emergency had been declared, is – according to the historians of states of emergencies – 'a demon still to be exorcised in the contingency planning community'.[2] 'At the time many of those in positions of influence looked into the abyss and saw only a few days away the possibility of the country being plunged into a state of chaos . . . this is the power that exists to hold the country to ransom: it was fear of that abyss which had an important effect on subsequent policy,' wrote the then adviser to the Chancellor of the Exchequer.[3] The demon was exorcised, the abyss bridged, by the development of the Civil Contingencies Unit, replacing the old, and discredited, Emergencies Organisation which had its origins in the late 1940s. Its main task was to ensure the availability of vital supplies and utilities during industrial action, a task it fulfilled with some success during the 1974 miners' strike – though the relative restraint of the miners' picket in that engagement was probably more important.

It was an irony that the CCU, brought into being as a reaction to the unpreparedness of the state to mass working-class power led by Arthur Scargill was not used when Scargill launched a much longer and more serious engagement. The reason for that was not that the Unit was not prepared: it was. It had close links with the chief constables and heads of the country's military districts, an army whose experience in Northern Ireland had made it increasingly sophisticated in riot control at its command.

But two developments were to mean that it became less crucial to the nation's continued well being in emergencies. First, it was not the only way in which government and the state prepared for a future engagement: the planning engaged in by politicians, civil servants and police officers was largely designed to pre-empt the state of affairs developing in which the CCU would have to be used. Second, developments in the country's infrastructure throughout the 1970s and early 1980s meant, on the whole, that it became less dependent on the centralised provision of services by a corporation dominated by a monopoly union. This was especially the case in the railways.

When Mrs Thatcher succeeded Heath as Conservative leader in 1975, she appointed Lord Carrington, who had been at Energy during the last strike, to head a group of former ministers to enquire into the causes of the Heath débâcle. The report presented to Thatcher stressed the waxing power of the unions, especially in the fuel and power industries. The army could not operate to mitigate that power. (The Ulster Workers' Council strike, coming soon after the Wilson government took power, was a better lesson than any provided in mainland Britain of this.) It called for better planning, and a better presentation of government's case, but at bottom it was fatalistic: no government could indefinitely withstand a strike by workers in the crucial utilities which was well supported. It was this assumption which was taken up in the most famous 'plan' – the 'Ridley Plan'. During and after the strike, it acquired a demonological status. Dog-eared photocopies of it were available on miners' picket lines; it was promoted by the union and the left as being the secret blueprint for the breaking of the labour movement.

That characterisation had something in it. The 'Ridley Plan' was the final report of a group of Conservative back-benchers who had been charged with drawing up a series of proposals on nationalised industries from which manifesto measures would be drawn. The group was chaired by Nicholas Ridley, now Environment Secretary, then a right-wing back-bencher. It had nothing directly to do with the miners. Most of it was concerned with getting the nationalised industries under control. The main mechanism proposed the government specifying a rate of return and being 'totally inflexible' in demanding to be adhered to. It called for vigorous denationalisation, the ending of statutory monopolies (as that of the NCB over coal production), and for state industry boards to be dominated by part-timers and made supervisory.

It was the annexe which made the news, when *The Economist* magazine made the leak of the report its lead story on 27 May 1978. In that, Ridley anticipated a 'political threat' from the Labour movement, which would of course be hostile to the denationalisation strategy: the most likely battlefield was held to be the coal fields. As reported by *The Economist*, the group believed that to deal with a coal strike a government should '(a) build up maximum coal stocks, particularly at the power stations; (b) make contingency plans for the import of coal; (c) encourage the recruitment of non-union drivers by haulage companies to help move coal when necessary; (d) introduce dual coal/oil firing in all power stations as quickly as possible.

'The group believes that the greatest deterrent to any strike would be to "cut off the money to strikers, and make the union finance them" . . . there should be a large mobile squad of police equipped and prepared to uphold the law against violent picketing. "Good non-union drivers" should be recruited to cross picket lines with police protection.'

The 'Ridley Plan' was prescient and showed a willingness to plan: but few ministers or civil servants even knew of its existence. Tim Eggar, the MP (now a Foreign Office minister) who took over chairmanship of the group when it reformed to perform the same task before the 1983 election, could not find a copy of it anywhere and finally borrowed one from Ridley, who himself had difficulty in finding it. It had no immediate practical value: its importance lies in the indication it gave that future ministers were capable of thinking what had been unthinkable, and in seeing that a mixture of authoritarianism and populism could be used to break a strike. But when the crisis seemed about to break upon the government in 1981, the famous plan was nowhere to be seen.

Instead, the publication then hasty withdrawal of the 'pit closure programme' of February 1981 was apparently a capitulation before any kind of action had been joined. The media, hyping itself and its audiences up for a new engagement of mammoth proportions, saw the cut and run tactics, inevitably, as a U-turn by a government then suffering from some unpopularity. Even those, like Arthur Scargill, who were not deceived into thinking it was any such thing, did not see that it and more importantly its aftermath marked the end of the NCB's unique position in British society: and on that unique position the power of the NUM very substantially depended.

The Plan for Coal had given the miners' union even more power than that it had secured under the Nationalisation Act and subsequent developments within the board. Sir Derek Ezra, chairman throughout much of the 1970s, had after the 1974 strike forged an ever closer alliance with Joe Gormley, the NUM president, to the annoyance of the harder men in both their camps. John Northard, now the board's operations director, recalls being told to reverse a decision on a pit closure in North Derbyshire when he was area director there because Gormley had 'had a word' with Ezra. Norman Siddall, the long-serving deputy chairman, had been the representative of disgruntled managers' views within Hobart House, and never had a good relationship with Ezra because of it, but the relationship won the approval of the Labour government. Efficiency, the managers believed, was being sacrificed to politics.

The Derek and Joe show, as it was known in Whitehall and beyond, was instantly threatened by the Conservative victory in 1979. David Howell, with a reputation for being a thinker of the new Conservatism, came in as Energy Secretary; John Moore, with a reputation to make, bounded in as Coal Minister. Both registered quiet but mounting horror over the NCB.

The most obvious problem, by 1981, was the drop in electricity and therefore coal demand after recession hit the economy in 1980. Coal consumption peaked in the Plan for Coal period at 129.4 million tonnes in 1979. Thereafter it declined to 123.5 million tonnes in 1980, 118.4 million tonnes in 1981, and around 111 million tonnes in 1982 and 1983. But coal production outstripped it progressively: it peaked in 1980 at 130.1 million tonnes, dipping to 127 million tonnes in 1981, 124.7 million tonnes in 1982 and 119.3 million tonnes in 1983 (showing the effects of the overtime ban). Yet overproduction was seen by the government as a symptom of a deeper cause. Moore says that 'it was fashionable to say in the industry that the recession came on too fast. It wasn't that . . . the basic underlying problem, the need to restructure the industry, was already there and was being ignored. Looking at the NCB, it seemed to me that there was an extraordinary combination of management and people potential on the ground, and terrifying ossification at the top . . . you had two static pyramids, the NCB pyramid and the union pyramid.'

Howell shared his view, calling the NCB in retrospect a 'funny old organisation – a lot of people in it were very weak.' But he wanted to go slowly: in the tripartite meetings which he had inherited from Labour he would argue consistently but not over-forcefully against following the targets in the Plan for Coal in a period of deepening recession, and press for more closures. Quite soon, four camps appeared: the NUM, which in theory would not tolerate any closures except through exhaustion; Ezra, who wanted the closure rate held to 1.5–2 million tonnes a year; Howell, who was pressing for 2.5–3 million tonnes a year; and the treasury, which wanted 4 million tonnes a year. As the figures worsened, the treasury won.

In 1980, the Coal Bill was published (known in the industry as the 'Closure Bill'), which enjoined break-even by 1984–5. It meant a rapid acceleration in the closure rate of around 1.5 million tonnes and also meant trouble. Ezra, who dismissed the criticism of him then and since by ministers as the carping of men who did not understand the industry or his handling of it, says he demanded three times to have a full-dress meeting with all ministers likely to be involved in planning for a coal strike. Each time, he says, he was refused. Others in the Energy Department at the time give credence to this. Many doubted that Howell raised the warnings from the industry in the cabinet, or if so, that he did so forcefully enough to command that attention be given to it. Says Ezra: 'What clearly happened was that they [energy ministers] didn't pass it on, and when this blew up I was personally attacked in parliament by some rabid Tory or another saying I had put a time bomb under the government. The truth was they didn't take any notice of what we said.'

Having exhausted argument, Ezra had to conform. A meeting of the board and the mining unions was set for 10 February 1981. It was carefully planned: it would be a difficult meeting, and the government, in coaching Ezra for the talks, stressed that on no account was he to mention a figure of pits to be closed. But he did, to the extent of indicating that between 25 and 50 pits might have to go in order to bring the board within its new external financing limits of £834 million for 1980–1 and £882 million for 1981–2. That would mean some 30,000 miners leaving the industry, half of which would be by 'natural wastage'.

Gormley's view of the matter[4] was that Ezra had been too reluctant to tell Howell the truth about the trouble that would come (Gormley believed he should have resigned to make the point), and that Howell 'didn't have the courage, or the seniority, or the plain nous to tell the cabinet that it was impossible to place the financial restrictions on the industry which they wanted.' Like any miners' leader, he was against pit closures. He argued that the 8 million tonnes a year overproduction would be balanced by cutting the coincidentally neat 8 million tonnes of coal being imported that year. He describes the meeting as one where 'all hell broke loose' once Ezra had talked of the need for closures, with 'the general cry being, "Tell us how many pits you're talking about." ' So great had become the chaos that Gormley had to cross to the other side of the table and co-chair the meeting with Ezra to get calm. From that vantage point, trading hard on the special relationship between them, Gormley said, as one old friend to another: 'You might as well tell them, Derek [*them*, not us]. You must *know* the numbers.' Thus Ezra produced the figures.

Says Howell: 'I don't think it was conspiracy or premeditation on the part of Gormley and Ezra – I may be naive, but knowing the people involved I don't think they think like that. I think it was all a splendid piece of bungling and, oops, sorry, I dropped the soup – that kind of thing.'

Whether the soup was dropped or was thrown, the drums beat hard and fast round the coal fields. Gormley came out of the meeting to say, 'I hope it doesn't lead to conflict but by God it *can* lead to conflict.' Two days later a special NUM executive decided unanimously – then still a rare event – to call a strike if the closure plan went ahead. A rousing delegate conference immediately after saw the leaders of the left on the executive received with huge acclaim by delegations not just from their own militant fields, but from the more conservative north-east, Midlands – even Nottinghamshire – areas as well. Peter Heathfield, then North Derbyshire area secretary, told the 350 delegates that 'It's all part of a grand design to reduce the impact and influence of the miners in the affairs of the British working class.'

By Monday 16th, as area strikes were declared one after the other, a meeting was arranged between Howell, Ezra and the miners' leaders. On Wednesday Scargill – who had stayed his hand – learned that the board wanted to shut four pits with the ultimate loss of more than 1,800 jobs, and called for a strike from the next Monday. He was, unusually, gazumped. Later that night, at the Energy Department, Howell threw in his hand: he told an astonished Gormley and Ezra that he was prepared to rethink the board's entire financial structure. Gormley recovered sufficiently to ask Ezra for a withdrawal of the 23-pit list: Ezra agreed. Looking back, Ezra comments that, 'We were completely taken aback. We assumed they would stand firm. We had warned, but not only were we not allowed to brief other ministers, there is no evidence they did it themselves.'

The prime minister had pulled the rug. Warned, especially by Prior (who kept open his lines to Gormley, and who had a quiet meeting with him on 21 January in which Gormley warned of the possibility of a strike if the closures were announced), she was quickly seized of the hopelessness of the position. A ballot would certainly have been won: even cautious area officials were talking of 90 per cent. The leaders of the steel and railway workers, Bill Sirs and Sid Weighell – friends of Gormley on the right of the movement and partners in the 'Triple

Alliance' of coal, steel and rail unions – declared their support. Prior's advice she might have instinctively distrusted, but Lord Carrington and the then Mr William Whitelaw talked in the same accents. Howell, feeling sore that he had, as he saw it, given constant warnings of industrial trouble if forced to move faster than he wished and was now being dished by those who had ignored him, said he thought they could let the situation run for a bit. The prime minister brusquely told him to get out: to give the miners and the board what they wished, but to get out.

It was the worst moment in Howell's career: he felt bruised and betrayed, his initial judgment that the treasury had pushed too far overridden, his later advice to stick it out brusquely dismissed. In the summer of that year, he was moved down to the Department of Transport, then dropped from government: Nigel Lawson moved to Energy.

But Moore, who stayed to be promoted to the treasury after the 1983 election as Financial Secretary, then, in May 1986, to the cabinet as Transport Secretary, was able to see a silver lining emerge even as he and Howell were being savaged by angry back-benchers. For the first time, he noticed, the serious papers, and other commentators and analysts, were beginning to pick over the flaws and deficits of the industry, and he detected a growing consensus for something to be done.

Most importantly, the government was itself galvanised by its 'defeat'. As Hoskyns puts it, the Macmillan dictum – never tangle with the Catholic Church, the Guards or the NUM – began to be questioned for the first time. Within months of the illusory U-turn, moves had been instituted which would ultimately render the next engagement one fought very largely on the government's terms.

Stocks at the power stations and the pitheads, around 29.9 million tonnes when the government came to power, grew to 37.7 million tonnes in 1980, 42.2 million tonnes in 1981, 52.3 million tonnes in 1982 and 58 million tonnes in 1983. Under Lawson, the government ensured that over half of that stock was held by the CEGB. Moore says of that time, during which the supposedly beaten government were having talks with the victorious mineworkers, that 'we were then able to build up stocks without challenge. We made the argument that we were building up the stocks to secure the viability of the industry, to take the coal off the industry's hands. And the NUM leaders went along with it. I couldn't believe it as it went on, month after month, that we weren't rumbled: I still can't.'

Ministers were fortuitously assisted by a long-standing dispute between British Rail and the train drivers' union ASLEF, which meant that some of the freight commonly shifted by trains went by road – including coal. Fatally for the long-term interests of the railway workers, and fortunately for the government's prosecution of the strike when it came, private hauliers were being introduced in ever-larger numbers to the coal market.

The main focus for the government's stepped-up contingency planning was the CEGB. Sir Donald Maitland, then the Energy permanent secretary, asked Glyn England, then chairman of the CEGB, to undertake a special piece of planning for a miners' strike – something which, Maitland stressed to England, was of a higher grade than the routine contingency work. By the end of that year, England's officials were able to produce a report for Lawson which had costed proposals for increased oil burning; for extra storage capacity at oil-fired stations; for improved facilities for receiving coal brought in by road; for taking treated water for the boilers from rivers; and for laying in extra supplies of hydrogen and chlorine.

From the government's point of view this was highly satisfactory, but England and Lawson grew increasingly disaffected with each other. The CEGB chairman, a former Labour Party member who had helped to found the Social Democratic Party, was no enthusiast for the government's views, and was spikily independent. He saw Lawson as a man over-keen to please the prime minister. He was prepared to collaborate in the stock build-up and in the contingency planning, but he did not want to pay for either. He told the government repeatedly that he would not have prepared in this fashion as a commercial matter, and that he should therefore have the extra costs defrayed from government funds. Since government and industry were then sniping at him for the high cost of electricity, and the government's settlement with the NCB and the miners in February had cut imports down from 2 million tonnes to 750,000 (with dearer UK coal being substituted at an estimated cost of £25 million) he felt he had a case.

By March 1982 it was clear that the government was looking for a new chairman. The day after April Fools' Day Lawson curtly announced that England's contract was not to be renewed, blaming a 'lack of information' from the board to the department, a complaint England dismissed as 'nonsense'. He left in July, to be replaced later that month by Dr Walter (now Lord) Marshall, chairman of the Atomic Energy Authority. The point was not lost on Scargill: he protested that it was aimed at 'weakening the power of miners and transport workers' – as indeed it was. Marshall pressed on with the stocking of his power stations, only calling a halt when the stations held 30 million tonnes of the then total of 55 million tonnes in August 1983, and had run out of storage space. Government compensation to the board for stocking costs was then running at £30 million a year.

The most important piece of contingency planning undertaken by government was the planning exercise conducted by an *ad hoc* committee, Misc (for miscellaneous) 57, which was composed of senior officials and met under the chairmanship of Mr (now Sir) Robert Wade-Gery, then chairman of the CCU and now High Commissioner in Delhi. It drafted in experts from all corners of government, concentrating on those with a detailed knowledge of mineworkers. For Hoskyns, it was a satisfying, if rare, example of a government confronting a problem early enough to do something effective about it. The 1981 débâcle, coupled with the fear of Scargill, had lifted long-range planning into an unusually privileged position.

The Wade-Gery committee trawled through the ground once more of what had happened during the Heath strikes. Like previous plans, it concentrated on securing the supply of electricity. Like previous plans, too, it called for larger stocks at pitheads, for the easing of cash limits on the CEGB to allow these to be paid for, for a switch from coal to oil burning, and for private hauliers to be substituted for trains in the event of a rail strike. The object was, first of all, to deter miners from striking. If that failed, it was thought that the hardship suffered might cause splits and encourage a drift back to work. And like other reports, too, it stressed that there could be no certainty. It never once assumed that the miners would attempt to mount strike action without a ballot, and was informed with the assumption that should a ballot come out for a strike, support from the rest of the union movement was more rather than less likely.

Every piece of contingency planning, every appointment made by the government in the period between early 1981 and early 1984 has been seen in retrospect as part of a wholly conscious plot leading to the miners' downfall. It clearly was not: rather it was a series of zig-zagging, often opportunist, sometimes accidental moves, though deserving the name of strategy because imbued with a common purpose: to render the government and the state as protected as it was possible to be from a miners' strike. But it was still an object of real and present dread.

As well it might be. Despite losing two ballots on industrial action Scargill was on the stump once more in the autumn and winter of 1983. A special conference imposed an overtime ban in protest at the board's 5.2 per cent wages offer in November. The president, however, needed all his rhetorical powers at the time. In some parts of the country there were mutterings over the ban's futility – especially among the winding enginemen, who in most coal fields had a sixth day of guaranteed overtime (while repair and maintenance work was done at the weekends) and resented losing it. Large numbers of miners, especially those over 50, were taking the redundancy terms being offered by the board. The centre of the industrial stage was being held by the National Graphical Association in its struggle with Eddie Shah over the maintenance of a closed shop at his *Stockport Messenger* freesheet – and by Christmas, the NGA had lost, as the TUC split in theatrical rage on left–right lines over support for the print union (deepening still further Scargill's contempt for the organisation). In January 1984 Heathfield whiskered in to his post as general secretary some 3,516 votes ahead of North Yorkshire agent John Walsh, a right-winger who opposed the overtime ban. Scargill welcomed the news of the election of 'my close friend' by saying that the 'ban is going better than we dreamed possible' – a heroic statement to be made at the end of a three-month period since the beginning of the ban which had seen the closure of 5 pits, the merger of 2 more and the planned closure of a further 6. The board *was* being hurt, to the tune of between £2 million and £3 million a month, but it was clearly not about to move on its offer.

That was never, though, the only or main point of the ban for the union leadership. It made the miners as a whole angry – and for the most part, the anger was, or could be, directed at the board and at the Aunt Sally figure of MacGregor. When the NUM president said it was working beyond his dreams, he was likely to have had in mind the complementary effect it was having on the preparations he and his colleagues had already made for the strike. For, though they had not put in the amount of time and energy into planning which the government had, could not command the resources and did not match the rigour of thought, they *had* planned in the expectation that a strike would come.

The most important part of that was the most obvious. Scargill had a huge, in retrospect clearly an exaggerated, belief in the power of propaganda (the importance he accords it in part explains his obsessive interest in, and hatred of, the press, radio and television). In an interview with one of the authors soon after taking office, he said that the *Miner*, then edited by the comfortable figure of Bob Houston, would be greatly expanded, put out regularly and push a consistent, militant line. That, said Scargill, would counter the 'filth of Fleet Street'. Houston – a talented Fleet Street journalist – was ditched; Maurice Jones, editor of the *Yorkshire Miner*, was brought in in his stead. Jones had himself attracted press attention when he had fled to East Germany in June 1977, following his arrest on the Grunwick picket lines, to claim political asylum. He claimed that police had made veiled threats against his daughter and his wife. Scargill and Owen Briscoe, the Yorkshire secretary, flew to East Germany and persuaded him to come back. Not surprisingly, the *Miner* under Jones's editorship instantly screwed up its pitch and launched itself against the board and the government.

But Scargill really trusted only himself. Correctly, he saw that no one else in the leadership's ranks could exercise the sway he could over the mineworkers at that time. He was greatly assisted by the fact that as well as being a miners' leader, he was a star – instantly recognisable, blessed by the constant unction of television. He wanted to appear to his people, and he did. From his election, he was continually on the move round the country, doing pit meetings, local labour party meetings, meetings arranged by left groups in and out of the party, galas, rallies, demonstrations and lobbies. For the two ballot votes, especially the first, he flogged himself round the country to give massive rallies in the coal fields. It was the first taste most reporters had of the mesmeric effect he could exercise over the miners who attended, of the efficiency of the left organisation in ensuring that the rallies were packed (though he was a considerable draw), and in the deployment of his main themes.

His first mass rally of the October 1982 campaign was in the Aberavon sports centre, near Port Talbot – two years later, he was to sit impassive as a noose dangled down from a catwalk over the head of Norman Willis on the same platform. It was a revelation to the few journalists who attended: a packed hall, a roaring crowd, a speech of some psychological complexity. He proposed a bond between leader and led, a bond he was to refer to again and again in the course of the strike – 'every miner in this industry has the right to say to me: fight for better wages, abide by conference decisions, ensure that our pit or workshop does not close. We too have the right, when the Coal Board treats this union with contempt, to turn round and demand your loyalty in the fight against the board.' He made the ante as high as he possibly could. The ballot was conducted on the twin basis of opposition to the then current 8.2 per cent basic pay offer, and to pit closures. He told the Welsh miners that they had to choose between loyalty to the union on the one hand and 'the Tory government's philosophy' on the other. He would never, he said, betray them, never go to the House of Lords (as Joe Gormley just had), always remain of them, responsive to their needs. Like every major Scargill speech made to mineworkers, it was terrifically emotive. Its hidden message was a command that they be bound to him as he was to them, a Bruderbond down through time. There was no half-way house: if not for, you were against, lost in the snare of Tory philosophy. For those in the Aberavon sports centre, and in Sheffield City Hall, and in Edinburgh's Usher Hall, the message got through: the people who ran the branches at the pits, who supported the union most heartily, were solid. Though the vote was lost, the cadres of the pits were won.

But it was precisely because Scargill and the left could only be certain that it was the cadres, and not the rank and file – who still read and perhaps believed the filth of Fleet Street and of the television studios – who were won that the second piece of preparation was essential. And that was aimed at getting a strike without a ballot: one of the most fateful decisions made within the Labour movement this century.

Towards the end of February 1983, Philip Weekes, the NCB's director in South Wales, decided he had to close a pit named Lewis Merthyr. The 'combination of a weak roof and a soft floor,' he wrote to the miners, had made its position 'hopeless'. But it was Des Dutfield's pit. Dutfield, a powerful 40-year-old, was the area's vice president and a gut militant somewhat out of step with the more disciplined leftism of Emlyn Williams and George Rees at the Pontypridd headquarters (Dutfield succeeded Williams as president early in 1986). Much to Williams's disgust, Dutfield staged a 'sit-in' down the pit. To Williams's alarm, he began to get support. Canny old warrior that he was, he put himself at the head of a movement that it appeared difficult to stop. He told a coal-field rally which had voted to hold a ballot on strike action that 'men and their families must realise this is the end of the road. We fight or we die.' The Welsh miners *did* vote for strike – but only by 55.74 per cent, a whisker more than the 55 per cent minimum required under rule, and there were some solid suspicions that the count had not been wholly rigorous. By the last day of February the 23,000 miners in the area were on strike. The day after, the Yorkshire area executive called their 55,000 men out on strike, followed by Scotland and Kent. In other areas – such as Lancashire, Durham and Nottinghamshire – the executives said they would call ballots with strike recommendations. Cowan, from Hobart House, issued a statement saying he welcomed the ballots in those areas which were holding them – a sign of the board's rooted belief that the rank and file would not vote.

It was a belief shared by the left of the NUM. On 2 March Scargill suggested in a BBC radio interview that no ballot was required to mobilise national support for a strike; that, under rule 41, areas could call their men out on strike (with or without a ballot, as their own rules dictated) and that this could amount to a national strike but called by different, though still constitutional, means. It was a controversial claim. In Yorkshire, miners at Grimethorpe, Shireoaks and Kinsley Drift demanded assurances that a ballot would be held before strike action, and in Cadley Hill pit in the Midlands they actually went on a 30-minute strike against the idea. Siddall said the apparent meaning of Scargill's statement could constitute a 'deplorable denial of the men's democratic rights'.

In the executive on 4 March, the left proposed that the strike be called without a ballot, under rule 41. In the last victory the right was to win the executive voted narrowly to put the issue out to ballot, on a motion put up by Jack Jones, the Leicestershire secretary.

Discussions went on within the left on the tactic – sharpened by the loss of the 4 March ballot call by 61 per cent of the vote. During a trip in August that year by all the mining unions to the Soviet Union, the NUM delegation took the opportunity of arguing the case through in the hotel lounges over drinks, deep into the night. Some – like Eric Clarke, the Scottish secretary – had qualms over the move. What, he said, would we do if the men would not follow the strike call without a ballot? Jack Collins, the Kent secretary whose amiability co-exists with a fierce loyalty to the Soviet Union and the Communist movement, had a simple sanction: drop them down the mineshaft, he said.

Between March 1983, when the no-ballot tactic was beaten, and April 1984, when it was rammed through, the left had prepared their ground well, and had become reconciled to it as the only way of getting the men out. There was no question in their minds that there had to be a strike: says McGahey, 'The miners had no alternative. The appointment of MacGregor was a declaration of war on the British miners and the mining industry by the government.'

The preparation for the no-ballot option is one example of the premeditation with which the NUM leadership approached the strike. There are two others. First, James Cowan, the board's deputy chairman throughout the strike and MacGregor's indispensable eyes, ears and intelligence in the coal fields, was given what he regards as an unmistakable warning of the strike's beginning and *even its manner of beginning* from the man who had been his respected sparring partner in Scotland during his directorship of the area – McGahey himself. Cowan met McGahey at a board function in December 1983. He took him aside and said that he believed the union was building up to a damaging strike, and that only McGahey's authority at national level could halt it. McGahey, on Cowan's recollection, shook his head and said: '*The dies are cast.*' He told Cowan it would be 'bloody', and it would start 'with Jack Taylor in Yorkshire'. Further, he said that Henry Richardson, the Notts secretary, would 'hold' Nottingham and that another leader – Cowan believes it was Jim Colgan, the newly elected Midlands secretary – would hold the Midlands, the two areas least likely to follow a militant lead.

Cowan believes now that McGahey gave him the warning in order to allow him to retire before the coming storm, keep his reputation intact and preserve his health, which had been bad. But, he says, it had the effect of making him wholly determined to see the strike through: 'The whole thing was calculated and planned. There was nothing spontaneous about it.' McGahey confirms the meeting and the warning, but says that Colgan's name was not mentioned. He says that, 'I spoke in the context of the appointment of MacGregor being the most provocative in British industry. I warned Cowan that he should face the fact that the inevitable consequence of that would be strike action.'

Among the best indicators that the NUM leadership had specifically prepared for a serious engagement came after the strike was over, from the painstaking work done by Michael Arnold, appointed as receiver of the NUM's assets in December 1984. Arnold discovered that a 'plan' existed, under which union funds would be transferred out of the country, or at least out of the apparent formal control of the union, in February of 1984 – some weeks before the strike was declared. In his report to the High Court in April 1986, Arnold wrote that his investigations 'generally indicated that, prior to the strike, in February and early March 1984 and subsequently, a plan had developed and been implemented under which the NUM would divest itself of the bulk of its assets either by transferring the same abroad or by placing them in the hands of some other person within the jurisdiction. The evidence indicated . . . that the motive for those divestments was to protect them from the likely consequences of defiance of the orders of this Court.'

Though the NUM leadership was preparing for war, at least some of their opposite numbers at the NCB still hoped for peace. MacGregor himself wanted to get his way by agreement. He did not dissent from the line being run by Ned Smith and Kevan Hunt, the numbers one and two in the Hobart House industrial relations department, that everything possible should be done to push Scargill back without giving him the chance of declaring a popular war. The chairman was running on more than one track in his efforts to achieve his end.

The first track, the public face, was sweetest reason, and was the one which he followed on the advice of his officials. In the mirrored cavern of Room 16, the room at NCB headquarters where the various consultative forums he so disliked are held – the Coal Industry National Consultative Committee and the Joint Policy Advisory Committee were the main ones – he heard again and again the complaints from Scargill that he had a 'hit list' which he refused to divulge. Finally, on 13 December he said, OK, let's look at the facts together at our next meeting. That next meeting – ultimately held on 6 March – was not welcomed by the officials or by the government, but was seen as inevitable by all. MacGregor believed that the facts could in the end convince anyone, if only they were faced: his officials worried about the kind of political capital Scargill would make of them.

The second track was MacGregor's own: it was his own instinctive dislike of the unions, his own – correct – appreciation that there could never be any agreement between him and Scargill. By mid-February, three weeks before the meeting on 6 March, he had given up on the project of securing an agreement with the unions. Speaking to one of the authors in Brussels, where he had gone on 14 February to deliver an after-dinner speech at a Conference Board seminar (on the need for lower wages to stimulate employment growth in the UK, a theme dear to the heart of the government), he said flatly that 'It has proved impossible to get any basis for agreement. I can't wait for the unions. I work for the government.' In effect, MacGregor was pulling out of the formal gavotte which he was expected to perform before the music stopped. The 'crucial meeting' of 6 March had already been dismissed in his mind as a waste of time, at least in terms of achieving what it was meant to – agreement on a joint approach.

MacGregor then knew, of course, the details of the budgets for the areas, which were being drawn up at the beginning of 1984. Government was very much involved in this. As the board had slipped into higher and higher deficits over the years, so the Department of Energy was impelled to become more and more concerned about both the budgets set and the closure implications which they carried. MacGregor's budgets carried closure implications which marked a significant increase on the rate set by Siddall – though not one wildly out of line with it – and had no chance whatever, he knew, of being agreed even as a basis of negotiation with Scargill.

Once the figures had been agreed between the board and the government, it remained for the office of the chief executive to pass the word down to the areas to put into effect the strategy of cuts. Four areas were identified as having to bear the bulk of the cuts: South Wales, the board's biggest lossmaker; the north-east; Scotland, which had already seen scatterings of industrial action and near strikes in protest against a pit closure programme energetically undertaken by its adamantine director, Bert Wheeler; and South Yorkshire. In meetings and phone calls over this period, Jim Cowan stressed to the area directors – Wheeler, Philip Weekes of South Wales, David Archibald of the north-east and George Hayes of South Yorkshire – the importance of going ahead with closures and going ahead fast.

Bert Wheeler's case was a clear example. Wheeler had pushed through closures at a faster rate than any of his colleagues. Between later 1982 and the beginning of the strike, he had announced the closure of Kinneil, Cardowan, Monktonhall, Bogside and Polmaise. In each case strike action had been threatened. The planned closure of Monktonhall sparked off an eight-week strike, called off in October 1983 for more talks (the closure never went ahead). But in February 1984, with the closure pending of Bogside and Polmaise, an area strike was again threatened – only to be ducked at a passionate area delegates' meeting in Edinburgh on 20 February, a bare three weeks before strike action flared across the country. It was a measure not just of Wheeler's success, but of demoralisation infecting the Labour movement, that the Communist-led Scottish miners, part of a labour movement which still retained a substantial strength in its society, should have seen its numbers drop from around 17,000 to 12,000 in three years, and yet (perhaps because) be unable to summon up defiance. 'We have not yet won the majority,' said McGahey, revealingly, as angry pro-strike miners shouted at him from behind the TV cameras.

Wheeler was proud of his record: he was reducing Scotland's legendary losses without encountering its legendary militancy. But his programme had been carefully phased. It was to a large extent known by the Scottish NUM leadership (though not of course agreed by them), and he believed that by sticking to it he could keep it that way. But Cowan told him to crack ahead faster, specifically to shut the last two remaining Ayrshire pits, Barony and Killoch. That, Wheeler thought, would unite the Scots miners, where his policy had been to keep them divided. Wheeler refused to move at Cowan's speed.

So too did Weekes and Archibald. In Weekes's case, with characteristic high spirits, he told Cowan that he could not hear what he was saying during the phone call telling him what to shut because of a bad line between London and Cardiff.

Hayes, less self assured than the other three men, was told to shut Brookhouse and Cortonwood. He did not want to. He questioned the decision at board level, but got the message that while he might get away with not closing both, he had to close one. One senior board official described his reaction as that of 'the good regimental sergeant major who asks – "are you sure sir?" – then carries out the order.' On 1 March he summoned the representatives of the three mining unions to his headquarters in Wath upon Dearne and baldly announced the closure. It could provide a spark for a fire – as Hayes knew well – for three reasons.

First, the South Yorkshire area was already in a dispute. An attempt by management to impose new mealtimes (snap times) at Manvers had resulted in a strike, for which area support had been sought (though 8 of the area's 15 pits refused to come out at meetings on 3 and 4 March). Bullcliffe Wood was also under threat of closure and men who had been transferred to next-door Denby Grange had been turned back by pickets.

Second, Hayes did not observe protocol. The meeting at which he made his announcement was a colliery review meeting, at which pits with 'problems' are raised for discussion. Though it is generally well known by all parties that the pits coming forward are probably marked for closure, the initial meeting does not consider it. But Hayes said it was to shut, by mid-April. All agree that was a blunder, few believe it was a set-up.

Third, it was an overtly economic closure. Hayes told the meeting that there was no market for Cortonwood coal. Yet the pit had earlier been thought to have had around five years' life in it still. Men from the closed Elsecar pit had recently been transferred to Cortonwood on that understanding. Over £1 million investment had recently been made in the pit. Says Jack Taylor, the Yorkshire president, who was at the meeting, 'You had to get your breath and we all sat back. This was the first one on uneconomic grounds, and they spelt it out in great detail, in a way a bit like a challenge.'

And so, by activating the mandate given them by a vote to take industrial action against closures taken in 1982, the Yorkshire area council on 5 March voted to oppose the closure of Cortonwood by strike action from Friday 9 March and to seek support from other areas at the national executive meeting on 8 March. By 5 March half the pits in Yorkshire were already out. At Yorkshire Main, managers trying to do safety work were stoned by pickets. The board was trying to recoup the situation. Peter Walker, as much taken by surprise by the Cortonwood decision as anyone, made sure that the board put out a letter to the 830 Cortonwood men stressing that the pit's future would go through the proper procedure – but too late.

In the commentary on the strike's beginnings, the announcement of the closure of Cortonwood in South Yorkshire on 1 March and the union's meeting with the board on 6 March are seen as co-equal. Indeed, Insight[5] says that if Cortonwood had not been scheduled for closure, 'the whole protracted strike would have taken a very different course, maybe never started at all'. We make a different judgment (a judgment is all it can be). That is, that Cortonwood was only part, though an inflammatory part, of a process which at some point would have led to a strike being declared – and declared, necessarily, in the same terms as it was.

The meeting of 6 March between board and unions had been well prepared for. The Thursday before – 1 March – MacGregor with his officials and Walker with his went over the planned output reductions to be announced to the unions. The figures already agreed by the board area by area produced a 4 million tonne cut in the planned output for 1984–5 on what had been achieved in 1983–4, but – as Scargill was to insist – an 8 million tonne cut on that latter year's *planned* output. The central objective was agreed between the two men and their advisors: avoid at all costs any aggregation of pit losses at national level; stress the continuing commitment to investment and voluntary redundancies, and to securing agreed closures at area level discussions; at the same time continue the (obviously fictional) progress towards an agreed basis for joint talks with government on a future Plan for Coal.

MacGregor stuck to his brief at the meeting. He took up a reasonable tone and attitude, going over again the slump in demand, the pressures from government to reduce the losses (the Select Committee on Energy had, the day before, published a report critical of the board's continuing huge losses), the determination of the board to look after the 'humanities'. He did not say twenty pits would close, but when Scargill deduced the figure from the capacity cut he said – well, more or less.

This was enough to allow Scargill to claim justification for the existence of a hit list, of which the twenty pits were merely part. Two days later, on Thursday 8 March, the national executive committee approved the calls from Yorkshire and Scotland for sanction for area strike action, approved in advance any such calls to be made subsequently and defeated, by 21 votes to 3 (Trevor Bell, secretary of the white collar section COSA; Roy Ottey, secretary of the Midlands-based power group; and Ted MacKay, secretary of the tiny North Wales area), a call for a national ballot. After some ineffectual attempts by Jack Taylor, the Yorkshire president, to limit his pickets to six within the Yorks boundaries, the area leadership recognised the *de facto* situation retrospectively as hundreds of Yorkshire pickets streamed joyously across the border to Nottinghamshire – hitting first Harworth pit in North Notts on the morning of 12 March – in order to force out men of whom they talked openly as 'scabby bastards'.

From the very earliest beginnings of the strike, the theme of 'miner against miner' was inscribed into its heart. The Yorks pickets at Harworth, and then elsewhere, were wholly uninterested in the Notts men's protests that no ballot had been held. They imposed a simple dualism: to turn back from the lines was good, to cross them treachery. Some Harworth men did turn back on that first day, few with any evidence of enthusiasm, a number with apparent resignation. More crossed over the lines into a pit whose entrance was broad and difficult to blockade without large numbers. About a dozen women kept up a barrage of obscene abuse aimed at the pickets from the estate across the road from the pit. The Harworth NUM committee looked and sounded ineffectual, trying to get the Yorks men to withdraw on the promise of holding a meeting of the men. It was a microcosm of what the coal field would become.

The one effort the right made to enforce a national ballot demonstrates the defensiveness of the group. Organised by McKay, Ottey and Jones, a gathering on 27 March was arranged at a day's notice at the Brant Inn, near Leicester. Most were nervous. Jones arranged police coverage in case pickets discovered the meeting. Joe McKie of the Midlands area excused himself from attendance on the ground there could be a 'backlash' in his area, and Sid Vincent said, when TV crews turned up at the event, 'I shall get bloody hung in my area.' (Revealingly, Jones routed a message to Chadburn to attend via Ned Smith at the NCB. Chadburn, in London at a court case, told Roy Lynk to attend, who pledged Notts' two executive votes for a ballot.) They were right to be frightened: most were later harassed by pickets, and a group burst into Ottey's Stoke-on-Trent office the next day to threaten him.

The meeting issued a statement calling on the national officials, 'being in the knowledge that at least 13 members out of 24 members of the National Executive Committee are in favour of a national ballot vote, to call an immediate meeting of the NEC towards organising the taking of an immediate *national ballot vote* [italics in original]. We can then concentrate on bringing public attention to the real issues facing the union and the industry.'

For all that the Brant Inn meeting was a fiasco, in which the main protagonists were seen as either scared or defensive, the NUM executive did have, by early April, a majority mandated for a ballot. Early in the fateful national executive meeting of 12 April, held with a crowd of some 2,000 fired-up, pro-strike miners outside expressing the crudest pressure, Henry Richardson made a heartfelt appeal for a ballot. According to Roy

Ottey, the Power Group Secretary, who has left an eye-witness account, Richardson said: 'The tragedy is . . . the members in Notts have tried everything and we are failing all down the line. There are 20,000 from 27,000 who have said "NO" and we here can't forget what is happening. The longer we go on the bigger the split.' He said in Cresswell village there had been daubing of doors and smashing of windows. 'Aren't they [the men] going to lose faith? It's no use saying it's a mistake because you are only making the situation worse. . . . I would hope we have a ballot. If we lose . . . are we in any different position to now? We are destroying trade unionism in Nottinghamshire.'[6]

But the left was not to be moved, and it had prepared for the fact that the majority wanted a ballot. When Jack Jones insisted on pressing a motion for a ballot, Scargill ruled it out of order on the grounds that a motion to that effect had been defeated at the previous executive on 8 March. He said that the special delegate conference called for 19 April would make decisions both on a ballot and on lowering the qualifying percentage needed for a strike call from 55 to 50 per cent. Ottey called the ruling 'nonsense'. Certainly there is no authorisation for it in the rule book, though the president has the power to interpret the rule and Scargill followed the correct procedure. But the constitutionality of the manoeuvre is beside the point.

Many on the left of the union have had second thoughts about a tactic in which the left-wingers on the executive all participated. Emlyn Williams frankly said it was wrong in an interview given on his retirement as South Wales president in February 1986. McGahey gives a series of defences of the no-ballot tactic: he says it functioned as a screen behind which those who were against the strike hid; that had the ballot result been lower than the 80 per cent then not working, it would have weakened the union; that all miners were not affected equally by the question of closures; that the left still remembered that fraud (as they saw it) of the ballot on incentive schemes in 1977. But at the end of that, he says, 'I believe we should have an analysis of the strike – which means, among other things, should we have had a ballot in the March–April period?'

Neil Kinnock, who had called for a ballot, heard about the executive decision while in North Wales, where he had been visiting South Wales miners from Cynheidre who were picketing Wylva power station. He had heard from them that the lorry drivers were not stopping; heard from the TGWU officials that their members would not stop for members of a union which could not get all its own men out. He thought the miners' executive would get the same point he was getting – that a ballot was the only hope of stopping the shambles affecting the union.

But he was bitterly disappointed. He had to endure months of taunts from opposition parties, and the justifiable pressure of his own colleagues, because he did not continue to press for a ballot. His own calculation that he could not give Scargill an alibi for losing the strike was the root reason why he did not. It meant a high price being exacted from the Labour Party and from Kinnock himself – though it gave both an even greater respect for the democracy of the ballot box.

6
Here we go

> 'Picketing of pits was both violent and intimidating. Most men arrived for work in ones and twos whereas the pickets often numbered fifty or a hundred. It takes tremendous courage for a man to force his way through a threatening line of pickets who outnumber him so dramatically.
>
> The men at W . . . colliery were afraid to go to work on the nightshift because, as they claimed, their vehicles left in the car-park would very likely be damaged by the pickets. The flying-squads of pickets in Yorkshire were highly organised and the men were paid for the days they spent going round the coalfields trying to stop other pits.'[1]

It might have been one of hundreds of reports which appeared in newspapers throughout the strike. In fact, it is the description by the former Coal Board chairman, Lord Robens, of events in the Yorkshire and Nottinghamshire coal field during unofficial action by miners in 1969 and 1970.

So when the young Yorkshire pickets from Markham Main colliery in the militant Doncaster area of Yorkshire converged on Harworth colliery on the first day of the strike in defiance of their area's instruction to stay out of other areas, they were following a traditional pattern. But the way they and others carried out that picketing was to colour and blight the dispute, ending hopes of support from a united miners' union and representing to many in the trade union movement, including its titular leaders in the TUC, the unacceptable face of trade unionism.

What made the picketing different in this dispute was not just its scale and ferocity but the way that the union's official national leadership, and the local leadership in many striking areas, deliberately encouraged it as an instrument of policy (sometimes it seemed the only policy) without qualification.

Early in the 1972 strike, which had seen far less violence, the then NUM General Secretary, Lawrence Daly, wrote to all areas under the heading, 'Peaceful Picketing'. Referring to reports in the press and television about disturbances involving pickets and people attempting to cross their lines, he said,

> Having regard for the size of the exercise that has been undertaken by the union, such incidents are minimal but unfortunately they attract maximum publicity, particularly when people are injured.
>
> In addition to the discomfort suffered by the unfortunate individual, there is the damage that such incidents inflict upon the good name of the union and its members, and that we cannot afford if we intend to keep public opinion on our side.
>
> Will you therefore impress upon the members who volunteer for picket duty that they are engaged on peaceful picketing and that physical contact with persons who attempt to pass through the line is illegal, and should be avoided, regardless of any provocation which our members may have to endure.

Twelve years later no instruction of that sort was ever issued from the NUM's national office or from the mouth of its spokesmen. One of the few pieces of advice for pickets came in a circular from Sheffield from the National Co-ordinating Committee on 26 June 1984. It said, 'all areas are requested to advise their pickets to be properly protected by the wearing of industrial type footwear and clothing, and, if possible, safety helmets. This advice to be offered in the light of the brutal and violent attacks we have witnessed by police on unarmed workers.' The tone could scarcely have been more different.

Arthur Scargill repeatedly made clear that he would never condemn actions by his members on picket lines. At Stoke on Trent on 30 November 1984, after the death of David Wilkie, the South Wales taxi-driver killed by pickets, his precise words were that the NUM dissociated itself from any acts of this kind 'which occur anywhere away from the picket lines'. It was one more clear break with the past.

For Scargill, himself the most celebrated flying picket commander in 1972, the picket line was both the symbol of the highest form of trade union commitment and the key tactical weapon. 'What is wrong', he demanded at the Brighton TUC in 1984, 'with asking Congress to support the basic tenet of trade unionism? When workers are on strike, trade unionists do not cross picket lines.'

But any strike? Any workers?

It was a question that Len (now Lord) Murray, the TUC general secretary, had put to him a few days previously in the intense midnight negotiations which had finally brought the miners and the TUC to an acceptable compromise on a conference resolution. What, asked Murray, if the EEPTU, a union deeply antipathetic to Scargill, was on strike at a coal-fired power station for union recognition and was offering a no-strike agrement deal (anathema to the NUM) as part of its bargain. Are you saying your members would not walk through a picket line?' Murray believed he got no real answer and in the event the TUC formula related not to picket lines but to the movement of coal.

But for Scargill the sanctity of the picket line was a vital weapon, particularly if it could be extended. ASLEF drivers had already broken new ground in 1972 by stopping for a picket banner draped over a railway bridge. It meant that a very few people could have a devastating effect. Take that further, as the NUM tried to do in a letter to all electricity supply unions in May 1984, and declare that all power stations should be 'deemed' to be picketed even when there was no line set up, and the possibilities were unlimited.

In practice the concept was rejected by the electricity unions and even where picket lines were physically established (and there were fewer than expected) they were mostly ignored, as they were in a number of other industries, principally steel. So with many workers refusing to accept the picket line 'basic tenet' argument, particularly in areas where miners had balloted to work, the NUM was thrown back on different forms of picket-line persuasion. But there were clear distinctions between the tactics, the number of pickets, and their behaviour depending on the areas and the pits they came from.

The heaviest picket was the final one at Orgreave on 18 June 1984 with about 10,000 according to police estimates, equivalent to about one in fourteen of those on strike. The smallest were those at isolated works and power stations at some distance from the coal fields. Many pits for most of the day had only the six set out in the code of conduct enshrined in the government's new trade union legislation, which was based deliberately on the NUM guidelines in 1974.

The most sustained picketing was in Nottinghamshire where in May there were never less than 11,000 pickets visiting a week, and one week as many as 18,000 in spite of the elaborate police road blocks. The record for an individual pit was at Harworth on the afternoon shift of 2 May 1984 when 8,000 pickets appeared and police were flown in by air from Hampshire.

Except at pits, where planks and tarpaulins made rudimentary picket shelters beside the obligatory brazier, there was little 24-hour picketing. Manning the lines outside power stations was not popular. As one executive member seeking to stiffen the arrangements put it, 'It was a boring job, dull, cold, and there were only a few lorries.'

It was frequently but un-checkably said that 95 per cent of the time picketing was peaceful. It was probably true because the moments of pressure were concentrated on the time something was happening, a shift change, or the arrival of vehicles. Then the action varied. There was ritual push and shove, often enjoyed by the young men on both the police and NUM sides. But there was also a long catalogue of vicious violence on display at the setpiece battles around Orgreave which many miners' leaders saw as their Waterloo, but perhaps most brutally evident in the villages of South Yorkshire in the bitter months in the second half of the strike when small pockets of men started to return.

One of the worst incidents was here at Rossington when on 9 July 1984 eleven Coal Board management staff (not NUM members and not on strike) went into the pit to carry out safety work. As camera teams watched, forbidden to film, pickets cut down trees and strung barbed wire and scaffolding from ransacked buildings across the entrance. Nails were hammered through conveyor belts which were then laid on the road against the rumoured arrival of police horses and vans while bottles from the pit canteen were filled with petrol for petrol bombs. Attempts were made to set fire to a Coal Board van, but as it was fuelled by diesel it resisted three attempts to ignite it.

Finally two police vans arrived to rescue the management staff and bundled them in under a barrage of missiles. But one unfortunate undermanager was left caught on the barbed wire. He ran back to the offices, locked himself in and telephoned for help. He was on tranquillisers for weeks.

On the other side, miners' leaders point to what happened in the village of Armthorpe next to the important pit of Markham Main in South Yorkshire on 22 August. Here, after two days of battles round the pit entrance, the police sealed off the village for about 45 minutes. Then, in some cases with drawn truncheons, they chased pickets through a housing estate, entering gardens and at least two houses in pursuit, breaking down doors and beating some pickets.

Different areas produced different kinds of picket behaviour. The small Kent area, heavily politicised, had some of the most resourceful. 'Semi-professional organisers' was their area secretary's description of them. South Wales picketed more power stations than anyone else and largely avoided mass picketing. Scotland had difficulty in raising enough pickets for its own needs and Scottish pickets only rarely crossed the border. Yorkshire provided the most and the most violent picketing. North-Eastern men spread out from their area and gave help to Scotland at Bilston Glen.

Most, but not all, pickets were paid. In Yorkshire they received £1 a day plus petrol expenses; in Kent and South Wales it was £3, later cut to £2; in Durham it was £1 a day for a pit and £2 elsewhere; Scotland paid nothing and Northumberland only for picketing outside the county. In some areas such as Yorkshire, where it caused endless wrangling, there was also money on occasions for repair of pickets' cars.

There was hardly any central co-ordination of picketing. A national co-ordinating committee was established in May and met weekly on a

Wednesday afternoon, but it made no important decisions and was described by one member as a 'fiasco'. It finally perished amid arguments about who paid its members' hotel bills after sequestration. There were few centrally arranged pickets. The exceptions included Orgreave and picketing at some East Anglian ports. Picketing was left as the responsibility of individual areas. There was some sorting out of zones of influence: South Wales withdrew from Leicestershire in favour of Yorkshiremen; Kent pickets left Didcot power station to the Welsh.

The cost was enormous. At the start, South Wales was spending £80,000 a week on picketing and sometimes as much as £100,000 on its 4,000 pickets. Some wags said the area would have gone bankrupt if it had not been sequestrated. As it was, it had spent £1.3 million by the time the court acted in August 1984. After Christmas the area set a limit of £35,000 a week. Tiny Kent, with 2,000 members, found itself spending £19,478 on paying members' fines. Durham spent £70,000 a week on picketing.

There were four main phases of picketing. First was the attempt by individual areas to make sure that their own pits came out. Quickly over in Yorkshire, South Wales and Scotland, it led on to the batle to bring out non-striking areas, particularly Nottingham. It was followed by the attempt to gain an industrial and psychological conquest at Orgreave, and then came the long and ultimately unsuccessful battle to prevent the return to work and the breaking of the strike. Each stage saw an escalation of violence beyond what had gone before, taking the action into territory which had not been reached in post-war industrial disputes.

Picketing was already a preoccupation for the NUM national executive when it met on 8 March and gave the areas carte blanche to take strike action under union rule 41 rather than proceeding to national action under a ballot as provided for in rule 43. The relation between areas which struck and those which might not was never spelt out, and members of the executive were in no doubt that that meant that striking areas, Yorkshire in particular, were likely to send pickets into other areas.

Three area secretaries who were sympathetic to the Yorkshire case were sufficiently alarmed by the prospects to try for deals with Yorkshire to keep them out until they had had time to persuade their own members at meetings. They were Gordon Butler in Derbyshire, Jim Colgan in the Midlands, and Henry Richardson in Nottingham.

An emergency meeting of the Yorkshire area executive had already resolved the day before that 'picketing must be restricted to collieries in the Yorkshire area, with numbers of pickets limited to no more than six'. But it was the inability of the Yorkshire leaders to control their members and stick to the agreement which many miners' leaders now claim cost them any chance of a united union and was a fatal blow to their chances of success.

But before this became apparent, there was great uncertainty even about whether other traditionally militant areas would support the strike, particularly South Wales, the union's third largest area after Yorkshire and Nottingham, and Scotland, even though the national executive had made action over Polmaise colliery official. There were recent and well-founded question marks over both areas. In Scotland the coal field had failed to come out over the closure of Polmaise only a couple of weeks previously.

In South Wales, the attempt almost exactly twelve months before to bring out the NUM nationally in support of the Lewis Merthyr pit had ended in failure. Welsh delegates who had visited every Yorkshire pit had been infuriated by their refusal to give support, with a particularly hostile turn-down from Cortonwood. Now they doubted whether Yorkshire itself would come out, and were bitter about being asked for support after it had been refused them.

Over the weekend of 10–11 March, with action called for the Monday, the doubts looked well justified. A number of Scottish pits heard calls for a ballot, with the largest, Bilston Glen, making fairly clear that it wanted to work. In South Wales there was a dramatic vote; lodges voted 18 to 13 against a strike. In both cases, the answer to the NUM leadership's problems was the same – picketing.

In Scotland, on the Monday morning, three pits worked, Killoch and Barony in Ayrshire, and Bilston Glen. The Ayrshire pits had been picketed out by the end of the first day, but Bilston Glen kept working on the Tuesday until pickets who had been brought in buses from Fallin Welfare in Fife, where Polmaise was situated, succeeded in stopping all but a handful of men going in.

In South Wales, the coal field was stopped after some smart freelance organisation by the union's research officer, Kim Howells, who was to become the NUM's picket organiser during the strike. Leaving the atmosphere of gloom which surrounded the union leadership after the result of the lodge vote became known, he telephoned round to arrange a meeting of representatives from a number of militant pits that following day. Held in the ambulance room in Hirwaun village, it brought together men from eight pits. A rush of organisation that evening meant that there were pickets on every South Wales colliery the following morning. At Deep Navigation colliery, a single picket turned back the coaches of miners arriving for work with the words, 'Official picket, boys'. In disciplined South Wales, that was enough.

By the end of the day, South Wales NUM leadership was sufficiently confident to start to send pickets by bus to other coal fields. With their experience of the previous year's unsuccessful campaign, they knew their way round every pit in the land. With a shrewd idea which pits were likely to be more sympathetic than others, they headed for their destinations including the Nottinghamshire coal field, which was at that moment becoming the target for a rather different sort of picket.

These were the men from the Yorkshire Doncaster area pits, closer to the Nottingham pits than to many of their fellow Yorkshire collieries. Doncaster's reputation was of the most militant in Yorkshire, but on this occasion the panel which ran its affairs had not, as it had done before, authorised picketing in defiance of the area. It was backing the union line of keeping out of other coal fields.

None the less on Monday morning forty Yorkshiremen were outside the border Nottingham colliery of Harworth. By the time the afternoon shift were assembling at midday, the picket had swollen to 250, most from Markham Main colliery at Armthorpe ten miles away. The Doncaster area agent, Frank Cave, appeared on the scene and appealed to them to disperse. About fifty women, wives of local miners, argued with them. It was a repeat of 1969, and Jack Taylor's words appealing to members to continue the 'dignified and responsible approach' of restricting picketing to their own coal field fell on deaf ears as he announced that the Harworth pickets were 'being ordered back into line'.

By the next day there were pickets at other Nottinghamshire collieries, including Ollerton, and Bevercotes which was closed by 200 pickets and the men sent home. By now they were from Rossington, Hatfield and Bentley, as well as Markham Main. Richardson, his deal with Taylor in tatters, appealed publicly for the Yorkshiremen to stay out: 'What is happening is not picketing but mass blockading. It will be counter productive and no union can sustain a strike under the circumstances.' But it was too late. The chairman of the NUM's Barnsley panel, Tommy Delamere, called for picketing to be stepped up, declaring, 'We want to hit as hard as we can.' The Yorkshire executive met to review the situation and backed the *fait accompli*. That night Yorkshire pickets were at most North Notts collieries by the late evening and on the following day, Wednesday, production was halted at eight collieries and reduced at the other six.

Yorkshire pickets were by now in Derbyshire where the big Markham pit was stopped. Gordon Butler, the area secretary, publicly accused Taylor of breaking a gentleman's agreement to keep flying pickets out. Later he would say that because the picketing had occurred before Derbyshire had had its chance to hold meetings on the strike, it had prevented a 55 per cent majority for strike action in the area.

Why Yorkshire failed to control its troops will be a matter of argument for years, but there are many in Yorkshire who place the blame on strong Trotskyist influence at pits like Markham Main, Rossington and Hatfield. It is not the whole story. These were the pits on the whole closest to Notts and with men arriving outside miners' welfare clubs in the early part of the week, eager to go picketing, it was difficult to send them home. None the less it seems clear that an element anxious to show militancy in the face of the leadership's more measured approach was a major factor. 'The Trots at Armthorpe (Markham) and Rossington', as one member of the Yorkshire executive put it, played a key role in an action which some believe prejudiced the whole course of the strike.

Henry Richardson, the Notts area secretary, who later lost his job for his support for the strike, says now, 'We got assurances from Yorkshire that they wouldn't come. But they lost control. Quite honestly one or two Marxist and Workers Revolutionary party men sent them down without the backing of the area. It was fringe elements that organised it.' But he is guarded about the effect. 'Had there been no picketing, I think Notts would still have voted against a strike because of the way branch officials canvassed for a no vote. Certainly the picketing didn't help, but I don't think it turned a win into a loser.'

Jimmy Millar, the Markham Main branch secretary, says the reason they picketed was because the branch had voted to do so. He dismisses the idea of Trotskyist influence as just 'two or three' people. He had tried to get the pickets assembled at Armthorpe to disperse around as many Nottingham pits as possible giving an element of surprise. But instead they had voted to go all together to the nearest pit – Harworth.

They knew, he said, that the union was holding the middle page of its *Miner* newspaper for an appeal for solidarity from the Nottinghamshire officials. 'But we didn't put a great deal of faith in that.' He is critical of both Arthur Scargill and Jack Taylor for having 'no plan whatsoever' for the picketing. 'It was just a free-for-all.'

In retrospect, the union vice president, Mick McGahey, says, 'I am not sure we handled it all correctly. The mass intrusion of pickets into Notts, not just Yorkshiremen; I accept some responsibility for that, and so will the left have to. I think if as an executive we had approached Notts without pickets, it might have been different. Because I reject, I have made this clear since the strike, that 25 or 30,000 Notts miners, their wives and families and communities are scabs and blacklegs. I refuse to accept this. We did alienate them during the strike.'

One of the pits affected was Cresswell. Here men talk about the way the first pickets appeared – not from Yorkshire but from South Wales. Roy Whitehead, who later became president of the branch, in the move which pushed out pro-strike men, describes how after being spoken to by the South Wales pickets, many, including him, turned back from work. When they went back to the pit the next day, the Welshmen said that they had been told Yorkshiremen were on the way. 'There'll be trouble,' they said, 'We'll be off.'

When the Yorkshiremen arrived in force and attempted to prevent men going in, after they had balloted to do so, most of the Cresswell men, including Whitehead, insisted on working to show they would not be intimidated.

Their determination was made plain when at the end of the first week, the ballot of Nottinghamshire men was held after a brief picketing lull, when pits closed so that the ballot could take place in a calmer atmosphere. Nottingham men voted heavily to stay at work. None of the areas which held a ballot on strike action produced the 55 per cent majority required by the rule book.

Still, at the end of the first week, picketing had secured some major successes. Scotland and South Wales had joined Yorkshire, and Durham was in the process of coming out through a mixture of mass picketing and persuasion. Looking around the coal fields at the end of the first week, as the ballot results were awaited, the picture had changed from one where there was scarcely a coal field in which some pits had not voted to work, to one where there was scarcely a coal field where any work at all was going on.

In Nottingham the picketing had at times been ferocious. Much of the action was in the darkness of late night and early morning. Stones were thrown, working miners' cars kicked, barricades built. With Harworth, the target of the first picketing, closed because of the weight of picketing until the ballot took place, Ollerton, thought to be the Notts pit with the strongest left-wing pro-strike feelings, became a focus. On the morning of 14 March pickets got into the pithead baths and outbuildings, and police moved in to clear them.

That night a Yorkshire picket, 24-year-old David Jones from Ackton Hall near Pontefract, was killed. The inquest returned an open verdict. Jones had died from crush injuries, but it was not clear how. It was a confused night. Bricks and bottles had been thrown at the night shift arriving for work. Jones, pausing himself like many for a drink at the pub, had given first aid to one working miner struck by a brick. Local people had gathered to shout at the pickets, and the pickets themselves had had to rush back to their cars when local youths started to vandalise them.

At ten to five the following morning the North Notts area director, Jack Wood, confronted the area president, Ray Chadburn, in his office. Wood, woken in the night after Jones's death, had driven through the pickets streaming away from Ollerton to nearby Thoresby colliery. Chadburn, greatly upset, asked Wood to shut down Nottinghamshire. Wood gave him a sharp answer, 'Your men want to work. I am not going to prevent them, and you should be leading them.' It was a clear signal of the board's determination to keep going. Although Ollerton closed as a mark of respect, it was only temporary.

But keeping the pits open only became possible by the biggest concerted police action seen in Great Britain since the end of the war. Chief constables involved still insist strongly that there was no national direction, that the National Reporting Centre established in Scotland Yard in the first week of the strike was simply a clearing house for their demands for extra men from other forces, and that they retained complete operational control in their areas.

But Arthur Scargill saw it as the arrival of George Orwell's '1984', announcing that they already lived in a police state. Casual passers-by and many middle-of-the-road politicians were shocked and alarmed by the virtual isolation of the Nottingham coal fields by road blocks on highly public motorways and in particular the stopping of pickets from Kent heading north through the Dartford tunnel in Kent for coal fields more than a hundred miles away.

Tellingly, the incident was not repeated. Outside Nottingham, two of the police forces most involved, South Yorkshire and Derbyshire, made a conscious decision not to use road blocks to turn pickets back.

The police attitude was markedly firmer than in the 1972 strike. Then, faced with hundreds of miners' pickets, plus local engineering workers and others on strike in support of the miners, the then chief constable of Birmingham, Sir Derrick Capper, agreed to close the gates of Saltley coke depot. It started the legend of Arthur Scargill and sent shock waves through the establishment. This time, it was made clear from the prime minister herself to chief constables who had themselves absorbed the lessons of Saltley, a very different line was expected. It was demonstrated first clearly in Nottingham and then at Orgreave. It involved using the police as a physical barrier, instead of mounting a legal challenge to the picketing by the Coal Board.

The result was bitterly criticised by many police officers who saw themselves as being used as the meat in the sandwich. As inspector Ronald Carroll of West Yorkshire police put it at the 1985 conference of the police's main trade union, the Police Federation, 'The police were used by the Coal Board to do all their dirty work. Instead of seeking the civil remedies under the existing civil law, they relied completely on the police to solve their problems by implementing the criminal law.'

Demanding that the 'government's policy' of keeping a low profile must go, he said, 'It is totally wrong to expect our officers to be incessantly abused, viciously assaulted, and then see many of the assailants go free in order to maintain a low profile for political purposes.'

That was one view of the police's role. Another was provided by a much-quoted letter in the *Guardian* from a police inspector on 6 June 1984. It accused the government of using 'the "thin blue line" as its battering ram against Arthur Scargill in an attempt to deliver the "coup de grace" to the trade union movement as a whole.' He contended that the police force was being used to 'pursue a political goal rather than one of public duty'.

There can be no doubt that it was only the police which prevented the miners' leadership from achieving its objective of halting all coal fields by picketing. In the process the miners' leadership, acutely aware of the way its public support had suffered from the picket-line violence, attempted to transfer the blame for that violence on to the police. It appeared to be an alternative to attempting to modify the behaviour of NUM members on picket lines. Although the public generally accepted that there had been cases of police bad behaviour, loss of control, and over-use of truncheons, particularly at Orgreave, where other senior police officers were critical of some of the police behaviour, the union's attempt failed. It never managed to shift the blame for picket-line violence on to the police in the way in which Arthur Scargill's public pronouncements attempted.

Once again Mick McGahey is frank about it. 'Anyone who makes an analysis of the miners' strike can't avoid this issue of violence. I'll argue that the Ridley plan, the mass use of police, the use of scab lorries and so on, contributed to the violence, the exasperation of it all. But I find it difficult to argue that there was not violence on our side, and that violence did not help us. It was played up to the maximum. Many people would say "the miners have a case but we can't have this business of harassment; the vilification of people; it's against the best traditions of British people." So we didn't have the mass support we had had in 1972 and 1974.'

In the first week of the strike there had been doubts about whether even the police presence could stem the flood of picketing. At Ollerton pickets had broken through police lines, and at Welbeck colliery they had got into the pit yard by overwhelming the half dozen police there. By the Wednesday the Nottingham chief constable, Charles McLachlan, had applied under the police's 'mutual aid' provisions (which allows them to ask for temporary reinforcements from other forces for assistance). Men from the north and Midlands were moved to Ollerton, and that day McLachlan had available 130 extra police support units from outside – about 3,000 men – larger than his entire 2,200 strong Notts force.

It was on that day that the National Reporting Centre was established on the 13th floor of Scotland Yard. The NRC became the subject of enormous comment and some deliberate misinformation during the strike. For the police it was a clearing house for the transfer of forces from different parts of the country to the coal fields and for information, for its critics it was an embryo national police force. The confusion was assisted by the fact that the chairman of the Association of Chief Police Officers, which ran it, was for much of the strike one of the chief constables most operationally involved in the dispute, McLachlan himself.

The idea of the NRC was born from the Conservative government's outrage at what had happened in the 1972 miners' dispute – flying pickets and Saltley in particular. It was fortified by widespread and violent hit-and-run picketing during the building workers' dispute, and 1972 ACPO, the Metropolitan Police Commissioner and the Home Secretary agreed to provide for the operation of an NRC if necessary. Described by the Home Office as a 'communications room at Scotland Yard', it has no permanent form, and in normal times equipment is merely stored in a Scotland Yard cupboard and then installed in a commandeered conference room as necessary. It was used during the inner city riots of 1981, the prison officers' dispute of 1980–1, and the Pope's visit in 1982. Its role is to process requests for aid from chief constables whose informal arrangements for assistance from neighbouring forces are insufficient to cope with the demands on them, and to pass them to other forces who can assist.

Peter Wright, chief constable of South Yorkshire, puts the strongly held police view in his report on policing the strike:

> The centre has been said to have acted as an arm of government and to have coordinated the largest scale police operation ever mounted in this country. In fact, the centre has only responded to requests for assistance from chief constables. . . .
>
> The strategy of policing the dispute in South Yorkshire has been the responsibility of the Chief Constable. All officers who have performed duty in the county, including those from other police forces, have been under the command of the Chief Constable and the direct operational control of his senior officers. . . .
>
> To remove [the NRC] would leave no viable alternative but the creation of larger police forces or national force. The manner in which the NRC has functioned in this dispute militates against the necessity for a national police force.

In general this was true. But in practice, particularly with vans of imported police arriving in the middle of a confused situation, sometimes finding themselves under sudden ambush, some important operational decisions were made without reference to the local force. Where large numbers of imports were on hand, it was also sometimes hard for the local officer to assert his authority, leading to the sometimes convenient complaint by pickets that their local policing was being overruled by strangers.

The police reinforcements were organised as Police Support Units, detachments of twenty men usually with two sergeants and an inspector with their own transport – a bus or two transit vans. They were generally drawn from the 10 per cent or so of the 140,000 police officers in

England and Wales who have had training according to the Tactical Operations Manual which covers public order problems and involves guidance on the use of long and short shields and other defensive equipment. But as the strike went on, less well trained officers were sent, some with no shield training, including on one occasion half a PSU of Thames River Police from the Metropolitan Police.

The first news of the deployment was given to officials of the Police Federation by the then chairman of ACPO, David Hall, the Humberside chief constable, as he went to London to set up the NRC. Tony Judge, the federation's spokesman, describes conditions then as 'absolute chaos'. Visiting the Notts training headquarters at Edwinstowe, close to Ollerton, he found 'officers sleeping on billiard tables or mattresses . . . men arriving in hired buses and transits from all over the country'.

The problems of accommodation and long hours, a distinct dampener on the huge sums of overtime, were to occupy the Federation for twelve months. Old RAF and army camps were pressed into use; men were billeted in drill halls and hangars. Later some were housed in holiday camps and university halls of residence, but at the beginning conditions could be appalling.

Some men were on duty sixteen hours a day. There were complaints of men coming off the picket line at eleven at night and being woken at three for breakfast. One West Midlands official of the federation told its 1984 conference of one camp: 'It was an old army transit camp. There were twelve men to each hut with a coke stove in the middle. There were blankets to keep out the holes in the windows but no blankets or sheets for the beds. The ablutions were so far away as to be useless. I thought this was bad, but the next place I saw was worse. There were twenty-four men jammed into a room which was not intended for more than ten. Two chaps were sleeping in a drying room, and two more in a mop room. They were all sleeping on li-los, in sleeping bags.' A Metropolitan policeman talked of 350 men in one hangar at RAF Newton, sleeping on camp beds 2 feet 6 inches apart.

Some accommodation was better, and things improved. At some camps there were extensive recreational and sports facilities. Everywhere there were endless video showings to beat the boredom which was the most constact factor for policemen. Not all the expedients were as ingenious as one detachment of police waiting for duty on the riverside wharves of the Trent, who occupied themselves with a Miss Coalfields 1984 contest with half a dozen brawny constables parading in little more than helmets and jockstraps.

Jokes apart, the conditions for police and the long hours were a poor preparation for remaining calm and good-humoured on picket lines. Senior officers were increasingly concerned about the way a strong group mentality was established, when recent emphasis on police training had been to encourage an officer's independence and sense of individuality.

With reinforcement assured, McLachlan now implemented the controversial policy of establishing road blocks at the entrance to the Nottingham coal field.

The police had started to stop coaches as early as the second day of the strike. McLachlan had been at a Home Office discussion group the previous month about inner city questions. When the treatment of the NGA dispute at Warrington had been discussed where Cheshire police had turned back coaches once disturbances had started, McLachlan put forward the view that there was a case for stopping them even if there was only a risk of disturbance, little thinking that barely a month later he would try his theory in practice. It was legally challenged in the High Court in November 1984 by miners stopped by police, but it was ruled by Mr Justice Skinner and Mr Justice Otton that 'if, on stopping vehicles the police are satisfied that there was a real possibility of the occupants causing a breach of the peace one and a half miles away . . . it would be their duty to prevent the convoy from proceeding further.' That coincided with the Attorney General's view expressed in parliament early in the strike.

McLachlan, who extended the intercept policy to cars by the weekend says, 'My view was that we had the power to apprehend breaches of the peace – not simply to stop them when they were already happening, but to prevent them. I took the view at first that we should turn back buses, coaches and mini-buses. My particular worry about coaches was that they could be like football coaches. There may be drink on board; you could build up this tremendous fighting spirit. Bearing in mind what had already happened in Nottinghamshire, I felt that if we could intercept them that would be a contribution to preserving the peace at the pitheads.'

As one picket leader put it, 'Police cars waited on roundabouts in Doncaster. People would then be stopped on the motorway and told, "either turn off or you will be stopped at the next roundabout and your car taken off you." Perhaps a tenth of our cars got through.' Some pickets who refused to turn back were arrested.

The complaints mounted. Tommy Delamere of the Barnsley NUM panel complained that police were smashing windscreens with truncheons. Nottingham police admitted to at least one incident where they said the windows had been broken because pickets had locked themselves in.

The vicar at the pit village of Goldthorpe in Yorkshire, Rev. Rodney Marshall, was stopped while in a car driven by a local NUM branch secretary, as they went into Notts. They were warned to turn back or be arrested because there was reason to believe they were going to picket. When the vicar got out and displayed his dog collar, the police were alleged to have replied, 'It doesn't mean a thing to me, it could be a miner in disguise.'

But there were also close links between local police and miners. In South Yorkshire, over 60 policemen had themselves been miners and many more came from mining families. Some police in South Yorkshire and Derbyshire actually helped to support their striking relations. When the restrictions of road blocks led to pickets on the M18 driving deliberately slowly in a tactic made famous by French lorry drivers, one of those arrested for obstruction was Tony Gibbons from Yorkshire Main colliery. Himself a former policeman, he found himself being arrested by his brother, Mick, who was still in the force. It was a comic moment in an increasingly bitter atmosphere between striking pickets and police.

In North Wales, the chief constable admitted having plain clothes men to gather information among pickets. A group from Kellingley colliery in North Yorkshire complained of being interrogated about their political beliefs when arrested in Notts. How had they voted? What if the choice was between Conservative and Communist? Who had they voted for as NUM president?

The explanation seems to be a questionnaire used by Nottingham police which did not include those questions but asked others to try to establish who was directing the pickets. Police intelligence on the whole was not very good. There was information that pickets were on their way from spotter cars at crossroads (sometimes violently attacked by pickets), but not so much information about where they were going.

Charles McLachlan says, 'We came under criticism for not establishing who was directing. In fact there were efforts made but it was very difficult, particularly as the pickets often received their directions by telephone. We did have teams of officers questioning the pickets, particularly at the time when they were obstructing the motorways. We were accused of political questioning. The Questionnaire asked questions like "Who's paid you for coming? Who told you to come?" A whole questionnaire trying to get to people behind the action. We carried it on but not to any great extent because we just were not getting anywhere. They realised they were going to be questioned and they were well briefed as well.'

Picket organisers went to some lengths to disguise their intentions in Yorkshire. Area agents agreed the targets at the daily Barnsley committee for the four areas and then passed them on at an evening meeting. Some branch secretaries thought this helped leaks but took precautions to keep their destination a secret. At Frickley pit, for example, often cars were simply told to muster and then followed the treasurer and delegate who drove the front vehicle. At the start Yorkshire destinations were handed out in writing, but later it was by word of mouth as any writing down was avoided.

When cases came to court, the pickets found another problem; bail conditions which kept them off the lines. One of the first cases to come up, on only the third day of the strike, was of a Yorkshire picket from Conisborough accused of threatening behaviour at the Notts pit of Thoresby. Bail terms were specific – he was not to visit any Coal Board premises except to go to work. The conditions varied a little; police chiefs liked to compare them with those imposed on people accused of offences at football matches.

In South Yorkshire, the police solicitors sought two conditions – that the accused should not go within one mile of the place of his arrest, and that he should not visit any premises of the National Coal Board, British Steel Corporation or Central Electricity Generating Board, except for his own place of work. The proviso did not exclude anyone automatically from picketing his own pit.

At the numbers arrested swelled, bail conditions helped to blunt the edge of the picketing. Kent men, as in previous strikes picketing small south-east ports which were easy destinations for coasters bringing in coal from the continent, were early casualties. After some large pickets at Wivenhoe in Essex, they withdrew. Area secretary, Jack Collins, says bluntly, 'We couldn't keep it up. Everyone was lifted and many of them had bail restrictions placed on them.' Here the conditions included reporting to a home police station. The National Association of Probation Officers complained of 'supermarket justice'.

But in Nottingham, which remained the key to the strike, the battle was far from over. Old hands in Yorkshire had estimated that it would take them about a fortnight to bring Nottingham out, though that was before the police effort reached such a pitch. Their men kept trying and Coal Board chiefs concede they were never certain of keeping Nottingham largely at work until into June.

In spite of the road blocks, the numbers of pickets in the coal field actually increased. Using back roads, on occasions leaving their cars and walking across the border through countryside, they carried on. Tactics changed again when the Coal Board ended nightshifts at many collieries because of the trouble in the dark, particularly after the pubs were open. The impact of drink on pickets in the early days was frequently obvious particularly in the big demonstrations in Sheffield, Mansfield and later London.

There was now more daytime picketing, with the advantage that picket cars were less obvious in the general mass of daytime traffic than in the isolated small hours.

As frustration mounted, sabotage became more common; conveyor belts were cut on tips, boiler switches interfered with.

A month into the strike, tactics changed again with single pits being targeted for saturation picketing. Cresswell was a favourite target, 2,000 one afternoon shift on 9 May, but the record was 8,000 at Harworth on 2 May.

Coal continued to be produced with shortfalls in production being made up from stocks. In the first week a usual average of about a quarter of a million tonnes in North Nottingham was cut by two thirds – down to 85,000 with half as much again lifted from stock. But in the second week, it was getting close to normal levels with just under 200,000 tonnes deep-mined supplemented by 40,000 from stock. In the first five weeks of the strike, North Notts sent nearly 900,000 tonnes into the market, compared with a normal 1.2 million.

By now things were beginning to settle into a pattern across the country, with implicit understanding between police and pickets in the majority of cases. But in some key areas the name of the game remained an attempt to outwit the police and bring things to a halt by sheer weight of numbers.

South Yorkshire police had been through the bitter 1981 steel strike as well as previous coal disputes. They saw a major difference this time in the refusal of NUM officials to give advance warning of their targets or sometimes to hold discussions with senior policemen about policing arrangements. Peter Wright's view of the reception accorded to his deputy and an assistant chief constable when they went to NUM headquarters to discuss the handling of the huge demonstrations outside the crucial executive and special conference meetings in March and April, is that 'they were given individuals to talk to who were dismissive of what they were trying to do . . . in my view they were not concerned with what went on.'

Another police view of the dispute is provided by a Northants inspector, Robert Bartlett, who was billeted in the Warwickshire coal field, which sets out the pattern which prevailed at many pits:

> The pickets were in the main quite affable. One afternoon the police played South Wales miners in a soccer match. The kickabout was followed by a sharing of police sandwiches and a long discussion about the intricacies of the dispute. The pickets lived, 27 of them, in a semi-detached house with a tent in the garden. Most were reasonable men, committed to what they believed to be their only way to protest, critical of violence, but quite agreeable to a bit of pushing and shoving.
>
> Those going to work were approached by the six pickets in the road (accompanied by 'minders' from the Police Support Unit) but most refused to stop or listen. Those who stopped were spoken to, in the main politely, with no swearing, no threats. 'Come on, if all the craftsmen come out, we can soon get a result.' The reply was usually along the lines of, 'I'll come out if it's done by the rule-book.'
>
> Both sides have firm, honourable men believing deeply that what they are doing is right, but there are some nasty men on the fringes.

> The six pickets stood in the drive of the pit on Coal Board property the result of a truly British compromise. The original line was outside a line of miners' cottages and the noise had kept children awake. A move up the drive, under a street lamp with a car park for the demonstrators was agreed.
>
> It was sensitive policing that ensured that the Chief Inspector in charge was referred to as 'Sir' by the pickets, who consulted him before they tried to visit the colliery officers. Newly-arrived pickets were introduced to the chief inspector, who greeted many of the regulars by their christian names. The Welsh miners invariably came and saw him before going home to Wales and usually informed him if they were to come back.[2]

Throughout the long hot summer of 1984 it was the pits which remained the focus of most picketing, although there were other targets as well. But one of the surprises was the failure to mount serious pickets at many power stations.

In Yorkshire in the first month there were some sporadic attempts at picketing power stations in some numbers, explained by local NUM President Jack Taylor as a switch to secondary targets because of the difficulty of getting through to Notts pits. In practice in Yorkshire there was no effort made to move coal into power stations, but there would have been a case for attempting to stop some of the other chemical supplies necessary for operations. This had been a crucial factor in 1972, since when the CEGB had built up much larger supplies and storage facilities, but they were not shortage-proof.

There was a bitter argument about it between the NUM's Doncaster area panel committee, which wanted the right to pick its own targets, and the Yorkshire area which was directing it. The Doncaster men wanted to spread their picketing to power stations in large numbers and also for pickets to go out more than once a day.

Late in the strike Yorkshire national and executive member John Weaver was detached to try to step up the power station blockade. But it was too late. Jack Taylor still insists that the reason they did not do more was the need to concentrate on the pits.

South Wales and Kent saw power stations as a much more crucial target. Kim Howells, who organised pickets in South Wales, was openly critical during the strike for the national leadership's unconcern about power station picketing. His men made power stations and ports a priority. South Wales miners could be found from Heysham in Lancashire to Fawley in Southampton Water.

It led to some jokes. Pickets arrived at Heysham, telephoned to say that they had found no coal after stopping all vehicles for two hours. It had to be pointed out to them that Heysham was a nuclear station. A plan was then drawn up to try to restrict gas supplies to nuclear stations.

At the big Pembroke oil-fired station there was another problem. It was potato harvest time, and pickets unsuccessfully trying to persuade power station workers who had passed rapidly from short time (and possible redundancy) to almost unlimited overtime, found themselves a target. Farmers invited them to join the harvesting, and relays of pickets sent up from South Wales headquarters ended up making good money in the potato fields.

Ports were another target. Kent men who had run the national picketing office in London in 1972 and 1974 went back to the south-east ports, and there were battles at Wivenhoe in Essex. But there were so many small ports and wharves that miners' attempts to prevent coal being imported largely for the domestic market would have been doomed to failure even if they had been better organised. As it was, the Trent wharves on the borders of Yorkshire saw some of the largest coal shipments, and Yorkshire pickets did little to stop coal from Flixborough wharf going to Scunthorpe to supplement and replace the Orgreave supplies. In 1984 coal imports doubled according to official port statistics from 5,295,000 tonnes to 10,049,000 tonnes. The NUM could see it happening but could not prevent it.

On 24 July a national circular on coal imports included a memorandum from Vernon Jones of the NUM's international department admitting the problem. 'Although we have had some success in the curtailment of imports,' he wrote, 'I believe the scale of the problem is worse than generally known. We are in a very difficult position in this office because area strike headquarters tend not to pass information to our control centre, only problems.

'Apart from the details provided by Scotland [which had listed ships unloading coal at their ports] none of our control centres around the country have kept any records or details of ship movements.

'However, they have been quick to point out that we are being inundated with imported coal.'

An early circular had expressed confidence that coal imports from Poland could be prevented. But the NUM had no effect and when Scargill, accompanied by the National Union of Seamen general secretary, Jim Slater, who had served on Polish ships during the war, went to the Polish Embassy, he got little change. Slater says the Poles replied that their contracts were not with Britain, but with a third party. They just had a contract to ship to Rotterdam.

The union's special conference on 19 April 1984 had resolved that 'future deployment of picketing, requests for solidarity action etc. shall be co-ordinated by the National Office.' A week later Peter Heathfield was writing to areas asking for numbers of pickets deployed and where, what 'additional forces' were available so that 'targets to be dealt with' could be identified and requests responded to more efficiently.

It was not to be. The centre never succeeded in co-ordinating picketing and bogged down on simple logistics. As one insider put it, 'our great failure was communications'. At the start of the strike a co-ordinating office had been established in London at the headquarters of the National Union of Seamen. There in a small room lined with maps which showed every railway line and siding in the country and, supplied with telephones, a member of the NUM national executive from Kent, Wes Chambers, took messages and requests for advice and assistance. It was not a huge operation, much was to do with co-ordinating support and fundraising in London, and giving advice to miners threatened with disciplinary action if they didn't go to work. It became yet another base for Kent pickets. But it benefited from the excellent communications system which the NUS employs to keep in touch with its members on ships travelling world wide and its fellow unions across the globe.

When the NUM decided to set up its own centre and moved it to Sheffield, the results were almost comic. There was no telex in the NUM office so any telex had to be sent to the NUS and then passed on. As Jim Slater, the NUS general secretary put it, 'It all had to be done third hand. If the NUM wanted to send a telex, Sheffield used to telephone one of the staff here who used to take it down in shorthand and then send it. When we got a message back, we had to relay it to Sheffield, and often it was very difficult to get through. We used to have to try again and again because everyone else, the media, other unions, were trying to get through.'

The problem was shared by other NUM centres round the country who attempted to liaise with Sheffield. The number sent out for them to ring in the 26 April circular was simply the main office number. In Sheffield the team manning the control centre 24 hours a day consisted of paid staff of the union such as Vernon Jones and Danny Connor of the pensions department, plus two seconded executive members, Wes Chambers and John Weaver from Yorkshire. Control centre is a grand word; much of the time whoever was in the building answered the phone. They found a great deal of their time taken up with individual casework queries about pickets being arrested and their legal rights, and worries from women whose husbands hadn't returned. There were some bizarre calls from well-wishers, including on one occasion an equestrian expert who advised miners to lie down in front of police horses to stop them. When that was passed on to Yorkshire headquarters, the reply came back that they had already had the same advice; someone had tried it, and been trodden on.

The most bizarre attempt to bring a measure of national co-ordination came when areas were circulated with a code with which to ask for assistance. Sent out by the union's administrative officer, Roger Windsor, who was dramatically aware of the dangers of phone tapping by the police and conspiratorially searched rooms for bugging devices, it suggested that pickets should be referred to as vegetables and requests for assistance couched in the language of grocery lists.

So pickets became apples, police potatoes, the railway was the freezer, NUR members mechanics and Seamen plumbers. Collieries were Tesco branches, power stations were Woolworths and ports were Marks and Spencer.

In an example given to guide strike centres a message declared, 'There are problems at Tesco Branch no. 414. They need apples urgently on advice note DLM/0500. There are potatoes in the market No. 1 at supplier No. 16. Woolworths Branch 4A has problems with the freezer, but the engineer will fix it. A broken window at Marks and Spencer Branch No. PSA is being repaired by the shopfitters.'

The translation was – 'Problems at Rufford colliery – send 500 pickets. Police on M1 at Junction 16. Little Braford power station receiving coal by railway but ASLEF advised. Coal arriving at Colchester Port but NUS (should be TGWU) are dealing with it.' The code brought a good deal of amusement to picket centres, but it does not seem to have been much used.

Heathfield's circular had stated that it was not the wish of the national officials 'to alter the present command arrangements' but to process requests and information to the appropriate strike HQ.

That in practice was a fair description. There were few attempts at national co-ordination – to the disgust of Jack Collins in Kent, who complained that they were still 'tied up with the cricket mentality', but to the relief of others such as Howells who mistrusted the centre's ability to organise. One such occasion was the despatch of pickets, including Durham men, to the East Anglian ports of Lowestoft and Great Yarmouth, where they were left without accommodation and had to sleep in fields and elsewhere and, worse still, failed to find any evidence of the ships bringing coal they had expected, until a solitary barge was located on Great Yarmouth docks.

But a second example was pivotal – the call by Arthur Scargill for a mass picket at Orgreave. It was an obvious target. For anyone driving off the motorway into Sheffield from the south, as the miners' president did so many times, the sight of the great gaunt rambling coke plant smoking darkly away amid the green fields as you approached the city was a graphic image of the strikers' inability to 'tighten the knot'.

Orgreave, which supplied coke to the big BSC steel plant at Scunthorpe, was an obvious place to pressurise the steel industry, particularly when highly visible lorry convoys were brought in. The plant was already a secondary target for Yorkshire pickets, a fall-back destination if they could not get through to Nottingham pits.

The first convoys began on 23 May. Between then and 18 June, when the huge 10,000 mass picket was held, there was an uneven series of pickets in which the levels of violence sharply escalated. A workmen's hut was set on fire, thousands of stones thrown, a telegraph pole rolled down towards the police, and of course, police horses employed in a way not experienced before in a recent industrial dispute.

When the final mass picket was mounted, the plant was known to be down to its last few days of supply, and vastly more coal was already coming in from ships on the Trent wharves. It became a symbol, and to Arthur Scargill it was a potential Saltley, the chance finally to win a big propaganda victory which would send a psychological shock through the country. Police and miners alike had no doubt that the closure of Orgreave would be the start of something big, and the leaflets and posters sent out to encourage miners to demonstrate there made the connection with Saltley explicit.

What foiled the plan to repeat Saltley were two factors – the determination of the police and the basic geography of the plant. The Saltley works had had a narrow entrance with a small square where pickets could muster surrounded by the walls and buildings of an old industrial city.

Orgreave could scarcely be more different. Set in open fields, with roads to take vehicles from the plant in two opposite directions and large open areas in the plant for assembling and parking vehicles, it made things very difficult for the pickets. In the month of battles round the plant the police were able to claim that the pickets did not succeed in stopping a single lorry.

The Orgreave plant is approached off the main dual carriageway running towards Sheffield along a narrow lane which runs downhill towards the works. It goes through a housing estate, over a narrow bridge (nicknamed by some 'a bridge too far') and then descends to the plant. There is a large field on each side of the lane and then the plant lies on the right with a disused chemical works on the left. The road then continues along the side of the plant with fields on the other side until it links up with another main road which provides access to the motorway.

In the words of one police officer at Orgreave, 'It was almost ideal for us. The only advantage the NUM had was that they were pushing downhill. We had a control room in the old chemical works overlooking the entrance, enough ground to keep the men away from any area of production. It wasn't a main road so it could be closed off without adding more than five minutes to anyone's journey, and it was so convenient to the motorways that we used it for most of the dispute as our base for keeping a reservoir of men.'

Many picket leaders also now question the assault on Orgreave. 'Our Waterloo' was one description, and the nature of the proceedings with charges across open fields against fixed positions has a curious symmetry with a nineteenth-century pitched battle.

Another picketing organiser describes it as 'a pickets' deathtrap, a mistake'. 'We took a lot of casualties. It was terrible. Even if we had stopped the lorries, you would still have had Scunthorpe steelworks working. Every hour coal was being moved. It was a drop in the ocean. Hundreds of wagons a day were going from Flixborough wharf and other places.'

Yorkshire had Orgreave as a relatively low priority – one among a number of picketing sites. It had at first refused to send men for a mass picket, and South Wales, who were to send thirty coach loads on the final day, had great doubts. Howells, who organised the Welsh pickets, says, 'Orgreave smelt from the start. We had had some experience of mass picketing already; we had sent 600 to Oldbury. But to organise that many, you had to go public. It couldn't be secret. We had already had a number of situations where we had realised that large numbers were being allowed into a spacious area and then surrounded by police. So we had turned to different tactics, trying to stretch the police by hitting seven or eight places at once.

'Orgreave was a turning point for the strike. They realised that they were not going to win by mass picketing. It was the proof of what we had already suspected, that the police were able to take on any number of pickets.

'The feeling after 18 June was horrible. We realised it was a disastrous policy. 1972 and Saltley was an age away. It was a government of a completely different order from Heath.'

Howells's remarks were not simply post-event wisdom. There had already been a big argument about mass picketing within the left-wing caucus which met before national executive meetings. As one long-serving NEC member put it, 'Arthur brought mass picketing to the meeting, and he didn't get it through. Then he went off and announced Orgreave.'

John Weaver, another NEC member, says, 'Orgreave was close to Sheffield and easy to get to; it became the fall-back destination for lads who went to picket Notts pits and couldn't get through.

'The lads were going to Orgreave, so Arthur went. Then he made the public announcement about the mass picket. It was just Arthur on the media.'

The final battle of Orgreave on 18 June marked a turning point. It was a clear indication that miners' own muscle and their push and shove were not going to bring victory; they needed help from elsewhere. But the way violence had escalated had huge ramifications for the conduct and outcome of the strike. The scenes at Orgreave bred a new determination amongst government and Coal Board that they could not compromise with such violent forces.

Meanwhile the level of the police response, with riot gear and horses used in an industrial dispute in a way that no one had witnessed before, raised major questions about the role of the police, and bred a resentment among many activist miners which showed itself in the ferocity of the battles in Yorkshire later. A Rubicon was crossed at Orgreave and there was no going back for the rest of the strike. But it is still an open question what its effect on industrial disputes in the future is.

Some critics of the police tactics at Orgreave have suggested that it marked a new stage in policing policy. The use of shields and snatch squads and horses, it is postulated, has broken the old mould of dealing with industrial disputes by push and shove between pickets and police in which the pickets have some hope of success. Because police were trained in a panic in more aggressive and impersonal tactics to deal with inner city riots, they have neglected the old methods, it is argued. With pickets deprived of hope of achieving results their reaction becomes more violent.

The analysis is set out by Dr Roger Geary in a study of the policing of industrial disputes from 1893 to 1985.[3] He quotes one NUM official as contrasting the old push and shove with 1985: 'Today you've no chance. There's a lot more of them and if you look like you're going to break through, hard guts are called in, them with shields and bloody truncheons. Well your unarmed picket can't compete with that sort of thing. I don't condone it, but I can understand why some of the lads start throwing things.'

Geary concludes that it was the very effectiveness of the Police Support Units which 'displaced violence from the picket line'. 'In short, conventional picketing has now become a set battle that strikers cannot win. Faced with certain defeat at the pit gates, hit and run tactics have become the only feasible alternative. Intimidation of working miners, the destruction of Coal Board property and attacks on police stations are evidence of a frustrated backlash.'

The problem, though not the analysis, is one admitted by senior policemen, conscious of the words of Sir Robert Mark, that the police have to succeed by not being seen to succeed.

But Peter Wright of South Yorkshire insists that his men were trained for the push and shove and regularly employed it. Strict instructions were given not to bring out riot gear until the situation demanded. At Orgreave, even if police had ended a morning's battles in riot gear, they started the afternoon watch in ordinary uniform.

Wright's view is this: 'I know that aggressive and ill-timed police action can provoke a situation that wouldn't otherwise arise, and you have to be very careful about that. But my policy was to achieve the old-style confrontation. The very nature of every instruction sent out was to say, "Now look, normal uniform, normal policing, normal actions," and then of course, once the need to protect my officers comes in, the only way is to withdraw them or bring out the riot shields. Given the first few stones – and I don't know any chief officer that would find it easy to count the stones – what level of tolerance do you need to have?

'If you say, when the pushing gets too heavy, what do you do then – there is only one source. It's mounted. That's what they are for. It's the football crowd control role. Now once you push them back you cause a distance between police and pickets which can only be bridged if you like by stones, so that is a factor which escalates itself. So given the numbers that were there, somehow you are on an automatic escalation, which may be out of control of both parties.

'The only way I see of stopping that is by reducing the numbers who go. Once the policy of mass picketing is followed, then I can see that mass pickets will not stand by passively. If they are going to travel great distances and come together in such numbers day after day and see their objectives not being achieved, you are automatically on an escalating course.'

Jack Taylor, who was at Orgreave, has this view of it: 'One of the things that trade unionists can never get round and nobody explains is that the chief constable will instruct his officers and they will carry out his instructions; the Coal Board director can instruct managers, but we *advise* our members what is the best thing to do. That has a fundamental effect, and it's the reason why you don't expect to conform to the same standards. People were saying "pickets three; police four". It was becoming a bit like football results. But we were talking about lads in running pumps with no shirts on in many cases, and fighting for jobs. On the other side, you were talking about men over five foot whatever in uniforms and big boots, doing it for money.'

The final picket at Orgreave was on 18 June, but it came after a month in which a pattern of confrontation and violence had been established. It was something many pickets were unhappy about – contemporary newspaper reports speak of many men who after the push and shove walked away from the scene once missiles started to be thrown with walls being demolished for ammunition and, on 18 June, a scrapyard ransacked for material to build barricades and start fires.

At the end of the battles of 18 June fires blazed and demonstrators hurled bricks in a desultory manner across the railway cutting at police, who did not bother to respond. Two demonstrators picked their way across the barricade of burnt-out cars and metal towards the police lines. 'Why don't you arrest them', the first man asked in a strong Scottish accent pointing to the stone throwers. 'They're no miners. They're agitators. We deplore them. OK we don't want to throw bricks, we don't want to hurt policemen. We have got respect for policemen. They are doing a hard job. Fair enough, we'll push youse; you push us back; that's all we want to do. What we are doing is wanting to fight for our jobs. Nothing else. You must remember that if the pits go, the steelworks go, the car industry goes, the people who produce safety clothing go, . . . you are not talking about 70,000 jobs . . . we're here to be a peaceful picket, nothing else.'

That was the culmination, but patterns had been established over the previous four weeks: the two pressure points morning and afternoon as the convoys left; the increasingly forlorn opportunity for six pickets to approach the lorry drivers, with a police decision not to push the main body of pickets back over the hill so that they could have clear sight of their colleagues speaking to the drivers; sometimes football matches between police and pickets in the long sunny interludes; an unofficial bargain, never spelt out but widely understood, that if pickets did not throw stones, horses would not be used.

On 1 June after another day of violence with miners injured in the crush being laid out for medical attention, BBC cameras filmed a poignant conversation between a mounted policeman and a picket. 'The bricks were coming over first as far as we were concerned,' said the policeman. 'We didn't want no bricks thrown', said the picket, 'because they were hitting us. We are up front having a good push. We know we aren't going to get through but we have got to try.'

Much of the discussion of Orgreave has centred on 18 June, the final mass picket. But it cannot be seen in isolation.

On that day about 10,000 pickets from all parts of the coal field converged on the plant. Picket organisers found it strange that police, who had on previous days discouraged them from reaching the plant, on this occasion directed them straight to it. The police explanation is that with such large numbers, it was better to marshal them all in one place, rather than have them still on the roads which the convoys would use.

Critics of police tactics concentrate their attack on two aspects, the use of horses and truncheoning, some of it indiscriminate. It is symbolised by the ITN television pictures of a Northumberland policeman repeatedly hitting a picket across the shoulders.

Some pickets like Keith Harris, a Derbyshire branch secretary, insist that police broke the unwritten rule, no stones, no horses: 'I will swear on my child's life that there was not a stone thrown before the police charged into that crowd.' But others, including Frank Harding, the cameraman who took the famous truncheoning picture, insist that before horses were sent in to charge the crowd, police had stood for a long time with stones being thrown at them, protected partially by a line of South Yorkshiremen with long riot shields in the front rank. The horses went in only after a number of warnings from assistant chief constable Tony Clement that he would use horses unless the bombardment stopped.

A number of camera crews were themselves hit by stones before the horses went in. John Bruce, a BBC sound recordist, recalls standing in front of the police horsemen and a policeman behind him being toppled by a stone which struck him in the groin.

The horses were employed in two different roles during the day. The first came as a mass of pickets pushed against the police lines. The horses were used in what Wright argues was their traditional football match function – to take the pressure off a dangerous surge. There is no doubt that the physical pressures were ferocious; crush injuries were common on picket lines, and already at Orgreave one striker had been given the kiss of life by a Manchester police sergeant after a particularly difficult shove. (Later in hospital the man had refused to meet the policeman, declaring that had the police not been out in such heavy numbers, none of it would have happened.)

Wright argues that using horses like this actually reduces injuries and arrests. Without them it becomes a much more drawn-out battle. What happened at this point at Orgreave was that the police lines opened and the horses cantered forward and then stopped. Their appearance was sufficiently alarming for pickets to break off their push. Staffs were not drawn and pickets not attacked as they were to be later. The stand-off in the lines then turned into persistent stone-throwing which was followed later by the truncheoning charges of horses followed by the snatch squads of policemen with short shields who used truncheons.

Many senior police officers who watched what happened on television take the view that truncheons were used far too liberally. A few had been drawn in the early push and shove, a tactic which the police themselves regard as counter-productive with identification and arrest being preferred. One of the ensuing difficulties was that as Wright had insisted that his own men should bear the brunt and be on the front line with long shields, the squads who ran forward later with short shields were largely from outside forces. Because South Yorkshire had little billeting in the county, most of the reserves had arrived only that day from elsewhere, and often there was insufficient time to brief them. This lack of control was appreciated as a problem both by the South Yorkshire police and their police committee. It was to become an important factor again, in the disturbances when men started to return to work in Yorkshire.

The 18th marked the end of the battles at Orgreave. It became clear that day that the BSC convoys would soon cease because the coke was running out – and BSC was getting plenty of coal from imports. When the convoys resumed much later, there was no return to mass picketing.

By then priorities had changed. Those picketing elsewhere had no doubt that Orgreave had been a costly diversion. On the 18th South Wales pickets at the important coal-fired Rugeley power station in the

Midlands counted over 1,000 lorry movements. The South Wales area decided to turn away from mass picketing and concentrate instead on winning public support and raising funds in a wide range of centres from Cardiff to Southampton and Basingstoke.

Crucially, Orgreave marked the end of the battle to bring Nottingham out. Picket appearances logged by the NCB in Nottingham had been running at over 10,000 a week up to the last week at Orgreave. After that, they never reached five figures again.

It also marked the end of the mass picket as an offensive tactic. Its use would be defensive when men started to go back later in the hitherto solid areas of Yorkshire and the north-east. But as miners' delegates gathered for their abbreviated annual conference in July, the talk was of other workers, particularly the dockers, doing their work for them, and of the pressure on power supplies and coal stocks as after midsummer's day the days imperceptibly started to draw in.

Orgreave was the first mass confrontation in Yorkshire since the strike began. Immediately, there was some fall-out. Miners at Yorkshire Main banned police from their welfare club and sports teams after seeing a local policeman apparently roughing up a miner in television pictures from Orgreave. More seriously there were outbreaks of violence between youths and police in Maltby and Barnsley; most did not appear to be miners and in Maltby the NUM branch secretary dissociated miners from what was happening. But the tactics, particularly the throwing of bricks at the police, appeared to imitate the picket line.

At this point in the strike, Coal Board attempts to get men back to work in striking areas were still hesitant. A concerted campaign in North Derbyshire was showing only slow, small returns, and when the north-east put on buses to take men to work, it ended in fiasco with only pickets travelling on them for a lift to the picket line.

Attitudes were ambivalent. Tony Judge of the Police Federation remembers a conversation at Orgreave with a senior Yorkshire policeman who remarked that he had a man who wanted to go back to work. 'It's one and a half miles through an estate and I can't possibly protect him.'

By August things had changed. Hopes of a settlement from the July talks or an industrial victory via the dockers had evaporated, and MacGregor believed it was only intimidation which was preventing men from returning. A concerted attempt was mounted to get men back even if it was only one at a pit.

It was a Coal Board decision but its effect appeared to draw the police unambiguously into taking sides in the dispute – something which their instruction manuals warn against. There were doubts among some police officers. As Tony Leonard, then Assistant Chief Constable of Derbyshire, wrote afterwards, 'the NCB often had unrealistic expectations of the police. We had to remind them that they frequently made decisions which were very proper for them to take as managers of an industry but which had consequences for people outside the industry.' Derbyshire police refused to escort back to work buses, to avoid being seen to take sides, but did sweep the road in front.

The biggest consequence, of course, was the impact on law and order of escorting a miner back to work in a hostile community. The National Council for Civil Liberties argued in its report on the dispute that the rights of individuals within the law should be protected, but there was also the need to preserve 'public tranquillity'. It was a legitimate use of police resources to ensure that working miners could travel to work, but not at any cost. (But its general secretary resigned after a meeting including striking miners and their supporters successfully argued against the report's assertion that 'freedom not to take part in a strike is as much a fundamental right as the right to strike.' By 415 votes to 139 it argued that strike-beating 'undermines the collective rights of others and cannot be supported as a fundamental freedom.')

The police saw the problem but many felt they had no option. Peter Wright in South Yorkshire says, 'my general principle was that Orgreave was an industrial complex which was entitled to work, wasn't on strike to start with and that lorries wanted to go in, and I had a duty to see that normality was going on there. Normality was not locking up plants to prevent breaches of the peace.

'Now when you swung that argument round to Armthorpe, there was a pit in the village that was strike-bound and a man who didn't live in the village deciding that he wanted to go back to work.'

Wright set out what he thought was his responsibility in two exchanges of correspondence with a local MP. 'I appreciate that the numbers wishing to attend work are not as great as those in Nottinghamshire and Derbyshire, but in my view the law has little value if it does not protect the rights of the individual. If I were to decide that I could not protect the one or two who wish to go to work, I would then be presented with the difficulty of defining the number that would need to attend before I should provide protection. I am sure you would agree that this would put me in an impossible situation.'

Taxed later with the suggestion that withdrawing his officers would end violence, he replied, 'Following such a move on my part I agree that the actual violence directed at or towards working miners and their families would effectively and quickly stop them exercising their legal right to work and the continued threat and lack of protection thereafter would maintain that position. I do not concede that such action, or more importantly inaction, would be in the public interest.'

Wright's official report records the period from 11 July to 19 August as the 'quiet summer', the quiet before the storm. Elsewhere there were many incidents. There were days of picketing at Bilston Glen in Scotland after working miners produced the first coal, but the numbers were vastly smaller – only about 350 with extra pickets being brought in from Durham at McGahey's request, and then complaining they were being used as the shock troops, with missiles thrown from the back by Scotsmen falling on their heads. There were disturbances in the villages of Fitzwilliam and Hemsworth in the West Yorkshire police area, and in South Wales on one single day 46 pickets were arrested at the entrance to the Port Talbot steelworks as coal unloaded at the works jetty and processed in its coke ovens left by lorry for foundries in Wales and south-west England.

But after Monday 20 August, when a single miner returned to work at Silverwood Colliery near Rotherham, the confrontation in Yorkshire reached new levels of violence and hostility.

A special police enquiry called for by the South Yorkshire Police Committee into the events of the following day unfolds a saga of mayhem and confusion particularly in the village of Armthorpe at the entrance to its local pit, Markham Main, which led assistant chief constable Terry Watson to conclude that many police officers 'will have found themselves on occasions frightened and mesmerised by the trauma that was taking place round them', and at least two Armthorpe residents to complain of police breaking into their houses and dragging out and beating pickets who took shelter.

The trouble had begun after a bus containing three working miners had driven through a nominal picket at the colliery. Elsewhere 1,000 pickets had appeared at Silverwood building barricades and setting vehicles on fire, and 2,000 at nearby Brodsworth, while battles raged throughout the morning at Hatfield colliery. At Armthorpe the trouble began when a convoy of PSUs entered the village and were stoned. When half of them subsequently tried to enter the pit, about 150 pickets threw a metal workman's hut in front of them, used a railway sleeper as a battering ram on another van, and hurled missiles which knocked one driver unconscious. Police deployed ready to make arrests but no command was given by the senior officer who had decided to adopt a low profile. A number of police units recorded their frustration at the softly-softly approach in their log books. Barricades were built at the colliery entrance but there was no police line drawn up. When two inspectors approached from the colliery to speak to the demonstrators, they were stoned. Assistance was then requested by radio to clear the demonstrators to get the working miners out. As two convoys of police vans with horns blaring and lights flashing approached the entrance from different directions, police with shields came down the pit lane. The demonstrators started to withdraw and hurled bricks and concrete through the van windows from about three feet away. Police saw one man swinging a wooden stave with a piece of concrete on the end like 'throwing the hammer' against one vehicle. The vehicles stopped to allow the police to get out. 'They did not have time to organise themselves into drawn up units but reacted to the turmoil they found themselves embroiled in,' says the report.

Police with shields then formed a cordon under persistent stoning, and once again some PSU commanders complained that the officer in charge was too passive, and left them exposed rather than attacking the demonstrators. With the help of an NUM official things quietened down, although at one point a pick-up truck arrived to deliver missiles to the demonstrators.

During the night extra police were again called to the colliery after attacks by about 30 marauding youths, and when picket numbers built up a deal between the policeman in charge, inspector Torvill, and NUM branch secretary Jimmy Millar, reduced police numbers and sent most pickets away.

With matters apparently quiet, the single PSU at the colliery was withdrawn about 6.30 in the morning for use elsewhere. Shortly afterwards pickets started to gather, smashed the television security cameras and commandeered a mobile crane to build a barricade. Two road vehicles were seized from the council road maintenance depot and the crane then set on fire. When a single PSU approached the colliery it found its way blocked by about 1,000 pickets.

Two columns of PSUs with about 400 men under a Greater Manchester superintendent were then brought in under a barrage of stones, bottles and metal bars, and as they debussed and started to disperse the crowd, they pursued them into the housing estate, houses and the village centre. It was then that residents complain people were sometimes physically hurt when they attempted to stop police breaking into their homes to seek out pickets.

Margaret Paul of Paxton Crescent received £105 in compensation for an incident in which pickets ran through her house and were followed by police who smashed a kitchen window and then truncheoned the men outside. Betty Tucker, who lived in the same street, let in six pickets and locked the door, but police in riot gear smashed her windows and dragged the men out. Both women complained of terrible verbal abuse from the police.

Twenty-four arrests were made; only eight were local miners. The police report sums up euphemistically, 'a positive attempt was made to arrest and deal with offences and to nip any recurrence of trouble in the bud. This operation may have caused a little consternation and concern to people who were not involved and had not seen the build-up, but the fact remains that within an hour there was no further trouble of any consequence and from then until the conclusion of the dispute, conditions have remained relatively peaceful at Armthorpe.'

The detail of the report suggests that the action was taken in the belief of many of the police officers present that the softly-softly low profile of the previous day, and what many believed had been a 'no arrest' policy, had backfired and a new approach was needed. The operation was under the control of Greater Manchester police, with only the most general guidance from the local incident room.

The local NUM saw the matter quite differently, as it made clear at a series of public meetings and in a demand, which was refused, for a public enquiry to Home Secretary Leon Brittan.

The Armthorpe affair is worth quoting in detail for a number of reasons. It illustrates just how far inhibitions had disappeared in the wake of Orgreave. It is a vast remove from 'push and shove' and some way from the days when a policeman was required to note in writing every use of his truncheon. It shows how local policing can be swamped by the *ad hoc* decisions of support units imported from elsewhere, and it illustrates the sheer panic and confusion which could prevail. Above all it shows how differently the pickets and the police could view things. The NUM officials were outraged by the appearance of a few working miners from outside the village in an armoured bus, with police vans, with hooters blaring, disgorging men in riot gear to break up their lines. From the police side, men arrived in a village they might never have seen before, uncertain of their directions, suddenly to be met with a hail of stones and iron bars and breaking glass before they could even get out of their vans.

Events such as Armthorpe were to set a pattern over the autumn and start of winter as the push to get more men back to work continued. There were more pitched battles, more flaming barricades, flares, petrol bombs, the throwing of paint stripper and other corrosive substances at police. Catapults were used to fire ball-bearings. At Cortonwood, where the return to work provoked particular outrage, the local cricket club roller was launched down the hill at police, while near Silverwood colliery a convoy of police dog handling vans was ambushed and two vans overturned with a police dog handler knocked unconscious, his dog attacking pickets and police alike. In a few cases, the picket line battle spilled over into smashing and looting of shops.

The police had started to use horses on the village streets, and took to beating their shields like a Zulu Impi as they advanced up streets. That dismayed the Home Office and was soon forbidden by the chief constable after strong protests by the South Yorkshire Police Committee. But it was a lasting image and nearly a year later the same tactic was to be seen from police in the Tottenham riots.

Violence reached a crescendo on Monday 12 November, the day when across the country nearly 2,000 men returned to work, encouraged by the Coal Board's offer of large Christmas payments. Ranked by the police with the last day of Orgreave for violence, it saw collieries entered by pickets, trees and lamp posts felled, power cables dragged down, oil spread on roads, vehicles set on fire and widespread damage and looting in Dinnington town centre, all in the early hours of the morning.

Numbers of pickets dropped at each site as more collieries became involved in the return to work. 'By the beginning of November the mass pickets were over and were to be replaced by intense violence by smaller numbers of pickets and increasing instances of intimidation towards working miners,' says the South Yorkshire police report.

But from the beginning of December picketing became light and generally peaceful in South Yorkshire. After Christmas, as the end of the strike became obvious and talks were taking place, the police record that 'violence on picket lines decreased markedly in the last two months of the dispute, but there was an increase in the number of attacks on working miners, their homes and property, probably because there were many more working miners to intimidate.'

Travelling through the Yorkshire countryside in the early hours of the morning in late 1984 was an eerie experience. Roads deserted, then sudden convoys of police transit vans headed by motorcycle outriders, their warning lights needlessly flashing. Down pit lanes, more transits spaced at intervals, engines running to keep the men inside warm. A few yards away a picket hut of corrugated iron, its wood and canvas door closed to keep in the heat and fug from a breeze-block stove like some First World War dug-out.

At Goldthorpe colliery, where a urinal had been demolished to prevent men using bricks from it to throw at police, pickets said they had been warned not to use cameras or binoculars at risk of seeing the picket hut demolished. At a nearby colliery, they claimed the hut had been destroyed by police. They saw little difference between the visiting police forces who had manned the colliery, although they felt some Welshmen had been more sympathetic.

With the qualifying time for Christmas payments past they were resigned to sitting things out and waiting for power cuts. 'Wait until the lights start to go out in January and the businessmen start to put pressure on Thatcher.'

Nearby at Askern colliery the bus bringing in working miners arrived just before four o'clock. Even then there were about 100 pickets, men and women, who had turned out to shout and have a mild push at the police. The police emerged from within the pit just before the bus's scheduled arrival, parking a van with riot gear outside the entrance.

(It was a common complaint by NUM officials that police had taken over the pit yards. If they wanted to talk to managers, they claimed, they had first to negotiate with police. Police manuals advise against using employers' premises in industrial disputes, as it appears to be taking sides. But here in South Yorkshire, chief constable Wright argued that unless he did so, the police presence would have been very provocative and visible, and it was the lesser of two evils, to keep men tucked away inside the pit and also able to use telephone communications.)

Over in the West Yorkshire area, the arrival of working miners was once again staggered between pit and pit to enable police resources to move from one pit to another without being stretched. It also enabled wandering pickets to do the same thing.

There's a big turn-out of police at the Prince of Wales colliery opposite Pontefract race course. And a chilling noise, the sound of barking police dogs being marched by their handlers along the skyline. Their job to deter pickets from cutting across the race course and the empty fields beside the pit.

A confident superintendent outlines his strategy, as pickets in twos and threes start to arrive, chatting casually, one explaining he has come here because he has been banned from picketing his own pit. 'I shall sweep down the road [before the bus comes] using ordinary uniformed police and put up a line to keep this lot back. If they get through, they are usually rather embarrassed and try to get back to their own side quickly. They are as good as gold really.'

He says he doesn't expect trouble unless there are 'visitors'. The previous night there had been and some bricks were thrown. 'It's not always so orderly,' says the picket, 'sometimes they have used dogs and horses to sweep down the road.'

Then comes an ancient National Bus – a shout of 'scabs', 'scabby bastards'. The police line is shoved back, quickly reinforced and heaved back into place. It takes about two minutes, police and pickets disentangle as if emerging from a rugby scrum.

People start to head off and on to the Big K, Kellingley, for the next arrival, a line of cars with waiting pickets parked along its approaches.

'Light picketing at all collieries with little or no violence' was the police verdict on that night in South Yorkshire. But the same night saw the killing of the first person by pickets in an industrial dispute for years.

In South Wales, a concrete block dropped from a bridge over the motorway killed taxi driver David Wilkie as he brought a working miner to the Merthyr Vale colliery. The area director had refused to use armoured buses because it was thought to be provocative.

There had been little mass picketing in South Wales. The battles at the gates of Port Talbot steelworks had been one exception. Many pickets were sent out of the Principality at the start of the strike. Later this was much reduced.

The area was also seized with the importance of reinforcing success, deploying men to support railwaymen who were refusing to move coal. Up until Christmas, there were never less than 400 pickets based at

Stoke, covering Midlands pits, but also the important Holdstock coal yard. Pickets were also kept in Leicestershire, although the coal field (apart from the so-called 'dirty thirty') was solid against the strike. A strong reason was to stiffen the resolve of the railwaymen at the key Coalville depot who were refusing to run coal for the important Didcot power station, and other destinations.

Welsh pickets saw themselves as being a bit different. When their union funds were sequestrated, they withdrew from Leicestershire, handing over to Yorkshiremen. They brought home stories of how on the day they had left Bagworth the pub they had used, the Eagle, had been smashed and vandalised by the arriving Yorkshiremen. Theirs, they insisted, was a different sort of picketing.

It was certainly more colourful. Pickets blocked the river Usk at Newport by taking over the transporter bridge to suspend the gondola in midstream and at the same time occupied the unloading cranes at the wharves at Port Talbot. As Kim Howells, the organiser, put it, 'Both occupations were peaceful and a conscious alternative to challenging lines of single-minded and well-equipped policemen, a tactic which had already been tried in most spectacular fashion at Orgreave.

'Unfortunately it was the latter type of tactic which came to dominate the headlines and capture people's imagination. It never stopped a single lorry nor a scab and taught us in South Wales a good deal about what to do to win friends and influence people during industrial disputes.'[4]

Another principal target for the South Wales miners became the ore and coal convoys, sometimes two hundred lorries at a time, which ran supplies the sixty or so miles between Port Talbot and Llanwern. They travelled the M4 and pickets made use of the bridges above the motorway to drop missiles on them in a way which was to be paralleled later in the killing of David Wilkie.

It was not a regular occurrence. Police checked bridges and lorry drivers had their own retaliation. Often using CB radios themselves, they could alert each other about pickets on bridges and on occasion detour to go over the bridge to intimidate the pickets themselves. There were widely told stories of lorries which had scraped along the sides of the pickets' parked cars.

But the miners themselves drew back. Early in the convoys, a meticulously planned ambush had been laid with eggshells painstakingly filled with a 60–40 per cent mixture of paint and turpentine. As the convoy passed, men emerged from bushes after a signal of whistles to bombard the convoy. When drivers switched on their wipers to clear the windscreen, the mixture was smeared across and then hardened. The results, according to one onlooker, were horrific, with lorries skewing wildly over the road. A decision was made not to repeat the episode. Instead efforts were concentrated on slip roads and silent pickets intended to unnerve drivers were mounted on bridges.

The concentration of action in the last months of the strike in and around the pickets' home pits brought police into prolonged daily contact not just with pickets, but the communities from which they came. It was this interaction which brought about some of the bitterest and most emotional reactions of the strike, and perhaps some of the longest-lived. It is the behaviour of the police in the villages, not so much in the heat of the picket-line confrontation, that many miners are most bitter about. Those who are critical blame the out-of-town police, often the London Metropolitan Police, for their behaviour.

There are many instances of police sharing sandwiches and jokes on the line, with men light-heartedly being plastered with 'We met the Met' badges in the push and shove.

Some miners' memory is partial. They remember the slagging-off of women by police on picket lines, without the accompanying taunting and slagging from some of the women themselves. But the way detachments from outside police forces 'occupied' villages, did damage relations between some mining communities, particularly in South Yorkshire and the north-east, and the police. One retired miner's son, returning to his native Easington, found his mother complaining that, 'The police were marching up the street. There was a lot of swashbuckling. There was the feeling that it is not your village, this is ours. The "off-picket" policing was intimidatory.'

The leader of the Easington council, John Cummings, was the secretary of a local pit mechanics' branch. Suddenly as a single man came back to work, he found his village closed off with road blocks and himself unable to get to his council meetings for the day. 'For the first time we saw villages laid siege to.' Cummings is critical of police behaviour. He speaks of police slagging-off women as they took their children to school, and of them teasing men on picket lines about what they would give their children for Christmas. 'They would show ten pound notes and talk about the bicycles they were going to give their children, and then roll ten pence pieces across the road to the pickets.' Cummings exempts the much-criticised Metropolitan Police from his criticism. In his experience they were gentlemen, handing out sandwiches and drinks on the line – 'the pigs' were others.

Another observer of the Durham scene, Huw Beynon, a university lecturer who assisted the NUM, was also at Easington. 'It was very scary. People were being picked up and it was thought they were going to be done on conspiracy charges. People were asked – "Who paid you?" and "Who told you where to go?" I know there were CID people in the village from August onwards.'

The South Yorkshire Police Committee reported that,

> most of the complaints arise out of incidents taking place when pickets are dispersing, or when detachments of police officers have gone into a mining village after recent picket line disorder. A common factor is that the police have been from outside forces and beyond the immediate supervision of a superior officer of the South Yorkshire police force.[5]

But it was convenient for blame to be put on visiting forces so that once gone, more normal relations could be resumed. A network of local consultative committees had been established in South Yorkshire before the strike and enabled some of the local grievances to be put at some bitter meetings. Miners felt they had made little progress, but the police believed that it 'allowed the release of tension'.

Local policing suffered. Crime detection rates went down and the police recorded an increase in damage to vehicles driven by local officers attending incidents unconnected with the strike. The police explanation was that

> in a dispute affecting such a large proportion of the community, there are no shades of grey nor any room for understanding the police role. To a striking miner everything is in black or white; if you are not with him, you are against him, and the police were clearly seen as against.

The South Yorkshire report went on,

> the wider community even in mining villages remained moderate in its actions, and from comments made by residents where serious street disorder occurred, it was apparent that the majority of people abhorred the violence and destruction and damage caused to their good reputations.
>
> Unfortunately these views were never publicly expressed because within these communities support for the miners was solid, and to give public support to the police would be seen as being disloyal to the miners.[6]

Local police claim things had started to return to normal by the end of 1985, much faster than they might have expected, and certainly than some of the rhetoric predicted. But the underlying questions about the police role and the way they were used to do the 'government's dirty work' according to one view, or to protect the rights of individuals and defend communities against self-invited outsiders according to another, still remained. And just as in the dispute patterns of behaviour once thought unthinkable became accepted, and the jumping-off point for new escalations, so the worries remained about whether what was seen in the mining dispute might become the basis for new norms.

McLachlan in Nottingham, where the police were warmly supported by most local miners, is concerned about the effect of the strike: 'I think that one of the problems is that very much against our will the police are becoming more and more a public order body rather than a law enforcement body. The difficulty about the sort of violence we saw in the miners' strike is that it leads to a lowering of perceptions generally about how serious the matter is. I think that every time that something like this happens, there is a coarsening of one's view of the situation. The seriousness is diminished. We are seeing a notching up of violence all the time.'

When West Country police later in the year sent in men with short shields and truncheons to smash the vehicles of the Stonehenge hippies' convoy; when the Metropolitan Police were seen to beat their long shields in the now familiar crescendo in the Tottenham riots; when demonstrators started to throw bricks and other missiles at police in Trafalgar Square anti-apartheid demonstrations; when Wapping seemed to re-enact picket scenes from the coal dispute – were these the signs of a new insensitivity and lack of inhibition bred by the miners' strike, or was there a wider explanation, a changing climate which itself had allowed such brutalism in the coal strike?

And was there also another effect, heading in contrary direction, from the fact that intimidatory picketing had not brought success. The determination of the National Union of Railwaymen to play things strictly according to the rule-book and to take members' views carefully into account in the guards' dispute, plus the willingness of other unions to make more use of the ballot, spurred on in part by pressure from their members – would that have happened if things had turned out differently?

They are complex and to some extent unknowable questions. The answers to them are entwined with the question of law and the rule of law which ran like a persistent refrain throughout the strike, sometimes dipping from sight, sometimes deliberately obscured, sometimes brought to a contrived crescendo, but with implications not just for industrial law, but for basic questions about civil liberties.

7
'No request for assistance'

Early in July 1983, eight months before the strike began, the Central Electricity Generating Board received a letter signed by the then general secretary of the NUM, Lawrence Daly. It wanted to know how the proportion of coal received by rail compared with the situation ten years before, at the time of the miners' strikes of the 1970s, and asked specifically whether figures were available for particular localities.

The executive secretary to the board in due course replied in a careful letter that there had been no significant variation at all. By return of post, the NUM wrote back to say it would appreciate some more specific figures on the tonnages transferred between pits and power stations by road and rail over the previous ten years.

The union at the time was trying to re-forge its links with the rail and steel unions in the 'Triple Alliance', but the letter put the CEGB sharply on its guard. Its message seemed clear. Just as in the 1970s, the NUM was looking to find ways to put pressure on other industries and other unions to achieve its goals.

Back in 1974 with a General Election pending over the miners' strike, other unions had been only too willing to row in with pledges of support. TUC guidelines were drawn up with unions pledging not to handle various materials brought to power stations and the NUM agreeing to limit picketing to six people.

It was a recipe for a rapid and orderly squeeze on power supplies. Ten years later, many miners were to look back at it with envy, for this time their leaders deliberately avoided calling on the TUC for organised support. Worse still, their inability to unite their own members and the resort to violent picketing discouraged many other trade unionists, unconvinced by their case, from risking their jobs on their behalf.

Why did the miners' leaders adopt this attitude, which once the strategy of forcing people out through picketing had failed, then effectively blunted the second weapon in their chosen armoury, the call on other unions to do their job for them by secondary action?

In part it was a distrust of the TUC, a justified suspicion that if a formal call for assistance was made, then conditions would be imposed from outside, in a demand for a ballot, or picketing guidelines or a hand in negotiations. In part it was Scargill's characteristic and obsessive determination to work only with those who would give him 100 per cent loyalty and control. Finally there was Scargill's personal antipathy to Len Murray and the TUC, an institution, as he saw it, still stained by its conduct in 1926.

The need for assistance from other unions had been recognised by the union before the strike even started. It had become traditional that at the onset of a dispute the miners called on the railway unions not to move coal. This time they were in touch long before. On 5 December 1983, soon after the NUM instituted its overtime ban, it had talks with the railway unions about not handling extra supplies of imported coal. Approaches were also made to the National Union of Seamen not to ship extra supplies which the NUM believed were about to be ordered from Poland.

It was an emotive moment. Bitter battles which included some deputations of miners were taking place around the Cheshire printing plant of Eddie Shah in a struggle over recognition of the National Graphical Association. When the union's assets were sequestrated for contempt of court, the TUC split down the middle but eventually refused to back the breach of the law. That evening Scargill denounced it in a miners' rally at Sheffield as the biggest betrayal since 1926. On the platform with him Bill Sirs of the Steelworkers, who had helped provide the narrow majority against the NGA, was howled down. The divisions within the movement were solidifying. It scotched any chance there might have been of Scargill himself going to the TUC for help, and it also cemented an emerging alliance, nicknamed 'the alternative TUC', which brought together prominent left-wingers on the General Council to give aid and support to the NGA while its assets were seized. This grouping included the miners, the Transport and General workers, the National Union of Railwaymen and ASLEF. Together with the printing union SOGAT and the Fire Brigades Union, it was to be the core of the NUM's industrial support, and would later attempt a similar job for the NUM's funds as it had for the NGA.

Among the key figures were Ray Buckton of ASLEF whose union had given the most unqualified support to the miners in 1972 and 1974; Moss Evans of the Transport Union; Jim Slater of the National Union of Seamen, whose brother was an NUM lodge secretary and, perhaps most important, Jimmy Knapp who, recently elected as general secretary of the NUR with left support, had helped swing its policies through 180 degrees from those of his right-wing predecessor, Sid Weighell.

Knapp and Buckton were already involved with the leaders of the

NUM in re-launching the Triple Alliance, the revival of the old 1920s link-up between miners, railway workers and steelmen. But with personal and political antipathies running high between the NUM and the steelworkers' leaders, the NUM leadership turned to the doctrinally sympathetic grouping rapidly transforming the loose alliance into a transport unions co-ordinating committee with the addition of the Transport union and the Seamen's union. The aim was to stifle industry by cutting off what supplies of coal were being mined.

The other half of the strategy, encouraging sympathetic action in the power stations, was not seriously attempted in the first months of the strike. Once again it appears to have been the antipathies of the miners' leaders for the predominantly middle-of-the-road or right-wing trade unionists whose unions dominated the power industry which was responsible. It would be difficult to think of two trade union leaders more opposed to the Scargill line than Eric Hammond of the Electrical, Electronic, Plumbing and Telecommunications Union, and John Lyons of the Electrical Power Engineers' Association, who bluntly told his members that the NUM policy of making his industry entirely dependent on coal was damaging to all electricity supply workers. But there was still room for winning some co-operation from other unions such as the General and Municipal which had the largest membership in power stations and whose general secretary, David Basnett, was anxious to get some purchase on the miners' dispute and would have traded industrial assistance to get it.

But it was exactly that fear, that going to the TUC would lose the miners total control, as well as an apparent belief that they could win on their own terms with a selected group of powerful industrial allies, which made them push the TUC aside.

On 16 March, at the end of the first week of the strike, Peter Heathfield wrote to the TUC informing it officially about the action in Yorkshire and Scotland. He said categorically, 'No request is being made by this union for the intervention or assistance of the TUC. Should such be required, I shall further contact you.' It was the clearest possible hands-off warning. A week later it was reported to the TUC's inner cabinet, which noted also that 'the NUM was in direct contact with certain unions in transport'.

Len Murray, the TUC general secretary, takes a clear view: 'Frankly it suited the General Council to have the letter, both the right and the left.

'The right didn't want to get drawn in, the left were thinking in terms of giving direct support to the NUM. They thought they could do it themselves and under the leadership of the NUM, challenging the position of the General Council as they saw it on industrial and political developments.

'So this bid by Scargill – because by then one is talking about Scargill

– this bid for direct assistance from trade union members directly bypassing the TUC, and indeed bypassing unions to a considerable extent, was Scargill trying to establish his leadership, his authority over the TUC, and in the face of the TUC.

'Well, we let him get on with it. I kept in touch invariably by phone with Peter Heathfield from time to time; that meant a couple of phone calls a month. I never remember Peter ringing me.

'At all times right from the beginning, I knew that the NUM had to come to us. In one way or another, informally, a phone call, a letter, a message through others; they had to come to us asking for help. The message never came.

'It was a condition of the TUC's involvement. If we had gone and said to the NUM in whatever words were used "We pledge support" or "What can we do to help?" he would have had us by the balls and we could not afford to put unions in that position. Because I did not believe that, although some unions might be jumping up and down, they could be taking members along with them, because of the attitude shown by the NUM and particularly the violence. The ballot in the first place, but also the violence.'

Ray Buckton, chairman of the TUC and one of the NUM's closest allies at the time, explains the NUM attitude partly in terms of what happened to his own union when the TUC called it in and ordered it to settle its 'flexible rostering dispute' which had disrupted the railways. Murray's view remains that that intervention followed strong nods and winks from ASLEF to get it off the hook, a view not shared by Buckton.

Buckton says, 'The real reason behind the letter was what happened to my own union. They believed that the TUC would take over negotiations and make a firm decision and instruct the union what to do, as they did with us.

'Actually there was a lot of sympathy for them. There was one period when the letter was still warm when I felt because of the atmosphere and talking to various unions that they could have got a decision of support. I told the miners that but I didn't interfere. They took the decision that there might be interference and they would end up like us; that was the words used many times.'

And the arm's-length treatment extended to the power industry unions too. A letter was sent to the EEPTU at almost exactly the same time as to the TUC. But its request was not for industrial help but for a register of coal stocks held by the CEGB, similar to one the union had provided in 1974. Eric Hammond, the union's general secretary elect, replied that fossil fuel stations had at least five months supply, but expressed concern about the NUM's picketing at power stations. He enclosed a circular referring to the picketing and possible boycotts of vital materials. 'Members are advised that there is no obligation whatsoever for any of our members to do other than to continue to carry out their norma duties,' it said tartly.

It wasn't until mid-May when, ten weeks into the strike, the NUM wrote to all fuel and power unions announcing that 'It is felt necessary to call upon the support of your union to bring this dispute to a speedy and just conclusion.' It announced, to the outrage of a number of unions, that 'all power stations are picketed or deemed to be picketed, and I am calling on all trade unionists not to cross those picket lines.'

The reply from John Lyons, as secretary of the unions' joint national committee for the Electricity Supply Industry, was that the proposals were so far-reaching as seriously to affect the whole country. They should therefore be discussed through the TUC. Once again, it was a stand-off.

But the NUM had in the meantime been pursuing its own direct action strategy. The letter to the electricity unions had come from a meeting of the NUM and the transport unions, the vehicle chosen by the NUM officials to run its campaign of secondary action.

It had considerable success, most notably on the railways, and, less important, at sea. The committee included the old Triple Alliance grouping, the NUR and ASLEF with the white-collar rail union Transport Salaried Staffs Association and the Iron and Steel Trades Confederation (though both later dropped out), plus the Transport and General Workers' Union and the National Union of Seamen. It was an alliance of the interlocking self-interest of the old heavy industries, with seamen's and railway unions, and to an extent the TGWU, arguing that fewer pits meant fewer cargoes and less employment for them, together with a more generalised industrial radicalism, with a political content.

As Moss Evans, general secretary of the TGWU put it, 'We had lost more jobs than anyone. Michael Edwardes at BL, MacGregor at Steel; we were losing membership and jobs left, right and centre. The miners came out on an issue some of our own members were not prepared to fight on. The only people who took a positive stand against closures were the miners. We thought that if the miners won, employers would think twice and so would the government.'

The committee was called together within a fortnight of the start of the strike but already Buckton and Knapp had been in close telephone contact with Arthur Scargill, just as Buckton and Gormley had in previous disputes. The rules were simple for ASLEF; if miners put even a token picket beside a line or on a bridge, drivers would stop. 'We knew pickets were on every coal depot. So therefore there was no movement there. Then of course it spread very quickly. Movements of coal in the network were stopped. It had to go into a place where they put pickets,' says Buckton.

But all did not go so smoothly. A large amount of coal, something like

9,000 tonnes, was imprisoned in the network almost to the end of the strike, the wagons rotting and deteriorating beneath it. But with large parts of the Midlands still mining coal, the NUR and ASLEF had difficulty in persuading their members not to move it.

The NUR had been less involved than ASLEF in previous NUM strikes, and, as a ballot of guards a year later was to demonstrate, was less militant at grass-roots level than its executive would suggest. Every attempt was made to encourage and protect members, particularly guards and signalmen who refused to work coal trains. A special allowance of £10 a day was voted by the NUR conference in June for members sent home 'as a consequence of carrying out loyally a decision of the executive'. ASLEF also made up its members' wages, spending eventually £273,655 on making up wages – roughly a fifth of the union's annual income.

At the height of the dispute British Rail estimated that it was running about 40 coal trains a day, compared with a normal 300. The equivalent of another 100 trains a day was going by road. Behind those figures lay a continuing game of cat and mouse, of pressure and counterpressure. It centred around the key depots in the Midland coal fields of Toton in Nottingham, Tinsley at Sheffield and Shirebrook on the Notts and Derbyshire borders. As a struggle went on in the villages between miners themselves about whether to work, Knapp and Buckton travelled personally to a meeting in June to urge railway workers not to shift the coal even if it was produced. It was a remarkable example of one union attempting to pull another's chestnuts out of the fire. Its partial success really meant failure.

Knapp remembers, 'They had made it plain that it was us they wanted to talk to. It was a very civilised meeting, no abuse. They raised all the natural questions. I had questions, for example, from a man who said he had two sons still digging coal. I spoke about the need to defend our own industry and appealed basically to the loyalty of our members. In the 1980s you can't take that for granted; but the amazing thing is that it did happen.

'There had been a feeling at the start that we were pulling the miners' coal out of the fire for them. There was a 17 to 5 vote on our executive for stopping the movement of coal, although some said the miners should have a ballot. From that day there was never a sign of a challenge in our union for nearly twelve months.'

But at ground level, the pressures were ferocious; men were warned that if they didn't move trains, they would be sent home for the shift. Police patrolling the coal fields kept a close watch on the railways, not always successfully. In April a locomotive near Cresswell pit in Derbyshire doing 40 mph ran into a steel pole thrown across the line. Attempts were made to derail another at Ollerton. In May a signalbox on the route to High Marnham power station was set on fire. British Rail instituted an anti-sabotage 24-hour manning of signal boxes, carefully not rostering men who wouldn't pass coal trains for the lucrative overtime duties.

Railway staff reporting for work became used to being stopped and questioned by police, who were also on hand in the offices as they clocked on. Eventually at Shirebrook about two thirds of the people worked. But it wasn't enough for BR to ship out even the coal that was being produced. The key Trent power stations of Cottam and West Burton were cut off from rail supplies, and a number of big pits such as Bagworth in Leicestershire and Daw Mill in Warwickshire would have been choked by lack of storage room, if their normal rail links had not been replaced by round the clock lorry movements.

But in spite of the prediction made by the rail union leaders after a transport co-ordinating committee meeting of June that by the end of the week no trains would be running, the miners' allies fell short of their aim of choking off supplies.

A key factor here was the attitude of British Rail management, and its decision to take what a number of other industries felt was a markedly soft line with railwaymen who refused to work coal trains. Instead of sending them home indefinitely and running the risk of provoking sympathy action on passenger services as well as freight, it restricted disciplinary action simply to the shift involved. Men were sent home but allowed to report back for their next shift almost as if nothing had happened. Such is the way that railway work is rostered that the following shift would often not involve coal movement.

Nowhere was the struggle watched more closely than at the regular morning briefing meetings held by the Energy Secretary, Peter Walker, at his Millbank office in London. Regular daily summaries of the situation were delivered to those meetings by a Department of Transport civil servant, and in the words of one of the participants – 'I used to know exactly when the signalman at Coalville was due to take his holidays.'

One major preoccupation of those meetings was to make sure that nothing was being done which might 'open a second front' and throughout the early weeks of the strike (before it became clear how large a substitute role road transport could play) the likeliest place for further action was the railways. Whitehall is acutely conscious of the impact of trouble on the trains. As another participant in Walker's briefings remarked, 'The British public can endure anything but inconvenience, so you are in bad trouble if the trains don't run, however much they are prepared to condemn the people who are doing it. They say, "The government must do something." But in this affair, that factor was never there.'

The reason was that both management and unions backed off from a confrontation – a battle which some of their supporters on both sides might have liked them to fight. British Rail was aware that its two main north–south lines had key sections controlled by signal boxes manned by very pro-miner signalmen – Warrington in the north-west and Doncaster on the east coast main line in the heart of the most militant mining territory. They were not challenged throughout the dispute until at the very end Doncaster came briefly out in support of Coalville men who the unions claimed had been victimised. The result: 98 per cent of British Rail's passenger trains ran during the dispute.

On the other hand, the unions were themselves not looking for ultimate confrontation. Ray Buckton says he knew that British Railways were worried about provoking a reaction that would have stopped the service. 'Everybody realised that if they did escalate there would have been a very serious position. We never provoked it.'

Jimmy Knapp says frankly, 'The miners never asked us to take strike action. I don't think feelings were ever strong enough to take that kind of action. What if we had tried it and got egg on our face? I don't think I could have called that action.'

By the end of the strike British Rail was summoning the unions and warning of tougher action if they didn't run coal trains. The union's refusal, it estimated, cost it £70 million during the year and a continuing loss of revenue as customers like steel and the CEGB continued with a percentage of road traffic after the strike. But during most of the dispute, it was the softly-softly approach. Privately some BR managers concede that they might have taken a harder line if they had known the miners' strike would have continued so long. But at the time, acutely conscious, as they saw it, of unions locally prodding them towards action, they kept a low profile with the full support of the government. This became embarrassingly plain in June, when the *Daily Mirror* published letters from John Gummer, a junior Employment Department minister who was also the chairman of the Conservative Party, making clear that BR should nod through its annual pay agreement at a comfortable but not out of the ordinary 5 per cent, to prevent another industrial front opening up.

This attitude was not appreciated by the British Steel Corporation. Coal's second biggest customer, it relied largely on the railways for supplies, and wanted British Rail to push the unions harder. It was a point frequently made by its managing director of personnal, Dr David Grieves, down the telephone to his opposite number at British Rail, John Palette. More colourfully, local Yorkshire management referred scornfully to their equivalents on the railways as 'chocolate teapots'. And it was steel which was to bear the brunt of the next assault from the miners.

'No request for assistance'

It was a very obvious target. Second biggest customer for coal, its stockpiles limited, it needed to process some of its blast-furnace coke in works outside the perimeters of its sprawling works. Its workers were part of the Triple Alliance and due a call for solidarity and repayment of the debt owed to some of the miners for their help in their picket lines in the 1980 steel dispute.

With no quick results from the trial of endurance in the power stations, steel, particularly as seen from the steel city of Sheffield, was an obvious target for a spectacular victory which would then impact on other industries. For, as the CBI kept repeating throughout the summer months, the dispute had so far had remarkably little effect on other industries, outside mining and its suppliers.

That was not quite how the steelworkers saw it. Under Ian MacGregor, before he had moved to the Coal Board, they had seen their own numbers diminish. Thousands had gone out on redundancy terms well below those offered to the miners. They were taking pride in the way their plants were performing and becoming competitive in Europe. Yet there was a cloud over it all; MacGregor and his successors had come to the reluctant conclusion that out of their five main integrated works, there was one too many. Only political and social considerations were holding back the closure of either Llanwern in South Wales or Ravenscraig in Scotland, with most people's money on Ravenscraig, arguably the most left-wing plant, as the target.

Steel-making is a complex business, with the blast furnaces which produce its first stage, iron, perhaps the most delicate. If one of those were to collapse as a result of not enough coke, or the wrong mix, the plant could be out for six months and might not be thought worth saving. So the argument ran, and it cut so deep that one member of the ISTC executive not involved with the big plants remarked with horror, 'They're all hoping in there that it's one of the other plants that goes.'

The miners, with Yorkshire to the fore, soon called on the steelworkers to cash in their cheque. Anxious to assist short of suicide, agreements were made in most works to run at lower production levels provided coal supplies were maintained.

Local Triple Alliance networks fixed up the deals, though not without difficulty. Local pits had traditionally relied on steelworks and keeping them going made sense for both parties. The management, although traditionally macho, went along with it to preserve the loyalty of the workforce. At Ravenscraig production was cut back from more than 90 per cent to 70 per cent. At Llanwern there were reductions as negotiations continued to bring in two trains a day.

The biggest cuts were at Scunthorpe in Lincolnshire, traditionally supplied by the nearby Yorkshire coal field. Production more than halved from 62,000 to 29,000 tonnes of liquid steel a week. The hard decision was made to abandon export orders and BSC struggled to find them from elsewhere.

But it wasn't enough for Arthur Scargill and for the Yorkshire area of the NUM. Scargill pressed Bill Sirs at a co-ordinating committee meeting in Knapp's London office to reduce steel production simply to a level sufficient to keep furnaces ticking over. Sirs riposted bitterly that it would mean the end of one of the five integrated works. Alex Kitson, there to represent the TGWU, replied, 'There will have to be casualties.'

Meanwhile agreed deliveries to Scunthorpe from Yorkshire were falling short, and the very crisis that the steelworkers had feared occurred. The Queen Mary blast furnace had a dangerous collapse of ore and coke. Urgent supplies of good metallurgical coke were needed for a sustained hot blow. The NUM Yorkshire area stalled and insisted Arthur Scargill be consulted too. The ISTC failed to get a reply. Then three days after the request, BSC moved lorries into its Orgreave coking plant on the borders of Sheffield and started to move in coke.

It was a turning point. Bill Sirs blames BSC for not giving the union early enough warning to agree something with the miners. British Rail still had hopes of persuading its men to take coke from Orgreave. But BSC, impatient with both, and with a crisis of possibly fatal proportions on its hands, took action.

The result was the collapse of all local agreements over steel supplies. Yorkshire miners had been critical of what they called the 'sweetheart deals' in Scotland and South Wales, where production levels were higher than at Scunthorpe, the one plant which traditionally had taken all its supplies from British pits. They wanted equality of sacrifice.

But it is not clear who made the decision to abrogate the deals. It was announced by Arthur Scargill himself after a meeting of the union executive. The South Wales president, Emlyn Williams, heard Scargill announcing the end of the deals on his car radio driving back to his Pontypridd office. Next week the South Wales executive found themselves lobbied by some hundreds of miners vigorously opposing any deals, and by a single vote agreed to abrogate the agreement.

The NUM sent an ultimatum to the ISTC: Meet us by 19 June to agree exact quantities of coal and coke to be delivered to steel plants. Sirs had been scandalised by an intemperate letter from Scargill. It accused him of displaying an attitude which 'can only be described as deplorable and one which is in violation of every basic principle accepted by the trade union and Labour movement.' It attacked the ISTC for accepting the use of blackleg labour to breach NUM picket lines and taking in coke which would be used to help defeat NUM members. 'The fact that you have acquiesced in the use of scab labour is something that will be on your conscience for the rest of your life. . . . I can only say that you are a disgrace to the very concept of the Triple Alliance and all that it was supposed to do.'

Sirs and his executive, determined not to be dictated to, ignored the ultimatum. But at a meeting of Scargill's substitute for the Triple Alliance, the inter-union co-ordinating committee, a new broadside was delivered. With Sirs's deputy, Roy Evans, attending, the other unions decided that they would halt not only all supplies of coal to steelworks, but also of iron ore.

It was, as Sir Robert Haslam, the BSC chairman was to say later, the lowest point for the steel corporation in the strike. Iron ore is such a weighty material, so much heavier than coal, that the corporation had considered it impossible to find enough vehicles to convey the material from its deep-water facilities in South Wales and Scotland to its plants at Llanwern and Ravenscraig.

But they did. Lorries poured in from England to Scotland and South Wales, and at times convoys of more than 150 vehicles surged along the 50 miles of the motorway from Port Talbot to Llanwern while frustrated miners' pickets for a while threw bricks and concrete and eggs full of paint at them. It was, said one miners' leader in South Wales, 'the destruction of the Triple Alliance in South Wales. Arthur's statement that there were bound to be casualties in a war was thrown at us every time we met the steelworkers. Everyone knew it was the wrong target.'

It was the end of hopes of support from steelworkers. There were eventually meetings – on 2 July between the two executives; on 21 September with the TUC steel committee representing a number of unions. But both sides were now entrenched. Bill Irvine, ISTC convenor at Ravenscraig, was the president of ISTC for most of the strike. Well to the left of Bill Sirs, he also found himself dismayed by the NUM attitude. 'We still wanted to help the miners if we could. We had an idea of a deal with all five plants reducing production. But they wanted no production at all.'

At the end of an icy TUC meeting Irvine spoke up: 'I said I didn't want the miners to go out of the room with the impression that they had no friends in the room. I was trying to get them to understand that they should get a deal they could realise. What I said was, "Ask us for something we can deliver, not something we can't." '

So once again the all or nothing approach of the NUM ended with nothing. Bill Sirs takes an understandably bleak view:

> The trade union movement should never allow control of a dispute to slip from its hands. The NUM's refusal to uphold the local coal supply agreements that steelworkers and miners had made around the country meant that British Steel stepped in, hired transport and took control. When union speaks to union, it must be on the basis of trust and mutual support. The NUM's unilateral withdrawal from

> honourable agreements it had entered into with a brother trade union was perhaps the beginning of the end for the miners.[1]

The attempt to starve British Steel of supplies had failed because of the availability of hundreds of extra lorries and the Transport Union's inability to prevent them taking the traditional railway traffic. But there was still another chance to prevent supplies reaching the steelworks, if they could be stopped at the docks.

The National Union of Seamen had done its bit by persuading its members not to ship coal but cargoes of both coal and iron ore were coming in in foreign-flag vessels to BSC's own wharves at Port Talbot in South Wales, on Teesside, at the Hunterston terminal in Scotland jointly manned by Transport union dockers and members of ISTC, and at the Humberside docks of Immingham for Scunthorpe. An attempt was made in South Wales to persuade tugmen not to berth the ships at Port Talbot, and turned brusquely down. Hunterston was to become a flashpoint only later, and it was at Immingham that the ingredients came together for the biggest challenge to the government's 'no second front' policy.

It came over BSC's use of trucks instead of rail transport. Under the provisions of the dock labour scheme which covered the port, BSC was specifically allowed to bring in a contractor with a front-loading shovel to fill trucks if railway transport was not available. The proviso was that a docker should accompany him, walking beside the vehicle. It was a typical agreement which made dock work some of the most protected in the country, heartily disliked by employers and the government, but an acknowledgment of the days when the dockers' power to cripple the country had been high on the worries of governments anxious to reform industrial legislation.

BSC maintains to this day that it did nothing wrong; that the shovel was accompanied in fact by two, not one, men though they later went off to a meeting. But the union accused BSC of a breach of the scheme, and called its men out.

With a network of provisions such as those covering the use of the shovel, port employers had been increasingly anxious for changes in the scheme. The union already believed that many breaches had occurred and had circulated a paper early in the year saying that this was the case and warning of attempts by the employers and government to re-write the scheme. Privately some employers had been anticipating trouble, and earlier in the year had marked off the autumn as a likely time for it.

So the flicker of a genuine industrial quarrel was there, and it was fanned into the flames by a desire of much of the dockers' militant leadership to give the miners a hand. Small in number the dockers may be, but their power within the TGWU is evidenced by the fact that both the chairman and the vice chairman of the union executive were themselves from the docks.

But just as the number of dockers had shrunk dramatically in recent years, so had the nature of their organisation. Much of the cargoes once laboriously loaded onto vessels by men at the quayside were now simply carried in large container lorries which drove on and off ferries.

Two of the principal ports for this traffic, fast-growing Felixstowe and the ferry port of Dover, were themselves, though unionised, outside the dock labour scheme. Leaving aside bulk cargoes, their omission from any action effectively destroyed it. Strenuous efforts were made to bring them out. The union argued that if employers could ride roughshod at scheme ports, how much more would they at non-scheme ports. The persuasion worked, and for a number of days, which coincided with the miners' truncated annual conference at Sheffield, the ports were out almost solidly. The Civil Contingencies Unit in Whitehall ran over its plans for use of troops in the docks, not employed since 1950, and the Transport Minister, Nicholas Ridley, and the Employment Secretary, Tom King, started a quickly discontinued series of regular morning meetings in the style of Peter Walker. For the miners at Sheffield it was the high point – they saw other workers giving support that looked like producing quick results and, as nights imperceptibly drew in, they believed that their fundamental hope of power cuts was drawing nearer.

For observers in London, it was the one moment that had the mixture of excitement, panic, and the element of the unexpected that was a feature of the industrial crises of the 1970s. In the international dealing rooms in the City of London a tape message of the calling of a national strike flashed across a screen and dealers shouted loudly across the room, 'Dock strike, a national dock strike'. The pound dropped immediately and within hours interest rates were jumping up a crisis 2 per cent, just as in the familiar July crises of the 1970s.

But it did not last. Lorry drivers at Dover, many of them foreign, infuriated by the blockade and seeing hundreds of holidaymaking cars allowed on to the ferries as dockers attempted not to alienate public sympathy, took matters into their own hands. They forced their way on to the ferries. Self-interest had overcome solidarity once more.

There was a further attempt at a dock strike, this time at Hunterston. It was made clear to British Steel that transport union members would not berth the huge ore carrier *Ostia* bringing supplies for Ravenscraig. This time there was no obfuscation, it was to be straightforward sympathy action to support the miners.

For nearly a fortnight BSC argued, even offering to take dockers to Ravenscraig to discuss matters with steelworkers there. But in the end BSC acted after an expensive public relations campaign which included full-page newspaper advertisements. Arguing that without large coal supplies the plant faced permanent damage, it went on, 'British Steel is not seeking a confrontation with the dockers or their union and has consulted with them many times over the past few weeks. But thousands of steel jobs, plus hundreds in the Scottish coal field, depend on Ravenscraig working normally.'

So the ship came in, moored by a union firm but one not usually employed at Hunterston, with a non-TGWU man directing operations from the bridge. It was an undeniable breach of the scheme.

BSC's tough line paid off. Having failed with one dock strike, the union couldn't climb the mountain a second time. It went through the motions. But ports were divided about working. Even London docks, the historical heart of dockers' militancy, saw a determined attempt to go to work by a sizeable number of dockers and the union had to resort to its heavy-handed disciplinary machinery. Meanwhile on the Humber, where the first strike had started, the union's national docks secretary, John Connolly, and its general secretary elect, Ron Todd, found themselves barracked when they attempted to bring them out.

The miners' leaders' attempt to get others to do the job their own divided members could not do, had led to them exporting the very same divisions into other unions. Even the question of the ballot, higlighted by the miners' own divisions, had become an issue. Dockers at Middlesborough demanded that they should have a ballot, even though, as harassed union officials pointed out to them, the union's rulebook made no provision for it – a docks delegate conference decision was binding.

Nowhere were the limits of solidarity more apparent than with the lorry drivers. The leadership of the Transport union had identified almost unreservedly with the miners. Moss Evans committed the union to the NUM 'without reservation' and his successor-to-be, Ron Todd, was one of the most regular speakers at miners' meetings. Yet the union, in spite of instructions issued both early in the strike and repeated very publicly after the September TUC congress, failed to deliver. It blamed a variety of factors – the increase in the number of owner-operators and small firms, people who belonged to other unions or no union at all. But there was no doubt that many of the lorries which effectively broke the strike were driven by its members. The union's leadership promised the miners that they could deliver something they were unable to. The question is how far the miners believed them and took it for granted in their strategy.

One of the puzzles about the TGWU's failure to deliver was the relative success of its lorry drivers' strike in the early months of 1979, which suggested to many that the union was better organised than it had thought. TGWU officials give a number of different explanations. Clearly drivers had been more willing to take action for an issue that affected them directly, their own pay. But second, since 1979 industrial recession had forced hundreds of firms to the wall, and many more were fighting to survive. For them, to sacrifice themselves for the miners was too high a price. There is another reason too, that by and large the long-distance drivers who were the backbone of the 1979 action are not those who were involved with the haulage of coal and bulk materials, for which most vehicles are tipper lorries.

Roger Hobby is the chairman of the Road Haulage Association's National Tipper Group. Himself involved with running coal during the strike, he described those involved like this: 'The large majority of small haulage operations in the tipping world are non-union. Tipper men are not like long-distance lorrymen with their Yorkie bar image. They have their own little clique. The long-distance man's attitude tends to be that the tipperman is a scruffy little bugger who goes in and out of coal pits. But he is an independent cuss, and independence was crucial in the strike. They were not going to be intimidated.

'Many felt that they were doing something that contributed to the country. There was a feeling that Scargill was wrong and they had the right.

'Many firms had been on the edge of bankruptcy. They had problems with mortgages, of wives and families. The strike was a saviour. They had to do it to stabilise and get security.'

The shaky state of many haulage companies had been due to the drop in business as industry declined with its obvious effect on haulage rates. Back in 1981, the rate for running a tonne of coal from the Nottinghamshire pit of Harworth to West Burton power station on the Trent had been £1.56. But by the time the strike began, it had dropped to a hardly economic £1.35. During the strike, the rate went up of course, but only to £1.50, an advantage magnified by the many extra journeys involved. As one Coal Board executive put it, 'We never understood the depth of the recession until we found how many idle lorries were available.'

Many people bought lorries to come into the trade. Owners with flatbeds hired tipper backs, companies double shifted, and Hobby says he knows of at least one case where one of his own subcontractors employed a striking miner to drive on the inconspicuous nightshift. Since the strike, many of those who came into the industry have been unable to find regular work, and rates have dropped even below the pre-strike levels, down to £1.25 a tonne for the Harworth to West Burton run.

So regional union organisers found themselves in difficulty. George Wright, the TGWU regional secretary in Wales, actually took disciplinary action against some firms in an attempt to halt the traffic and stiffen the resolution of railwaymen at Margam, who were wavering about their refusal to supply Llanwern when they saw so much traffic going by road. He had some success, but the big Llanwern convoys ended by being organised by an English firm, E.J. Meek of Mansfield in Notts, from an area where miners were working.

Wright also points to a more organised operation by hauliers, following lessons learnt during the 1981 steel strike. He claims that several hundred drivers who refused to cross picket lines during the steel dispute have not worked since. 'Drivers wanted to make sure that if they didn't cross picket lines, they wouldn't be permanently shut out of contracts.'

It was in South Wales that some of the heaviest employer pressure came. A Forest of Dean firm, George Reads, was responsible for taking the NUM to court, a case which resulted in sequestration of the assets of the South Wales area, for action they had taken to prevent them loading at the docks.

But the failure by the TGWU was not understood by the miners. In December, the union's north eastern regional secretary, Joe Mills, went to a miners' meeting at their Northumberland headquarters. In his pocket he had a £2,000 cheque for the miners' welfare fund. But far from being welcomed, he found himself mobbed by miners demanding to know what he was going to do about his members. On another occasion he had been abruptly summoned back to his office from holiday to meet 400 miners who had come to protest. Once again he had to explain the position before they would leave, taking an office clock with them.

The other side of the coin was meetings with drivers at which union officials were pressed to give men guarantees that they would keep their jobs if they refused to work. 'What they were asking the union was in the event of the company being put against the wall, because of the many scab operators, what would the union do? We couldn't give any guarantees.'

Sometimes the turn-down was more blunt. Another TGWU officer, arguing with men in Cumberland where a company was leasing 40 wagons to owner-drivers to operate the Ravenscraig run, was told by the men that if he forced the issue they would simply tear their union cards up.

Perhaps the most revealing comment comes from the TGWU general secretary, Moss Evans. Acknowledging the union's failure, he says, 'When we went to Scotland for a conference, we could see from our hotel window the convoys of lorries going to Ravenscraig, and there was nothing we could do about it.'

Joe Mills raises another issue. Pointing out the way that miners had been promised so much, particularly when Arthur Scargill went to Transport House on 7 June 1984 and met all the executive and regional secretaries and was assured of support, he says, 'I think the movement greatly misled Arthur Scargill. He went into situations believing that his tactics could be determined by all the support behind him. But the movement let him down because they promised things they couldn't deliver. But I think he might have realised that if he had had a better informed network of his own areas.'

On 29 December 1984 the Energy Secretary, Peter Walker, announced that, 'There will be no power cuts during the whole of 1985 with the coal production that has now been achieved.' It was a shrewd, if predictable, blow. But it was turned into one of the most decisive moments of the strike by Arthur Scargill's response – probably the most ill-considered he was to make during the twelve months of the dispute. To general amazement, as much among his own members as anyone else, he declared that he had 'never suggested' that there would be power cuts. In fact, of course, he had. Most famously on 26 June 1984 he told the NUR conference that he had learnt from a 'high-level mole' in the CEGB that there were secret government plans for power cuts at the end of August.

But even if he hadn't done so in so many words, anyone who had sat in picket huts, or argued the case with miners in pubs, or read the union's newspaper with its ritual reference to the assistance available from General Winter knew very well that the object of the striking miners' hopes was that the union would achieve what it had done in 1972 and 1974, to put the lights out through cutting the supply of power.

The government and the Central Electricity Generating Board knew it well enough. Caught in February 1981 with stocks too low to resist a strike, they had taken corrective action. Stocks had steadily been built up. (A computer prediction at the start of the strike estimated that they could run for 22 weeks.) In addition extra storage had been provided at power stations for oil and such chemicals as hydrogen and chlorine. The blockade of chemicals had been one of the causes of the power reductions in the strikes of the 1970s.

Perhaps most important, a number of new burners had been installed in the big coal-fired power stations enabling them to replace coal with oil. Called Firefly burners, they allowed the generators to produce as much as a third of their power simply by use of oil alone. Coupled with other measures, this meant that the CEGB doubled its capacity for generating on oil during the strike, and some of the burners were actually installed during the dispute, most crucially at Didcot in Oxfordshire. Oil is regularly used to light up coal furnaces, and is also mixed with poor quality coal to improve its ability to burn. But this was a measure of a different order, whose importance the miners had failed to appreciate.

Another change from the 1970s had been a dramatic contraction in the number of power stations with the phasing out of a scatter of smaller units. They had been replaced by a smaller number of big stations including what had been nicknamed the white elephants, a line of four large oil-fired plants across the south of England and Wales, built to run on expensive oil and placed next to refineries. At least one of these, at the Isle of Grain, recently completed after a saga of industrial relations difficulties, was under serious discussion as a candidate for conversion to coal. The last stage of its commissioning took place in the early months of the strike, and in the event it was Grain, with nearly 18,000 gigawatt hours supplied to the National Grid, followed by two other oil-fired stations, Littlebrook and Fawley, which produced the most electricity during the year.

The CEGB lives by contingency planning and careful studies had been made of how to operate in a number of emergencies, including a miners' strike, on the assumption of receiving no coal supplies at all.

Compared with this, the NUM's planning had been rudimentary or non-existent. In 1974 and 1972 its success had been based on denying coal to power stations. With no fresh coal being mined, it had been simple to ask power station workers not to accept it. Given the political climate too, in the election atmosphere of 1974, power unions had been anxious to co-operate to keep matters as orderly as possible.

This time, with the miners themselves split and substantial supplies of coal being delivered from working pits, there was all the more reason to contact power station workers. Yet, as miners' leaders were to complain later, no groundwork had been done. The miners had put all their eggs into the leaky basket of denying coal to the generating board by use of the transport unions.

The unions who comprise the employees' national committee of the electricity supply industry are a close-knit group. They work together with the generating board and the various area boards under the auspices of the Electricity Council. Although both sides would deny it is a cosy relationship, it is certainly far different from the licensed antagonism that prevails in sections of British industry and certain coal fields. They share a common commitment to the efficient performance of the industry and a determination expressed frequently in the miners' strike that its awesome ability to bring the nation rapidly to a halt should be guarded responsibly and not be at the mercy of any outside group which cared to use it.

They had met together at the end of the first week of the miners' strike at the EEPTU college at Esher to discuss the threat of privatisation to the industry. With the coal-field situation still uncertain, an attempt was made to get a joint declaration that would carefully not involve them in any dispute and simply tell members to stick to their own work. It failed.

One union would not agree. Fred Howell, national officer for the TGWU, with heavy membership in power stations in Yorkshire and the north-west, wanted a more active role.

So after the unions agreed to go their separate ways, he called in his full-time officials and sent a circular to his shop stewards. No coal was to be accepted to replenish existing stocks, no extraordinary transfer of coal was to be made from one stockpile to another within the stations, and members should give maximum co-operation so that picket lines were not breached. It was still pretty generalised stuff, and there was one key omission. It said nothing about oil. Howell is frank about its absence, 'I knew that as far as we were concerned we would be very ineffective. If I attempted to attack oil, I would probably fail, and would put our industrial members in a most difficult position. But I advised officials to limit the use of oil only for lighting-up.'

The TGWU's strength in the big coal-fired Yorkshire stations along the river Aire was hardly tested. There was no local coal available and the decision had been made that there was no need to take coal from pit stockpiles. The stations, which had something like eight to twelve weeks' supplies, were given a very low load factor and used as stand-by stations and not in their normal function as part of the base load. 'The objective,' says one CEGB executive, 'was to do nothing to provoke a reaction.' Across the Pennines, the big Fiddler's Ferry power station near Liverpool has one of the most abrasive union set-ups in the country. But with some Lancashire pits working, it was still theoretically possible to supply it by train. This time it was the Warrington signalmen who said no, threatening to stop all passenger traffic if it went ahead. After a few days of pressure by BR for a change of heart, the attempt was dropped. Given the union attitude at the station, it was decided not to supply it by road.

A broadly similar pattern emerged in strike-hit South Wales at Aberthaw, and at Didcot in Oxfordshire which was supplied by coal from the Midlands, which train crews refused to pass.

The CEGB quickly classified its power stations into two categories – the haves and the have-nots, stations which could get coal in and those which could not. A sustained effort was mounted with the long-run objective of turning the have-nots into haves.

The CEGB chairman, Sir Walter (now Lord) Marshall, kept in the closest touch with the Energy Minister, Peter Walker. He usually saw him every Tuesday morning after spending most of the morning being briefed by his staff. A crucial consideration was to get the stock figures and to check that they were as accurate as possible. Power in his case really did depend on knowledge.

Walker kept the figures tightly in his control. At the special cabinet committee MISC 101 which met weekly to monitor the dispute, he even drove Norman Tebbit, the Industry Minister, to complain that he couldn't get the figures. But the board and the government believed it paid off and took some satisfaction when City analysts' deductions of the autumn coal stocks proved to be well under-estimated.

In parallel, the unions were kept closely in touch. John Lyons, secretary of the Employees national committee could probably have got the figures from his own members manning the most sensitive parts of the CEGB network as power engineers, but the CEGB took care to brief him. A research assistant was given details every Friday afternoon.

Lyons was horrified by the regular Scargill predictions of imminent power cuts and took care to brief Norman Willis when he became TUC general secretary about the true position, even on occasion giving coal supply figures to a TUC general council meeting. 'What I tried to do with the information on the coal stocks was to try to tell the miners the truth; they were being lied to systematically by Arthur and the *Morning Star* about the coal stocks. I thought that was scandalous.'

As the miners' leader continued to insist that his version, assisted by his 'mole' in the CEGB, was correct, another attempt was made to get the real facts across. South Wales NUM research officer Kim Howells was told by an unknown caller to attend a London telephone booth, where he was given a print-out of CEGB figures. Finding them markedly different from the Scargill version, he passed them on to Sheffield where they were apparently pushed aside as unhelpful.

Along with situation reports, union leaders were also consulted closely about how far their members in individual stations would be prepared to go in the various measures being taken to beat the strike by varying the burn, and accepting and moving different supplies, particularly coal, by road. By and large there was little problem with oil stations as the piped-in supplies were controlled by Lyons's power engineers, professionally dedicated to keeping the system running. The battle ground was the stations mainly supplied by coal.

Altogether there are 43 of these. The 12 biggest, with a capability of 1,000 megawatts or more, were concentrated in 3 main groupings: on the edge of the Yorkshire coal field; in a crescent roughly along the line of the Trent from north Nottingham to the Midlands; and on the river Thames at Didcot (supplied by rail) and downstream in the estuary fed by the historic collier run by sea from the Tyne.

With question marks about the Yorkshire stations and the other two northern giants at Fiddler's Ferry and Blyth in Northumberland, and oil – even at the full blast allowed by the government decision three weeks into the strike to give a blank cheque to keep supplies going – only able to provide for less than 40 per cent of the demand, it was the Nottingham and Midland stations which became the key, with a war of nerves along the Thames to get coal by lorry from the Midlands.

The first part of that battle was to get enough coal out of the pityards cut off from rail links. Even with the flood of lorries enticed by unlimited work and a marginal jump in rates for short-run traffic, the problem became how to turn round them fast enough.

The answer in many cases was to put railway sleepers over the rail tracks and build ramps so that vehicles could be loaded directly from the railway loading chutes. To cut weighing delays, it was agreed by the Coal Board that lorries should be weighed not at both ends of the journey, but only at the customers'. 'Plimsoll lines' were painted on vehicles to make sure that, unweighed, they were not overloaded for traffic regulations.

The daily tally of tonnages moved by road was a staple at Walker's morning meeting. Through the summer, something over 400,000 tonnes a week was being moved on average by road and rail into the power stations, and a big drive was then mounted in the autumn with CEGB deliveries pushed up to a regular 600,000 tonnes a week plus.

For the CEGB, there was then a delicate game of persuasion to make sure the coal was used. It had predictable success in Nottingham and the Midlands where miners were working and power workers naturally took the local view; strategically vital success in the Thames estuary where a battle at West Thurrock over installing larger oilburners obscured the fact that coal was steadily coming into the stations by road; while it decided not to try anything in Yorkshire and at Fiddler's Ferry.

As one electricity industry executive put it, 'It was a question of trial and error, trying to see what the reaction was. In general people went on working normally. When they were asked to do extra things, it was judged very carefully. The policy was to avoid pushing station staff to the point where they had grounds for not handling coal-stocks or taking sympathetic action. Managers were very effective; they knew just how far to press.'

Nowhere was the battle between management pressure and union determination to assist the miners seen more clearly and drawn out so long as at Didcot. One of the big twelve coal-burning stations, set in the flat Thames river plain south of Oxford, its supplies reached it from the Midlands, at the southernmost end of the supply chain. Picketed at first by a small detachment of Kent miners, it was then taken over as the responsibility of the South Wales miners, with men from Mardy and Merthyr Vale collieries establishing a base in Oxford for fund-raising and support.

The unions in the power station were a mixture. Though predominantly members of GMBATU, there were also TGWU members, and AUEW members (generally responsible for maintenance), as well as the power engineers of the EPEA who ran the station. What happened at Didcot was an example of how local trade unionists in broad sympathy with the miners' case, assisted and encouraged by sympathetic full-time officials, were able to take action that affected electricity supplies. But it was also a demonstration of the determination and persistent pressure from management which kept power supplies running and in the end frustrated the miners. In the process Didcot became the first 'have-not' power station to be turned into a 'have'.

What went on was largely outside national attention, but within the industry its importance was not in doubt. According to one informed observer, 'Didcot was pivotal. It was the cauldron in which everything was fought out. Both sides were willing to make it the cockpit.'

The power station had no tradition of militancy. Most of its 475 manual workers were organised by the middle of the road GMBATU which had 315 members and the maintenance union, AUEW, with about 80. Otherwise there were a handful of TGWU, who would prove significant, and some EETPU members.

At the start railwaymen refused to cross miners' picket lines, and a line of coal trains backed up down the line. Then Didcot, like a number of big Yorkshire stations, was shut down during much of the summer to conserve its stocks. The annual maintenance shut-down was lengthened from six weeks to two months. The reason was that new burners were being fitted with the ability to operate on much greater proportions of oil.

No attempt was made to bring in coal by road until 28 June, three months into the strike when management proposed it. A mass meeting held jointly by the unions voted three to one not to accept it. Then in October it became clear that more oil was being brought in than the usual quota of about one large tanker a week. Union officials attempted to persuade men from a mix of unions to stop handling it. Although 19 GMBATU men agreed, 3 transport union men said they would handle the oil. It was the first crack in the solidarity.

Three weeks later coal lorries started to arrive. The shift walked off and went to sit in the canteen. But a later shift started to unload the ten lorries until the intervention of a convenor. Negotiations followed and it was agreed that the vehicles should be unloaded but their coal stored separately from other stocks, and no other lorries brought in. A few days later the union members met and once more reaffirmed they would not handle coal.

But managers kept up the pressure. Three days later it was announced that a number of men who had been approached individually were prepared to marshal lorries in the stock yards, although not to unload them or use their coal.

By this time, huge quantities of oil were arriving at the station with something like 200 tankers a day. It was effectively running on oil. But a stream of coal lorries were also arriving, sometimes as many as 400 a day. They were being marshalled and directed by two of the five shifts.

Pressures were now building on the workers and with the death of the Welsh taxi-driver David Wilkie at the end of November there was a sharp swing of opinion against the NUM. Opinion polarised and there were a number of incidents, including the tipping-up of tea and arguments in the canteen. The GMWU convenor, Roy Allen, described the atmosphere as 'like a barrel of dynamite'.

By now there were two piles of coal in the station – one 'white' and one 'black'. When two operatives on one shift agred to load some of the 'black' coal, the engineering workers threatened to stop all maintenance if it was used. Management backed off until after Christmas. Then with more miners returning to work, it pushed again.

By now nearly 500 lorries a day were arriving. The mountain of 'black' coal had reached 200,000 tonnes. Finally on 7 January AUEW members decided they would not object to management moving or burning any coal at the station. Faced by that decision the GMBATU members largely ceased their opposition, although a small group, led by the convenor Roy Allen, continued to sit in the canteen refusing to handle coal brought by lorry until many weeks after the end of the strike.

It had been a long struggle. It was influenced by external factors: the return to work by many miners; the failure of other power stations to make similar sacrifices, particularly in oil-fired stations; and the emotional change which many from both sides comment on as a result of David Wilkie's death.

Ian Keys, who was the full-time GMBATU official responsible for the power station, sums it up: 'We held for six months, and only after substantial management pressure, and pressure from other workers in the station did it begin to break.

'Then we failed on oil, but we held it on coal for just under three months more.

'The significance of Didcot was that a number of people were extremely dedicated to what the trade unions and those representing the railwaymen were doing. They were refusing to deliver what Walter Marshall said could be delivered and were therefore subjected to huge amounts of pressure.'

Didcot also showed what even a traditionally moderate union could do given determined local leadership, and the groundswell of sympathy for the miners. The problem was that it could not be sustained.

And in many key places, notably in the Midlands mining areas, there was less sympathy for the striking miners, and worries about their tactics. Gavin Laird, general secretary of the AUEW, who had pledged support for the miners when they at last came for assistance to the TUC congress in September, blames various factors for the lack of support for the striking NUM among his electricity supply members: 'They were undoubtedly influenced by the lack of a ballot. We are a union which lives by the electoral process and our members expect a vote.

'Then there was the attitude of the NUM over nuclear power where many of our people work. They were aware that it was Scargill who had moved the motion to try to change the TUC's energy policy in order to oppose nuclear power. They knew what affect that would have on jobs.

'Then the violence thing militated against us. It was always bubbling about. Remember that at Saltley in 1972 it was largely our members who had come out in support of the miners. But when I went round this time to branches and districts (and I did a lot of that because I was involved in my own election), there was no question that violence was a feature. There was regret that the miners had allowed things to deteriorate.'

One of the GMBATU's national officials most closely involved in trying to step up the sympathy action says bluntly, 'Mass picketing was counterproductive. When our people saw pickets coming, they expected them to give them trouble, even though 95 per cent of picketing was peaceful.'

When the miners at last came to the TUC in September, formal attempts were finally made to get a co-ordinated response by the supply unions. But two refused – the EEPTU, which held a ballot of all its workers in electricity supply (half not in the power stations) and got a resounding no to action, and the EPEA. John Lyons (whose union hired a bodyguard to protect him during the TUC congress, so fearful were they of violence from miners and their supporters) was perhaps the most outspoken opponent. 'Congress has voted', he wrote in his union journal, 'to support the NUM down to the last worker in the steel and electricity supply industries.'[2]

Lyons was totally antipathetic to Scargill, accusing him of running a strike which had nothing to do with pit closures: 'It was essentially a revolutionary strike, intended to mobilise the trade unions to take power by industrial means. That was my analysis from the beginning. That was based on statements Scargill had made. He always made it quite clear; he was looking for virtually any cause to get his members out.'

A generally similar view was taken by Frank Cottam, the GMBATU national officer for electricity supply. Cottam insisted throughout that his members had little appetite for action and clashed famously at Brighton with his own general secretary, David Basnett, who wanted more done to bring pressure on the government and Coal Board to reopen talks.

With leaders like these, the miners' reluctance to make a national approach was perhaps explicable, but in trade union terms, the decision not to go through the normal formalities and to rely instead on appeals and threats to men in the power stations and steelworks via speeches and television broadcasts was guaranteed to get the worst results and raise the hackles of those from whom the NUM most wanted support.

Lyons argued that a more pro-NUM attitude by the officials would not have helped: 'If we had given a militant lead to our members, it would not have made any difference, except perhaps at the margins. It would only have destroyed our unions. The key people in the power stations would not have followed. I was getting twelve letters to one in support, something I have never had before. People saying, "You mustn't do it; we won't let you." '

Cottam believes that his view about the general reluctance of his members to take sympathy action was borne out by the failure to get a markedly more militant response after the TUC congress. His own union's research department did produce plans to limit power supplies. One key paper proposed a series of measures which included limiting oil-burn and taking no fresh coal from Nottingham. Although it robustly talked of realistically being able to deliver half its restrictions, it failed to do anything like that, and the approach was vitiated by estimates of coal stocks which were too low and of the crisis margin for stocks which was too high.

One key GMBATU official claims that movements of stock between power stations were restricted and that places like Didcot did manage to restrict deliveries of fresh coal for a time, but it was too late. A crucial factor remained the reluctance of workers in oil-fired stations, who had had little overtime for months and feared redundancies, to take any action which interfered with their new lease of life.

There was some activity. At West Thurrock, picked by the CEGB as a battleground, workers successfully refused to use new oil-burning equipment installed during the strike, and a small oil tanker was blacked by the NUS and left moored without a crew, blocking the berth.

But Fred Howell appeared to have a realistic measure of things when he advised a handful of TGWU members at West Burton in Nottingham, who wanted to take action, not to put themselves at risk in the face of the attitude of both management and their colleagues.

He tried one last throw, arguing at a TUC meeting of the supply unions that they should try to affect the oil-fired stations in the south. But it was far too late. He found himself apologising to the indefatigable Jimmy Knapp who turned up to a well advertised meeting for power station workers in Rochester to be greeted by an audience of about four people: 'But our members just stayed away from the meetings. To be fair there was very little they could do in the oil-fired stations with the power engineers controlling things. But meetings were boycotted, shop stewards didn't turn up; a lot were anti-Scargill because of the media.

'You could almost cry when you saw what the miners and their families were going through and we had the chance of getting a negotiated settlement. But we never could for want of that extra little bit.'

There were still alarms for the CEGB, but its paper exercise in August about moving stocks from strike-bound pits was never needed, and the NACODS scare came to nothing. John Lyons had however taken the time to warn the government that his members would not tolerate the use of troops if they had been considered in the threatened NACODS crisis.

The alarms came with voltage reductions on 5 and 6 November 1984.

Soaking wet coal in the furnaces had combined with the normal crisis point of the aftermath of the end of Summer Time to produce difficulties. As a precaution, supplies had been cut to two major works, Llanwern steelworks in South Wales and the British Oxygen plant on the outskirts of London, both of whom had special low tariff arrangements on the basis that supplies could be interrupted with notice.

But that was the last time it happened. Although it was precautionary and CEGB engineers maintain that the general supply was never in danger, Energy Minister Peter Walker took a different view. Furious that it might give aid and comfort to the miners, he directed the CEGB not to repeat the exercise again.

They did not. On 8 January the board faced the largest demand it had ever had – 44,748 megawatts. In an almost symbolic gesture, the controllers turned to the largest power station in Yorkshire – Drax – to take them over the top and meet the demand. In the fortnight that followed that record was broken three more times. It was the clearest signal that the miners' attempt to use other unions to win the victory they could not attain on their own, had failed.

8
'The right to go to work'

The mineworkers were beaten by no foe so deadly as their own members, and their own members found no better weapon than the courts. The euphoric contempt Scargill demonstrated for the courts in the early days – 'I'm papering the walls with the writs,' he would tell all who asked – ground into the apologies to the court which a weary executive forced him to authorise – though not, personally, to *say* – in order to regain control of their depleted funds.

The individuals who took the NUM to court stumbled on a central fact of British justice: that it is based on the individual's, not the collective's, rights. Unions have always found this irksome: as collective organisations they must inevitably impose collective disciplines, and are always liable to challenge from a disaffected individual or groups of individuals. The Employment Acts of 1980 and 1982, and the 1984 Trade Union Act, deliberately built on this, encouraging the individual union members to challenge collective authority where that authority did not permit the individual ballot vote. These Acts were not much used during the strike: but the common law was to prove flexible enough to serve the purpose of the dissident miners. The favouring of the individual over the collective was imbued in its practice.

Lord Wedderburn, the most eloquent exponent of this case, says of the judiciary that it 'tends not to understand the nature of employment. Confronted by an individual employee they will frequently respond with sympathy – but because he is an individual, not because he is an employee. They may draw the conclusion that he needs protection. They do not draw the conclusion that he needs to *combine* in order to be protected from his subordination. . . . Protection *from* the union is more readily understood by judges than protection *through* the union.'[1] The workplace relationship, as Wedderburn remarks, is a power relationship, in which collectives confront each other. It was the legitimacy of these collectives' powers over their members which was fought through the courts of the country in the strike.

The social democratic balance struck in the quarter of the century after the Second World War included, near its heart, an acquiescence by most of society's powerful forces in the relatively large power of the trade union movement. It *was* a balance: in the later 1940s and 1950s at least, union leaders gave general support to the mixed economy, tripartite structures and orderly bargaining. In that period, most industrial action took place in the pits and nearly all of that was at pit level, over piece-work payments. On the other side, employers did not impede, and even at times encouraged, the spread of trade unionism. Above all the industrial relations system was *voluntary*. The celebrator of this system, Otto Kahn Freund, described it in the midst of war in terms that stood for twenty years after it: 'British collective labour law is in one respect unique among the labour systems of the larger industrial countries . . . [it] was achieved . . . by purely industrial as distinct from political and legislative action. . . . The proud edifice of collective labour regulation was built up without the assistance of the law.'[2]

This happy balance was disturbed from the late 1960s for the next two decades. Both Labour (1966) and Conservative (1970–4) governments attempted to inculcate 'responsible' behaviour through a tighter legislative framework. Both were defeated by the opposition of a union movement neither dared defy too long. The social contract period (1974–9) was one in which collective bargaining was strongly supported by legislation – but also one in which unions cast away the gains they had won, or had been given, in the 'winter of discontent'. At the end of it, James Callaghan, the Labour prime minister, asked in despair: 'How can any government govern the country without provoking a destructive reaction from the trade unions?' The labour movement did not have an answer, and so one was given to them by the Thatcher government.

Though the members of that government differed sharply about the speed of reform, they agreed the broad objective: to 'redress the balance of power in British industry'. The 1980 and 1982 Acts substantially narrowed the immunities enjoyed by unions – and (importantly for the miners' strike) opened union funds to civil action. Running throughout these acts, at the very heart of the 1984 Trade Union Act, was the principle that union members themselves take action against their unions – an explicit opposition to the legalistic controls which the 1970–4 government had attempted. Much of Scargill's contempt for the TUC derived from its collective inability to slough off the legislative chains which were weighing it down. The TUC's special conference at Wembley in 1982 was the co-incidence of interest between those who thought the unions capable of again humbling a government and those who simply disliked learning to live in a new environment. Only Scargill had the will and the troops to attempt the first task.

The Wembley debate was among the most fateful conferences ever mounted by the British labour movement – because it was full of fury and could deliver little or nothing. For the TUC, a major power in the land, to be revealed to all to have so little of its old authority was a severely wounding blow. It is plain in retrospect, and should have been clear to responsible leaders then, that the kind of campaign called for – intensely political and even potentially insurrectionary – could only be undertaken with a very large degree of public support by a self-confident movement. But only Eric Hammond, the general secretary of the electricians, had the gall to speak into the gale of militant words to remind the delegates that 'there is little feeling among the membership for a confrontation. Many members will respond initially out of loyalty to the union, but how far can we strain that loyalty?' Scargill was to show him how far *he* would strain that loyalty, as he took on, in action, the 'enemy' before which most of his other labour movement colleagues merely danced in rage. Throughout the strike, Scargill rubbed home remorselessly that he was conducting a fight on the movement's behalf against the panoply of laws which, they had all (or almost all) agreed at Wembley would destroy them if left unchallenged. In so doing, he made these predictions come true: the law did, progressively, enclose him, choke out his union's militancy, and finally exact from him an acknowledgment of its authority – an acknowledgment he was forced to make by his executive colleagues less willing to carry on life with the union in receivership than he was. 'There is not', intoned Justice Mervyn Davies on 22 October 1985, 'one law for Mr Scargill and another for everyone else.' The British judiciary had saved up for that remark for over a year and a half.

The use of the law against the NUM by its members was not preordained. It was the result of deliberate calculation, in which two men, both millionaire farmers, played important parts. The first was Peter Walker, Secretary of State for Energy; the second was David Hart, a property developer and farmer whose consuming passion is politics. Without their endeavours, it might have gone quite differently.

Walker's care, from the early days of the strike, was to keep government as far away from the strike as it was possible to make it appear. That meant *not* permitting the 'Tory laws' to be deployed against the miners.

On Wednesday 14 March, two days after the effective start of the strike, as Yorkshire pickets flooded into Nottinghamshire in defiance of guidelines issued, then withdrawn, by their own area leaders, the National Coal Board applied for and was granted an injunction restraining the picketing. Walker heard of it just after the NCB got to court. It was a move which could not be allowed – though there was a considerable irony in this, since the Act under which the injunction had been granted was precisely drawn up in response to public alarm over mass picketing and the 'rule of the mob'. What Walker did then, and what he continued to do, was to ensure that none of the state corporations most affected by the strike – the NCB itself, the British Steel Corporation and the Central Electricity Generating Board – used the Acts put in place to give relief to employers in just such an eventuality as confronted them.

The 1980 Act, in sections 16 and 17, narrows the definition of lawful picketing to that which takes place at or near the pickets' place of work. Picketing outside that definition, and any picketing which was not peaceful, loses immunity and is open to action from employers, customers, suppliers and anyone else adversely affected – including those workers who wish to pass through picket lines to work. It was brought in with the 'winter of discontent', a memory kept fresh by the government. Less fresh in most minds (though certainly still green in those of some of the cabinet) was the trauma of Saltley Gates, where the police had abdicated the task of keeping the coke lorries running in the face of mass picketing. Picketing had already been seen by the government before its members took their seats at the Cabinet table as the 'rule of the mob'. The strike was to give them no cause for revising that judgment. Why then did Walker not allow the industries under the government's ultimate control to use the law his government had brought in for their relief from 'the mob'?

Simply because he saw clearly the absolute necessity of avoiding the politicisation of the strike in the first place. Later, when it became obvious to him that the Nottinghamshire miners would not join their comrades elsewhere in the striking coal fields, the policy of no recourse to the law became even more tightly policed, lest a case in court of a state industry v. the miners be seized upon by the NUM as a rallying point for all miners to come to the aid of the union under threat.

It was the state industries who were the main target of the mass pickets: the pits themselves, the steel plants, the power stations. Yet their owner, who had spent much of the late 1970s inveighing against lawlessness in industrial relations and brought in, once in government, a raft of legislation designed to remedy such a state of affairs, absolutely prohibited its chairmen from using these laws. Walker pulled MacGregor back from the brink of action. The injunction granted against the Yorkshire pickets was never activated. When BSC managers came under pressure from their own workforces to use the Employment Acts to lift the gauntlet of pickets which the steelmen had to face every morning at Ravenscraig, Llanwern and Port Talbot, the request was sent up the line – and refused. Norman Tebbit, then Trade and Industry Secretary, told Sir Robert Haslam, then BSC chairman, to stay his hand, just as MacGregor was doing.

And so, by government design, the 'little men' stepped in to fill the breach left by the government itself. Action from below was encouraged by the absence of action from above. When two Gloucestershire truck companies and a few apprehensive Nottinghamshire, Derbyshire, Lancashire and South Wales miners took (in both cases) the South Wales NUM to court to restrain pickets at pits and steel plants, they were redeeming a pledge given by the government itself. A few naive souls – the Police Federation, speaking for the hard-pressed police officers on the picket lines; the steelworkers; the Alliance parties; some Tory back-benchers – pressed for the law to be used, but the message, passed down quickly through the upper layers of the political and industrial establishment, soon got home, and most took the point. This was not one for the government: it mustn't be seen to be involved.

George and Richard Read are brothers, with two independent transport companies working out of the Forest of Dean, heavily dependent for their living on the Port Talbot steel plant. At the time of the strike, about half of George Read's 10 trucks and 8 of Richard Read's 22 trucks were dedicated to hauling coke from Port Talbot to various parts of the country in George Read's case, or to Commonwealth Smelting at Avonmouth in the case of Richard Read. They had built their businesses up from scratch, and were both wholly involved with them. When, in the first week of April, his drivers came back to the depot without loads because pickets had turned them back, George Read jumped into the cab of one of his trucks on 11 April and drove through the picket lines himself.

Read and the pickets round the Port Talbot main gate nearly came to blows. In his affidavit, sworn two days later as part of his successful effort to obtain an injunction against the pickets, Read said that the pickets had told him he would be 'blacked' and then 'asked me who I was, and I told them I was the owner of the vehicle. I was then subjected to personal abuse including foul language. I told the pickets that they were unlawfully there and that I intended to issue a summons against the union. One of them replied that that does not bother us. Another picket told me that I had better make sure that I did not try to load again out of South Wales. The atmosphere became heated and I deemed it wise to leave.'

Both Richard and George Read got the injunctions they applied for on 17 April. Two days later, copies of them were nailed to the door of the NUM's office in the engineering union's building in Sardis Road, Pontypridd.

The Read case, heard before Mr Justice Park in the High Court on 30 July, found that these injunctions had been breached, that the breaches had interfered with the plaintiff's business, that the pickets' conduct had been authorised by the NUM and that the union officials gave no evidence of revoking the instructions to picket.

The case was to prove unusual in that it *was* 'Tory law' which provided the remedy to the Reads' complaint. Section 16 of the 1980 Act narrowed the definition of legal picketing to peaceful persuasion at the picketers' place of work. The pickets were not peaceful and were not at their workplaces. Much more importantly, though, Section 15(1) of the 1982 Act deprives unions of immunity for unlawful acts where these acts had been authorised or endorsed by senior officials, or where, once committed, they were not repudiated by a responsible official.

This section, opening up unions to action and to damages – in the South Wales case, Park imposed two separate fines for the contempts of £25,000 each – had early been identified as a dangerous measure for the unions. The TUC, in its analysis presented to the 1982 Wembley Conference, said it could 'revive one of the most controversial and fundamental issues in British Labour law'. Invoking the Taff Vale case – where the railway union was sued for striking, convincing many doubters that the unions needed their own voice in parliament – the TUC said that the Act would 'enable and indeed encourage employers and others to seek to bankrupt unions through claims for damages, which is likely to lead to a repetition of the bitter conflicts of the Industrial Relations Act period.'

It has not yet done the latter. Indeed, its effect during and since the miners' strike has less been to inflame union temper than to suppress it. The inexorable toll which the courts took on the NUM's funds at area and national level – the Reads' case was the first in the chain – fatally weakened it.

The case was also of great importance in the interpretation offered of what constituted a 'repudiation' of the action. Park saw that as a highly active matter. It was not enough, he said in his judgment, merely to declare that the official in question had 'done his best' to stop the proscribed activities: 'The only exception to that proposition is where the court order itself only orders the person concerned to "do his best". But if a court order requires a certain state of affairs to be achieved, the only way in which the order can be complied with is by achieving that state of affairs.'

Park's judgment was remarkable in another way as well. He referred twice to newspaper reports, once to a report in the *Guardian*, where Williams was quoted (indirect speech) as saying he offered to cut the pickets to a minimum because he feared a fatal accident. This was adduced as crucial evidence that the South Wales president was in control of the pickets, and could reduce or enlarge them as he wished. Second, and even more crucially, he referred to a report in the *Daily Express* which claimed that the union was seeking to escape payment of fines by transferring its funds into the officials' private accounts. This was taken as the sole justification for allowing the Reads to issue a writ of sequestration. Of course, the absence of the NUM meant these could not be challenged, but it is an index of how tough judges were prepared to be with the unions that a writ of sequestration be permitted on such speculative grounds. After the strike, there were many on the anti-NUM side who reflected thankfully on the general complaisance of the judges to their cases. This was not, as Scargill and others in the NUM saw it and still see it, simply a demonstration of the interlinked oppression of the ruling class. Rather it was an instance of the fact that judges, especially perhaps British judges, were very alive to the seriousness of contempt and – as Wedderburn observed – very much more sympathetic to the rights of the individual than to those of the collective.

The Read case established that the courts could be used successfully to challenge the tactic of picketing, but it was the use of the courts by *miners* for the same end which was of more immediate importance to the conduct of the strike. The centre of these actions was, of course, Nottinghamshire, and here the figure of David Hart assumed a central role. It is true to say that the working miners' legal actions proceeded from their own initiatives: but it is also the case that Hart shaped their initially uncertain moves, linked them to powerful sources of financial and other support, and helped them feel they were part of a crusade.

Hart's role in the strike was portrayed in the course of it as a mixture of a conspiracy and a mystery. In fact, in so far as his actions sprang from a simple, single cause, they were those of a man with a mission. He took up the challenge posed by Scargill in both personal and ideological terms. He both forged a strong personal bond with the working miners' leaders, and he saw the struggle as that of freedom versus tyranny, libertarianism against authoritarian Marxism. He led MacGregor to see it in those terms, too: from initially regarding it as a 'shootout on the other side of town', the NCB chairman ended the strike paying homage to the working miners as freedom fighters, characterising the strike as a test of British democracy itself. That perspective was largely Hart's.

He is a wealthy man. His father, 'Boy' Hart, co-founded the merchant bank Henry Ansbacher. In 1974, during the secondary banking crash, Hart declared himself bankrupt. He was discharged in 1978, and recovered to run a successful property business from an office in Brook Street. He has a country house of real beauty and some luxury, Coldham Hall, near Bury. When in London, two or three days a week, he rents a suite in Claridges or stays with his mother in her Chelsea house. What distinguishes him from other wealthy men with a comfortable niche in life is a powerfully extrovert personality which is split – though in no very anguished way – between the active and the reflective. He has published one novel, in 1982 – *The Colonel* – and was working on another after the strike ended. In January 1985 the radical right Adam Smith Institute published a pamphlet by him, *The Soul Politic*. He is an occasional contributor to *The Times*.

But he is too much of a social and political being to resist high-level dabbling in politics. He is well connected, through the right-wing advisor network, with the Reagan White House and with right-wing policy circles in Washington. He takes a particular interest in defence, touring US bases and taking upon himself the role of an ambassador for the Strategic Defence – Star Wars – Initiative. Most importantly it is clear that – in spite of his own reticence in admitting it – he has developed and retained a relationship with the prime minister which permits him to offer advice on a range of matters – defence, social policy, policing and at times, though surprisingly infrequently, the miners' strike.

His wealth and position gives him the possibility of moving in the highest circles. His nerve secures him introductions and interest. His convictions and ideology, mixed with a willingness to attend to practical details and if necessary fund, or find funding for, causes ensures his influence. By the end of the strike, David Hart could be found in the chairman's office as often as the chairman. At one point towards the end of 1984 when MacGregor was abroad, Hart issued orders in MacGregor's name.

He defines himself not as a Conservative, but as a Libertarian:

> Libertarians recognise that men and women express themselves through free decisions. Animals can be fed and provided for, their material needs anticipated and met. Men and women assert their individuality by the *choices* they make. . . . Libertarians recognise that men and women achieve moral growth only through the exercise of responsibility. For the libertarian freedom to make choices must be a fundamental aim of public policy. They hold that man has another self than the purely material. This other self inspires the will to freedom. This is the unique distinction between libertarianism and all the other political philosophies at work in the latter part of the 20th century.[3]

His belief in the moral basis of libertarianism was strengthed by the miners' dispute. He wrote that the growth of the state had fostered the creation of interest groups who further restrict liberty in their own interests: 'When individuals or groups of individuals object, if they speak their mind fearlessly, or if they refuse to co-operate, physical violence is often used to persuade them. This has characterised the miners' dispute.' Above all, though, what animates Hart in his 'soul politic' is idealism, pure and unashamed, but an idealism the opposite of that which drives socialists. Hart calls it humility: the idealism of the non-interventionist:

> Libertarians believe that the institutions that have a benign influence on humanity are not and cannot be the creation of single minds, but are the result of the interaction of many minds upon one another over long periods of time. They believe that the spontaneous order which results from this interaction is far superior to any order which can be planned or conceived by any one person or group. This spontaneous order represents a process of millions of trial-and-error discoveries, accumulated over countless years. It is the product of a society that has survived where others have not. It represents the highest wisdom of that society.
>
> For this reason and because of the profound respect they bear for their fellow men, a respect that in any other age would be called love, libertarians approach with extreme caution any intervention in the lives of others, as they do in the institutions that others, with the help of time, have evolved.[4]

There could scarcely be a more explicit opposite to Scargill and to Scargillism, and Hart saw himself, in shaping a strategy to win, as matched against the miners' president. However, he fell into his role in the strike somewhat by accident. Fascinated by it, he secured a letter of accreditation from *The Times* as a feature writer and toured the coal fields, driven about in his large Mercedes by his chauffeur/minder, a former policeman named Peter Devereux. He excited the initial suspicion of several of the NCB regional press officers to whom he applied for help. They were accustomed to reporters looking scruffy and acting cynical – the apparition of a large, rich idealist was not in their frame of reference.

On 8 June 1984 Hart turned up in Shirebrook, in Derbyshire, one of the most bitterly divided of the pit villages. He asked a policeman if anyone was having a rough time. The policeman directed him down the street. There he met a woman whose husband was working and whose son, by a previous marriage, was on strike. Bricks had come through her windows, she and her husband (who did not want to talk) were ostracised and she hardly dared go out to shop. Hart felt real anger and determined to assist. It made him feel good in two ways: first, he was exercising altruism, and second, he knew what he was doing was right – never before in his life had he been so sure of his actions, so determined in taking action, than during the miners' strike.

He did two things. First, he got himself invited to a party at which he knew MacGregor would be present. He had a reason for introducing himself because his brother Tim had worked with MacGregor at Lehmann Bros, the US investment bankers. MacGregor at that time thought the strike would be over in a month or two, and appeared to Hart to have little conception of the political challenge which was being offered. Hart stuck around MacGregor after that, proving himself at first useful and then indispensable.

Second, he contacted the tiny group in Nottinghamshire which was trying to organise working miners' resistance to the NUM. The working miners became Hart's real base. In a sense, he developed into their representative, bringing them down for a meeting in Claridges (which was the subject of the first leak of his influence, in Paul Foot's column in the *Mirror*), apprising MacGregor and the prime minister of their importance, giving their early meetings both a coherence and a strategy. When they needed money Hart either used his own or persuaded rich friends to donate it. From the onset the expensive battles in the courts drew their funds from starkly contrasting sources: the NUM's from moneys donated by left-wing unions or supporters, or from the Soviet Union; the working miners' from many thousands of individual donations sent in to their lawyers from up and down the country, and from wealthy businessmen or public figures, most of who remained anonymous, though Sir Hector Laing, chairman of United Biscuits, did begin a public fund for the working miners in August. His appeal circulated among chairmen and executives headed by a quotation from Edmund Burke: 'All that is needed for evil to triumph is that good men do nothing.'

The working miners whose names became familiar were only the publicly visible of the 24,000 Notts miners – five-sixths of the total – who continued working throughout the strike. Most did not demonstrate their feelings other than by working, though nearly half – an estimated 11,000 – turned up at the Berry Hill, Mansfield, offices of their area union to protest against the pro-strike stance still being adopted by their official leaders. But they became, in that delicate period, the unofficial leadership, constituting themselves as a committee, meeting sometimes behind police protection in pubs, often taking over the functions of the branch officials who were on strike in pits which were largely working. Most were soon replaced as the leadership of the Notts area by men who had been officials before the strike began, but had, unlike Ray Chadburn and Henry Richardson, president and secretary of the Notts area, taken the side of the working miners. These were Roy Lynk, David Prendergast and later Neil Greatrex, a Bentinck branch secretary who continued to work. But the earlier dissenters from the official NUM line – most prominent were Colin Clarke, the delegate to area council from the Pye Hill branch, and John Liptrot, former secretary of Sherwood branch – turned to the law as their main weapon. Hart's tactic, which was followed through brilliantly, was to encourage case after case taken by the working miners, with the aim of tying up NUM leadership time and energy and attacking their funds.

Clarke was the key man. A slow-spoken careful man (whom Hart, with typical hyperbole, describes as a 'saint'), he had already gone to the law before Hart arrived on the scene, incensed by the way in which it seemed to him his area and national leaders were flouting union rule and practice. On 15 May, with Liptrot and Howard Shooter, also of the Pye Hill branch, he issued writs in the High Court against the NUM, at area and national levels, to lift the instruction given by the area officials on 20 April that the strike in Notts was official and had to be obeyed. On 25 May Justice Megarry ruled in their favour. Two days before that judgment Clarke had threatened further writs against the area leaders if they delayed the holding of branch elections.

The winning of the case, and the threatening of further writs, secured in Notts both the illegality of the strike call and the holding of elections, which resulted in a pro-working miner majority replacing the strikers on the area executive. It showed the way to miners in Lancashire and South Wales, who also secured declarations that the strikes in their areas were unlawful. In neighbouring North Derbyshire, too, working miners were stirred into taking action. That case, taken by three miners from different North Derbyshire pits, was one of the most important of the strike.

The prime mover in this case was Albert Taylor, a surface engineer from Shirebrook. With John Roberts, a quality control inspector from the area's central workshops, and John Phillips, a mobile plant driver from the Williamthorpe complex, Taylor took a case on the simple grounds that the strike nationally and at area level was unlawful.

Taylor had not responded to his union call to strike. He had voted against it in the area ballot organised on Friday 16 March, as had 4,322 others; 4,307 had voted for a strike, giving those in Albert Taylor's camp a slim, 50.1 per cent, vote against a strike (though the North Derbyshire rules had the then standard qualifying level of 55 per cent for a strike). He had gone to work at Shirebrook whenever he could, but on many days the pit was picketed out by masses of Yorkshire pickets. He saw bricks thrown (at him), bales of hay dragged out on the road and set on fire to stop the working miners, pickets pushing at police as though to push them under the buses roaring in to work. In his riven village, his family was the focus of hatred from the activists on strike and their families. His wife was threatened, and he stayed at home for four weeks because of the harassment. He went back when he saw that other men were doing so. Roberts was picketed out for nine weeks, then returned. His 10-year-old was abused at school, and he moved his family out of the area for a time, away from the jeers and curses of his neighbours. Phillips, working at different pits, got plenty of abuse, but little harassment away from his work.

As the national union moved towards its 19 April declaration that the strike was 'official', the Derbyshire union, a tradition of left leadership embedded within its officials and activists, strove to marry an adverse vote from below and orders to advance from above. On 19

March, a special meeting of the area council voted, by 12 to 2, to call for an all-out strike on the coal field in defence of jobs and in opposition to pit closures. On 6 April Gordon Butler, the area secretary, got a letter from Heathfield, his long-time associate in North Derbyshire, making the area strike official in accordance with the NEC decision of 8 March. That same day the area executive met and 'expressed grave concern at certain instances where a minority of men were continuing to work'.

On 19 April the special delegate conference in Sheffield set the seal on the strike. Scargill, speaking at the Derbyshire area conference on 1 May, said that his 'final message to you in Derbyshire [is to] make sure that every striking miner is a picket not only in the Notts coalfield but also at power stations, docks and factories.' Three weeks later, the Derbyshire executive met to decide that, following its decision on 6 April, it would expel 'for an indefinite period . . . those members who have not conformed to NUM policy during the period of the present dispute, and who have offered themselves as scab labour.' Albert Taylor saw himself jobless, and went to the law.

The three Derbyshire miners had to wait until 29 September, when Mr Justice Nicholls pronounced the strike, at national and Derbyshire area levels, unlawful. Nicholls made the judgment on the national strike as a by-product of his judgment on Derbyshire. He said that, 'It is as plain as a pikestaff . . . that the strike call by the Derbyshire Union and by the NUM was in breach of the rules of the Derbyshire Union and of the NUM and hence invalid. No national ballot has been held so the strike call cannot stand as a lawful call for a national strike . . . the plaintiffs are entitled, without breaching any rule or obligation they owe the Union, not to strike, and to disregard the call to strike and to cross . . . picket lines.'

The complaints, brought by Taylor, Roberts and Phillips were not 'mere technicalities, lawyers' quibbles on nice points of interpretation of obscure rules.' They were, instead, over the way in which union members should be governed: 'The rules are the constitutions of the unions. They exist for the benefit and the protection of all the members. The rules regarding strikes are explicit, but for a period of over six months now, the officers of the NUM and the Derbyshire Union have chosen to disregard the constitutions under which they hold office, and to ride roughshod over their members.'

The case taken by the South Wales miners against their own area union to restrain it from organising the pickets which harassed them as they returned – the first of the very few who broke the strike in South Wales – to their pits resulted in a complex judgment whose importance is still a mater of some dispute. It was taken after the most dramatic cases had been heard, but it appears to have set a powerful precedent on the numbers of those who can peacefully picket, and the distinction – or lack of it – between a picket and a 'demonstration'.

The plaintiffs were drawn from five pits, all of which had, by November/December of 1984, a few men back at work. Picketing, token or non-existent at most South Wales pits before, was stepped up sharply. The men got a rough ride in (though not as rough as that suffered by their working colleagues in Yorkshire, or in the north-east). One (Sheehan) claimed that up to 50 pickets assembled outside his house on two evenings, 8 and 9 November. On a third instance, some 30 picketed the Cross Keys Technical College where he was taking a course. Another (Fjaelberg) said the entrance to his estate was picketed 3 out of 5 working days.

The case concerned that central issue in the strike: the right to work. The working miners said it was endangered by the pickets, who were, they claimed, acting unlawfully. Mr Justice Scott agreed with them in part, disagreed in part. He held that picketing was lawful at common law (a useful judgment for future picketers: the law was not clear); he refused to issue general injunctions prohibiting picketing; refused to grant an injunction against either the South Wales NUM or the NUM nationally to stop them calling strikes or industrial action which might result in civil wrongs, or torts (and noted in passing that the South Wales strike was called according to the area union rules).

But he deemed it to be plain, in a passage at the core of his judgment, that 'the picketing at the colliery gates is of a nature and is carried out in a manner that represents an unreasonable harassment of the working miners. A daily congregation on average of 50 to 70 men hurling abuse and in circumstances that require a police presence and require the working miners to be conveyed in vehicles do not in my view leave any room for argument. The working miners have the right to go to work. Neither they nor any other working man should be required, in order to exercise that right, to tolerate the situation I have described.'

This particular judgment was to restrain the South Wales union from organising the picketing – he had found, on ordinary common law principles, that it was vicariously liable for the acts of its lodges and lodge officers – except under strict conditions. The injunction granted restrained the South Wales NUM from inciting, procuring, assisting, encouraging or organising members of the union or others to congregate or assemble at or near the entrance to the colliery (a) otherwise than for the purpose of peacefully obtaining or communicating information or peacefully persuading any person to work or abstain from working and (b) otherwise than in numbers not exceeding six.'

The first of these conditions ruled out 'demonstrations' separate from pickets which, the NUM had argued, were present near the pit gates in a different capacity from the picketers. Scott said that there was 'no legitimate distinction to be drawn between so-called pickets who are stationed close to the gates of the colliery and the rest, so-called demonstrators, who stand nearby.'

The second is a precedent of considerable weight. Scott restrained the South Wales NUM from setting more than six pickets. In doing so, he relied on the 1980 Code of Practice on picketing, issued under the 1980 Employment Act. The Code, a child of a decade just past which had seen picketing become the prime weapon of industrial power, observed that (para. 29) 'the main cause of violence and disorder on the picket line is excessive numbers' and recommended that 'pickets and their organisers should ensure that in general the number of pickets does not exceed six at any entrance to a workplace.' In doing so, he has enshrined in common law the principle that pickets exceeding six may be intimidatory. From being a guide, the Code had become a limit.

The cases taken in the first months of the strike can be seen, in retrospect, as preparing the ground for the case which, more than any other, forced the NUM leadership to come to terms with the law of the land. Ironically, it came from two Yorkshire miners, though both, while working in the Yorkshire area's boundaries, lived in Nottinghamshire. Ken Foulstone and Bob Taylor are big, powerful men who worked in the Manton Pit. Both are family men, who stressed their 'ordinariness' and 'decency' – a presentation made more delicate by a robbery charge which hung over Foulstone's head, and of which he was convicted after the strike ended. But in the summer of 1984, Foulstone's home, up a secluded lane on water board land outside the village of Minton near Newark, was a peaceful place – though its peace was guaranteed by the presence, round the clock, of half a dozen police officers who had reinforcements within a few minutes' call. They were there to protect the Foulstone home – and the Taylor home three miles away – from the kind of attack which had seen windows smashed, homes burned and women and children terrified.

Foulstone and Taylor were genuine enough, but they did not burst upon the world unprepared. Hart, by this time holding regular meetings with the Working Miners' Committee and keeping MacGregor closely in touch, put the Foulstone and Taylor lawyers, David Payne and Andrew Fearn of Newark-based Hodgkinson Tallent, in touch with David Negus of Ellis Fermor in Nottingham, who had handled most of the Working Miners' Committee cases (Foulstone and Taylor were reluctant to be seen to be in touch with the Committee).

At a press conference arranged by Payne in London on 9 August, after smuggling them down to London to avoid the press discovering what they were doing, the two men presented an inexpert but straightforward front. They were treated sympathetically by the largely anti-NUM press – and no wonder, for they said some telling things. Said Taylor: 'I've been on strike for half a year – and no progress has been made.' Said

Foulstone: 'The only person that's given anything is the NCB, and the only person who hasn't given anything is the leader of the NUM.' Said Taylor, confronted with the view that they were lone voices: 'If the NUM is certain that we don't have any support, let's have a ballot and have it all settled.' Foulstone said the 'moderates' on the NUM national executive appeared to have gone 'into hiding' rather than stand up for their principles, thus leaving it to the rank and file – a complaint which was to be repeated over and over again.

The two men – especially Taylor – had been out of step with the leadership of their area for some time. Back in January 1981, when the NCB, pushed by the government, made a move to shut down unprofitable pits, the South Yorkshire pit of Orgreave was on the list of 25 which the board wished to close. A ballot was held, asking if the members would give the area 'authority to take various forms of action (including strike action if necessary), to stop the closure of any pit except on the grounds of exhaustion'. In the vote, 85.6 per cent of those voting said yes. When the Board proceeded with closure a two-week strike ensued; when it pulled back, the strike ended.

That majority was not repeated. In the three subsequent national ballots – January 1982, October 1982 and March 1983 – the Yorkshire vote for strike action declined from 66.5 per cent to 56 per cent to 54 per cent. In each case, they were out of step with the national majority, which voted against action by 55 per cent, and by 61 per cent twice.

But come the 1984 strike, the Yorkshire area derived its mandate for the strike from the January 1981 ballot. When the Manvers pit in South Yorkshire went on strike on 20 February over a 'snap-time' dispute, the South Yorkshire panel declared a strike from 5 March – a week before the rest of the coal fields. Taylor and Foulstone worked on that Monday, but on Tuesday they were withdrawn from underground and given police protection past howling pickets. From 7 March they were 'on strike'. As they were doing so, George Hayes, their area director, had announced the closure of Cortonwood pit. That same Monday 5 March, the Yorkshire area council met and passed a motion which said that 'in conformity with the 1981 Yorkshire area individual ballot vote of 85.6 per cent' a strike would be declared from Friday 8 March. It called on the NUM's national executive to ratify its call for an area strike under rule 41, a request gladly granted on 8 March in Sheffield. 'Area by area will decide,' Mick McGahey said before that executive, 'and in my opinion it will have a domino effect. . . . We will not be constitutionalised out of a defence of our jobs.'

Bit by bit, Foulstone and Taylor came to the view that *they* had been manipulated out of their jobs. Taylor, who had been in the small majority to vote against the strike mandate in 1981, who had been in the countrywide majority to vote for the Conservative Party in 1983, led the disaffected group at his pit in demanding a branch meeting. These had been suspended by the branch committee once the strike began. Early in May he began to talk to other miners, and found 'hundreds' who felt as resentful as he did about being on strike. He got three signatures (including his own) for a recalled branch meeting on Friday 11 May and there, at a meeting in Worksop packed with miners, the 'moderate revolt' which had been (unwisely for the rebels) trumpeted in the press failed. Taylor and Foulstone were howled down. The 'hundreds' from the pit's 1,300 men did not materialise, and the demand that a vote be taken on a return to work was ruled out of order.

It was a repetition at branch level of the tactic used by Scargill in the executive meeting of 12 April, to rule 'out of order' a decision which might be lost (though the Manton meeting, unlike the executive, would probably have achieved the right result for the strikers). It was an effective and simple tactic. It stamped the authority of the leadership on the event; it bred, in the right conditions, the most ferocious discontent.

Foulstone and Taylor, deprived of the democratic route by – as they held – terrorism, fell to plotting, and to the law. Their case, which Fearn and Payne dropped all else to prepare for them, and which finally came to court on 25 August, demanded a number of 'reliefs': for the holding of Yorkshire branch elections, due on June 1984 but indefinitely delayed by national executive fiat; for the restraint of the application of 'rule 51', the rule passed by the special conference in August which set out a complex procedure whereby members of the NUM were to be disciplined; for a declaration that the strike in Yorkshire was unlawful: and for the holding of a ballot on strike action.

Mr Justice Nicholls granted all but the last relief. He believed that, on balance, the NUM rule 43 which laid down that 'a national strike shall only be entered upon as a result of a ballot vote of the members' did not contain a 'positive obligation entitling a member to compel the NUM to hold a ballot'. In theory, and at the time, Nicholls's decision appeared a large setback to the plaintiffs and to working miners as a whole. A ballot might have ended their dilemma once and for all, and would certainly have held to the test the contentions of both sides on the strike's support, or lack of it. But in practice, it hardly mattered. Any such order would have been disobeyed, and the orders which *were* allowed the NUM leadership to proclaim defiance and thus to suffer the same consequences as defiance of the order to ballot would have entailed.

Nicholls, giving judgment immediately after dealing with the Derbyshire case, said that the national strike's unlawfulness was 'self-evident'. The plaintiff's contention that the Yorkshire strike was merely part of a 'dressed up' national strike was supported. The Yorkshire area strike did not comply with the area's rule 53, which is the familiar area rule laying down a 55 per cent ballot vote of the membership for strike action. As for the 1981 ballot, it was 'too remote in time [with] . . . too much change in the branch membership of the Area since then for that ballot to be capable of justifying a call to strike action 2½ years later.'

The union, he said, had a remedy in its own hands for declaring an official strike – ballot the members. Taylor and Foulstone, living behind police guards, needed protection. An injunction was granted restraining the NUM or the Yorkshire area from seeking to persuade its members not to cross the picket lines.

The crucial distinction between the Derbyshire and the Yorkshire judgments was in this: that where in the Derbyshire case, Nicholls had declared that the national and area strikes were unlawful, and that the instructions issued by the unions were in breach of their rules, in the Yorkshire case he specified that the Yorkshire and the NUM officials be restrained from 'describing or treating the strike or any picket line in the said Yorkshire area as "official" or words to the like effect.'

The judgment was made on the Friday before the beginning, on the next Monday, of the Labour Party conference in Blackpool. That same evening, Scargill went on Channel 4 News to say that, whatever the courts said, the strike in Derbyshire, Yorkshire and everywhere else was official: 'and I'm going to say this, quite clearly: that any miner in this union and any official in this union who urges or crosses a picket line in defiance of our union's instructions runs the risk of being disciplined under the rules. . . . There is no High Court judge going to take away the democratic right of our union to deal with internal affairs. We are an independent democratic trade union.'

Payne and Fearn were ready for this, their video recorder spinning as Scargill spoke. On Saturday they prepared affidavits and applied to the High Court for leave to give notice of contempt proceedings forthwith. The orders were issued early on Monday morning, and the lawyers were faced with a dilemma. They had to have them served on Scargill that day, or their validity would expire, but could not get to Blackpool in time to do so. Here Hart stepped in. He chartered a helicopter, had it delivered to Coldham Hall, flew to the London Heliport to collect the process server, landed him at Blackpool Airport in the company of a *Daily Express* photographer, got him in to the conference with a false press pass and had the notice of motion and accompany documents served while Hart strolled about Blackpool looking like a Spitfire pilot.

The NUM president immediately called an emergency executive which again supported his defiance. He told the press that 'We will continue to support the decisions of our members. If that brings us into conflict with the law, then so be it.' He picked out the threat in the motion to commit him to jail, repeating in interviews and meetings that he expected to be jailed and was willing to be so. At a rally organised by the ultra-left *Labour Herald* newspaper, where he was received in roaring rapture by the delegates, he spelled out his position 'specifically and categorically' once more: the strike remained official.

If there was a choice, he said, between betraying one's class and going to prison, then 'there's no choice as far as I'm concerned. I stand by my class, by my union – and if that means prison, so be it. We have come too far, we have suffered too much, for there to be any compromise with either the judiciary or the government.'

It was a moment of the purest excitement. The rally had before it the only man in the country willing to translate its rhetoric into action, and now, as his action bit, the forces of reaction began to unsheath their claws, to wheel into the light their instruments of repression. Scargill was stripping away the veneer, the social blurring which had fooled the masses for so long. He was a catalyst for revolt, and the masses need do nothing, risk nothing, but the health of their throats. At that same conference, three days before, the harsh whine of Eric Hammond's cockney had drilled into the outrage of the delegates to tell them, once again, that they were deluded. He slammed picket line violence (to be drowned in booing, as was everyone else who did so), and told them the decision to support the miners would take the party further from power and further from its supporters. Most delegates at the conference, certainly most from the constituency parties, appeared to regard him as a freak. It did not occur to them, at least not in public, that the microphones through which both he and they abused each other were able to amplify their voices because of the practical, tacit agreement between Hammond and the power – and other – workers.

As if in another world, the legal wheels ground down on the union. On 10 October, the week after the Labour Party conference, the NUM was fined £200,000 and Scargill £1,000 for contempt (the latter subsequently and anonymously paid). Nicholls, his small mouth pursed together as he peered down from his high chair into a court seething with reporters but with no presence from those flouting his orders, said that the orders of the court had been 'openly and repeatedly defied. . . . If the orders of the court are to be set at nought in this way – where is the rule of law?' Scargill came out on the steps of the union headquarters in Sheffield to read a statement saying that 'The official strike action will continue until the National Coal Board withdraws its pit closure programme, agrees to keep open those pits currently under threat and provides a basis for resolving this dispute in line with the Plan for Coal.'

Two weeks later the time to pay the fine ran out. On 25 October, Nicholls noted sadly that the NUM officials persisted in 'regarding the laws of this country as applicable to others and not to itself'. At root, he said, was their refusal to recognise that their members had rights against the union which the law should be as ready to protect as the union's rights against its members, and against others outside.

Nicholls ordered sequestration of the NUM's assets, appointing four partners in the City chartered accountancy firm of Price Waterhouse to do so. The sequestrators found difficulty in tracing, and in obtaining control of, the NUM's £8 million assets, largely because the courts in Ireland, Luxembourg and Switzerland, to where the assets were traced, were uncertain of their status and refused to release the funds into their hands. The working miners were not to be baulked. Colin Clarke prompted by Hart and with 15 other members of the Working Miners' Committee, came back to court to call for the 25 members of the union NEC to be made personally liable for the £200,000 fine, and for the NUM trustees – Scargill, Heathfield and McGahey – to be replaced by a receiver appointed by the court. On 30 November, the union's assets, wherever they were, passed into the control of Mr Herbert Brewer, a Derbyshire solicitor (who turned out to be a stalwart Conservative and member of the Institute of Directors, and who was hastily replaced by the less politically embarrassing figure of Mr Michael Arnold).

The application for receivership marked the first time the NUM leaders showed even a limited appreciation of the damage threatening the union. They appeared in court and argued, through their counsel, Mr William Stubbs QC, that the receivership should not be imposed because they were willing to give an undertaking – personally signed by Scargill – that that part of the funds discovered to be in Luxembourg (some £4.63 million) would not be touched until a full hearing of the case in a week's time. But they once more ran up against the hard fact of legal life that conditional compliance with court orders was not enough. Justice Mervyn Davies asked if they were prepared to submit to the authority of the court. Mr Stubbs had to reply he had no instructions to that effect. The receivership was imposed.

We have seen how the union leadership prepared for the strike, and how it made what preparations it could to protect its funds once the strike was on its way. But the imposition of the sequestration and then of the receivership stimulated a new bout of frenzied monetary activity during the 'twilight period' when foreign banks and courts still preferred to deal with the people who appeared to have title to the funds – the NUM. In English law, however, the NUM leaders had no control. The sequestrator had been appointed to take charge of all monies in order to pay the £200,000 fine and the plaintiff's costs. The receiver replaced the union's trustees – Scargill, Heathfield, McGahey, together with the then Nottinghamshire secretary Henry Richardson and the Yorkshire vice president Sammy Thompson.

Nevertheless, on 8 and 23 November and on 20 December 'persons purportedly acting for the NUM' (as a receiver's report of November 1985 has it) made a contract to sell £4 million at a fixed exchange rate on 25 January, then reversed that and countermanded part of the original instruction in order to *buy* £2 million, then $500,000, at fixed rates. At the time, these transactions were effected, the funds were sequestrated, or both sequestrated and in receivership.

Later, Scargill was to claim that his overseas dealings had made the union money. He said up to $1 million had been earned in interest and in exchange rate dealings. The receiver demurred: his November report said that his 'calculations reveal that the funds would have fared far better had they been invested in England in conformity with the relevant investment powers.'

The union had to have money. It came from three main sources – inside the union, from some of its constituent areas; from other unions; and from abroad. Two areas – the Cokemen's area and Yorkshire – 'loaned' £107,673 and £42,752 respectively to the national union. At the same time, however, as the national union was defying the courts, some areas were quietly making their own arrangements with the receiver to gain access to those funds which they paid each week to the NUM, part of which was then released back to them for certain types of expenditure. This account, known as the 'imprest' account, is essential to area unions' continued solvency, and from May 1985, eleven of them – Cokemen, the white-collar group COSA, Cumberland, Derbyshire, Leicestershire, Midlands, North Wales, Lancashire, Power Group, South Derbyshire and Yorkshire – gave a pledge that they were not improperly financing the national union in order to gain access to it.

Other unions gave money clandestinely, and thus no final estimate has yet been made. The Transport and General Workers' Union, the largest in the country with 1.5 million members, is thought to be the largest contributor: estimates vary between £2 million and £4 million. The National Union of Public Employees and the National Union of Railwaymen also gave. Others did too, but the figures are impossible to discover. Much of the money was said to have been passed over, in cash form in carrier bags, to Scargill in the Barbican flat the NUM kept for him. More went via Scotland where the NUM strike was lawful.

The Soviet Union was the main contributor from overseas. The huge publicity which ensued from the trip by Roger Windsor, the NUM's chief executive, to Libya, produced more headlines than cash. It was an index of how far the union leadership was prepared to go in its search for money that the Libyan government, a funder for terrorist groups and particularly reviled in Britain because of the shooting, in 1984 of policewoman Yvonne Fletcher by Libyan 'diplomats', should be seen as a legitimate source. Such an initiative made the funds received from the Soviet Union seem quite staid. Some of this – as much as £1 million – was openly advertised as gifts from the Soviet Union, especially the mineworkers. However, British secret service estimates supplied to the government put the contributions as high as £7 million. The reports said that the money was routed via the Confédération Générale de Travail, the Communist-dominated, and largest, French trade union centre.

Scargill and his colleagues did not attempt to disguise many of these transactions (though the *Sunday Times*'s revelations of the Libyan connection met a wall of hostility and silence when put to NUM leaders). Indeed, the miners' president gained strength in *not* dissimulating. Where a Zinoviev letter (and that a forgery perpetrated by the right) could ruin Labour's election chances in 1924, the same connection could shock British public opinion because it was not treated as a matter to be disguised by those receiving it. One of the many achievements of Arthur Scargill was his ability to convince enough people that his enemy's enemy should be his friend.

Yet it was the noose which the sequestrators and the receiver drew round the union and the areas which in the end forced Scargill to bow to the court, and come back, at least (and probably only) in form within the law. By September of 1985 those areas which, like the north-eastern unions and Scotland, had made no deals with the receiver, were beginning to find themselves running into huge debt. At an executive meeting in Sheffield on 10 October, a number of them ganged up on him, George Rees, the South Wales Secretary, Eric Clarke, the Scottish secretary, and Denis Murphy, the Northumberland president, taking the lead. Murphy told him that 'if it means bending the knee, you've got to do it.' But no vote was taken at that meeting, and Scargill did nothing, hating as poison the thought of bowing the knee to courts which had assisted in beating him.

But at an executive held in London's County Hall on 28 October, before a special conference on the position of the sacked miners, a vote *was* taken, and by 11 votes to 7, bending the knee, or purging its contempt of the court, became union policy. On 14 November, before the impassive Justice Nicholls once more, the NUM's QC Gavin Lightman tendered 'the apology of the NUM for the contempt and request that the writ of sequestration be lifted.'

It was part, said Lightman, of the 'human condition' that circumstances arose where a person might feel bound to act in accordance with the dictates of his own conscience, and thus in defiance of the law. The courts could not approve but might recognise their sincerity. 'That is the position of the NUM. They recognise their conduct was unlawful and that it was their legal duty to obey. They do apologise. The sequestration order has achieved its purpose. The rule of law has once more prevailed. The union has paid dearly for what it has done and its members should not be further punished.'

Thus it was that sequestration, and the contempt, was ended with three men in the court – Scargill, Heathfield, McGahey, the troika –

arguing that they had done as personal conscience dictated. It was a curious apology for men, especially for Scargill, who had argued, with some justice, that their actions proceeded not from the higher court of their own judgment but from the higher court of their union's collective decisions, to which they as servants were bound. It was cunningly designed to conform to the individualist sympathies of the court and of the judge, and perhaps it did, for Nicholls released the union from sequestration without putting the union leaders – as they had feared – through an examination of the murkier points of where the moneys had gone. In the end, the espousal of the collective will, the revolutionary creed which Scargill had championed so ably, collapsed into the plea of the conscientious objector.

9
Inside Hobart House

'The Area Directors met on Monday with the four full-time board members. Moses from North Derbyshire keeps saying he has had the best-ever attendance, but he is out of line. David Archibald from the north-east says there may be a groundswell in our favour in a couple of weeks. But George Hayes says the television programme about the violence at Kiveton Park has had the worst effect of anything. There is now much less confidence about a return to work. Bert Wheeler from Scotland takes the hardest line; he is quite incredibly hard. Philip Weekes from South Wales was the most blunt about the pressures. He said there was no break at all; not a flicker.'

That contemporary account of a meeting when the strike was six months old is a sharp reminder of how uncertain its outcome appeared to be through long periods of stalemate through the hot summer and autumn of 1984.

In retrospect there seems a logical progression in the Coal Board's ultimately successful conduct of the strike. A strong push for a ballot combined with a concerted effort to keep men working led into talks in mid-summer and then further negotiations in the autumn. Their breakdown was followed by a refusal to talk which encouraged the return to work. But it was far from obvious at the time.

In fact most of the key participants were struck by the way the Coal Board line wavered and changed over all sorts of issues: the use of the law; possible negotiating concessions; the return to work; inconsistencies which both hawks and doves in the board saw as reflecting the inconsistencies in the approach of the chairman himself.

Yet at the end of the day it was MacGregor's determination, shorn of some of his closest aides, which was triumphant, though at a cost which still has to be quantified. His chief lieutenant, Jimmy Cowan, said bluntly, 'We didn't have the will, the stamina to contain a strike until MacGregor came. There wasn't the capacity to absorb pressure that he had, and if he did anything it was to make management very direct and he was to my mind an essential part in not losing the strike.'

'Not losing' sums up the Coal Board's attitude at the start of the strike. Throughout it remained as set out by Ned Smith on MacGregor's arrival, 'Scargill must not be allowed to win – ever.' For all the loose talk in Whitehall about the Coal Board's chumminess with the unions from ministers who were quick to back down when individual pits threatened to become flash points, most area directors felt that the board had not been strong enough in the past and welcomed the stronger line, first from Siddall and then MacGregor.

Bert Wheeler, who took a notably uncompromising line in Scotland, said, 'We were in it to win. We had a lot to lose if we had lost. The whole country had a lot to lose.' It was a sentiment shared by Jack Wood of North Notts, establishing his emergency control room, ringing up in the middle of the night if the trains stopped, typifying a no-nonsense conservative breed of mining engineer.

Even Philip Weekes, the Labour-supporting South Wales area director who met his union officials regularly throughout the strike saw no room for compromise. He had clashed earlier with Ezra because Weekes wanted to close pits more quickly, and during the strike he earmarked coal faces he would never open again. In the need, as they saw it, to prevent Scargill, rather than the miners, succeeding there were no dissenters. Where the arguments came was over the methods.

Here a major problem was that however stage-managed the confrontation, the board went into it without clarifying its lines of command and with the crucial changes in personnel which would be part of the MacGregor revolution neither thought through nor effected. Instead they were carried out piecemeal through the strike; a recipe for confusion on both a practical and philosophical level.

MacGregor's brief was to bring the abrasive attitudes of international private enterprise to bear on a traditionally inward-looking and conservative industry. So the industrial relations department with its close union links would be confronted by a new 'management has the right to manage' imperative; marketing challenged by the chairman's favourite world views about the markets for coal; industrial relations, excellent at its press relations, forced to accede to the thinking of advertising agencies and opinion samplers who for the Conservatives had become an essential part of the new kind of campaigning.

How quickly these changes would have occurred without the steamhammer pressure of the strike must remain a matter for conjecture, but the strike began before the impact of MacGregor's new thinking had made itself felt.

Perhaps the most striking thing about MacGregor's conduct of affairs was that well before the end of 1985 the only one of the five full-time directors still in post was MacGregor himself, while of the five directors general and director of public relations only two remained, Malcolm Edwards in marketing (not by coincidence praised by the government for keeping supplies moving during the strike), and Mike Butler in finance. By contrast the union side, as Scargill remarked with a smile, was relatively unaffected.

It brought plenty of tensions. The new chief executive office arrangements meant people found themselves by-passed, particularly in industrial relations, with Cowan, Merrik Spanton, the director responsible, and Ned Smith not always aware of what the other was doing. Then Smith in particular complained about the influence on the chairman of David Hart and Saatchi and Saatchi advertising executive Tim Bell, who were often to be found in MacGregor's office. Meanwhile the devolving of some matters to areas meant that there were inconsistencies which nearly proved fatal when they caused the NACODS dispute.

Many of these tensions were still below the surface as the dispute began, and even when they did surface the board was able still to cling to one unifying factor – that it was not prepared to let Arthur Scargill win. He united the board as much as he divided his own side. But the question remained – what did winning and losing mean?

On the surface MacGregor had no doubts, telling the NUM negotiators early on, 'This is like poker. Do you understand poker? You'll know that there is only one winner.' Yet in practice he sometimes terrified his own side by his willingness to compromise.

Smith had tried to remonstrate with him, once, a few weeks into the strike when MacGregor told management unions that the closure programme could go slower, and again on Maundy Thursday, after the NUM conference rejected calls for a ballot and also dropped the percentage needed for strike vote from 55 per cent to just over 50 per cent. Smith told friends later that he had to 'shove a yard of steel up his backbone'. MacGregor had wanted to increase the wages offer.

More fundamentally the chairman bounced the idea off some associates in mid-summer that having stood up to the miners long enough, they could settle on terms, making sure only that they protected themselves in the small print. It was the possibility ministers perhaps feared more than anything else.

In July as the talks lengthened at the nearby Rubens Hotel, the Energy Department anxiously tried to reach MacGregor as reports of the formula seemed dangerously close to capitulation. As one person on the government side said, 'The difficulty was that the closure of uneconomic pits was not always obvious from the text. For example, what does the "right to manage" and other formulations mean?

'If the words had been picked up in July there would have been a fair amount of sucking of teeth in government because you always had this vision of Scargill coming down the steps first and saying, "Victory." God knows how long it would have taken the Coal Board to get its act together and in front of a TV camera. We knew that given 24 or 36 hours you would get the media right, but it's the immediate thing.'

In the event it was never put to the test. Arthur Scargill demonstrated his refusal to compromise once more. But he also showed the same appreciation as MacGregor that by that stage, whatever the words, the chances of bringing men out again were remote.

But at the start, on 12 March, it was still far from certain that anything like a national strike would ensue. Memories were fresh of the failure to bring Scotland out over the closure of one of its own pits only a few weeks before, and the ballot defeat almost exactly a year before over national action on the Welsh pit of Ty Mawr-Lewis Merthyr. What was not appreciated was the conscious way the left had rejected the practical Gormley doctrine that the NUM could not fight as a split union, and therefore a unifying ballot was necessary once sporadic action had started.

This time, with Yorkshire on strike and picketing aggressively, any board calculations about ballots or lengths of strike were submerged by the urgent necessity to do something to stop the rapid shut-down of most of its pits.

But how? The first question was whether to use the law. By temperament, MacGregor backed the view that the law should have been used more in industrial relations, and had approved the government's still cautious moves to regulate trade union rights including making picketing away from the place of work unlawful, though not a criminal offence.

But there were difficulties, practical and strategic. Would the pickets pay any attention? Would it be necessary to name individual pickets whose places could then be taken by others? More important, would legal action lead to a repetition of the scenes which defeated the 1971 Industrial Relations Act when sympathetic action by other workers had resulted in the release of jailed dockers from Pentonville Prison? Would action by the board have the effect of uniting the union and bringing out in sympathy the very miners whom the action was intended to protect?

These were the questions for board and government as they strove to achieve their twin objectives: to keep as many men as possible at work, and to avoid a 'second front' with other groups of workers.

But almost before the government knew, the board appeared in court seeking an injunction, and quoting the government's new employment laws in support of it, to restrict picketing by the Yorkshire area. It had been an almost knee-jerk decision fully supported by the areas which were feeling the brunt of the picketing.

In North Nottingham, Coal Board officials had been out all night on the second night of the dispute (Tuesday 13 March) gathering evidence. In a co-ordinated operation, managers in Yorkshire noted pickets' registration numbers as they drove off. At six in the morning Wood oversaw the signing of affidavits which went to London on an early train. That afternoon, Mr Justice Nolan, after a half-hour hearing, granted the injunction restraining the Yorkshire NUM leaders under Section 16 of the 1980 Employment Act.

It had little effect. Yorkshire pickets briefly withdrew from Nottingham, but only to re-group after their area executive officially took control. The board had to decide in earnest what to do. Two days later on Friday 16 March, it went back to court for permission to bring a contempt of court action the following Monday. But in the event it never did.

On the Monday, MacGregor had held a lengthy meeting with his staff. By mid-morning the signs were that the action would go ahead. But then as hundreds of Yorkshire miners surrounded their Barnsley headquarters against the possible appearance of the bailiffs, the NCB backed away from direct legal confrontation. It effectively meant it was a closed option for the rest of the strike, much to the disgust of officials of the Police Federation who claimed their members were being used to do a job which the legal process should have achieved.

In court, the board announced it was not proceeding because of 'important events over the weekend'. It was a flimsy line. The only change was the much greater supply of police available and the ballots in moderate areas in its favour; the picketing was unaffected.

What had happened was two-fold. The argument of the industrial relations specialists in the board had triumphed, and the government had made clear that while it was strictly a matter for the board it did not believe that contempt proceedings would be helpful.

That was the line taken by Peter Walker, although he had some difficulties convincing his cabinet colleagues. As Geoff Kirk said later to colleagues, 'The matter was taken out of our hands.' Later on a radio programme Mrs Thatcher was to say that it was entirely a matter for the board.

The board's industrial relations team had argued that legal action could backfire in moderate areas and impede efforts to get a national ballot with a result favourable to the board. Both Smith and Hunt had indications from some Notts NUM men that they believed it would be harder to keep men working if the union was seen to be under direct attack. They also cautioned that once launched on the legal process there would be no going back, and that martyring the NUM might encourage other unions, so far lukewarm in their support, to back the NUM effectively.

But the decision upset many in the board. Jack Wood was one. 'I signed the affidavit and I think it should have gone ahead. Definitely. Trying to ameliorate with Scargill is not on. I said to Mr MacGregor and others, this man is never going to come to an agreement with you. I don't believe an injunction would have turned Notts miners against the board. They had been so battered and subjected to abuse that it made them more determined to go to work. They developed as vehement a determination to go to work as the pickets to stop them.'

More fundamentally, looking at the pressures later from court actions by individual miners, senior Coal Board figures believed that earlier action would have drained the union's funds and energies, and tied up Arthur Scargill in his procession from rally to adoring rally, at a key stage. They believed that the spectacle of the union defying the law which affected NUM members' support in the autumn would have had a much more decisive effect earlier on.

On the other hand, the context of early 1984 was of a Scargill whose hour had come. This was after all the man who had routinely announced for years from every TUC and Labour platform that he was prepared to be the first to go to jail. It was judged to be altogether too high a risk. But two years later, as a result of the events of the miners' strike, and perhaps because of that initial caution, employers, even in nationalised industries, were much more prepared to use the law.

Shorn of this recourse, the board now pinned its hopes on a national ballot. Smith and Hunt were daily in contact with the 'moderates' on the executive trying to encourage them and get some cohesion out of their disarray. Like Neil Kinnock in the Labour Party, or civil servants in Whitehall, or indeed many ordinary miners in the coal fields, they could never quite believe that there would not be a ballot.

So when that option was finally knocked on the head by the special delegate conference on Maundy Thursday, 19 April, it was perhaps the lowest point of the strike for the board. MacGregor's reaction was to try to find some sweetener for the union, suggesting an improved wages offer, something which some NUM leaders thought might have helped during the overtime ban, but which clearly made no sense now. But he was persuaded by Smith and Hunt to stay his hand and shortly went off to Chicago for a mining conference. In combative mood when he returned, he told the colliery managers' conference that he was prepared to sit out the strike indefinitely. The board launched the first of its big press publicity campaigns to get men back to work, and the NUM, its procedures completed by the delegate conference, wrote to the NCB for the first time during the strike to say it was prepared to sit down to discuss the industry's future.

It brought no immediate response. It had become an industrial trial of strength. As no clear advantage immediately emerged but both sides continued to hope for one, no one was hurting badly enough to be pushed into talking.

It was a time not for the Hobart House generals but for the battalion commanders out in the field, the NCB's area directors, together with the supply and commissariat experts, the men with the crucial job of keeping coal supplies flowing to power stations and industrial plants, in the face of the choking off of the normal supply routes, the railways, by the miners' trade union allies.

The way different directors tackled the job reflected the different approaches of their union areas and the traditions of the coal fields. But the preoccupations were the same: to keep men at work and encourage others to return; to produce coal, and, at very least, to keep pits safe.

For Wood in North Notts it was a question of keeping pits open and encouraging men to come in. He spent hours liaising with police and trying to keep up the morale of working miners. As large numbers of cars and some houses were being damaged by pickets, arrangements were made through the board's pension and insurance section to pay for repairs.

He was assisted by a decision he had taken during the overtime ban. Expecting it to lead to more, he took a deliberately conciliatory line, avoiding punitive action and keeping as many men working as possible even when a rope was being changed: 'The object of the overtime ban was to get everyone steamed up and then to say, "We're fed up with all this shilly-shallying; let's once and for all sort it out." I thought it was the start of something bigger and that we would need support.'

In Yorkshire the problems were markedly sharper. Some pits had already been on strike because of an argument about synchronising mealtimes because of the overtime ban. The NUM refused any safety cover, and on occasions tried to prevent management getting into the pit for safety work. The pit deputies, NACODS, relying on guidelines from previous strikes, did not pass difficult picket lines. In many cases, they arranged a rendezvous with strikers, were warned off and went home on pay. Even when hundreds of men were back in some Yorkshire pits by the end of the strike, many could not go underground because of the continuing lack of NACODS members. During the strike the management men carrying out safety work had to be supplemented by office staff and senior area officials from headquarters.

In South Wales by contrast, with many small, difficult pits, safety cover was provided. Area director Philip Weekes, a Welshman himself, though exasperated by the way that the coal field had been picketed out, recognised the traditional solidarity of the union in the principality and worked with it. He met the NUM leadership frequently and secretly and arranged for coal from stock to be prepared for schools and hospitals and, at the start, to keep the big Llanwern steelworks, a symbol to both sides of continuing Welsh industrial importance, supplied with its traditional feedstock.

With some hundreds of safety men, nominated by the union, employed, it was another source of funds to the union, but also a source of division. It cut both ways. While Weekes was criticised in Hobart House for keeping the very uneconomic pits which the board wanted to close in apple-pie order, there were rows in the NUM executive when the Welsh and Scots were attacked for providing safety cover by some areas which were not.

It was much more hard-fought in Scotland. There the strong line from Bert Wheeler affected both the NUM and NACODS, and on occasion he switched power supplies off if men did not do safety work. Essential for ventilation to keep pits clear of gas and for pumps to remove water, this was a major sanction, and it worked. Men came back, although one pit, Polkemmet, was lost after a flood when the NUM prevented management going in.

As for NACODS, Wheeler was unyielding: 'It was up to management to do its job seven days a week, twenty-four hours a day. If the attitude was taken that they couldn't do it, senior management couldn't be expected to do it, so we switched power off.

'The manager was in control. He could lose a pit in four hours if it didn't break. You sit it out. We were asking people to go to work. We must have the courage to take it to the ultimate.'

Wheeler's determined approach meant that something like 1,000 men, 7 or 8 per cent of the union's membership, were involved in safety work in Scotland. Again it divided the union membership, and reduced numbers available for picketing. Wheeler also used it in a crucial way. Getting safety men down the pit involved winding enginemen being on hand. That meant that working miners could also get down and coal come up the shaft. There were tussles with the union which at times withdrew winding enginemen. At the key pit, Bilston Glen, where Wheeler concentrated his efforts to break the strike, only one winder was prepared to work after the union withdrew its men, and there was a hiatus while another was trained up from a working miner.

Bilston Glen, the largest and most modern pit in Scotland, had become the focus because of the determined group of men who were prepared to work, and made a point of returning and walking through the gate even when they had been beaten up the previous day. Other miners recommended by the men were contacted by telephone by the managers and encouraged. Local managers met them and then Wheeler himself went to larger meetings at a public house on the outskirts of Edinburgh. The men were encouraged to bring their wives along and talk about the problems of going to work. It soon emerged that, as in other coal fields, one of the biggest worries was what would happen to their houses and families, and the importance of a 24-hour police watch on their homes.

1) Portent of things to come. Ian MacGregor (far right) is flour-bombed during a visit to Brodsworth colliery in Yorkshire during the NUM overtime ban in November 1983.

2 (a) Wish they hadn't. (i) Arthur Scargill salutes his supporters with gesture Fleet Street used against him (*Sheffield Newspapers*)

(b) Wish they hadn't. (ii) Ian MacGregor covers his face with a plastic bag as he arrives for talks at Edinburgh. (*Scotsman Publications*)

3 Battle over the ballot
(a) Nottinghamshire miners call for a ballot. (*Sheffield Newspapers*)

(b) NUM strikers demonstrate against Nottinghamshire members. (*Sheffield Newspapers*)

(c) 19 April 1984. NUM executive members arrive for the delegate conference which voted against holding a strike ballot. (*Sheffield Newspapers*)

4 Here we go. Chesterfield 1984
(a) Derbyshire area rallies support. (*Sheffield Newspapers*)

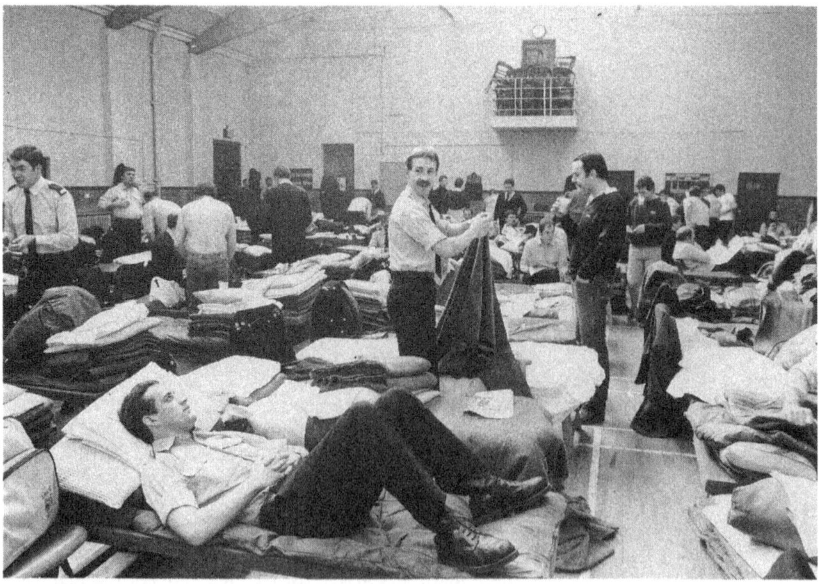

(b) Police support units in temporary accommodation. (*Sheffield Newspapers*)

5 Casualties
(a) and (b) Picket and President. Orgreave June 1984. (*Sheffield Newspapers*)

(c) Carrying a colleague to safety. Rossington. October 1984. (Ron Richardson)

6 (a) (b) (c) Orgreave–pickets' view. (*Sheffield Newspapers*)

7 (a) (b) Orgreave–police view. (South Yorkshire police)

8 Pit village solidarity.
(a) Police at Armthorpe. 21 August 1984. (Ron Richardson)

(b) Back-to-work miner's vandalised house. (South Yorkshire police)

(c) Cortonwood colliery marches back. March 1985.
(*Sheffield Newspapers*)

It was a very slow process. Not until 20 June, more than three months into the strike, did the first coal emerge from the pit. Even then it had taken two days to get it to the surface. On the first day men moved it to an underground bunker from the face; on the second, the same men manned different conveyor belts to get it to the surface. It was a highly symbolic moment of which the Coal Board made maximum publicity. But it was achieved by just over 30 men out of a work force of about 2,000.

Publicity was very much the name of the game in North Derbyshire. Often styled as the barometer area because of the way its NUM vote usually reflected the national result, its miners were split almost equally over the strike. But in spite of the divisions, it was many months before even the voting split was reflected in the figures of men working, and then only after a campaign of almost military-style proportions.

Ken Moses, the area director, a small combative Lancastrian who was promoted after the strike to become technical director of the board, together with his neighbour John Northard in the adjacent western area (who became the operations director later), worked out the detailed strategies for persuading the men back, ploys which caused distinct unhappiness to the traditionalist industrial relations men like Ned Smith.

Moses announced his intentions in a letter to miners on 18 May. Saying there were two possible solutions, a negotiated national settlement of which he could see little hope because of the 'entrenched positions' or 'seeking a reversal of the domino effect by which the strike spread.'

The whole basis of the strategy was then to put pressure on men who lived outside mining communities at some distance from the pit, who might be less committed to the strike and realistically at less risk if they returned. (This had also been a factor at Bilston Glen, which drew its men from a wide area.) On a BBC *Panorama* programme on 17 September he demonstrated his planning, indicating maps with circles at 5- and 10-mile distances from pits with the numbers in different places identified. It was explained how the board contacted people on the periphery with managers themselves knocking on doors, and then moved steadily in.

As Moses put it, pointing to the maps on which miners' homes were marked in colour, 'We know where they all live; whether they are next to a working miner and so on. We have found that the most likely person to return to work is the man who is married, wife not working, lives in a house where he's paying mortgage, and who has had a very good attendance record.'

But what was perhaps more striking was that by then, after six months, in an area where half the men had voted to work, only about 800 out of 10,500 were at work, half of them at Bolsover colliery where hundreds had defied the strike call throughout.

As the description of the directors' meeting at the beginning of the chapter shows, there was scepticism even among some area directors about the approach. They continued to meet regularly and glumly with pressure throughout the summer for things to be done to try to take the heat off the Midlands coal fields. The push in North Derbyshire plus the diversion at Orgreave had some effect, while in Scotland Wheeler tied up both Scottish pickets and the forceful figure of the union's vice president, Mick McGahey.

But as autumn began, the success of the back-to-work strategy was by no means obvious. Trade and Industry Secretary Norman Tebbit joshed Peter Walker in cabinet committee about how many years it would take at the current rate to get all the men back.

As the North Yorkshire area director, Michael Eaton, put it, 'At the area directors' meetings I don't think any of us knew what we were doing. There was a firm strategy of encouraging people to come back and break the strike. By the end of August we knew we were in for a big fight, but there was still talk of whole pits going back. Then it was obvious it was going to be a long strike. We had all been forecasting it would be over by September.' Moses described it as 'a long, lonely summer' in North Derbyshire as his men trickled back with agonising slowness.

There was ambivalence too about the return to work. While an obvious necessity in areas where many men were already working, the benefit of getting men back into pits in ones and twos was much less obvious to local managers. They risked alienating communities and preventing what they still hoped for, a concerted return by a large group or a whole pit.

In the militant left-wing coal field of Kent, Irene McGibbon, a militant right-wing Conservative Party member who had led a wives' revolt during a car workers' strike at Cowley, was now living in Deal. Her husband, Bob, had left the motor industry to work at Betteshanger pit. She recalls clearly being dissuaded by local managers from a return to work in the early weeks.

An argument about the subject was in process at Hobart House, where the familiar Scargill tactic of keeping things going and simply hanging on was beginning to foster increasing strains in the board, not least on MacGregor's patience. So as Scargill hung on throughout the summer, tightening the ratchet of industrial pressure, MacGregor was back to the shotgun technique of spraying out a variety of options.

In the process he pointed up the differences between the traditional Coal Board style and the way he himself was prepared to examine almost any expedient with a willingness to break established custom and practice and damn the consequences. It was at odds with Ned Smith's cardinal principle of doing nothing which would interfere with their ability to manage the industry afterwards. MacGregor's view was different. He had come to break the mould, and was looking for a way to win the strike now.

Just how different things were to be emerged only after the strike was over. Miners returning to work in striking areas found whole networks of local agreements and pit deals about allowances and winding times unilaterally abrogated and the union branch excluded from traditional consultations.

In parallel, MacGregor increasingly sought advice from outsiders. Smith had assured him of his loyalty, describing himself, in a phrase which made MacGregor chuckle, as his 'praetorian guard', but friends of MacGregor outside coal were alarmed to hear the bitterness with which MacGregor privately ran down his Coal Board team.

So the figure of Tim Bell, a key figure in the Saatchi and Saatchi advertising agency in its successful promotion of Mrs Thatcher in the 1979 election, appeared in the board's corridors. Extensive opinion sampling in mining areas was carried out by Gallup and ORC, helping buoy up the board.

There was to be a rapid clash between Smith and the new man Bell and David Hart over the decision in June to send a letter under MacGregor's name to all miners. But before then the new Coal Board approach had been tested, and the strains revealed in the first talks with the NUM.

During the twelve-month strike, there were six cycles of talks, three of them in the summer: a one-day fiasco in London on 23 May; a two-week cycle from 31 May to 13 June split between Sheffield, Edinburgh and Rotherham; and a further two weeks from 5 July to 18 July in London and Edinburgh. It was the breakdown of this cycle which brought the government into the open.

The groundwork for the first talks had been laid by Peter McNestry, the new general secretary of NACODS, closer to Scargill than his predecessors but worried by the deterioration of pits as the strike went on. From the end of April he shuttled between the two sides, unpublicised, finally achieving talks on 23 May after, in what was to be a familiar ritual, MacGregor had first objected that an NUM letter ruling out negotiations on pit closures or job losses was seen as dictating the terms.

After a stagey withdrawal of Kent pickets, from the front steps, the two sides met at Hobart House with the full NUM executive in attendance. Scargill told his executive there would be no discussion unless the board agreed to withdraw the closure programme, and the NUM greeted the board team with wisecracks asking MacGregor whether he had 'just come off Concorde', declaring that the industry was 'under the control of the stars and stripes' and McGahey taunting the chairman that he was too old to be running the industry. Cowan fired back, a little ambiguously, 'Imagine leaving the industry to you. An even worse disaster.'

The board then deployed its arguments, concentrating on Plan for Coal, insisting that it retained its spirit in building a new industry from old, but warning that the immediate outlook was bleak with £875 million loss projected for the year just ended, £200 million from the NUM's overtime ban.

The NUM listened in silence, then Scargill insisted on the need to withdraw the closure programme before any substantive talks. He asked MacGregor directly. MacGregor, arms characteristically clasped across his chest, stared ahead, and said, 'I have no comment.' Little more was said apart from an offer by Cowan to meet the NUM officials about the industry's future.

The board then withdrew, and the NUM executive concentrated more on their problems in Nottingham than anything from the meeting. 'People are saying they don't want to belong to the union; they want one of their own,' said one executive member, while the moderate Roy Ottey[1] warned they would lose more strikers if they didn't continue talking. But Peter Heathfield retorted, 'It would be headlines tomorrow "Scargill agrees to talk about pit closures; MacGregor stands firm". We can't talk about anything.' It was to be only one of many occasions when the press was used as a disciplinary force on the executive.

But MacGregor was not standing firm. Smith and his colleagues defended his 'No comment' remark while conceding that they might have conducted matters less stiffly, adopting a more vigorous 'come off it, Arthur' approach. In a post-talks press conference MacGregor said publicly that the projected 4 million tonne cutback could be 'up for discussion'. He was persuaded to take a more flexible line, commenting on *TV Eye* the following day that he saw 'a degree of realism entering into the picture', while the prime minister said in the Commons that an offer of further talks by Cowan was 'very wise'.

A week later serious negotiations were under way. It was a strange atmosphere. They were interspersed with calls from Arthur Scargill for mass picketing at Orgreave, by increasingly bitter scenes there, and even the arrest of Scargill himself. The NUM leader would go from apparently useful meetings almost directly to shout the odds at rallies, declaring at one London demonstration that as the winter approached the NUM's demands increased.

The formal talks were interspersed with long informal chats over meals with both sides yarning about coal industries in other countries, with Scargill at one summer session introducing Cuban mines into the conversation, to be told by an icy MacGregor, 'Those were my mines your friend Castro nationalised.'

Nothing was written down in the formal sessions. The words were worked out by each side in the adjournments with the NUM thumbing through *Roget's Thesaurus* and a dictionary and on occasion ringing their Sheffield office for advice.

A brief meeting without MacGregor at the Monk Fryston Hotel near Selby, at which Scargill detected signs that the board was prepared to be flexible, was followed by a session at the Norton House Hotel near Edinburgh airport, which both sides were pleased with.

At Edinburgh, the board shifted away from its insistence that 4 million tonnes capacity be cut, and that the final formula be explicit about closing uneconomic pits. Scargill thought he had also got an assurance that the five pits would not be a problem. The two sides agreed that pits could close for two reasons: exhaustion and severe geological difficulties. That left a third category and it was at Edinburgh that the search for a phrase to cover the board's demand for an explicit agreement that pits shut for economic reasons, and the NUM's explicit refusal to countenance that, had begun its lengthy and fruitless journey.

The temperature changed abruptly at the next session at the Carlton Park in Rotherham. On the morning before, an interview with MacGregor had been published in *The Times*. Its details, talking of a rewritten Plan for Coal and fewer if better-paid miners, and its tone, infuriated the NUM leaders. Scargill, seeing MacGregor's comment that he would 'regain the management of the industry' as 'suggesting that they mean to exclude the trade unions from all processes of consultation on the industry's future', had sat up all night after getting an early copy to produce a twelve-page paper stating all the NUM's negotiating demands over the previous few years.

The meeting was a fiasco. Both sides were upset because television cameras were waiting for them. It was pure fluke; BBC crews were using the hotel as a base from which to cover the Orgreave disturbances. But both thought they had been set up by the other.

The NUM entered the room with remarks like 'Who's the Director?'; 'I can only see the stooges for Maggie Thatcher.' As for the *Times* interview, Ned Smith's view at the time was that, although awkward, it wasn't decisive. 'We could have had a good up and downer about it. If people of that calibre wanted to progress, it was a pretty forlorn reason why they should build brick walls ten feet high with bloody glass bottles on the top.'

In the event Scargill never presented his paper, coming out to announce that MacGregor had had further instructions from Mrs Thatcher.

But there were none. Thatcher did meet MacGregor privately on 3 July. It was later reported as a 'ticking-off' session. Walker, however, thought the meeting would encourage a chairman then very depressed by the continuing strike and the high level of violence. He had felt it necessary to give the chairman, now beginning to be seen as a liability by many on the government side, public support on the Jimmy Young radio programme of 22 June. But the prime minister took the opportunity to ask MacGregor about his strategy and express concern about the public face of the board.

By now MacGregor's associates agree that he was greatly affected by the violence and intimidation. Even though the American scene was much tougher, 'This was different. This was Britain.' He was also soured by his negotiating experience. 'He was sitting through hours and hours of dialogue where whatever he put forward was being combated by what he saw as the negative side – we must withdraw the March 6 proposals or. . . . He insisted that, whatever came out on paper, the issue could not be fudged. His view was, "You can't shade the issue or weasel-word it. That's no goddamn good." He was alarmed by what he thought was prejudice and bias from the other side. He was used to doing deals with hard-nosed trade unionists who understood the balance sheet and would bargain and set aside rhetoric.'

With talks in ruins, he reverted to an old idea, that of the NCB holding its own ballot. He had succeeded in a ballot backing his survival plan, and cut-backs, at steel in spite of opposition there from the union with the biggest membership, the ISTC. But now the idea alarmed Peter Walker and horrified Ned Smith.

Smith argued that at this stage, with most men on strike, it would simply play into the union's hands, allowing it to manipulate the result. More, that it would discredit ballots in the industry for good, removing an essential management tool. None the less he was sent to see Seamus Burke, the secretary of the Electoral Reform Society, which had counted miners' ballots for years. In the event Burke refused.

He argued that it would discredit them and imperil the relations (and the fees) which went back 100 years with the NUM. 'I felt, as a national body, we should be prepared to offer a ballot facility but on balance it would not be advantageous to the board. It would certainly threaten the position of the society and do no good for industrial relations as far as our machinery was concerned.'

MacGregor pressed. There was discussion about a university department giving the NCB advice on running its own ballot, but eventually the idea was dropped. Meanwhile, with Tim Bell's advice, he was drawing up a letter to every miner. Smith was horrified. He had prided himself on the Coal Board's success in persuading miners to defeat Scargill in two previous ballots, but was now told he was 'not a professional communicator'. Soundings of his mining relations convinced him that a personal letter from MacGregor, whose 'butcher' image had been greatly believed by striking miners, let alone one beginning preposterously, 'Dear colleague', would be counter-productive. But times were changing. Although Smith managed to alter the draft, the letter was sent.

But Smith kept up the pressure for talks. On 5 and 6 July the two sides met a few yards from the NCB headquarters at the Rubens Hotel. Then it was back to the Norton Park at Edinburgh on 9 July.

As a signal of the advances made, both sides released the texts of their proposed draft agreements. The wordings were often identical. A quick reading suggested they were getting close. But in fact they were merely refining the core of their differences.

The first clauses promised to 'revise' the 6 March proposals according to the NCB, or to 'withdraw' them according to the NUM. Clause 2 of the board's proposal would have made the five named pits 'the subject of further consideration' while the NUM's words would have had them 'kept open'. But the key difference was in the board's Clause 3c.

This talked of a joint agreement between the two sides that a colliery should be deemed exhausted after a mining engineers' investigation by both sides showed that there were no further minable reserves 'that are workable or which can be beneficially developed'. The NUM's wording was almost identical except that it omitted the word beneficially.

It was on that word that the whole weight of the case by the board that uneconomic pits should shut now rested. The night before the last session of talks on 18 July, MacGregor had told his eleven-man board that he had no choice but to extract a formula to allow him to close uneconomic pits. In the past five years 58 pits had closed without appeal, many on economic grounds tacitly accepted by the union.

His board backed him unanimously. It was a sign of the shakiness in the chairman's position that he saw the need to stress that backing at a news conference on the eve of the talks which the next day, predictably, failed.

The MacGregor tactic had been to concede a great deal verbally, but on the calculation that so long as a fig leaf had been preserved to cover the unmentionable concept of 'uneconomic pits', once agreement had been signed the board could proceed to close pits in the knowledge that a workforce on strike for upwards of two months would not be mobilisable again in the near future. He told his advisors early on that it would be over in a few weeks, that it could be settled by apparently large concessions, but that once ended the closure programme could proceed with renewed vigour. As one of those advisors said, 'His view was that after two or three months, the Coal Board would have shown that it could stand up to the miners; there was no need to show it any more. They could then protect themselves in the small print.'

'Beneficial' was pretty small print. Both McGahey and Scargill knew it was a white rabbit word. It meant what one said it meant. And the one saying what it meant after the strike would be MacGregor.

This was Scargill's strongest justification for the adamantine stance he took. He understood the tactic and knew that if he permitted the 'protection of the small print', he would ultimately lose. The NCB concessions were paper ones. Because Scargill did not trust MacGregor any more than MacGregor trusted him (and both were right to feel so) an agreement on MacGregor's terms was always, for Scargill, an impossibility.

The government came to understand this too, though Walker had to soothe anxieties about talk of concessions. As one senior official put it, 'I am sure MacGregor believed that he never would, nor would his bankers ever have allowed him to, foreclose on the position that he could shut uneconomic pits. The difficulty was that it was not always evident from the text. It was asked, "Where does it say that Scargill is agreeing to close uneconomic pits?" It took a fair amount of education over some long time to suggest that it was not there and never would be there until hell froze.'

The verbal war continued through the summer. The peace camp in the NCB was weakened by the contemptuous rejection by the NUM special delegate conference of 10 August of the Rubens offer. Smith confessed himself 'quite forlorn'. MacGregor began to shift further.

David Hart was partly responsible. As he became more drawn in, he was concerned to insert his own moralistic view of the strike into MacGregor's mind. Convinced it was a battle between tyranny and freedom, he found MacGregor thought of it simply as winning an industrial battle. He put the working miners' case, as he saw it, in opposition to the concern of the professional industrial relations men about not disrupting relations which they would have to re-make with the NUM after the strike. He also rubbed home the violence inflicted on working miners by strikers, a message which MacGregor became strongly seized of in early August.

In an interview with the *Financial Times* on 2 August he said, 'We have an enormous enclave of fear, built up and controlled within our society by new dedicated militants. Perhaps I am naive. I thought this was a law-abiding country, but within the last few weeks, criminal acts have been happening every day and nothing can be done about it. How many of the people arrested suffer any particular sanction? Again that's part of the tolerant society. People who are engaged in doing harm to others and enormous damage to property have been given suspended sentences or let off with a fine that's less than a fine for speeding on the highway. This is part of the tolerant society which makes it vulnerable to criminal actions.'

At this time the political rhetoric grew sharper. Walker seemed to invoke a theory of genetic politicisation when he wrote in the *Sunday*

Express of 12 August of Scargill as 'the son of an active Communist'. MacGregor, cutting the first turf for a new Vale of Belvoir mine, suggested miners' leaders could be prosecuted for criminal conspiracy, an opinion echoed by the retiring electricians' union secretary, Frank Chapple.

But there was still an ambivalence about the board's attitude to working miners. While it wanted them back, the working miners' groups, often critical of each other, were not always encouraged. Merrik Spanton, as a former Notts area director himself, was worried about splitting the Notts men into factions, and advised MacGregor to be careful that the emerging Notts NUM under Lynk and Prendergast (which would become the UDM) was not split by the Working Miners' Committee.

MacGregor announced at one point that there was plenty of money for legal actions by working miners and was thought by some to donate some personal money to the National Working Miners. But the principal case against the NUM, which resulted in sequestration, was brought by Foulstone and Taylor without the Coal Board's knowledge and support. Its finance came first from the funds of Chris 'Silver Birch' Butcher and then by the result of a further newspaper appeal which brought in over £40,000 in hundreds of mainly small contributions.

It was Butcher's tour round the country, assisted by the *Mail on Sunday* newspaper, which turned up the case and took the working miners' cause outside the central coal fields where it had largely been concentrated. As Jack Wood put it, 'He did create an image; a peg or something to follow for people in other coal fields. A peg for others to hang a bit of hope on because don't forget that men in other coal fields were frightened to death. There were reports even of pickets saying to men going to work, "For Christ-sake, continue, because you are the only hope we have got." '

But there are still people in the board who wonder whether the board's strategy from August to encourage any little pennypackets of men to return was the right one. It took pressure off the Midlands and released some coal stocks. But the strike only broke in the six weeks before Christmas when considerable numbers started to return, particularly in the north-east, and finally when South Wales decided that things could be held no longer.

Merrik Spanton says, 'If we had concentrated on areas where people wanted to go back and left others alone, it might have prevented all the violence it created, which was a minus for Great Britain. It helped encourage people to defy the law and perhaps kept things going longer than if we had let them get bored stiff. One couldn't think it could have gone on much longer whatever we did.'

Little happened in August as the miners prepared for the TUC, but the start of the Yorkshire return to work began to throw up the problems which led to the NACODS dispute.

Labour's energy spokesman, Stan Orme, endlessly patient, shuttled between the two sides with formulae. One, drafted by Kinnock, reworked 'beneficial' with a clause about reserves which 'could be worked to the benefit of the colliery, the workforce of the colliery and the national interest.' The board said it could live with it; Scargill, to Kinnock's profound disappointment, said No.

Meanwhile Cowan, MacGregor's right-hand man, was concentrating, in his own words 'in blinkers', in trying to keep pits running and the thin momentum of the return to work moving. He saw victory lying in local battles. It was here he believed that the propaganda battle should be fought and won; and it was the audience of miners returning to work, or thinking about returning, who would be decisive. The national battle for public opinion was less crucial.

So Cowan was perhaps the closest to indifference when a series of public relations disasters from August to early November culminated in the departure of both Ned Smith and the public relations director, Geoff Kirk. In retrospect the two events seem less cataclysmic than they appeared at the time. The NCB still had the capacity to lose the battle, but not, like Jellicoe during the First World War, in a single afternoon. The currents were beginning to run in its favour as the flow of coal supplies was improved.

But still the impact was considerable. Public relations was one of the government's principal concerns, and businessmen were alarmed at what looked first like incompetence and then managerial disarray at the board. Some at the CBI conference even suggested that MacGregor should go forthwith.

The train of public fumbling had been set off by the live TV debate on 22 August on Channel Four between MacGregor and Scargill. Smith had been briefed to do it; then in late afternoon MacGregor asserted his chairman's prerogative, cancelled it, and then after Smith had gone home in a huff, did it himself. Coached by Hart up to and inside the studio, MacGregor was bested by Scargill who led him down a maze of back-to-work figures and accused him of rejecting Stan Orme's latest initiative of which MacGregor denied knowledge. Orme later confirmed it, and MacGregor had to issue an embarrassing explanation about a misunderstanding.

Then ten days later, on the eve of the TUC congress, talks were suddenly on again. Smith was suddenly summoned home from the golf club which abuts his house and discovered his wife on the telephone discussing the filling in of a bingo card with a man called 'Bob'. Smith found himself talking to the newspaper proprietor, Robert Maxwell, who had already been in touch with MacGregor to arrange fresh talks and was ringing from Scargill's room at the Curzon Hotel in Brighton.

A meeting was arranged for Catterick on the Wednesday. Smith was horrified. In his judgment negotiations with a Scargill hotfoot from standing ovations at the TUC were unlikely to succeed. MacGregor too became alarmed when early editions of the *Daily Mirror* crowed about the talks. When he rang Smith expressing concern he was told sharply, 'He is your millionaire, not mine.'

The talks were called off after a row between Smith and Heathfield, then set up again after an exchange of letters when both sides merely restated their positions. They were urged on by the anti-Scargill electricians and engineering managers, who were opposing the Scargill line at the TUC but none the less phoned the electricity council to warn that other unions in power stations might harden their position if talks did not ensue. John Lyons, the managers' leader, believes it brought a 'major change'.

So began a farcical time. MacGregor's last throw for a fudged solution, one which many believe came very close. On 9 September talks started in Edinburgh. Entering the Norton House Hotel, MacGregor hid his face behind a plastic bag. It was said to be a joke; if so, it backfired and became a graphic image of the chairman's lack of touch.

The two sides talked first at the Allersley House Hotel where at one stage Peter Heathfield lunged across the table at MacGregor, index finger jabbing at his nose, and had to be hauled back by Scargill. Heathfield had believed MacGregor had back-tracked on a deal reached in conversations to withdraw the uneconomic pit closure formulation in 'Plan for Coal'. In the adjournment the NUM side had produced a form of words quoting MacGregor as saying so, which had led to a furious denial by MacGregor. But the board side insist that the offer had only been to abandon the form of words, not the principle.

The disaster was weathered, and the two sides met again at the Monk Fryston Hotel near Selby. But the NUM motorcade was followed, and the hotel so besieged by press and camera crews that MacGregor and Scargill appeared side by side on the steps to issue a joint statement complaining of press harassment, and passed on to Doncaster and the offices of British Ropes, where they talked till two in the morning.

Smith and Hunt believe that meeting saw a virtual breakthrough, only prevented by a failure to keep talking and the NUM's reaction to the words in the cold light of day. But it seems difficult to believe now.

There had been an extraordinary number of draft formulae during the week. 'A small parcel of coal' from the NUM, subsequently defined as 'sufficient for a few months'; 'no further mineable reserves'. The board on the other hand proposed cases where 'further investment of human and financial resources could not be justified'. Later it had offered to replace 'beneficial' with 'satisfactory' or 'acceptable'. Then it talked of no further reserves for the board to develop 'in line with their responsibilities'.

But at the rope factory, verbal commitments appeared to have been given by both sides to forms of words which, when written down, were deemed unacceptable. All sides admit they were weary, and decided to break off as adjournments lengthened. Merrik Spanton says now, 'Scargill was never going to settle on anything we were.' The judgment is correct. The fundamental lack of trust and the fundamentally different aims meant that no deal was possible, and no deal ever was possible.

But there was still to be one more attempt, forced on board and government by people they did not expect to break, the members of the National Association of Colliery Overmen, Deputies and Shotfirers (NACODS). It was small (16,000 strong), middle-of-the-road, careful and respectable. Its members were promoted from the NUM, acting effectively as foremen. Their families were interlocked, but their differentials were resented by the NUM and the deputies prized their status, having their own rooms at the pit and their own clubs, like a sergeants' mess. Their crucial function was to carry out the safety checks underground on heat, air and water without which the pits would have by law to be shut down.

They had just elected a new general secretary, Peter McNestry, the 41-year-old branch secretary at the big Yorkshire pit of Kellingley. To the left of his predecessor, he was impressed by the Scargill warnings that the board were planning cutbacks, which would, of course, also affect NACODS jobs. He had sought leverage for some time. His opportunity came when on 15 August Spanton told the NACODS executive that regardless of the old guidelines that they could return home on pay if they met a difficult picket line, they would now be expected to go to work regardless, in the board's reinforced buses. It was a direct result of the return to work; miners were coming back and there was no one to supervise them.

McNestry had been away on holiday when Spanton made the announcement. On his return, he encouraged the executive to hold a ballot for strike action, and had long discussions with Scargill at Brighton. The ballot produced an 82 per cent vote. Ironically, as the TUC failed to crank up power and other unions to do significantly more to help the NUM, the pit deputies had been pushed by the board into contemplating industrial action for the first time in the union's life.

The government was immediately seized of the danger and made clear to the board that they must buy off trouble. The TUC also saw the possibilities. NACODS was a godsend to it. The union had had a ballot. It had a comprehensible list of demands. Its leaders were reassuringly modest on television. Norman Willis leapt at them as the one real lever he had.

Unfortunately for the TUC, NACODS quickly got all they wanted.

The new guidelines were withdrawn and tentative agreement reached on a new colliery review procedure establishing an independent body to adjudicate on any pit the union wished to keep open. But McNestry, with TUC support, did not settle immediately. He demanded that the issue go to ACAS and that other pit unions be involved.

It was a symbolic moment. The Thatcher governments dislike fudge, finding it overcloying for their sharper, harder taste, but they let ACAS, a Labour government creation, live on because it had achieved bipartisan support and it kept disputes away from ministers. But getting the coal dispute to ACAS was for the TUC tremendously reassuring, a reassertion that the instruments of the corporate state were still, if battered, in place and capable of working. MacGregor was not pleased. More Thatcherite than Thatcher, he disliked having matters removed from his control. 'This place stinks,' he said as he entered, a remark loyally put down by Kirk to a smell of paint others failed to notice.

In Sir Pat Lowry, the ACAS chairman (a former BL personnel director) and Denis Boyd, its chief officer, ACAS had two men of endless patience and experience. They attempted to shift matters away from Clause 3c and 'beneficial' and concentrate instead on the concept of 'Plan for Coal'. The NUM got as far as accepting a review of collieries 'in line with Plan for Coal'; the NCB one which was 'in line with the principles of Plan for Coal'. MacGregor's saving grace had come to that. But once more it fell apart, and the Coal Board team with it.

Smith, increasingly disaffected, had walked out of the Coal Board after a meeting on 18 October where MacGregor, apparently unfazed by the NACODS strike vote, had declared he was going to have a fight with 'goddamn NACODS' and break them. Smith felt it was no coincidence that Hart and Bell were also there.

Scarcely had Smith departed when MacGregor summoned down the North Yorkshire area director, Michael Eaton, as the board's new spokesman. The move had been under consideration for some time. The prime minister, lobbied hard by her supporters to improve the Coal Board's PR, had asked her press secretary, Bernard Ingham, whom he would suggest. He had come up with three names on a plane back from York – Moses, Wheeler and Eaton, whom he pointed out she had met at Selby and was known to her parliamentary private secretary, Michael Allison, as a local MP.

Eaton was reassuring, with a plain face and plain rather slow speech, given to Yorkshire expressions. He had been in his time the youngest area director, the first to welcome MacGregor publicly, but a discreet critic of the conduct of the strike. Hart and Bell studied videotapes, and choosing between Moses and Eaton found Eaton blinked less, which the technical manuals said suggested greater honesty.

So he was summoned down by Cowan, but met by Hart who took him to his Bond Street office and talked of 'screwing Scargill'. Eaton objected that he must do things his own way. For Eaton the job was appealing. He had been depressed like his colleagues with the board's poor showing, and he was also ambitious. In a difficult conversation on the telephone with the NACODS president, Ken Sampey, he asked what could be done, and suggested to a suspicious Sampey that they might get rid of the 'old man'.

Over the weekend the newspapers had a field day with the appointment, styling Eaton as 'Mr Fixit' and the man for compromise. It infuriated members of the board who blamed the public relations director, Geoff Kirk, though Kirk, under ferocious journalistic pressure, had continued to insist that Eaton was not to be a negotiator, only a spokesman.

The board did agree to further talks with NACODS. Smith, with Walker's encouragement, was brought back, but Eaton, on the insistence of Smith and Cowan, was kept off the negotiating team.

There were two elements in the reaction – personal pique, and serious industrial relations. Neither wanted it to look as if the NCB line was softening. Smith regarded Eaton as too soft and a man who should have taken a firmer line with NACODS in his area.

Cowan says he was swamped by telephone calls when the appointment was announced: 'The strike was going our way. Perhaps there were some who thought our publicity could be better. I subscribed to that view. I was one who recommended Eaton because he had such a nice way with him and was such a nice man.

'But when it came out on the Sunday that he was there to "fix it", my phone never stopped ringing. People from Notts and elsewhere that we were going to sacrifice them. Arthur Scargill would destroy them. I actually had a miner from Yorkshire call me. He knew the people involved and said, "Have you sold the pass?" I said No. He told me he was on strike; he was virtually in tears. He said, "Don't let this evil man win." I said, if you go to work, you can prevent it. He said he was frightened to go back to work. That was at ten o'clock at night. God knows how he got my number.

'The people who were coming back to work were absolutely alarmed and that's why I took the action I did; Mike will be no part of the negotiations. That was to keep the confidence of the areas. Maybe it sounded hard. But I was absolutely adamant.

'If we had had a soft approach then, we would have lost it. People were going back on strike. It was an absolutely critical time.'

The return of Smith, who was trusted by NACODS in a way the others were not, helped to settle the dispute. The document was less a formal agreement than a conciliatory letter, but became, in Walker's and the prime minister's words, sacrosanct, although post-strike MacGregor tried hard to wriggle out of the revised review procedure. It stressed 'understanding and trust' between the two sides as 'a major component in the management of the industry' and reinstated the old picket-line guidelines.

The core was of course the revised review procedure, which was to apply specifically too to the five named pits. The reference of any disputed pit closure would go to 'an independent body' to whose findings 'full weight', but not automatic compliance, would be given by the board.

But even as it was being agreed, the TUC team arrived at ACAS and tried to persuade NACODS to unstitch the deal to achieve the real prize, settlement of the NUM dispute as well. But NACODS stood firm, having got all they wanted, and their executive backed it, to the scorn of the NUM, the following day.

Scargill dismissed it as worth less than the draft agreement he had already been offered and rejected, and declared the references to the market and production opportunities were 'a clear departure from the Plan for Coal'.

There was one more ACAS try with the NUM and NCB, which foundered on 31 October after yet another possible ACAS formula talking about the 'broad strategy of the Plan for Coal' instead of the 'principles'. It had aroused some interest among the NUM but the board had rejected it.

In the meantime the board had lost another stalwart. Geoff Kirk had arranged a series of interviews for Eaton with senior industrial correspondents on the day following the sensational announcement of the NUM'S approach for help to the Libyan leader 'Colonel' Gaddafi, whose men had recently gunned down an English policewoman. In mid-morning MacGregor ordered the interviews cancelled so that nothing should impair the Libyan sensation. But as the gag was applied in the middle of the interviews, it had precisely the opposite effect. Kirk objected strongly and then the following day blew his top when he found MacGregor breaking his own prohibition and giving an off-the-cuff interview to a radio reporter who just happened to phone in. By lunchtime Kirk had been told by Cowan, on MacGregor's instructions, to take indefinite leave. He returned briefly, but rejected an offer to continue and took early retirement, announcing at a remarkable press conference as he left that MacGregor 'resents someone who questions his judgment'. A farewell party for Kirk was held at No. 10 Downing Street by his friend and admirer, the prime minister's press secretary, Bernard Ingham.

Kirk's departure had a symbolism about it. Deeply trusted by Siddall, who made a point of attending his funeral after he died some months later in a boating accident off Skye, he had found himself given progressively less information under MacGregor though supporting him loyally. He had been particularly upset by the transfer of the board's advertising campaign in October away from CM Partnership to Lowe Howard-Spink, whose chairman Tim Hart shortly afterwards became. But a retrospective glance at the early NCB advertising shows a great difference between its ponderous, 'To keep the record straight; here is the National Coal Board's side of the story' plus a series of complex and minuscule graphs, and the later, crisper reading with headlines like 'It'll pay every miner who's not at work to read this'. Peter Walker himself, unbeknown to Kirk, had suggested a change of agency. So there were cogent reasons for changes, but to many in the board, throughout which Kirk's wryly humorous figure was well known and liked, it seemed a switch from an era of honesty to one of manipulation.

The final sessions at ACAS turned out to be the last substantial negotiations of the strike. They established the fact that the gulf was unbridgeable, though that had to be rubbed in more deeply before the TUC would publicly acknowledge it.

Afterwards the board reverted to the strategy which many of its area directors like Bert Wheeler had been urging – no more talks. It was welcomed by the hardline back-to-workers like Irene McGibbon in Kent. She had been bending everyone's ear, including Mrs Thatcher's at a Downing Street reception, about the way men promising to return would ring her up and back off when any talks seemed remotely possible.

But now the strategy worked, helped by the carrot of the big Christmas bonuses. In the first full week after the breakdown of talks, 2,100 men came back. The bonus offer kept the momentum up throughout the month. The working percentages rose to 15 per cent in the hitherto almost solid north-east; to 22 per cent in Scotland; 42 per cent at last in North Derbyshire, and 78 per cent in the Western area by its end.

The TUC officials privately wrote off the miners. 'That was his last chance of peace with honour,' said one. 'After that it all moved to operation extrication. It became apparent that the government was confident about power stations and we believed them.

'There was no chance of industrial support. Winter was coming in. The miners were in a bad way. There was no problem with coal supplies from abroad. And the penny finally dropped that Arthur was not going to settle in anything like a traditional industrial relations way.'

So in the end the return-to-workers won. In the process the board had been shaken almost to pieces, the mould well and truly broken. MacGregor had his opportunity to reshape the industry, sweeping away traditions of national and local co-operation, deliberately encouraging a breakaway union.

The men he chose to assist him were the successful field generals of the strike, Northard, Moses and Wheeler. Eaton was never forgiven for his interventions. Continually clashing with MacGregor, over relocation of working miners from hostile areas for instance (MacGregor discouraged it at first), and over MacGregor's backtracking on NACODS, he was disappointed in his over-optimistic hopes for the deputy chairman's post. Working more and more away from the office, he finally resigned and was taken to hospital with severe stomach ulcers. He had departed, he said, because he could not stand 'that man' any longer. Not long afterwards it was Jimmy Cowan's turn to take his overdue retirement. His view was quite different. Without 'that man', he believed, the strike could not have been won by the board.

Another, more subtle, view came from one of the Whitehall mandarins most closely associated with the strike. 'Under a more thoughtful and accommodating chairman, the long strike might have been avoided. With a less confrontational chairman, Arthur Scargill might have been less exposed. The MacGregor factor made the strike more bitter and longer but also as a result made Scargill more discredited. He was forced by the existence of MacGregor as a symbol to behave as a symbol himself and that made him hang on to the bitter end. If the strike had been shorter and more accommodating, Arthur Scargill would have been disruptive longer, so that's down to MacGregor.'

10
'The government is not involved'

Few episodes in the Thatcher government's life went so well for it as its handling of the miners' strike. It won its main objectives: it faced down the weightiest constitutional challenge it was likely to face on the UK mainland (Northern Ireland is a separate matter) and it wholly secured the right to make the coal industry – and thus any other industry, since that was the strongest bastion of non-market production – profitable and market-oriented. The chancellor, Nigel Lawson, was correct when he said, in the Commons on 1 August 1984, that it was a 'worthwhile investment': for the Conservative Party, and for free market principles, there have been few better. Politically, it appeared to have given the Conservatives little help once it ended, for they were sinking in the polls towards its dénouement. But it gave them a huge store of ammunition to use against Labour come an election: a store only a little less rich for having to be shared with the Alliance parties.

The *manner* of handling the strike was all important in achieving these desirable, and in many cases unlooked-for, objectives. Peter Walker, Secretary of State for Energy throughout the strike, was the keystone of the arch the government threw over the disputes. The prime minister intervened rarely, if powerfully. The junior energy ministers, Giles Shaw (to September 1984) and David Hunt (from September 1984) busied themselves to effect in the background. Leon Brittan, the home secretary, provided unlimited support to the police. Norman Tebbit, at Trade and Industry, steadied the nerves of the few industrialists who got windy and kept the British Steel Corporation management away from the courts. Tom King at the Employment Department kept out of active involvement, but provided a discreet shoulder for some trade unionists to weep on over the iniquities of the miners' leadership. Other ministers – including surprisingly senior ones – attempted freelance dabbling to no great effect. But the government was in general able to carry off the illusion that it was not deeply involved.

This sounds contradictory. How could so many senior ministers have so much to do with the dispute yet the government collectively never appear involved? In part it was done by insisting that authority was devolved. The government took care to stress that the NCB was in charge of negotiations, that the police were responsible for order, the courts for the law, public and private corporations for securing their own supplies of labour and materials. It worked. The mask slipped occasionally, as when the *Mirror* revealed on 6 June 1984 that Mrs Thatcher and other ministers had been closely concerned to ensure that the British Rail pay offer did not make the miners' offer look bad. But otherwise it stayed in place because, in essence, it did not have to hide *too* much. The government was *not* running the strike in the way governments have before. It *was* doing its damnedest to defeat the NUM leadership, but through the agency of others.

This approach was not stumbled upon. A number of object lessons of the past decade had burned themselves on the Conservative consciousness, and had indeed greatly assisted in producing what has come to be known as Thatcherism. We have already noted Saltley Gates. No other incident was so important in establishing the absolute need for the strong assertion of the rule of law. But the other lesson learned from the Heath period, particularly from the 1974 strike, was the absolute need *not* to become engaged in the day-to-day business of industrial disputes. Mrs Thatcher made clear from the outset that beer and sandwiches at Number Ten was out. That she did not order either for the miners was an index of her determination not to follow Edward Heath down his lonely trail of defeat.

It is an open question, on the well documented Heath period,[1] whether or not the imperatives of a statutory pay policy, conflated with the crisis engendered by the Middle East war, dictated government intervention – or if the style of government was anyway so interventionist that it would have entered the frame as the dominant actor sooner or later. Norman Tebbit had resigned, in 1973, as a PPS largely because he disagreed with the statutory pay policy. Reflecting on the period now, he says that while he was split over Heath's tactics, he 'could not see it was right to get into statutory control of pay, prices and incomes. That has remained my view, and I think once or twice recently that we have been extremely fortunate not to be in that position, of having even an informal policy, or anything of that kind.' The fortune lies, in Tebbit's view, in *not* being in control, or seen to be in control.

The lessons taught by the 1973–4 crisis were that a government, where it put itself forward as the negotiator of first resort, can too easily be seen as the villain of the piece even where the majority of the public agreed with its objectives (most polls showed that Heath did enjoy majority support). Government, in an at least potentially anti-statist society like Britain, is generally safer being modest in its endeavour to control social forces directly. Margaret Thatcher never met the miners' leaders and only met the TUC when the miners were clearly beaten, and then only to repeat, with a few minor alterations, the surrender terms. Instead of the government, the various forces of civil society competed for control of aspects of the dispute. As far as possible it sought to ensure that those it wished to win, won, thus ensuring that in the end, it did.

Three years after the fall of the Heath government, in the midst of a Labour government's difficult term of office, the massing of pickets outside the Grunwick film processing laboratories in Cricklewood provided another lesson, this time in how the courts could assist in establishing the 'right to work'. The Grunwick strikers, led by the gentle yet stubborn figure of Mrs Jeyaben Desai, marshalled by the talented organisation of Jack Dromey (now a senior TGWU official) and supported by a spectrum which took in Mrs Shirley Williams and Arthur Scargill, put up a powerful case for union recognition which attracted much sympathy – but they lost. The combination of a determined employer and, in the National Association for Freedom, a strongly politically motivated group which saw itself as carrying out a mission to free the country from the grip of union power, had been shown to be a powerful one.

Throughout the 1970s, as battles raged for the possession of the Conservative Party's soul none was more important than the battle for a hawkish position on the unions and labour law. Sir John Hoskyns, working full time at the Centre for Policy Studies from 1977, had the brief to work out the objectives of a future Tory government. Together with Norman Strauss, a Unilever executive, he identified union power as the central issue, especially in the public sector. In a paper to the shadow cabinet at the end of 1977 Hoskyns posed the alternatives as he saw them: are you going to go into the next government pledged to do nothing about the unions? Or will you adopt a sensible, step-by-step approach of whittling away their power? Mrs Thatcher, William Whitelaw, Keith Joseph and Geoffrey Howe bought the Hoskyns line early. Other shadow ministers, like John Biffen, only swung round during the 1978–9 'winter of discontent', and only then did Jim Prior, the shadow employment secretary, agree with reluctance to a first bill limiting picketing, secondary action and the closed shop.

Prior stuck to his gradualist line under great pressure, especially when the 1980 steel strike, beginning on the second day of the year, was fanned up into a conflict much more bitter than the steel union's right-wing leadership expected or wished, as mass picketing on the private steel works which continued to work grew more and more violent. When on 26 January the Lords overturned an earlier Court of Appeal injunction against the secondary picketing of the private plants, the judgment triggered a motion, signed by no fewer than 100 Tory backbenchers, calling on Prior to stiffen the terms of his then Employment Bill by eliminating all secondary action from immunity. The Prime Minister was on their side, having just lost a cabinet battle for a bill to deal with secondary picketing which would open up union funds to damages claims. Prior made it clear that if such an idea were endorsed, he would resign.

It delayed these measures, which were ushered in by Norman Tebbit in his 1982 Employment Act, but Prior never recovered from his misreading of the mood of his prime minister, the most active part of his party and, even, the country. Sent to Northern Ireland in 1981 (after public agonising on resignation) he finally *did* resign from the cabinet in 1984. Reflecting on this period in a Channel 4 interview in December 1985, Prior admitted that he was pushed further and faster than he wished, but that that had been 'my mistake'. He continued: 'Norman Tebbit actually got his legislation through, again a good deal more quietly than I would have expected. It's almost inconceivable to someone like myself who did actually see the passage of the Industrial Relations Act and all that happened subsequently to recognise the difference that there was between '79 and the present day, where the mood of the country has changed. The union leaders had vastly exceeded their authority in the eyes not only of the public generally, but also of their own members, and therefore the mood was right for rather more legislation, and after all quite a lot more union bashing than I ever thought would be justified or politically acceptable.'[2]

In making that mistake, Prior weakened greatly the 'wet' position, lost control of industrial relations policy to Tebbit (who, though a good deal more cautious than his image, still pushed ahead more boldly than Prior could have done), and ensured that when the miners did take on the government, their funds would not be protected. The steel strike, settled by a fudge on wages, was followed by rapid closures under Sir Charles Villiers then, later in 1980, Ian MacGregor. The main union, the Iron and Steel Trades Confederation, still likes to claim it 'won' (or at least did not lose) the 1980 strike, but while it secured a wage award (after arbitration), it lost control of bargaining at national level, and could do nothing about the further rationalisations of capacity, the speed-up of the work rate and the rapid reassertion of managerial hegemony over the workforce. The steel strike showed the governing party that union muscle could be pretty flabby: it gave many in it a taste for stronger law.

The 'phoney war' with the miners in February 1981 was of supreme importance in jolting the government into making the necessary preparations for the real thing. But it was the dispute between the National Graphical Association and Mr Eddie Shah's *Stockport Messenger* group which gave everyone a little dry run for what was to come – an exercise which the miners' leadership, and many of their supporters, chose to ignore or simply misinterpret.

The Shah dispute was over the maintenance of a closed shop in his group. The NGA had steadily increased picketing throughout the autumn of 1983. It came to a climax on 29 November when thousands of NGA members and others – including Scottish miners – attempted to blockade, then to break in to, the plant. Some 2,000 members of the Cheshire police force – whose chief constable, George Fenn, had been told by the Home Office to ensure that Shah's papers came out that night – fought all night around the plant to keep the pickets at bay. In the words of one observer, 'Soon the road round the back of the plant looked like an Ulster riot – with burning barricades, felled telegraph poles and groups of riot police with clubs chasing after pickets. There was brutality on both sides as the police cleared the area. Some members of the Tactical Aid Group in full riot gear clearly enjoyed the night out. But individual acts of police thuggery were in part provoked by the impersonal violence of the missiles which hailed down from the [pickets]. . . . It had been one of those rare, but uncomfortable, reminders that even in a mature democracy the struggle for industrial power can still involve a literal battle, and that the law ultimately remains underpinned by physical force.'[3]

Len Murray found some discomfort in the issue as well. After a meeting of the TUC employment policy committee on 10 December agreed to take a 'sympathetic and supportive attitude' to the NGA's call for secondary (and probably unlawful) industrial action in the national press on 14 December, the TUC general secretary repudiated the majority decision and got too-close-for-comfort backing from the general council for his contention that the funds of the TUC could not be placed in jeopardy by support. It was an act of great courage which badly weakened him, and very largely alienated the TUC left wing.

The clearest warning had been given that the police were possessed of the necessary will to clear pickets away, no matter how numerous. In the 1960s and 1970s, provincial newspaper publishers found that the police would not clear pickets away from blockading their plants during a dispute because of fears of being seen as 'political'. The government made clear that their fullest support for the 'rule of law' was defined as the right of Shah to bring out his paper. He was later made much of by the prime minister, and set out to show the Fleet Street barons how to do their job. Second, the TUC had an inbuilt majority against adventurism, and though many on that majority resented Murray's actions, they backed him not just because he was the general secretary but because they thought the NGA was wrong. They had demonstrated that the 'Wembley Principles' of 1982 did *not* give automatic backing to strike action, even where it could be defined as taking on the government's law as well as an employer. The NGA/*Stockport Messenger* clash showed a divided TUC and a determined government – but since the NUM leadership had contempt for both, it paid these lessons no heed.

The strike was expected to come but a surprise when it did, and for its first two months the best advice government was getting predicted a ballot. Common sense seemed to dictate it: the 'domino tactic' had found the Midlands fields difficult to topple, and the NUM leadership had proposed to put to the 19 April special delegate conference the lowering of the percentage vote required to sanction a strike from 55 per cent to a simple majority, with the apparent aim of seeking national sanction for the action. Polls taken in mid-April in the expectation of a ballot showed majorities for a strike: 55 per cent in a Harris poll for *Weekend World* and 65 per cent in a Mori poll for the *Sunday Times*, both published on 15 April.

The first imperative for government was to be seen to be doing as little as possible. Any actions by a hardline Conservative government would only serve to unite the clearly divided mineworkers against it, and produce in the expected ballot a majority for strike action. The calling of the strike thus opened phase one of government involvement: the stage of denying involvement without lying too much. A senior official concerned with the strike puts it this way: 'The Government's actions from an early stage do belie the argument that was used in the first months, that it was a matter entirely between the board and the union.

'That said, I admire the success with which the government stuck to that line, certainly until July. But of course with the numbers one was talking about, in terms of the deficit grant to the industry, it was quite inconceivable for the government not to care. But the government had no choice but to give the objectives it did and to try to ensure that the management stayed on top of the situation; and tactically it was also wise in the early days to stay away and not give the aspect of a political strike.'

Walker quickly emerged as the man in charge of not being involved in the strike. The prime minister had no interest in repeating the mistakes of Edward Heath, while the only other possibility, Tom King, never made a serious challenge to gather the reins of power at his Employment Department. His department did, however, make a large contribution. Douglas Smith, one of King's two deputy secretaries, proposed a committee of senior officials drawn from relevant departments to brief Walker on a daily basis as to the progress of the dispute. The need, Smith felt, was for information. There was, at that stage, no general danger to life, limb or supplies, and thus the Civil Contingencies Unit was inappropriate (as well as being cumbersome). So the daily briefing committee began its work, in mid-April. Meeting early in the morning, it brought together such senior men as Smith himself (later replaced by Ted Whybrew, an assistant secretary at Employment, when his work burden became too heavy); Ivor Manley, a deputy secretary from Energy whose responsibilities included coal; Robin Goodfellow from the Transport Department and David Hilary from the Home Office. David Brandrick, the laconic NCB secretary, usually attended, as did Malcolm Edwards, the marketing director (or Laurie Penser, his deputy), and Ned Smith, the industrial relations director general.

Walker would say little at these meetings, listening instead as each official reported the latest moves on his front, or anticipated what was to come that day. There were few papers: Walker, one of the longest-serving ministers in the government, was able to absorb large amounts of information orally and retain the vital facts. It did not deal with the detail of NCB negotiations, but it *did* go into considerable detail on how the rest of the country's infrastructure was coping with the strain of the miners' strike. The rail network was a particular concern: at least one session of the gathering got down to talking about the holiday rotas of the railwaymen manning the vital Shirebrook, Derbyshire, signalbox.

One thing for which Walker is famous – his critics say, the only thing for which he *should* be famous – is his public relations skill. That being so, much of the discussion centred on how the strike would *look* in the press and more importantly on television. The pictures from the picket lines were good news to the men gathered in Walker's room overlooking the Thames.

Walker also operated in other forums. From Monday 16 April, a cabinet committee – Misc 101 – of senior ministers – Mrs Thatcher, Walker, King, Tebbit, Brittan, with Sir Michael Havers the attorney general, Michael Heseltine from Defence, Nigel Lawson the chancellor, Nicholas Ridley the transport secretary and George Younger from the Scottish Office – was formed to monitor the dispute, a sign that the government was prepared to slog it out over the distance. Both in that committee and in the Commons, however, the energy secretary dominated his colleagues. He had the information at his fingertips – and, as time went on, he became increasingly confident over power supplies. He was a skilled Commons performer, not just on the floor of the house (where a defensive Labour Party had a too-decent-to-be-dangerous shadow energy secretary, Stan Orme, and rarely got the better of him), but more particularly with back-benchers. Tim Eggar, who took a close interest in the coal industry, says that 'there was very little murmuring in the party. As a party we were kept well informed by Walker – he went out of his way to do that. He wrote to every back-bencher, using good solid arguments of the kind we could use. . . . It was extraordinary that the feeling on the [Tory] back benches was that everything was under control. It was almost as though it [the strike] didn't exist. It was taken for granted that we were going to win at some stage and so we could get on with other things.'

Walker alone among ministers saw MacGregor or talked to him regularly by phone – often early in the morning, Walker from the kitchen of his home, MacGregor virtually alone in the fastness of Hobart House. The two men got on less and less well as the dispute went on: MacGregor resented any interference from the front office, Walker thought the chairman – not, after all, his choice – cantankerous, hasty in judgment, and poor in presentation. But he could do little except leave him be in most things, and while Walker was at times anxious over the chairman's grasp of negotiations as they unrolled themselves through spring, summer, then into autumn, he now says that there was no offer made, no form of words concocted, that did not have his approval. Like MacGregor, Walker took the view that any phrase, no matter how mild, would suffice so long as it could be interpreted as safeguarding the NCB's position on closing uneconomic pits.

Walker also now identifies two phases in Scargill's tactics. In the first months to July, he believes, the miners' leader attempted to run the strike as one between the unions as a whole and the government's trade union legislation. Walker says that he kept himself away from the public limelight – despite daily entreaties from the media – because to go public would have been to demonstrate to the other unions that Scargill's line that it *was* a fight against a reactionary government would gain some underpinning. Many on the right did not share Walker's view: Sir John Hoskyns met Whitelaw to lobby him for a more public stance, believing that the public would respond to a clear lead against a threat which could easily be identified as unconstitutional.

That line never won out, but after the collapse of negotiations in July Walker says he judged that the phase in which the government's legislation was identified as the main enemy has passed, and the government political profile could be raised. This was not at all clear at the time. Indeed, officials from Walker's department – clearly, as it seemed, mirroring the view of their political master – made it known that the government was in despair over MacGregor's handling of the media battle, and simply snatched the public presentation of the strike out of his hands as soon as the July round of talks failed.

Whatever the reasoning, the ministers were let slip after the collapse of the July talks. Over the succeeding days, Peter Walker, Nigel Lawson, Leon Brittan, Norman Tebbit, Tom King, John Selwyn Gummer (then Tory Party chairman) and others gave speeches and interviews which attacked the NUM leadership, and Scargill in particular, for launching an attempted political coup. Tebbit repeated the call for a ballot. Walker, in a 20 July piece in *The Times*, talked of 'Scargill's challenge to us all'. Gummer, with others, called directly for a rank-and-file revolt against the leadership. Alex Fletcher, a junior trade and industry minister, went further than most, claiming there was 'a strong similarity between Mr Scargill and General Galtieri [the Argentinian dictator at the time of the Falklands invasion]. They both believe in intimidation, in substituting the force of persuasion with the persuasion of force. I predict that Mr Scargill will suffer the same fate as General Galtieri. His threats, his lies, will not even save his own job. He will fail and he will be ousted.'

Characteristically, the prime minister was most controversial. In a speech to the 1922 (Conservative back-bench) Committee she talked of 'the enemy within', contrasting that with the Argentinian 'enemy without'. The internal enemy, she said, was just as dangerous to liberty, and the country was witnessing an attack on democracy and the rule of law. The 'enemy within' was immediately interpreted as a reference to the mineworkers as a whole, and was snatched into the political debate and flung against Thatcher in the Commons by Michael Foot and others. In fact, the prime minister had been talking about the miners' leaders and the core of activists across the coal fields – which Neil Kinnock was later to estimate numbered no more than 2,000 – who drove the strike. But the phrase stuck and, like Harold Wilson's much more deliberately insulting designation of the Northern Irish Protestants during their strike a decade earlier as 'spongers', it was worn with pride, soon appearing on badges and stencilled on T-shirts.

MacGregor did not like what the 'front office' was doing in 'politicising' the strike. He had Cowan appeal to the NUM executive the day after the Rubens breakdown to 'carefully examine our proposals'. He let it be known that he thought Scargill willing to get a settlement, and that the politicians' cries could torpedo these hopes. His officials' advice was that the executive could yet rise up against the national leaders and demand acceptance of the deal: murmurings within the left seemed a hopeful sign. But that, like the hopes of Heathfield's pragmatism, was to prove illusory.

The politicians had a further reason for coming out: the supply of coal was improving markedly. By 22 July Walker could appear on *Weekend World* to tell his viewers that coal supplies would last well into 1985. The key movements of coal had gone up over the past months from 500,000 to 670,000 tonnes a week; the stocks stood at around 16 million tonnes in the power stations (with 22 million tonnes at the pithead); oil was being burned in the stations at the rate of around 400,000 tonnes a week and coal was coming in to small ports and harbours at an annual rate of 10 million tonnes. The position was clearly wide open to damage from other workers, and thus ministers took aim at the weakest side of the strike – its 'undemocratic' nature, its attendant violence, and its political dimension – in order to scare off support from the trade unions.

As those closest to MacGregor constantly told us, it is a mistake to equate the chairman's considerable willpower and strength of mind with consistency of line. He could be influenced over a long period of time by people, like Ned Smith, whom he was later to dismiss as romantics. For the first eight months of the strike – until the last round of negotiations in October – MacGregor stuck to the line that the strike could be won on a formula which was close to meaningless. But David Hart, by October his closest adviser, was warning him strongly against this line. In a note written for MacGregor on 10 October Hart told him that the strike was clearly political, and that its outcome was no longer the exclusive concern of the board's management – if it ever had been. Where the national interest clashed with the narrower interests of the board, Hart wrote, the former must take precedence. It was *not* in the national interest for a settlement to be reached, because any agreement could only be secured by the NCB – and therefore the nation – surrendering to Scargill. Hart was attempting to wrest MacGregor out of his own definition of himself as a simple industrialist confronted with a strike, and replace it with one of a statesman. He advised better public relations, an end to all negotiations, withdrawal of the commitment to no compulsory redundancies after November, the sacking of all miners convicted of offences, and the closure of pits in danger. Only the first two of these proposals were fully implemented, but some of Hart's message did get through. The chairman grew tougher, less concerned to present the face of compromise (though this was not consistent) and his speeches, in the closing months and even more in the aftermath of the strike, grew much more overly political, picking up on some of Hart's themes of individual liberty and the war against tyranny. Walker did not like what he heard of Hart's involvement, and may have resented his influence with the prime minister as well as the chairman. On the one time they talked (on the telephone) Walker said he did not wish to see the strike run from Claridges – though Walker plays down the importance of this while Hart sees Walker's opposition to him as sustained and at times vitriolic.

It probably was Walker who first saw the importance of the TUC to the government's strategy – even though, in part *because* – it had wholly failed to offer even a fraction of the total support promised at its September Congress. The TUC had suffered greatly over the five years before the strike because of its loss of influence on government. Since the war, when it was encouraged to play the role of social partner, it had depended on at least being listened to by successive governments, on having its claims of hegemony over the working class being unquestioned. The Thatcher government was not just questioning these claims but in some areas disposing of them. It had bred among union leaders a mixture of defiance (to which there was too little response from members) and accommodation (to which there was too little response from government). Now there was a national crisis, caused at least in part by the actions of its affiliate. Now was a time to recoup some power and influence.

David Basnett tended this flame the longest. The general secretary of the General Municipal and Boilermakers' Union – he retired early in 1986 – was the only surviving major union leader on the council who had been active and influential through most of the 1970s. The weak leadership of the TGWU, and the occupation of a strong right-wing stand by Terry Duffy of the engineers, meant that Basnett emerged in the 1980s as the central figure on the general council, holding the chair of its economic committee. A decent and reasonable man who had to cope with the personal blow of his son's paralysis during the last two months of the strike, he had spent the period of his leadership of the council striving for unity by trying to discover a central position between left and right camps. It produced short-term gains, but it never amounted to a strategy which others could follow. In the strike his continued insistence, first, that the TUC should get involved fell on stony ground, and when the TUC did get involved his pleas that it must draw the government into the act were also ignored for months.

By November the three-man TUC liaison group of Basnett, Buckton and Willis had grown to a group of seven (naturally known as 'magnificent') with the addition of Jack Eccles the TUC chairman, Moss Evans the TGWU general secretary, Bill Keys the Sogat 82 general secretary, and Gerry Russell an executive councillor of the engineering union AUEW. These last two were as shrewd a pair of old pros as the movement possessed. Keys, an emotional leftist who thrived in the tortuous, shady, boozy world of newspaper negotiations, had the open-handed approach of the London working-class lad made good (he was born in Elephant and Castle in poverty) which characterises many of the well-off Fleet Street printworkers. Russell was a sharp Merseysider who had matured in engineering union politics in Liverpool toolshops, making it on to the AUEW executive as the only member not tied to either the powerful left or right-wing machines. Keys made or had links with many of the left-wing leaders in the NUM: his wife, Enid, was a miner's daughter, and his son, Ian, a GMBU officer, was responsible for persuading the men at Didcot power station in Oxford to refuse supplies. As the year wore on, he found his NUM friends growing more and more desperate: in clubs and hotels in London and in the coal fields, they would confide in the endlessly sympathetic Keys their anxieties over the strike, the hardship – and 'Arthur'. The print union leader had himself tried to fix a settlement, and over Christmas thought he had got Mick McGahey's backing to push a draft through the three national officials – but at a meeting with the three in Sheffield it was rejected. Russell had no such contacts, but he shared the deep scepticism of his right-wing colleagues on the engineers' executive about the NUM leadership. Time and again, during the endless meetings arranged between the 'seven' and the 'three' Russell would cut through the talk in his nasal lilt and ask: What's the strategy? What will you do about the violence? What have you got going for you?

As the heart went out of the strike, figures on all sides got involved in freelance, or at least clandestine, efforts to pull a settlement out of the fire. Near Christmas 1984, with parliament in recess and the prime minister in the Far East, Keys was called at home late one night and asked to a meeting at the House of Lords. He went to find his host was Lord Whitelaw, deputy prime minister: joining him a little later came David (now Lord) Young, then still chairman of the Manpower Services Commission on which Keys sat as a TUC representative. It was a gracious occasion: Whitelaw had taken the time to ascertain that Keys liked a glass of wine, and had laid on a bottle. Both men impressed on Keys the desire of the government to get a settlement, and Whitelaw told him the initiative had the blessing of the absent prime minister. Together, Whitelaw and Keys agreed that a settlement could and should be found short of total capitulation – though any settlement would have to include a firm written agreement to the closure of uneconomic pits. Keys thought that some of the NUM executive would buy it – he believed, for example, that McGahey would settle on a formula which was also acceptable to the government and the board. But that idea, with others like it, smashed against the rock of Scargillite opposition.

Though the TUC was itself against going to government – What would we go with? Willis would ask Basnett – a majority of the seven gradually came round to it because nothing else seemed to work. Out in the coal fields, the three national officials belted out a fundamentalist message at mass rallies. Kinnock refused to attend, and Willis, condemning violence in the midst of an otherwise supportive speech in Aberavon on 13 November, was howled into inaudibility as a noose dangled above his head. So the seven had a secret meeting with Walker on 5 December. Walker was of all the cabinet the least antipathetic to unions. In whatever department of state he has worked he made it clear that unions would be welcome to talk to him. He could see, in the TUC's increasing desperation, a way of assisting to bring the strike to an end – an end which he feared could be infinitely delayed by the actions of the NCB chairman.

The private meeting took place without the board's presence. Walker was quite charming: he told the TUC leaders that he believed the problem to be centred on Scargill, that he was quite unlike other union leaders, that the government had no choice but to see him off. It was not government's choosing; a reasonable deal could have been done with the miners which could have left its leaders looking good. But with Scargill – just hopeless. The energy secretary doubted if the TUC could bring him to his senses – but he encouraged them to see what they could do and come back any time.

Basnett thought that Walker was playing politics, but he saw his invitation to drop in again as encouraging. Willis was much less optimistic: he had seen Len Murray, his predecessor, being made into the fall guy for the NGA a year before; he knew the movement's history well enough to be acutely conscious of the can of 'betrayal' which had been tied to the TUC's tail after the 1926 miners' strike. He did not want to be the patsy and a deal cooked up between government and the TUC looked a prime route to that. But the left now wanted off the hook: Keys was getting his messages, Buckton's support for the miners was costing the union large sums, since ASLEF paid its members who did not work driving coal trains the wages they lost. Willis put Graham and Monks to work drafting out fudges. They established friendly enough relations with officials at the Department of Energy. Scargill remained aloof from the process, though Heathfield gave discreet encouragement to it.

The fruits of their endeavours were presented to Walker at a further meeting with the TUC on 14 December, this time with full attendant publicity. Willis told Walker – who had with him Tom King and David Hunt, the Coal Minister – that the TUC had come up with yet another scheme: drop entirely the attempt to get a definition of 'uneconomic', and instead get a return to work on the explicit understanding that a revised Plan for Coal would be renegotiated on that return. The 4 million tonne cut and the closure of the five named pits would be dropped (as had already been essentially agreed). Walker went through his piece: the offer to the NUM was unparalleled in British industry; the government wished to see the industry expand; two of the three mining unions, and more than one third of NUM members, were at work; no strike ballot had been taken – and anyway, what could the TUC deliver? As he put it after the meeting, 'The TUC had nothing to bring to this meeting in the way of suggesting a change in the NUM attitude.'

That, in effect, was Walker's challenge to the TUC: come back when you can get Scargill to sign. It was a reasonable, corporatist bargain: if the TUC was to be taken seriously by government once more, it had to show it could deliver. Willis did try. Working largely on his own in the first month of 1985, he put out feelers to the Coal Board as well as to the department. Drafts of agreements, some put up by Stan Orme, began to be thrashed through once more.

But the shades were gathering fast. Willis found the board's, and government's, attitude hardening by the day. MacGregor now insisted that talks could not begin again without a crucial precondition: that the NUM leaders committed themselves in advance to discuss – in some versions, to agree to – the closure of uneconomic pits. Though there was real confusion on whether the board meant 'discuss' or 'agree' (David Hunt tended to say the first, Eaton the second) the NCB and government had at last patched up a reasonable act for public consumption. The prime minister put it most clearly. She told the Commons, on the same day the executive met, that there should be 'a clear settlement. After seven rounds of negotiations it is important that the next round be entered into on a clear basis so that there can be no fudging whatever.' A little late for that – the board had spent much of the previous year fudging as much as it could, but it was now carefully herding these bolted horses back in through the stable door. As Thatcher spoke, the board sent a letter to the NUM executive requiring a 'written indication that the union is prepared to help resolve the problem of uneconomic capacity' and 'co-operate with the essential task of closing loss-making pits'.

Through the further intervention of ACAS, Heathfield met Merrik Spanton in London five days later, to be told the familiar story that he had to agree to closures before talks began. On 30 January, a now-jittery NUM executive were told that the pound's slide was due to the effects of the strike, that there had been a series of unreported power cuts, and that the strike still had some life in it.

Ned Smith was the one remaining dissentient from the NCB line. Over Christmas, this man who had once been a miner, and a Labour Party parliamentary aspirant, found himself increasingly convinced that the hard line was both damaging and cruel. Talking to Walker after a Christmas party at the Energy Department, he said that the miners who were then flooding back to the pits would all come out again after the New Year once they had secured enough money to buy presents for their families. Walker, who liked Smith personally, saw that the industrial relations director's deep involvement and beliefs in an 'honourable settlement' were affecting his judgment.

Smith was also convinced that he could pull off a deal. TUC negotiators who met Smith were convinced that he did not differ fundamentally from a point of view often expressed by Heathfield (the two men had kept in touch throughout most of the strike): that there was no need to write down that uneconomic pits should close. It was, said Heathfield many times, unprecedented. No other union had been asked to sign away its objections to redundancies in advance. To that point of view Smith felt himself inclined.

Smith and Heathfield met on 16 January at the Cavendish Square headquarters of the Coal Industry Social Welfare Organisation, and agreed to meet again on 21 January. MacGregor was consulted and agreed, another remarkable example of his privately accommodating style, especially at a time when his public stance had hardened against all talks. There is evidence that he later regretted it, and when Walker heard of it he was enraged. By the time the talks ended, lobby correspondents were receiving a briefing from Ingham which dismissed them. Eaton was on television soon after suggesting that Smith had exceeded his brief.

What Smith had done was act according to his convictions. He produced a draft in which both sides stated their position: the board that it would shut loss-making pits, the union that it would oppose such closures. It safeguarded the principles of both, gave both a way out, allowed a settlement to the strike. It could not be allowed to run at a time when total victory was in sight.

Though the NUM executive approved it on 24 January as a basis for talks, it was swept from the table by board and government.

Willis's contacts with the board now intensified. In private meetings with MacGregor and Cowan (Smith retired on 3 February) he and his officials began to refine a draft agreement, mostly dictated by the board, but with the corners softened by TUC pressure and argument. By Friday 15 February the process had gone as far as it could. At a specially convened meeting of the NUM executive Willis presented the document, cast in the form of a draft agreement. It was, as he knew, non-negotiable.

It was also, compared to what had been on offer before, awful, reflecting the continuing shift in the balance of power (around 45 per cent of the miners were then working). The NUM had to 'recognise it is the duty of the NCB to manage the industry efficiently'. Discussions on a new Plan to Coal would be undertaken on a return to work, to be completed within six months. Pits could close in that time. Pits would close on exhaustion or geological faulting – or 'where there are no further reserves which can be developed to provide the board in line with their responsibilities with a satisfactory basis for continuing operations.' The board would make the final decision on closure. The discussions about a new Plan for Coal would focus on the markets available. The sops were few: a clause saying that the agreement did not constitute a no-strike deal; another saying that 'community responsibility' would be part of the closures' criteria; a commitment to reconciliation. But it was a surrender document. Scargill called it 'a blueprint for the closures of pits' and refused to discuss it.

His executive staged a flurry of revolt. Emlyn Williams, the South Wales president, led a move which attempted to get changes in the document – though the changes left in most of the harshest clauses. But the board, knowing when the NUM was on the run, reiterated what it had told the TUC: the draft was not negotiable.

The prime minister was the final throw. Granting the unions an audience on 19 February before flying to the USA, she met a body of men who were of roughly the same mind over Scargill as she was. She handled the meeting with great skill – inquiring thoughtfully after Basnett's son, taking care with their names, neither lecturing nor showing scorn. She simply reasserted that the deal had to be clear. The miners, she said, must not be deceived any longer. Willis, who did most of the talking, thought it a clever but unremarkable performance.

Basnett invested it with greater significance, seeing it as an opening to the TUC for a new relationship which could be built on after the strike. Later, though, he concluded that the opening had closed.

Further, Walker had kept his lines open to Peter McNestry of NACODS and Alan Wilson of BACM. The latter was particularly influential with the energy secretary, since he could and did command respect throughout the industry. But the more Walker listened to these men the more MacGregor was infuriated. Wilson complained bitterly that the reorganisations effected by MacGregor in creating the office of the chief executive, and the distance maintained between MacGregor and Cowan in the office and management down the line, had been responsible for endless misunderstandings, while McNestry urged again and again that talks restart, and that the conditions be softened. Both McNestry and Wilson regarded Walker and Hunt, the coal minister, as their allies against MacGregor, and the chairman knew it. So when, in the shuttling to and fro between Congress House and the Energy Department in the closing weeks of the strike, Walker signalled a willingness to soften the terms to get agreement, MacGregor blew his top and threatened resignation. The politician and the industrialist did not talk for days, and Tim Bell had to act as a go-between until relations were resumed.

The softening in the document – to specify that no pits would close while the revised review procedure was being agreed – did go in the final settlement, though it was ignored by the board after the strike ended. But it failed to attract support from the NUM executive. When Willis presented it to them on 20 February, after a late-night meeting with Walker, he found they were all willing to adopt Scargill's line that the agreement was worse than it had been before – a judgment which the NUM president appeared to make in minutes, and which Heathfield accepted without appearing to read more than the first page.

The TUC leaders were furious. Not only had their climactic efforts been in vain, but their negotiating skills had been insulted. Walker had succeeded brilliantly – though he was greatly aided by Scargill in this – in achieving a common view of Scargill, albeit unspoken, between the government and the TUC. That is not surprising. The left-wing Tory and the union leaders, differing in much, still shared the root belief in a society run by agreement between powerful interest groups. Since Scargill was one of the TUC's own, and since they could not deliver him to a deal, their anger was naturally more directed at him than at Walker, or even the prime minister, both of whom gave every appearance of sympathy with their plight. When, on 3 March, the miners' special delegate conference adopted the South Wales way of ending the strike – without an agreement – the miners were alone.

11
No other industry could do it

On 11 October 1985, seven months after the end of the strike, a group of miners waited, enjoying the last of the autumn sunshine, before going underground at Yorkshire Main colliery in the village of Edlington near Doncaster. It was a poignant moment. One of the most militant collieries in Yorkshire, which had been on strike in advance of the main dispute, its union branch had voted, with just 3 of the 1,300 men against, for its closure even though it had plenty of coal in the ground.

This was the last official production day, although 1,000 metres below the ground men were already starting the business of salvaging, removing mining equipment from the tunnels and roadways.

As they waited, some about to go underground at the pit for the last time, the question was asked by a television interviewer, 'Was it all for nothing?' There was a variety of different replies.

'Yes definitely,' said one man taking redundancy after thirty years in the pit. 'We have not won anything. We are all going up the road. . . . But it's all coming true as Arthur Scargill said; it's all happening.' Close by another man burst out, 'That's what happens when you follow donkeys . . . this leadership. They were right what they said about them being donkeys, and they are.' Beside him, another miner said warningly to him, 'Don't let them show your face.'

A few yards away another group of young men were explaining how after managing for a year on their wits without any strike or social security pay, they were now going to go redundant, when they would at least have unemployment benefit to help them along.

Amongst those opting for redundancy were many of the branch committee who had organised the picketing and the supplies of food and money during the strike. At that moment the former branch chairman was talking to his bank manager arranging the purchase of a seaside off-licence with his forthcoming redundancy money. Already some others of the strike activists were refusing to talk to him because he was, in their phrase, 'selling his job'.

The scene was a microcosm of the terrible and conflicting pressures which tore mining communities during the strike, or more accurately mining families, because as both sides became well aware, not all miners lived within the narrow corral of a mining community close to the pit.

It was a strong mixture, of a spirit of sticking together in the face of hardships no one had expected or experienced; of a time of stronger community in some places than perhaps ever before; of great excitement for young freebooting pickets enjoying a game of cat and mouse with the police in a splendid summer setting far preferable to the grimy caverns below the ground; of women from an essentially male chauvinist society finding themselves carrying much of the burden of the strike and making their voices known in a way which sometimes perplexed their men; of men and women from enclosed communities finding themselves travelling the length and breadth of the country.

But it was also a time of acute hardship and misery; of a situation which one NUM leader described as '130,000 men sitting at home quarrelling with their wives'; of people who found themselves first on strike to their bewilderment and then unable or too frightened to go back; of men afraid to discuss the merits of the strike in case they were overheard and accused of being scabs; of shopkeepers gladly giving money and supplies and others who paid up simply for fear of their windows being broken.

And it was a time of brutalities too; of people who had not been in trouble with the law before tussling with police and finding themselves forced into vans and up on criminal charges; of others carrying out lootings and burnings in a paroxysm of bitterness which engulfed them; of men in areas like Nottingham dredging up the courage to go to work across barriers of physical and verbal attack.

The worst hostilities surrounded those who went to work in divided communities, or risked the condemnation of the mass mentality of mostly solid areas. They were the most obvious casualties of the strike, they and their families abused, windows broken, homes daubed. A year on most have moved, many, probably a majority, have left the industry, and even some who have shifted away from mining villages to other places have been visited since by unforgiving strikers.

A proper chronicle of these experiences is impossible. It would have to cover 200,000 people and their families and neighbours. So too no examples can be typical. This chapter will therefore look at some common themes, fleshed out by a more detailed description of the experiences of four men from a single pit; three of them strikers, one a manager who had to run the gauntlet of the pickets every day to keep the pit in shape. Three out of the four have now left the industry. Without the strike they would probably all be still mining.

When the strike began, nobody expected it to last for many weeks.

For many men it was a relatively welcome interlude from the pit, and with talk of a ballot, they expected matters to be resolved before long. With the last pay cheque not coming until a week into the strike, and some men with pit savings put by for an interruption of work, the first weeks were relatively free from the financial worries that crowded in after a month or so on strike.

Miners had a reputation in the communities around as happy-go-lucky spenders but also with building societies and hire-purchase companies as those who paid their bills regularly. There were few problems about arranging to alter mortgage payments to interest-only payments, while some local authorities waived rent payments for strikers.

But a month into the strike and the strains were starting to show. On 13 April the *Sheffield Star* recorded that a striking miner from Edlington had received a conditional discharge for causing actual bodily harm to his common-law wife. 'It all blew up,' he explained, 'because we were short of money. There is only £20 a week coming into the house and she accused me of squandering money on drink.' He had lost his temper and kicked her on the side of her head causing her to fall off her chair.

By now mining families were discovering the impact of the new government legislation which 'deemed' that the households of strikers were receiving £15 a week from the union. (Later in the year it rose to £16.) 'Where is my £15?' was a complaint that union officials were to hear from numerous bemused and resentful men. The NUM did not pay strike pay, because it would have required enormous funds which would have been quickly exhausted. The payments were for picketing, and some areas did not pay even for that. It encouraged picketing; some Nottingham men, amazed to be encouraged by some pickets to keep working, found themselves being told that they were their only hope for an end to the strike, and the only reason they picketed was to get some money.

Under social security regulations strikers received no money but their wives and children could. So in early April the Citizens Advice Bureau in Stainforth in South Yorkshire gave these figures: a married striker with two children under 11 paying £15 a week in rent received in theory £21.45 a week for his wife, £9.15 for each child, and the £15 for his rent, making a total of £54.75. But from this was deducted child benefit payments of £6.50 for each child and the £15 'deemed' to have been paid by the union – result £26.75 a week.[1]

The way people managed was explained by a striking Derbyshire miner, Stuart Asher, in an interview with the *Sheffield Star*.[2] He had three children including a 16-month-old baby. His family was receiving £33.47 from social security plus some family allowance. They calculated they could spend 70p a head per day on food. The baby had been switched from expensive baby food to toast and soup. Milk was coming from the supermarket rather than the milkman because it was cheaper. Cereal was reckoned to be too expensive for breakfast so they had gone on to bread or toast and treacle. Tea was soup and potatoes, with meat occasionally.

The children benefited from the free school meals provided even in the holidays by many local councils, and he himself could have a free lunch at the miners' welfare. His wife meanwhile was eating mostly bread and doing a lot of baking. By mid-summer they had run out of anthracite – and cold for many miners in the autumn and winter was to be a major preoccupation. The couple no longer went out, but Stuart himself would be bought a pint or two by his father on a Sunday night. It was a bleak description, but one in which it seemed the miner suffered less than his wife.

Even social security payments were not always regular or guaranteed. Many strikers complained that payments were held up, or less than they had calculated. When they tried for extra payments for clothing or shoes for their children, they were often disappointed. Many mining families came to rely on in-laws and relations who assisted by inviting them round for meals and buying children clothes or birthday presents.

One persistent headache was the regular payments to building societies and electricity and gas boards. A number of NUM officials were surprised by the number of their members who still lived in privately rented accommodation where rent payments could not be postponed or waived as they could be in council houses. Faced by this a number of men borrowed money from money-lenders, sometimes with dire results. John Burrows, the administrative officer of the Derbyshire NUM, found the money-lenders much more intractable than the building societies. He found himself unable to prevent one man losing his house to a finance company; the best he could do was to fix the family up with accommodation from the sympathetic local council.

In County Durham, the Trustee Savings Bank allowed hundreds of miners to run up huge overdrafts to pay their principal outgoings such as electricity bills or insurance payments. In the village of Murton, for example, where about 600 miners banked with the TSB, about 350 took advantage of the overdraft facility and ran up debts of an average of £1,300 which were then converted to personal loans to be paid off in the two years after the strike.

Many miners got by only with the assistance of their wives' often part-time jobs. One miner's wife in Upton in Yorkshire told Professor Hilary Rose of Bradford University of the week she had to pay the electricity bill or be cut off. 'That week my wages (£22 for part-time work) plus the supplementary benefit had to go on the bill. We had £13 child benefit to live off that week. I was in a terrible state.

'I went down to the supermarket. I must spend £5 and no more. But I had to get the tea, bread, butter, sugar and milk. I got to the cashier and it was £8. I went outside and sat down and for about ten minutes broke my heart because I'd spent £8 instead of £5. My weekly bill used to be £40. That week I fed everyone on beans, eggs and spaghetti. My husband's mother bought us some meat for the weekend.'[3]

So union branch secretaries found themselves striking deals with local utilities. In Yorkshire an arrangement was made for families to pay the Yorkshire Electricity Board £1 a week to keep supplies going, with the rest to be made up after the strike. But even so, the YEB, seen as some sort of government agency, found its showrooms and pylons and vans sometimes the target of physical attack in the bitter Yorkshire autumn.

The worst off were single miners. They were not entitled to any supplementary benefit and were early recognised as a problem. At Yorkshire Main colliery they were all paid £2 a week, but that was exceptional. Jack Collins, the Kent NUM secretary, also saw them as a priority for food parcels: 'Some of our people said those who were not active were not entitled to food parcels. I said the ones who were picketing should take second place, because we had already won them over.' It was these single men who were amongst the chief recipients from the special food kitchens set up by the burgeoning women's support groups.

The changing role of women in the mining communities in the strike has been widely publicised. They lived in a very male-dominated society. Down the pit was one of the few working environments in Britain where there were no women at all, although they were to be found in the pithead offices and canteens. An anguished letter in the Trotskyist newspaper *Socialist Worker* early in the strike complaining about the miners' shout to women sympathisers, 'Show your tits for the miners,' demonstrated how little affected most had been by the women's movement. One woman in Upton put her differences with her husband like this: 'It's like, if there's a chop, Bob and his mother would think he ought to have it. But me, I'd give it to the children if there wasn't enough to go round for everyone.'

It was against this background that the women's support groups were established, soon after the beginning of the strike. The groups were to play a big role in welfare and in keeping the communities' morale going, but they had a wider political significance.

In the past, the pressure from wives of strikers was often for a return to work. Individuals and groups who expressed this point of view could be sure of a hearing and sometimes front-page publicity from popular newspapers opposed to the strike. A famous example was the appearance of wives outside the British Leyland Cowley plant in the frequent disputes of the 1970s urging a return to work. Indeed one of those closely involved there, a Conservative, Irene McGibbon, appeared as a major campaigner for the working miners in 1984. (Her husband, sickened by the uncertainties and interruptions to pay in the industry, had returned to his native Kent and become a miner.) In mining itself, wives of Nottingham miners had appeared on picket lines in the 1960s, as they did in 1984, in large numbers to shout at Yorkshire pickets trying to stop the pits and encourage their men to go through.

So the purpose of support groups, which were encouraged and sometimes led by political activists, was to demonstrate both to communities and the media that the women in mining communities were behind the strike. So, miners' wives from Kent travelled by hired bus to the Midlands coal fields very early in the dispute to demonstrate support for the strike and encourage men there to join it.

During the strike, individuals from the support groups travelled widely, often far more widely than they had done before, speaking for the striking miners' cause, and also collecting money to keep their welfare activities going.

The South Wales women's support group, which was an umbrella organisation covering groups with about 1,000 members gave this description for a survey conducted by the Labour Research Department:

> More women are becoming politically aware and want to carry on the women's movement after the strike. Our women in the various groups have visited Germany, Denmark, Austria, France, Belgium, Sweden, Holland, Spain, Norway, America and Canada. Contacts have been made with union organisations, socialist groups, miners' families and communities and ordinary people. A great flow of clothes, food, toys and chocolate cake came at Christmas, with vast sums of money. Many lasting friendships were made. People from these countries have visited the mining communities.[4]

The importance of the activists in the groups was appreciated by Arthur Scargill, whose wife, Ann, appeared on many picket lines and marches, while Betty Heathfield, the wife of the NUM general secretary, who had been active in the Communist Party for years, was a major organiser and speaker on behalf of the groups. So at the Edinburgh television festival, she complained that they had not been given sufficient attention and read from some of the writing and poetry of women in the groups which were an off-shoot of the strike.

The NUM leadership even went so far as to try to bind the groups into the union by proposing a change in the union rules to allow an affiliated membership. But this was resisted by areas who believed that this would dilute the union and bring in outside political and sectional interest groups not subject to the disciplines of the union.

It was certainly the case that support groups in general (and not just women's) were targets for groupings, always hovering on the edge of the strike, particularly the Workers Revolutionary Party and the Socialist Workers Party. After the strike some support groups have disbanded, but others have continued, in some cases becoming more political and engaging in arguments with the union leadership. So in Yorkshire by the end of 1985 there was a rift between the official union leadership and activists in groups running a save-our-coal-fields campaign on whose platforms no branch officials were sometimes to be found.

But as far as the women's support groups were concerned, the main drive was to provide welfare assistance for the communities, as well as giving women an active focus. The prime activity was providing midday meals for miners and children and food parcels for families.

So the 50 women in the Barnsley Women Against Pit Closures organised 16 kitchens, each providing 300 meals; the 15 women in Frickley Ladies Action Group in Yorkshire, whose members raised between £1,500 and £2,000 a week from street collections down in London, provided over 3,000 meals a week; while the 25 or so women in the Cynheidre group in South Wales fed 1,200 families, providing 750 food packs a week to 10 different villages (LRD Survey).

The support that these groups could muster was shown in the rally held at Chesterfield football ground in Betty Heathfield's home town at the end of the strike – about 2,000 attended. But the active membership of the support groups was often very small, with 15 or 25 out of villages where the pits employed over 1,000 men.

It is this disparity between activists and the mass of the mining community which makes description so difficult. One miner's son, returning to the pit town of Easington in Durham where his brother and nephew were on strike, described the different groups in the village: an active 40 or so committed union men around the branch officials; then a wider group of middle-aged men who would go picketing but were anxious that it should be responsible and were unhappy about taking his nephew along because he was seen to be too hot-headed; then a much larger body of men who did not picket and stayed at home, but were anxious not to break a strike which appeared to defend the jobs they were particularly concerned about in the north-east.

In the nearby village of Murton, a mechanic described the way there was little discussion at branch meetings because a group of active strike supporters would take up the front rows and shout 'scab' at suggestions of criticism. He had been little concerned about the strike in the early days, seeing it as not much more than a break from the pit. But as the months went on, he came under family pressures to earn some money for coal to heat the home: 'There were no casual jobs to be had; any that there were had gone already, and if I went on to the tip to forage for coal, I risked being arrested and losing my job.' In the end his relations helped out, though he ended with over £1,000 of debts.

His branch secretary, John Cummings, who was also the leader of Easington District Council, also found himself deeply in debt for the first time in his life at the end of the strike. But he had much happier memories, of playing cat and mouse, trying to mislead the police about the destination of picketing, of raising a penny rate to be spent on food vouchers for the Salvation Army to feed people, of a camp for miners' children during the summer in Teesdale where they were taught to hunt and snare rabbits.

The pressures in the communities to conform were intense. In the Yorkshire coal field miners from Hatfield colliery wrote to all local businesses asking for aid in March. The proprietor of a fish and chip shop who was thought not to be helping miners sufficiently received a postcard through his door which said, 'We will see you bankrupt, watch out for your windows.' The catch was that he was himself a striking miner.[5]

In April posters appeared in the village of Goldthorpe announcing that a local baker was the only shop which had not contributed to the Dearne Miners Food Fund. The shopkeeper hurried to the miners' headquarters to explain that she had not refused, but said she was too busy at that moment. The posters came down.[6]

At the same time, a club entertainer in Mexborough called Gerry Graham had said that he did not agree with the way the strike was handled. It was announced that 29 clubs had said they would not be engaging him.[7]

Businesses in mining areas were badly hit, though the Federation of Small Businesses in North Notts and South Yorks complained that things became even worse throughout the rest of 1985 once the strike was over. Miners were left with such debts that they could not afford further consumption. Things became so bad after the strike that they met government ministers in an unsuccessful plea that help designed to start up businesses should be switched to keep them going. The problems ran through all kinds of businesses, from clothes shops, to butchers, to electricians and the small engineering firms which serviced the board and its suppliers.

In Barnsley one publican moved ostensibly because of the strike, but the local secretary of the Licensed Victuallers, Melvin Hepworth, said towards the end of 1985, 'Things didn't go down as much as we expected during the strike. Trade is now worse than during the strike, because during the strike what money they had, they spent. Now they are hard at work, they are having to pay what they owe.'

Some of the hardest hit businesses were small electrical and building firms, who found themselves vastly undercut by the numerous mining craftsmen, qualified electricians and bricklayers employed to do those jobs at the pit. The public relations officer of the South Wales NCB was having an extension built on his house and returned one day to find an unfamiliar face wiring up the new building. Asked who he was, he turned out to be a pit electrician. In South Yorkshire 1984 was a fine time to have bricklaying done. A brickie could be found for £40 a week instead of the usual £150 or so, and painting and oddjobbing was available at similar rates.

One of the biggest sources of income was from coal plundered from NCB stockyards and tips. During the strike householders in South Yorkshire became accustomed to a knock on the door and the offer of coal at around £50 a ton compared with the usual £80 or so. It was usually delivered from vans in fertiliser sacks. The bitter disturbances in Grimethorpe in the autumn of 1984 followed attempts by the police to crack down on what was becoming very large-scale plunder of coal from pithead stocks.

For an active younger man in Yorkshire, picketing at £1 a day plus transport expenses and possibly a free meal could be supplemented by odd jobs if he could find them.

At the Coalite plant at Grimethorpe, owned by a private company but supplied by the NCB, operations continued during the strike largely because it was one of the few sources of smokeless fuel for miners' pensioners and such institutions as schools and hospitals. But an informal levy was extracted – a bag of coal from every load – and each picket received a bag a day worth about £4.

The small Kent area with only about 2,000 miners, the size of a single large Yorkshire pit, was one of the best off for funds because of its proximity to London and sympathisers on the continent. Its secretary Jack Collins described how they operated: 'We started by drawing up a list of all the children. Some people didn't want to bring them to the communal feeding places because they felt it was a bit of a stigma, so we attempted to bring the food to them.

'I remember one woman coming in wanting some food for the children. An organiser was saying in a loud voice, "Get the kids down and we'll feed them." But he said if she didn't bring them down, there would be no food for them. So I asked how many children she had. She said three under 7. I said, "I can understand you not wanting to bring them down."

'In the very first fortnight we bought food, corned beef, beans and so on. Very early on people were bringing in second-hand clothes, but they were not needed then. Later on we had teams of men cutting down trees for logs. Various people allowed us to cut trees on their land.

'At Betteshanger, they had a little workshop in the welfare (they called it the garage) where they repaired cars and got them ready for MOT. When they packed up, they would estimate the value and buy an equally ropey old banger instead. I authorised many strange things. We even bought washing machines.'

Kent was a fortunate area. With small numbers, well organised and early into the field collecting money, it had more resources per head than any other area. Other areas joked that they were raising enough money to buy their three pits. But elsewhere, and particularly in the big Yorkshire area, fund-raising was more difficult. It was much less organised than the picketing which the area saw as its priority and would have much greater demands made on it.

One of the keys was support from local authorities. South Yorkshire, the north-east and to a great extent South Wales have a life that is almost entirely dependent on the public sector. Jobs, housing and welfare depend to an enormous extent on the Coal Board and on municipal and local health authorities which provide both services and employment. For example, when the Cortonwood pit, which had sparked the strike, closed in October 1985, the local village of Brampton saw it as the beginning of a wind-down which included likely cuts at the municipalised bus company, Yorkshire Traction, and the closure of a local school.

Just as many of the pits link up underground, mining the same coal reserves, so the villages which adjoin them in South Yorkshire butt against one another, stretching for miles over ridges lined with municipal terraces. Most of the housing is either erected by the Coal Board or local authority. So traditionally many of those who sit on the authorities, Labour-controlled in perpetuity, have been miners, anxious to look after the interests of miners.

This close link led early in the strike to a conscious effort by miners and their sympathisers on local authorities to use whatever resources they legally could to assist the strikers. In Durham, the NUM detached a local councillor to try to maximise the assistance they could get even from non-Labour councils.

The first steps were taken early when local councils such as Doncaster, Barnsley and Chesterfield announced that they would give free school meals to miners' children. That was soon extended to providing them in the holidays as well. In April Doncaster was feeding over 4,000 children in the school holidays at a cost of £12,000 a day. That was followed by an offer by the education committee to provide vouchers for free shoes to miners' children. Chesterfield voted £50,000 for miners' welfare in early May. Strathclyde made interest-free loans of over £1 million under local Scottish legislation.

One of the biggest contributions which councils made was over the collection of rates and rents. Rates were largely waived, while rents were reduced or foregone completely. In parallel, as it became obvious that the strike was to be a long one, huge funds and, more often, provisions in kind, were made available by trade unions, often in spite of misgivings about the conduct of the strike by their leaders. Hundreds of thousands also came from sympathetic groups such as local Labour parties who twinned with pits and a variety of support groups, as well as from overseas.

It is impossible to know how much money and supplies were received by the NUM. Some of it went to the union's national solidarity fund and was then distributed to areas and pits; much went directly to areas and individual collieries.

It came from an extraordinary variety of sources, from the £1 million plus from the official trade union movement of the Soviet Union to the contributions of the eleven Lesbian and Gay Men's Miners Support groups which were established. Their London group raised £5,650 at a single 'Pits and Perverts' concert where a South Wales miner told the audience, 'You have worn our badge, "Coal not Dole", and you know what harassment means, as we do. Now we will pin your badge on us. We will support you. It won't change overnight but now 140,000 miners know that there are other causes and other problems. We know about blacks, and gays, and nuclear disarmament, and we will never be the same.'[8] It was a graphic measure of the way the search for funds and support had broadened the outlook of mining communities.

The biggest contributions came from the trade unions, many compensating for their unwillingness fully to support the aims of the miners' leadership by instead providing succour to their communities. The General, Municipal and Boilermakers gave over £1 million including £210,000 in food vouchers at the rate of £7,000 a week, plus a loan of £½ million interest free.

But a number of unions made sure that their money should not be diverted into paying for picketing and other expenditures by contributing only or mainly in kind. So the ISTC, made responsible by the International Metalworkers Federation for distributing its contribution of £450,000 in kind and cash, made sure that it all went in the form of food parcels and toys.

It led to some amusing incidents. John Foley, the ISTC's man in South Wales, had ordered 3,000 turkeys and was suddenly rung up by the farmer to ask where he wanted the birds delivered – live. Jim Slater of the Seamen got a message from New Zealand that a container of frozen lamb carcasses was on its way to his offices. He quickly arranged with the Co-op to distribute an equivalent amount and re-routed the container to them.

The printing unions were particularly effective and experienced fund-raisers. Tens of thousands of pounds were donated from Fleet Street, particularly assisting Kent miners who were all supplied with Christmas turkeys so large that some could not fit into their ovens. All told, SOGAT branches are estimated to have raised over £1 million in cash and kind for the miners with about £35,000 coming from central funds. On one occasion a convoy of eleven lorries took deliveries up to Barnsley. Miners afterwards attempted to return the favour when the printers employed by Rupert Murdoch were sacked a year later.

But the supplies were not shared equally. Yorkshire was markedly less supplied than some other areas per head. Jack Taylor, the Yorkshire president says, 'The sad thing about the dispute was the tremendous hardship people suffered in Yorkshire. The union could not provide for that. You would never have dreamt that the hardship people suffered would take place. We ought to have had more people collecting money, but the lads saw it as their duty to picket. Perhaps the union was not organised enough.' By the time Yorkshire got round to organising, most of the best lucrative big city centres were being worked by other areas.

Kent were by far the most successful money-raisers, but their success was resented. Jack Collins says, 'We were criticised by a number of other areas and women's groups who said we had had thousands of pounds and kept it to ourselves.

'But we did send money to other areas. We sent £50,000. We also looked after other miners. We had their children for holidays. We put them with our people and gave them a couple of pounds each.

'The *Morning Star* carried stories of French miners handing us over £20,000. Actually it was £2,000 and we were the only area printing the thousands of leaflets for the London meetings. We said that since we had nowhere else to collect we would do it in London for 20 per cent. That was not accepted. But after all we had set up the organisation in London. We were responsible for the picketing there. But other people came into London and thought it was all for collecting money. We said there was really no need to send people to collect money; we should have been trusted.'

Kent also benefited from the fact, much noticed, that there was a lot of money and support to be had from the south, from places far removed from mining areas but from individuals and groups such as local Labour parties who were anxious to give support to the miners because they saw them as resisting Thatcherism, and were, of course, touched by the suffering and the general romanticism about miners.

A number of trade union leaders ironically noted that when it came to workplace collections and sympathy for the miners, often it was those farthest away from mining areas which produced the most. Closer to home, other groups of workers, who had experienced redundancy in their own industries with payments far less than those on offer to the miners, were more critical.

The South Wales NUM, for example, found that it raised more money (£110,000) in Oxford than it did in Cardiff, and that per head of population it got most out of the Southampton/Portsmouth conurbation on the south coast. Basingstoke was another fruitful area for Welsh collecting, and the way that individuals identified with their cause was shown by the donation by one old lady of jewellery worth £12,000.

Another such was Andrew Bain, a wealthy businessman in the Sussex commuter belt town of East Grinstead. Bain, who was 74, describes himself as the only 'socialist capitalist' in the town. His father knew Keir Hardie. His business is the manufacture of vacuum cleaner parts, and he and his vans drive up and down the motorways to collect them from manufacturers and distribute them to his supply depots. In the process they visit and pass through mining areas. During the strike he used them to distribute supplies to the miners, loading them with meat and vegetables, or bringing a hundredweight of dripping to cook the potatoes.

Bain, who has no formal party affiliation, is frank about his motives about helping the miners. 'It was mainly because I got a great kick out of seeing them and striking a blow against such a stupid government.'

Bain's introduction to the strike was on a visit to Edlington, near Doncaster, to pick up some parts from a local engineering workshop. Fancying a drink at the conclusion of his business in mid-morning, he suggested the nearby miners' welfare club. There he was astonished to find a large group of men already inside. When he asked why, it was gently explained to him that they were on strike. The first £50 of the £6,000 or £7,000 he was to contribute to the NUM cause was handed over to buy them beer.

Bain's contribution spread wide. He put up £750, half the money, for a record in aid of the miners to be cut by Kellingley Colliery Band. He also visited and assisted pits in Ayrshire in Scotland and in Durham, using a personal letter from Arthur Scargill thanking him for his help over the record as an introduction.

Edlington, where Bain encountered the striking miners, is a big sprawling village about four miles out of Doncaster, and contiguous with the ribbon development which stretches out from the town. Off the main street stretch lines of municipal-style Coal Board and council housing, of varying ages, some of them with their façades covered with an artificial stone fronting, which is popular among miners.

There is a ridge behind the pit from which you can look across the flat plain of the Don, past the pits around the town of Doncaster and away to the smoke and steam arising from the chimneys and cooling towers of the huge power stations out to the agricultural east which take their power from these collieries.

The pits here are little different from those in Nottingham, a few miles south. Large and with good reserves, their lack of productivity when compared to their neighbours was a continuing source of irritation and frustration to the Coal Board throughout the 1970s and early 1980s. In temper, the area is militant, with a tradition of sudden strikes at a number of pits at a time.

Yorkshire Main, the Edlington colliery, was typical. Its miners claimed it was making a small profit before the strike, but relations between men and management were bad. The pit was on strike for a fortnight before the national action began over an internal dispute where men refused to work a new heading which they believed to be wrongly planned and unsafe. It was a bitter disagreement, with pickets on the gates and managers stoned when they attempted to go in.

There follows the account of four of the men involved: David Windle, who was the branch chairman; Mick Hassett, the treasurer who was also secretary of the large and active Miners' Welfare Club which stood next to the pit; Jim Kelly, a young Scotsman who was an enthusiastic picket and took Hassett's job as treasurer of the branch; and George Smith, the personnel manager, who had been at the pit for fourteen years.

Windle, who comes from an old mining family (his father was branch secretary at the old Orgreave pit) starts the story: 'I was proud to be associated with this branch. There was always something going on. The officials were available all the time and that was appreciated by the members. The pit had a very low scab rate because no one could accuse us of being unhelpful. We cared and shared and even staff [white-collar] members were treated the same.

'Before the strike this pit was making a lot of money. It was a profitable pit in a loss-making area. A lot of men were working very hard down the pit and yet pits which were losing were taking home five or six times as much bonus. I think one thing led to another.

'Once the main strike started I took the full brunt of much of the picket organising. I would come down to the Miners' Welfare at one in the morning in order for people to be in Notts by 4.30. On the wall we had a chart of everyone who had a car, his name, address and phone number, and those men would have a regular car full.

'We would say to the driver, be at the Welfare at eight o'clock at night. He would then get hold of the others to be at the Welfare at 2 a.m., but we still wouldn't tell him where he was going until he actually came. Then we would say to another lot of cars, we want you here at nine o'clock and they might go somewhere quite different. Mick Hassett, our treasurer, would go over to Brodsworth the previous evening and get the instructions from the area agent. They were given by word of mouth.'

Jim Kelly describes the start of picketing at a time when the Yorkshire area had instructed men not to go into other coal fields: 'We were already in dispute. At one of our meetings it was said that all those who wanted to go picketing, would go. We were formed into teams. We knew they would be carrying on in Notts, so we were organised to cover all shifts.

We were deputed to cover the night shift.

'On the Monday, Barnsley had told us to keep away from Notts so as not to interfere with their ballot, but the message never came over until the morning. By then a lot of lads had turned up at 4.30 in the morning, all ready with flasks and snap tins and very enthusiastic. They were told by the branch officials that they wouldn't be going. But some of them decided, "We're here; we're going."

'Then as the week progressed, it was decided that we were going out. We were reorganised and we were given Newstead to picket.

'We went there on the same morning that the trouble flared at Ollerton. It was quite happy. We stopped the afternoon shift. As men got off the buses, we spoke to them – myself and our spokesman. Many said they were not going to cross a picket line, then one decided to go over in a car without asking anyone, and knocked one of our lads over.

'It had been very good up to then. We were even using the pit canteen. But then one or two lads chased after the car and the police got involved. Five or six van loads from a different division appeared.

'After that we started to have difficulty getting into Notts. [Note: the roadblock policy was established by police later that week.] We did get in; but it was pretty difficult getting to the pit of your choice. So we moved down to Leicester pits on the night shift. But we couldn't get anywhere near the pit. Villages would be policed to stop pickets getting through.'

Kelly did manage to get through to the control room in one pit, but he was pursued by a policeman and taken back: 'He spoke pleasantly enough to me across the yard, but once we got over the white line and amongst his colleagues, he said loudly that he would "have me" if I ever crossed the white line again.

'After that, because of the difficulties, we were set to picket Harworth. We left our cars and walked across the fields.'

Kelly then took part in a pre-arranged ruse to get Yorkshire pickets into Notts. He travelled down in mid-May to the big demonstration at Mansfield. But instead of returning, he took an ordinary bus service to the village of Blidworth where he and about 40 others were put up in houses and, in his case, a tent in the garden.

'The people in the houses were on strike. It was about 60/40 there with the sixty per cent working. But it was slowly changing; more were going back. So they had asked for some Yorkshire people down there because we were not getting through. They were saying that the spirit of those who had stayed out had ebbed away, and so they wanted some encouragement.'

They were discovered by police the next day, and finally ordered to leave three days later. 'We were only on £4 a day so we couldn't afford to go to the pub. We were lazing about, playing cards and going to the pit for shift changes.

'At the end of the week, we were invited into houses and given home-made beer and wine. While we were there one of our lads had to go back to the tent to get his jacket. When he got there, he found a policeman already in it. He asked what he was doing, but he made an exit and disappeared.

'He looked where he had been and found a torch with a police number on it. So he hid it because he thought the police were going to come back under the excuse of looking for stolen property.

'Then the police came. There must have been about ten vans. They blocked off the end of the street, and when we tried to leave for the shift change, they said if we left the gardens they would get us for trespassing. They arrested our leader for stepping onto the street. They really came down heavy on us, and the following day we got an ultimatum; either go or we'll arrest you. So we left.'

A different view of the picketing was taken by George Smith, the personnel manager, after his experiences when the pit was on strike before most of the rest of Yorkshire. Smith, a cheerful, good-natured man, liked and respected by men at the colliery, has this to say: 'We would all meet in the pub yard of the Cecil, about a mile away and leave our cars there. We came down in the van on the first day and there must have been about a thousand pickets strung across the gate. The police inspector had told us that he didn't want a head-on clash but the NUM secretary said we were not going through even though there was already a management night shift in the pit. So the inspector said we should go round the back and climb over the tip.

'We got up the side and under the screens. There must have been a foot of mud. Then all of a sudden a great group of people converged on us; there must have been 300 of them. They were baying "kill the bastards". They were throwing all sorts of things and the deputy mechanical engineer stopped a brick in the side of his face. We ran back out again and there was a single police constable there. When they saw him, they stopped. The van was down at the bottom of the tip and we went straight to the police station. They took a look at the engineer and said "it's a stitching job", and took him to hospital in a police car.

'We didn't get into the pit, but they decided to let the others out. So then the area director went on television and said they were pulling all the plugs out; all machinery would be stopped and the pit would accumulate gas. We were back in the pit within 24 hours.

'After that it calmed down, but even so it lasted a year, and as soon as I started to approach the picket line from the Cecil my heart used to start pounding and I never got over it.

'During the strike we were split into three shifts and I was in charge of one. There were only five of us on the back shift. We had to check the methane, the boilers, the ventilation and the compressors. It was terrible. You never did go out; all you did was shout.

'People picking coal were like ants. They were coming in all over the place with bags. If you saw anyone, you went to the phone. You constantly found that your cars were scratched. You got nails in your tyres. I had been through 1972 and 1974 and there was nothing like this.'

Meanwhile Windle and Hassett on the union side were busy organising welfare for their 1,300 members. Windle says: 'During the strike I seemed to be everybody's father and mother. It was very hard physically and emotionally. I was very proud of my wife. I don't know how she managed. We have four children and the door was ever open; the phone was never still. I knew everybody and I suppose people thought, and rightly so, that I would understand the problems that families were having.

'At the start of the strike there were many babies imminent. So we advertised for baby clothes, cots, prams and so on. We got a tremendous response. I used to go and collect the stuff, often from people who would say, "We don't believe in the strike, but we don't like to see babies suffering hardship."

'I also got on surprisingly well with Coal Board officials. If people were really in trouble, and I knew that they were suffering, something would be done about getting fuel to them. But the management of the pit itself wouldn't do anything.

'Socially we did a good job, covering every aspect of it. We tried to make support non-political because you could forfeit support talking politics.'

Windle also went to Belgium accompanying 50 children from the Yorkshire area and used the opportunity to raise funds: 'I could see a lot of the people there were not politically motivated. I tried to keep as much as possible on the social welfare aspect. They took us very much to their hearts and invited us over again. And people from there would come over with big car loads of food and clothing.'

Mick Hassett had a key role in organising the welfare side. For some years he had run not only the union benevolent fund but also a pithead shop for the miners. It had considerable funds and it would also buy large items, like washing machines, which miners wanted from stores in Doncaster, allowing men to pay back over a period. Its funds, and ability to make advances, were to come in very handy during the strike. Hassett bent his attention to seeing what money in the village might be available for the hardship fund he rapidly established and pulled together about £3,000.

'From the first meeting of the strike we decided to form a hardship committee. Our first aim was to see to the single miners. They got nothing from social security. To start with we paid each single miner £2 a week. But we had to stop paying after some months because we had such a lot. It was a young pit with an average age of about 36.

'As the strike went on, we received money allocated from the national fund on a membership basis. It came either as cash or food vouchers.'

The distribution of the food took place at weekend branch meetings held in the miners' welfare club. 'We had as many as a thousand people to meetings. Branch policy was that members must attend a meeting. We always had packed meetings, and had to put extra loudspeakers in the overflow bar.'

At the meeting, there would be a draw for food parcels: 'Every member had a card with his name and his lamp number on it, specially printed. The cards from all those at the meeting would be placed in a drum and someone from the floor was called to draw them. There would be about 300 food parcels, and the winning cards would not go into the drum the following week. So everyone was guaranteed a parcel about once every three weeks.

'They were mainly meat parcels to a value of £5 though they were a bargain. We had a very good butcher. You got six or seven items – chops, sausages, mince, liver, bacon and so on. Each week we would also get food from the contact point at Doncaster and those parcels would also go into the draw. But we would draw the meat first.'

There was no women's support group as such in Edlington until quite late in the strike. Even then it was outside the union, as the NUM branch insisted on controlling what was going on. It organised its own meal centre run by wives and mothers. 'We had three-course meals, always meat. We used to feed between two and three hundred. Funnily enough, we hardly ever had children. It was used by people on picket-lines and single men. There was a very good response by traders in the village. but we couldn't compare with some other places. We didn't have the facilities.

'Altogether we received about £50,000 from national and area level. We assisted with rent, with electricity bills. We liaised with the Yorkshire Electricity Board. People used to pay in a pound a week. The Doncaster council were very good. We had rates paid and part of the rent. But I was surprised by the number of people in private accommodation who could only be helped with money.

'We used to vet people every week. We had the shop facilities. When people said they couldn't afford things they needed, we said we can make you an advance and you repay it.

'You got some individuals who were always coming and asking. I would never take it on on my own. That's why we had the hardship committee. So the responsibility wasn't one person's.'

Jim Kelly, with two children, described how he managed: 'My wife was working part-time at the hospital doing cleaning. That was the only way we were managing. She brought in about £35 a week. The children of course got free school meals. My father-in-law was a deputy, and not on strike, so we would go up there on Sunday for lunch. They also looked after the kids although we didn't ask for anything. How many people had working wives? I don't know. Probably less than half.'

Life continued in this way through the summer of 1984, one in which many miners liked to describe as the time they 'went through the pain barrier' and found themselves learning to cope. In Edlington the pit was peaceful. 'For many months', says Windle, 'we were always welcome in the pit yard to discuss on a man-to-man basis.'

Jim Kelly says, 'We didn't need to picket so we used pensioners and others. The local police used to give them Mars Bars and so on. There was no anti-strike feeling among them. But later the outside forces they brought in just didn't care.'

The change came at the end of the summer when the first men started to return to work, initially from outside the village.

George Smith was closely involved in the arrangements for the NCB: 'Amongst the first to come back were the more elderly with the intention of taking redundancy. Just prior to the strike I had approached the union about the number of men who wanted to go, and there was about 90.

'The first man actually in the village to attempt to come back was in October. They surrounded his house and put his windows in. He gave them a promise that he wouldn't go back. They told me that a shop had put up a sign saying he and his wife were not welcome on the premises.

'The next man to come in had his house burnt [though Windle claims it was an electrical fault associated with contractors' work]. We saved a bit of his furniture and kept it in the stores.

'It seemed to put the others off. Then we had two men come in over the tip. Later they contacted us on three occasions and tried to come in but each time they found their houses were being watched, so they didn't come in.

'Then there was the blacksmith. But he got beaten up in a fight and we didn't see him again.'

Windle and Hassett had been responsible for persuading the first man not to return. Windle describes the event: 'We had just returned from getting the picketing instructions. We heard there were a lot of people up at his house and we took it upon ourselves to go up. We found about 300 round the house. There were five or six police there and we asked the inspector if we would be allowed to go into the house if we dispersed the crowd, which we did.

'We then went in and saw him. We asked if he was in difficulties and a very amicable situation was reached. There was no bribery and no threats. We invited the inspector to come in with us, but he didn't. He hovered in the next room, but I think he was earwigging. He was a bit courteous.'

Windle says he asked the man whether he was going back because of hardship and asked why he had not approached the union for help. 'He replied that he was not that sort of man. I said that it was not a matter of giving, but of helping each other. So I appealed to him and I said I would go into the shop thirty yards from his house which had put up his name saying he would not be served, and ask them to take the sign out of the window.'

Kelly took a harsher view of the affair. 'There were two schools of thought. Some said that as he had gone back, he should be treated like a scab. Others that he wasn't a scab because he had come out again. My feeling was that he could carry on going back.'

In September the branch prepared a letter to men who returned to work. Signed by the secretary, Ian Ferguson, it said, 'If you continue with your present strike breaking action, the end of the strike will without doubt be the beginning of considerable difficulty for yourselves. Have you considered the prospect of facing the men you have betrayed and caused to hate you in a way that I have never known in my long experience as a branch official?

'We believe that the NCB have made you certain promises and assurances that they can not fulfil and I therefore ask that you agree to discuss the matter with me as I consider that it is in all our interests to do so, more for you than for us.

'If you agree, let the bearer of the letter know and I will come in and we can discuss the matter objectively.'

Kelly went out trying to spot returning miners: 'Our pit is quite a cosmopolitan pit. Quite a lot of people come from different places outside the village. There was a section who lived in one area of Doncaster who went back to work.

'We would try to spot them. We would drive around what we thought the route of the bus would be and every so often local people would say, "We think so-and-so is going in." We would send out a car looking for lights on in the morning. Sometimes we would get names and addresses and we would park up to see if a police car, or an unmarked car, came.

'We had about fifty back and we spotted about half. The branch officials tried to approach them but it was never any good. If you asked someone, "Are you going back to work?", most of the reaction was, "No, I am not".'

The return of working miners brought a much bigger police presence to the pit. It was also used because of its good facilities as a staging and reserve post for police. Windle was greatly upset: 'We were very heavily policed. Sometimes there were too many to get into the pit yard. There were some local sergeants inside the buildings but the rest were Metropolitan police in the main.

'Their behaviour was scandalous. A lot of shops refused to serve them and put up signs saying police on picket duty would not be served. They used to call out obscene things to women as they passed and people used to be pushed out of the way by them in shops. The police in charge were OK. But then the Mets came and if there was no senior men around they would be all over the place, hitting and kicking and truncheoning.'

Both Windle and Kelly were arrested on the same day, 31 August, the day after the first man returned to work. Kelly says, 'They used to have Metropolitan police inside the pit. The others would be outside when the bus arrived, then afterwards when we were dispersing, the Metropolitan police would sometimes come out, shout something and pull a couple of pickets out. On that day, they were coming out and jumping over the wall by the entrance. Three of them got me and I was being kicked on the ground until some of our lads set about them.' He spent a day and a night in the cells accused of criminal damage, threatening behaviour and breach of the peace, but the case was later dropped.

Windle says, 'The bus had just gone in and I said to the Superintendent, "I am going to leave six on the top and bottom gates." There was a big crowd to disperse and I did that. I was making my way back to the top gate when suddenly hordes of police came over the wall from inside. My view was that they were trying to show some justification for having so many police there for just 250 pickets.

'I looked at the bus-shelter and there must have been six of them on one man, hammering him and banging his head against the wall. The next thing I felt was being strangled with my arm bent up my back. There were two lads on me.

'I was dragged through the top gate, but the most terrifying thing about it in all my 23 years at the pit was when I was taken through an outer door into the conference room. It was quite different. It was full of chairs and tables and police eating. As we were being dragged through, the police threw tea and half-eaten bread at us. I don't know what stopped me crying.

'The man in front was dragged through a reinforced glass fire door which shattered. They were saying things like, "Oh what a nasty little accident." I found that the Met constables were telling South Yorkshire sergeants what to do, as though they regarded them as nothing, saying, "It's my collar" and so on.'

The case against Windle was later dismissed because of lack of evidence. But the event has scarred him: 'What the strike has done has been to leave a lot of genuine people with no trust at all in the police. I used to think the Irish were nutters and the blacks had a chip on their shoulder but if that's the type of person who is policing those areas, then God help Britain.'

After the strike, the pit failed to revive. Management took a tough line, cancelling local deals about extra payments, and men complained that they spent weeks on clearing up and taking inventories of material down the pit, and that they were unable to earn bonus pay. A new production target was set but when after several weeks the pit had only got about half way there, the board proposed its closure. By a very big majority the men agreed, the first pure economic closure in Yorkshire since the strike. It was not surprising when Cortonwood took the same decision a few days later.

'Sitting and thinking about the strike now,' says Jim Kelly, 'it could have been handled differently. But at the time we weren't concerned. I was proud to have been part of it. I was solid to the end. The only sad thing was that my colliery got caught up in redundancy fever because they had so many debts. But I was astonished at the way branch officials took redundancy.' Kelly has stayed in the industry, the only one of the four not to leave.

George Smith, the manager, said as he watched the men come up the shaft after coaling for the last time officially, 'I was disgusted by the hypocrisy of it all. For twelve months, men stood on picket lines abusing you and saying they were fighting for their jobs, and against pit closures.

'I know people who had abused us and threatened us on the picket line and then were the first to put in for redundancy. I put up a notice asking for men to apply for a form if they wanted redundancy. I had 300 vacancies and I got 520 applications, 7 of them from the committee. After the strike it was never the same. We started to manage and they didn't like it.'

David Windle says, 'I would never have thought of redundancy if it had not been for the strike. But I would never have thought of transfer to another pit either. Our pit could have been a great pit. I came here from Orgreave when it closed. I have seen four people killed down the pit. But I still think it's the most enjoyable, finest job you could have. I have worked with the finest people you could ever meet. I have had the most fantastic working life one could ever imagine.'

The final word might be left to John Weaver, a member of the NUM national executive throughout the strike, who came from Yorkshire Main colliery. Looking back at the strike he says, 'I don't think you will ever see the like of it again. There isn't another industry which could do it.'

12
'Our enemies' front-line troops'

On 25 October 1984 Mr Justice Nicholls, sitting in a court in the crypts of the High Courts of Justice in the Strand, started to hear the case for contempt of court against the NUM.

As the case began, counsel passed forward a television video cassette, neatly tied up in legal pink ribbon like some early Christmas present. Perched a few feet away was a large television set, specially installed for the day, from which in due course there burst a blast of over-amplified sound, followed by the voice of Arthur Scargill.

It was a graphic illustration of the way that presentation of the dispute in the media, and particularly the television coverage of it, came to obsess the parties involved, with the messenger frequently blamed because their message did not come across to their satisfaction, and on occasions both sides believing that the delicate chemistry which might have produced a settlement had been upset by excessive media interest and disclosure.

In his Sheffield headquarters, Arthur Scargill would keep the Ceefax news service flickering endlessly across the screen, switching to each news broadcast as it appeared. A hundred and fifty miles south, the Department of Energy, under Peter Walker, was paying £1,000 a week at one stage for a monitoring agency to record any broadcast on the strike and facsimile the text to the department.

In any major public sector strike, the battle for public opinion is seen as of crucial importance. Even when the cause appears unpopular, governments are watchful for the moment when antipathy to those taking the action causing inconvenience turns instead to a compulsive belief that enough is enough and that something, anything, must be done by the government to end the mess.

And there are occasions, more rare, when public opinion suddenly solidifies into accepting the justice of the case put by one side or the other. For the miners, there was obvious precedent in the 1972 strike when the public became aware of the low wages being paid for the miners' difficult job, and even the Conservative *Daily Express* demanded, 'Give them the money.'

It is never simply a matter of argument. There is another dimension – the conduct of the dispute which can colour and overshadow the argument. This was true above all in the miners' strike. Television's portrayal, night after night, of the violent scenes on the picket lines, deliberately intimidating from the first days of the strike and rising to unimagined crescendos of violence involving both pickets and police as matters progressed, were, many would argue, the crucial factor preventing public opinion ever swinging unambiguously to the miners' side.[1] It led the Labour Party and the TUC when they entered the propaganda battle late in the game to differentiate sharply between the miners' aims – 'The Case for Coal' – and the methods sometimes used to promote them, while the government's supporters were moved to insist that there could be no surrender to conduct of this violent sort.

In the process, the media came to be ranked undifferentiated alongside the police, judiciary and government by Arthur Scargill as the shock troops of the Establishment against the striking miners. Deliberately and as a matter of routine identified as 'vermin' in the warm-up part of almost every Scargill speech, reporters and, more particularly, television crews felt the imprint of miners' fists and boots in a way rare in other disputes. Equipment and vehicles were sabotaged and smashed. Yet ironically miners would spend hours videotaping the scenes from the picket lines they had rushed home to see. 'Never', said one member of the NUM executive at the end of the strike, 'have I watched so much television news.' In part it was necessity; appearances on the media were one of Arthur Scargill's most used ways of passing messages to his membership.

So to an unprecedented extent in a British industrial dispute, the media became itself an issue. Its roles varied – a messenger boy, its missives, electronic or typographical, scrutinised microscopically by both sides; on occasions a mediator, arguably even a participant and actor on the stage dominated by two of the wiliest manipulators of the media of their breed. One was Arthur Scargill, combining remarkably mastery of two key but often contradictory techniques, swaying a mass meeting and also dominating a small-scale television interview. The other was not Ian MacGregor but Energy Minister Peter Walker. Sometimes belittled, unfairly, by his cabinet colleagues as simply a 'journalist', his relatively rare public appearances before the government dropped its 'hands off' pretence in July, belied the fact that presentation of both the Coal Board's and the government's case had been and continued to be a matter of daily discussion, planning and personal briefing by him throughout the strike.

Arthur Scargill has never been one to underestimate the impact of the media. From the time when he gave journalists lifts in his bronze Ford Zodiac and enthused about the banners coming over the hill at Saltley in 1972 to his elevation to Yorkshire president, his public relations sense was acute. But he has always gone to great lengths to ensure that it is on his own terms. As Yorkshire president, all press enquiries were channelled through him and he was almost the only national executive member of the time whose telephone number was not generally available to journalists covering the union's affairs.

At national executive meetings and Coal Board negotiations his stock-in-trade was to leave meetings first in order to give his figures or his interpretation of what had been proposed. The practice infuriated the then president, Joe Gormley, whose press conference would be held in the executive room after the executive had left. Nowadays, in the Sheffield tower block which houses the NUM offices, Scargill heads straight for a separate press briefing room and his press conference is given usually before the rest of the executive have emerged eight floors below.

When he became national president, the casual openness of the NUM's London office became tightly constrained. All calls into the building were logged, identifying who called whom. Instructions were given for all press calls, even about routine time and place information, to go to a newly appointed press officer, Nell Myers. Others, not even the editor of the union's newspaper, were not empowered to speak in her absence. For a while some journalists managed to short-circuit the system by using direct-line numbers, but with the move to Sheffield and the replacement of most of the senior office staff this soon ceased.

In the 1972 and 1974 strikes the NUM headquarters had been open house for journalists who could talk to officials and the Kent pickets manning the control centre, drinking with them later in the pubs in the streets behind. It was in keeping with the gregarious style of the national officials, Gormley and general secretary Lawrence Daly. But in 1984–5 matters were tightly controlled. Few national journalists went to the Sheffield headquarters except for the fortnightly executive meetings. There was no open access to the eighth floor offices. On occasions selected newspaper journalists got off-the-record briefings from Scargill, but they were rare.

At press conferences, a new combative atmosphere prevailed. NUM staff with video cameras filmed the proceedings, including the questioners. On some occasions demonstrating strikers were allowed in to listen, applaud and sometimes heckle. There was particular applause when Scargill told one reporter complaining that he had not answered a question about violence that he had asked the question three times, and although it was not the answer he wanted, it was the one he was going to get.

This approach was possible because Scargill's domination of the executive and the running of the strike, and his personal charisma meant that the media were beating a path to his door. Every day there was a rally at which he could lay out the agenda he wanted in a speech, and, if he wished, answer questions on issues which came up during the day. At the same time, his staff would be receiving a stream of requests for interviews. Like Peter Walker (from July onwards) he could pick and choose which he wanted to do, knowing the words would be picked up everywhere else.

From early on it became a practice for the NUM president to say he would only be interviewed live (so that his words could not be edited or shortened) or 'as live' (where an interview, though recorded in advance, had to be shown in full). It was a demand rarely acceded to by BBC TV News – which had few live interviews except at lunchtime – rather more often accommodated by ITN News on ITV, but most provided for by current affairs programmes with a regular discussion format such as the BBC's *Newsnight* and ITN's *Channel Four News*, which had longer running times. By the end of the dispute, the NUM president had added a further demand. He was trying to insist on a minimum period of time, asking, for example, for a full ten minutes on one occasion on *Channel Four News*.

Predictably it was *Newsnight* and *Channel Four News* which were picked out for praise by Scargill in his speech to the Edinburgh Television Festival in 1984. Current affairs, he said, had touched on the facts, the implications and what it meant to human beings at the centre. It was news that was the problem. It was 'not news at all, pure unadulterated bias.'

The difficulty for him was that news audiences were vastly larger – 6 million or so in the early evening in June 1984, going up to 8 million later at night. By contrast *Newsnight* could draw a million viewers and *Channel Four News* about 600,000.

The other key bulletin was the BBC Radio Four morning *Today* programme. It had an audience of only about 1.2 million at its morning peak but they included a disproportionate number of opinion-formers including, regularly, the prime minister herself. It also enabled interviewees to set the tone for the day, and to know that what they said would be picked up by evening papers and broadcasts throughout the day.

Considerations like this were meat and drink to Peter Walker. One government minister who had been closely associated with the coal industry described a politician's relationship like this: 'Politicians are so much the children of the media. They see it as a reflection of public opinion. But they themselves are an odd combination – at once both creation and master of it.'

Walker's way of dealing with the conundrum was direct. Another minister who went to work for him described his amazement at the width of Walker's contacts and found him ringing round Sunday newspaper editors on a Saturday afternoon. There was even a story of one long-serving Sunday editor who left a space on his front page for something big because he had failed to get his regular call from Walker who, he assumed, must be up to something. A hurried fill-in had to be arranged when Walker telephoned late in the afternoon to explain he had been shopping with his wife.

Walker's practical appreciation of the way the media operated was in action from the start, putting the government view in a subtle way, and limiting the damage caused by the ineptness of the Coal Board spokesmen until he decided to discard the fig-leaf of non-involvement four months into the strike. His morning meeting covered 'media events' as a matter of course, as well as what was happening in Parliament or on picket lines. As one key participant put it, 'It dealt with details, like how many trains were running; signals about *Newsnight* tonight; did we need to field someone? The media was seen as tremendously important. Public opinion is a very powerful factor on how any government handles a dispute. It's a very chancy thing.'

This was basic Whitehall prudence. But the system was still better than in most post-war industrial disputes. Where Walker made a qualitative difference was in his personal contact with influential journalists and his regular weekend briefing. He was, quite simply, friends with a number of editors. Sir David English of the *Daily Mail*, a key contact who was also in touch with other Fleet Street editors, lived in the same short street, a couple of doors away. Andrew Neil, recently appointed to the *Sunday Times*, which regularly pointed to good coal stock figures and ran an embarrassingly fulsome profile of Walker during the strike, had once worked for Walker. Rupert Murdoch, the owner of the *Times* newspapers and the two biggest circulation papers in their class, the *Sun* and the *News of the World*, was at least an acquaintance, though relations with the *Sun* editor, Kelvin Mackenzie, were cool. Even Robert Maxwell, who had at first offered help to Scargill when he took over the *Mirror* group, later became close to Walker. Sir Alastair Burnet, on the ITN board, presenter of *News at Ten* and also a director of the *Times*, was another friend on occasion rung by Walker.

It was a formidable list of connections and not left to gather dust. As one associate put it, 'It was marvellous. Here was a man who could spring from his seat and ring a friend in the cause. Of course it wasn't so good for the journalist; he would find his editor had got a bee in his bonnet.'

There are plenty of examples, some trivial, of Walker's influence, and, perhaps more significant, of editors' own concern not to rock the boat.

So a story in the *Daily Express* about the launch of a new boiler which could switch from fuel to fuel was dropped because it might suggest concern about coal supplies. On another occasion, after a telephone call, a paragraph was inserted in a popular paper story about talks stressing the NCB's new determined line. Most famously, an indiscreet remark about privatising pits from Treasury Minister, John Moore, was taken out.

Walker's particular target was the Sunday press. In particular he often selected the unfashionable *News of the World*, whose traditionally lurid coverage of sex and violence had brought it the long-established nickname of the 'screws of the world'. This was the paper which in 1984 regularly carried signed articles by the Energy Minister. It had the largest Sunday readership and was popular among miners. As a Walker aide put it, 'It was the miners we were worried about. We weren't addressing a great audience of politically alert people. That was another game.'

The Sunday market had another appeal. Ministers believed it helped set the tone and the terms for coverage for the following week. So Walker regularly called in a number of Sunday paper political correspondents on a Friday for briefing. They included Paul Potts, political editor of the *News of the World*, and the two Joneses, Michael Jones of the *Sunday Times* and George Jones of the *Sunday Telegraph*. Significantly it was these he chose to brief and not the industrial correspondents who by contrast on the daily papers were carrying the burden of the coverage and were regarded by some in government as inclined to be too sympathetic to the miners.

The briefing would cover government attitudes, coal stocks (although actual figures were kept very close), and often a rebuttal of various Scargill statements. The department pressed its arguments and facts and drew on a detailed combing of past Scargill statements instituted by Walker which demonstrated what he saw as his Marxist utterances over the years.

It was a subtle approach which complemented the footslogging daily press relations of the NCB which was wrestling with the increasingly severe problems of its public spokesmen.

The board had started the dispute with a marked residue of goodwill and trust for its press department among industrial journalists. Under Geoff Kirk, who had been in charge since 1970, its reputation was of arguably the best press department in private or public industry with which they had to deal. The marks of that were that it would tell the truth even if inconvenient, and was kept informed through access to heads of departments. It had a wide selection of facts and figures, would dig for more, rapidly and efficiently, if asked, and it knew what was going on. It was complemented by sizeable groups of press officers in six other UK locations, who were also responsible for working on the NCB newspaper, *Coal News*. This was published monthly and sold, not given away, to miners, and some of the sales price went to a nominated pit charity. The argument was that it should be worth reading and worth buying, a valuable asset for the board particularly as its detailed tables on wage offers and redundancy payments were treated as gospel by many miners. In April 1984, a month into the strike, its print order was increased from 150,000 to 230,000 and the board took to posting it to every miner's home. Since the strike the board has sent it free to every miner. It was a token of a shift to more obvious propaganda, and as the strike continued, the NCB press office began to find it markedly more difficult to find out what was happening.

Even so the NUM was unable to put up a matching effort. Its own newspaper, the *Miner*, produced by a single person, its editor Maurice Jones, was closely supervised by Arthur Scargill himself. Its print order steadily increased from an initial 200,000 to 400,000 and its obsession with Fleet Street was obvious with regular attacks on the national media. It was the single national publication of the NUM, printed every ten days or so, at a cost of what must have been £5,000 or £6,000. It was a trivial amount compared with the other sums being spent and its appeals for cash helped defray the cost. But inexplicably from the end of August, ostensibly on the ground of cost, its print order reverted back to around the 200,000 mark and letters were sent to journalists and others to say it could only be received on payment of subscription in advance. More oddly still, any orders had to be approved formally by the national office. Only authorised subscribers were allowed to receive it, and the printers were not allowed to despatch copies without authorisation even to the support groups which sprang up in different parts of the country.

It was yet another example of the tight control of media relations under Scargill. The NUM could not match the Coal Board's press office effort. Press enquiries went to Sheffield's congested telephone. Often journalists would be told that the solitary press officer, Nell Myers, was not available, in a meeting, or had just slipped out. Usually there was no alternative person to talk to. There was a black list of journalists who were not phoned back. A suggestion that press officers should be seconded from other unions to help carry the load was rapidly dismissed by the NUM leadership, but in the north-east a journalist was attached to the Durham area for the duration of the strike.

There was one marked exception. In South Wales the union's research officer, Dr Kim Howells, who was also the picketing organiser, himself held a National Union of Journalists card and was a helpful and accessible source of information. He enjoyed the confidence of the South Wales NUM president, and was able to put across the area's views. As the strike lengthened, he became an increasingly valuable source about the national scene for national journalists, and ideas about an organised return to work without agreement which eventually ended the strike were first floated from South Wales through him, to the fury of Scargill, who made him a bitter telephone-call.

The NUM's disarray over press relations meant that Coal Board assertions, and particularly its figures, were never convincingly challenged. Early on Scargill attacked figures about pits working, particularly the ludicrous phraseology of 'working normally' when sizeable numbers of men were clearly on strike or picketed out, with some success. But when the return to work began, NCB figures, sometimes audited by accountants, could rarely be matched by union branches who had depended on the NCB even for the addresses of their own members. At Bilston Glen in Scotland, reporters had to take union return-to-work figures off pickets at the gate. For all the cracks about the Coal Board even counting the colliery cat, the union was not equipped to answer back.

On picket lines, local branch secretaries were often vocal, but at the big setpieces in Yorkshire they were often outdone by a smooth police operation, particularly in South Yorkshire where chief constable Peter Wright had laid down that chief officers on the spot should always speak to the press without waiting for an after-the-event press conference. So at Orgreave, while assistant chief constable Tony Clement gave regular updates on how he saw the situation, including his version of the incident when Arthur Scargill was injured, journalists often searched in vain for an NUM official to give a similarly coherent view. They were hampered too by hostility from the pickets themselves.

So on the climactic day at Orgreave on 18 June 1984, before the charges of mounted police, a BBC camera crew saw Arthur Scargill apparently directing operations with a walkie-talkie, and decided to try for an interview. The police line parted with some amazement to let them through. But then, as the sound recordist John Bruce describes, 'We hadn't got more than twenty yards when someone shouted at us. A huge man rammed me with his belly; another grabbed the camera cable and a third jumped onto the cameraman's back. We told them we were trying to get through to Arthur Scargill, but it made no difference. We ran back and the police lines opened. The police were laughing all over their faces.'

In Nottingham at the start of the dispute cameramen had often found themselves corralled by police some way from the action, a restriction they did their best to avoid. At Orgreave, after initial limitations, the police allowed them almost unlimited freedom, a factor which some senior officers believed had a restraining effect on the handling of pickets.

By contrast there were always great difficulties in filming among pickets. Even where persuasion worked with one group, the inchoate nature of the crowd meant that others could take a different view and attack the crew, frequently yanking out the cable connecting camera and sound recorder which had the effect of pulling over the cameraman.

Remonstrating with Arthur Scargill after an incident of this sort, one of the BBC's most experienced cameramen, Bernard Hesketh, who had filmed the Falklands war, argued that it did not help the NUM cause if he could not be interviewed because his men had damaged his camera. The Scargill reply was to the effect that if he had suffered at the hands of the media as his men had, he would do the same thing.

The attacks had started before the dispute was under way. Crews outside a Bilston Glen meeting in Scotland, where men were demanding a vote, were set upon, and as television reporters went into the Sheffield headquarters for the executive meeting which was to call the strike, a group of men tucked into a corner started to barrack, 'Here comes the lie machine.'

Bob Prabhu, a BBC sound recordist, was at Ollerton in the darkness of the third morning of the strike. 'The light came on and because they were pushing the police they didn't like being photographed. They broke the line and went in. We were trying to film it and they threw a big plank at us. It missed and instead it hit a striking miner on the nose.

'One shouted, "Don't you film this, who asked you to film?" Another miner charged up to the cameraman and pushed him off his feet. Then the police asked us to move saying we were provoking the miners on the picket line. But we hadn't even been there at the beginning. We had seen the pushing and shoving and then gone in. My view was that they didn't want us there so that they could do their own thing.

'When daylight broke, we could film from about thirty yards away and local people urged us to film the scene.

'As the dispute went on, basically there was a handful of people always wanting to have a go. That was the difference between the mining dispute and what happened when I was filming the Indira Gandhi funeral when the crowd as a whole went for us.'

Other camera teams who did regular stints in the Yorkshire coal fields claimed to recognise members of a group who appeared on numerous picket-lines inciting others to have a go at press and television.

A number of camera cars were overturned, many suffered dents and smashed windows, and cameras were smashed as well. At the particularly bitter rally in Mansfield in May, an ITN engineer attempting to fix a transmission dish was knocked down and urinated on by a group of demonstrators and as the BBC News outside broadcast van left the town, a brick smashed through the side window of its cab, luckily diverted by a suitcase on the passenger seat. Incidents of this sort were played down at the time as camera teams and reporters attempted to get on with their jobs, and police offers to take action were generally discouraged.

Considerable efforts were made to reach some *modus vivendi*. In the dark mornings, the use of lights meant that lighting men (nicknamed torchies by the miners) were an obvious focus for hostility; efforts were made to film both with and without them. There were endless arguments too along the lines that if miners wouldn't put their case, it would go by default.

But journalists covering picket lines and mining villages found difficulty in getting natural reactions. If an interview with an individual was begun, it was usually interrupted by an official anxious to give the authorised version. Ralph Smith, the BBC Radio Northern correspondent, himself living among miners near Wakefield, said, 'There seemed to be a very good early-warning system in the villages. If you approached anyone in the street, you would be very quickly passed onto the strike committee. In other places, they would be on you in a matter of seconds, not wanting to give you the party line but telling you to clear out.'

Two major broadcasting changes also meant that events on the picket line were brought to television far more vividly and immediately than in previous disputes: the use of electronic news-gathering cameras, and the advent of Breakfast Television.

ENG coverage using videotape cassettes instead of more cumbersome film, particularly in the hands of cameramen experienced in Northern Ireland or Beirut, meant that material from picket lines was available for immediate use without waiting for processing and also that clear images could be obtained with far less light. The availability of this action early in the morning was a gift to often news-starved Breakfast Television. But some would argue that the extra demands of immediate material and instant judgments plus sheer fatigue crowded out some more long-term approaches. Often the fullest and more diverse coverage came in lunchtime news bulletins with later newscasts, under pressure from events later in the day, and the inevitable battle of words between the protagonists, reducing the picket-line coverage to highlights, sometimes voiced by people who had not been there.

These were problems appreciated by the broadcasters, conscious of the constraints of their timeframe. Miners inevitably believed that they had a better opportunity to set out their case on the current affairs programmes. They enjoyed the chant of 'Channel Four, Channel Four' to bait other crews. The irony was that the same ITN crews who were being abused were those who were shooting the Channel Four pictures, just as their BBC counterparts were being used by *Newsnight*.

The most innovative coverage was the *Channel Four News* brainwave of providing Scargill and MacGregor with the technical facilities to set out their case. Characteristically Scargill emphasised the human arguments about communities, doing interviews and delivering a piece to camera on a picket line without a fluff, while MacGregor demonstrated his case with graphics, emphasising his belief that cold facts are the best persuaders.

But the problem for Scargill was that, dominate the airwaves by his rhetoric as he did, he could do nothing about the daily diet of scenes from the picket lines, and it was the violence here that helped decide the strike.

Scargill was not the only one who complained. At the Police Federation conference in 1984, inspector Ronald Carroll complained that the media showed 'many violent situations in which the police were involved, but failed to show the events leading up to that situation' and talked of putting 'the police on trial by way of their journalistic licence'. Working miners' groups also worried that the violence on television dissuaded more from joining them, and producers and reporters found working miners much less anxious to co-operate than striking miners in making programmes.

Opinion polls consistently showed the public concern. Trade unionists from other industries spoke of the worry of their members that if they were picketed by miners, violence would follow. Only a minority of striking miners went picketing, many dissuaded because of the violence they saw.

Scargill's reaction was all-out attack. His words at Edinburgh could scarcely have been more uncompromising: 'By arranging this debate you reveal a serious concern about media coverage about the miners strike. What is the nature of this concern? Is it guilt about bias and distortion? Is it anxiety that the truth be seen and heard, that balance be maintained or that principles and ideals should not be sacrificed to government policies and state interference? Not at all.

'You are anxious and concerned because you are under attack.'

There were tactical elements in the onslaught, a typical whole-hogging Scargill approach which allowed for no compromise, but which he must have known would encourage even more people from the media to beat a path to his door.

He was obsessed with the coverage. At the ACAS talks a special television set had to be found so that the NUM side could watch. In Jimmy Knapp's office at the NUM at an early meeting of the transport unions, Scargill was to be found watching the picket lines on television. When Roy Evans of the steelworkers attempted to remonstrate with him, telling him to get his facts right and to realise that Sir Charles Villiers had been responsible for more steel cuts than MacGregor, Scargill put his hands over his ears and went on watching.

But his relationship with the media was a symbiotic one. Each lived and drew sustenance from the other. Scargill used the media to communicate with his members and other workers. The calls to picket Orgreave or to end coal supplies for steelworks, or to call on electricity workers to come out in sympathy, were primarily made in speeches which would be picked up on television and radio. Both NUM leaders and officials in other industries complained that instead of being approached directly the appeals were made over their heads.

The speech was an ideal opportunity for ringing assertions which could not be satisfactorily denied by the other side. For example at the Mansfield rally Scargill buttressed his claim to be making great headway by quoting figures to show that North Notts had lost 65 per cent of its usual output in a recent week. Two national newspapers printed the claim; what they did not find out was that the week involved had been cut to three days because of Easter holidays.

The media also fulfilled another function. As he travelled from rally to rally, picket line to picket line, Scargill was largely amongst adoring friends. The only people he was confronting in direct argument for much of the time were journalists, putting questions which others uninvolved in the dispute were posing. Even confrontation with politicians was frequently within the setting of a studio. For much of the time, the only people not on his side with whom he was in daily contact were journalists.

There was a revealing moment at the TUC conference in 1984 when, after following the coal story throughout the week, a group of industrial correspondents were eating lunchtime sandwiches in a bar in the conference centre. Suddenly Scargill appeared without his delegation or assistants. With the bar to choose from, it was the journalists he chose, and talked about the strain and boredom of his constant car journeys, and how, rather improbably it seemed to some of his listeners, he most missed not going to football matches because of the strike.

So just as the rhetoric about 'vermin' hid a more complex relationship, so that attack on bias in the press, hugely justified in relation to most of the popular press, concealed some considerable successes. Apart from the way that his outright attacks brought the miners' leader offers to 'state his case', and printworkers sometimes insisted on replying to attacks on the miners, he was afforded some remarkable opportunities, particularly by the *Daily Mirror*.

Traditionally this paper has been a committed supporter of the Labour Party, even exchanging staff with Labour governments, but at the start of the strike its attitude to the NUM stance, like much of the Labour movement, was ambiguous. Worse still for the miners, it did not appear very interested – a key absence when rivals like the *Sun* were prepared to use almost anything against Scargill including a picture of him saluting his supporters which made it look as if he were giving the Nazi salute.

But when Robert Maxwell took it over in July 1984 things changed. He asked the long-serving industrial editor, Geoffrey Goodman, why the paper had not done more about the strike, and what it could do. There followed a typical newspaper stunt – a seaside day out for miners' children. But this led to strains as the NUM leaders objected to the way money was sent directly to Maxwell.

Goodman then suggested a seminar with the miners' officials. A meeting was arranged in the Hallam Towers, a four star hotel close to the Sheffield University campus and a few minutes' drive from the NUM headquarters near the city centre.

Maxwell travelled up in his own helicopter and sat directly across the table from Scargill who was accompanied by Heathfield and McGahey. The *Mirror* team included Goodman, the political editor Joe Haines, and the chief feature writer John Pilger. Maxwell invited Scargill to expound his case and then pronounced himself anxious to achieve an honourable settlement for the miners.

After the NUM side went over negotiating details, Maxwell offered Scargill some advice; when he next went on television he should make clear he was against violence. It was one single issue on which he was losing public support. This brought an immediate change in Scargill's attitude, according to those present. He stiffened up and went straight into the attack, castigating police violence. Maxwell, rather taken aback, reacted by suggesting that Pilger should go into some mining villages and write about what he found and also about violence against striking miners. So the meeting ended, and the Pilger articles later appeared.

Maxwell went on to act as mediator, trying to organise talks at the TUC in September, but came to see more of Walker than Scargill as the energy minister made sure his views were known to the *Mirror*, a paper well read by miners.

The Maxwell case highlights the opportunities available to the miners, and those which were not. Although Heathfield addressed an editor's meeting of *Guardian* journalists, there was little attempt by other editors or proprietors to be in direct touch with the miners' leadership.

Mostly the miners' leaders were in contact with industrial correspondents (typed later by Nell Myers as 'along with broadcasting technicians basically our enemies' front-line troops') and with producers and editors of television programmes. On occasion these were supplied with special NUM information under an embargo so that it could be displayed to maximum advantage. *Channel Four News* spelt out what the NUM claimed were secret proposals for major cutbacks in the north-east which came from documents given to them by Scargill. Less successfully, the Glyn report challenging the NCB's uneconomic pit calculations was given as an exclusive to *Newsnight* during the 1984 Labour Party conference. The problem was that newspaper journalists, many of whose papers needed copy by late afternoon for publication the following day, did not receive it till early evening and were professionally irritated by the way it had been handed out exclusively elsewhere. The argument rumbles to this day with Scargill complaining it was ignored and newspaper journalists, heavily involved in conference coverage, retorting that they had inadequate time but that it still received a considerable number of column inches.

From the opposite perspective, many employers and Conservatives believed that Scargill was given far too much broadcasting time and were despairing of the Coal Board's response. One argument to be heard was that Scargill had moved the goalposts in the dispute so far to the left that the traditional down-the-middle, give-both-sides-a-hearing approach of some broadcasters had been shifted decisively to the left, assisted by the failures of the Coal Board to respond.

Why was the Coal Board so bad? Ian MacGregor's mistrust of the British media was well-known at the Steel Corporation. There he gave few on-the-record interviews, and he moved to the NCB with little experience of public exposure to the British media. After one early meeting with the NUM, Geoff Kirk asked whether he wanted to say anything to balance the briefing given by Scargill. His reply, in the tough American style he favoured, was a pithy piece of advice: 'Never get into a pissing contest with a skunk.' It amused Kirk greatly but it was a nostrum which he and others in the Coal Board team were to wish MacGregor had stuck by.

MacGregor's handling of the press was always erratic. Early in the dispute, after addressing a luncheon meeting at a hotel, he was approached by three journalists, all of whom he knew on first-name terms, and responded by fleeing down a concrete back staircase and jumping into his car, concealing his face behind a newspaper.

The problem was that there was no one in the NCB hierarchy to take his place. Cowan was so taciturn that he sometimes failed to complete his sentences, ending with a shrug when he thought his meaning sufficiently conveyed. With no other directors suited either, the ebullient Ned Smith took some of the weight, but his obvious relish for the role was at odds with his professional view that the man responsible for the delicate nuances of negotiation should not also be the public spokesman. Even the arrival of Michael Eaton by no means solved the board's problems. Apart from the NACODS fiasco, the board still could not get its timing right. Scargill had become a past master at appearing on the steps of various meeting places only minutes before a news broadcast was due, to ensure his points got across. By the autumn he was so assured that when a swearing altercation broke out behind him between two journalists, he simply paused, smiled at the camera and said, 'Shall we start that again,' knowing that extraneous sound would have made his answer unusable.

The NCB meanwhile could spend two hours after a meeting deciding what to say and whether to say it at all. By this time each side was monitoring each other's words to such a degree that sometimes they would not appear until they had checked the other's statement. The concentration on the immediate, the unwillingness to miss a trick, to blame the other side for not talking, or breaking off talks, reached its apogee at the 1984 TUC when the miners' leaders refused to give their reaction to the NCB's final letter on talks until they could check that the letter distributed to journalists was identical with the one they had received. A BBC despatch rider had to be sent to bring a copy of the NCB letter.

Meanwhile the Department of Energy had engaged a monitoring firm, Modern Media Monitoring, and insisted it installed a facsimile machine to rush them any broadcasts by the miner's leaders. With a four minute item costing between £30 and £40, the department's bills must have reached £1,000 some weeks, with the total sum exceeding £20,000. The company had offered the same service to the NUM but given the chaos of the Sheffield message-taking system no reply was received.

The obsession with the immediate, hanging on every press report while lambasting the press at every opportunity, did not please all NUM leaders. Mick McGahey said sharply at one point that he would like to put a lock on Scargill's mouth; others questioned whether a different strategy might have paid dividends.

Writing in the NUJ newspaper in January 1985 Howells was openly critical: 'All too often the news gatherers have been used as whipping boys by miners leaders who quite clearly are venting their frustration at being unable to mobilise wider trade union support for the NUM.

'The NUM has displayed extreme symptoms of the malaise which afflicts virtually the whole of the trade union movement. It assumes that somehow the "truth" about the dispute is going to fall out of the sky and land neatly on news desks, ready packaged for consumption.

'Union press statements are almost non-existent or often are so predictable as to be virtually unusable.'

He went on to claim that South Wales officials had been more open about discussing the dispute publicly, but he also blamed journalists for not giving more attention to pit closures, investment strategy and energy policy, claiming they were held in 'universal mistrust' by many working people.

Jack Collins, the firebrand leader of the Kent miners, was also critical: 'We lost the publicity battle. Maurice Jones should have had half a dozen assistants working with him and flooded the coal fields with literature. The Dutch socialist party would have run off all the leaflets we wanted. But as it was, if we wanted any more literature, we had to pay for it.'

A more partial view comes from Keith Bill who runs the Union Communications PR agency. Bill, who worked both with Scargill's opponent Sirs and his ally Jimmy Knapp is also critical: 'If we had been given £2 million from the NUM, we could have won the strike for them. We would have set the objectives and run a PR campaign fronted by reasonable and acceptable people. But my only contact was three months before the end of the strike. I was asked to arrange a press conference about striking miners who had been beaten up. I refused. I told them it was just too late.'

The obsession of Arthur Scargill about the media was a key element in the strike, and his super-sensitivity had huge consequences for the union's conduct of the strike. Put bluntly, he used the media and the threat of exposure in the media as a disciplinary force on the executive, which was reluctant throughout the strike to have any discussion which might disclose differences of opinion. When Peter Heathfield said in May that the executive could not resume talks with the board after their first meeting with it, because 'it would be headlines tomorrow – "Scargill agrees to talk about pit closures – MacGregor stands firm" ', it was but one example.

Jack Taylor, the president of the Yorkshire NUM, indicates vividly the way miners' leaders were throughout looking over their shoulders for fear of being accused of betrayal: 'One of the big difficuties on the NEC was that you could never have an in-depth honest discussion because people ran to the media. Half of them weren't on strike anyway. Comments on the NEC were being given to the press and so therefore there was never the required discussion needed to run a strike of that nature.'

It is a powerful indication of the way that Arthur Scargill, with his rhetoric about those who betrayed the union being 'stained to the end of time', was able to operate virtually without challenge from a body to which at other times he would insist he was answerable.

Politicians and trade unionists often tend to over-emphasise and over-blame the media's role, but in this dispute, its use was a central preoccupation. At times, it even seemed to take attention away from the issues of the strike itself.

For an elected government, ever-conscious of the realities of an election ballot, persuading and gauging public opinion is a major and proper obsession. For Scargill, too, it was crucial. In his early defeats as president in ballot votes he had picked issues carefully, linking pay and pit closures in a major campaign. He had gone from one adoring rally to another, but then been overwhelmingly rejected in the vote. An obvious explanation was the press, which in some cases had advised miners specifically to vote the other way. In our view, it may have been a contributory but was scarcely a sufficient reason.

But for unions which rely voluntarily, or now by law, on holding ballots the media will become an increasingly important issue, and also, as in the miners' dispute, a political target, even more so after Wapping. But the pressure for ballots is likely to become greater not less after the chaos caused in the NUM by its absence.

In this dispute press and media relations were not a sideshow. They were one of the central battlegrounds, and the continued failure of the NUM leaders to swing public opinion, including that of their own members, decisively to their side, in spite of the self-inflicted wounds of the Coal Board, was a key factor in their defeat.[2]

13
Enough of being spat at

Trade unionism is ultimately defined by the willingness of workers to take collective action in defence or pursuit of collective gains. Collectivism can only work through unity of action: its enemy is self-evidently individualism, where the collective's units – people – follow their own rather than the collective's interests, where the two conflict.

Strike action is the supreme example of collective activity in the labour movement, and thus the strike-breaker, or 'scab', is the acme of individualism. Soon after the strike began, the South Wales area of the NUM put out a fearsome little one-page handbill, with the headline 'a strike-breaker is a traitor'. Reproduced below was a terribly poignant photograph. It showed three miners, faces black from work, being escorted down a village main street in front of two columns of police. Villagers stood on both sides of the street, and at their windows, watching them. Two of the miners stared, faces set, in front of them; the third, shoulders slumped as he walked, looked to one side. The police, by contrast, looked jolly and hearty; in the front ranks, some were smiling at colleagues who stood on the pavement. The caption below read: 'Blacklegs in the Garw valley of South Wales in 1929.' Below the caption, another headline: 'Jack London's definition of a scab.' It read:

> After God had finished the rattlesnake, the toad and the vampire, He had some awful substance left from which he made a scab. A scab is a two-legged animal with a cork-screw soul, a water-logged brain, a combination backbone of jelly and glue. Where others have a heart, he carries a tumour of rotten principles. . . . Esau sold his birthright for a mess of pottage, Judas Iscariot sold his saviour for 30 pieces of silver. Benedict Arnold sold his country for the promise of a commission in the British army.
>
> The modern strike breaker sells his birthright, his country, his wife, his children and his fellow men for an unfilled promise from his employer. Esau was a traitor to himself; Judas Iscariot was a traitor to his God; Benedict Arnold was a traitor to his country. A STRIKE BREAKER IS A TRAITOR to his God, his country, his wife, his

family, his class. A REAL MAN NEVER BECOMES A STRIKE BREAKER.

At the end of the strike, close on 60 per cent of the NUM were, on a strict definition, strike-breakers or scabs – though in practice the NUM leadership declared a moratorium on calling them so after Christmas 1984. But the core of strike-breaking, its inspiration and its moral justification, was to be found in Nottinghamshire.

Many on the left accused Nottinghamshire miners of original sin: of behaving as they did because of their birthright. Almost everyone has invoked 'Spencerism' as a parallel for what has happened in Nottinghamshire, and in the creation, largely by its anti-strike leadership, of the Union of Democratic Mineworkers. So the uneasy figure of George Spencer, and his union, has to be understood before it is appreciated how much more important the modern successor is – and how much more profound an effect it will have on the Labour movement, even if the UDM itself does not survive, or fails in its self-appointed task of replacing the NUM.

Spencer was general secretary of the Nottinghamshire Miners Association, a constituent area of the Mineworkers Federation of Great Britain. He was also Labour MP for Broxtowe. By October 1926, when some 70 per cent of the Association's 34,000 members were back at work, he broke with the MFGB on the issue of separate negotiations with the (Notts) coal owners, and in November did a back-to-work deal on terms much more favourable than most other districts received.[1]

A.J. Cook, the MFGB secretary, made no attempt to keep Notts within the fold. In a speech in Bootle on 8 November, the man whom Scargill rightly saw as his forerunner said: 'I would rather see the organisation [the MFGB] broken down and built up again than we should sign away the conditions our men ought to have.' In neighbouring Leicestershire, however, the MFGB leadership put up with a return to work on compromise terms negotiated by the Leicestershire leadership – and did not support a breakaway union of the left formed by Jack Smith, an agent loyal to the strike, who claimed, with justice, that he was following MFGB policy.

The split in Notts was more overt, and was in any case linked to a movement current in the unions at the time from which it drew temporary strength: the non-political union movement.

Tracing its roots to the British Workers League, founded in the early years of the century on a platform of anti-socialist trade unionism, the non-political trade union movement was started in 1926 by Havelock Wilson, secretary of the National Union of Seamen, whose 310,000-strong union had signed a no-strike deal with the ship owners in return for a closed shop. He appealed to all those employers who 'value peace and goodwill in industry' to subscribe funds for his movement, designed to oppose 'foreign-controlled Communist domination'. Some 93 companies subscribed, including 30 shipping firms and nine coal companies. It was more or less a complete failure: the 1928 annual report of the Chief Registrar of Friendly Societies – the forerunner of today's Certification Officer – showed that, outside of mining and shipping, only four 'industrial unions' existed. Two of these – the Government Workers Industrial Union and the Railways Salaried Staff (non-political) Association had no members listed. A third, the Shipbuilding, Shiprepairing and Engineering Industrial Union, based in Liverpool, had 683; and the last, the Industrial Union of Engineering Workers, had 10.

The position taken by the NUS under Wilson was a powerful and evidently shameful memory in the minds of the union's left-wing leadership in the 1980s. Jim Slater, its general secretary, who worked hard to assist the NUM during the strike, talked afterwards of the union having 'vindicated itself' for the non-political period.

Within the mining industry, the Notts and the South Wales unions grew strongest (in both areas, around 50 per cent of the miners were in *no* union in the 1920s). Elsewhere, most other coal fields had a few hundred, or even a few dozen, 'Spencerists' – but none took root. The Notts industrial (Spencer) union grew from 12,853 in 1927 to 17,179 in 1937; at the same time the NMA dropped from 16,624 to 9,700. South Wales began with 6,435 in 1927, but had sunk to 589 by 1937. The leaders of the NMA wanted to run Spencer out: the MFGB leadership knew they could not. After a bitter struggle between the Association and the industrial union at Harworth pit, a settlement was reached which made Spencer the president of the two merged unions in Notts; restricted political business to special meetings, continued the existing wage agreements for five years, during which time there were to be no strikes; and continued a pension fund jointly financed by union members and coal owners (taken over by the NCB and still in existence).

The Spencer union's relationship with the generally liberal employers varied. Some insisted on membership, and sacked men who stuck to the NMA; others tolerated the Association. The industrial union *did* operate as a 'normal' union. Spencer kept the wages higher than those paid to miners elsewhere (the Notts field was among the richest in the country) and branch officials, elected in the usual way, were replaced by the men if they had not done a sufficiently good job in representing their grievances. His advocacy of district agreements won wide support in Notts, whose members knew they had been held back by national agreements. Spencer never tried to become a national figure – that was Havelock Wilson's role, and he died in 1929.

Spencer, and it can be assumed many of his members, were fiercely anti-Communist. The Communist Party, then much more the target of press 'scares' than now (it was, of course, an overtly revolutionary party in that period) had trumpeted its part in the General Strike – to the alarm of the TUC. In a speech in July 1927, Spencer said that 'non-political trade unionism is not a new movement as is often supposed . . . it is seeking to return to the line of action and modes of expression which characterised the movement before the Communist elements got a hold of it.' From his distrust of left politics flowed his acceptance of a market economy, and the unions' place in it: in a further speech that year he said that 'in my view there can be no improvement in the lot of the worker unless and until there is co-operation between the two [workers and employers], but while I am co-operating with the owners, I shall see to it that the workers get their share of the wealth that the joint efforts create.'

Spencer's 'treachery' was, in the acts of other union leaders, mere pragmatism. The Leicestershire leaders, playing it more cannily, acted in precisely the same way as Spencer (with the full support of their members) throughout the 1920s and 1930s, yet remained in the MFGB. 'We have,' said MFGB president Herbert Smith at the June 1927 MFGB conference, 'got to take our Leicestershire friends as they are.' Nearly sixty years later, the NUM leadership took a similar view, and stayed out of Leicestershire as its secretary, Jack Jones, persuaded his men to stay in the NUM by telling them that Scargill didn't count for much any more.

Notts' position as a right-wing area remained in place after the formation of the NUM in 1944 – but it was, of course, not alone. Neighbouring Yorkshire was on the right, too, as were the other Midlands fields, and Northumberland and Durham. It remained, however, more wedded than the poorer, more rapidly declining fields to separate area agreements. Len Clarke, the area president in the 1970s, fought hard for four years in the national executive and in conferences to get through an incentive bonus agreement, which was unpopular in most other areas and was rejected several times in national ballots (only Notts of the large areas produced big majorities for it). The last ballot, taken after a court case brought by Jack Dunn, the Kent secretary, and supported by the left against the executive to stop it, produced a majority of 55.75 against a national scheme – much to the left's amazement. It was the action of the NEC majority in sanctioning, in December 1977, area agreements which lay behind much of the bitterness many leading leftists felt for Gormley and for Notts.

The area was not insulated from the move to the left in the late 1960s and 1970s. Joe Whelan, a Communist, was elected an area official in the early 1970s, and Henry Richardson was elected general secretary in 1981. The area voted by nearly 78 per cent in favour of strike in 1974. By the early 1980s the area council was largely left-wing. When Ray Chadburn, the right-wing area president, ran against Scargill for the national presidency in 1981 (after much doubt) he could not get his own council's nomination: it voted 15:9 to nominate Scargill, leaving Chadburn to scratch up a nomination from tiny Cumberland.

But Nottinghamshire's leftism was activist-deep. Unlike areas such as South Wales, Scotland, and more recently Yorkshire, there was little membership depth to it. The left had not had the time, or the will, to change the traditions in the area, and their belief that they could force militancy upon them has broken the NUM. 'We've never had', said George Bolton the month after the strike ended, 'any significant, powerful, organised left progressive leadership in the Notts coal field. Indeed, the strike was something of a tragedy, because the left had just begun to emerge in Nottingham over the course of the last two years, just before the strike. But it tended to be at a certain level, at a branch leadership level, or in the shape of Henry Richardson.'[2]

Here was wisdom after the event. If it had been seen that leftism was so shallow in Notts, why was the left incapable of acting upon that evident fact during the strike? The answer lies in the deep sectarianism which characterises the left, and which found a ready echo – indeed, was often surpassed by – the national president's supporters in the executive and in the activists' ranks. 'We tended to assume that Nottingham was much worse than it really was,' said Bolton, putting it mildly. That assumption had only been possible because a vastly overconfident left, having secured the NUM's three national posts, assumed that all else would follow. It was, in microcosm, a pointer to what had happened in the Labour movement as a whole.

Albert Sparham, a former branch secretary from Clipstone, near Mansfield, found a few weeks after the start of the strike that the man who got the biggest vote in the NUM's history had no supporters in the Notts miners' clubs. 'He's running the union for political ends,' he said then. 'I believe this union was better when the executive was split 14:13, like it was with Joe [Gormley]. That's better than unanimity with Arthur. It was a healthy debate and Joe then ended up doing a good bit of what the 13 (the left) wanted.'

The collapse of the right after the assumption of the presidency by Scargill meant that its leaders were discredited and made a revolt from below a necessity. Though Chadburn and Richardson both called repeatedly for a national ballot and warned of the divisions in their area both inside the national executive and publicly, both of them ultimately took the view that their loyalties lay in obeying executive and delegate conference decisions. After the 12 April executive, where the most determined push for a ballot vote was defeated, Chadburn was badly roughed up by elements in the crowd outside. In the drive back to Mansfield with Richardson, who had bravely shielded him from the worst effects of the violence, both men determined to regulate their ambiguous position by telling their area members to 'get off their knees' and strike.

It was an uncomfortable position to take. Six days before, on 5 April, the Notts area delegates had voted, by 186 to 72, to reverse an earlier decision by the left-dominated Notts executive to observe picket lines. Some of the delegates had shouted for their area officials' resignation. Three weeks before *that*, the Notts area had, in its ballot, registered a vote of 20,188 to 7,285 against striking. All over the coal field the majority of Notts miners were going to work through columns of jeering Yorkshiremen (and some of their own comrades). The perception of a split in the union, based on Notts, was common even then. James Cowan, in an interview with the *Financial Times* on 10 April, talked of two unions as 'an emerging possibility', one of which the board was 'not afraid . . . we can work with it. It would help in some ways and hinder in others.'

On 17 April the Notts area delegates voted against the proposed rule change to bring the strike majority down to 55 per cent, against Chadburn's and Richardson's advice: again, the meeting ended with shouts for their resignation. At the delegate conference in Sheffield two days later, it was Lynk who spoke for Notts, telling the booing conference that 55 per cent was needed to make a strike solid. The strike was declared official as Notts men kept on going in to work. By the end of April, the board counted 5,388 of the 30,000 men on strike, going down all the time (the Notts NUM claimed 12,000: it was the beginning of a war of figures between union and board).

As happened in 1926, Notts took the brunt of the attack while Leicestershire, with South Derbyshire and much of the Midlands area, worked on without producing the political challenge Notts was to do. Neither Toon nor Jones, nor the majority of their area executives, instructed their members to strike. Nearly all crossed the picket lines throughout the strike. In Leicestershire, the strikers numbered 30 (they became known as the 'Dirty Thirty', and did a good business for the strike fund selling Dirty Thirty badges, mugs and vests). In South Derbyshire, Nick Wroughton, one of the handful of strikers, was amazed to discover at the strike's end that there had been as many as 17 on strike throughout.

The first two months of the strike saw Notts in sullen revolt, its two senior leaders divided from the bulk of the workforce and their delegates. In other areas opposition to the strike was fragmented, leaderless at area level. In Yorkshire, for example, John Walsh, the unsuccessful candidate of the right for the general secretaryship, did or said nothing during the strike to constitute a focus of dissatisfaction. Initially, at least, the collective will as defined by the left held sway, and held down the opposition of individuals.

Intimidation of working miners was a large feature of that. In October 1984 the National Working Miners Committee released a 25-page glossy pamphlet – *The Miners' Dispute: A Catalogue of Violence* – which gave some picture of what went on. It still makes grim reading, even allowing for the fact that most of the material was lifted from unchecked newspaper reports. (Many involved in the strike believe press reports understated the depths of bitterness, and thus violence, between striking and working miners.) Some examples: '26 March – a young miner opposed to the strike was found hanged after being branded a scab. Ian Tarren, 25, was discovered dead by his fiancée Denise Atkinson in their flat in Peterlee, County Durham. Her father said that Mr Tarren had been mercilessly taunted and continually threatened because of his views on the strike'; '10 May – police began watch on the house of a Warwickshire miner who received an anonymous note threatening to damage the kidney dialysis machine which keeps his son alive'; '17 August – the pregnant wife of a Staffordshire working miner collapsed with shock after a piece of concrete was thrown through a window at their home and landed in a cot.' As Henry Richardson had reported to the 12 April executive, this kind of attack merely hardened the resolve of the Notts miners to work.

But there was another force at work, too: miners in Notts, and elsewhere, often wanted the freedom to leave the industry in return for large redundancy payments, even though they were – as the union constantly reminded them – 'selling jobs'. The temptation held out to mineworkers who wished to leave the industry was a redundancy package which no other manual workers approached. The new rates introduced by the government on 1 April gave miners £1,000 for each year of service up to 50; above that, the miners who wished to leave would get lump sums of up to £20,000 plus pension benefits which would, with their state entitlements, give an income of over £100 a week. A man of 40 could get £25,000 if he had worked all of his life for the board. It was more money than he could hope to save, a tremendously powerful attraction for a man who felt able to start a second career, or do a 'bit on the side'.

The board and the government, in reshaping their policies to cope with a period of contraction, had fashioned a redundancy package which appealed to the individual miner but which was bound to get the opposition of the union. The case was repeated throughout British industry, especially the public sector, in steel, in the shipyards, in British Telecom. Everywhere, the employers found workers ready to take the sums offered, in spite of the opposition of the union. Indeed, union officials found that if they expressed their opposition too forcefully they met the anger of their members.

The NUM, under the left leadership, was the most hostile to individualism of this kind. Its definition of collective responsibilities and of the need for struggle necessarily conflicted with the short-term, family-bounded horizons of many of its members: and where other unions would simply back off with a shrug from taking on what their officials saw to be 'human nature', the NUM leadership's ambitions *were* high enough to choose to take on that nature. The Notts men, and miners everywhere less exposed than they, increasingly sought a collective identity less unsparing on its members' individualism, one which could accommodate their priorities and horizons to its own. The rallying cry for the dissident miners was the lack of the ballot, but beneath that other dissatisfactions were already in place which gave force to that cry.

And thus organised resistance began. On 1 May the working miners of Nottinghamshire marched on their own union office, in the Berry Hill district of Mansfield, some 7,000 of them, kept apart from the 1,000 pro-strike miners by a four-deep wall of police. In place of comradeship was brutal language and actions. The workers held up pay checks and sang, 'We're going to work tomo–or–ow, we're going to work tomo–orow', 'Pay day on Friday, pay day on Friday' and 'You're beat, you're beat, you're fucking beat.' From the working miners, came the familiar call to 'Fight like men' and the obscene insults: 'You filthy fucking sheep' and 'Fucking scabs'. 'We've had paint sprayed at us, and brake fluid,' one Rufford miner told Philip Bassett of the *Financial Times*. 'Pickets have taken car numbers going in every day, and then they've gone round the estates ripping tyres and causing damage. But now we've had enough of going in and being spat at. We've had enough. They [the strikers] don't want work, they're just tap room men.'

On the balcony of the Berry Hill office Ray Chadburn tried unavailingly to be heard as he shouted, 'We're fighting for our jobs.' As he did so, his members talked of setting up their own union – 'We can do it, we've got the majority in the pits.' From among the officials on the balcony, Roy Lynk detached himself and took the microphone: 'They can't fetch you out without a ballot and whatever decision you take I shall support.' The strikers threw stones and spat at him, but he had put down a marker.

In that month of May the Notts working miners came together and produced their *own* activists and officials. They began to meet, in pubs and clubs, often (like their neutered counterparts on the NUM executive) behind police protection and certainly with NCB approval. A working miners' committee, begun at Bevercotes pit by John Blessington, who became its secretary, began to meet. It had three aims: to co-ordinate information on working miners' groups; to give financial aid to working miners who had suffered damage to their cars or houses from strikers; and 'to reaffirm democracy within the NUM, but not to break or replace it.' In some pits where the NUM branch committee were all on strike – as Blidworth, Cresswell, Ollerton and Thoresby – the working miners activists effectively replaced the committee in representing the majority of men who were working.

Early in July the semi-clandestine nature of their existence ended with the election of many of them to branch office, to the area council and even to the executive. More than 100 branch officials were changed, 18 delegates to the 31-man area council were replaced, and the 10-man executive lost 8 of its members. A few left-wingers remained, but these were men who had bowed to the wishes of the majority early in the strike and had themselves gone in to work. They had a tide behind them. In the pits the votes for the new officials were typically in the order of 6 or 7 to 1. Chadburn, still turning this way and that in his attempts to square hopelessly conflicting imperatives from above and below, pointed in horror to the existence of liberals, social democrats, 'even Tories' on the new area council. But he comforted himself by saying that 'I think that at the end of the day they realise the implications of trying to form a breakaway union.' At the same time as these results were known, the board reported that Notts working was 'almost normal': coal production from the field rose to 300,000, then to 500,000 tonnes and beyond. Where train drivers refused to carry it, it went by road to the string of big power stations in the Trent Valley. With the assistance of imported oil and the unlikely aid of Polish miners (who had failed in *their* efforts to found an independent union, and whose government was now shipping coal to the UK in the name of hard currency), the Notts miners were breaking the strike.

They also reached out into other areas. The most flamboyant expression of this was Chris Butcher, who took the nickname Silver Birch from his prematurely greying hair. A (then) 33-year-old blacksmith at Bevercotes, he had been active in setting up the Notts Working Miners' Committee after the 1 May rally at Mansfield. Then, in late July, he set off on a trip round other coal fields, accompanied for part of the time by Christopher Leake, industrial editor of the *Mail on Sunday*, to test out what disaffection existed in other coal fields. Butcher was of value to the working miners' movement. His very thirst for publicity was an advantage at a time when the movement needed to be taken beyond the Nottinghamshire borders. He was able to contact groups of men who wanted to return and in some cases later formed back-to-work groups of their own. But his individualistic style and suspicions that he was 'in it for himself' set him apart from other working miners' groups, and he ended the strike a rather embittered man, complaining to reporters who had once fought to interview him that he had been passed over. He was right, but his place in the strike is an important one, not least for his encouragement of the Foulstone and Taylor case which ultimately crippled the NUM, and his donation of £10,000 to it as 'seed capital' from his fighting fund.

Colin Clarke and John Liptrot had played a large part in beginning the flood of legal actions in the court. Through the National Working Miners' Committee, they linked up with men from other fields who were prepared to operate more or less openly to break the strike. The committee was heavily influenced by Hart, who helped to raise funds for it. He persuaded the reclusive multi-millionaire John Paul Getty II, a patient in a London Clinic, to contribute almost £100,000. In all, Hart raised several hundred thousand pounds for the committee, mostly for legal fees, but also to defray the costs of press advertisements, designed by Tim Bell. MacGregor knew of the involvement, approved of it, but did not himself contribute, nor did he use Coal Board funds as the NUM alleged. At one stage Hart tried to organise an abortive meeting between the group and Lech Walesa. At another, he invited a number of them down to Claridges.

The meetings were clandestine. The committee met in hotels all over the Midlands, several times at Hambledon Hall, near Oakham, whose proprietor, Tim Hart, was David Hart's brother and a former colleague of MacGregor's. They adopted false names: Hart was known as David Lawrence, Liptrot as John Joseph. The Hart connection meant that a number of would-be recruits, and others who had been part of the group – such as Bob Copping of the Barnsley winders – shied away. But Hart did impart some of his own sense of mission to the group, all of whom were wholly inexperienced in operating on the national stage.

The NUM leadership, contemptuous (at least publicly) of the Notts men at first, were gradually forced to respond. Their first response once it was clear that mass picketing would not deliver Notts to them; Jack Taylor, typically honest, said as early as 30 March that it would not work – was to discipline non-strikers by the use of the rule book. For that, the rule book needed to be changed.

The NUM rule book bears all the stamp of the 1944 conference which formed the union. It was a rule book for a union with very largely independent areas. Crucially, miners did not join the NUM, but joined the *area* union; by doing so, they then became NUM members. The national rules which were in effect when the strike broke out had no disciplinary rule over individual members – its disciplinary powers extended over areas, in the event of arrears of contributions. In the model area rules, there were powers over individual members who fell into arrears – including expulsion from the union – and for 'misconduct', defined as a wilful breach of the rules. A member disciplined by suspension or expulsion had the right of appeal to area council and to the national executive.

The flaw for the national leadership was that disciplinary action could only be initiated by the area, and if the area leadership was itself composed of working miners there was no possibility of action against others working in the area. Rule 51 was the answer to that.

It must be said that the national leadership has always denied that its intent was to discipline Nottinghamshire, and other, working miners – a claim which was made the more forcefully as the Notts rebellion gathered strength in 1985. Scargill said repeatedly that the move had been planned for two years. He also claimed that the move initiated in Notts, a claim the Notts leadership later denied. But even if this were so, the introduction of the rule at a special delegate conference in Sheffield on 11 and 12 July was accompanied by repeated calls by delegates to use the rule against the 'scabs' from Notts. As the Notts delegates entered and left the hall they were subjected to a barrage of abuse and obscenities, while Ken Toon of South Derbyshire caused most delegates to walk out when he told them a ballot should have been held.

Thereafter, Rule 51 (so called because it became the 51st rule in the book: when new rules were adopted in July 1985, it became rule 30) became the most potent recruiting agent for the working miners they were to have. It was very long – 21 clauses – and complex. It was also very sweeping: a national disciplinary committee was empowered to hear a complaint on a range of matters, including 'that a member has done any act (which includes any omission) which may be detrimental to the interests of the union and which is not specifically provided for in this rule.' The disciplinary committee was to be presided over by the vice president and the appeals committee by the president. It was quickly represented in the press as 'Scargill's star chamber'. Expulsion from the union would probably have meant loss of the job, for, while there was no formal closed shop, a working assumption before the strike was that any non-member attempting to work would stimulate a walk-out by his colleagues – and thus bring on his own dismissal if peace were to be restored. For this reason, Ned Smith made a statement after the conference that miners' 'employment was not at risk out of loss of trades union membership'.

The passing of the new rule – by 116 votes to 62 – was in the first instance futile because of an injunction granted to 17 Notts miners barring discussion of the rule because strikers had prevented a meeting of the Notts delegates earlier in the week at Berry Hill from discussing their position. A second delegate conference on 10 August passed it once more – this time, in the absence of Notts, Leicestershire and South Derbyshire – by a card vote of 167,000 to 22,000.

Back in their own area, the Notts working leadership determined to make its own rule change. It put to its branches, and got past in mid-December, a resolution that rule 30 in its area rule book be deleted. This time a court challenge from the NUM seeking to block the change failed. Rule 30 laid down that 'in all matters in which the rules of this union and those of the national union conflict, the rules of the national union shall apply and in all cases of doubt or dispute the matter shall be decided by the national executive committee of the national union'. Igor Judge, the Notts barrister, argued in court that the introduction of the rule 51 disciplinary provision had been the catalyst, together with amendments to other rules which established the NEC's precedence, for the change. Its passing meant that the area was, arguably, virtually independent.

Lynk had already anticipated that. He persuaded the area council, keen to end the 13-month overtime ban (for which Notts, like all other areas, had voted) to delay a decision to do so in favour of seeking a fresh mandate on the ban from the membership. He did not want the area to give the NUM a hostage to fortune, he wanted to be *seen* to be loyal. For the same reason he resisted pressure to settle unilaterally with the board on its still outstanding 5.2 per cent pay offer. But he knew where the union was heading. In an interview with one of the authors the day after the area council 29–2 vote to delete rule 30, he said that he and his colleagues were ready to run a wholly autonomous union if they had to: 'Once you have started down a road, you have to be prepared to follow it through.'

Both the NUM and the Notts area were locked into combat. The national leadership proposed early in 1985 a further delegate conference to consider two issues: first, the expulsion of Notts from the union, and second, the adoption of a new structure for the NEC itself. The move was to founder on a mixture of internal dissent – growing by that time on the left – and the hectic events around the closing weeks of the strike. But it illuminated an issue of central importance, one which was close to the heart of the weakness of Scargill's strategy.

The 1944 rule book had laid down that the national executive was a conclave of regional barons. Every area, no matter how small, would have representation by virtue of rule 12 which specified that every area union with a membership up to 22,500 would have one executive member. Areas with a membership of between 22,500 and 55,000 would have 2 members; areas with more than 55,000 would have 3. In proportional terms, this produced a nonsense executive: Harry Hanlon sat on the NEC throughout the strike, as his membership in his 'area's' one pit, Haig, dwindled from some 750 before the strike to 150; Trevor Bell's 16,500 white-collar workers got the same representation. Yorkshire's three left-wing votes for the 55,000 membership counted for less than the four right-wing votes which some 7,000 miners in Cumberland, Leicestershire, North Wales and South Derbyshire could command. Long before becoming national president Scargill had identified this as an evil to be changed. In his pamphlet, *Miners in the*

Eighties, he wrote that, 'to have a democratic union we must have a democratic NEC and for this the system of representation must be altered. . . . The answer is to introduce the same voting structure within the NEC as already applies in the national conference (where one delegate represents 1,000 miners, thus ensuring proportional representation).'

His staff drew up a more proportional structure, which would merge the Cumberland, North Wales and Lancashire areas into a Western area; the Leicestershire, South Derbyshire, Power Group and Midlands area into a new Midlands area; the Scottish area with the Scottish craftsmen (Group No. 2) and the Durham area with the Durham craftsmen (Group No. 1). The right wing, concentrated in the smaller areas, lost out. But the move also aroused the latent hostility in all area leaders to the national centre, and the plan was very substantially modified before it came back, in July 1985, in a different form in the new rule book.

Len Murray, seeing Scargill advance to national power, had from an early date recognised that a central project was to centralise power through a reconstruction of his union, and shrewdly reckoned that that might prove his undoing. Scargill had correctly grasped, from the late 1960s, that with the imposition of more or less equal rates of pay across the country with the national power loading agreement of 1967, the miners would feel more of a national body because they would be equally treated. He said in the *New Left Review* interview that 'the one thing that Alf Robens [the then chairman] forgot or ignored was that by his very act, with the support incidentally of the left, he was creating and the left were creating a situation where unity could be the order of the day . . . no longer would we have Scotland, Wales, Nottinghamshire, Derbyshire, Yorkshire on different rates of pay. At the end of the 1960s everybody would be on the same rates of pay and the frustration was growing in the coal fields.' But the president had in his turn forgotten or ignored the enduring strength of local area feeling, and the resentment, especially in Nottinghamshire, of the loss of a privileged position which could still be available to it.

Growing in confidence, the Notts area leadership sacked Richardson soon after the strike ended for 'gross misconduct'. Richardson lost a court battle for reinstatement when Mr Justice Mann, in the High Court, found that 'it would be quite wrong for this court to impose on a trade union an official in whom it has no confidence.' Chadburn stayed on, ignored. The NUM executive voted by 10 votes to 9 on 14 May to dismiss Lynk and reprimand Prendergast. Lynk said he would ignore the decision. The three working areas of Notts, Leicestershire and South Derbyshire had formed a 'democratic alliance'. Their leaders met regularly.

As Notts was growing in strength, the left was losing it. By the summer of 1985 the tensions which were surfacing as the strike ended, and which had been below the surface from an early stage in the strike, finally took concrete form. In the June executive meeting, Emlyn Williams told Scargill, whom he had grown to dislike heartily, that he was the NEC's 'servant', not its master. In both South Wales and Scotland the Communist or Communist-trained leadership were beginning the sober analysis of defeat which their training prescribed, and they rejected as puerile Scargill's continuing claims of victory. McGahey, in a delicate position as at once the national vice president and president of the Scottish area, was now really concerned about the loss of Notts. In North Derbyshire, Gordon Butler, the area secretary who had succeeded Heathfield, had come to quiet accommodation with his area management and found his president's talk of further strike action absurd. Even the loyal Yorkshire leaders mumbled and grumbled – though usually supported Scargill in a push. All area leaders were concerned with the sacked miners – especially Scotland, which had over 200 from a national total, in July, of around 600. But Scotland found that the despised arts of negotiation and quiet deals could win reinstatement for some of their men where rhetoric merely confirmed their banishment.

Before all the area leaderships, as the July annual conference drew near, was a complete new rule book, drawn up by their indefatigable president after the strike. The disciplinary rule remained unchanged, but the plan to merge areas had been dropped, replaced with a rule for the national executive which set a minimum of 1,000 members as a qualification for a representative on the NEC, and allowed two representatives for all areas over 18,000 members and three for any over 40,000. It preserved representation as it was – except for Harry Hanlon of Cumberland. But that was barely controversial any more.

Instead, attention focussed on rule 11, on the president. 'The President', it said, 'shall preside (but shall have no votes in any capacity) at all meetings of the NEC, Annual Conference and special conference.' The parenthesis was critical: it meant that Arthur Scargill was complying with Tory law, and wished to remain president for life.

The 1984 Trade Union Act specified periodic five-yearly balloting for all members of a national executive who held a vote. Its other two provisions were to specify ballots on strikes, and on the maintenance of political funds. The NUM *had* always elected its president and its general secretary by ballot, but for life. The vice-president, elected by the conference, had to stand for re-election every two years. But the left had been vehemently against the life presidency, seeing it as corrupting, removing a man from his members. Scargill was enthusiastically for it, arguing that it kept a president in touch. Like Tony Benn, to whom he drew closer as the strike went on, Scargill had believed in the efficacy of inner union or inner party democracy. Both, perhaps, based their support at least in part on a shrewd belief that, in an activist democracy, their kind of charismatic fundamentalism would tend to be well received.

But in the aftermath of the strike, the calculation changed. Scargill argued that the new rule 11 merely regularised a situation which had existed for years. The president did not have a vote, he said, except when chairing a meeting of the executive and even then only when there was a tie. He claimed he had never exercised his vote. Behind this lawyer's argument was a dispassionate assessment that, if he had to face the membership in the near future, the vote he could expect would be a good deal lower than the 70.3 per cent he got in December 1981. Indeed, with a good candidate against him he could lose.

The left was outraged. In South Wales, where the area executive now contained very few Scargill supporters, a decision was taken to vote down the rule.

The rules went further than that, though. Rule 5a widened the scope of membership to include almost anyone whom conference wished: associate membership, which Scargill wanted to confer on the members of the women's support groups, allowed the NEC to admit into (non-voting) membership anyone at all. Rule 5D specified that the NEC allocate members to areas – this fundamentally changing the relationship between the miner and the union by making him a member first of the national, then of the area, union. Rule 16 indemnified the three national officials, retrospectively, 'in respect of every act done as such a national official so long as such act was not contrary to the policy of conference or the NEC'. Other rules indemnified in the same way NEC members and area officials. Rule 17B specified that membership of an area may be broader than the area itself, and rule 17D gave the conference powers to 'create, dissolve, merge, combine or amalgamate areas'. Rule 26C gave the NEC 'power to call industrial action by any group of members whether in one or part of one or more than one area' (assuming that the NEC had already been made aware of industrial action in one of the areas called out). Rule 29 specified a grievance procedure of great length, which prohibited any reference to the courts until it was exhausted.

The rules were leaked to the press by the Notts area leadership. They attracted a storm of adverse comment. Defending them, Heathfield termed them 'minor' and claimed the press reports that they were fundamental and far-reaching as 'totally and dangerously untrue'. But the Notts men no longer believed him. They asked Igor Judge, the QC who had defended the area union leadership against Richardson's charges that he had been unfairly dismissed, to analyse them.

Judge's judgment was trenchant. He conceded that Scargill's 'presidency for life' rule change was 'not illegal nor is it a change'. It would mean, however, that 'the president elected by the membership of the union under one system of rules which gave them a degree of control over him would continue in office under new Rules which would reduce the members' control over him while extending his control over them, their own constituent unions and the NUM itself.'

The net effect of the new rules would be, he wrote

> to allow the inclusion in the NUM of large numbers of diverse members who are not engaged in either the mining industry or ancillary undertakings and who are not members of the present area unions;
>
> to enable the NEC to reallocate the members of the area unions from one to another area union at any time, and to include in an area union persons not engaged in the mining industry;
>
> to greatly increase the power of the NUM as against the area unions, and in particular the power of the NEC and the president;
>
> to enable the NEC to call out on strikes, which it could declare official, any group of members in one or more areas without a ballot and without court interference of the type recently seen;
>
> to reduce the legal rights of the members to apply to the courts for redress of grievances;
>
> to give wide indemnity provisions for past and future acts for the benefit of the national officials, members of the NEC and area officials;
>
> to reduce the area unions to something close to mere branches of the NUM so that any meaningful local autonomy would become an illusion.

In summary, said Judge, 'the question of control by the members, together with the autonomy and independence of the constituent unions, remains the most important aspect of the proposed changes. The recent dispute inevitably looms large in the thoughts of all members of the union and their reaction to it is likely to affect their reaction to the rule changes.'

Notts went to the July conference – as did South Derbyshire and Leicestershire – primed to vote against all or most of the rules. A ballot of the area members in May had produced a 15,000:6,500 vote against the rule changes. South Wales, still terribly reluctant to be seen as 'supporting the right', approved most of the rule changes but baulked at presidency for life, associate membership and increased powers to the NEC to call one or more areas out on strike. The Scottish area delegates voted to leave decisions on the rules to the delegation, on the understanding that it would support a reference back of all the rules to the executive if proposed by another area. The move, a half-hearted one, reflected the concern felt by McGahey and Bolton that pushing through the rules would cause a split.

The non-Scargill left were caught in a painful position. They had supported the national leadership throughout the strike. They had assisted in adumbrating the strategy which drove the strike. They were under attack from the board, the government and from the putative split within their ranks. Scargill was the union's president, put there by the left. The word went out among the left: the changes may be unwise, but any move to defeat or defer them would be seen by Scargill as an attack upon him, and lead to greater damage than their passing.

The Communist Party worked hard at replacing that line with one more hostile to Scargill. During and especially since the strike it had moved sharply away from supporting the president. Its mining advisory group, meeting throughout the strike, had sounded warnings over its conduct for the latter half of it. At a meeting in Chesterfield a week before the conference, Peter Carter, its iconoclastic industrial organiser, put to the 50 Communists there that the change would divide when unification was paramount; that if they were defeated by the right they would be seen to herald the defeat of the left as a whole; and that an analysis of the strike, warts and all, must be undertaken. Its line was winning in Scotland and South Wales – but not in Yorkshire, or in the north-east. Still, a reference back of the rules might succeed.

Scargill, master of the procedure, slapped it down before it had time to rise. The rules, he told the press on the eve of the 1 July opening of the conference, would be put to the conference *en bloc*. If accepted by a simple majority, they would then form the established rules of the union. Thereafter, any amendments, including deletions, would require a two-thirds majority to succeed in changing them. This reversed what had been thought to be the natural order – that the new rules would themselves require a two-thirds majority to replace the old. The left, hoping that the right would do some of the job for them, were rocked back. In the event, the only substantive rule that was lost was that ushering in associate membership.

But before that happened the 15 delegates from Notts had walked out of the hall. They had been treated as lepers for the three days they had attended: bussed in every day from Mansfield, with a police escort, they had been placed deliberately at the front of the hall, where their every vote (usually against the majority) was noted and attracted catcalls and shouts of 'scab'. Chadburn and Richardson, perched at the end of the row, hardly looked at their colleagues. At one point Chadburn had to intervene in what threatened to be a fist fight between Richardson and Lynk. They were surrounded by TV lights and cameras and reporters at every turn, a factor which increased the dislike from the rest of the hall. When George Liddle, the Notts vice president, gave a carefully worded speech identifying the mistakes of the strike – 'Any general worth his salt knows that the timing of the commencement of a battle is crucially important; even more important is that the enemy should not be allowed to choose the battleground' – he was booed and hissed (though he said nothing which many of the left leaders had not already concluded for themselves). On 3 July, in closed session, the conference voted, by 81:13

and 81:13, to dismiss from their posts both Lynk and Prendergast – a hardening of the NEC decision to remove Lynk but reprimand Prendergast. Both men remained NUM members, and remained delegates from their area to the NEC, but their £18,000 salaries and expenses, paid by the national office for fulfilling area duties, would be cut off.

In fact, both men were safeguarded against such an eventuality. When appointed to their posts as respectively general secretary and financial officer earlier in the year, they had signed contracts with the Notts area executive. Lynk said after the closed session that 'I will continue doing my job for the Nottinghamshire miners.' Next day the Notts men were bussed back to another closed session in which 75 per cent of the 132 delegates voted in the new rule book. They promptly walked out again, boarded the bus and went back to Mansfield. Two days later, on Saturday 6 July, at the Berry Hill offices Notts delegates voted by 228 to 20 to leave the National Union of Mineworkers after 41 years.

The growth of the 'breakaway' was thereafter relatively rapid. From the beginning, it drew close to the 1,500-strong Colliery Workers and Allied Trades Association, based in Durham and composed largely of Durham craftsmen thrown out of the NUM for 'scabbing' during the strike – a hostage to fortune which even Scargill tried to stop. The two other areas in the 'Democratic Alliance', South Derbyshire and Leicestershire, were also expected to go independent; in the event, only South Derbyshire did. The three 'areas' voted on 18/19 October to merge to form a new union – the Union of Democratic Mineworkers. Notts got a 72 per cent majority in a 90 per cent poll, the CWATA (naturally) a near 100 per cent, and the South Derbyshire miners a scraped-through 51 per cent.

In other areas other pits were looking to the UDM too. Daw Mill, a highly productive pit in Warwickshire which had worked throughout the strike, voted to ballot on leaving the NUM in August. It was followed by Agecroft and Parsonage in Lancashire, and Chase Terrace and Trenton Workshops in Staffordshire. In Durham, a group of white-collar (COSA) men formed the first UDM white-collar 'area'. By early 1986 the UDM could plausibly claim over 30,000 members. All over the country, Lynk said, NUM members were quietly joining.

The NCB, closely in touch with its leaders throughout the strike, had not been surprised to see it emerge and quickly agreed to negotiate with it. Cowan says he knew before the strike started that its creation was on the cards. There were possible problems with the Coal Industry Act 1946 which lays a duty on the NCB to consult and negotiate with organisations representing 'substantial' numbers of staff (could the UDM be termed 'substantial'?). The National Reference Tribunal, the final arbiter on national awards, chaired by Stephen Sedley QC, delivered a judgment in

December 1985 that the NCB had been wrong in recognising the UDM without consulting the NUM, but MacGregor was hardly likely to take any notice of *that*.

By the end of October the Notts area, followed by South Derbyshire and the CWATA, approved a 5.9 per cent pay offer made up of a 4.5 per cent rise on basic rates and the remainder on bonus. They also agreed to a series of pit level incentive deals designed to favour the face worker and to widen the differentials between him and his other colleagues underground and on the surface. The NUM, with Scargill huffing and puffing about the meagreness of the offer and the dictatorial tactics of the baord in demanding the NUM sign an agreement to negotiate on productivity (which it was pledged not to do) before making an offer, was dragged along, willy nilly, behind the UDM.

The introduction of productivity deals on a pit-by-pit basis has been the intention of MacGregor since joining the board. In doing so, he builds upon a movement away from the equalised payments imposed on the industry by the power loading agreement of 1967, once the strikes of the early 1970s made clear that the system stimulated national wage militancy. In talks with miners in the Midlands – especially on a series of visits to Daw Mill, some of whose miners took up a MacGregor invitation to visit US mines – MacGregor spoke warmly of the benefits miners could reap from a much higher output linked to payment by results. His proposals chimed in well with the government's insistence that wages should reflect the market; they also met a ready welcome in the Midlands coal fields where the equalised wage had held back earnings for decades.

Between them, the Coal Board and the UDM constructed a new approach to wages and to work tailor-made for the board's strategy of moving miners out of the older, unproductive pits to the thicker-seamed new super pits. At an early stage in the UDM's life, its officials and those of the board agreed that it did not matter if the NUM remained strong in the older, declining areas of South Wales, Scotland and the north-east – so long as the UDM was attractive to miners in the highly productive complexes planned in the Vale of Belvoir, Warwickshire, Notts and Oxfordshire.

It sought to be so by returning to the past in its rules. The UDM rule book, with only 14 rules against the NUM's 32, specifies a 55 per cent vote for industrial action, as the NUM rules used to do before April 1984; any industrial action requires the assent of all members; areas' autonomy is guaranteed. An innovation in the rules reflected bitter recent experience: no members in one area (or 'section') can picket the members of any other. Where the NUM's new rules make strikes easier to call, the UDM's makes them very difficult indeed.

From its inception, the UDM declared it would remain loyal to the

Labour Party and would wish to affiliate to the TUC. Both of these bodies made clear that their constitutions would not allow them to admit it – but neither was anxious to embark on a campaign against it. Neil Kinnock knew it would not go away; indeed, he believed it could grow to become the majority union over time, and that the only thing which could save the NUM would be a Labour government which could knit the two unions together. For the TUC's part, it had no intention of being drawn, as Scargill wished it to, into a denunciation of the UDM. When the electricians' union, the EETPU, met the UDM leaders at a well publicised conference in January 1986, the TUC declined to accept the NUM's invitation to discipline the electricians.

In an internal report in November 1985 for the finance and general purposes committee the TUC recognised with respect the UDM's strengths: 'The problem facing the NUM is that the new union has a solid base in Notts, the second largest coal field, where it enjoys majority support . . . but as developments at Daw Mill, Agecroft and elsewhere show, the union has the potential to attract miners in other areas, particularly those who worked through the strike. . . . The UDM is therefore solidly based in Notts with the potential to expand elsewhere, particularly in the most productive collieries. In these circumstances there seems to be the most limited scope, if any, for a further campaign to be mounted by the NUM, supported by the TUC, against the new organisation.'

Within the NUM leadership, Mick McGahey now pushed hard for a new approach. Much more openly critical of Scargill than he had allowed himself to be throughout the strike, and with the knowledge that he had behind him the majority of the executive, he developed a strategy which depended on the union making clear to its areas that there would be no central interference with area business; that there would be no use of disciplinary or other procedures; and that, most importantly of all, there would be no efforts to use industrial action.

McGahey was proposing nothing less than a union much less centrally directed than it had been under Gormley, and light years away from the new model army which Scargill had made it his business to construct since his presidency began. Unity, McGahey reminded his 'young friend', is all, the individual nothing. For the sake of the British miners, Scargillism was to be set aside. And the implication was clear: if it was not, then Scargill himself would be.

The UDM's growth was halted when, in January 1986, a ballot in Leicestershire produced a majority against the area's affiliation to the new union. Jack Jones, the right-wing Leicestershire secretary, had campaigned hard in his four pits for continued membership of the NUM, claiming to have turned down both UDM and NCB blandishments to play a leading role in the then fast growing union. Roy Lynk, who had proved more than equal to the task of wresting the area union away from a leadership out of touch with the mood of its members, was less able to tackle the problems of growth. Within the Coal Board, the feeling among senior officials developed that Lynk was not the man for the job, but he could scarcely be replaced. Hart, who continued to take a close interest in the UDM, thought that a man was wanted who could project a moral intensity as white hot as Scargill's – but of course in defence of different causes.

'Spencer has returned to the coal fields,' said Peter Heathfield when the UDM was formed. But it was not Spencerism, for though elements in the NCB encouraged the UDM's formation and existence, it had erupted from below against the opposition of the bulk of the area leadership, it did not rely on the management enforcing membership by refusing jobs to those who were not in the union and – as McGahey pointed out to his executive colleagues – it was not part of a larger movement hostile to the Labour Party and to the TUC. Indeed, McGahey's close interest in working-class history allowed *him* to discriminate carefully between the new and the old breakaway movements, and in doing so, he disciplined himself, and tried to discipline others, into forgoing any insults to the Notts miners. They were, he insisted, miners like any others.

Others than McGahey grew to appreciate that, and with it to grasp, too late for their members, that the world had changed since they turned it part upside down in the early 1970s. They and others came to see that the verities of the Labour movement, which for decades had reserved, from a mixture of respect and guilt, a place of honour for the mineworkers, now could no longer afford to act on such sentiments.

By early spring of 1986, the NCB privately reckoned that the UDM was losing as many members as it was gaining. Without a further leap forward, it seemed to have shot its bolt and was vulnerable to a revival in the NUM's fortunes. Both unions were thinking of mergers – the UDM with the electricians, some left leaders of the NUM with the transport workers (Emlyn Williams mooted the thought publicly during a valedictory interview when retiring as South Wales president in February 1986 – an interview bitterly hostile to Scargill).

But the UDM had by then demonstrated, as Spencerism did not, that *in extremis*, any union is fissile; that the imposition of the collective will had to recognise clear limits and constraints within a democracy; that weapons such as the law, and the press, and the employers themselves, would be turned against union leaderships when members felt they needed protection. That lesson is unlikely to be forgotten.

14

'Your members have yet to be heard'

As little as a year after the miners' strike ended, Arthur Scargill was seen to have been correct: the strike *had* politicised the unions. It had turned the bulk of the leaders and the activists away from policies which were, explicitly or implicitly, revolutionary. It had helped replace vanguardism – the practice of leadership by a core of activists and professionals – by a plebiscitary democracy which yielded uncertain results. Left leaders like Ron Todd, Rodney Bickerstaffe of the public employees, Jimmy Knapp of the railway workers – all of whom had supported the NUM to the hilt during the dispute – now found themselves edging into a separate camp as Scargill remained a purist ever, on the far left. They accepted that victory for *their* kind of socialism came only through an electoral gain, and if that could not be achieved, they had to make the best of the world as they and their members found it.

The miners had thus played the neatest of roles within a decade and a half. In the early 1970s, as union power grew and its exercise of it became less and less inhibited, the miners showed the movement what might be achieved: the destabilisation of the government, no less. More, it could be argued that it achieved its collapse, its defeat. Industrial power was seen – wrongly, but seductively – as the real arbiter of the country's future; if the organised labour did not accept government policies, then they could not, in the end, be implemented. It was a perception common to left and right.

Trade unions had been seen as the organic expressions of working-class power, with real and deep roots inside the class. Harold Macmillan's dictum – that the three forces against which a government could not prevail were the Catholic Church, the Brigade of Guards and the NUM – had been widened in the 1970s to include the trade unions as a whole, with the NUM, of course, as *their* Brigade of Guards. It was a state of affairs highly advantageous to the unions and their organised expression, the TUC. By preserving a judicious ambivalence over obedience to the law, it had won great victories under it.

The unions approached Thatcher's laws with history apparently on their side. The Wembley Principles were the unions' way of reminding the government that they were boss where they cared to be. But they failed: the demos were poorly attended, the strikes non-existent, the working class not touched after all. The serious people moved in, impatient with the wetness of the TUC; they, the NUM, would show what could be done. But they needed the working class behind them, too, as they had been before, and they did not move for them, either – worse, many turned against them.

Since the late 1960s, union power had been the dominant issue in British political life. But that phase – the phase of 'semi-syndicalism' – was closed by the miners, who had given it such confidence as it took off. In trying to gain all, they had lost much: most of all, they had lost, for themselves and their comrades in the movement, the great illusion of possessing an irresistible power.

In doing so – in failing so obviously and cruelly – they laid ghosts for the rest of the Labour movement; one in particular, the ghost of 1926. Scargill had been explicit in drawing parallels between the two events: it had been his root justification for refusing to approach the TUC for aid, as Len Murray perceived.

But the manner in which Scargill refused to accept aid, or conditions, or counsel – yet hugged to himself the right to determine at what tempo the resistance to government should be made – was 1926 not like this too? Was the TUC's action in calling off the General Strike in all of the mines not merely an overdue recognition that the struggle was hopeless – and that the miners' leadership, A.J. Cook in particular, was as driven and impossibilist as the other Arthur 60 years later?

After the 1926 miners' strike, the TUC were seen by the miners and the left as traitors in two senses: first, in letting down the miners by calling off the General Strike, and second, by collaborating with employers and government after the strike in creating an industrial relations structure and atmosphere which put negotiation and compromise above the political aims of the movement, to achieve the suppression of capitalism and the hegemony over society of the working class.

Yet in their industrial policies, the TUC leaders did not differ much from George Spencer, the reviled leader of the Nottinghamshire breakaway union. In the weakened years after the General Strike, as TUC affiliates' membership fell from under 4.4 million in 1926 to under 3.3 million in 1934 before it began to rise again – the canniest leaders drew the lessons of defeat and sought to make the best of a bad job. The Baldwin government, in spite of much pressure for revenge from its right wing, did attempt to promote reconciliation between employers and unions – though the passing of the 1927 Trade Union Act, which narrowed the lawful grounds for strike action and proscribed the 'contracting in' to the political levy, aroused union hostility. Under prompting from the prime minister a group of industrialists led by Sir Alfred Mond, chairman of Imperial Chemical Industries, proposed talks on the establishment of a national industrial council. The TUC, under the chairmanship of Ben Turner, agreed to the talks and a council was established. 'We realise', said Mond in a letter to the TUC, 'that industrial reconstruction can be undertaken only in conjunction with and with the co-operation of those entitled to speak for organised labour.'

The TUC leaders were pleased with their progress. The report to the 1928 Congress was fulsome: 'for the first time in history the representatives of organised labour have been invited to meet a group of important industrialists to discuss the finance and management of industry, new developments in technology and organisation . . . these are the things the trade union movement has been claiming for years to have a voice in and for years it has been denied that voice.'

The left judged 'Mondism' a sham. No one was more vociferously opposed than A.J. Cook. In two pamphlets – *Mond Moonshine* (March 1928) and *Mond's Manacles* (August 1926) Cook tore into the compromise with capitalism which the meetings represented. The second of these pamphlets ended with the flat statement of belief which unites the two miners' leaders down through the decades: 'There can be no peace with poverty and unemployment. There can be no peace with capitalism.'

The myth of betrayal of the miners has lasted well, better than the assessment made at the time by those involved. Walter Citrine, beginning his distinguished stewardship of the TUC in the year of the strike (as Norman Willis was to do nearly 60 years later) wrote in his diary as the strike ended – 'never again will the Congress undertake the custodianship of any movement without the clear, specific and unalterable understanding that the General Council, and the General Council alone, shall have the free and untrammelled right to determine policy. How can we, with the millions of interests and considerations to review, allow our policy to be dominated by the considerations of one union only?' Far from thinking that they had betrayed the miners, the other union leaders believed that the miners had badly mishandled their strike and that industrial adventures should now be ruled out of court. Sir Denis Barnes, former permanent secretary to the Department of Employment, comments that 'the use of industrial power for political purposes was discredited until the 1970s . . . the possibility of the TUC's exercising authority or even effective influence over individual unions, except on limited domestic issues and in very special circumstances, was destroyed. Individual unions had surrendered their powers to the General Council with disastrous results – for them – and they would not repeat the operation.'[1]

Bevin and Citrine, with other leaders like C.T. Cramp of the railway workers, and George Hicks of the building workers, put the TUC and its unions on a new basis; it turned its back firmly on any adulteration of industrial pursuits by political aims, grew ever more strongly reformist, and developed new joint forums for collective bargaining. Though the recession and wage cutting meant that relations between the unions and employers were rarely smooth, the 1930s saw the establishment of trade boards in a number of industries and greater use of government-appointed conciliation officers. It seemed to work: in 1937, Frank Gannett, head of the US newspaper chain which still bears his name, visited Britain to study its industrial relations and wrote later that 'the British have been blessed with little of this conflict between capital and labour'. A consensus had been reached, based on the supremacy of capital, but with an acknowledged place for organised labour – with disciplined collective bargaining as its cornerstone.

The historical parallels illuminate by contrast as well as by similarity. In the 1980s, as in the 1920s, few union leaders expect much from the TUC other than central services and a certain lobbying presence with government: the NUM ambitions to destroy the Thatcher project of curbing union power had themselves been curbed. 'New realism', a more collaborative style *vis-à-vis* government and employer, on the implicit understanding that the TUC is now the junior of the social partners, was all that was available.

But where the new order after 1926 was forged by leaders who gradually underpinned TUC authority by asserting collective discipline through strong, centralised leadership, the post-1985 order owes its inspiration to men who base their appeal on turning decisions of all kinds over to their members to take. The miners' strike had shown that the individual could, when pushed, destroy collective discipline that was felt to be illegitimate. Those attempting to re-legitimise trade unionism in the late twentieth century were ready to take advantage of that lesson by elevating the individual member to a position of authority he had not previously been told he could enjoy.

The TUC did not, as some of its leaders and officials expected, suffer a sustained charge of betrayal after the strike from the NUM or even the bulk of the left. Scargill, on the day (3 March) a special delegate conference called off the strike, said that a major reason why most of his members had returned to work was 'that the trade union movement in Britain, with a few honourable exceptions, have left this union isolated. They have not carried out TUC congress decisions, to their eternal shame.' But they didn't *feel* shame; indeed, most felt only relief, and settled back to business as usual. Quite quickly, the waters closed over the head of the miners' strike; disputes on the London Underground, the railways and the schools occupied the time of the General Council.

But two men knew that business could not continue as usual, nor did they wish it to. Eric Hammond and Gavin Laird had both come up through the ranks of skilled workers after the war: both had begun their political trajectory on the left (Laird in the Communist Party), both had explicitly and consciously rejected it. Hammond had taken over the general secretaryship of the Electrical Electronic Telecommunications and Plumbing Union from the formidable former Communist anti-Communist Frank Chapple in 1983. Laird had followed the equally protean figure of (Sir) John Boyd to the secretaryship of the Amalgamated Union of Engineering Workers in 1982. They claimed between them a membership of more than 1.3 million workers.

They were to become the public exponents of the '*new* new realism', but they could not have done so were they not products of two forcing-houses for right-wing labourism. The AUEW right, organised, disciplined and influential, maintains with some of the same vigour and idealism more commonly found on the left a style of union work which emphasises gradual change, fidelity to the Labour leadership and anti-Communism. As the union movement – and the AUEW itself, for 10 years under the presidency of Hugh (now Lord) Scanlon – went to the left in the 1960s and 1970s, the citadel of the right in the union was guarded by a succession of hard-minded general secretaries: Jim Conway, from 1964 to 1975; Sir John Boyd, from 1975 to 1982; and Gavin Laird, from 1982. The AUEW right had constantly to prove itself against a left wing in which the Communist Party was strong and active, and which could produce at the same time national figures like Scanlon and Jimmy Reid, the Clydeside leader who gripped the country's imagination when he became the public face of working-class opposition to Tory policies in the early 1970s through the 'work-in' at Upper Clyde shipyards. The union had developed a two-party system more advanced than any found in any other union. It was one which produced bitterly-fought elections, but also a certain respect: the Communist Jim Airlie, Jimmy Reid's comrade on the Clyde and executive member for Scotland from 1983, said of the majority of his colleagues on the right that 'they represent something deep in the union; a political tradition that has roots. I *also* represent a political tradition with roots.' Common to both strands in the union was a class consciousness which was free from ideological meaning, but laden with class and craft pride. Conway told an interviewer in 1964 that the union's then greatly increased representation in Parliament through sponsored MPs was 'a matter of prestige. We are the most important union in Britain. And the men we send to Parliament are *authentic* working class men.'[2] The 'authenticity' of the AUEW's working-class credentials has proved vital to their project of swinging the Labour movement to the right.

The EETPU has had a more sensational trajectory. The ballot-rigging scandal organised by the Communist-dominated executive in the late 1950s, the replacement of the CP group by a group led by Les Cannon, then Frank Chapple, both former Party activists, is well known at least in outline. Under Chapple's leadership over 20 years to 1983, the right wing has asserted a hegemony over the union which has rarely appeared to face serious challenge.

The new leadership, many of them former Communists, progressively dismantled the left-activist bases within the union – such as the district committees – replacing them with industrially-based branches and, more importantly, replacing the pyramidal structure of voting for executive members with direct, postal balloting. Like the AUEW, the EETPU's executive is full-time, elected by members in a given geographical region; as in the AUEW, the postal ballot vote became an article of faith.

Both unions' leaderships accepted, reluctantly, the TUC's adoption of the Wembley programme in April 1982. Terry Duffy, then president, made a rather confused, short speech, in which he pledged support while clearly his heart was not fully in it. He reminded the delegates that in spite of an agreement to oppose government legislation, 'it remained the prerogative of individual unions to do as they like'. It would obey the injunction not to take government cash for ballots – but he reinforced his union's attachment to them: 'If you want democracy you take orders from the bottom.'

Hammond was less accommodating, indeed, his speech was not in support of the TUC policy at all. He asked: 'Will a policy of massive confrontation serve us best in achieving this objective [of changing the government at the next election] or might we and they be better served to undertake the best possible damage limitation?' Breaking the law in an advanced democracy like Britain's, said Hammond – amplifying Duffy's point – was a wholly different matter from the defiance of 'arbitrary law' in Poland, Russia, South Africa and Chile. 'In Britain, it is a rejection of democracy itself – and that is the only real means we have to change bad law.'

The Wembley Principles were a more or less complete failure. Few trade unionists marched or demonstrated; a majority voted for parties other than Labour a year after the Wembley conference. Its decisions remained on the TUC 'statute book' – but only the National Graphical Association sought to test the unions' commitment to the Wembley Principles, to find that the majority leaned heavily on the caveat entered by Murray that the General Council could give no union a blank cheque.

The 1984 Congress, with its motion pledging 'total support' for the miners' struggle to save pits, jobs and communities and its appeal to other workers to make the dispute more effective by banning the movement of coal or oil substituted for it, was a patent attempt to bring the NUM leadership to the negotiating table and keep them there. It was sold to the right wing on that basis, with the further sweetener added in the motion that support would only be delivered 'after detailed discussions with the general council and agreement with the unions which would be directly concerned'. The EEPTU and the Engineering Managers' Association, alone among the unions in the power industry whose support was crucial, refused to toe the line.

Hammond gave a largely inaudible speech, drowned by bellowing from the floor and even more from the gallery. 'Can [the miners] not hear the back-stage whispering?' said Hammond. The motion was 'an expedient to get us through the week but it will be at the cost of credibility and confidence for years to come'. In an attack on his own TUC colleagues as pointed as Chapple had ever made, Hammond said that they were supporting the motion from 'fear of being politically attacked by the 57 varieties of political extremists who have attached themselves to the miners' cause, or fear of being branded right-wing. . . . The General Council has spoken in this statement: today Congress will speak. But I tell you, brothers, your members have yet to be heard. In their name, I oppose the statement and the motion.'

John Lyons, of the Engineering Managers – rising after Derek Fullick, president of the train drivers' union ASLEF had expressed his 'disgust' at Hammond's speech – told the congress that if it carried the motion it would be 'in the knowledge that, one, it will not work; two, you are pretending to the miners already on strike for six months that support is coming when it is not; and three, you will do so, most of you, safe in the knowledge that you bear no responsibility whatsoever for the outcome of what you are deciding.' The industrial leverage of the power workers – the capacity, as Hammond had put it, to ensure that 'all industrial activity and the means of civilised life will end' – could not be used and democracy survive. Both Lyons and Hammond believed that their putative control of the industry meant they had a large responsibility in the preservation of the constitution. 'There can', concluded Lyons, 'scarcely ever have been a more important motion for the General Council, for the Congress, to throw out than this.'

But the AUEW executive *had* bought the resolution – though it was touch and go. Gerry Russell, the only executive councillor not tied to either the right or left machines, was their senior TUC councillor. He argued strongly for support of the motion with his colleagues. They were doubtful, but the caveats in the motion – that support would be dependent on 'detailed discussions with the General Council and agreement of the unions who would be directly concerned' – convinced them that there was no need to threaten TUC unity. They had had their arms twisted by Murray and Basnett and others, who really believed that TUC-assisted negotiation could solve the dispute. Though the instincts of some of them – Laird, Duffy (then a sick man) – was that Scargill would not settle, they were prepared to leave judgment on that to those more centrally involved. Laird stood up to say that, yes, 'we have been very critical of the fact that the NUM saw fit for all too many months to ignore the General Council', and, yes, 'there is no excuse for violence on the picket line' but that, yes, 'from today . . . the AUEW and its 943,000 members are at one with the NUM and we will resolve this dispute on the basis of victory.'

Long before it was resolved on the basis of defeat, Laird, and the majority of his colleagues, had decided they had no longer any use for false unity with the TUC. First the engineers, then the electricians, deliberately determined to break ranks with the Wembley Principles at the point which was at once their weakest link and, for these two unions, their most irksome aspect. They decided to apply to the government for money to fund their ballots.

To take state aid for ballots – available under the 1980 Employment Act – was one of two explicit prohibitions under the Wembley Principles; the other was holding votes on the maintenance of a closed shop. Both were adopted in the Wembley spirit of a refusal to bow the knee to the demands of a government seen as interfering in internal union affairs, but both were terribly vulnerable to an awakening desire among union members to make use of these parts of Tory legislation which gave them voting rights.

Both the AUEW and the EETPU were principled proponents of a voting system based on the individual making decisions in his or her own time, free from any possibility of activist manipulation. (Both Laird and Hammond carried their search for the fairest possible ballot into the political sphere, and supported some form of proportional representation because it avoided the inequities of the traditional British 'first past the post' system.) Their decisions to drop further adherence to the Wembley Principles in this regard were taken against this broad philosophical field, but the thrust of their attack was both stimulated and strengthened by the experience of the miners' dispute. They believed that the strike saw the denial of individual rights in favour of a democratic centralist approach with which the rest of the Labour movement acquiesced, if not actually approved. The ending of the strike in defeat, and the low opinion in which Scargill was held by many in the Labour movement by its end, were necessary to the launching of the initiative and to its ultimate success.

As the miners' strike ground to defeat in November of 1984, the AUEW executive held a ballot of its membership on whether or not to take the ballot money. The government had set a time limit of February 1985 to apply for aid retrospectively to March 1981, when the fund first became available. The membership delivered a 12:1 vote in favour, but next April the policy-making National Committee, though right-wing dominated, voted that the ballot be run again – with this time the arguments against taking the money to be put as well as the arguments for. The National Committee, right or left, were activists alarmed by the danger, obvious from that time, of TUC discipline being exerted against the AUEW. Duffy had to accept the vote, but said, 'Even if the TUC votes for our expulsion, which I do not think they will, we would have to accept that sadly.'

In June, the Certification Officer handed over £1.2 million in ballot money to cover polling between March 1981 and September 1984. As he did so another application for funds, from the EEPTU, was lodged. The smaller union claimed some £200,000. Hammond, even more combative than the AUEW leaders because less constrained by internal union pressures, told his conference in July that the research department had come up with some 100 cases of unions holding ballots on the maintenance of closed shops – the other specific proscription of the 'Wembley Principles'. The right-led AUEW and EETPU were being singled out for censure with a 'special spite', he said. 'There is hardly a major TUC policy that has not been breached by one or more of the unions.'

The 'ballot row' grew till, by the September Congress, it filled most of the space available. The TUC had boxed itself in: its finance and general purposes committee had voted 13:1 in July to discipline the AUEW. From then on, the train was on the rails and could not be stopped. Willis, still bogged down in talks with the NUM leadership and struggling to impose his authority on a Congress House bureaucracy which he did not quite trust, was trapped between a gut feeling that the engineers were running with the tide, and his job as upholder of Congress policy which they were clearly flouting. When a miner, Tommy Barrett, told him on a Radio 4 phone-in on 27 August that the balloting provisions of the 1984 Act were 'pro-union . . . I *demand* the right to choose my leaders', Willis responded warmly that 'there will be many speeches made next week [during Congress] on that subject, but I doubt if there will be any better ones than that.' At the same time, though, he told the *Financial Times* in an interview that 'if you want one national centre it must be effective. If there is any solution, it must have the element of recognition of TUC authority.'

It did not. The AUEW and the TUC were caught in a game of facing each other down. As was said *ad nauseam* at the time, the AUEW blinked first. A week of hectic meetings behind the stage of Blackpool's Winter Gardens, the Imperial Hotel and the AUEW's base at the Clifton Hotel resulted in a TUC team composed of Willis, Keys, Basnett and Ron Todd of the Transport Workers producing a fudge which deferred any decision on suspension of the AUEW until after its second ballot in

November. The fudge got a 35:7 majority on the General Council. The agreed statement laid down that the AUEW would put on its ballot paper that 'the AUEW as an affiliate of the TUC acknowledge the authority of Congress and accepts that under the direction of the general council the consequences of a yes vote will mean suspension from the TUC.'

The General Council had backed away in the face of irresistible force. For the past three months, it had been clear that the EETPU, and some in the AUEW, were wholly reconciled to being expelled from the TUC and to forming a rival centre outside it. Laird talked confidently of being 'able to stand on our own feet'. Hammond, more specific, itemised the non-TUC affiliated unions – which organise some 2 million workers – as being a solid base on which to start recruiting for a new, moderate force. He was the man of the congress. He told a hostile audience on 3 September, during the debate on employment law, that 'I must put my union's position beyond doubt. Put us out of the TUC, declare open season on our membership, and we will not lie quiescent waiting to be carved up. We will do what is necessary to survive. Unthinkable pacts on union membership, a free for all. *You ain't seen nothing yet.*' The General Council didn't want to see it.

Hammond was only in part talking of the ballot fund issue. More important for his union, and much more important for both the Labour movement and the UK economy, was the underlying movement he was seeking to stimulate. The EETPU, followed in this case by the Engineers, had adopted a new industrial philosophy which it intended to implement, with or without the TUC. It was immensely ambitious: it sought to replace the class-based trade unionism in which conflict was seen as endemic, even a good, with a co-operative style of working in which industrial action was all but impossible. Starting with an agreement signed with Toshiba in Plymouth in 1980, the EETPU developed an off-the-shelf industrial relations system which promised the reconciliation of potential disputes without striking, in return for a substantial concession of influence and control by workplace representatives over the organisation of production, marketing, investment and manpower policy. Central to most of such packages was 'pendulum arbitration' – an agreement that, in the event of a dispute, both sides would abide by the decision of an arbitrator who would decide between either the union's claim or the employer's offer, rather than attempting to find a compromise in the middle. This would, it was held, force both parties closer together in their initial positions. A necessary component of such deals was that they were signed between employer and one union only, thus cutting out the multi-unionism typical of UK industry and hated by employers.

It was inspired by Japanese practice. Roy Sanderson, the EETPU national engineering officer was an enthusiast for Japan, regarding it as egalitarian and efficient at the same time. It was Japanese companies who pioneered the adoption of the EETPU practices: Toshiba, Hitachi, Sony and Sanyo all signed. When Nissan finally determined on a site near Washington New Town in the north-east for its Datsun assembly plant, it made clear to the competing unions that it, too, wanted a no-strike agreement with a single union. The AUEW clinched the deal in April 1985 with an agreement copied from the EETPU. It laid down that both sides would seek to resolve all disputes without recourse to industrial action, but if they could not, ACAS would be called in and pendulum arbitration used. Workers would be trained to be wholly flexible between skills; supervisors would be given enhanced authority; all conditions of work would be common, all staff salaried. 'What we are attempting to do,' said Peter Wickens, the Nissan personnel director, 'is eliminate the need for industrial action.'

The deals were popular with many employers – though not all, as the EETPU pointed out. Many were 'too conservative', in the union's words, to concede to union members the range of decisions which the package called for as a *quid pro quo* for peace. As importantly, strikes were no longer a major problem: the strike rate for 1985 – 813 stoppages – was among the lowest for 30 years. But where a company was in trouble, it would often reach for a new-style deal to save it. Borg Warner, the US-based transmission company, saved a 600-job plant in West Glamorgan by concluding a deal with the AUEW which specified complete flexibility between trades and a *six*-year pay agreement. Shell Chemicals cut its workforce from 1,200 to 700 at its Carrington Plant, near Manchester, and got more flexibility by agreement with all of its site unions. Ian Brown, the craft unions' convenor, later ran for an EETPU executive post (unsuccessfully) on a left-wing ticket. In those instances and others, companies effectively said to their workers: this is the only way we can save the plant; if you don't want to save it, don't agree.

The electricians' ambitions took them even to Fleet Street. Eddie Shah's taste for a national presence had been whetted by his blooding at Warrington in 1983. He had been made much of by some of the great of the land and grown mightily in confidence. In the spring of 1985 he set up an office near Victoria in London and began prospecting the chances of a new national paper. By July, the EETPU leadership and Shah had agreed, in outline, a no-strike, single-union deal for the paper. Fleet Street managers, feeling the balance of power shifting since Warrington, leapt on the bandwagon. Robert Maxwell got rid of more than 2,000 of the 7,000 Mirror Group jobs by agreement with the unions as the EETPU stood in the wings, waiting to sign if they did not; and Rupert Murdoch, peripatetic Australian owner of *The Times*, *Sunday Times*, *Sun* and *News of the World*, put up a legally binding, no-strike, wholly flexible, management rules draft agreement which *only* the EETPU was prepared to talk about – even the AUEW backed away from that.

The electricians' union overreached itself slightly with Murdoch: in colluding with his News International Company to supply members to his new printing plants at Wapping in London and in Glasgow, it earned the condemnation of all TUC General Council members and had to back off from signing an agreement with the company which would have excluded the other print unions.

The symmetry between the EETPU, the AUEW and the UDM became clearer as the miners' strike receded. Their leadership styles were all in part a reaction against the left: in the case of the latter two, a revulsion from the left, which took concrete form as an attachment to ballot-based democracy, a populist stress on individual membership supremacy. Their rhetoric was as comfortably employed in defence of individual freedom, individual choice, as in the services of the collectivist virtues – though all adhered to these, too, at times.

Their industrial posture was frankly and openly what most unions were covertly: an acceptance of the marketplace and a determination to do well in that marketplace for their members. But in their frankness in espousing market principles they went further than a grudging acquiescence, they became enthusiastic proponents of efficiency and productivity. Laird and Hammond saw British industrial problems in much the same way as senior managers did. They believed in flexibility at work, for example, not just as a counter to be conceded in return for higher wages or greater consultation, but as desirable in itself. The EETPU, followed by the AUEW, set up training courses for their members to prepare them for the electronic age because employers were too tardy in doing so. In April, the union got Norman Tebbit, then Trade and Industry Secretary and former hammer of the unions, to open the second technology centre at Cudham, in Kent. Hammond, whose grinding nasal working-class accent is similar to Tebbit's, joked that 'some of our colleagues felt that having you here would be a clear signal to the world of our softening our attitudes.'

There was nothing starry-eyed about any of this: the EETPU and the AUEW were in business for members. They increasingly saw themselves *as* businesses attracting members on the basis of the package it could offer them. The EETPU used the most advanced computer facility in the union movement to keep in touch with its membership and tailor information and services for them. The training programmes were designed to allow the union to 'follow the job' when plants changed over from mechanical or electro-mechanical production techniques to electronic equipment; without such training, the electricians would lose out to the technicians unions like ASTMS and Tass. The union leaderships knew, too, that at a time of waning union power, they could not bludgeon employers into conceding recognition; rather they had to market themselves better than the next union, offering employers, as well as members, a service if they signed a deal rather than trouble if they didn't.

They did not, of course, put it in this way, but Laird, Hammond and their colleagues had adapted to post-Thatcher life quite well. Indeed, they liked parts of it; they liked the 1984 Trade Union Act, seeing it as a vindication of their own practice. Because of that, they were able to use it.

The AUEW's second ballot on taking government money produced an 8:1 majority in December. The EETPU's first ballot produced a 9:1 majority on a 41 per cent poll, higher than most returns on the electricians' postal ballot system. Hammond turned the knife as he announced the results, saying that the most difficult question he had to answer from his members was 'What does the union get from being a member of the TUC?' He capped that by saying, 'If we made a cold calculation, we would have more members if we were outside the TUC than inside.' In February 1986 a special TUC conference dropped the policy of opposition to taking ballot money.

As the TUC did so, so the individual unions were quietly dropping their initial bravado in flouting the Acts. Jimmy Knapp, leader of the railway workers, admitted after the collapse of a London Underground strike in May 1985 that the 1984 Act had stimulated an expectation among his members that they be balloted before a strike (they were not in the tube strike). In August, when his guards were faced with British Rail demands to introduce driver-only operated trains, he got his left-dominated executive to accept that a ballot would have to be held, then campaigned for it like a presidential candidate. BR responded in kind, and Knapp lost his strike ballot, but said afterwards he would not revert to a strike call without a ballot. In January 1986 the TGWU and the AUEW together called a strike at Ford over a two-year deal which, the company claimed, gave some 15 per cent in return for improved productivity and flexibility. The two unions prepared meticulously; after mass meetings, booths were set up in the workplace for secret voting. This time, the unions won, by 2:1. The age of the car-park meetings with the (often disputed) show of hands appeared to be over.

The UDM's industrial posture of encouraging productivity-based bargaining was as consonant with the EETPU's no-strike flexibility agreement as its anti-Scargillism was in tune with the larger union's anti-leftism. The two organisations struck up close links during the miners' strike. Prendergast was vice president of a right-wing union grouping called Mainstream, whose powerhouse was the EETPU's research director, John Spellar, a former MP for Birmingham Northfields. The day after the NUM executive called on the TUC to censure the electricians' union for its contacts with the UDM – 10 January – the top officials of the two unions met to talk about energy policy, and found they agreed that it should be a mix of coal, oil and nuclear power (the NUM is wholly anti-nuclear). 'Some of us', said Tom Breakell, the EETPU's emotional president, 'saw in the mining dispute, not completely and not directly, images of the Communist dictatorship of the electrical trades union. We were beginning to think that perhaps we better start fighting again.' Less high-flown comment had it that the electricians were looking for a takeover of the new miners' union. Both leaderships denied it but both had thought of it. For the UDM, it was an insurance policy if it ran out of steam, or money.

For the unions, the miners' strike made thinkable, then do-able, a series of manoeuvres and actions which might have never been attempted, or would have been at issue between left and right. By removing the position of total defiance by showing that it resulted in catastrophe for the union which attempted it, it united left and right in pragmatism. It meant that the hyperbolic positions taken at Wembley, to which the left before and during the strike were demanding absolute fidelity, were universally seen as irrelevant and damaging. In the AUEW, Bill Jordan, a strong right-winger, became AUEW president in April 1986 following the death of Terry Duffy in November 1985. At the General and Municipal Workers, John Edmonds, a man of the pragmatic centre, succeeded David Basnett as general secretary in January 1986. Even at the TGWU, a left redoubt since the 1950s, the right began to recover confidence, as the postal ballots for the union's general executive council began to replace the left-wingers with centrists or right-wingers. Ron Todd, its leftist general secretary, swung the full support of Kinnock, especially in his campaign to rid the Labour Party of the Trotskyist Militant Tendency. Everywhere, trade union officials began to speak of the need for efficiency and profitability.

The strike cauterised all illusions that the leadership and activist groups who necessarily run unions necessarily speak for their members. The Tory challenge to the unions' hegemony over the working class, for so long unquestioned, met its greatest test in the pit dispute, and won.

For the Labour Party, and for its leader especially, the strike had and will continue to have for many years an effect greater than any event since the war. Frozen during the strike in a posture of support which varied from the very grudging to the very gung ho, Labour since has had to reassess and come to terms with the ambiguity in the party, one which has run through it from its earliest days: is it a party of revolt or of reform? does it overthrow the existing order, or amend it? The question is in practice capable of every sort of deviation and fudge, and will always be so as long as there are socialist parties in democracies, but at times – the miners' strike was one of them – the cadres of such a party are forced to express, even if only to themselves, their allegiance, fundamentally, to the evolutionary or revolutionary route.

Tony Benn, since early 1983 the MP for Chesterfield, with Denis Healey Labour's longest serving former cabinet minister, put himself at the head of the latter route in the aftermath of the 1979 Labour defeat. He would deny it on two counts: first, he insists that the cult of the personal leadership is dangerous, and that he merely articulated and helped shape a growing current which flowed from the working class itself through the Labour Party; second, that he and his group were revolutionaries 'in the sense of taking over the BBC one morning and getting rid of Timpson and Redhead' (the *Today* programme's presenters). One of the few opinions he shares with Neil Kinnock is that there are no revolutionaries in Britain; he goes on to say that those in the various far left groups are merely putting forward different analyses of capitalism's nature, attempting to shed some illumination in a world darkened by media obscurantism.

But revolutionary change does not depend on undergoing a re-run of the Bolshevik seizure of power, or Castro's eventual victory over Battista. In the UK context in the late twentieth century, revolutionary change would be a politics which replaces capitalist or mixed-economy relationships with fully socialist ones; which radically alters the UK's network of international alliances, particularly within the Common Market, NATO and *vis-à-vis* the United States; and which replaces in fundamental ways, powers and prerogatives of Parliament and the cabinet by powers exercised by parties or by organisations such as – applicable in this case – trade unions.

Neil Kinnock had said goodbye to all that publicly when he refused to vote for Benn during the 1981 deputy leadership elections, though when in October 1983 he was elected leader of the Labour Party over Roy Hattersley, he retained enough of what came to be known as 'soft left' support to freeze out the rather limp challenge from Michael Meacher on the far left, and to confine Hattersley to the centre and right. He inherited a party which, under the leadership of Michael Foot, had in the 1983 election polled a little more than a quarter of votes cast; a part of whose right had formed the Social Democratic Party which, with the Liberals, rarely dipped below a 25 per cent rating (Kinnock thought little, probably far too little, of David Owen, its leader, but genuinely regretted the loss of Shirley Williams, its President); which had a membership of over 250,000; an organisation near bankruptcy and badly run; a network of constituency Labour Parties often – especially in London and other large cities – controlled by the far left; 210 MPs; and a need to win between 130 and 135 seats at the next election if it was to gain power again.

All Labour leaders who won elections have conformed to what seemed to them the inexorable logic of British politics; they began as left-wingers and clawed in to the centre. MacDonald, Attlee and Wilson had little else obviously in common, but that they should share that confers upon the rightwards move which Kinnock instituted a certain traditional benison. It had some success: the polls began to swing Labour's way, the inner party struggles abated, and the soft left rallied to the new leader, progressively isolating those who would not come with them into a hard left represented in the Commons by the Campaign Group.

Kinnock, who did not like Scargill, and who had come close to hitting him during a *Panorama* programme immediately after the deputy leadership elections in which the then Yorkshire area president lectured him on the nature of the Labour Party, nevertheless made it his business to see him first of all union leaders after his assumption of the leadership. He did not underestimate the Yorkshireman: he had witnessed his campaign for the national presidency, saw him sweeping through the right-wing areas.

The first meeting between the two men, within three weeks of Kinnock taking over in October 1983, went well. The Labour leader knew there was a good chance of a strike soon, and wanted to offer counsel that it must be properly prepared for, and played long. Public opinion had to be brought on to the miners' side: the Surrey housewife had to be made to feel sympathetic as well as support maintained in the coalfields. Scargill agreed. When he came back to see Kinnock a few weeks later he brought with him Nell Myers, his press and publicity officer, and talked of a leaflet campaign and the need to make the case for coal. When the strike was called in March the next year, Kinnock was appalled. He thought, and believes still, that Scargill – who had wished to play it long – felt he was losing control of the Yorkshiremen and panicked.

Kinnock met Scargill and Heathfield at the end of March, a few weeks after the strike began. He asked him insistently: what is your strategy? But Scargill did not answer directly, preferring instead to concentrate on the weakness of the board and government. The two did not meet again for more than two months. Kinnock believed that a ballot would be called – registered public disappointment when it was not – then seemed to draw back, concentrating his parliamentary fire on accusations that the government was manipulating negotiations.

He was privately horrified by the strike's leadership; he thought they had boxed themselves in so securely with arguments about why a ballot should not be held that they did not have the courage to break out and hold one, even when logic dictated they should. He visited picket lines discreetly. At the Wylfa power station in North Wales – where his brother-in-law was in charge of the pickets – he heard that the miners were experiencing decreasing success in turning back the lorries, driven by TGWU members (Kinnock's own union) because the drivers objected to taking supportive action on behalf of a union in which the lack of a ballot had encouraged some members of it to work.

But he voiced no public criticism. As he faced his colleagues in the shadow cabinet room next to his office each Tuesday and Thursday, he found himself doing what he hated most – back-pedalling, excusing. His overriding imperative was: don't give Scargill an alibi; don't pull the plug on him in a way that would enable the miners' president to blame Kinnock, and the parliamentary party, for the strike's failure (which Kinnock saw as inevitable from an early stage).

He worked away with Stan Orme at getting a settlement. The shadow energy secretary was one of the nicest men in the Labour Party: straightforward, warmhearted and (for a senior politician) remarkably free from malice. He was in touch with everyone in the strike and was trusted by most; he never appeared to lose faith in the possibilities of negotiation. When Kinnock refused to be bounced into appearing in the series of rallies in November 1984, planned to gather fresh support for the flagging strike, Orme unfussily went to three of the five, and got a big hand from the miners at all. But he accomplished nothing.

Kinnock did appear with Scargill at a rally, but it was on his own terms: at a rally organised by the Labour Party itself, in Stoke on Trent, on 30 November. That morning, David Wilkie, driving a working miner to Merthyr Vale Colliery near Aberfan, had been killed when a concrete block smashed through his minicab's roof. Kinnock's difficult task was, for the most ghoulish of reasons, made a little easier. 'We meet here tonight', he said, speaking after an exhausted Scargill, 'in the shadow of an outrage.' He was heckled: some of the NUM's far left supporters had got in to the ticket-only affair and began screaming in rage against a man they believed had betrayed the cause. Kinnock, his own fury barely under control, described them as 'living like parasites off the struggle of the miners'; they were manhandled from the hall. But most of his speech was well prepared; it was, as Willis's had been in Aberavon a month before, aimed at rehabilitating the struggle within the bounds of normal industrial relations. The dispute, he said, 'does not originate in any political motives. It is not fuelled by any ambition to harm democracy in this country. British democracy is strong. Its values and institutions have never been threatened from below by any social mood, industrial dispute or political movement, for it has always been the subject of democracy that has advanced liberty and tried to sustain that acheivement.'

He could not leave it there. The NUM was left, after the strike, with a legacy of sacked miners. The executive, before the July 1985 conference, agreed a motion for the TUC and the Labour Party which called for the reinstatement of all sacked miners, the reimbursement of all monies fined or sequestrated during the strike, a review of all cases of miners jailed and an end to all pit closures other than on grounds of exhaustion. The

TUC general council urged its rejection; Willis lobbied hard against it, even putting his own job on the line over it; but a waffling speech from the TUC general secretary and a confident performance from Scargill secured a victory by a whisker at the Congress (4.649 million votes to 4.585 million) and a more solid victory at party conference (3.542 million to 2.912 million). Kinnock had been assured that the TUC would defeat it. In Blackpool when the vote was taken, he instantly disassociated himself from it. At Bournemouth, in the antiseptic new conference centre, Kinnock let himself go.

The conference debate saw Kinnock turn the tables on Scargill: he lost the vote, but won the day. Scargill was cramped into a ten-minute speech from the rostrum (which ended when his microphone was switched off as he explained the class nature of the strike). He recalled that Kinnock had earlier in the week said that principles without power were sterile: 'As a socialist all my life I urge that power without principles is unthinkable.'

Kinnock came back with a speech which he had prepared for the past 18 months. It was the most passionate speech of his career, all the more remarkable for following, the previous day, a tremendous oratorical performance in which he used the phrase 'enabling state' as a forerunner of the party's renewed commitment to liberalism, and tore into the 'obscenity' of Militant-dominated Liverpool council politics. It was precise, concentrating on the practical ways of assisting, for example, the mineworkers still then dismissed for proven or alleged offences committed during the strike. It was also shot through by the repressed rage which Kinnock had had to suffer during the strike. When interrupted by a heckler who asked him how he had assisted the miners during the dispute, he roared back, 'Well I was not telling them lies. That is what I was not doing during that period' – a clear reference to his view of the NUM president's stance. As the 16-minute speech went on, it became more and more of an indictment of the NUM leadership (Eric Hammond had earlier characterised the miners as 'lions led by donkeys'; Kinnock, who had publicly rebuked him for the phrase, said in essence the same thing). The strike had 'left the management of the National Coal Board with a power, a prerogative, a force that no mining management in Britain has enjoyed for one day since 1947.' Quoting a lodge official in his own Islwyn constituency, he said that, 'The fact . . . that it [the strike] was called without a ballot denied to the miners unity and denied to the miners the solidarity of so much of the rest of the trade union movement [Applause]. On top of that . . . we were given continued, repeated promises that coal stocks were on the verge of exhaustion, and it was never true.' Kinnock continued his quotations of the lodge official, who sounded terribly like the leader of the Labour Party: 'The strike wore on. The violence built up because the single tactic chosen was that of mass picketing and so we saw policing on a scale and with a system that has never been seen in Britain before. The court actions came, and by their attitude to the court actions the NUM leadership ensured that they would face crippling damages as a consequence. To the question: "How did this position arise?" the man from my lodge in my constituency said: "It arose because nobody really thought it out." ' Kinnock managed, in that speech, to load the blame not just for the strike's failure, but for much else, on to the NUM leadership. For example, by blaming violence on the tactic of mass picketing, he made police action (which he had often criticised) dependent on the prior violence caused by a leadership tactic. It was as complete a repudiation of Scargill as was possible.

It depended for much of its content on Kim Howells, the South Wales NUM's research officer, who became a Kinnock confidant. Howells, as sharp and charismatic as Kinnock himself, emerged in the latter stages of the strike and after it as the fiercest critic of Scargill from within the miners' ranks. He helped Kinnock with that and other speeches, and supplied position papers on coal and energy policy to him. Kinnock tried to persuade a sceptical Howells to run for a Labour seat. Howells was a little embarrassed when *Private Eye* revealed he had helped Kinnock on the speech – but not *too* embarrassed. His employers shielded him from the wrath of Scargill. He enjoyed the sudden access to power and country-wide popularity with Labour and other groups that his actions gave him, and, in the end, he believed he was right.

Kinnock's speech drew tremendous acclaim from across the spectrum (Heathfield curtly dismissed it as 'diabolical'). By the support it was shown to gain from the conference (though it was loudly heckled), it enabled Kinnock further to hem in the hard left, detaching its more doubtful members like Michael Meacher from it (Meacher backed Kinnock in the crucial national executive vote to oppose the miners' motion, which went through by 15 votes to 14: Kinnock was working on him even while the vote was taken). That was of great importance in the other struggle within the party – that over Militant, and its grip on Liverpool Council. Kinnock's first speech of the conference, his parliamentary report, contained a root-and-branch attack on the Militant council leaders. With the support of the soft left, the party agreed in November to launch an inquiry into their practice in Liverpool's Labour politics.

Kinnock's style, inevitably dubbed 'Rambo-ism' from the Sylvester Stallone film released around the same time, faced the left with a gruesome choice: could they oppose him and claim to care about the next election? Could they support him and retain their left credentials? The Labour Co-ordinating Committee, which had by then evolved away from its Bennite roots to become a soft left body, underwent much private and public agonising during the party conference but finally decided in its newsletter of 3 October that 'those who decide to fight Kinnock are saying they do not care about the winning the next election'.

The Labour leader, by this time, cared little for their support: oddly, he appeared to be more impressed by the positions taken by a small and declining party which was facing convulsions even more fundamental (for it) than those taking place in the Labour Party. The Communist Party of Great Britain, which for much of its history could claim it had as much effect on the miners' politics as Labour, had come out of the strike in terrible shape.

Very many of the miners' leaders on the left had been in the party: Horner and Paynter; Abe and Alex Moffat, both Scottish NUM presidents; Jock Kane from Yorkshire; Daly and McGahey; Scargill himself. But McGahey was unusual in staying in: as Labour turned to the left, the CP lost its hold over militants, especially young working-class activists.

In the 1970s the current known as Eurocommunism swept through the West European parties. Produced very largely by the Communist Party of Italy under the late Enrico Berlinguer, Eurocommunism built on the work of the Italian Communist and Marxist political scientist Antonio Gramsci in turning away from a revolutionary seizure of state power by a vanguard party to a strategy of widening the arena for democratic advance, with the working class seeking alliances with other social movements. The PCI embraced what Communists had called 'bourgeois' democracy, recognising that it embodied gains for which workers themselves had striven and from which they benefited.

The CPGB, never a mass party and by the 1970s down to a membership in the 20,000-30,000 mark, stayed clear of the controversy which raged round Eurocommunism for a time, but in the end, was drawn into it. Within the party a pro-Soviet wing, angered by Eurocommunism's increasingly open attacks on the Soviet Union, split to form the New Communist Party in summer 1977; other pro-Soviets remained in, hoping to steer the party away from its flirtation with liberalism back to the correct, proletarian internationalist line. Factions began to form. The 'hard-liners', or pro-Soviets, had bases in the *Morning Star*, the CP newspaper which was controlled by a front organisation called the People's Press Printing Society, together with the British Soviet Friendship Society and Marx House, the CP-founded library. The Eurocommunists had a strong influence on the leadership and the executive, and controlled the monthly theoretical journal, *Marxism Today*.

Marxism Today, under the talented editorship of Martin Jacques, became something of a house journal for the 'soft' left. It coined the word 'Thatcherism', by which it meant a kind of Conservative politics quite different to that which had gone before, to which a new response from the left was called for. Professor Eric Hobsbawm, the party's most distinguished intellectual and an internationally respected modern historian, wrote in September 1978 an essay on 'The Forward March of Labour Halted', that a working class no longer cast in the mould the left assumed would no longer respond in the way it wished. Stuart Hall, whose essays formed a constant bedrock of *Marxism Today*'s thesis, wrote in 'The great Moving Right Show' (in *The Politics of Thatcherism*, 1983) that Thatcher's populist style 'is no rhetorical device or trick, for this populism is operating on genuine contradictions, it has a rational and material core'.[3]

Kinnock let it be known that he liked this kind of thing. When Hobsbawm was the star turn at a Fabian Society meeting on the eve of the 1983 Labour Party conference, Kinnock chaired the meeting and openly admitted his debt to the surprised Hobsbawm. The hard-liners in the party seethed. Mick Costello, the party's industrial organiser, lighted on an article by Tony Lane in the September 1982 issue of *Marxism Today* which criticised shop stewards as going beyond the pale. His infuriated comments appeared in the *Morning Star*, and Costello was later dismissed from his job, to be replaced by Peter Carter, a former official of the building workers union UCATT.

The miners' strike appeared to unite the warring wings of the party, but as it dragged on the fissures reappeared. McGahey and George Bolton, the Scottish area vice president who was party chairman, grew more and more critical of their national president. In a *Marxism Today* round table in July 1984 Bolton, together with Alan Baker, the Communist branch secretary at Oakdale pit in Kinnock's Bedwellty constituency, voiced guarded criticism.

Carter, a bolder spirit, wanted to go further. He wrote a pamphlet deeply critical of Scargill's leadership, but had to agree to its suppression for the sake of 'unity'. Still unpublished, it was a remarkable document for a Communist Party official to write in the middle of a miners' strike, and showed how deep the gulf was growing between the CP and the NUM leader.

The pamphlet does not mention the NUM president by name as the object of its criticism, but he is. Pointing out that the political scene has shifted drastically since the early 1970s – a cornerstone to the characterisation of 'Thatcherism' – Carter says that this inability to learn 'led to the idea that the miners could win the strike alone through a re-run of Saltley Gate. There were too many illusions in the movement about the power of industrial muscle alone. . . . There was a lack of political clarity on how to develop the struggle in a way that the strike could have been won. Under such conditions unity becomes problematic and sections of the movement will respond in a narrow and sectarian way. . . . This approach represents the classic ultra-left response to the problems of encouraging mass working-class activity. In spite of its grass-roots pretensions, it is essentially politics from above, not below. If only trade union leaders would stick to a socialist line and the most militant form of action, the workers will follow and win through. This line was revealed during the miners' strike with a consistent refusal to take on the difficult but essential task of winning wider political support, concentrating instead on empty fanciful rhetoric for escalation to a General Strike. . . .

'All this suggests some vital lessons for the working class as a whole. In the present economic and political climate, even the best organised and most militant sections of the movement will face considerable difficulties if they cannot present their demands in terms capable of winning considerable support and building alliances. . . . The central task facing the left in the aftermath of the struggle is not to further open the wounds of the labour movement through revolutionary rhetoric and denunciation. Instead the crucial task is to preserve the unity and organisation of the NUM, to learn the potential lessons of industrial struggle under Thatcherism and prepare the ground for a widely-based political challenge to this government's assault on the coal industry, and other sections of British industry.'

In May the CPGB's 39th Congress was dominated by the strike. It debated, deeply divided over, but finally passed a motion written by Carter which pointed to the 'disunity, the Government's thorough preparations, [which] meant that both wider industrial action and broad public sympathy and support were essential for victory. Neither were forthcoming on the necessary scale and a sober analysis of the reasons why is essential. . . . Because the new features of the Thatcherite strategy were not grasped from the start, a coherent counter strategy was not found and implemented. . . . In [its] absence the concentration increasingly became the use of centralised mass picketing [which] . . . tended to internalise the struggle, hardening the division of miner against miner.' It was a rejection of Scargillism, a nail in the coffin of the myth of Saltley Gates.

Scargill deeply resented what he saw as the party's betrayal of him. In a meeting with party leaders in December 1985, he told Gordon McLennan, the CPGB general secretary, that he was the better Marxist of the two. McLennan, who believes that the CPGB is the only vehicle for Marxism in the UK, flared up at him in rage. McGahey, also at the meeting, sat silent, smoking, looking at the floor.

Only one figure of national stature stood with Scargill at the end. Tony Benn saw in the miners' president many parallels with himself. Both were abused by the media to the point of harassment and beyond; both had seen the desertion of allies; both saw themselves as serious challengers to the existing order and as men who could neither be corrupted nor bought. Benn accepted that the argument over the ballot was a 'red herring', believing that Nottinghamshire would not have come out on any count. He believed that the allegations of violence levelled against the miners had been disposed of by the Orgreave 'trials', in which miners accused of riot and violence against the police were acquitted as the ill-prepared police cases collapsed. He saw Scargill, alone among left trade unionists, as willing to take seriously the political battle against the Tories. Like Scargill, he scorned the CP's analysis of the mistakes made; like Scargill, he loathed Kinnock's march to the right, seeing in it a capitulation to the establishment from which he believed himself to have broken.

But he believed that the setback of the miners' strike was temporary: 'there's a great deal of feeling there, and you'll see it come out at the next election. The miners' strike was the greatest piece of political radicalisation I've seen; there have never been so many socialists in the country in my lifetime.'

It was an uncommon perception: that, in Benn's words, 'We're only half-way between Dunkirk and D–Day.' In his mind, as in Scargill's, was undimmed a vision of a time when the world would change to fit the pattern of history they claimed to be able to interpret better than their colleagues in the movement. As the strike confirmed Kinnock's commitment to the constitutional road, so in them it bred a deeper belief in the struggle's ultimate victory – once there had been a little lapse of time to end the period of confusion. They had historical parallels – Benn used Churchill, solitary in the mid-1930s; both could invoke the tiny band of Bolsheviks, mostly exiled, after the failed putsch of 1905; the remnants of the beaten Chinese Communists on a seemingly hopeless Long March; the tiny Castro forces hiding in the hills; the Viet Cong facing the might of the United States. History had moved their way: could it turn again for Arthur Scargill, and the forces he helped unleash, in Britain once Margaret Thatcher lost her grip on it?

Postscript

At the end of April 1986, thirteen months after the strike ended, Ian MacGregor announced a new title for the National Coal Board. It would now trade as 'British Coal', a symbol that 'the past is behind us and this will be our future'.

■ But as he departed from the Board two months later, freshly knighted in the Birthday Honours List, the uncertainties which have perpetually surrounded the industry still pressed upon it. A precipitate drop in oil prices, which at one stage had been cut by half, once more threatened the viability of pits struggling to improve their performance and led to a new cut-price deal for their coal to continue to supply the power stations. Then part way into the trauma came news of the dreadful accident at Chernobyl, questioning as never before the future of coal's nuclear competitor, and leading to a fresh look at mothballed plans for new coal-fired power stations. Coal was back on the roller-coaster.

■ MacGregor's own view, set out in a *Sunday Express* interview, was that the industry had been made safe for the foreseeable future, protected by the big cuts in capacity and productivity improvements since the strike. Of the strike he said, 'It's not generally understood how near the abyss we came. We could so easily have gone down the tube. This country was that close to disaster. Total.' But his own account, sometimes detailed, sometimes curiously vague, was greeted with surprised disbelief by some of those most closely involved.

■ He left behind an industry which he claimed was transformed. In 1985–6 its results were the best for seven years; a loss apparently of only £50 millions, with the last quarter in profit. But it was still an industry heavily dependent on government subsidy – £1.4 billion worth of deficit grants, social payments and redundancy payments. Even the final figure benefited from a credit of £342 millions for strike recovery costs carried over from the previous year.

■ A year on, and coal was still in the red. The arrival of the new chairman, Sir Robert Haslam, had coincided with the result of the cut-price deal for power station coal. The industry estimated it would cost it £400 million a year. 'The fiercest competitive conditions I have ever encountered in any industry,' was Sir Robert's description, and with some hyperbole, 'the most difficult . . . and turbulent business environment ever experienced in British Coal's history.'

■ In an all-too-familiar pattern, real losses for the year 1986–7 were down – to £288 millions – but breakeven was still over the horizon, now predicted for 1988–9. As Sir Robert acknowledged, it was still 'jam tomorrow'.

■ Haslam himself, a deceptively quiet-spoken, affable man, with a wide range of contacts in all sorts of industries, and unions too, was a contrast to MacGregor. No pushover, determined under the charm, he tried to map a consistent course.

■ He had privately met a number of the NUM leaders, though not Arthur Scargill, before taking up his chairmanship. Now he moved quickly to settle the wrangle over pay, imposing a settlement which the union reluctantly accepted and instituting a review of the cases of sacked miners.

■ At a managerial level MacGregor's innovation – the office of Chief Executive – was abandoned and committee discussions restored to the board's top management. Senior men felt free to see journalists openly without having to arrange meetings far away from the office.

■ In the coalfields, productivity, helped by concentrating on highly mechanised, heavy-duty faces, shot up by almost 50 per cent in two years, an achievement, Sir Robert declared, 'probably unmatched by any other industry'. From a record of 2.59 tonnes per man shift before the strike, the record had reached 3.76 tonnes by early 1987, after it had been broken fifteen times in a year.

■ It was helped by a big reduction in the workforce and the number of pits. In the two years following the strike, 42 pits closed and the workforce was almost halved. Not one pit was saved by the elaborately worked out review procedure. The number of people employed by the NCB had shrunk from over 234,000, when the strike had begun, to little more than 143,000 in May 1987. At collieries, the decline was steeper: from 181,000 to 108,000. The rush to take redundancy had been hastened by the official end of the government's special redundancy arrangements for coalminers at the end of March 1987.

■ To keep productivity booming British Coal looked for ways of changing the old mining customs, wishing to alter the 1908 Hours of

Work Act, to allow six-day working and longer shifts for new high-investment pits, and some existing ones, like those going miles out under the North Sea in north-east England. Without six-day working, Haslam warned 'nobody in their right mind would put such expensive equipment underground and only use it part of the time'.

■ The rush for redundancy had done most to undermine the position of the NUM. Even some of its executive team during the strike had opted to take redundancy and departed. At the NUM conference in Tenby in 1986, Arthur Scargill appealed for action, 'sooner rather than later'. The strike, he said, 'had dramatically slowed down' the board's 'programme of butchery' and given determination and inspiration to striking printers and teachers. He concluded 'we can either surrender or fight back, there is no middle ground'.

■ He was heard in bemused silence. There was no roaring, standing ovation; some delegates did not applaud at all.

■ As time wore on, Mick McGahey and the South Wales leadership increasingly despaired about what they thought was his refusal to face reality.

■ Open warfare finally broke out among the left at the start of 1987 when British Coal unveiled firm plans for a new mine at Margam in the west of the South Wales coalfield. It would be the first new pit in the area for more than a decade, and provide 800 jobs for men who had watched half their pits go since the strike. There was one hard condition – the new demand that men should work it six days a week, taking time off on a new shift pattern, which could mean them working only three weeks a month. The South Wales area, desperate to halt decline, voted to talk, promising an eventual pithead ballot.

■ But for Scargill it was betrayal of the union's old battles over working hours. He attacked the South Wales leaders as 'collaborationists'.

■ As Mick McGahey approached retirement, he continued to insist on the paramount need to bring the UDM back into the fold, warning 'colleagues', by which he meant Scargill, against laying down harsh conditions.

■ Scargill retorted that it was a 'tragedy that people from the far north should pontificate about what we should be doing to win back members for the NUM'.

■ And although some Scargill supporters lost their seats in national executive elections in 1987, it was the Scargill candidate, Yorkshireman Sammy Thompson (reflecting the way that his county increasingly dominated NUM voting, after Nottingham's departure), who defeated the Scottish secretary, Eric Clarke, to take over the Vice-Presidency from McGahey. Thompson's platform was 'no change' and opposition to new working hours.

■ For the moment, Arthur Scargill's personal position remained unassailable. The left had however finally backed moves to make him stand for re-election every five years, and the victorious Conservative government still held him in their sights. Proposals for more trade union reform seemed particularly directed against him, and the actions of his union during the strike. They included election for all trade union leaders – whether with votes or not – every five years; the right of all union members to inspect the union's books and see how their money was spent; and a commissioner for trade union affairs to help union members take their union to court.

■ The union was in terrible shape. Of over £9 million of assets held before the strike, the Receiver estimated that about £1.7 millions was still available when the Receivership was finally lifted in the summer of 1986.

■ Union general secretary, Peter Heathfield, warned of a horrendous £2 million deficit unless remedial action was taken. Plans for the union's new headquarters were scaled down by over a million; executive members were allocated less expensive cars; and a series of other economies were made. Reluctantly NUM delegates agreed to raise subscriptions by roughly a half.

■ In the pits themselves there was a mixture of realistic adjustment to the new situation, and sullenness. Even after the review commissioned by the new chairman, 373 of the 1,014 sacked during and after the strike for a variety of offences (from those punished with prison sentences to others so trivial that industrial tribunals ruled that they had been wrongly dismissed) were still out.

■ Even when tribunals had come down in their favour, the Coal Board, which had clearly targeted certain individuals, had often judged it cheaper to pay them off than to take them back or pay redundancy entitlements.

■ The case of the sacked men helped to keep resentments alive. After ten months of talks, the NUM, at Scargill's insistence, flatly refused to accept new wage-bargaining arrangements which would have given the UDM a position. As Sir Robert Haslam imposed a pay settlement for the second year running, he spoke of a big increase in what he termed 'rag-outs', lightning strikes which stopped pits. In the previous year they had cost the industry £20 millions; only 15 pits had been free of them. Two thirds were in Yorkshire – an indication of continuing guerilla war, which meant miners were still 30 times more likely to take action than other workers.

■ But the activists who had opposed the NUM leadership were not in happy shape either. The UDM demonstrated its virility in 1987 by balloting against a pay offer, and then winning a better deal. However its membership was stagnant. Many of the leaders of the back-to-work movement were out of the industry. In the largely striking areas, those who had gone back in small numbers had mainly left, or, in the case of some hundreds, been transferred to largely working areas. Colin Clarke's view was that 'the Coal Board was not able to keep its promise of no intimidation'.

■ Of Foulstone and Taylor, who had taken the most celebrated and effective case against the union, Foulstone was back in the industry, but transferred to a Nottingham pit, after a jail sentence for burglary which had led to his sacking. Taylor was running a small business on the south coast.

■ In militant Kent, only a couple of the 32 return-to-work miners were still employed. Most had left the industry; some transferred to the Midlands. Bob and Irene Fitzgibbon, the lightning conductors among them, were gone, taking his redundancy money of £8,000 for him to start yet another new career, as a chiropodist in Nottinghamshire. They left behind a house daubed and vandalised a dozen times since the strike, sold eventually to nominees of an unknown buyer.

■ The Kent coalfield itself, predicted by everyone for post-strike closure, still retained two of its three pits after a remarkable jump in productivity which bespoke a realistic understanding between miners and managers which was at odds with the rhetoric in many areas.

■ As the industry appeared to be settling down, there was talk of what had been unmentionable for years – of privatisation of whole, or part, of the industry; no longer deterred by dread of the NUM's power. The Commons Select Committee, turning its searchlight once more on the industry, suggested joint ventures between public and private capital and a raising of limits on private operations, above the 30 men underground permitted. It was a lively talking-point both within British Coal and the big private companies which did opencast work or development work for British Coal below ground. One prominent Coal Board executive during the strike, Michael Eaton, even bought a share of two small Welsh private mines in collaboration with a bigger mining company. It was a futher challenge to the spirit of nationalisation – a measure of the NUM's weakening grip.

■ But the uncertainties remained. The Central Electricity Generating Board announced a growing energy gap, and decided to order the first new coal-fired power stations for years – two of them. But at the same time it won approval for a new generation of nuclear-powered plant – the American style PWR.

■ The future seemed obscure and as difficult to read as ever. For the coal industry, the market and the economics remained as uncertain as they had been before the strike.

Notes

1 The choice

1 See Michael Crick, *Arthur Scargill*, Harmondsworth, Penguin, 1985; Geoffrey Goodman, *The Miners' Strike*, London, Pluto, 1985; Insight Team, *Strike*, London, Coronet, 1985.
2 *Marxism Today*, April 1981.
3 Patrick Cosgrave, *Thatcher, the First Term*, London, The Bodley Head, 1985. For a fine and objective account, see Peter Riddell, *The Thatcher Government*, London, Martin Robertson, 1985.

2 The coal question

1 Anthony Sampson, *Anatomy of Britain*, London, Hodder, 1962, p. 539.
2 Lord Gormley, *Battered Cherub*, London, Hamish Hamilton, 1982, p. 176.
3 Andrew Glyn, *The Economic Case against Pit Closures*, Sheffield, National Union of Mineworkers, 1984.

3 'There's only one Arthur Scargill'

1 Nina Fishman, untitled, unpub. doctoral thesis, Birkbeck College, University of London, 1986.
2 Fishman, op. cit., p. 3.
3 Fishman, op. cit., p. 4.
4 *Marxism Today*, February 1982, p. 17.
5 V.L. Allen, *The Militancy of British Miners*, Shipley, Yorkshire, The Moor Press, 1981, pp. 166–7.
6 Joe Gormley, *Battered Cherub*, London, Hamish Hamilton, 1982, pp. 76–7.
7 Allen, op. cit., p. 172.
8 Lord Robens, *Ten Year Stint*, London, Cassell, 1972, p. 173.
9 Gormley, op. cit., p. 211.
10 V.L. Allen, 'Miners' Man', *New Society*, 24 January 1985, p. 136.
11 There is an excellent discussion of this in an untitled, unpublished paper by Eddie Heevy, a research fellow at the London School of Economics.
12 Gormley, op. cit., p. 170.

13 Roy Ottey, *The Strike*, London, Sidgwick & Jackson, 1985, pp. 54–5.
14 Allen, 'Miners' Man', op. cit., pp. 136–7.
15 Arthur Horner, *Incorrigible Rebel*, London, Lawrence & Wishart, 1960, p. 72.
16 Paul Foot, *An Agitator of the Worst Kind*, London, SWP, 1986.

4 'A hoary old bastard who only wants to win'

1 Michael Edwardes, *Back from the Brink*, London, Collins, p. 42.

5 Fear of the abyss

1 D. Barnes and E. Reid, *Governments and Trade Unions*, London, Heinemann/PSI, 1980, p. 228.
2 K. Jeffery and P. Hennessy, *States of Emergency*, London, Routledge & Kegan Paul, 1983, p. 235.
3 R. Harris and B. Sewill, *British Economic Policy, 1970–74, Two Views*, London, Institute of Economic Affairs, 1975, p. 50.
4 Joe Gormley, *Battered Cherub*, London, Hamish Hamilton, 1982, pp. 170–82.
5 Insight Team, *Strike*, London, Coronet, 1985, pp. 41ff.
6 Roy Ottey, *The Strike*, London, Sidgwick & Jackson, 1985, p. 98.

6 Here we go

1 Lord Robens, *Ten-Year Stint*, London, Cassell, 1972, pp. 34–5.
2 *Police Review*, 25 May 1984.
3 Roger Geary, *Policing Industrial Disputes 1893 to 1985*, Cambridge, Cambridge University Press, 1985, p. 143.
4 Kim Howells, in *Digging Deeper: Issues in the Miners' Strike* (ed. Huw Beynon), London, Verso, 1985.
5 *Policing the Coal Industry Dispute in South Yorkshire*, Sheffield, South Yorkshire Police, 1985. (This includes the official report of the Chief Constable as well as the report of the enquiry on policing policy during the strike by a special sub-committee of the South Yorkshire Police Committee, also a police reply to it.)
6 *Ibid*.

7 'No request for assistance'

1 William Sirs, *Hard Labour*, London, Sidgwick & Jackson, 1985, p. 42.
2 *Electrical Power Engineer*, vol. 66, no. 6, October/November 1984, p. 198.

Notes

8 'The right to go to work'

1 Lord Wedderburn, 'The New Policies in Industrial Relations Law', in P. Fosh and C. Littler, *Industrial Relations and the Law in the 1980s*, London, Gower, 1985, pp. 29ff.
2 Otto Kahn Freund, 'Collective Agreements under War Legislation', *Modern Law Review*, vi, 1943, p. 143; quoted in G. Bain, *Industrial Relations in Britain*, Oxford, Blackwell, 1983, p. 367.
3 D. Hart, *The Soul Politic*, London, Adam Smith Institute, 1985, p. 6.
4 *Ibid.*

9 Inside Hobart House

1 Roy Ottey, *The Strike*, London, Sidgwick & Jackson, 1985, p. 122.

10 'The government is not involved'

1 For a recent fine survey, see P. Whitehead, *The Writing on the Wall*, London, Michael Joseph, 1985.
2 Quoted in the *New Statesman*, 20 December 1985, pp. 13–14.
3 D. Goodhart and P. Wintour, *Eddy Shah and the Newspaper Revolution*, London, Coronet, 1986, pp. 12–13.

11 No other industry could do it

1 *Sheffield Star*, 7 April 1984.
2 *Sheffield Star*, 25 May 1984.
3 Hilary Rose, 'The Miners' Wives of Upton' in *New Society*, 29 November 1984.
4 *Solidarity with the Miners*, London, Labour Research Dept, 1985.
5 *Sheffield Star*, 29 March 1984.
6 *Sheffield Star*, 26 April 1984.
7 *Sheffield Star*, 21 April 1984.
8 *Solidarity with the Miners*, LRD.

12 'Our enemies' front-line troops'

1 Three MORI polls during the dispute asked the question 'Who do you support, the miners or the NCB?' Support for the miners was 35 per cent in June, 30 per cent in August and 31 per cent in December. For the NCB it was 41 per cent in June, 46 per cent in August and 44 per cent in December. But the figureheads for both sides did badly. Asked whether they were running things well or badly, 49 per cent said MacGregor was doing badly in June, 47 per cent in August and 62 per cent in December. Scargill was even less popular, 76 per cent saying he was running things badly in June, 79 per

cent in August and 82 per cent in December.

2 For a fuller discussion of press and broadcasting coverage, including judgments on the authors' own performance, studies include Alastair Hetherington, *News, Newspapers and Television*, London, Macmillan, 1985; G. Cumberbatch *et al.*, *Television News and the Miners' Strike*, Aston University, Broadcasting Research Unit, 1986; Nicholas Jones, *Strikes and the Media*, Oxford, Blackwell, 1986.

13 Enough of being spat at

1 This account relies heavily on 'The Non-Political Trade Union Movement' by A.R. and C.P. Griffin, in *Essays in Labour History*, vol. 3, eds John Saville and Asa Briggs, London, Croom Helm, 1977.

2 *Marxism Today*, April 1985, p. 23.

14 'Your members have yet to be heard'

1 D. Barnes and E. Reid, *Governments and Trade Unions*, London, Heinemann/PSI, 1980, pp. 6–7.

2 Irving Richter, *Political Purpose in Trade Unions*, London, Allen & Unwin, 1973, p. 66.

3 Stuart Hall and Martin Jacques, *The Politics of Thatcherism*, London, Lawrence & Wishart, 1983, pp. 38–9.

Index

Index

Index

Index

Index

Index

For Product Safety Concerns and Information please contact our EU representative GPSR@taylorandfrancis.com Taylor & Francis Verlag GmbH, Kaufingerstraße 24, 80331 München, Germany

Batch number: 10725800

Printed by Printforce, the Netherlands

First published 2012 by Psychology Press

Published 2018 by Routledge
2 Park Square, Milton Park, Abingdon, Oxon, OX14 4RN
52 Vanderbilt Avenue, New York, NY 10017

First issued in hardback 2018

Routledge is an imprint of the Taylor & Francis Group, an informa business

ISBN 13: 978-1-138-47561-8 (hbk)
ISBN 13: 978-1-84872-775-5 (pbk)

EUROPEAN JOURNAL OF WORK AND
ORGANIZATIONAL PSYCHOLOGY
2012, 21 (5), 629–656

Time and change in teams: Where we are and where we are moving

Robert A. Roe[1], Christine Gockel[2], and Bertolt Meyer[3]

[1]School of Business and Economics, Maastricht University, Maastricht, The Netherlands

[2]Department of Psychology, University of Fribourg, Fribourg, Switzerland

[3]Institute of Psychology, University of Zurich, Zurich, Switzerland

In this introduction to the special issue on Time and Change in Teams, we argue that the field of team research shows signs of a problem-method misfit with respect to the study of processes. Drawing on the distinction between differential and temporal (or variable vs. process) research, we scrutinise recent theories and research practices in the field, aiming to better understand the lack of congruence between research objectives and methods. We also discuss ways in which the gap between theory and method can be narrowed, and how the five studies making up this special issue contribute to this. We conclude with suggesting some future directions for the study of time and change in teams.

Keywords: Teams; Time; Process; Dynamics; Methodology.

While the study of work teams is almost a century old, the interest in how teams function and what determines their success has never been as great as today. Teams have become a common form of organisational collaboration (Salas, Cooke, & Gorman, 2010). Teams are known to be more effective than individual workers in dealing with complex tasks and information processing requirements (Hinsz, Tindale, & Vollrath, 1997), and tasks

---

Correspondence should be addressed to Bertolt Meyer, Institute of Psychology, University of Zurich, Box 15, Zurich, 8050, Switzerland. E-mail: bmeyer@sozpsy.uzh.ch

The authors gratefully acknowledge the financial support of the European Association of Work and Organizational Psychology (EAWOP) to the Small group Meeting on Time and Change in Teams, held in Chemnitz, Germany, on 24–25 February 2011, from which this special issue emerged.

requiring creative solutions (van Knippenberg, De Dreu, & Homan, 2004). As teams are very well suited to coordinate the performance of tasks under variable conditions and high time-pressure, they are frequently used in fields as diverse as science, medicine, and emergency services (Sundstrom, McIntyre, Halfhill, & Richards, 2000). All this is reflected in a plethora of recent studies on team processes and team performance.

All work teams, regardless of whether they are spontaneously formed or formally installed, exist for a certain period of time. Their members meet at certain moments to exchange ideas, to solve problems, or to perform tasks during longer or shorter time-spells. While doing so they forge relationships, develop trust and perhaps friendships, generate and manage conflicts, and so on. Over time, teams change in composition, in relations among team members, in what they pursue, in how they function, and in cohesion and capabilities. Although the temporal footprint of what we designate as teams is hugely different, it is obvious that teams can neither be defined nor understood without reference to time. Time and change are inherent in teams.

With a history of about a century, one would expect that the psychological study of work teams had produced a large and comprehensive body of knowledge about "what happens in teams", and that by now psychology would be able to answer such questions as how teams form and develop, and how they function and perform. This expectation would be particularly justified in view of the critique by well-profiled organisational scholars on older research that lacked a time-perspective, and their empathic call for temporal theory-building and empirical research (e.g. Ancona, Goodman, Lawrence, & Tushman, 2001; George & Jones, 2000; Mathieu, Maynard, Rapp, & Gilson, 2008; Mitchell & James, 2001; Ployhart, Holtz, & Bliese, 2002). However, the reality of today is rather different, and this has, in fact, been a major reason for publishing this special issue on Time and Change in Teams (and for the organisation of the small group meeting on the subject that sparked it).

As we will explain below, there has been no lack of research on team dynamics, team processes, team performance, and the like during the past decades—on the contrary, there is a large volume of studies on these topics. However, this research has not quite produced the results and insights that might have been expected. We are inclined to attribute this to an incompatibility between the phenomena investigated—mainly "processes" occurring inside teams—and the methods used—mainly addressing how teams differ from each other. In other words, we believe that team research suffers from problem-method misfit (Edmondson & McManus, 2007). The problems team researchers are interested in relate to processes such as collaboration and conflict, which unfold over time, and call for a process-oriented or temporal approach. Yet, most of the methods applied derive from a variance-oriented or differential approach and focus on differences between teams in such characteristics as diversity, trust, or the typical level of conflict, which are assumed to be stable over time (Roe, 2008b; Van de Ven & Poole, 2005). The notion of "process" can been defined in various ways (Rescher, 1996; Seibt, 2003). We refer to a process as a changing state of the subject of study defined with reference to a certain time interval.

The temporal approach starts from the idea that "everything changes" (Heraclitus's *panta rei*) and focuses on how phenomena develop over time within a subject[1] and on "what influences what" along the timeline. In contrast, the differential approach focuses on individual differences between subjects and compares them with the help of variables. The study of blood pressure in humans provides an example. To study variations in blood pressure during the day, one would follow a temporal approach; to distinguish people with high blood pressure from those with average or low blood pressure, one would follow the differential approach. The two approaches are orthogonal and complementary: a person's average systolic blood pressure provides no information about the changes in systolic blood pressure within a day, or vice versa.

The aim of this special issue is to demonstrate how team research can profit from a sharper distinction between the two approaches. We will first review how the field of team research has dealt with temporal dynamics and where it is today. Next, we will expand on the differential and the temporal approach. This will allow us to clarify the problem-method misfit that has characterised much of team research in recent decades, and show what can be gained from moving towards a temporal approach. It will also enable us to systematically explore the intersection of the two approaches, and discover how temporal and differential analyses can be combined in a theoretically and methodologically sound way. Subsequently, we will introduce the various articles in this special issue, describing how they represent steps to move away from a differential towards a more temporal approach, and how they help in narrowing and resolving the gap between problems and methods.

LOOKING BACK

It is apparent from the research literature on teams and groups[2] that team researchers have always been interested in dynamic processes. The very

[1]We use the term "subject" in a methodological sense, that is, to designate the "subject of study". When referring to team research, we will speak of teams or team members rather than subjects. When addressing general methodological issues that also apply outside the domain of team research, we will use the term "subject".

[2]In line with the current idiom, we prefer to use the term "team" as a generic label for groups characterised by a common purpose and a sense of cohesion. When speaking of teams we thus refer both to groups as defined in the older literature, see for example McGrath & Gruenfeld (1993), and teams as defined more recently by Kozlowski & Ilgen (2006).

existence of the term "group dynamics" introduced by Kurt Lewin in the 1940s is a noteworthy indicator of this. It refers to processes inside and between groups that distinguish people working in groups from individuals. However, it is fair to say that various scholars before Lewin and several of his contemporaries studied group processes as well (e.g. Bion, 1946; 1952). At that time, researchers tended to pay explicit attention to time in their studies. For instance, the famous study by Lewin and colleagues about leadership styles in youth clubs plotted levels of aggression in teams over time as a function of the changes in leadership style (Lewin, 1947). Time is also clearly visible in the work of Bales (1950), who studied the interactions of members in small groups using observational methods. His work was one of the roots for later stage models of group development (Tuckman, 1965; Wheelan & McKeage, 1993), which postulate that groups pass through a series of stages with typical member interactions and experiences during their lifetime.

Time and change are also very salient in the many publications of Joseph McGrath (e.g. Arrow & McGrath, 1993; McGrath, 1964; 1984; 1988; 1993; McGrath, Arrow, & Berdahl, 2000; McGrath & Kelly, 1986; McGrath & Rotchford, 1983; McGrath & Tschan, 2004). Probably more than any other scholar, he pleaded for incorporating time in social psychological theory and for using longitudinal research designs. His own research, conducted in collaboration with many others, demonstrates the feasibility of this approach (Arrow & McGrath, 1993; Arrow, McGrath, & Berdahl, 2000; Harrison, Mohammed, McGrath, Florey, & Vanderstoep, 2003; Kelly, Futoran, & McGrath, 1990; Tschan et al., 2009). It sheds light on how teams develop over time and how they respond to changes in composition and adapt to external changes.

With the advent of survey methods and the widespread adoption of associational (correlation, regression) statistics in the 1970s, the treatment of time in team research began to change. Researchers remained interested in team processes but rather than studying processes in a direct way, they increasingly treated processes as quasi-traits that could be measured with multi-item questionnaires. It became customary to speak of "process variables" and to use statistical methods such as correlation, regression, and analysis of variance that analyse differences between teams, in order to investigate the relations between input variables, process variables, and output variables. The prevailing conceptual model became the "input-process-output" model (I-P-O model; McGrath, 1964; McGrath & Altman, 1966), which implied an analogy of the team with an information processing unit.

This approach to the study of team processes, which is still quite popular, is beset with conceptual difficulty and has been rather unfruitful in producing greater insights in team dynamics. The main reason is apparent from the expression "process variable", which to us seems a *contradictio in terminis*. A process is a changing state of a subject defined with reference to (a certain period of) time, whereas a variable is a fixed attribute of a subject that differs between subjects belonging to the same class. Thus, for example, conceiving team task conflict as a process variable and measuring it with items such as "We had task-related disagreements", "How much conflict of ideas was there in this team?" and "We often disagreed about work things" (Jehn, Greer, Levine, & Szulanski, 2008) without a specific reference to time is in contradiction with the notion of task conflict as a process that increases, stabilises, or decreases over time. Processes and variables are ontologically different, and studying them requires contrasting epistemologies (Roe, 2008b; Solinger, 2009; Van de Ven & Poole, 2005). It is logically impossible to obtain knowledge about how a team changes by comparing different teams with each other. This explains why research based on the I-P-O model has helped little in gaining a better insight into process dynamics.[3]

STATUS QUO

Taking a brief look at the status quo in the field of team research from the perspective of temporal dynamics, three conditions strike the eye, namely, a high degree of temporal rhetoric, problematic conceptualisation and operationalisation of temporal facets of team life, and inconsistent use of methods. We elaborate on each of these three issues in the following.

Temporal rhetoric

A haphazard sample from the recent team literature gives the impression that the focus of current theory and research is on what happens in teams over time. For instance, one journal article states:

> When time is provided periodically during a team's life cycle for sharing feedback and guidance is provided for problem-solving group interpersonal processes, the differences in performance between culturally diverse and culturally nondiverse teams have been shown to diminish ... We expect similar findings between such teams when both types of teams have experienced periodic feedback regarding their task performance and interpersonal processes (Watson, Johnson, & Merritt, 1998, p. 166).

Another article states:

> Time serves as a medium for collaboration in teams, allowing members to exchange personal and task-related information. We propose that

[3]The same limitation applies to the Input-Mediator-Output-Input model, proposed by Ilgen, Hollenbeck, Johnson, & Jundt (2005).

stronger team reward contingencies stimulate collaboration. As time passes, increasing collaboration weakens the effects of surface-level (demographic) diversity on team outcomes but strengthens those of deep-level (psychological) diversity (Harrison, Price, Gavin, & Florey, 2002, p. 1029).

A time perspective is also apparent in the following quote:

According to team development theory, as team members interact socially in the initial formation phase of team development, they come to understand the values of their team members, reflect on their own values, and upon comparison develop perceptions of values-based person–team fit. Individuals seek and develop inter-personal knowledge about other team members to reduce social ambiguity and create a mutual understanding among team members regarding their individual value structures (DeRue & Morgeson, 2007, p. 1243).

A final example is:

This research aims to better understand the circumstances that underlie the effectiveness of self-managing multi-cultural teams as they develop over time. We focus on the composition of cultural value diversity, theorizing that specific compositions of cultural value orientations at different stages of team development can compensate the lack of formal leadership (Cheng, Chua, Morris, & Lee, 2012, p. 390).

We have selected these quotes to illustrate a rhetoric style that is characteristic of recent team research—not, of course, to criticise specific researchers. The quotes display linguistic forms suggesting that the research examines what happens in teams as time unfolds, although this is not the case. In this sense, they give an inadequate impression. Time and change are rarely studied in current team research. What is written in research publications about how teams or team members act and respond, how teams change from one state into another, how early developments influence later ones, how "inputs" exert their influences, and how the team produces "outputs", reveals what the researchers *think* rather than what the research actually investigates.

Close reading may sometimes inform readers that authors are, in fact, not dealing with time and change in teams, because they use expressions such as "We examined the *associations* between task and relationship conflict with team performance and team member satisfaction" (De Dreu & Weingart, 2003, p. 742; emphasis added), or "Mean levels of learning orientation in teams will be positively *related* to backing up behavior" (Porter, 2005, p. 813; emphasis added) or "Teams that *have* positive beliefs about their capability tend to perform more effectively" (Collins & Parker, 2010, p.1003; emphasis added), which indicate that researchers are dealing with inter-team differences. References to "prediction" and to "mediators" or "moderators" are also indicative of non-temporal research approaches, as we will explain below.

Problematic conceptualisation and operationalisation

Another issue is that many articles, acknowledging the importance of time and the dynamic nature of team processes, conceptualise and operationalise behavioural phenomena in terms of stable individual differences. Time is thus noticeable but stripped from its essence, i.e. the capacity to flow. Typical examples are: time urgency, polychronicity, pacing style, time perspective and time pressure (e.g. Chong, Eerde, Rutte, & Chai, 2012; Gevers, Rutte, & van Eerde, 2006; Souitaris & Maestro, 2010; Waller, Conte, Gibson, & Carpenter, 2001). They are treated as variables that describe teams' or team members' characteristics, or they are used to define temporal diversity variables that are supposed to represent stable characteristics of teams (e.g. Mohammed & Nadkarni, 2011; Mohammed, Tesler, & Hamilton, 2012). Such characteristics may be stable over certain periods of time, but evidence for this is rarely presented. A similar practice has developed with regard to the notions of team processes and emergent states. Examples include team communication, team conflict, and intra-team trust. While these are dynamic in nature, that is, unfolding over time, they are typically treated as quasi-traits that are considered as being stable within the team and varying between teams. This inconsistency between the dynamic nature of the core concept and the non-dynamic form chosen for its operationalisation, which allows for subsequent differential analyses, has not remained unnoticed. For instance, Marks, Mathieu, & Zaccaro (2001) state:

> Even when authors observe teams over more extensive periods, in their analysis they usually aggregate process data gathered over time into a summary index that portrays direct process -> outcome relationships (e.g. Barry & Stewart, 1997). Thus, variance across time is collapsed into a static indicator of teamwork process as though it occurs at a single point in time. The result is that temporal factors are eliminated from further examination (p. 359).

However, it seems to us that Marks et al.'s way of classifying team processes inadvertently invites researchers to continue this practice because it designates the processes as "dimensions" that refer to attributes on which teams could and should be compared rather than as changing states manifesting themselves along the timeline. The review by LePine, Piccolo,

Jackson, Mathieu, & Saul (2008) shows that this is exactly what happens when researchers start using the taxonomy. They use the dimensions as variables to compare teams, not as processes occurring within teams.

Inconsistent methods

Given the inconsistencies identified above, it comes as no surprise that research designs and methods of analysis are often also inconsistent. Researchers use cross-sectional designs to study the relationships between inputs, processes and outputs. Whereas team processes are thought to be dynamic or are at least described as such, inputs, process and outputs are all treated as variables that are assumed to show stable inter-team differences. This state of affairs does not only follow from a questionable conceptualisation of processes as outlined above, but also from entrenched methodological practices that are common in all social science research. One is the tendency among us researchers to speak of "prediction" of one variable from another one, based on cross-sectional correlations or regressions. Many team researchers uncritically use the notion of prediction to suggest that particular ("input") variables predict process variables or that these predict certain other ("output") variables. They fail to acknowledge that prediction simply means that teams "high on A" are likely to be also "high on B", and that this has no bearing whatsoever on whether "rise in A" forecasts a "rise in B". This also applies to longitudinal designs in which there is some time interval between A and B. The prediction is based on differential logic and has no implication for the within-team prediction in the sense of a "forecast".

There is a similar issue in mediation analysis, which is generally believed to extract information about "what influences what" from "what is associated with what" (Roe, 2012). There are numerous team studies, particularly in connection with the I-P-O model, that have used mediator analysis to pursue the logically impossible objective of revealing where team interactions, conflict, trust and other processes and emergent states come from and lead to (see e.g. Han & Harms, 2010; Leach, Wall, Rogelberg, & Jackson, 2005; LePine et al., 2008). Some researchers have used longitudinal designs with two or more measurement points, assuming that this would resolve the problem (e.g. Dierdorff, Bell, & Belohlav, 2011; Greer, Jehn, & Mannix, 2008; Tekleab, Quigley, & Tesluk, 2009). Unfortunately, in most cases, it does not. The compression of processes into stable individual difference variables remains problematic, regardless of how data are gathered and analysed. Using regression-based analyses—as in mediator analysis—implies that one still draws upon between-teams covariance of variables, and not on within-team covariance over time. If the goal is to understand what happens in teams and why, there is no alternative to gathering time-series data and analysing these with proper techniques for within-team analysis.

Evaluation

Based on the foregoing, one cannot but conclude that there are shortcomings in how team processes have been studied in the past decades. Many studies show a discrepancy between the way of writing about team processes and the way of investigating them. A possible explanation is that—as in other fields of social science research—researchers have not been fully aware of the temporal-differential distinction and of its implications for theory-building and empirical research. Given the difficulties of doing team research in organisations and of collecting data from a sufficiently large number of teams over longer periods of time, this would make it understandable why researchers have opted for studying process variables with differential methods. We would not like to suggest that all team research has been affected by this problem-method inconsistency, nor that all differential research would be without value. There are plenty of team studies that have been differential in problem and methods, and that have produced useful insights into how team characteristics are associated with team effectiveness (see e.g. Mathieu et al., 2008; Richter, Dawson, & West, 2011) – under given temporal constraints. The literature also provides examples of studies that have opted for a temporal dynamic route; we will discuss these studies later.

Taking these points together, we are apt to conclude that team research is in need of change. Both the temporal legacy of Lewin, Bales, McGrath and others and the calls for temporal theorising and research by contemporary scholars have made team researchers aware that something must change. In our view, two developments are augmenting the pressure. One is the publication of an increasing number of studies that actually collect and analyse time-series data (see below). Although still small in number, they deliver the proof that temporal research is feasible. The second is the reflection of organisational scholars on the fact that the ecology and content of work—and thereby of teamwork—are changing. Two very recent publications are worth mentioning in this respect. The first is a special issue on present-day teams, and how they differ from teams in former times, in the *Journal of Organizational Behavior*. The authors point at the virtual nature and the accelerating changes in teams and what these mean for the study of teams. Wageman, Gardner, and Mortensen (2012) refer in their lead article to the teams that we always studied as "archetypical". The second is an issue of *Industrial and Organizational Psychology,* with a lead article by Tannenbaum, Mathieu, Salas and Cohen (2012b) entitled "Teams are changing: are research and practice evolving fast enough?". With all this emphasis on temporal dynamics, it is obvious that issues of time and change can no longer be ignored, and that the concepts and methods derived from the differential paradigm have lost part of their value.

FROM A DIFFERENTIAL TO A TEMPORAL APPROACH

To give the reader a better understanding of the temporal approach and the way in which it deviates from the well-known differential approach, we now briefly describe these approaches, based on Van de Ven & Poole (2005) and Roe (2008b). Although the epistemological and methodological issues are more general, our focus will be on team research. After contrasting the approaches, we will describe how the differential and temporal approaches intersect, with (between-team) differences in (within-team) processes as common ground. Next, we will outline how team-research may profit by moving from a differential towards a temporal approach. Such a move implies the adoption of dynamic concepts, dynamic measurement, dynamic research designs and dynamic analysis. As we will explain below, these steps are reflected in the contributions to this special issue.

Differential approach

The differential approach starts from the assumption that all teams, like individuals and other social entities, differ with regard to the conditions in which they find themselves, their characteristics, their behaviours, and the effects of those behaviours. It studies variations of these variables between teams and the covariation among them. The variances and covariances are calculated from data that are collected from sufficiently diverse samples with or without repeated measures. The methods propagated are (co)variance analysis, correlation analysis, regression analysis and various extensions, such as multilevel analysis (which deals with entities at different levels, e.g. individuals and teams). Characteristic for the differential approach is the focus on variance and the proportion of variance "explained" by other variables. Hence Van de Ven & Poole (2005) speak about a "variance-based approach". When a sufficient degree of variance is explained, variables can "predict" other variables, which means that the score of a team on one variable can be transformed into an expected score on another variable, using the appropriate regression function. In the differential approach, the notions of prediction and explanation are treated as synonymous. Wherever a substantial amount of covariance is observed, it means that the researcher can predict, and by the same token that the researcher can explain. This is of course a mere *statistical* explanation and *not a causal* one, although researchers sometimes seem to believe the latter to be so (Hackman, 2012). A causal explanation requires that change in the explaining variable precedes change in the explained variable, and that alternative explanations for this change can be ruled out.

Temporal approach

The temporal approach, in contrast, assumes that everything in the life of people, that is, the conditions in which people find themselves, their characteristics, their behaviours, and the effects of those behaviours, is subject to change. Again, this holds at the level of individuals as well as that of groups and organisations. It proposes studying phenomena as they unfold over time, looking at their dynamic features (onset-offset, duration, and patterns or trajectories) and their dynamic interrelations. Van de Ven & Poole (2005) speak about a focus on "process", Roe (2008b) about a focus on "what happens". The information for this can come from a single subject or from multiple subjects (here: a single team or multiple teams), but unlike the differential approach there is no need for a multi-subject (multi-team) sample. The counterpart of the sample in the differential approach is a time-series, drawn from the lifespan as a whole. The preferred methods are all based on trajectory analysis, tracing the development of the phenomenon (process) over time. However, as trajectories have many characteristics (onset, offset, duration, and dynamic features such as increase, decrease, frequency, amplitude; Roe, 2008b) there are many ways to describe or parameterise them and to analyse their dynamic interrelations.

How the differential and temporal approaches intersect

The use of the differential approach is not restricted to between-subjects (between-teams) variation at a single moment in time, and neither is the use of the temporal approach restricted to time-series on a single subject (team). Multiple observations of variables over time and multiple observations of phenomena in different subjects (teams), represented by a three-dimensional data matrix with variables × time × subjects (teams), allows for complementary and even combined analyses. We will therefore now discuss options for exploring the common ground of variance and process, or between-variation and within-variation.

We first consider the *differential approach*, which, in spite of its explicit focus on variance, can also be used to study cases where variables are measured more than once, with some time interval in between. Due to an ambiguity in its conceptual apparatus, this possibility has given rise to considerable confusion among researchers. The ambiguity becomes manifest in two common practices, i.e. the use of conceptual models showing the postulated links between variables, and the very use of the notion of variable (Roe, 2005). Conceptual models typically show variables as boxes (or latent variables as ellipses) interconnected by arrows. Such models show a logical order (variables on the left are supposed to influence variables on the right) and not a temporal order (in reality, most variables are simultaneously observable), but they can easily be misunderstood in that respect. The concept of variable does not permit one to distinguish between within-subjects (within-teams) and between-subjects (between-teams) associations of variables. This is misleading and makes many team researchers (see for example the review by van Knippenberg et al. [2004]) believe that the observed covariation of variables between teams also holds within teams, which is not the case. The fact that a variable "predicts" and "explains" across subjects, does not mean that it "predicts" and "explains" over time. Logically and mathematically, there is no connection.[4]

Besides, the notion of prediction itself is confusing, as it suggests that one automatically bridges a time-interval when making a prediction. When variables are measured at the same time, this is obviously not the case. However, with distinct measurement moments it is not necessarily the case either, because the statistical association is established *post hoc* in a given set of data. Crossing time only occurs when an established regression function is applied to new data, collected from teams not included in the sample in which the regression function was derived; a rare situation in team research.

Starting from the differential point of view, the proper analytical approach to examine change over time is that of (non-)linear growth modelling. It fits a common temporal regression function to the data, and explores whether individual variations in regression parameters (intercept, slope, higher order polynomials) would increase the fit. The differential logic shows in the fact that the covariance-matrix in the sample as a whole determines what the temporal regression function for the sample and a fortiori for each of the teams will look like.

The *temporal perspective* offers a different approach to the common ground. Here, change trajectories are established first for each and every team separately. The rationale is that it would make no sense to let the trajectory of a particular team be influenced by the trajectories of other teams. For example, the development of conflict in a given team should not be determined by the development of conflict in other teams. However, trajectories can afterwards be compared and grouped according to their similarity, using clustering techniques such as latent cluster growth modelling (Nagin, 1999; 2005) and general growth mixture modelling (Muthén, 2004;

[4]Mathematically a relationship can only be established under the so-called "ergodicity assumptions", which imply homogeneity (each subject follows the same model as the population) and stationarity (the process has constant characteristics over time; see Molenaar & Campbell [2009]). These assumptions are very stringent and unlikely to be met in social behaviour.

Reinecke & Seddig, 2011). These techniques offer a way to bridge the gap between the differential and temporal approach, as they allow the number of trajectory groups to be chosen. With fewer groups, more weight is given to the differential logic, with more groups to the temporal logic.

Temporalism: Key notions and requirements for research

In the temporal approach as presented by Roe (2008b), the key notion is that of *phenomenon,* defined as an observable event or series of events happening to a particular subject (e.g. individual, group, or organisation) during a certain time interval. Examples of team phenomena include communication, collaboration, conflict, trust, etc. To study such phenomena one must specify one or more attributes that can vary in intensity and a time interval that spans either the whole lifespan or a part of it. The focus of the study is on features of the trajectory by which the phenomenon unfolds over time.

Two important conjectures are being made (Roe, 2008b; 2009). The first is that all phenomena have a beginning (onset) and an end (offset), a duration, and a trajectory of growth and decline. Thus, for example, conflict does not just exist at any point in time, but starts and ends within an interval bounded by the creation and the termination of the team. Some phenomena (e.g. trust) will manifest themselves continuously, but others (e.g. performance) will be interrupted by breaks, daily meals and night rests, changes in tasks etc. (Roe, 2008b). The second conjecture is that trajectories will have multiple appearances depending on the time window through which they are looked at. A wide window with few observation points will produce a different trajectory compared to a narrow window with a fine-grained observation scale. Changing the "zoom level", that is, the length of the observation interval and the resolution of the timescale will therefore reveal different trajectories and hence lead to a different understanding of what happens (Collins, 2006; Zaheer, Albert, & Zaheer, 1999).

Roe (2008b; 2009) sees three aims for temporal research. Applied to teams, these can be summarised as: (1) describing temporal phenomena in teams,[5] (2) studying the temporal and causal relationships among multiple temporal phenomena in the same teams, and (3) establishing long-term constancy and change in phenomena and their interrelationships. These aims involve different types of research questions, which highlight distinct dynamic features. The descriptive study of phenomena seeks answers to such questions as: When does personal conflict start and how long does it last? How fast does trust develop and vanish? What is the rhythm of task activity? When does team performance peak? How stable is team temporal diversity? The study of relations between phenomena addresses questions such as:

[5]Of course, this can be extended to inter-team relations or multi-team systems.

How does a change in team composition affect coordination among team members? Do variations in task monitoring produce more stable task performance over time? Does an increase in shared cognition lead to more stable performance? How does rate of decline in trust relate to rate of decline in situational awareness? Does variable task complexity lead to an increase in cognitive flexibility? Does teams' confidence building coincide with or follow their conflict management activities? The study of long-term stability and change deals with questions such as: Does our knowledge on the onset, duration, growth, stability, frequency, and rhythm of such phenomena as task activity, coordination, conflict, cohesion and performance in teams, and on their interrelations, hold for teams that were studied in for example the 1950s, the 1980s, and the 2010s? Which findings are stable? Which ones reveal trends? Can these trends be explained from changes in demographics, economy, technology, or politics? It should be noted that these exemplary questions are much broader in scope than the research questions that drive current team research. This underlines that conventional team research leaves many dynamic issues unaddressed.

Doing temporal research generally differs from doing differential research in a number of ways—this also applies to team research. First, the phenomena must be defined in ways that bring the dynamic aspects to the foreground. That makes nouns such as conflict, trust or performance less suitable than *verbs* such as opposing, bullying, or producing. In the context of team research, this is illustrated by the work of Kozlowski and colleagues on how teams learn, develop and adapt (Kozlowski & Bell, 2008; Kozlowski & Chao, 2012).

Second, one must choose a *time frame* and a *timescale* with a number of time points, as the findings of the study will depend on them. These choices must be made explicit and be justified. If multiple time scales are explored, each of these must be spelled out. This is particularly important because the timescales at which certain phenomena manifest themselves may not be the same. For instance, teams may be engaged in multiple interweaving threads of interaction (task-related, relational, topical) that involve different timescales (Poole & Roth, 1989) and team-level and individual-level processes are associated with different timescales (Kozlowski & Klein, 2000).

Third, one must indicate *when* the study is being done, that is, in which year, quarter or month, and how long it lasts. Explicit information on these time markers is needed to assess the influence of exogenous time-related factors (e.g. market forces, organisational rhythm, industry cycles, and the long-term trends mentioned above), and to evaluate long-term stability and change. It is also needed for making informed decisions about generalisation to an overall population or generational cohorts.

Fourth, one needs *measurement* methods that are suitable for repeated measurement, which means that they are temporally sensitive and robust against reuse (Roe, 2008a). The instruments should capture both time and the intensity of the attributes covered by the phenomenon. Instruments that are well suited for differential measurement, such as multi-item questionnaires and tests, may be less suitable in this context, because they are made to reliably differentiate between people and not to pick up change. Administrating such instruments on multiple occasions may lead to beta and gamma change (Golembiewski, Billingsley, & Yeager, 1976). The more items are used, the more these instruments are vulnerable to lack of measurement equivalence over time. An alternative is to develop single item measures, e.g. using graphic scales.

Fifth, one must choose *research designs* with a clear time-dimension that allow conducting within-team analyses, possibly combined with between-teams analyses. This rules out purely cross-sectional correlation and regression analyses, as well as conventional moderator and mediator analysis, and limits the choice of analysis of variance models. The designs will have to be different from traditional longitudinal designs, in which time points (and intervals) are arbitrarily chosen and few in number. Finally, appropriate *analyses* must be chosen that allow making the needed inferences about the dynamic phenomena. There are many techniques that can be used for temporal analysis, including descriptive modelling and clustering, sequential analysis, random coefficient modelling, latent growth modelling, latent class analysis, event history analysis, time-series analysis, dynamic modelling, event history analysis, survival analysis, and so on. The recent research literature provides several examples of how these techniques may be used (e.g. Broström, 2012; Cordery, Morrison, Wright, & Wall, 2010; Dickter, Roznowski, & Harrison, 1996; Fu, 2009; Fuller et al., 2003; Russell, 2001; Sacco & Schmitt, 2005). In cases where dynamic phenomena have been sufficiently charted and parameterised, researchers may also use selected parameters (such as onset, duration, frequency, initial level, lowest/highest level, ultimate level, slope, number of inflections, amplitude) in regression-based analyses or analyses of variance to establish relationships with parameters of other phenomena or extraneous factors.

Opportunities for discovery

Although the price of temporal research is high, in terms of the effort and resources required and the long time-to-publication (cf. Ancona et al., 2001), it pays off by considerably extending the opportunities for discovering hitherto-unknown aspects of team life and for resolving long-lasting theoretical problems. We mention just a few of these opportunities.

First of all, researchers can answer the recent call (e.g. Wageman et al., 2012) for a more *dynamic conceptualisation* of key constructs, such as for example interaction, adaptation, conflict, trust, interdependence, cohesion, efficacy, and temporal diversity. The work by Kozlowski and colleagues (Kozlowski, 2012; Kozlowski & Bell, 2008; Kozlowski & Chao, 2012) on team learning and adaptation is exemplary in this respect. Seemingly stable attributes, such as for example team size, might also be conceived dynamically.

Second, with more dynamic concepts, it becomes easier to study the development *trajectories* of team phenomena. There are already good examples from studies on team efficacy (DeRue, Hollenbeck, Ilgen, & Feltz, 2010), person-team fit and person-role fit (DeRue & Morgeson, 2007), and on team mental model convergence (McComb, Kennedy, Perryman, Warner, & Letsky, 2010).

Third, explicit consideration and variation of *time frames and timescales* allow resolving certain controversial issues, such as the dispute about stage and phase models. The question whether Tuckman (1965) or Gersick (1988) was right may have made sense in the differential context; it does not in a temporal context, because the phenomena and their time brackets are not the same. Depending on the type of teams, their overall lifetime, and the study's time frame and scale, the development of team members' social structure and climate (Bion, 1952; Tuckman, 1965; Wheelan & McKeage, 1993) is likely to show a different dynamic than the development of a team's task-related activities (Gersick, 1988; see also Ito & Brotheridge, 2008; Marks et al., 2001) or communication activities (McComb et al., 2010; Swigger, Hoyt, Serçe, Lopez, & Alpaslan, 2012). Only repeated studies using the same conceptual and temporal research apparatus can establish which model gives the best description of what (e.g. Chang, Bordia, & Duck, 2003).

Fourth, it becomes possible to investigate patterns of team activity *over longer time periods* and to examine the stability of teams and team process or roles. In differential research, stability was often assumed present, or "proven" by evidence of retest-reliability. Today it is understood that a requirement for proving stability is measurement equivalence over time, which calls for a test of a nested set of models in latent growth structural equation modelling (as in Lance, Vandenberg, & Self, 2000). In temporal research, stability should be established as one of many forms of development: *stability is a special case of chan*ge (Roe, 2011). Whether or not stability will be found is always conditioned by the time frame and scale of the study (e.g. Landis, 2001). Given the conjecture of phenomena's limited lifetime, long-term stability appears to be very unlikely.

Fifth, it will become possible to study the *path dependency* of team phenomena (and of patterns of interrelated phenomena). This is a particularly important distinction with differential research where teams are supposed to exhibit an identical or similar growth trajectory as the whole sample. As we have noted, this is still a characteristic of conventional latent growth modelling. Temporal research allows studying growth trajectories in their own right, that is idiosyncratically, and to take into consideration the special conditions applying to the singular case.

Finally, it becomes possible to enrich team research with the study of interruptions and other events, either of an external origin or emerging from within the team (Uitdewilligen & De Jong, 2012; Zellmer-Bruhn, 2003), which may shed a new light on the *dynamics of performance*.

THIS SPECIAL ISSUE

The recognition of the limitations of a purely differential approach and the change towards a temporal approach, stimulated by the emergence of virtual teams and the availability of electronically gathered data, is likely to change the landscape of team research. This is already visible from the recent research literature, for instance in the studies on activities in resuscitation teams by Tschan et al. (2009) (also: Hunziker et al., 2012; Tschan, Vetterli, Semmer, Hunziker, & Marsch, 2011) and on communication patterns by McComb et al. (2010) and Swigger et al. (2012). Recent technological advances such as the automatic detection and recording of behaviours within teams (e.g., Curhan & Pentland, 2007; Sanchez-Cortes, Aran, Schmid-Mast, & Gatica-Perez, 2012) also provide rich sources of longitudinal within-team data. Yet, the change from differential to temporal research does not come easily, and involves many different steps. It is also manifest in the contributions to this special issue.

Accordingly, we see the five papers in this special issue as exemplifying steps from a differential framework towards a temporal approach in team research. The papers highlight different ways of changing the way we, as researchers, develop theory and conduct studies. Therefore, all papers incorporate temporal aspects, but they do so in different ways. They also reflect different scientific approaches brought to the study of time and change in teams and offer different theoretical and methodological insights. These papers are not only taking steps towards a more temporal view on teams, but also represent a variety of research questions and methodological approaches that contribute to our understanding of team processes.

The first paper by Arman and Adair (2012) is a conceptual paper about temporal diversity in teams. The authors explain how members from different cultural backgrounds can differ in their perceptions and use of time and how this characteristic can influence team processes and outcomes in multinational teams. Arman and Adair take time into account as it relates to individual team member characteristics and the composition of the team. An interesting issue for future research would be the stability and change of temporal diversity, particularly in relation to the acculturation that is likely to take place as team members collaborate for longer periods of time.

It would also be worth investigating differences in trajectories of temporal diversity over time, for example in function of entrainment enhancing events or changes in team composition.

In the second paper, Cleveland, Finez, Blascovich, and Ginther (2012) examined the effect of teammate performance on team member evaluations of resources and demands over a period of four weeks with four measurement points. They found that team members working with inferior teammates perceived fewer resources and exhibited a physiological threat response and that team members working with superior teammates perceived more resources and exhibited a physiological challenge response. In their study, they used cardiovascular measures that can (theoretically) be applied several times without the risk of beta or gamma change. Although their analysis is a differential one, they do present a new method for eliciting temporal within-team data. This research might be extended with studies into intra-team dynamics of resource perceptions and physiological responses, as prolonged interaction between team members might alter the findings. It would also be interesting to explore the effects of changes in team composition or team size.

Within-team temporal data can be analysed in a temporal way with the intra-team longitudinal approach introduced by Li and Roe (2012) in the third paper. Their approach is quite different from traditional inter-team longitudinal approaches, such as random coefficient modelling. They follow a cases-to-sample order of inference and measure each team's change trajectory before using it in additional analyses as either outcome or predictor. The added value of this new intra-team approach is that the temporality of the data is maintained. It shows how data from new studies can be analysed or even data from previous studies re-analysed. The method allows comparing temporal trajectories between teams with different characteristics, which implies a combination of the temporal and differential approach.

In the fourth paper, Zijlstra, Waller, and Phillips (2012) also analyse sequential within-team data in a temporal way. They investigated whether communication patterns in teams that emerge at the very beginning of the team's lifespan are predictive for later team performance. More specifically, they examined whether the performance difference between high-performing and low-performing flight crews is reflected in differences between communication patterns during the pre-flight phase. Thus, the paper includes several temporal aspects. First, the conceptual framework and the resulting hypotheses make explicit reference to temporal dynamics. Communication at the beginning of a crew's short lifespan is hypothesised to influence performance at a later point in time. Second, the methodology captures the sequential and dynamic nature of team interactions. Reoccurring communication sequences were detected using pattern analysis of behaviour-coded sequences of communication acts. An interesting issue for further research would be whether the information gathered about teams' early interaction patterns would allow forecasting teams' performance at a later time.

The last paper of the special issue is another example of a temporal conceptual approach combined with a temporal design and analysis: Ramos-Villagrasa, Navarro, and García-Izquierdo (2012) conceptualise teams as complex adaptive systems (CAS) and argue that correspondingly, team interactions and outcomes should be viewed from a chaos-theoretic perspective. Drawing from chaos theory, they hypothesise that high-performing teams should exhibit temporal dynamics that are characterised by low-dimensionality chaos, while low-performing teams should exhibit a high dimensionality of chaos. In a sample of professional basketball teams, the authors test their hypothesis with chaos-theoretic measures that they compute on the basis of time series analyses, thereby fully reflecting the temporal and dynamic nature of team performance. Here again, it would be interesting to examine to what degree the method would allow forecasting teams' later performance.

LOOKING AHEAD

Although there are other important issues in team research, such as the need for greater conceptual clarity about what teams are, the relationship between team-level and individual-level phenomena, or the role of context (e.g. Tannenbaum, Mathieu, Salas, & Cohen, 2012a), we believe that resolving the temporal problem-method misfit has the potential to significantly advance the study of teams. Moving towards a temporal approach can expand the equipment for conceptualisation and research, but will not automatically lead to new and better theories. Referring to the work presented in this special issue, we believe that new research efforts can stimulate theory development in a number of ways. One way is by engaging in observational and descriptive studies of teams in their concrete real-life environment, precisely recording the processes and changes that are taking place and labelling them with new concepts—if possible verbs rather than nouns—that do not carry a legacy from former differential research. Although this runs counter to the common mantra that research should be driven by theory, we believe it is needed to first develop ideas about the dynamic aspects and particularly the timing of team phenomena that earlier research has failed to produce. It will not only promote new notions of "what happens" but also about "when it happens", "how often", "at what rate", "in what rhythm", "for how long", etc. It is precisely this information that researchers are lacking when they set up temporal studies and have to decide which time frame and how many observation points to use (Zaheer et al., 1999).

We believe that diary methods and electronic activity records, which are routinely generated in many contemporary teams, can help in documenting and exploring the emergence of new types of teams and the disappearance of older teams, as well as the ways in which new teams function. These are issues that team researchers are increasingly interested in (e.g. Hackman, 2012; Wageman et al., 2012). New data will likely stimulate the development of new concepts and new theories about "what teams are" and "how they function". Particularly important in this context is how to conceptualise the relationship between the team and its members, and its dynamic aspects. With the growing popularity of multi-level methods in team research it is important to understand what levels are and which processes at lower level influence the higher level and vice versa (Kozlowski & Klein, 2000). As Murase, Doty, Wax, DeChurch, & Contractor (2012) point out, we cannot assume that teams are homogeneous sets that remain stable over time; rather they resemble dynamic networks. This raises the question how team-level properties can be derived from individual-level perceptions. Instead of compositional approaches, team researchers may need to adopt compilational ones (meaning that team-level phenomena do not resemble the elemental content visible at the individual level), while taking account of changes over time. The relationship between teams and their members take on new forms when people are involved in multiple teams at the same time, devoting a variable amount of time to each of them (Espinosa, Cummings, Wilson, & Pearce, 2003; Maynard, Mathieu, Rapp, & Gilson, 2012). Also worth investigating are relationships between members from different teams that interact periodically, such as top managers and middle managers (Raes, Heijltjes, Glunk, & Roe, 2011), or on an ongoing basis, as in multiteam systems (Zaccaro, Marks, & DeChurch, 2012).

In addition, we see an opportunity for infusing team research with dynamic concepts from other theoretical domains that were not compatible with the dominant differential mode of thinking in the past. As an example we think of using theoretical notions from European action theory which, starting from a conception of human work as goal-directed action, can describe and explain the cognitive mechanisms and processes involved in generating actions. Notions from action regulation theory (Bergman & Richter, 1994; Frese & Zapf, 1994; Hacker, 2003) have already been applied to teamwork by Tschan (2002). We think that further work along this line would add to the efforts of Marks et al. (2001) to gain a better understanding of "teamwork" activities (e.g. planning, coordination, monitoring) by which teams shape their "taskwork". Another example would be applying notions from the realm of individual time management to the working of teams (Claessens, Roe, & Rutte, 2008; Gevers, van Eerde, & Rutte, 2009).

A different issue that team researchers will need to address is the agency of team members and teams. The point has been articulated by Hackman

(2012), who suggests that team research should give up its preoccupation with causal analysis and try to identity conditions that would facilitate teams to "chart their own courses". This idea of action research is by no means new. It has been advocated by many before, in connection with change and development of organisations as well as teams (Argyris, 1982; Greenwood & Levin, 1998; Van de Ven, 2007). But the detailed study of what teams actually do, why they do it, and what they see as their goals may be enriching team research.

The potential to build better theories also holds a promise for practice. More detailed and empirically supported knowledge about how (that means, by which trajectories) teams emerge, develop, learn, perform, and adapt, and about how they are influenced by and exert influences on their environment, will constitute a wider and firmer base for interventions. It will help practitioners in identifying which knowledge elements can be applied and what to expect. We see several areas of application where time-based team research may prove beneficial. An obvious area is that of team training, where evidence about how team-level knowledge emerges in an interactive process that involves the team level and the member level helps to achieve better, more reliable, and more adaptive performance (e.g. Kozlowski & Chao, 2012). A specific example of how findings on temporal aspects of collaboration have been successfully applied is training in medical settings, for example in resuscitation teams (Hunziker et al., 2011). A novel and more general opportunity for applying temporal knowledge lies in the timing of interventions. Future research may provide guidance on when to intervene, as teams show communication breakdown, failure to learn, declining performance, or disruptive conflicts. The proper timing (and dosage) of interventions may not only be useful with regard to feedback, instruction, guidance, coaching, and retraining but also for more drastic measures, such as changing a team's composition or disbanding it altogether, in order to avoid negative spirals or catastrophic events.

CONCLUSION

We conclude from our evaluation of the literature that team research is in need of transition. The period in which a majority of researchers routinely used differential methods to investigate team processes may come to an end, as it becomes clearer that these methods are fundamentally unfit for this purpose and that more time-sensitive methods are required. To understand how teams emerge, develop, learn, perform and adapt, one should study them from a temporal perspective. However, embracing time and change as inherent ingredients of teams is not easy; not just because collecting and analysing temporal data is resource-intensive and effortful, but also because researchers need to adopt new ideas and routines that differ markedly from those stemming from the differential approach. We hope that the following studies will be helpful in this respect and that this special issue may be one of the signs marking the transition.

REFERENCES

Ancona, D. G., Goodman, P. S., Lawrence, B. S., & Tushman, M. L. (2001). Time: A new research lens. *Academy of Management Review*, *26*, 645–663. doi:10.5465/AMR.2001.5393903.

Argyris, C. (1982). *Reasoning, learning, and action: Individual and organizational.* San Francisco, CA: Jossey-Bass.

Arman, G., & Adair, C. K. (2012). Cross-cultural difference in perception of time: Implications for multinational teams. *European Journal of Work and Organizational Psychology*, *21*, 657–680.

Arrow, H., & McGrath, J. E. (1993). Membership matters: How member change and continuity affect small group structure, process, and performance. *Small Group Research*, *24*, 334–361. doi:10.1177/1046496493243004.

Arrow, H., McGrath, J. E., & Berdahl, J. L. (2000). *Small groups as complex systems: Formation, coordination, development, and adaptation.* Thousand Oaks, CA: SAGE.

Bales, R. F. (1950). *Interaction process analysis: A method for the study of small groups.* Reading, MA: Addison-Wesley.

Barry, B., & Stewart, G. L. (1997). Composition, process, and performance in self-managed groups: The role of personality. *Journal of Applied Psychology*, *82*, 62–78. doi:10.1037/0021-9010.82.1.62.

Bergman, B., & Richter, P. (1994). *Die Handlungsregulationstheorie. Von der Praxis einer Theorie.* Göttingen: Hogrefe.

Bion, W. R. (1946). The leaderless group project. *Bulletin of the Menninger Clinic*, *10*, 77–81.

Bion, W. R. (1952). Group dynamics: A re-view. *The International Journal of Psychoanalysis*, *33*, 235–247.

Broström, G. (2012). *Event history analysis with R.* Boca Raton, FL: CRC Press.

Chang, A., Bordia, P., & Duck, J. (2003). Punctuated equilibrium and linear progression: Toward a new understanding of group development. *Academy of Management Journal*, *46*, 106–117. doi:10.2307/30040680.

Cheng, C.-Y., Chua, R. Y. J., Morris, M. W., & Lee, L. (2012). Finding the right mix: How the composition of self-managing multicultural teams' cultural value orientation influences performance over time. *Journal of Organizational Behavior*, *33*, 389–411. doi: 10.1002/job.1777.

Chong, D. S. F., van Eerde, W., Rutte, C. G., & Chai, K. H. (2012). Bringing employees closer: The effect of proximity on communication when teams function under time pressure. *Journal of Product Innovation Management*, *29*, 205–215. doi: 10.1111/j.1540-5885.2011.00890.x.

Claessens, B. J. C., Roe, R. A., & Rutte, C. G. (2008). *Time management: Logic, effectiveness, and challenges.* In R. A. Roe, M. J. Waller, & S. R. Clegg (Eds.), *Time in Organizational Research* (pp. 23–41). London: Routledge.

Cleveland, C., Finez, L., Blascovich, J., & Ginther, N. (2012). For better of for worse: The effect of superior and inferior teammate performance on changes in challenge/threat cardiovascular responses. *European Journal of Work and Organizational Psychology*, *21*, 681–717.

Collins, L. M. (2006). Analysis of longitudinal data: The integration of theoretical model, temporal design, and statistical model. *Annual Review of Psychology*, *57*, 505–528. doi:10.1146/annurev.psych.57.102904.190146.

Collins, C. G., & Parker, S. K. (2010). Team capability beliefs over time: Distinguishing between team potency, team outcome efficacy, and team process efficacy. *Journal of Occupational & Organizational Psychology*, *83*, 1003–1023. doi: 10.1348/096317909x484271.

Cordery, J. L., Morrison, D., Wright, B. M., & Wall, T. D. (2010). The impact of autonomy and task uncertainty on team performance: A longitudinal field study. *Journal of Organizational Behavior, 31*, 240–258. doi:10.1002/job.657.

Curhan, J., & Pentland, A. (2007). Thin slices of negotiation: Predicting outcomes from conversational dynamics within the first 5 minutes. *Journal of Applied Psychology, 92*, 802–811. doi:10.1037/0021-9010.92.3.802.

De Dreu, C. K. W., & Weingart, L. R. (2003). Task versus relationship conflict, team performance, and team member satisfaction: A meta-analysis. *Journal of Applied Psychology, 88*, 741–749. doi:10.1037/0021-9010.88.4.741.

DeRue, D. S., Hollenbeck, J., Ilgen, D., & Feltz, D. (2010). Efficacy dispersion in teams: Moving beyond agreement and aggregation. *Personnel Psychology, 63*, 1–40. doi: 10.1111/j.1744-6570.2009.01161.x.

DeRue, D. S., & Morgeson, F. P. (2007). Stability and change in person-team and person-role fit over time: The effects of growth satisfaction, performance, and general self-efficacy. *Journal of Applied Psychology, 92*, 1242–1253. doi: 10.1037/0021-9010.92.5.1242.

Dickter, D. N., Roznowski, M., & Harrison, D. A. (1996). Temporal tempering: An event history analysis of the process of voluntary turnover. *Journal of Applied Psychology, 81*, 705–716. doi:10.1037//0021-9010.81.6.705.

Dierdorff, E. C., Bell, S. T., & Belohlav, J. A. (2011). The power of "we": Effects of psychological collectivism on team performance over time. *Journal of Applied Psychology, 96*, 247–262. doi: 10.1037/a0020929.

Edmondson, A. C., & McManus, S. E. (2007). Methodological fit in management field research. *The Academy of Management Review, 32*, 1155–1179. doi: 10.2307/2015936.

Espinosa, J. A., Cummings, J. N., Wilson, J. M., & Pearce, B. M. (2003). Team boundary issues across multiple global firms. *Journal of Management Information Systems, 19*, 157–190.

Frese, M., & Zapf, D. (1994). Action as the core of work psychology: A German approach. In H. C. Triandis, M. D. Dunnette, & L. M. Hough (Eds.), *Handbook of industrial & organizational psychology: Vol. 4* (pp. 271–340). Palo Alto, CA: Consulting Psychologists Press.

Fu, F. Q. (2009). Effects of salesperson experience, age, and goal setting on new product performance trajectory: A growth curve modeling approach. *Journal of Marketing Theory & Practice, 17*, 7–20. doi: 10.2753/mtp1069-6679170101.

Fuller, J. A., Stanton, J. M., Fisher, G. G., Spitzmüller, C., Russell, S. S., & Smith, P. C. (2003). A lengthy look at the daily grind: Time series analysis of events, mood, stress, and satisfaction. *Journal of Applied Psychology, 88*, 1019–1033. doi:10.1037/0021-9010.88.6.1019.

George, J. M., & Jones, G. R. (2000). The role of time in theory and theory building. *Journal of Management, 26*, 657–684. doi:10.1177/014920630002600404.

Gersick, C. J. G. (1988). Time and transition in work teams: Toward a new model of group development. *Academy of Management Journal, 31*, 9–41. doi:10.2307/256496.

Gevers, J. M. P., Rutte, C. G., & van Eerde, W. (2006). Meeting deadlines in work groups: Implicit and explicit mechanisms. *Applied Psychology: An International Review, 55*, 52–72. doi:10.1111/j.1464-0597.2006.00228.x.

Gevers, J. M. P., van Eerde, W., & Rutte, C. G. (2009). Team self-regulation and meeting deadlines in project teams: Antecedents and effects of temporal consensus. *European Journal of Work and Organizational Psychology, 18*, 295–321. doi: 10.1080/13594320701693217.

Golembiewski, R. T., Billingsley, K., & Yeager, S. (1976). Measuring change and persistence in human affairs: Types of change generated by OD designs. *Journal of Applied Behavioral Science, 12*, 133–157. doi:10.1177/002188637601200201.

Greenwood, D. J., & Levin, M. (1998). *Introduction to action research: Social research for social change*. Thousand Oaks, CA: SAGE.

Greer, L. L., Jehn, K. A., & Mannix, E. A. (2008). Conflict transformation: A longitudinal investigation of the relationships between different types of intragroup conflict and the moderating role of conflict resolution. *Small Group Research, 39*, 278–302. doi: 10.1177/1046496408317793.

Hacker, W. (2003). Action Regulation Theory: A practical tool for the design of modern work processes? *European Journal of Work and Organizational Psychology, 12*, 105–130. doi:10.1080/13594320344000075.

Hackman, J. R. (2012). From causes to conditions in group research. *Journal of Organizational Behavior, 33*, 428–444. doi: 10.1002/job.1774.

Han, G., & Harms, P. D. (2010). Team identification, trust, and conflict: A mediation model. *International Journal of Conflict Management, 21*, 20–43. doi: 10.1108/104440610 11016614.

Harrison, D. A., Mohammed, S., McGrath, J. E., Florey, A. T., & Vanderstoep, S. W. (2003). Time matters in team performance: Effects of member familiarity, entrainment, and task discontinuity on speed and quality. *Personnel Psychology, 56*, 633–669. doi:10.1111/j.1744-6570.2003.tb00753.x.

Harrison, D. A., Price, K. H., Gavin, J. H., & Florey, A. T. (2002). Time, teams, and task performance: Changing effects of surface- and deep-level diversity on group functioning. *Academy of Management Journal, 45*, 1029–1045. doi:10.2307/3069328.

Hinsz, V. B., Tindale, R. S., & Vollrath, D. A. (1997). The emerging conceptualization of groups as information processors. *Psychological Bulletin, 121*, 43–64. doi: 10.1037/0033-2909.121.1.43.

Hunziker, S., Johansson, A. C., Tschan, F., Semmer, N. K., Rock, L., Howell, M. D., & Marsch, S. (2011). Teamwork and leadership in cardiopulmonary resuscitation. *Journal of The American College of Cardiology, 57*, 2381–2388. doi:10.1016/j.jacc.2011.03.017.

Hunziker, S., Semmer, N. K., Tschan, F., Schuetz, P., Mueller, B., & Marsch, S. (2012). Dynamics and association of different acute stress markers with performance during a simulated resuscitation. *Resuscitation, 83*, 572–578. doi:10.1016/j.resuscitation.2011.11.013.

Ilgen, D. R., Hollenbeck, J. R., Johnson, M., & Jundt, D. (2005). Teams in organizations: From Input-Process-Output models to IMOI models. *Annual Review of Psychology, 56*, 517–543. doi:10.1146/annurev.psych.56.091103.070250.

Ito, J. K., & Brotheridge, C., M. (2008). Do teams grow up one stage at a time?: Exploring the complexity of group development models. *Team Performance Management, 14*, 214–232. doi:10.1108/13527590810898491.

Jehn, K. A., Greer, L., Levine, S., & Szulanski, G. (2008). The effects of conflict types, dimensions, and emergent states on group outcomes. *Group Decision and Negotiation, 17*, 465–495. doi: 10.1007/s10726-008-9107-0.

Kelly, J. R., Futoran, G. C., & McGrath, J. E. (1990). Capacity and capability: Seven studies of entrainment of task performance rates. *Small Group Research, 21*, 283–314. doi:10.1177/1046496490213001.

Kozlowski, S. W. J. (2012). Groups and teams in organizations: Studying the multilevel dynamics of emergence. In A. B. Hollingshead & M. S. Poole (Eds.), *Research methods for studying groups and teams: A guide to approaches, tools, and technologies* (pp. 260–283). New York, NY: Routledge Academic.

Kozlowski, S. W. J., & Bell, B. S. (2008). Team learning, development, and adaptation. In V. I. Sessa & M. London (Eds.), *Work group learning: Understanding, improving & assessing how groups learn in organizations* (pp. 15–44). Mahwah, NJ: LEA.

Kozlowski, S. W. J., & Chao, G. T. (2012). Macro cognition, team learning, and team knowledge: Origins, emergence, and measurement. In E. Salas, S. M. Fiore, & M. P. Letsky (Eds.), *Theories of team cognition: Cross-disciplinary perspectives* (pp. 19–48). New York, NY: Routledge Academic.

Kozlowski, S. W. J., & Ilgen, D. R. (2006). Enhancing the effectiveness of work groups and teams. *Psychological Science in the Public Interest, 7*, 77–124. doi:10.1111/j.1529-1006.2006.00030.x.

Kozlowski, S. W. J., & Klein, K. J. (2000). A multilevel approach to theory and research in organizations: Contextual, temporal, and emergent processes. In K. J. Klein & S. W. J. Kozlowski (Eds.), *Multilevel theory, research, and methods in organizations* (pp. 3–90). San Francisco, CA: Jossey-Bass.

Lance, C. E., Vandenberg, R. J., & Self, R. M. (2000). Latent growth models of individual change: The case of newcomer adjustment. *Organizational Behavior and Human Decision Processes, 83*, 107–140. doi:10.1006/obhd.2000.2904.

Landis, R. S. (2001). A note on the stability of team performance. *Journal of Applied Psychology, 86*, 446–450. doi:10.1037//0021-9010.86.3.446.

Leach, D. J., Wall, T. D., Rogelberg, S. G., & Jackson, P. R. (2005). Team autonomy, performance, and member job strain: Uncovering the teamwork KSA link. *Applied Psychology: An International Review, 54*, 1–24. doi:10.1111/j.1464-0597.2005.00193.x.

LePine, J. A., Piccolo, R. F., Jackson, C. L., Mathieu, J. E., & Saul, J. R. (2008). A meta-analysis of teamwork processes: Tests of a multidimensional model and relationships with team effectiveness criteria. *Personnel Psychology, 61*, 273–307. doi: 10.1111/j.1744-6570.2008.00114.x.

Lewin, K. (1947). Frontiers in group dynamics: Concept, method and reality in social science; social equilibria and social change. *Human Relations, 1*, 5–41. doi: 10.1177/001872674700100103.

Li, J., & Roe, R. A. (2012). Introducing an intratram longitudinal approach to the study of team process dynamics. *European Journal of Work and Organizational Psychology, 21*, 718–748.

Marks, M. A., Mathieu, J. E., & Zaccaro, S. J. (2001). A temporally based framework and taxonomy of team processes. *Academy of Management Review, 26*, 356–376. doi: 10.5465/amr.2001.4845785.

Mathieu, J., Maynard, M. T., Rapp, T., & Gilson, L. (2008). Team effectiveness 1997-2007: A review of recent advancements and a glimpse into the future. *Journal of Management, 34*, 410–476. doi: 10.1177/0149206308316061.

Maynard, M. T., Mathieu, J. E., Rapp, T. L., & Gilson, L. L. (2012). Something(s) old and something(s) new: Modeling drivers of global virtual team effectiveness. *Journal of Organizational Behavior, 33*, 342–365. doi: 10.1002/job.1772.

McComb, S., Kennedy, D., Perryman, R., Warner, N., & Letsky, M. (2010). Temporal patterns of mental model convergence: Implications for distributed teams interacting in electronic collaboration spaces. *Human Factors, 52*, 264–281. doi: 10.1177/0018720810370458.

McGrath, J. E. (1964). *Social psychology: A brief introduction.* New York, NY: Holt, Rinehart and Winston.

McGrath, J. E. (1984). *Groups: Interaction and performance.* Englewood Cliffs, NJ: Prentice-Hall.

McGrath, J. E. (1988). Time and social psychology. In J. E. McGrath (Ed.), *The social psychology of time: New perspectives (SAGE Focus Editions)* (pp. 255–267). Newbury Park, CA: SAGE.

McGrath, J. E. (1993). Introduction: The JEMCO workshop: Description of a longitudinal study. *Small Group Research, 24*, 285–306. doi:10.1177/1046496493243002.

McGrath, J. E., & Altman, I. (1966). *Small group research: A synthesis and critique of the field.* Oxford: Holt, Rinehart, & Winston.

McGrath, J. E., Arrow, H., & Berdahl, J. L. (2000). The study of groups: Past, present, and future. *Personality and Social Psychology Review, 4*, 95–105. doi:10.1207/S15327957PSPR0401_8.

McGrath, J. E., & Gruenfeld, D. H. (1993). Toward a dynamic and systemic theory of groups: An integration of six temporally enriched perspectives. In M. M. Chemers & R. Ayman (Eds.), *Leadership theory and research: Perspectives and directions* (pp. 217–243). San Diego, CA: Academic Press.

McGrath, J. E., & Kelly, J. R. (1986). *Time and human interaction: Toward a social psychology of time*. New York, NY: Guilford Press.

McGrath, J. E., & Rotchford, N. L. (1983). Time and behavior in organizations. *Research in Organizational Behavior*, *5*, 57–101.

McGrath, J. E., & Tschan, F. (2004). *Temporal matters in social psychology*. Washington, DC: American Psychological Association.

Mitchell, T. R., & James, L. R. (2001). Building better theory: Time and the specification of when things happen. *Academy of Management Review*, *26*, 530–547. doi:10.5465/AMR.2001.5393889.

Mohammed, S., & Nadkarni, S. (2011). Temporal diversity and team performance: The moderating role of team temporal leadership. *Academy of Management Journal*, *54*, 489–508. doi: 10.5465/amj.2011.61967991.

Mohammed, S., Tesler, R., & Hamilton, K. (2012). Time and team cognition: Toward greater integration of temporal dynamics. In E. Salas, S. M. Fiore, & M. P. Letsky (Eds.), *Theories of team cognition: Cross-disciplinary perspectives* (pp. 87–116). New York, NY: Routledge/Taylor & Francis.

Molenaar, P. C. M. & Campbell, C. G. (2009). The new person-specific paradigm in psychology. *Current Directions in Psychological Science*, *18*, 112–117. doi:10.1111/j.1467-8721.2009.01619.x.

Murase, T., Doty, D., Wax, A., DeChurch, L. A., & Contractor, N. S. (2012). Teams are changing: Time to "think networks". *Industrial and Organizational Psychology: Perspectives on Science and Practice*, *5*, 41–44. doi: 10.1111/j.1754-9434.2011.01402.x.

Muthén, B. (2004). Latent variable analysis: Growth mixture modeling and related techniques for longitudinal data. In D. Kaplan (Ed.), *The SAGE Handbook of Quantitative Methodology for the Social Sciences* (pp. 345–368). Thousand Oaks, CA: SAGE.

Nagin, D. S. (1999). Analyzing developmental trajectories: A semiparametric, group-based approach. *Psychological Methods*, *4*, 139–157. doi:10.1037//1082-989X.4.2.139.

Nagin, D. S. (2005). *Group-based modeling of development*. Cambridge, MA: Harvard University Press.

Ployhart, R. E., Holtz, B. C., & Bliese, P. D. (2002). Longitudinal data analysis: Applications of random coefficient modeling to leadership research. *Leadership Quarterly*, *13*, 455–486. doi:10.1016/S1048-9843(02)00122-4.

Poole, M. S., & Roth, J. (1989). Decision development in small groups IV: A typology of group decision paths. *Human Communication Research*, *15*, 323–356. doi: 10.1111/j.1468-2958.1989.tb00188.x.

Porter, C. O. L. H. (2005). Goal orientation: Effects on backing up behavior, performance, efficacy, and commitment in teams. *Journal of Applied Psychology*, *90*, 811–818. doi:10.1037/0021-9010.90.4.811.

Raes, A. M. L., Heijltjes, M. G., Glunk, U., & Roe, R. A. (2011). The interface of top management team and middle managers: A process model. *Academy of Management Review*, *36*, 102–126. doi: 10.5465/amr.2011.55662566.

Ramos-Villagrasa, P. J., Navarro, J., & García-Izquierdo, A. L. (2012). Chaotic dynamics and team effectiveness: Evidence from professional basketball. *European Journal of Work and Organizational Psychology*, *21*, 778–802.

Reinecke, J., & Seddig, D. (2011). Growth mixture models in longitudinal research. *AStA: Advances in Statistical Analysis*, *95*, 415–434. doi:10.1007/s10182-011-0171-4.

Rescher, N. (1996). *Process metaphysics: An introduction to process philosophy*. New York: State University of New York.

Richter, A. W., Dawson, J. F., & West, M. A. (2011). The effectiveness of teams in organizations: A meta-analysis. *The International Journal of Human Resource Management, 22*, 2749–2769. doi: 10.1080/09585192.2011.573971.

Roe, R. A. (2005). No more variables, please! Giving time a place in work and organizational psychology. In F. Avallone, H. Kepir Sinangil, & A. Caetano (Eds.), *Convivence in organizations and society* (pp. 11–20). Milano: Guerini.

Roe, R. A. (2008a, September). *Time and the study of behavior in organizations: Implications for assessment, selection, and development.* Paper presented at the meeting of SHL Seminar, Thames Ditton, England.

Roe, R. A. (2008b). Time in applied psychology: The study of "what happens" rather than "what is". *European Psychologist, 13*, 37–52. doi:10.1027/1016-9040.13.1.37.

Roe, R. A. (2009). Perspectives on time and the chronometric study of what happens in organizations. In R. A. Roe, M. J. Waller, & S. R. Clegg (Eds.), *Time in organizational research* (pp. 291–313). London: Routledge.

Roe, R. A. (2011, February). *Studying time in teams: Why and how?* Paper presented at the EAWOP Small Group Meeting on Time and Change in Teams, Chemnitz University of Technology, Germany.

Roe, R. A. (2012). What is wrong with mediators and moderators? *The European Health Psychologist, 14*, 4–9.

Russell, C. J. (2001). A longitudinal study of top-level executive performance. *Journal of Applied Psychology, 86*, 560–573. doi:10.1037/0021-9010.86.4.560.

Sacco, J. M., & Schmitt, N. (2005). A dynamic multilevel model of demographic diversity and misfit effects. *Journal of Applied Psychology, 90*, 203–231. doi:10.1037/0021-9010.90.2.203.

Salas, E., Cooke, N. J., & Gorman, J. C. (2010). The science of team performance: Progress and the need for more. *Human Factors, 52*, 344–346. doi: 10.1177/0018720810374614.

Sanchez-Cortes, D., Aran, O., Schmid-Mast, M., & Gatica-Perez, D. (2012). A nonverbal behavior approach to identify emergent leaders in small groups. *IEEE Transactions on Multimedia, 14*, 816–832. doi:10.1109/TMM.2011.2181941.

Seibt, J. (Ed.). (2003). *Process theories: Crossdisciplinary studies in dynamic categories.* Dordrecht: Kluwer Academic.

Solinger, O. N. (2009). Capturing the dynamics of commitment: Temporal theory, methods, and an application to the organizational commitment attitude *(Unpublished doctoral dissertation)*. Maastricht: Maastricht University.

Souitaris, V., & Maestro, B. M. M. (2010). Polychronicity in top management teams: The impact on strategic decision processes and performance of new technology ventures. *Strategic Management Journal, 31*, 652–678. doi:10.1002/smj.831.

Sundstrom, E., McIntyre, M., Halfhill, T., & Richards, H. (2000). Work groups: From the Hawthorne studies to work teams of the 1990s and beyond. *Group Dynamics: Theory, Research, and Practice, 4*, 44–67. doi: 10.1037/1089-2699.4.1.44.

Swigger, K., Hoyt, M., Serçe, F. C., Lopez, V., & Alpaslan, F. N. (2012). The temporal communication behaviors of global software development student teams. *Computers in Human Behavior, 28*, 384–392. doi: 10.1016/j.chb.2011.10.008.

Tannenbaum, S. I., Mathieu, J. E., Salas, E., & Cohen, D. (2012a). On teams: Unifying themes and the way ahead. *Industrial and Organizational Psychology: Perspectives on Science and Practice, 5*, 56–61. doi: 10.1111/j.1754-9434.2011.01406.x.

Tannenbaum, S. I., Mathieu, J. E., Salas, E., & Cohen, D. (2012b). Teams are changing: Are research and practice evolving fast enough? *Industrial and Organizational Psychology: Perspectives on Science and Practice, 5*, 2–24. doi: 10.1111/j.1754-9434.2011.01396.x.

Tekleab, A. G., Quigley, N. R., & Tesluk, P. E. (2009). A longitudinal study of team conflict, conflict management, cohesion, and team effectiveness. *Group & Organization Management, 34*, 170–205. doi: 10.1177/1059601108331218.

Tschan, F. (2002). Ideal cycles of communication (or cognitions) in triads, dyads, and individuals. *Small Group Research, 33*, 615–643. doi: 10.1177/1046496402238618.

Tschan, F., McGrath, J. E., Semmer, N. K., Arametti, M., Bogenstätter, Y., & Marsch, S. U. (2009). Temporal aspects of processes in ad-hoc groups: A conceptual schema and some research examples. In R. A. Roe, M. J. Waller, & S. R. Clegg (Eds.), *Time in organizational research* (pp. 42–61). London: Routledge.

Tschan, F., Vetterli, M., Semmer, N. K., Hunziker, S., & Marsch, S. C. U. (2011). Activities during interruptions in cardiopulmonary resuscitation: A simulator study. *Resuscitation, 82*, 1419–1423. doi:10.1016/j.resuscitation.2011.06.023.

Tuckman, B. W. (1965). Developmental sequence in small groups. *Psychological Bulletin, 63*, 384–399. doi:10.1037/h0022100.

Uitdewilligen, S., & De Jong, B. (2012, April). *Isn't it about time we start taking events in teams seriously?* Paper presented at the Seminar on Development and Utilization of Human Resources, Maastricht University, The Netherlands.

Van de Ven, A. H. (2007). *Engaged scholarship: A guide for organizational and social research.* Oxford: Oxford University Press.

Van de Ven, A. H., & Poole, M. S. (2005). Alternative approaches for studying organizational change. *Organization Studies, 26*, 1377–1404. doi:10.1177/0170840605056907.

van Knippenberg, D., De Dreu, C. K. W., & Homan, A. C. (2004). Work group diversity and group performance: An integrative model and research agenda. *Journal of Applied Psychology, 88*, 1008–1022. doi: 10.1037/0021-9010.89.6.1008.

Wageman, R., Gardner, H., & Mortensen, M. (2012). The changing ecology of teams: New directions for teams research. *Journal of Organizational Behavior, 33*, 301–315. doi: 10.1002/job.1775.

Waller, M. J., Conte, J. M., Gibson, C. B., & Carpenter, M. A. (2001). The effect of individual perceptions of deadlines on team performance. *The Academy of Management Review, 26*, 586–600. doi:10.2307/3560243.

Watson, W. E., Johnson, L., & Merritt, D. (1998). Team orientation, self-orientation, and diversity in task groups: Their connection to team performance over time. *Group and Organization Management, 23*, 161–188. doi:10.1177/1059601198232005.

Wheelan, S. A., & McKeage, R. L. (1993). Developmental patterns in small and large groups. *Small Group Research, 24*, 60–83. doi: 10.1177/1046496493241005.

Zaccaro, S. J., Marks, M. A., & DeChurch, L. A. (Eds.). (2012). *Multiteam systems: An organization form for dynamic and complex environments.* New York, NY: Routledge/Taylor & Francis.

Zaheer, S., Albert, S., & Zaheer, A. (1999). Time scales and organizational theory. *Academy of Management Review, 24*, 725–741. doi: 10.2307/259351.

Zellmer-Bruhn, M. E. (2003). Interruptive events and team knowledge acquisition. *Management Science, 49*, 514–528. doi: 10.1287/mnsc.49.4.514.14423.

Zijlstra, F. R. H., Waller, M. J., & Phillips, S. I. (2012). Setting the tone: Early interation patterns in swift-starting teams as a predictor of effectiveness. *European Journal of Work and Organizational Psychology, 21*, 749–777.

EUROPEAN JOURNAL OF WORK AND
ORGANIZATIONAL PSYCHOLOGY
2012, 21 (5), 657–680

Cross-cultural differences in perception of time: Implications for multinational teams

Gamze Arman and Christopher K. Adair

Department of Psychology, DePaul University, Chicago, IL, USA

Members of multinational teams likely have different perspectives on a variety of factors stemming from their different cultural backgrounds. The use and perception of time is one of the specific cultural values that differ cross-culturally and may have implications for the group dynamics and team effectiveness in multinational teams. Concepts such as time orientation, punctuality and pace of life are influenced by time-related differences among cultures. In the present article, it is argued that temporal diversity in multinational teams may serve as an input within the Input-Mediator-Output-Input model of team effectiveness (Ilgen, Hollenbeck, Johnson, & Jundt, 2005) and influence the team processes and outputs. Implications of cross-cultural differences in perception of time on multinational team functioning are discussed within the framework of the Marks, Mathieu, and Zaccaro (2001) taxonomy of team processes, which consists of 3 higher order team processes (i.e., transition processes, action processes, and interpersonal processes) that encompass 10 distinct, more specific processes. Propositions regarding the impact of temporal diversity on many of the distinct team processes and outcomes are put forward to help provide a temporal lens to future research on multinational teams.

Keywords: Culture; Multinational teams; Temporal diversity; Time.

Increased cultural diversity has become a prominent characteristic of the workforce. Employees of large organizations are no longer necessarily from

Correspondence should be addressed to Christopher K. Adair, Department of Psychology, Byrne Hall 420, DePaul University, 2219 N. Kenmore Ave., Chicago, IL 60614, USA. E-mail: cadair1@depaul.edu

The authors contributed equally to this article, and would like to thank Suzanne T. Bell, Eileen Linnabery, Peter Rekdahl, and the anonymous reviewers for their valuable insight and comments. An earlier version of this paper was presented at the 27th Annual Conference of the Society of Industrial and Organizational Psychology, San Diego, CA, USA.

the same or similar national backgrounds (cf. Shore et al., 2009). Multinational teams (MNTs) are defined as teams that are composed of members representing multiple nationalities. The members have interdependent tasks and goals, and they are mutually accountable to each other to achieve these goals, similar to other types of teams in organizations (Earley & Gibson, 2002). MNTs serve as a means of sharing and transferring knowledge across international boundaries and they are necessary for effective functioning of organizations that want to reach a global market. MNTs are usually geographically dispersed virtual teams (Joshi & Lazarova, 2005) and as a result of the increased opportunities they provide, those teams appear to be the norm for international businesses all over the world (Wright & Drewery, 2006). Cross-cultural differences, including the effects of the differences in perception and use of time, among MNT members constitute the basis of the present discussion, and their implications for MNTs serve as the focus of this article.

The literature on the impact of diversity in teams lacks consistent findings (van Knippenberg & Schippers, 2007). However, MNTs may benefit from positive impacts of diversity such as increased innovation and higher quality solutions to global business problems (Maznevski & Peterson, 1997). Results of a recent meta-analysis revealed that culturally diverse teams have higher creativity and team-level satisfaction compared to homogeneous teams (Stahl, Maznevski, Voigt, & Jonsen, 2010). MNTs inevitably face specific challenges as well. Given that nationality influences individual values, cognitive schemas, and behaviours, cultural differences among team members may result in different expectations regarding group dynamics (Hambrick, Davison, Snell, & Snow, 1998; Kirkman & Shapiro, 2005). These differences may result in conflict and low levels of trust among team members (Maznevski & Peterson, 1997). Meta-analytic results show that MNTs experience more conflict and lower levels of social integration, compared to homogeneous teams (Stahl et al., 2010). As a part of cultural differences in perception, people from different cultures also have different conceptualizations of time (Hall, 1983; Levine, 1997).

McGrath and Rotchford (1983) introduced time as a component of group research that constitutes the basis of the social entrainment perspective. This perspective viewed interpersonal interaction among group members as leading to entrainment of individuals' internal rhythms to one another, and that collective entrainment and synchronization of internal rhythms of individuals and groups could serve as external pacers effecting the individual rhythms (McGrath & Kelly, 1986). On the basis of this perspective, it was claimed that group researchers should pay attention to the timing of data collection, temporal patterns of group behaviour (e.g., sequences of actions, sudden shifts), and dominant themes of group dynamics at different times in groups, in their studies (Ballard, Tschan, & Waller, 2008). In their review of workplace temporality research, Ballard and Seibold (2003) emphasized that dimensions of time such as scheduling and scarcity can strongly influence the level of task interdependence, use of workplace technologies, and feedback cycles, and they likely have effects on teams as well (Ballard & Seibold, 2004).

Teams are special types of groups in work settings. Thus, given that the experience of time in groups and organizations is an important area of research, effects of time on teams should be also studied. Within the context of MNTs, cross-cultural differences in perception of time serve as a determinant of temporal diversity of a team, and should be examined as potential factors influencing team dynamics, processes, and outcomes (Maznevski & Peterson, 1997; Saunders, van Slyke, & Vogel, 2004). With this purpose, the current article addresses the potential effects of cross-cultural differences in perception of time on MNT effectiveness by discussing their specific implications for the processes and outcomes of MNTs, and offering propositions to guide future research.

CROSS-CULTURAL DIFFERENCES IN PERCEPTION OF TIME AS INPUTS IN MNTS

The Input-Process-Output (IPO) framework of team effectiveness (Hackman, 1987; McGrath, 1964) suggests that inputs consist of individual-level factors (e.g., member skills, attitudes, personality characteristics), group-level factors (e.g., structure, level of cohesiveness), and environment-level factors (e.g., group task characteristics, reward structure). Inputs influence group processes (e.g., coordination) and these processes influence outputs (e.g., performance quality, member satisfaction, group cohesiveness). To further explain team effectiveness, Ilgen, Hollenbeck, Johnson, and Jundt (2005) modified and extended the IPO framework, and developed the Input-Mediator-Output-Input (IMOI) model in which they emphasized that emergent states (e.g., trust) and team processes (e.g., goal monitoring) are mediating variables serving the transmission of inputs to outputs, and outputs serve as future inputs in recurring feedback loops. According to both models, inputs and processes play a crucial role in team effectiveness. As a team composition input, diversity based on demographic factors, functional factors, personality, and attitudes has been examined in several studies of team effectiveness (cf. Mathieu, Maynard, Rapp, & Gilson, 2008). Diversity was defined as a complex input factor, which might have positive, negative, or neutral effects on team processes, emergent states, and team performance (Webber & Donahue, 2001).

Hofstede (1991) defined culture as a mental programming, which is learned over time and determines people's thinking, feeling, and potential acting patterns. In an MNT setting, cultural backgrounds of team members can be interpreted as one of the individual-level inputs influencing group processes and outputs. Within a multilevel lens, cultural backgrounds can thus be understood as a compilation variable (in contrast to a composition variable; cf. Bliese, 2000). Compilation variables (such as demographics) reflect team inputs that are not considered to be isomorphic (or identical) with a higher level construct. Rather, the higher level construct is represented by the specific configuration of individual-level observations and represents a unique property of the group that is not readily apparent from any single individual observation. Given that intergroup variability is assumed, it is not necessary to demonstrate agreement between team members in order to aggregate to the team level.[1] It is thus important to remember throughout the following discussion of cultural backgrounds that a team-level representation refers to the unique configuration of the individual-level backgrounds.

Several researchers have been interested in cross-cultural differences in perception and use of time. For example, Levine and Norenzayan (1999) found differences in pace of life across cultures, and other research has found cross-cultural differences in the use of time in negotiation (Macduff, 2006), and the practice and effectiveness of time management (Nonis, Teng, & Ford, 2005). From a broader perspective, culture may affect present, past, or future focus in perspective and planning (Kluckhohn & Strodtbeck, 1961), conceptualization of time on the basis of clock time versus events (Levine & Norenzayan, 1999), perception and practice of punctuality, interpretation of silence (as positive or negative), and distribution of work versus leisure time in general and also task versus social time during the work day (Brislin & Kim, 2003).

MNTs may consist of team members from various different cultural backgrounds in several combinations, and cultural diversity may serve as a basis for temporal diversity in MNTs. Some researchers (e.g., Eisenhardt, 2004) claimed that temporal diversity among team members can provide a basis for better analysis of complex, dynamic, and uncertain environments by introducing different approaches and it can result in increased efficiency by balancing performing requirements such as speed, quality, and long-term versus short-term demands. On the other hand, based on McGrath and Rotchford's (1983) social entrainment perspective, it was also argued that temporal diversity can lead to problems in interpretation of paces of work and in planning of activities, thus it may result in conflict among team

[1]Although cultural background is assumed to be a compilation variable, this brings up a problem concerning missing data. That is, any missing data means that an accurate team-level representation cannot be adequately obtained. For the purposes of this discussion and the ensuing article, we are assuming that complete team data is available. We thank one of our reviewers for this valuable insight.

members, decreased timeliness, and lower quality outputs (Mohammed & Nadkarni, 2011).

Within the IMOI framework, temporal diversity, serving as an input, may influence team processes such as conflict, knowledge management system, and empowerment strategies (Gibson, Waller, Carpenter, & Conte, 2007). These processes, in turn, may determine the outcomes, such as the performance (Mohammed & Nadkarni, 2011), innovativeness of knowledge created, speed of knowledge creation, and speed of knowledge transfer (Gibson et al., 2007), which in turn influence future inputs. The potential influences of diversity in time perceptions on team processes in MNTs will be discussed in the following section.

MNTS AND TEAM PROCESSES

As mentioned earlier, team processes serve as mediating variables in transmitting inputs to outputs within the IMOI framework (Ilgen et al., 2005). Processes are typically understood as interdependent activities that convert inputs to outcomes and require interpersonal activity between team members (Driskell, Hogan, & Salas, 1987; Hackman, 1987). Specifically, effective team processes transmit each member's task-related contributions to other team members, enhancing outcomes such as performance and perceived satisfaction (Bettenhausen, 1991; LePine, Piccolo, Jackson, Mathieu, & Saul, 2008). For the purposes of this article, the Marks, Mathieu and Zaccaro (2001) taxonomy of team processes will serve as the organizing framework for this section.

A brief description of the Marks et al. (2001) taxonomy will facilitate the understanding of how team processes are enacted in MNTs and influenced by time perceptions (i.e., inputs). Three higher order processes, namely transition processes, action processes, and interpersonal processes, encompass 10 distinct, more specific processes. Transition processes are when teams evaluate activities to guide future behaviour, and action processes are direct attempts towards goal attainment. Interpersonal processes can occur during both action and transition phases, and may emphasize the effectiveness of the specific processes within each of these categories (Marks et al., 2001). These processes focus on team member emotions and ongoing interpersonal conflict. Processes such as strategy formulation, coordination, and affect management are distinct processes within transition, action, and interpersonal processes, respectively. The hierarchical factor structure of team processes has been meta-analytically supported elsewhere in the literature (LePine et al., 2008).

Each of the distinct processes will be discussed within the context of its broader process. Doing so will contribute to our understanding of temporal influences on team processes and provide a more thorough and nuanced description of team processes and how they function within MNTs. Table 1 demonstrates the interconnected nature of various temporal concepts and each of the broad processes, namely transition, action, and interpersonal. Each of the specific processes is included as an additional reference. Very little research has been done on the influence of culture and time on team processes. Accordingly, various propositions are put forward to encourage future studies.

Transition phase processes

Not all interactions within a team are focused on active task completion. Although the scope may vary between teams, many teams need to evaluate and plan prior to working toward a goal. These processes, referred to within the Marks et al. (2001) framework broadly as transition phase processes, focus on evaluative and planning interactions between team members. Here, teams take inventory on how well they performed during a previous performance episode, prepare for the upcoming episode, and derive performance gaps that need to be addressed. Developing strategies based on these analyses will guide future performance goals and team member interactions. Research has shown that following a temporal pattern of planning, executing, and terminating is associated with higher team performance (Tschan, 2002). As such, these processes are likely to occur in MNTs at the beginning of a project team's task (e.g., kick-off meeting before engaging in the work). Because transition-phase processes involve a measure of foresight and planning, it seems reasonable that time orientation will be heavily influential. For instance, time orientation can vary

TABLE 1
Summary of the relationship between team processes and temporal concepts

	Process	*Temporal concept*
Transition processes	1. Mission analysis	Time orientation
	2. Goal specification	Time orientation
	3. Strategy formulation	Polychronic and monochronic time use
Action processes	1. Coordination	Punctuality
	2. Goal monitoring	Time efficiency
	3. Systems monitoring	Time as a symbol
	4. Backup behaviours	Dealing with periods of silence
Interpersonal processes	1. Affect management	Pace of life
	2. Motivation & confidence building	Dealing with periods of silence
	3. Conflict management	Dealing with periods of silence

Many of these temporal concepts are borrowed from Brislin and Kim (2003).

significantly in terms of what type of behaviour is valued (House, Hanges, Javidan, Dorfman, & Gupta, 2004). Additionally, an MNT that is able to engage in multiple activities at once (e.g., polychronicity) may be more effective at planning and strategizing than an MNT that cannot. The following discussion will go into more detail concerning these temporal issues in relation to the specific transition phase processes.

First, mission analysis is likely to be influenced by the MNT's time orientation. Generally, this process describes when a team identifies its main tasks, the resources available for executing these tasks, and verbally ensures that all team members have a shared vision of the team's mission and objectives (Marks et al., 2001). A shared vision of the team's objectives is akin to mental model similarity, which has been shown to be a positive predictor of team performance (Lim & Klein, 2006). Given that team members should have an understanding of the main tasks and mission prior to engaging in a task, it is likely that this process will occur at the onset of a performance episode.

Time orientation may influence the effectiveness of this process for MNTs. Kluckhohn and Strodtbeck (1961) suggested that past-oriented cultures value traditions and compare current conditions to past conditions to estimate the value or quality of current conditions. These cultures also prefer taking long-term perspectives, avoiding risk, and emphasizing stability across time. Present-oriented cultures, on the other hand, are concerned with current conditions and the immediate future, with a preference for taking short-term perspectives that stress time efficiency. Finally, future-oriented cultures are concerned with the more distal future and thus prefer long-term perspectives for problem solving. This concept has been included as a part of more recent conceptualizations of broad cultural dimensions (Hofstede, 1991; House et al., 2004).

Teams that are composed of predominantly past-oriented members (e.g., little variability in individual-level time orientation) will be more likely to compare the current mission to those handled in the past. Past-oriented MNTs will value traditions and compare their current condition to past conditions (Brislin & Kim, 2003). Future-oriented MNTs, on the other hand, examine a mission from a more macro perspective, determining the distal outcomes associated with the mission. This stands in sharp contrast to mission analysis in present-oriented cultures, where the main concern is the mission's influence on the immediate future. It is possible that some orientations may be better suited for specific MNT missions. For instance, an MNT with a predominantly present orientation may perform better in response to time-sensitive matters due to their more short-term focus. As such, a preference may be put towards addressing proximal goals (e.g., accomplishing the task at hand) as opposed to distal goals (e.g., aligning tasks with a strategic vision). A predominantly future-oriented MNT, on the other hand, may be better for determining a new business-wide strategic plan because of their focus on broader, more distal objectives.

> *Proposition 1:* Time orientation influences the effectiveness of MNT mission analysis, such that proximal objectives are effectively addressed by a present orientation while distal objectives are effectively addressed by a future orientation.

Goal specification is another transition phase process that is influenced by time orientation. Here, teams identify and prioritize goals that are aligned with the overall vision and mission. Challenging and specific goals are the most effective (Locke & Latham, 2002), and teams effectively engage in goal specification when they assign these goals with respect to appropriate time and resource constraints. Because one quality of successful goal specification is that goals are aligned with the overall mission, it is likely similarly influenced by time orientation. The espoused (or, identified) goals of MNTs may differ greatly based on their orientation with respect to time. Different goals (e.g., proximal and distal) may carry different weight based on the cultural perspective of the MNT. Future-oriented MNTs may set more distal than proximal goals because these align with their preference for a macro perspective. Conversely, proximal goals may be favoured in present-oriented MNTs because these are goals that can be quickly attained.

> *Proposition 2:* Time orientation influences MNTs goal specification, where future-oriented MNTs favour distal goals and present-oriented MNTs favour proximal goals.

Finally, strategy formulation and planning may be particularly influenced by cultural differences in time perception. This process describes "the development of alternative courses of action for mission accomplishment" (Marks et al., 2001, p. 365). Teams that are effective in this process consider a variety of inputs and resources (e.g., time, team member experience, etc.) that are likely to be influential. The concept of polychronicity is likely strongly influential for this process. Polychronic time use is defined as the tendency to work on multiple tasks at a time and it is observed more frequently in North American cultures (Brislin & Kim, 2003; Hall, 1983). This is consistent with North Americans' conceptualization of time as a commodity that should be used efficiently and saved. In contrast, monochronicity is defined as focusing on a single event at a time. It is more likely to be adopted in Latin cultures, as a result of the prominence of paying undivided attention to the only task. Time can be viewed as a valuable resource in some cultures (Arrow, Poole, Henry, Wheelan, &

Moreland, 2004), and MNTs that treat time as such may be more prone to strategize using polychronic, as opposed to monochronic, time use.

Polychronic time use may come from other sources than culture: It could be a strategy, or it may arise from time pressure from ineffective earlier processes. The connection between strategy formulation and polychronic versus monochronic MNTs is made clearer when considering that Marks et al. (2001) included three different forms of strategy formulation: deliberate planning, contingency planning, and reactive strategy adjustment. Truly polychronic MNTs will engage in multiple tasks at once during deliberate planning because this serves as the principal course of action for fulfilling the team's mission. Teams that deliberately plan to use a polychronic approach know that they are responsible for multiple tasks at a time, and it is not a last-second effort to complete a task before a deadline. Contingency planning involves formulating alternatives for strategy a priori. MNTs may plan for their behaviours to become more polychronic as a deadline approaches, even if they are not composed of highly polychronic members. Finally, reactive strategy adjustment offers the potential for ineffective time use. Teams that adjust their strategy in response to unanticipated events or problems may find that individual differences in time orientation can have a heavy influence. Individual time-oriented behaviours may vary significantly within a team facing strong time pressure (Waller, Giambatista, & Zellmer-Bruhn, 1999), and this difference is likely heightened for MNTs due to strong cultural differences on time-oriented behaviours. Therefore, reactively adjusting from a monochronic to a polychronic time use within an MNT may cause team members to behave in less of a unified manner.

Proposition 3: Polychronic MNTs will be more effective at deliberate planning and contingency planning than reactive strategy adjustment, while the monochronicity of an MNT will not influence their strategy formulation process effectiveness.

In sum, the various transition phase processes are mostly likely useful for MNTs either prior to active task completion, or in between performance episodes. Mission analysis is likely effective prior to active task completion, where teams should ensure that all members have a similar time orientation. MNTs that may have a variety of time orientations at the individual level should address this during mission analysis to ensure that the mission objective and resources (e.g., time) are similarly understood by all. Goal specification is also influenced by time orientation, as proximal and distal goals may be differentially favoured depending on the MNT time orientation. Finally, strategy formulation is a multifaceted process that is heavily influenced by the polychronicity versus monochronicity of the team.

As with mission analysis, MNTs should do their best to establish their time use a priori using deliberate planning in order to plan for any individual differences in time-oriented behaviours.

The aforementioned propositions assume a high level of agreement within the MNT in terms of time orientation. Recall that recent literature on temporal diversity has suggested that it can negatively influence team effectiveness by causing problems in interpretation of paces of work and in planning of activities (Mohammed & Nadkarni, 2011). Within-team variability on cultural time concepts will be discussed more in the next proposition.

Action phase processes

Whereas transition phase processes are focused on ensuring the team understands the mission or objectives, action phase processes occur when teams actually engage in behaviours to achieve stated objectives. The processes that occur during an action phase are all focused on working toward a shared goal. It is especially important for distributed MNTs that these processes are verbally communicated, because communication for distributed teams tends to be less fluid (Hightower, Sayeed, Warkentin, & McHaney, 1997). In other words, distributed MNTs should ensure that interactions such as feedback are explicit, since the communication medium is less rich and is less easily transmitted by factors such as nonverbal communication. Open communication is particularly important for MNTs and virtual teams (Hinds & Mortensen, 2005). Time concepts such as punctuality and time efficiency (Brislin & Kim, 2003) are likely to be influential for these processes. Indeed, past research has suggested that temporal dimensions such as scheduling, precision, and pace contribute to team members' temporal experience (Ballard & Seibold, 2003). The three specific action phase processes discussed here are coordination, goal monitoring, and systems monitoring. The fourth action phase process, backup behaviour, will be discussed later with interpersonal processes.

Coordination involves a team engaging in behaviour focused on task completion by synchronizing the timing of their behaviours and sharing pertinent information (Marks et al., 2001). All teams, including MNTs, successfully coordinate when they are able to structure their behaviour in such a way that all team members contribute to accomplishing the goal. Because this requires a level of synchronization, time can heavily influence this process. Specifically, punctuality can be very influential for effective MNT coordination. Punctuality is highly related to use of clock time rather than event time (Brislin & Kim, 2003). In Western European countries, people tend to value being punctual, and feel bad if they fail to adhere to a set meeting time by even a few minutes. However, in countries such as

Turkey, punctuality is not taken as seriously, with some degree of tardiness existing as an expected part of life. A lack of punctuality is not a serious problem in countries using event time, as people in these cultures wait for an event to end before attending another regardless of the time set for the upcoming event.

Although some literature has suggested ways in which temporal diversity can benefit team effectiveness (e.g., Mohammed & Nadkarni, 2011), benefits are unlikely to emerge from differences regarding punctuality. MNTs that have different, culturally determined opinions about punctuality may struggle to manage their tasks within a performance episode. A high degree of within-team variability in punctuality may result in members having different schedules, and thus create ambiguity about how tasks are best accomplished. Recall that following a temporal pattern of planning, executing, and terminating a task is associated with higher team performance (Tschan, 2002). Thus, teams that fail to develop a shared collective cognition concerning punctuality will likely develop priorities and pacing styles that are discordant, which may be destructive to ultimate team performance (Mohammed & Nadkarni, 2011).

Proposition 4: MNTs need to have a large degree of agreement concerning punctuality in order to effectively coordinate.

Goal monitoring is another action phase process, and involves a team-level discussion of the progress towards a goal. For instance, a single member checking how he/she is progressing does not satisfy the requirements for this process. Rather, a verbal discourse is required among team members about progress and any changes that need to be made. Goal monitoring typically involves identifying performance gap through a comparison of the actual state and a desired state, which is similar to self-regulation (e.g., Gevers, van Eerde, & Rutte, 2009). Time efficiency (Brislin & Kim, 2003) is particularly influential for goal monitoring, since this process in many ways assumes a deadline. An increased level of time sensitivity in American and some European cultures results in focusing on deadlines and rewarding the employees who finish first. Other (e.g., Asian) cultures tend to value patience and focus on the quality of outcomes over speed. As teams monitor their progress towards a goal, their understanding of how to use time efficiently will influence their self-regulatory behaviours. Teams that are sensitive to the scarcity of time will have less patience and feel more urgency to accomplish their shared goal. The lack of patience may influence the team's desired state and in turn how the team monitors the effectiveness of their progress. Virtual teams that are culturally heterogeneous tend to be less satisfied and cohesive than teams that are culturally homogeneous (Staples & Zhao, 2006). One possible explanation for this observation may be differences in how time is interpreted. The cultural determinants of time may be evidenced through the process of goal monitoring by how an MNT shrinks their performance gap.

Proposition 5: MNTs that view time as a scarce resource engage in more goal monitoring than those that are less concerned with time.

Finally, teams can also monitor the external and internal resources with which they operate (Marks et al., 2001). Systems monitoring is particularly important for teams, especially when time is viewed as one of the valuable resources that a team needs to monitor. As mentioned earlier, time can be viewed as a finite, external resource for teams, especially for teams operating under a deadline (Arrow et al., 2004). In looking at time in this light, an MNT is placing a type of symbol on time. The use of time as a symbol may differ across cultures to influence MNT functioning (Brislin & Kim, 2003). For instance, the conceptualization of time as a symbol of money is prevalent in American culture, evidenced by the American practice of basing payment on an hourly rate. When time is viewed as a valuable resource as well as a symbol of money, an MNT is likely to monitor time because a monetary value has been placed on it. MNTs that do not use the "time as money" symbol will likely be less concerned with monitoring this resource. Time also serves as a sign of importance, such that people think that spending more time on one task over another shows that the former is more important. Each of these symbols may vary between cultures, influencing MNT functioning.

One way to observe how attaching a symbol to time influences MNT systems monitoring is through an examination of how companies use alternative work arrangements such as telework. Because systems monitoring also requires teams to monitor internal resources such as technologies and personnel (Marks et al., 2001), it may be influenced by how MNTs handle the differentiation between task and social time. Increasing technology has facilitated the implementation of distributed MNTs and teleworking (Wicks, 2002), but questions about how to separate work and leisure time arise from these added technologies. For instance, the United States and Japan are typically used as examples of cultures in which working for long hours and having very limited vacations is the norm (Brislin & Kim, 2003). These countries place a symbol on time that implies it has high value (e.g., "money"), and thus expect that the majority of time is spent on work rather than leisure. In contrast, the majority of European cultures value leisure time and their employees can take significantly more vacation days. The difference of European cultures may also arise from the less valuable symbols placed on time, in addition to the value they put on leisure time.

This association between work and leisure time is quite similar to work–family conflict, which has a wealth of research in a variety of contexts (cf. Greenhaus & Allen, 2011). However, research on work–life balance in a cross-cultural context is very limited, although research has suggested that various cultural dimensions are influential (Peters & den Dulk, 2003). For instance, manager uncertainty may increase along with an increase in worker time–spatial flexibility, given that employees have increased discretion on how they spend their time. As such, cultural differences in work–leisure time expectations as well as the value placed on time may influence the extent to which MNTs engage in systems monitoring. MNTs may need to place an additional emphasis on monitoring how individual team members expect work and leisure time to be separated.

Proposition 6: MNTs that place a high value on time will engage in frequent systems monitoring in order to ensure that sufficient time is being spent on work-related activities.

In sum, cultural influences of the perception of time can strongly influence each of the action-phase team processes. Various categories put forth by Brislin and Kim (2003), such as time efficiency and punctuality, may influence both the incidence of various processes as well as the perceived need of each of these processes. The propositions put forth offer a more narrowed scope for future research. The next section will discuss the final group of processes.

Interpersonal processes

Unlike action and transition phase processes that tend to occur in distinct periods of team member interactions, interpersonal processes are suggested to occur across both phases (Marks et al., 2001). In general, a high degree of within-team variability on any temporal concept is likely to negatively influence interpersonal processes. For instance, recall that Mohammed and Nadkarni (2011) suggested that temporal diversity with regard to pacing and time perspective may cause ambiguity and conflict. This relates directly to the interpersonal processes put forth by Marks et al. (2001), which include affect management, motivation and confidence building, and conflict management.

The first interpersonal process, affect management, involves controlling for team member emotions during task planning and completion (Marks et al., 2001). This process can take a variety of forms, as interpersonal affect can be highly variable. For instance, teams may seek to enhance social cohesion as a way of regulating team member emotions. Social cohesion is positively related to team-level outcomes (e.g., Beal, Cohen, Burke, &

McLendon, 2003). Time pressures can affect team member emotions, especially if individual members of an MNT have different perceptions of deadlines (Waller et al., 1999). The cultural category of "pace of life" is noteworthy here, as affective conflict may arise from different paces and MNTs must accommodate appropriately. Fast and slow pace of life (i.e., tempo of life) has been studied within a cultural context, by examining walking speed of people, speed of service at post offices, and accuracy of public clocks in 31 countries (Levine & Norenzayan, 1999). Speed of life is faster in places where the economies are healthier, the degree of industrialization is higher, or culture emphasizes collectivism rather than individualism. Thus, pace of life is likely to differ across countries depending on a variety of social, economic, and cultural characteristics. For example, the comparison revealed that pace of life was fastest in Switzerland, Ireland, Germany, and Japan and slowest in El Salvador, Brazil, Indonesia, and Mexico. Similarly, pacing styles are likely to differ within MNTs at least partially due to these varying paces of life. An MNT composed of members from Switzerland and Brazil may find that their pace of life influences their behaviour surrounding time-sensitive materials. Pacing styles differ with respect to how deadlines are approached and how temporal resources are allocated (Gevers, Rutte, & van Eerde, 2006). Indeed, research on pacing styles in general is abundant, and has shown that high intrateam variability can create strain and dissatisfaction (Jansen & Kristof-Brown, 2005).

> *Proposition 7:* Similar conceptualizations of pace of life within an MNT result in less need for affect management than when within-team variability is high.

Motivation and confidence building is another interpersonal process that can be heavily influenced by cultural factors. Additionally, there is a high level of conceptual overlap between this process and team backup behaviour, so these two processes are likely influenced by similar factors. Team backup behaviour may take the form of verbal reassurances offered to other members, assisting another member with his/her role, or providing feedback with the intention of working towards the shared goal (Marks et al., 2001). Recall that cultural differences may result in low levels of trust among MNT team members (Maznevski & Peterson, 1997). This may require a greater need for MNT confidence building to accommodate for the lower baseline levels of trust, or it may influence team member comfort with assisting other team members with his/her role (i.e., backup behaviours).

How an MNT perceives long periods of silence is another culturally determined temporal variable that is applicable to this discussion. Long periods of silence are not acceptable in American and Western European cultures, and people from these cultures feel the need to fill any experienced silent time (e.g., during a business meeting) with some sort of verbal discussion. People from Asian and Eastern cultures, on the other hand, are comfortable with such silent moments and perceive them as opportunities to focus on their thoughts before sharing them with others.

MNTs may be composed of team members with various comfort levels with respect to silence (Brislin & Kim, 2003). For instance, MNTs that have a predominantly "Western" interpretation of silence may fill this time with some form of discussion. This discussion may range from some form of off-task discussion to verbal reassurances and offers of assistance among team members. This desire to fill silent time with communication may not be shared by MNTs that interpret silence as many Asian cultures do. MNTs with a predominantly "Eastern" interpretation of silence thus may be comfortable with independently working towards the shared team goal and may not perceive a need for motivational discourse. In other words, the extent to which MNTs engage in motivation and confidence building may be influenced by how they handle periods of silence. This is partially due to this process being heavily verbal, such that teams need to communicate with each other to motivate, build confidence, or back up other team members (Marks et al., 2001).

Cultures that are less comfortable with periods of silence, such as many Western cultures, may fill that time with confidence building or backup behaviours. Teams composed of predominantly Western members may give "pep talks" or give feedback about individual progress and success. Personal feedback of this kind significantly influences self-efficacy in Western cultures (Earley, Gibson, & Chen, 1999), and individuals from Western cultures tend to seek feedback more than individuals from Eastern cultures (Morrison, Chen, & Salgado, 2004). Similarly, team backup behaviours are positively associated with collective efficacy beliefs (Porter, Gogus, & Yu, 2011). Because motivating and backup behaviours are often focused at the individual level (Marks et al., 2001), seeking these behaviours may follow a similar trajectory to general feedback. That is, Western team members may seek out and provide this type of communication more than their Eastern teammates.

On the other hand, cultures that do not perceive silent periods as problematic, such as many Eastern cultures, may not perceive a need for such motivational discourse. An example provided by Blackburn, Furst, and Rosen (2003) helps clarify this point further. In their example, an Asian member of a virtual MNT did not voice his feelings of disagreement with the team's progress, instead remaining silent in accordance with his cultural heritage. The other (presumably Western) members of the team in turn used this time to seek more information about potential sources of conflict from this team member. Although this example involves conflict rather than motivation, it helps demonstrate how the cultural makeup of an MNT may determine how members handle periods of silence. Further, although members may fill periods of silence with various forms of off-task discourse, we propose that one way in which MNTs may fill this time is through the on-task, cooperative discourse presented previously.

Proposition 8: MNTs that are uncomfortable with periods of silence will use this time to engage in more motivational, confidence building, and backup behaviour processes than MNTs that are comfortable with periods of silence.

Conflict management involves how a team handles conflict that has either already arisen or may potentially arise in the future (Marks et al., 2001). The conflict management literature is extensive, and time offers a variety of influences on how teams handle conflict. While there is some overlap with the previous discussion of coordination, the influence of temporal coordination on conflict management is important to note. Research has found that the general synchronization of tasks, or temporal coordination, significantly moderates the relationship between various forms of conflict management and performance (Montoya-Weiss, Massey, & Song, 2001). MNTs may have difficulties with temporal coordination because members may have different perceptions of time that are culturally determined (e.g., clock time, punctuality, fast/slow pace).

Additionally, Marks et al. (2001) pointed out that there are multiple types of conflict management. Teams engage in "preemptive conflict management" by establishing conditions to prevent team conflict before it occurs, and they engage in "reactive conflict management" by addressing existing interpersonal disagreements. Many of the conflict management strategies addressed in Montoya-Weiss et al. (2001) involved reactive approaches (e.g., accommodation, compromise). Thus, it appears that temporal coordination is influential chiefly on reactive approaches. However, all teams should do well to focus on preemptive conflict management, as it has positive effects on team-level outcomes (Behfar, Peterson, Mannix, & Trochim, 2008). Preemptive conflict management may take the form of other strategies, such as effective planning and strategizing. MNTs can address conflict before it occurs by effectively planning contingencies, managing deadlines, and synchronizing their behaviours.

Proposition 9: MNTs that are able to temporally coordinate their behaviours and processes report less need for conflict management (both reactive and preemptive) than MNTs that are unable to do so.

The previous discussion of the interpersonal processes highlights the interconnectedness with the transition and action phase processes. For instance, successful temporal coordination may preemptively lead to decreased levels of interpersonal conflict. Teams that address differences in MNT member perceptions of pace of life can also control for team member emotions during task planning and completion.

IMPLICATIONS FOR OUTCOMES

The IMOI framework suggests that team processes mediate the effects of inputs on outcomes in teams (Ilgen et al., 2005) and any problem in team processes may influence the quality of outcomes negatively. The previous discussion showed that in an MNT, significant differences on time perceptions may lead to misinterpretations, conflict among team members, and problems in team functioning. Thus, problems in processes arising from these differences may result in errors, low performance, member dissatisfaction, and low group cohesiveness. Increased diversity in perceptions of time urgency and pacing styles hinders performance in teams consisting of members from the same culture (Mohammed & Nadkarni, 2011), and their effects might be more negative in MNTs, when combined with other differences among team members.

> *Proposition 10:* Time-related cultural influences on team processes (Propositions 1–9) influence shared MNT outcomes, such that problems experienced in the processes lead to decreased member satisfaction, performance, and group cohesiveness.

CONCLUSION

We sought to consolidate and extend the extant literature on MNTs. Specifically, the diversity in perception and use of time was considered as an input, which we argue influences team processes and outcomes. Propositions were provided with the intent of spurring future research on this topic. As businesses grow ever more global, such research is increasingly necessary for better comprehension of group dynamics and team effectiveness in MNTs, with regard to the cultural differences among team members. However, before discussing the implications of the proposed relationships for research and practice, a few important issues regarding other aspects of MNTs and influences of culture should be emphasized.

MNT-related considerations

First, leadership in MNTs should be considered for several reasons. Increased temporal diversity among team members with regard to perceptions of time urgency and pacing style require special temporal leadership skills to prevent the negative effects of diversity on team performance (Mohammed & Nadkarni, 2011). In addition, leadership behaviours and managerial style are also influenced by the time perceptions of leaders, which may vary as a function of the leader's cultural background. Thus, leaders from different cultures may have different foci with respect to planning (i.e., long-term vs. short-term; Ayoun & Moreo, 2009) and level of attention paid to time management (Zwikael, Shimizu, & Globerson, 2005). Consequently, leadership and managerial style may vary within MNTs depending on the cultural background and time-related practices of the leader, and this style may or may not be consistent with the expectations of team members from different cultures. Time perceptions may play a role in interactions between the leader and the MNT members as well, as members may attach different meanings to time and time-related practices. Such differences and different interpretations of situations (e.g., meaning of silence) may lead to problems like misunderstanding and conflict (Brislin & Kim, 2003).

The second important issue is the virtual nature of the majority of MNTs (Joshi & Lazarova, 2005). Although the focus of the previous discussion was the effects of cross-cultural differences rather than the challenges in virtual teams, unique time-related characteristics of virtual teams are also relevant. Due to the lack of synchronous communication arising from the differences in time and space, coordination may be a significant challenge as virtual teams suffer from delays in responses and feedback (McGrath, 1991). Another challenge might be recognizing potential differences in time-related perceptions of members of virtual MNTs. In general, using technology and communication to address the potential problems and avoid complications have great potential to contribute to the soundness of team processes and consequently improve long-term outcomes in virtual teams (Maznevski & Chudoba, 2000).

Culture-related considerations

The previous discussion focused on the application of a specific cross-cultural difference (differences in use and perception of time) to a specific type of teams (MNTs). Members of MNTs might be working in the same location (i.e., office) all the time, in the same country but in different locations, or in different countries all the time, depending on their level of virtualness. However, it should be highlighted that there are many other cultural differences (e.g., individualism/collectivism, power distance) that may be influential on team processes in MNTs (Connaughton & Shuffler, 2007; Kirkman & Shapiro, 2005; Maznevski & Peterson, 1997). The effects of all types of cultural differences should be considered in any culturally diverse organizational setting, as well as the MNTs. For example, an MNT member from a collectivistic culture might be more likely to pay attention to the opinions of other team members compared to an MNT member from an individualistic culture (Maznevski & Peterson, 1997). Such differences also play a crucial role in team processes (e.g., coordination) and emergent states (e.g., trust). Several studies have focused on the effects of those differences in MNTs; however, temporal diversity appears to be an underexamined topic in the study of cultural diversity in teams. Therefore, future research building on the proposed relationships has the potential to broaden our understanding of culturally based dynamics in MNTs.

Perceptions and use of time can be heavily influenced by national culture, and any individual difference should be considered in MNTs. However, cultural norms should not be applied too strictly. First, even though culture may serve as a strong basis for individuals' mindsets, there are always other influential individual differences. In other words, we suggest caution in labelling all people from a culture as, for example, polychronics or monochronics, as there is also intranational variability on these factors (Nonis et al., 2005). Second, people working within the same organization also share an organizational culture (cf. Schein, 1993), which may define or change the perception and use of time within that organization regardless of the national cultures in which that organization operates. In relation to the effects of organizations, it has been argued that workplace technologies may influence employees' construals of time, or their present versus future time orientation (Ballard & Seibold, 2003). Also, higher firm-level global integration may lead to lower time perspective heterogeneity in MNTs (Gibson et al., 2007). As mentioned before, although the majority of MNTs are also virtual teams, they may be also functioning in a location existing within a main national culture (e.g., same office or same country). In this case, the dominant national culture may also influence the team members' experience of time (Ballard & Seibold, 2003).

The study of temporal diversity in MNTs is a promising endeavour, as long as we attempt to control potential confounds to the highest possible extent and avoid rigorous categorizations of people on the basis of their national backgrounds. We do not argue that temporal diversity is more important than other types of diversity, or temporal diversity is more important for MNTs in comparison to other types of teams. However, the literature on the effects of diversity in teams can be enriched by the inclusion of temporal diversity. The study of the temporal diversity with regard to cultural backgrounds might be a good starting point, as culture is a strong determinant of time perception.

Implications for research and practice

The present literature on MNTs does not involve any empirical studies focusing on temporal diversity in MNTs and their implications on team processes and outcomes. The propositions listed in this article are based on a compilation-based conceptualization of cultural backgrounds, such that they are considered to be unique individual-level contributions to a team-level representation (cf. Bliese, 2000). Using this as a basis for future research, the propositions can be tested in future studies. For example, quantitative data from several MNTs can be collected to test the effects of differences in punctuality, time orientation, and other time-related variables on team processes such as coordination and planning.

Future studies may wish to address more general research questions on this issue. For example, studies may incorporate time, processes, and leadership into a dynamic model. Such research may examine which team processes are more likely to suffer or benefit from differences in time perceptions of members and leader of MNTs. Future research may also discuss if organizations should consider differences in time perceptions while selecting members and leaders for MNTs (Mohammed & Nadkarni, 2011). Studies may focus on how leader and organizational factors influence team member time perceptions. For instance, this research could examine which factor among leader's perception, perceptions of majority of team members, or organizational culture is most influential in determining the team-level perceptions of time in an MNT.

Examination of time-related differences among MNT members has the potential to contribute to the effort to improve efficiency in MNT functioning in practice. Training programmes for MNT leaders, for example, can aim to improve their skills for appraising potential differences across team members, while taking measures to avoid and minimize problems (Joshi & Lazarova, 2005). On the other hand, cultural awareness training programmes targeting improvements in cultural intelligence of team members may also be beneficial to minimize potential conflict and misunderstandings among team members (Earley & Gardner, 2005).

In conclusion, examination of temporal diversity in MNTs can improve our theoretical understanding of team effectiveness in those teams. In the long term, building on the findings of scientific studies, we can improve the methods for increasing team efficiency in MNTs in practice.

REFERENCES

Arrow, H., Poole, M., Henry, K., Wheelan, S., & Moreland, R. (2004). Time, change, and development: The temporal perspective of groups. *Small Group Research*, *35*, 73–105. doi:10.1177/1046496403259757

Ayoun, B., & Moreo, P. (2009). Impact of time orientation on the strategic behavior of Thai and American hotel managers. *Journal of Hospitality Marketing and Management*, *18*, 676–691. doi:10.1080/19368620903170224

Ballard, D. I., & Seibold, D. R. (2003). Communicating and organizing in time: A meso-level model of organizational temporality. *Management Communication Quarterly*, *16*, 380–415. doi:10. 1177/0893318902238896

Ballard, D. I., & Seibold, D. R. (2004). Communication-related organizational structures and work group temporal experiences: The effects of coordination method, technology type, and feedback cycle on members' construals and enactments of time. *Communication Monographs, 71*, 1–27. doi:10.1080/036345204 10001691474

Ballard, D. I., Tschan, F., & Waller, M. J. (2008). All in the timing: Considering time at multiple stages of group research. *Small Group Research, 39*, 328–351. doi:10.1177/1046496408317036

Beal, D. J., Cohen, R. R., Burke, M. J., & McLendon, C. L. (2003). Cohesion and performance in groups: A meta-analytic clarification of construct relations. *Journal of Applied Psychology, 88*, 989–1004. doi:10.1037/0021-9010.88.6.989

Behfar, K., Peterson, R., Mannix, E., & Trochim, W. (2008). The critical role of conflict resolution in teams: A close look at the links between conflict type, conflict management strategies, and team outcomes. *Journal of Applied Psychology, 93*, 170–188. doi:10.1037/0021-9010.93.1.170

Bettenhausen, K. (1991). Five years of groups research: What we have learned and what needs to be addressed. *Journal of Management, 17*, 345–381. doi:10.1177/014920639101700205

Blackburn, R., Furst, S., & Rosen, B. (2003). Building a winning virtual team: KSAs, selection, training and evaluation. In C. Gibson & S. Gibson (Eds.), *Virtual teams that work: Creating conditions for virtual team effectiveness* (pp. 95–120). San Francisco, CA: Jossey-Bass.

Bliese, P. D. (2000). Within-group agreement, non-independence, and reliability: Implications for data aggregation and analysis. In K. K. Klein & S. W. J. Kozlowski (Eds.), *Multilevel theory, research, and methods in organizations: Foundations, extensions, and new directions* (pp. 349–381). San Francisco, CA: Jossey-Bass.

Brislin, R., & Kim, E. (2003). Cultural diversity in people's understanding and uses of time. *Applied Psychology: An International Review, 52*, 363–382. doi:10.1111/1464-0597.00140

Connaughton, S. L., & Shuffler, M. (2007). Multinational and multicultural distributed teams: A review and future agenda. *Small Group Research, 38*, 387–412. doi:10.1177/10464964 07301970

Driskell, J. E., Hogan, R., & Salas, E. (1987). Personality and group performance. In C. Hendrick (Ed.), *Group processes and intergroup relations* (pp. 91–112). Thousand Oaks, CA: Sage.

Earley, P. C., & Gardner, H. K. (2005). Internal dynamics and cultural intelligence in multinational teams. In D. L. Shapiro, M. A. von Glinow, & J. L. C. Cheng (Eds.), *Managing multinational teams: Global perspectives* (Vol. 18, pp. 3–31). Oxford, UK: Elsevier.

Earley, P. C., & Gibson, C. B. (2002). *Multinational teams: A new perspective*. Mahwah, NJ: Lawrence Erlbaum Associates, Inc.

Earley, P. C., Gibson, C. B., & Chen, C. C. (1999). "How did I do?" versus "how did we do?" Cultural contrasts of performance feedback use and self-efficacy. *Journal of Cross-Cultural Psychology, 30*, 594–619. doi:10.1177/0022022199030005003

Eisenhardt, K. M. (2004). Five issues where groups meet time. In S. Blount (Ed.), *Time in groups: Research on managing groups and teams* (Vol. 6, pp. 267–283). New York, NY: Elsevier.

Gevers, J., Rutte, C., & van Eerde, W. (2006). Meeting deadlines in work groups: Implicit and explicit mechanisms. *Applied Psychology: An International Review, 55*, 52–72. doi:10.1111/j.1464-0597.2006.00228.x

Gevers, J., van Eerde, W., & Rutte, C. (2009). Team self-regulation and meeting deadlines in project teams: Antecedents and effects of temporal consensus. *European Journal of Work and Organizational Psychology, 18*, 295–321. doi:10.1080/13594320701693217

Gibson, C. B., Waller, M. J., Carpenter, M. A., & Conte, J. M. (2007). Antecedents, consequences, and moderators of time perspective heterogeneity for knowledge management in MNO teams. *Journal of Organizational Behavior, 28*, 1005–1034. doi:10.1002/job.445

Greenhaus, J. H., & Allen, T. D. (2011). Work-family balance: A review and extension of the literature. In L. Tetrick & J. C. Quick (Eds.), *Handbook of occupational health psychology* (pp. 165–183). Washington, DC: American Psychological Association.

Hackman, J. R. (1987). The design of work teams. In J. Lorsch (Ed.), *Handbook of organizational behavior* (pp. 315–342). Englewood Cliffs, NJ: Prentice-Hall.

Hall, E. T. (1983). *The dance of life: The other dimension*. New York, NY: Anchor Press/ Doubleday.

Hambrick, D. C., Davison, S. C., Snell, S. A., & Snow, C. C. (1998). When groups consist of multiple nationalities: Towards a new understanding of the implications. *Organization Studies, 19*, 181–205. doi:10.1177/017084069801900202

Hightower, R. T., Sayeed, L., Warkentin, M., & McHaney, R. (1997). Information exchange in virtual work teams. In M. Tan & M. Igbaria (Eds.), *The virtual workplace* (pp. 199–216). Hershey, PA: Idea Group Publishing.

Hinds, P. J., & Mortensen, M. (2005). Understanding conflict in geographically distributed teams: The moderating effects of shared identity, shared context, and spontaneous communication. *Organization Science, 16*, 290–307. doi:10.1287/orsc.1050.0122

Hofstede, G. (1991). *Cultures and organizations: Software of the mind*. London, UK: McGraw-Hill.

House, R. J., Hanges, P. J., Javidan, M., Dorfman, P. W., & Gupta, V. (2004). *Culture, leadership, and organizations: The GLOBE study of 62 societies*. Thousand Oaks, CA: Sage.

Ilgen, D. R., Hollenbeck, J. R., Johnson, M., & Jundt, D. (2005). Teams in organizations: From input-process-output models to IMOI models. *Annual Review of Psychology, 56*, 517–543. doi:10.1146/annurev.psych.56.091103.070250

Jansen, K. J., & Kristof-Brown, A. L. (2005). Marching to the beat of a different drummer: Examining the impact of pacing congruence. *Organizational Behavior and Human Decision Processes, 97*, 93–105. doi:10.1016/j.obhdp.2005.03.005

Joshi, A., & Lazarova, M. (2005). Do "global" teams need "global" leaders? Identifying leadership competencies in multinational teams. In D. L. Shapiro, M. A. von Glinow, & J. L. C. Cheng (Eds.), *Managing multinational teams: Global perspectives* (Vol. 18, pp. 281–302). Oxford, UK: Elsevier.

Kirkman, B. L., & Shapiro, D. L. (2005). The impact of cultural value diversity on multicultural team performance. In D. L. Shapiro, M. A. von Glinow, & J. L.C. Cheng (Eds.), *Managing multinational teams: Global perspectives* (Vol. 18, pp. 33–67). Oxford, UK: Elsevier.

Kluckhohn, F. R., & Strodtbeck, F. L. (1961). *Variations in value orientations*. Evanston, IL: Row, Peterson.

LePine, J., Piccolo, R., Jackson, C., Mathieu, J., & Saul, J. (2008). A meta-analysis of teamwork processes: Tests of a multidimensional model and relationships with team effectiveness criteria. *Personnel Psychology, 61*, 273–307. doi:10.1111/j.1744-6570.2008.00114

Levine, R. (1997). *A geography of time*. New York, NY: Basic Books.

Levine, R., & Norenzayan, A. (1999). The pace of life in 31 countries. *Journal of Cross-Cultural Psychology, 30*, 178–205. doi:10.1177/0022022199030002003

Lim, B., & Klein, K. J. (2006). Team mental models and team performance: A field study of the effects of team mental model similarity and accuracy. *Journal of Organizational Behavior, 27*, 403–418. doi:10.1002/job.387

Locke, E. A., & Latham, G. P. (2002). Building a practically useful theory of goal setting and task motivation: A 35-year odyssey. *American Psychologist, 57*, 705–717. doi:10.1037//0003-066X.57.9.705

Macduff, I. (2006). Your pace or mine? Culture, time, and negotiation. *Negotiation Journal, 22*, 31–45. doi:10.1111/j.1571-9979.2006.00084.x

Marks, M. A., Mathieu, J. E., & Zaccaro, S. J. (2001). A temporally based framework and taxonomy of team processes. *Academy of Management Review, 26*, 356–376. doi:10.2307/ 259182

Mathieu, J., Maynard, M. T., Rapp, T., & Gilson, L. (2008). Team effectiveness 1997–2007: A review of recent advancements and a glimpse into the future. *Journal of Management, 34*, 410–476. doi:10.1177/0149206308316061

Maznevski, M. L., & Chudoba, K. M. (2000). Bridging space over time: Global virtual team dynamics and effectiveness. *Organization Science, 11*, 473–492. doi:1047-7039/00/1105/0473

Maznevski, M. L., & Peterson, M. F. (1997). Societal values, social interpretations, and multinational teams. In C. S. Granrose & K. Oskamp (Eds.), *Cross-cultural workgroups* (pp. 61–89). Thousand Oaks, CA: Sage.

McGrath, J. E. (1964). *Social psychology: A brief introduction.* New York, NY: Holt, Rinehart & Winston.

McGrath, J. E. (1991). Time, interaction, and performance (TIP): A theory of groups. *Small Group Research, 22*, 147–174. doi:10.1177/1046496491222001

McGrath, J. E., & Kelly, J. R. (1986). *Time and human interaction: Toward a social psychology of time.* New York, NY: Guilford Press.

McGrath, J. E., & Rotchford, N. L. (1983). Time and behavior in organizations. In L. L. Cummings & B. M. Staw (Eds.), *Research in organizational behavior* (Vol. 5, pp. 57–101). Greenwich, CT: JAI Press.

Mohammed, S., & Nadkarni, S. (2011). Temporal diversity and team performance: The moderating role of team temporal leadership. *Academy of Management Journal, 54*, 489–508. doi:10.5465/AMJ.2011.61967991

Montoya-Weiss, M. M., Massey, A. P., & Song, M. (2001). Getting it together: Temporal coordination and conflict management in global virtual teams. *Academy of Management Journal, 44*, 1251–1262. doi:10.2307/3069399

Morrison, E., Chen, Y., & Salgado, S. (2004). Cultural differences in newcomer feedback seeking: A comparison of the United States and Hong Kong. *Applied Psychology: An International Review, 53*, 1–22. doi:10.1111/j.1464-0597.2004.00158.x

Nonis, S. A., Teng, J. K., & Ford, C. W. (2005). A cross-cultural investigation of time management practices and job outcomes. *International Journal of Intercultural Relations, 29*, 409–428. doi:10.1016/j.ijintrel.2005.05.002

Peters, P., & den Dulk, L. (2003). Cross cultural differences in managers' support of home-based telework: A theoretical elaboration. *International Journal of Cross Cultural Management, 3*(3), 328–346. Retrieved from http://ccm.sagepub.com/

Porter, C., Gogus, C., & Yu, R. (2011). Does backing up behavior explain the efficacy-performance relationship in teams? *Small Groups Research, 42*, 458–474. doi:10.1177/1046496410390964

Saunders, C., van Slyke, C., & Vogel, D. R. (2004). My time or yours? Managing time visions in global virtual teams. *Academy of Management Executive, 18*(1), 19–31. Retrieved from http://journals.aomonline.org/amp/

Schein, E. H. (1993). Defining organizational culture. In J. M. Shafritz, J. S. Ott, & Y. S. Jang (Eds.), *Classics of organization theory* (5th ed., pp. 360–367). Fort Worth, TX: Harcourt.

Shore, L. M., Chung-Herrera, B. G., Dean, M. A., Ehrhart, K. H., Jung, D. I., Randel, A. E., & Singh, G. (2009). Diversity in organizations: Where are we now and where are we going? *Human Resource Management Review, 19*, 117–133. doi:10.1016/j.hrmr.2008.10.004

Stahl, G. K., Maznevski, M. L., Voigt, A., & Jonsen, K. (2010). Unraveling the effects of cultural diversity in teams: A meta-analysis of research on multicultural work groups. *Journal of International Business Studies, 41*, 690–709. doi:10.1057/jibs.2009.85

Staples, S., & Zhao, L. (2006). The effects of cultural diversity in virtual teams versus face-to-face teams. *Group Decision and Negotiation, 15*, 389–406. doi:10.1007/s10726-006-9042-x

Tschan, F. (2002). Ideal cycles of communication (or cognition) in triads, dyads, and individuals. *Small Group Research, 33*, 615–643. doi:10.1177/1046496402238618 van Knippenberg, D., & Schippers, M. C. (2007). Work group diversity. *Annual Review of Psychology*, *58*, 515–541. doi:10.1146/annurev.psych.58.110405.085546

Waller, M., Giambatista, R., & Zellmer-Bruhn, M. (1999). The effects of individual time urgency on group polychronicity. *Journal of Managerial Psychology*, *14*, 244–256. doi:10.1108/02683949910263765

Webber, S. S., & Donahue, L. M. (2001). Impact of highly and less job-related diversity on work group cohesion and performance: A meta-analysis. *Journal of Management*, *27*, 141–162. doi:10.1016/S0149-2063(00)00093-3

Wicks, D. (2002). Successfully increasing technological control through minimizing workplace resistance: Understanding the willingness to telework. *Management Decision*, *40*, 672–681. doi:10.1108/00251740210438508

Wright, N. S., & Drewery, G. P. (2006). Forming cohesion in culturally heterogeneous teams: Differences in Japanese, Pacific Islander and Anglo experiences. *Cross Cultural Management: An International Review*, *13*, 43–53. doi:10.1108/13527600610643475

Zwikael, O., Shimizu, K., & Globerson, S. (2005). Cultural differences in project management capabilities: A field study. *International Journal of Project Management*, *23*, 454–462. doi:10.1016/j.ijproman.2005.04.003

EUROPEAN JOURNAL OF WORK AND
ORGANIZATIONAL PSYCHOLOGY
2012, 21 (5), 681–717

For better or for worse: The effect of superior and inferior teammate performance on changes in challenge/threat cardiovascular responses

Christena Cleveland[1], Lucie Finez[2], Jim Blascovich[3], and Nicole Ginther[4]

[1]Department of Psychology, St. Catherine University, Saint Paul, MN, USA

[2]Laboratory of Applied Psychology, University of Reims, Champagne-Ardenne, France

[3]University of California, Santa Barbara, CA, USA

[4]Psychology Department, Pennsylvania State University, PN, USA

Although much research has investigated the consequences of working with teammates, little research has addressed the effect of team processes on changes in motivational states and associated cardiovascular responses. Filling this gap, we utilized the biopsychosocial model of challenge and threat to examine the effect of teammate performance on evaluations of resources and demands in a team performance situation. It was hypothesized that, assuming team identity engagement, individuals who worked with superior teammates would perceive more resources available to them and exhibit a challenge response (a physiological change that indicates relatively high perceived resources), whereas individuals who worked with inferior teammates would perceive less resources and exhibit a threat response (a physiological change that indicates relatively low perceived resources). For four weeks, 38 teams completed team-building exercises and competed in an anagram tournament, during which measures of cardiovascular reactivity were collected. Participants teamed with two confederates who were either inferior or superior performers. The results of the study revealed that despite the fact that they were the best performers on their team, individuals who worked with inferior teammates were threatened. However, individuals who worked with superior teammates were challenged. Explanations of the observed findings and applications for work/organizational contexts are discussed.

Correspondence should be addressed to Christena Cleveland, Department of Psychology, St. Catherine University, Saint Paul, MN 55105, USA. E-mail: christena.cleveland.03@alum.dartmouth.org

Keywords: Cardiovascular reactivity; Challenge; Motivation; Team building; Team identity; Threat.

Many organizations have moved towards utilizing work groups instead of simply individual workers, therefore teamwork has become an increasingly important topic of study. In fact, research has shown that more than 65% of knowledge workers in the United States and Europe are members of at least one work group, if not more (O'Leary, Mortensen, & Woolley, 2011). Due to the prevalence of teams in the workplace, it is imperative to investigate the elements that make a successful team. Many constructs have been researched, such as surface and deep level diversity (Bell, 2007), learning behaviours and psychological safety (Edmondson, 1999), and team mental models (Mohammed, Ferzandi, & Hamilton, 2010).

The current research examines the effect of teammate performance on an individual's motivation. Given that the necessity and usefulness of teamwork is context dependent, past research has focused on determining the circumstances in which teammate performance affects motivation. For example, research has shown that, in some circumstances, high performing teammates can have a positive effect on motivation gains (Messé, Hertel, Kerr, Lount, & Park, 2002) and, in other circumstances, a negative effect on motivation (Williams & Karau, 1991). The results of these studies provide insight into the ways in which working with inferior or superior teammates affect *strength* of motivation (e.g., absolute increases or decreases in motivation) during team tasks, but offer less insight on how this factor can affect the *type* of motivation (e.g., differing motivational states that are informed by expectations of success and failure). Other research has shown that an individual's expectation of success, coupled with information about ingroup and outgroup performance levels, predicts motivation (Festinger, 1942a, 1942b). However, this research does not offer insight into how these variables relate to each other in a team context. Indeed, few studies have examined how working with inferior or superior teammates can affect expectations of success or failure during team tasks or investigated the conditions that may lead to challenge motivation or threat motivation, both of which may have lasting implications for the workplace. In today's technologically dependent, fast paced, global economy it is increasingly important to understand how to form work teams that are less likely to experience burnout or stress-related health complications.

The present research examines the effect of teammate performance on challenge/threat motivation. Blascovich and colleagues (Blascovich, 2008; Blascovich & Mendes, 2000; Blascovich, Mendes, Tomaka, Salomon, & Seery, 2003; Blascovich & Tomaka, 1996) posit that *challenge* and *threat* represent anchors on a bipolar motivational dimension that involves affective and cognitive, conscious and nonconscious processes. Challenge occurs when evaluations of resources outweigh evaluations of situational demands. Threat occurs when evaluations of situational demands outweigh evaluations of resources. The question of whether working with teammates affects challenge/threat motivation is complex in that it may depend on many variables such as teammate performance and team identity. Indeed, past research suggests that these variables may moderate the consequence of working with teammates on challenge/threat motivation (Cleveland, Blascovich, Gangi, & Finez, 2011).

This investigation has both theoretical and practical implications. From a theoretical perspective, this research allows us to understand the variables that may affect an individual's appraisals and motivation as he/she works on team tasks, how the perceptions of team resources affect calculations of individual resources, and the effect of team identity on resource calculations. From a practical standpoint, this research can help us determine which precautions (with respect to performance ability) we should take when composing work groups. For example, is it important to incorporate teambuilding exercises on heterogeneous teams (e.g., teams composed of individuals with different levels of ability)? How can managers assess the positive and negative effects of working on heterogeneous (with respect to ability) teams? How can managers help team members avoid the negative effects (threat motivation) of being paired with superior teammates?

A potentially relevant approach to team composition from the extant literature is seeding (Humphrey, Hollenbeck, Meyer, & Ilgen, 2007). Humphrey and colleagues (2007) proposed that teams should be assembled (seeded) based upon the theories of supplementary and complementary fit. Certain traits are best matched based upon creating teams whose members have similarities (i.e., supplementary fit), whereas other traits are better matched based upon creating teams whose members complement each other (i.e., complementary fit). The authors theoretically explored how personality characteristics (i.e., extraversion and conscientiousness) could affect team composition, but actual variations in teammate performance ability were not explored in regards to work group seeding. The current research will seek to provide insight into how teammate performance levels can be taken into account when seeding and also how team composition, with respect to performance levels, can affect motivational states. Additionally, the present effort may help to elucidate the implications of doing team-building interventions in conjunction with team tasks.

The present study examines team identity and teammate performance and their effect on challenge/threat motivation (changes in physiological responses from baseline to task) during a 4-week long paradigm that included multiple team-building interventions and team performance tasks. The goal is to broaden our understanding of how collaboration with superior or inferior teammates increases or decreases an individual's expectations of success during collective work. However, this question is difficult to test in an experimental setting because participants' self-presentational concerns may make it challenging to obtain reliable measures of self-reported challenge/threat motivation. For example, research on claimed self-handicapping suggests that participants may inaccurately report high perceptions of situational demands so that they have a ready-made excuse to use in the event of failure (Finez, Berjot, Rosnet, & Cleveland, 2011). Participants may also hold self-presentational concerns related to sandbagging (i.e., feigned demonstration of inability used to lower observers' expectations for one's performance; Gibson & Daniel, 2000) or social desirability (i.e., wanting to appear ambitious or modest). Thus, depending on self-presentational concerns, individuals may inaccurately report their perceptions of resources and situational demands and thus inhibit this investigation of the effect of teammate performance on challenge/threat motivation.

The biopsychosocial model of challenge/ threat (Blascovich, 2008) is well-suited for an investigation of the ways in which teammate performance affects perceptions of resources and demands. The primary advantages of applying the biopsychosocial model to the study of team environment are methodological ones. For example, within the context of a motivated performance situation, challenge and threat can be assessed with physiological measures that are not limited by self-report. Physiological measures are collected on-line, continuously, and covertly during the task and do not require the participant's conscious attention. These characteristics allow investigators to avoid problems potentially associated with self-report measures. First, people may not have the ability to reflect on and report their inner states (Nisbett & Wilson, 1977). Second, even if they can, some people might not choose to accurately report these states (Mendes, Blascovich, Lickel, & Hunter, 2002). Third, even if they are willing and able to self-reflect and report accurately, interrupting and asking participants to do so may interfere with the exact processes that they are attempting to report. By utilizing the biopsychosocial model, we can assess motivational states while individuals are engaged in them.

THE BIOPSYCHOSOCIAL MODEL OF CHALLENGE/ THREAT

The biopsychosocial model of challenge/threat (Blascovich, 2008; Blascovich & Mendes, 2000; Blascovich et al., 2003; Blascovich & Tomaka, 1996) posits that *challenge* and *threat* represent anchors on a bipolar motivational dimension that involves affective and cognitive, conscious and nonconscious processes. Challenge and threat have typically been investigated in *motivated performance situations*—situations that are goal relevant, require active coping, and require that one act instrumentally to achieve a self-relevant objective. In the context of work teams, a motivated performance situation could include making an oral presentation, conducting an important business negotiation or conducting a risky emergency or police intervention.

Blascovich and colleagues maintain that challenge/threat motivation arises when a task is self or goal relevant and, hence, engaging or task involving. An individual who lacks a goal or does not care much about the task is not motivated and, hence, is neither challenged nor threatened. Goals can be self-relevant for a variety of reasons and individuals can experience both tangible and intangible consequences for reaching or failing to reach the goal. For example, members of a surgical team who are tasked with successfully completing a surgical procedure are likely to be engaged in the task because the patient's health is at stake, their professional reputations are at stake, and they possess a desire to succeed in their work.

Given task engagement, the extent to which an individual experiences challenge or threat is determined by the relative balance of the individual's evaluation of his or her coping *resources* and the evaluation of situational *demands*. Factors that influence these evaluations include: skills, knowledge, and abilities; dispositions; external support; danger; uncertainty; required effort, etc. For example, in the context of performing a surgical procedure, surgeons may consider the presence or absence of their own skills, knowledge and abilities in the context of the surgery, any dispositional characteristics that are relevant to the situation (i.e., high self-efficacy), external support (i.e., reliable ancillary staff), danger and uncertainty (i.e., the necessity of using a rare or risky procedure), and required effort when calculating resources and demands. Evaluations of resources and demands can be influenced by factors outside of conscious awareness. Individuals are challenged when their evaluated resources outweigh their evaluated demands of the situation. Individuals are threatened when their evaluation of the demands of the situation outweigh their evaluation of the resources. Essentially, individuals are challenged when they are subjectively prepared to cope with the situation and threatened when they are subjectively ill-prepared to cope with the situation. Challenge and threat represent opposite ends of a continuum, such that relative differences in challenge and threat (e.g., greater vs. lesser challenge) are meaningful (Blascovich, 2008).

Blascovich and colleagues have demonstrated that distinctive patterns of cardiovascular responses that are sensitive to sympathetic adrenal medullary (SAM) axis and/or hypothalamic pituitary (HPA) axis activation index challenge and threat. Three physiological recording techniques are used in their assessment: (1) electrocardiography, which measures electrical signals associated with the actions of the heart muscle; (2) impedance cardiography, which measures blood flow in the thoracic cavity; and (3) blood pressure measurement. By utilizing these techniques, one can measure or calculate four cardiovascular measures that identify task engagement and differentiate challenge from threat: heart rate (HR), expressed in beats per minute; ventricular contractility (VC), a chronotropic index of the left ventricle's contractile force; cardiac output (CO), the amount of blood pumped by the heart in litres per minute; and total peripheral resistance (TPR), an index of net constriction versus dilation in the vascular system.

Task engagement is indexed by changes in heart rate and ventricular contractility from baseline to task such that larger increases indicate greater task engagement. Individuals who are challenged exhibit positive changes in cardiac output and negative changes in total peripheral resistance, whereas individuals who are threatened exhibit little change in cardiac output and little change or even positive changes in total peripheral resistance. As such, physiological changes that result in relatively higher cardiac output and lower total peripheral resistance indicate relatively greater challenge or lesser threat.

These cardiovascular changes are the result of differential activation of the sympathetic adrenal medullary and hypothalamic pituitary axes. Both challenged and threatened individuals exhibit heightened sympathetic adrenal medullary activation and experience an increase in heart rate and ventricular contractility. However, threatened individuals also exhibit heightened hypothalamic pituitary activation which inhibits vasodilation and, hence, the cardiac increase and total peripheral resistance decrease—mediated by the release of epinephrine—that would otherwise occur.

Following Dienstbier (1989), the sympathetic adrenal medullary activation that occurs during challenge is adaptive for a situation in which coping resources meet or exceed demands. This is evidenced by the fact that the relatively short half-life of epinephrine released by the adrenal medulla results in relatively short-lived bursts of energy. These short-lived bursts of energy are fuelled by energy reserves and are well-suited for expectations of successful and presumably short-lived coping. The challenge response functions to increase blood flow (greater cardiac output), to skeletal muscles and dilate arteries to accommodate the increased blood flow (lower total peripheral resistance), which prepares the body for potential activity. The accompanying hypothalamic pituitary activation that occurs during threat is appropriate for a situation in which demands exceed coping resources. This is evidenced by the fact that the relatively long half-life of cortisol results in relatively long-lived bursts of energy. These long-lived bursts of energy are fuelled by energy reserves and are well-suited for expectations of an extended struggle. The threat response results in constriction of arteries (higher total peripheral resistance), which is characteristic of a vigilance response (Hunter, 2001) and is also well-suited for an extended struggle. Consistent with Dienstbier, it is logical to infer that the challenge/threat response was designed to prepare the body for a physical threat, whether one exists or not. As such, the challenge response—with its corresponding increase in cardiac performance and blood flow to the arms and legs—provides much needed energy for active goal pursuit (e.g., to fight off a physical threat). The threat response, on the other hand, is designed to help one survive an extended, losing struggle with a physical threat. Threat partially facilitates the approach-motivated goal of challenge (e.g., in order to keep one engaged in the task), but also prepares the body for loss of action or withdrawal. Accordingly, while the heart works harder during threat than at rest, the increase in total peripheral resistance (e.g., vasodilation), prevents increased blood flow and potentially down-regulates the cardiovascular system (see Seery, 2011).

It is worth noting that in theory, challenge and threat relate to the approach-avoidance constructs. Elliot and Trash (2002) define *approach* as the energization of behaviour directed towards positive or desirable stimuli and avoidance as the energization of behaviour directed away from negative or undesirable stimuli. In a chapter on approach-avoidance motivation and challenge/threat, Blascovich (2008) asserts that challenge/threat map onto approach-avoidance motivational states, albeit in unexpected ways. If adult individuals, like infants perhaps, were solely motivated to approach pleasurable states and avoid negative states, on a moment by moment basis, then challenge and threat would perfectly correlate with approach and avoidance, respectively. However, that is not the case; motivational states and their associated goals are far more complex. Both Blascovich and Elliot and Trash point out that many goals are hierarchical in nature. As such, movement towards a positive superordinate but distal goal (e.g., entering a profession) requires movement towards a negative subordinate proximal goal (e.g., preparing for difficult exams). In this way, many goals involve movement toward both positive and negative states. With this in mind, Blascovich argues that predictably, challenge correlates with approach avoidance. However, he adds that threat also involves approach motivation, albeit towards an undesirable state, as well as an element of avoidance motivation (see Blascovich, 2008). The challenge/threat model complements the family of approach-avoidance theories by providing data on motivated performance situations in which individual's exhibit approach behaviours towards negative states (as opposed to only positive states) and by revealing the (potentially negative) physiological effects that can occur when individuals approach negative states.

The cardiovascular indexes of challenge and threat have been used to examine the role of challenge and/or threat motivational processes in many studies (for reviews, see Blascovich, 2008; Blascovich & Mendes, 2000; Blascovich & Tomaka, 1996). For example, individuals who have stable high self-esteem have been shown to exhibit challenge after receiving negative feedback, whereas individuals with unstable high self-esteem exhibit threat after receiving negative feedback (Seery, Blascovich, Weisbuch, & Vick, 2004). This model has also recently been used to investigate the effects of teammate performance on challenge/threat motivation on recently formed teams (Cleveland et al., 2011). In this study, participants worked with superior teammates on a task before they undergone the process of depersonalization. As such, the participants in this study had not yet adopted a team identity and were not challenged when working with superior teammates (as predicted by social identity theory). Rather, these participants acted as individuals and engaged in individual-to-individual social comparison processes with their teammates that led to threat. This study suggests that team identity is necessary in order for teammate performance to be included in an individual's calculation of resources. The present research tests this hypothesis and extends the Cleveland et al. (2011) findings.

TEAM IDENTITY AND PERCEIVED RESOURCES AND DEMANDS

Social identity theory enables us to make predictions about the circumstances in which collaborating with teammates may lead to challenge motivation or threat motivation. Social identity theory suggests that team participation may make one's identity as a team member more salient than one's identity as an individual. Classic research such as Heider's balance theory (1958) states that, in the interest of cognitive consistency, observers perceive two objects as similar when the relationship between them is positive. Accordingly, team members on cohesive teams should perceive their teammates to be similar to themselves. More recent theories such as self-categorization theory and social identity theory offer additional insight into the ways in which team identity, once engaged, can impact the relationship between team factors such as teammate performance and team member's cognitive appraisals. Even though these theories were formulated with the more general concept of groups in mind, they can inform the current research as teams are a type of group.

The process by which individuals begin to perceive themselves as similar to teammates and adopt a team identity has been labelled depersonalization (Turner, 1985). Depersonalization is considered to be a basic process underlying group phenomena (Turner, 1985) and involves "self-stereotyping" whereby people come to perceive themselves more as interchangeable exemplars of a social category than as unique individuals defined by their differences from others (Turner, 1985). Depersonalization has been investigated within the framework of self-categorization theory, a theory that seeks to explain group behaviour as a reflection of the depersonalization that occurs when ingroup/outgroup categorizations are salient (Turner, 1985). According to self-categorization theory, antecedents of depersonalization include: group formation, interdependence amongst group members, shared outcomes (Sole, Marton, & Hornstein, 1975), shared success (Adair, 2004; Platow et al., 1999), shared threat or common enemy (Turner & Giles, 1981), group cohesion (Carron, 1982; Heider, 1958); intergroup conflict or competition (Brewer, 1979; Turner & Giles, 1981), accessibility of group categorization and perceived fit of group categorization (Turner, 1985).

Once achieved, depersonalization greatly affects the team environment, culminating in the formation of team identity. One consequence of depersonalization that is relevant to the current research is that the self is evaluated via intergroup comparison processes rather than intragroup comparison processes. Once team identity is engaged and maintained, an individual's self-esteem is closely related to team identity such that intergroup comparisons inform self-esteem much more than intragroup comparison between fellow team members (Tajfel & Turner, 1986). Consistent with this idea, Gardner, Gabriel, and Hochschild (2002) found that individuals were not threatened by close others who were superior performers because they did not engage in the upwards social comparison processes that typically result in decreased self-evaluations. Similarly, Cialdini and DeNicholas (1989) found that individuals treated the characteristics of a connected other as if they were positive or negative features of their own selves. This effect occurred whether the connection was superficial or not. In a similar manner, if one's social identity as a team member is salient, one is considering one's teammates' abilities in addition to one's own abilities. This simple act of "basking in reflected glory" decreases the likelihood that an individual is threatened by superior teammates and enables him or her to draw upon the teammates' abilities rather than simply relying upon personal resources when evaluating resources (Cialdini et al., 1976). On the other hand, working with teammates who are inferior performers should result in decreased resource evaluations because one is considering one's teammates low abilities when calculating resources.

Research by Aron and colleagues (Aron & Aron, 1986; Aron, Aron, & Smollan, 1992; Aron, Aron, Tudor, & Nelson, 1991) supports this notion by demonstrating that in close relationships, the self often includes overlapping connections with those close to the individual. As such, the other individuals are treated as similar to the self. Smith, Coats, and Watling (1999) add that these processes of self–other overlap extend to important group memberships. When the self is expanded to include others as part of the self, the outcomes of social comparison processes are altered. Rather than being threatened by a close other who outperforms one in a relevant domain, as the self-evaluation maintenance (SEM model; Tesser, 1988) would posit, one can essentially bask in reflected glory. Brown, Novick, Lord, and Richards (1992) found that when individuals are competing on a team with superior performers, self-appraisals tend to be enhanced rather than diminished. Similarly, Brewer and Weber (1994) found that individuals who were members of distinctive ingroups exhibited more positive self-evaluations following exposure to a superior ingroup member, but less positive self-evaluations following exposure to an inferior ingroup member.

Taken together, the research on social identity supports the hypothesis that competing on a team with superior performers can lead to increased perceived resources because the teammates' superior abilities inform the individual's calculations of resources, whereas competing on a team with inferior performers can lead to decreased perceived resources because the teammates' inferior abilities inform the individual's calculations of resources.

In terms of challenge/threat motivation, social identity and social categorization research suggests that once team identity is salient, teammate performance has an effect on an individual's evaluations of demands and resources. When team identity is salient, superior teammate performance should produce more challenge motivation because the individual is drawing upon the high resources of her teammates' abilities as she evaluates resources and demands. In other words, the individual should perceive that she has more resources to succeed in the performance situation. Additionally, inferior teammate performance should produce lesser challenge (and greater threat) because the individual is drawing upon the low resources of her teammates' abilities as she evaluates resources in the performance situation.

STUDY OVERVIEW AND HYPOTHESIS

In the past, groups and teams researchers have studied existing, real world teams or one-time, lab-based team in nonlongitudinal paradigms. However, there are limitations associated with each of these paradigms: Studies using existing, real world teams typically lack experimental control and studies using one-time, lab-based teams often lack ecological validity (as evidenced by low perceptions of group cohesion and group identity). With these limitations in mind, we designed a longitudinal study in which lab-based teams reconvened on a weekly basis for four consecutive weeks. The length of the study, multiple team-building interventions, and intergroup competition all contributed to greater ecological validity, and the lab-based paradigm helped to maintain experimental control.

The study was conducted in four phases, each phase occurring a week apart for four consecutive weeks, and was organized around a competitive anagram-solving tournament among lab-based teams (see Figure 1 for a summary of each phase). Each team consisted of one participant and two confederates. The participant did not know the confederates prior to the

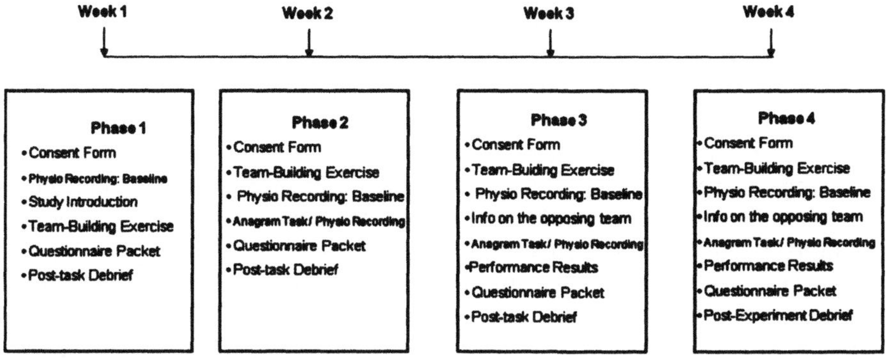

Figure 1. Longitudinal study timeline.
Note: Locations

- Consent form, Questionnaire and Debriefing occurred in the preparation room while the participant was alone
- Baseline physiological measurements were taken while participant was in the experimental room with the confederates, except during Phase 1 (when the participant was alone)
- Team-Building Exercises took place in the experimental room with the confederates except for Phase 4 which took place in the University Center,
- Anagram tasks took place in the experimental room with the condeferates
  Information on the opposing team and the performance results were given in the experimental room with the confederates.

start of the experiment. Teams were told that they would compete against three other teams and that the team with the highest point total at the conclusion of the tournament would receive a monetary prize.

Phase 1 consisted of a brief study introduction that emphasized the importance of teamwork and team cohesion, and a team-building intervention. Phase 2 consisted of a second team-building intervention and a team practice session. Phase 3 consisted of a third team-building intervention and one round of tournament competition. Lastly, Phase 4 consisted of a fourth team-building intervention and one round of tournament competition. After Phase 4, participants expected to compete against the third and final team in the tournament the following week; however, the study terminated after Phase 4.[1]

Two teammate performance conditions were examined: a superior teammate performance condition in which confederates performed substantially better than the participant (i.e., double the score); and an inferior

[1]Participants were told that they would be competing, returning to the laboratory for a third competition round (Week 5) in order to maintain task engagement during the second competition round (Week 4). If participants expected the second round of the competition to be the last one, they may have disengaged as they may have perceived that they would not win the tournament.

teammate performance condition in which confederates performed substantially worse (i.e., half the score) than the participant.

The hypotheses for the proposed study were based on research concerning social identity theory and self-categorization theory. We hypothesized that the participants in the *superior* condition would exhibit a change in cardiovascular responses that is consistent with a challenge response because they would draw upon the resources of their superior teammates and that participants in the inferior condition would exhibit a change in cardiovascular responses that is consistent threat response because they would include their teammates' inferior performance in their calculations of perceived resources and demands. Specifically, we predict that relative to baseline (Phase 1), participants in both conditions will exhibit increases in heart rate and ventricular contractility in Phases 3 and 4. Relative to baseline (Phase 1) participants who are paired with superior teammates will exhibit a challenge response (increases in cardiac output and decreases in total peripheral resistance) during Phases 3 and 4. Relative to baseline (Phase 1) participants who are paired with inferior teammates will exhibit a threat response (decreases in cardiac output and increases in total peripheral resistance) during Phases 3 and 4. As such, over the course of time (four consecutive weekly experimental sessions), we predict significant changes in cardiovascular reactivity, consistent with the hypotheses.

METHOD

Design

The independent variable was teammate performance (superior vs. inferior) and the primary dependent variables were the challenge/threat responses (i.e., changes in cardiovascular responses between baseline and the respective anagram tasks) in the team competitions rounds (Round 1 and Round 2). Participants were randomly assigned to the between-subjects factor so that there were at least 18 in each condition.

Participants

Thirty-eight female undergraduates at the University of California, Santa Barbara, participated in the study in exchange for introductory psychology course credit or 50 dollars.[2] Ten female confederates served as teammates on four to six teams each and spent a total of 4 hours with each team.

[2]A total of 45 participants completed the study. Seven participants completed all elements of the study but were excluded from analyses: four participants yielded cardiovascular data which were impossible to score reliably due to poor impedance cardiograph signal quality (i.e.,

Setting

The study took place in a social psychophysiology laboratory. The laboratory consisted of a control room and two recording suites. The former contained physiological equipment, video monitors and recorders connected to two cameras in each experimental room, and an audiotape player and intercom system connected to speakers in the experimental rooms. Each of the recording suites was divided into a preparation room and a recording room. In the preparation room, participants completed forms and an experimenter applied sensors to participants. The data collection occurred in the acoustically and environmentally controlled recording room that measured approximately 3.0 × 3.5 m and contained physiological, audiovisual, and computer equipment. Participants received additional instructions and interacted with the experimenter through an intercom. Participants sat upright in a comfortable chair throughout the experiment. All team-building activities and competitions that occurred in the lab were video recorded.

Tasks

During Phases 2 (practice round), 3, and 4 (first and second round of the tournament), the participant and the two confederates completed three different but equally difficult versions of an anagram task. During the anagram task, scrambled five-letter words were presented in succession on a computer monitor. The goal of the task was to solve the anagram with both speed and accuracy. The participant and the confederates alternated solving the anagrams and saying them aloud such that the participant solved one anagram and said it aloud, then a confederate solved the next and said it aloud, and another confederate solved the next and said it aloud. All three individuals in the group continued alternating in this manner throughout the anagram task. Each team member was given the opportunity to complete 12 anagrams. Participant responses (speed and accuracy) were recorded. The two versions of the anagram task that were presented during the two competition rounds (Phases 3 and 4) were counterbalanced. We chose this task because performance tasks that require speaking have been shown to exhibit challenge/threat responses (e.g., Mendes et al., 2002; Mendes, Blascovich, Major, & Seery, 2001). Furthermore, although the task is an individual task, the participants were completing the task in a team context. Not only are there various types of interdependencies exhibited in teams

ambiguous aortic valve opening); two participants were excluded due to experimenter error in conducting the study; one participant was excluded because she was suspicious of the use of confederates in the study and reported this suspicion during the debriefing.

(i.e., task, goal, and outcomes), the level of interdependence exhibited in teams can vary. The task utilized in the present study was high on both goal and outcome interdependence, such that the team members had a common goal and were subject to the same outcomes/consequences (Gully, Joshi, Incalcaterra, & Beaubien, 2002). Therefore, in conjunction with the team-building exercises, a team context was clearly created in this study.

Measures

Physiological measures. Cardiovascular measures were recorded noninvasively, following commonly accepted guidelines (Sherwood et al., 1990) and utilizing a Minnesota Impedance Cardiograph (Model 304B) and a Cortronics (Model 7000) continuously inflated blood pressure monitor. Signals were conditioned using Coulbourn amplifiers (Models S75-11 and S79-02; Coulbourn Instruments, Allentown, PA) and were stored on a desktop computer.

Impedance cardiograph (ZKG) and electrocardiograph (EKG) recording provided continuous measures of cardiac performance. The impedance cardiograph utilized a tetrapolar aluminum/mylar tape electrode system to record basal transthoracic impedance (Z0) and the first derivative of basal impedance (dZ/dt). Two pairs of band electrodes completely encircled the participants' bodies. Two inner electrodes were placed at the base of the neck and at the xiphisternal junction (approximately midchest); the two outer electrodes were placed on the upper neck and abdomen, separated from the respective inner electrodes by a distance of at least 3 cm. EKG signals were detected through the band electrodes. The Cortronics blood pressure monitor collected continuous noninvasive recordings of blood pressure from the brachial artery of participants' nondominant arm. In combination, ZKG and EKG recordings allowed computation of HR, VC, and CO; the addition of blood pressure monitoring allowed computation of TPR. Prior to collecting physiological measures during each performance task, a 5-minute baseline of resting physiological responses was collected. The baseline physiological data enabled to determine cardiovascular reactivity by giving resting values against which to compare values during the performance task. Cardiovascular reactivity values during the performance task were calculated by subtracting the baseline value—the last minute of the preceding rest period—from the value obtained during the performance task. The recorded data was scored using an interactive MS-DOS software program (Kelsey & Guethlein, 1990); scoring was performed blind to condition.

Ventricular contractility (VC) was calculated by multiplying changes in the duration of preejection period by -1; preejection period denotes the time in milliseconds in the cardiac cycle from the beginning of the ventricular depolarization to the opening of the aortic valve and initial ejection of blood. A larger VC value indicates greater contractility. Cardiac output (CO) is the product of stroke volume and heart rate. Total peripheral resistance (TPR) was derived by multiplying mean arterial pressure by cardiac output and multiplying the total by 80 (Sherwood et al., 1990). It is expressed in dyne/s/cm^{-5}. Once all four measures were calculated using these equations, reactivity scores for each measure were calculated by subtracting baseline resting levels from levels exhibited during the anagram task. For example, heart rate (HR) reactivity was calculated by subtracting the HR score during the baseline from the HR score during the task.

Self-report ratings. At the conclusion of each phase, participants completed two questionnaires: Group Environment Questionnaire (GEQ; Carron, Widmeyer, & Brawley, 1985), and a team identity questionnaire (Dimmock, Grove, & Eklund, 2005). The GEQ was used to measure the participants' perceptions of psychological closeness and group cohesion. Example questions include "I enjoy being a part of this team" and "If given the opportunity, I would develop friendships with people on this team." The team identity questionnaire was used to measure the extent to which participants are categorizing themselves as members of the team or as individuals. Example questions include "When my team fails, I feel depressed" and "I think of my team as part of who I am." Internal consistency was high for both the GEQ (Cronbach's $\alpha = .79$) and the team identity questionnaire (Cronbach's $\alpha = .86$).

Procedure

Each participant and two confederates arrived at the lab for 1 hour per week for four consecutive weeks. Prior to signing up for the study, participants were informed that the study would last 5 weeks, and that they would form a team, engage in team-building activities, and compete in a tournament. They received course credit or monetary compensation for each hour that they spent in the lab. At the beginning of each phase, the same procedure occurred: one participant and two confederates arrived waited in the hallway outside the laboratory; then, the experimenter greeted the participant and the confederates and took each individual into separate rooms where they signed consent forms.

Phase 1. After the participant signed the forms, the experimenter told her that she needed to collect the participant's baseline physiological data before they continued with the teams study. At this point, the experimenter applied physiological sensors to the participant and collected 5 minutes of physiological baseline data. At the conclusion of the data collection, the participant's sensors were taken off and the team was reunited for a study introduction.

During the study introduction, the experimenter briefly explained that the purpose of the study was to investigate the factors that contribute to team dynamics and that, throughout the study, the teams would be asked to participate in activities that are similar to those in which sports and business teams engage. The experimenter stressed the importance of attending the team session each week, of maintaining confidentiality, and of being as honest as possible when completing the questionnaires at the end of each team session. The team was also told that at various points of the study, their physiological responses would be recorded again to provide more information.

The participant and two confederates were instructed to spend the next 20 minutes choosing a team name based on a characteristic that they all had in common, choosing a team T-shirt colour, and creating a team banner. They were given the materials needed for accomplishing this team-building task. The team-building intervention was intended to foster team identity by increasing team distinctiveness and group cohesion (Carron, Spink, & Papavessis, 1997; Gaertner, Mann, Murrell, & Dovidio, 1989). Once they completed this task, they completed a series of questionnaires and left the laboratory.

Phase 2. Prior to arriving in the lab, each participant received an email and telephone call instructing her to come to the lab prepared to share a story from her personal life that illustrates something about her character, motives, or desires that are unknown to her teammates. The participants were given examples of appropriate stories, so they knew how to prepare. Additionally, a lab assistant contacted each participant via telephone to confirm that she had prepared a story.

Prior to Phase 2, all of team banners were posted in the laboratory and remained posted for the remainder of the 4-week study. After the participant completed the consent form, the experimenter retrieved the confederates from the other experimental rooms where they were ostensibly completing their consent forms.

Once all three of the participants were seated together, the experimenter gave them instructions for the team-building task: a 10 minute personal-disclosure mutual sharing exercise. The Personal-Disclosure Mutual-Sharing intervention (Holt & Dunn, 2006) has been shown to increase commitment to the team, teammate understanding, group cohesion, and perceptions of team invincibility. The exercise was conducted according to the guidelines outlined by Holt and Dunn (2006), during which each team member shared a personal story and answered questions concerning her story. The confederates were instructed to listen attentively and ask questions about peripheral aspects of the story, rather than central aspects. In this way, they gave the impression that they were interested in the story without prying too much and potentially making the participant feel uncomfortable.

At the conclusion of the team-building exercise, the experimenter escorted the confederates to separate rooms and returned to the participant's room. Then, the experimenter asked the participant to put on her team shirt and the experimenter applied the physiological sensors to the participant and asked the participant to sit in one of three chairs in the recording room. Next, the experimenter retrieved the other two "participants" from their "respective preparation rooms" (the confederates had already changed into their team T-shirts and applied counterfeit sensors to themselves in the control room).

Once both confederates were seated in their chairs and ostensibly connected to the physiological recording monitors, all three individuals heard recorded audio instructions welcoming them to the lab and asking them to sit quietly for the next few minutes. During this time, 5 minutes of baseline cardiovascular data were recorded.

Next, the participants heard recorded instructions explaining the nature of the tournament. They were told that there were a total of 40 lab-based teams in the study, but that the teams had been divided into 10 four-team clusters. They were told that they would compete against the three other teams in their cluster and that they would have the opportunity to play all three teams throughout the course of the experiment. They were also told that at the end of the tournament, the team with the best win/loss record in their cluster would receive a monetary prize of $75.00 to be divided equally amongst all three team members. Then they were told that for the next 20 minutes, they would have the opportunity to practice the competitive task in order to prepare for their first contest the next week.

The purpose of the team practice was to reduce threat that may result from simply competing with or against others on a novel task (Blascovich et al.,1999). This idea is further supported by Driskell, Salas, and Johnston's (1999) finding that stress leads to a loss of team perspective. The stress that participants might experience by simply competing with or against others on a novel task might negatively affect perceptions of team identity. Additionally, team practice sessions are related to increased teamwork and team identity salience (Cannon-Bowers, Tannenbaum, Salas, & Volpe, 1995) and to increased perceptual readiness to use team identity as a salient self-identity (Turner, 1985). Last, the team practice session was included to increase the ecological validity of the study; real-world teams are often given the opportunity to practise and prepare for their competition.

At the beginning of the practice session, the participant and confederates heard instructions explaining the anagram task. They were told that they must each take turns solving the anagrams that were presented on the computer screen, and that they would have up to 12 s to solve the anagram on the computer screen before they lost their turn and the screen automatically advanced to the next word. Also, they were told that each member of the team would have the opportunity to solve 12 anagrams and that team scores would be based on both accuracy and speed. After receiving these instructions, the team completed the practice round of the anagram task. Participant's cardiovascular reactivity was assessed while she was performing the anagram task.

In the superior teammate performance condition, the confederates solved each of their anagrams in *half* the time it took the participant to solve her anagrams. For example, if the participant solved the anagram in 4 ss, then each confederate solved the subsequent anagrams in 2 s. If the participant did not solve her anagram at all, the confederates were instructed to solve their subsequent anagrams in 6 s. In the inferior teammate performance condition, the confederates solved each of their anagrams in *twice* the time it took the participant to solve her anagrams. For example, if the participant solved the anagram in 4 s, then each confederate will solve the following anagram in 8 s. If the participant did not solve her anagram at all, the confederates were instructed not to solve their subsequent anagrams either. Prior to the start of the experiment, all confederates underwent extensive training in which they memorized the anagrams, practised saying them at various speeds, and learned to accurately keep track of time. All confederates participated in both the inferior and superior conditions. During the experiment, the experimenter monitored the confederate's performance via intercom to ensure that all confederate performance was consistent with the randomly assigned condition. No confederate errors were observed.

Upon completion of the contest, the participant and the confederates were instructed to complete a series of questionnaires. However, in order to ensure privacy while completing the questionnaires, the confederates were ostensibly escorted into their respective preparation rooms. Once the participant completed the questionnaires, the experimenter removed all sensors and completed a brief exit interview with the participant, in which she checked for suspicion or discomfort, and reminded the participant that confidentiality was very important.

Phase 3. Once the team members had completed their consent forms, they reconvened in one room and received instructions about the team-building task. They were informed that the researchers were interested in the reasoning processes in which teams engage when they are asked to make important decisions in a relatively unfamiliar situation. They were asked to imagine that they had survived a crash landing on the moon and needed to travel 200 km by foot in order to reach another spaceship. Then they were given a list of 15 items and were asked to rank the items in order of importance, with 1 being the most crucial for their survival on the moon and 15 being least crucial for their survival on the moon. They were also asked to justify their top three choices. Each team was given 10 minutes to complete this task. Team-building interventions that involve group problem solving enable the team to communicate and work together, thus fostering team cohesion (Levine & Moreland, 1998; Miller, 2004).

Once the team had completed the team-building intervention, they were taken into separate rooms so that they could have their physiological sensors applied and change into their team T-shirts. The experimenter applied the physiological sensors to the participant and seated her in one of the chairs in the physiology recording room. Next, the experimenter went to retrieve the two "participants" from their "respective preparation rooms". (The confederates had applied counterfeit sensors to themselves in the control room.) Once both confederates were seated in their chairs and ostensibly connected to the physiological recording monitors, all three individuals heard taped audio instructions that welcomed them to the lab and asked them to sit quietly for the next few minutes. During this time, 5 minutes of baseline cardiovascular data were recorded.

Next, the team was told that they would be competing against The Party Animals, a team that ostensibly performed the anagram task the previous day, and that they would have the opportunity to view the opposing team's picture and hear information about its performance, prior to competing against them in an attempt to best the opposing team's score and win the week's contest. Teams were told that the Party Animals had successfully completed 27 of the 32 anagrams. They were also told that the Party Animals had completed each anagram in 3.1 s on average. As such, the lab team was competing against a high performing team during which the resources of high teammate performance would be a valuable resource. In addition, the opposing team's banner was prominently displayed in the team's picture. Once the team viewed the opposing team's picture and heard its performance statistics, they completed one round of the anagram task. Participant's cardiovascular reactivity was assessed during the anagram task.

Teammate performance was also varied during the anagram task in Phase 3. However, teammate performance in Phases 3 and 4 was operationalized differently than in Phase 2. This is due to the fact that at the conclusion of Phase 2, two participants expressed mild suspicion that their teammates' performance seemed to closely mirror their own. As a result, the teammate performance manipulation used in Phases 3 and 4 is much more complex than that of Phase 2. In the superior teammate performance condition, the confederates solved their first two anagrams in 2 s, regardless of how well the participant did. Then they solved their *third* anagram in half the time it took the participant to solve her *second* anagram, and so on and so forth. In the inferior teammate performance condition, the confederates did not solve their first two anagrams, regardless of how well the participant did. Then they solved their *third* anagram in twice the time it took the participant to solve her *second* anagram, and so on and so forth.

As in Phases 1 and 2, upon completion of the contest, the participant and the confederates were instructed to complete the series of questionnaires in their respective preparation rooms. Once the participant completed the questionnaires, the experimenter removed all sensors and completed a brief exit interview with the participant, in which they checked for suspicion or discomfort.

Phase 4. After the participant completed the consent form, the participant and two confederates reconvened in one room and were given instructions about the week's team-building intervention. The experimenter explained that part of being on a team includes spending time together outside of the performance context. The experimenter gave each team a short scavenger hunt list and asked them to complete the scavenger hunt at the University Center, the campus student centre. The team was told that if they completed the task in 10 minutes or less, each team member would receive a candy bar at the conclusion of the experimental session. They were also instructed to stay together as a team and to refrain from running. The two confederates ensured that the team followed these instructions. Each team successfully completed the scavenger hunt within the 10 minute allotment. The team-building intervention was designed to mimic team building that occurs in the real world and allow teams the opportunity to interact outside of the performance environment. Informal activities outside of practice and competitions have been found to increase team unity, team spirit, social support, and personal bonding (Yukelson, 1997).

After the team returned from the scavenger hunt, the experimenter took the participant into the preparation room where the participant put on her team T-shirt. In this room, the experimenter applied the physiological sensors to the participant and asked the participant to sit in one of three chairs in the recording room. Next, the experimenter retrieved the other two "participants" from their "respective preparation rooms". (The confederates had changed into their team T-shirts and applied counterfeit sensors to themselves in the control room.)

Once both confederates were seated in their chairs and ostensibly connected to the physiological recording monitors, all three individuals heard recorded audio instructions welcoming them to the lab and asking them to sit quietly for the next few minutes. During this time, 5 minutes of baseline cardiovascular data were recorded. Next, the team was told that it would be competing against the Gauchos, a team that had ostensibly performed earlier in the day, and that they would have the opportunity to view the opposing team's record and performance statistics, prior to competing against them in an attempt to best the opposing team's score and win the week's contest. Teams were told that the Gauchos had successfully completed 29 of the 32 anagrams. They were also told that the Gauchos had completed each anagram in 3.9 s on average. As such, the lab team was competing against a high performing team. In addition, the opposing team's banner was prominently displayed in the team's picture. Once the team viewed the opposing team's picture and heard its performance statistics, they completed one round of the anagram task. The teammate performance manipulation in Phase 4 was identical to the one in Phase 3. Upon completion of the contest, the participant and the confederates were instructed to complete a series of questionnaires into their respective preparation rooms. Once the participant completed the questionnaires, the experimenter removed all sensors and the participant was told that the study was over, that she would not be competing during the fifth week, and was fully debriefed. One participant reported suspicion about the use of confederates and was excluded from the analyses (see Footnote 2).

RESULTS

Analytical strategy

In preliminary analyses, we scored the raw cardiovascular data, and tested the manipulation check, the quality of performance in the anagram task, and task engagement (heart rate and ventricular contractility reactivity) during the anagram task. In primary analyses—corresponding to our predictions—we tested challenge/threat during the anagram task. We used *t*-tests and multivariate analysis of variance to test the effects of teammate performance and time on the dependent variables (see Footnote 3).

Preliminary analyses

Manipulation check. Recall that, depending upon the condition, confederates were instructed to perform better or worse than the participant on the anagram task. We conducted a series of *t*-tests to assess whether participants' perceptions of teammate performance differed between the better and worse teammate performance condition in Phases 2, 3, and 4. Confirming the intent of the manipulation, during Phase 2, participants who were paired with superior teammates perceived that they performed worse than their teammates ($M = -1.26$, $SD = 0.618$) relative to those participants who were paired with inferior teammates ($M = -0.07$, $SD = 0.828$), $t(38) = 7.077$, $p < .0001$. During Phase 3, participants paired with superior teammates perceived that they performed worse than their teammates ($M = -1.24$, $SD = 0.654$) relative to those participants who were paired with inferior teammates ($M = 0.33$, $SD = 0.849$), $t(37) = 8.797$, $p < .0001$. During Phase 4, participants who were paired with superior teammates perceived that they performed worse than their teammates ($M = -1.15$, $SD = 0.702$) relative to those participants paired with inferior teammates ($M = 0.34$, $SD = 0.911$), $t(37) = 7.794$, $p < .0001$. However, while the relative difference between both experimental conditions is significant, the means for the participants who were paired with superior teammates indicates that they were reluctant to report that they had performed substantially better than their teammates. Rather, they reported that their performance was approximately equal to that of their teammates. However, during the debriefing session at the conclusion of the study, these participants were asked if they had performed better or worse than their teammates and they sheepishly admitted that they had, in fact, performed better. This anecdotal evidence further confirms the intent of the manipulation, even if participants were reluctant report so.

Group cohesion (Group Environment Questionnaire; GEQ). Participants were asked to complete a group cohesion scale at the conclusion of each phase. At the end of Phase 1, participants reported group cohesion ratings that were well above the midpoint of the scale ($M = 0.826$, $SD = 0.490$). For Phase 2, an independent-samples t-test was conducted to evaluate the effects of teammate performance condition on the participant's ratings of group cohesion. The t-test did not reveal a significant effect, $t(38) = 0.211$, $p = .834$. Indeed, participants who cooperated with inferior teammates did not rate their group as more or less cohesive ($M = 0.891$, $SD = 0.463$) than those who cooperated with superior teammates ($M = 0.868$, $SD = 0.485$). For Phase 3, an independent-samples t-test was conducted to evaluate the effects of team status and teammate performance on ratings of group cohesion. The t-test did not reveal a significant effect. Further, the independent-samples t-test to test the effect of teammate performance on group cohesion in Phase 4 was also nonsignificant. Overall, participants who were paired with inferior teammates did not rate their group as more or less cohesive than those who were paired with superior teammates.

A 2×4 mixed model ANOVA with one between-subjects factor: teammate performance (superior vs. inferior); and one within-subjects factor: phase (first, second, third, and fourth) was conducted to evaluate the effect of phase on group cohesion. The means and standard deviations for group cohesion are presented in Table 1. The results of the ANOVA

TABLE 1
Means and t-tests from zero (centre of scale) for perceptions of group cohesion

Phase	*Superior teammate performance*	*Inferior teammate performance*
1	0.77*	0.77*
2	0.87*	0.80*
3	0.33	0.27
4	0.27	0.30

All condition means were tested against zero to determine differences from the centre of the scale. $^*p < .05$.

indicated a main effect of phase, Wilk's $\Lambda = .359$, $F(3, 37) = 38.71$, $p < .001$, multivariate $\eta^2 = .64$. Follow-up polynomial contrasts indicated a significant linear effect with means decreasing over time, $F(1, 38) = 87.20$, $p < .001$, partial $\eta^2 = .57$. Participant ratings of group cohesion were highest during Phase 1 and slightly decreased over the course of the four week experiment (see Table 1 for group means). However, ratings of group cohesion remained high during the first two phases and decreased in the final two phases. Essentially, once teams began competing against high performing teams, their ratings of group cohesion decreased.

Team identity. Participants were asked to complete a team identity scale at the conclusion of each phase. At the end of Phase 1, participants reported team identity ratings that were above the midpoint of the scale ($M = 0.531$, $SD = 0.484$). For Phase 2, an independent-samples t-test was conducted to evaluate the effects of teammate performance condition on the participant's ratings of team identity. The t-test did not reveal a significant effect, $t(75) = -0.527$, $p = .600$. Indeed, participants who cooperated with inferior teammates reported ratings of team identity ($M = 0.552$, $SD = 0.467$) that were equal to participants who cooperated with superior teammates ($M = 0.602$, $SD = 0.338$). For Phase 3, an independent-samples t-test was conducted to evaluate the effects of team status and teammate performance on ratings of team identity. The t-test did not reveal a significant effect. Further, the independent-samples t-test to test the effect of teammate performance on team identity in Phase 4 was also nonsignificant. Overall, participants who were the best performers on their team did not differ in their perceptions of team identity relative to those who were the worst performers on their team.

A 2×4 mixed model ANOVA with one between subjects factor: teammate performance (superior vs. inferior); and one within subjects factor: phase (first, second, third, and fourth) was conducted to evaluate the effect of phase on team identity. The means and standard deviations for team identity are presented in Table 2. The results of the ANOVA indicated

TABLE 2
Means and *t*-tests from zero (centre of scale) for perceptions of team identity

Phase	*Superior teammate performance*	*Inferior teammate performance*
1	0.56*	0.52*
2	0.56*	0.55*
3	0.41*	0.40*
4	0.39*	0.41*

All condition means were tested against zero to determine differences from the centre of the scale. $^{*}p < .05$.

a significant main effect of phase, Wilk's $\Lambda = .824$, $F(3, 36) = 4.706$, $p = .005$, multivariate $\eta^2 = .18$. Follow-up polynomial contrasts indicated a significant linear effect with means decreasing over time, $F(1, 68) = 8.37$, $p = .005$, partial $\eta^2 = .11$. In other words, all participants reported high levels of team identity in Phase 1and Phase 2 compared to Phase 3 and Phase 4. However, participants reported decreasing levels of team identity over the course of the 4 week study; higher order polynomial contrasts were nonsignificant.[3,4]

Scoring cardiovascular raw data. Using an interactive MS-DOS software program (Kelsey & Guethlein, 1990), each EKG and dz/Dt waveform was inspected in order to ensure that the physiological data were properly collected. Next, the EKG and dz/Dt waveforms for each minute were averaged together so as to create one EKG waveform and one dz/Dt

[3]We also examined intragroup comparisons to determine any effects of individual or paired confederates on cardiovascular reactivity. Although we lacked adequate power to detect differences less than Cohen's $d = 1.20$, we did not observe any differences between confederates that suggested that our results were driven by any one confederate or any confederate pair.

[4]*Anagram performance.* Recall that each participant was given the opportunity to solve 12 anagrams during each competition. Anagram performance was assessed by calculating the number of anagrams that were correctly solved as well as the average amount of time in milliseconds it took for the participant to solve each anagram. A single anagram performance index was calculated by converting the number of anagrams correctly solved and the average time to complete each anagram into *z*-scores and summing them. For Phase 2, an independent-samples *t*-test was conducted to evaluate the effects of teammate performance condition on anagram performance. The *t*-test did not reveal a significant effect, $t(38) = 0.888$, $p = .378$. Participants who were teamed with inferior teammates did not perform significantly better or worse ($M = 0.1356$, $SD = 1.24$) relative to those who were teamed with superior teammates ($M = -0.1325$, $SD = 1.16$). For Phase 3, an independent-samples *t*-test was conducted to evaluate the effect of teammate performance on anagram performance. The results of the *t*-test did not reveal any significant results ($M = -0.0012$, $SD = 1.300$). For Phase 4, an independent-samples *t*-test was conducted to evaluate the effects of team status and teammate performance on anagram performance. The results of the *t*-test did not reveal any significant results ($M = -0.0008$, $SD = 1.111$).

waveform that represent the average EKG and dz/Dt waveforms for the minute in question. Next, three points in the averaged waveforms were marked: "Q", the point in the EKG wave that signals the onset of ventricular contraction; "B", the point in the dz/Dt wave in which the aortic valve opens; and, "X", the point in the dz/Dt wave in which the aortic valve closes. These three points were marked by the scoring software program but can be manually altered if the program commits an error. Occasionally, participants yield cardiovascular data which are impossible to score reliably due to poor impedance cardiograph signal quality (i.e., ambiguous aortic valve opening). When this occurs, those beats that are impossible to score are deleted and the remaining beats in the minute are used. The locations of Q, B, and X, and the accompanying blood pressure values, enabled to calculate raw HR, VC, CO, and TPR scores during baseline resting periods and task minutes (see, e.g., Blascovich et al., 2003).

Computing cardiovascular task reactivity. Cardiovascular reactivity values were calculated by subtracting the Phase 1 baseline value—the last minute of the baseline rest period—from the value obtained during the anagram task in each phase. Values that were more than 2.5 *SD*s from the mean ($p = .001$ in a normal distribution) were classified as extreme and were winsorized by assigning them a value 1% higher than the closest nonextreme value (Tabachnick & Fidell, 1996). As a result, the influence of the extreme values was minimized while the rank order of participants in the distribution remained.

Task engagement in the anagram task. Due to the fact that task engagement is a prerequisite for challenge and threat, we concluded that participants in the sample were, on average, engaged in the anagram task before testing for TPR and CO differences. We used *t*-tests to determine whether HR and VC increased significantly from baseline. Testing Phase 2 sample means with *t*-tests revealed that HR reactivity ($M = 3.94$, $SD = 6.90$) was significantly greater than zero, $t(38) = 4.85$, $p < .001$, as was VC ($M = 5.47$, $SD = 7.14$), $t(38) = 6.49$, $p < .001$. Testing Phase 3 sample means with *t*-tests revealed that HR reactivity ($M = 5.61$, $SD = 8.48$) was significantly greater than zero, $t(37) = 5.26$, $p < .001$, as was VC ($M = 7.07$, $SD = 8.06$), $t(37) = 6.97$, $p < .001$. Testing Phase 4 sample means with *t*-tests revealed that HR reactivity ($M = 5.53$, $SD = 7.59$) was significantly greater than zero, $t(36) = 6.23$, $p < .001$, as was VC ($M = 9.16$, $SD = 12.32$), $t(36) = 6.35$, $p < .001$. These findings suggest that participants were engaged in the task during the three anagram rounds. This demonstration of task engagement met the assumptions of the biopsychosocial model and enabled us to assess challenge and threat (Blascovich, 2008). We also completed a series of *t*-tests to assess whether task engagement differed by condition. All *t*-tests were nonsignificant (all *ps* > .05). These findings suggest that competing with inferior or superior teammates did not affect task engagement.

Primary analyses: Challenge and threat in the anagram task

Following Blascovich, Seery, Mugridge, Norris, and Weisbuch (2004), we calculated a single challenge and threat index for each cardiovascular term in the model (i.e., baseline and anagram task for each phase) by converting each participant's total peripheral resistance (TPR) and cardiac output (CO) values into *z*-scores and summing them. We assigned TPR a weight of -1 (i.e., TPR was reverse scored) and CO a weight of $+1$, such that a larger value corresponds to greater challenge for reactivity terms. Differences in TPR and CO reactivity are consistent with relative differences in challenge and threat. Further, both differences in TPR and CO reveal relative differences in the extent to which underlying sympathetic adrenal medullary (SAM) versus hypothalamic pituitary (HPA) axes are activated. As such, combining TPR and CO reactivity has the effect of creating a single measure out of two. Although this yields only relative challenge and threat differences—losing the absolute meaning of TPR and CO—it does allow us to assess the pattern of cardiovascular reactivity in a single analysis. Further, since challenge and threat exist on a continuum, such that greater challenge equals relatively lesser threat, we believe that an index that yields relative challenge and threat differences is most informative. Using this index allowed us to maximize the reliability of the cardiovascular measures and simplify the analyses. The absolute values of correlations between the three index scores and their component TPR and CO values ranged from $r = .94$ to $r = .98$, indicating that the index accurately represents the TPR and CO values. The challenge/threat unitary index is a commonly accepted tool for assessing and presenting challenge/threat reactivity (e.g., Seery, Weisbuch, Hetenyi, & Blascovich, 2010).

For Phase 2 (practice round of the tournament), an independent samples *t*-test was conducted to evaluate the effects of teammate performance condition on the participant's challenge/threat response during the anagram practice task. The *t*-test did not reveal a significant effect of experimental condition on challenge/threat cardiovascular reactivity, $t(37) = -1.062$, $p = .29$. Participants who were paired with inferior teammates were not more or less challenged ($M = -0.204$, $SD = 0.128$) than those who were paired with superior teammates ($M = 0.264$, $SD = 0.238$). Phase 2 participants were not challenged or threatened, as neither of the group means differed from 0.

For Phase 3 (first round of the tournament), an independent samples *t*-test was conducted to evaluate the effect of teammate performance on the

TABLE 3
Means and *t*-tests from zero (centre of scale) for challenge/threat unitary index

Phase	*Superior teammate performance*	*Inferior teammate performance*
3	1.22*	−1.21*
4	1.14*	−1.07*

Higher numbers represent challenge and lower numbers represent threat. All condition means were tested against zero to determine differences from the centre of the scale. *$p < .05$.

participant's challenge/threat response during the first round of the anagram tournament. The *t*-test indicated a significant effect of teammate performance, $t(37) = 9.78$, $p = .003$. Participants who were paired with inferior teammates were threatened ($M = -1.21$, $SD = 0.179$) relative to those who were paired with superior teammates ($M = 1.22$, $SD = 1.72$). In the same way, in Phase 4 (second round of the tournament, the *t*-test indicated a significant effect teammate performance, $t(37) = 4.59$, $p < .05$. The participants who paired with superior teammates were significantly more challenged ($M = 1.14$, $SD = 1.01$) than those who were paired with inferior teammates ($M = -1.07$, $SD = 0.99$) (see Table 3).

In order to evaluate whether challenge/threat responses differed from Phase 3 to Phase 4, a paired-samples *t*-test (with $\alpha = .30$) was conducted. The results of the *t*-test did not reveal a significant difference, $t(37) = -1.11$, $p = .78$. Challenge/threat responses in Phase 3 did not differ from challenge/threat responses in Phase 4.

Taken together, these findings illustrate that participants' cardiovascular responses did not differ in the training round (Phase 2) but that they differed during the two competition rounds of the tournament such that those who competed with inferior teammates were threatened while those who competed with superior teammates were challenged. Further, this pattern was the same at both times (Phase 3 and Phrase 4) that it was measured.

DISCUSSION

The present study examined the effect of teamwork on challenge/threat motivation with the goal of enhancing our understanding of the factors that affect individual motivation in work and organizational teams. In accordance with social identity theory, it was hypothesized that participants on teams with superior performers would exhibit a change in physiological responses (from baseline to task) that is consistent with challenge and participants on teams with inferior performance would exhibit a change in physiological responses (from baseline to task) that is consistent with threat. The results of the study support this hypothesis.

Teammate performance and challenge/threat motivation

Participants' challenge/threat motivation was greatly affected by their teammates' performance during the team performance situation. When participants had high teammate performance resources (e.g., when their teammates were superior performers), they were challenged. When they had low teammate performance resources (e.g., when their teammates were inferior performers), they were threatened. Thus, teammate performance seems to influence challenge/threat responses more than participants' own performance. Indeed, participants were challenged even though they were the worst performer of the team and participants were threatened even though they were the best performer of their team. Self-report data are consistent with the physiological responses. While completing the team identity questionnaire, participants were asked if they felt that they could depend on their teammates to win. The analyses for this particular question revealed a marginally significant difference (i.e., $p < .10$) existed between participants who were paired with inferior teammates and participants who were paired with superior teammates. Participants who were paired with inferior teammates reported lower ratings than participants who were paired with superior teammates. These data suggest that teammate performance resources are particularly important when one is working to achieve team goals (e.g., performing well). The processes that appear to be operating in this team situation are consistent with those outlined in both social identity theory and self-categorization theory.

Even though team identity ratings remained significantly high (relative to the midpoint of the scale) even until the end of the experiment, they steadily decreased each week. We believe that this is due to the fact that the teams repeatedly competed against and lost to high performing teams. It is worth noting that these findings are consistent with some aspects of social identity which posits that group failure can significantly decrease depersonalization and its associated effects, such as team identity salience. One such instance has been termed cutting-off-reflected-failure (Snyder, Lassegard, & Ford, 1986) and is defined as the act of responding so as to make it appear unlikely that one is associated with a group that has failed. Snyder and colleagues found that individuals in groups who had received negative false feedback after completing a group task were less willing to represent the group in front of a panel of judges and less willing to wear a team badge. The experience of group failure led participants to resist depersonalization. Instead, they sought to maintain their individual identities as a way of avoiding association with the group and its negative identity.

However, as mentioned earlier, participants did maintain a significant, albeit steadily decreasing, level of team identity during this 4 week experiment. We believe that there are several reasons why participants in this study maintained relatively high perceptions of team identity in the face of group failure. One plausible reason is that the experimental manipulation fostered a high degree of team identity while simultaneously making it relatively difficult for participants to disengage. Great lengths were taken to increase the likelihood that participants form close bonds with their teammates. Over the course of four weeks, participants completed numerous team-building interventions that were designed to build team identity. Further, because participants were committed to participating on their teams for the duration of the 4 week experiment, it is likely that it was difficult for them to disengage from their respective teams, even if they wanted to. These two factors likely worked in tandem to create an environment that cultivated team identity and group cohesion in all experimental conditions.

The results suggest that the team-building intervention worked as intended and that intergroup comparison processes, rather than intragroup comparison processes, were most dominant in this situation. In a previous experiment (Cleveland et al., 2011), we found that when team identity is not engaged, intragroup social comparison processes prevail during cooperative team tasks. As a result, participants who were paired with superior teammates were threatened, rather than challenged, relative to those who competed as individuals in an interindividual competitive task. However, that was not the case in the present investigation. During the anagram competitions (Phases 3 and 4), participants did not exhibit a threat response when paired with teammates who were superior performers. Indeed, they exhibited a challenge response. These results may be due to high team identity as the ratings in both conditions remained relatively high. This too is consistent with social identity theory, which proposes that, once group identity is engaged, intragroup social comparison processes give way to intergroup social comparison processes (Turner, 1985). More specifically, it also is consistent with research that shows that superior members of one's ingroup are not threatening (Gardner et al., 2002) and can even enhance one's self-evaluations (Brewer & Weber, 1994; Brown et al., 1992; Smith et al., 1999). However, we acknowledge that a definitive conclusion that intragroup social comparison processes did not play a role in this team situation would require an interindividual performance condition with which to compare those who competed in teams/on teams.

Limitations

The present research suggests that teammate performance affects individual perceptions of resources and demands. Nevertheless, these interpretations must be tempered by two factors. First, the fact that teammate performance was relative, rather than absolute, is a limitation in this study. Recall that confederates performed twice as well (i.e., faster) or half as well (i.e., slower) *as the participant* during the anagram task. There are benefits to using this particular teammate performance manipulation. For example, the relationship between the participant performance and confederate performance remained constant. This controlled for one more variable within the team situation. However, this teammate performance manipulation also presents limitations. Most importantly, because teammate performance was relative to that of the participant, team resources were also relative. In other words, teammate performance was confounded with team resources. It is possible that participants whose performance was more discrepant than that of their teammates may have perceived greater or lesser team resources, relative to participants whose performance was more similar to her teammates' performance. For example, if a participant who was the best person on a team solved her anagram in 1 second, her teammates were instructed to solve their anagrams in 2 seconds. Even though her teammates were objectively inferior performers, they were still performing at a high level and could have been perceived as resources, rather than demands.

Second, the fact that all of the teams in this study were composed of women presents questions about the generalizability of these findings to male teams. Traditionally, social psychologists have asserted that males and females relate to the world in different ways. Indeed, there are a considerable number of reports of gender differences in communal behaviours. Women are more attentive and express more agreement with what others have said (Carli, 1989); from young ages, girls use more techniques than boys to bind and continue social relationships (Maccoby, 1990; Zarbatany, McDougall, & Hymel, 2000); women interacting with women are more communal than men interacting with men (Moskowitz, Suh, & Desaulniers, 1994); and women interacting with women are less quarrelsome than men interacting with men (Moskowitz et al., 1994).

The lack of clarity concerning gender differences in interpersonal style limits the findings of this study. Based on Bakan (1966) and Maccoby's (1990) theories, it would be logical to infer that men would be more likely to engage in social comparison processes and less likely to engage in social identity processes than women during the team situation. However, social role theory (Eagly, 1987) suggests that gender differences will vary according to current social roles. Due to the fact that current gender roles, particularly among university students, are more egalitarian and less limiting than before, it would be reasonable to conclude that men and women would act similarly during the team situation. If Eagly (1987) is correct in asserting that gender roles are context dependent, then it would be useful to examine how gender affects the interpersonal processes that are operating in the team situation—a situation that uniquely requires both agency *and* communion. Previous research (Cleveland et al., 2011) has demonstrated that there are no gender differences in cardiovascular reactivity or group cohesion ratings when men and women compete on same-sex teams. However, the Cleveland et al. (2011) study consisted of one-time, lab-based teams that were essentially minimal groups. Whether these findings would replicate in a more long-term team situation remains an empirical question. In addition, Holt-Lunstad, Clayton, and Uchino (2001) found that while the participant's gender does not seem affect cardiovascular reactivity during competitive tasks, the competition's gender does. Specifically, they found that both male and female participants showed higher levels of cardiovascular reactivity when competing against a male, relative to a female. The possibility that men would show higher levels of cardiovascular reactivity in the current paradigm requires further research.

Future directions

Kozlowski and Ilgen (2006) note that most team processes are assessed in static ways that fail to capture teams' inherently temporal dynamics. The present study attempts to address this gap in the literature by showing temporal changes in cardiovascular responses between the resting period (baseline) and the participation in the anagram competitions. Follow-up research should focus on studying micro changes in challenge/threat motivation that may occur while collaborating with teammates in a work and organizational setting. In the context of work teams, individuals may be paired with teammates that are sometimes superior performers and sometime inferior performers. These changes in performance can vary from hour to hour, minute to minute, or even second to second. The biopsychosocial model would enable researchers to study these fluctuations within a work task (i.e., during a negotiation).

Additionally, the fact that each participant completed the same questionnaires four times may have contributed to multiple treatment effects. Future research would eliminate this possibility by utilizing each questionnaire once at a critical time in the experiment. In a related manner, it is likely that many social psychological processes are contributing to the findings of this study. The current study makes little attempt to differentiate these processes or their interactive effects. It is critical to begin examining possible individual factors within the team situation. For example, the current study manipulates team status, teammate performance, and team resources, among other unknown factors (i.e., self-esteem level and stability, achievement goals, group size, the nature of the team-building intervention). It is unclear how these factors are individually affecting the resulting challenge/threat responses. A series of studies investigating individual factors will greatly enhance our understanding of these processes.

Last, for a number of reasons, future research should extend the paradigm to existing teams or groups (i.e., already formed outside of the lab). One, the results of such a study, if consistent with the data presented here, could be used to validate the team manipulation. Two, data from these studies would offer insight into the processes that occur on real-world teams. Even though the present laboratory investigation made an ambitious attempt to create a psychologically real team environment, it is unrealistic to presume that it did so in a perfect manner (particularly, due to the use of confederates). It is logical to infer that individuals who are on real-world teams and are confident in their continued membership on a team will be even more likely to engage in social identity processes than those who participated in this study. As such, their challenge/threat motivation might be even more pronounced. Three, the use of the biopsychosocial model of challenge/threat among real-world organizational teams can enable leaders and managers to assess motivation in a rich manner. As mentioned earlier, to date, much of the team motivation research has focused on motivation gains and losses. By assessing challenge/threat states as they unfold in the team situation, managers can gather information about the ways in which team members perceive situational resources and demands. This information can also provide additional insight into how teams should be seeded. Four, the use of existing teams would enable researchers to assess challenge/threat responses at the team, rather than individual level. For example, researchers could collect cardiovascular reactivity for every team member and test hypotheses concerning the extent to which competing against inferior or superior teams affects each team member's challenge/threat motivation. Following, Mizruchi (1991), it is likely that team success and/or team status will positively affect challenge/threat responses. Future studies could assess the interaction of team success and teammate performance on all team members' cardiovascular reactivity.

Practical applications and conclusions

Previous research has purported that the ability level of the strongest team member is the most crucial factor for performance outcomes in situations in which tasks (e.g., problem solving tasks) are being solved (Steiner, 1972); the present effort has demonstrated that there are other important elements to take into consideration, such as team identity and team member perceptions of resources. The present study demonstrates that when team identity is high, teammate resources such as superior teammate performance enhance, rather than diminish perceptions of resources and lead to challenge. Previous findings show that when team identity is low, teammate resources such as superior teammate performance decrease perceptions of resources and lead to threat (Cleveland et al., 2011). Building on these findings, it seems that cost-effective team-building exercises such as the ones that we utilized in the present study (e.g., self-disclosure activities, noncompetitive cooperative tasks, etc.) can lead individuals to adopt a team identity and begin to include their teammate's resources in their calculations of resources and demands. In a work and organizational context, the use of high teammate resources can enable individuals to accurately evaluate the demand and resources of a task (i.e., by taking in consideration not only one's resources but also the resources of one's work partners). Further, it may enhance work effectiveness. For instance, it could help individuals and teams make appropriate decisions (e.g., while managing emergency events; van der Haar, Sigers, van den Bossche, & Jehn, 2011). Thus, when a recent team is created for a specific task and the task success depends on team members drawing upon their teammates' resources, it seems useful to have the team members participate in team-building exercises. Additionally, the fact that inferior and superior teammate performance has been shown to affect an individual's perception of resources can inform decisions related to personnel selection and seeding. It is important for managers to consider the effects that teammates can have on perceived resources as they work to create effective and motivated teams.

Over the past decades, a great deal of time and effort has been devoted to examining the ways in which others influence appraisals and motivation. A significant amount of information has been unearthed, but little research has explored the ways in which team status and teammate performance influence motivation within the team situation. The present research has attempted to reveal the various team environment processes that influence motivation and perceptions of resources and demands, particularly in competitive situations. Utilizing theory-driven physiological measures to assess motivation and perceptions of resources and demands can continue to shed valuable insight on the social processes that operate among teams

REFERENCES

Adair, J. (2004). *The concise Adair on teambuilding and motivation*. London, UK: Thorogood.

Aron, A., & Aron, E. A. (1986). *Love and expansion of self: Understanding attraction and satisfaction*. Washington, DC: Harper & Row.

Aron, A., Aron, E. A., & Smollan, D. (1992). Inclusion of other in the Self Scale and the structure of interpersonal closeness. *Journal of Personality and Social Psychology, 63*, 596–612. doi:10.1037//0022-3514.63.4.596

Aron, A., Aron, E. A., Tudor, M., & Nelson, G. (1991). Close relationships as including other in the self. *Journal of Personality and Social Psychology, 60*, 241–253. doi:10.1037//0022-3514.60.2.241

Bakan, D. (1966). *The duality of human existence: An essay on psychology and religion*. Chicago, IL: Rand McNally.

Bell, S. T. (2007). Deep-level composition variables as predictors of team performance: A meta-analysis. *Journal of Applied Psychology, 92*, 595–615.

Blascovich, J. (2008). Challenge and threat. In A. J. Elliott (Ed.), *Handbook of approach and avoidance motivation* (pp. 431–445). New York, NY: Psychology Press.

Blascovich, J., & Mendes, W. B. (2000). Challenge and threat appraisals: The role of affective cues. In J. P. Forgas (Ed.), *Feeling and thinking: The role of affect in social cognition* (pp. 59–82). Paris, France: Cambridge University Press.

Blascovich, J., Mendes, W. B., Tomaka, J., Salomon, K., & Seery, M. D. (2003). The robust nature of the biopsychosocial model of challenge and threat: A reply to Wright and Kirby. *Personality and Social Psychology Review, 7*, 234–243. doi:10.1207/S1532795 7PSPR0703_03

Blascovich, J., Seery, M. Mugridge, C. Norris, R. K., & Weisbuch, M. (2004). Predicting athletic performance from cardiovascular indexes of challenge and threat. *Journal of Experimental Social Psychology, 40*, 683–688.

Blascovich, J., & Tomaka, J. (1996). The biopsychosocial model of arousal regulation. *Advances in Experimental Social Psychology, 28*, 1–51. doi:10.1016/S0065-2601(08)60235-X

Brewer, M. B. (1979). Ingroup bias in the minimal intergroup situation: A cognitive-motivational analysis. *Psychological Bulletin, 86*, 307–324. doi:10.1037/0033-2909. 86.2.307

Brewer, M. B., & Weber, J. G. (1994). Self-evaluation effects of interpersonal versus intergroup social comparison. *Journal of Personality and Social Psychology, 66*, 268–275. doi:10.1037/ 0022- 3514.66.2.268

Brown, J. D., Novick, N. J., Lord, K. A., & Richards, J. M. (1992). When Gulliver travels: Social context, psychological closeness, and self-appraisals. *Journal of Personality and Social Psychology, 62*, 717–727. doi:10.1037/0022-3514.62.5.717

Cannon-Bowers, J. A., Tannenbaum, S. I., Salas, E., & Volpe, C. E. (1995). Defining team competencies and establishing team training requirements. In R. Guzzo & E. Salas (Eds.), *Team effectiveness and decision making in organizations* (pp. 333–380). San Francisco, CA: Jossey-Bass.

Carli, L. L. (1989). Gender differences in interaction style and influence. *Journal of Personality and Social Psychology, 56*, 565–576. doi:10.1037/0022-3514.56.4.565

Carron, A. V. (1982). Cohesiveness in sport groups: Interpretations and considerations. *Journal of Sport Psychology, 4*, 123–138.

Carron, A. V., Burk, S., & Prapavessis, H. (2004). Self-presentation and group influence. *Journal of Applied Sport Psychology, 16*, 41–58.

Carron, A. V., Spink, K. S., & Prapavessis, H. (1997). Team building and cohesiveness in the sport and exercise setting: Use if indirect interventions. *Journal of Applied Sport Psychology, 9*, 61–72.

Carron, A. V., Widmeyer, W. N., & Brawley, L. R. (1985). The development of an instrument to assess cohesion in sports teams: The Group Environment Questionnaire. *Journal of Sport Psychology, 7*, 244–266.

Cialdini, R. B., Borden, R. J., Thorne, A., Walker, M. R., Freeman, S., & Sloan, L. R. (1976). Basking in reflected glory: Three (football) field studies. *Journal of Personality and Social Psychology, 34*, 366–375. doi:10.1037/0022-3514.34.3.366

Cialdini, R. B., & DeNicholas, M. E. (1989). Self-presentation by association. *Journal of Personality and Social Psychology, 57*, 626–631. doi:10.1037/0022-3514.57.4.626

Cleveland, C., Blascovich, J., Gangi, C., & Finez, L. (2011). When good teammates are bad: Physiological threat on recently-formed teams. *Small Group Research, 42*, 3–31. doi:10.1177/ 1046496410386245

Dienstbier, R. A. (1989). Arousal and physiological toughness: Implications for mental and physical health. *Psychological Review, 96*, 84–100. doi:10.1037/0033-295X.96.1.84

Dimmock, J., Grove, R., & Eklund, R. (2005). Reconceptualizing team identification: New dimensions and their relationship to intergroup bias. *Group Dynamics: Theory, Research, and Practice*, *9*, 75–86. doi:10.1037/1089-2699.9.2.75

Driskell, J., Salas, E., & Johnston, J. (1999). Does stress lead to a loss of team perspective? *Group Dynamics: Theory, Research, and Practice*, *3*, 291–302.

Eagly, A. H. (1987). *Sex differences in social behavior: A social-role interpretation*. Hillsdale, NJ: Lawrence Erlbaum Associates, Inc.

Edmondson, A. (1999). Psychological safety and learning behavior in work teams. *Administrative Science Quarterly*, *44*, 350–383.

Elliot, A. J., & Trash, T. M. (2002). Approach-avoidance motivation in personality: Approach and avoidance temperaments and goals. *Journal of Personality and Social Psychology*, *82*, 804–818.

Festinger, L. (1942). A theoretical interpretation in shifts in level of aspiration. *Psychological Review*, *49*, 235–250.

Festinger, L. (1942). Wish, expectation, and group standards as factors influencing level of aspiration. *Journal of Abnormal and Social Psychology*, *37*, 184–200.

Finez, L., Berjot, S., Rosnet, E., & Cleveland, C. (2011). Do athletes claim handicaps in low ego-threatening conditions? Re-examining the effect of ego-threat on claimed self-handicapping. *The Sport Psychologist*, *25*, 288–304.

Furhnam, A., & Yazdonpanahi, T. (1995). Personality differences and group versus individual brainstorming. *Personality and Individual Differences*, *19*, 73–80.

Gaertner, S. L., Mann, J., Murrell, A., & Dovidio, J. F. (1989). Reducing intergroup bias: The benefits of recategorization. *Journal of Personality and Social Psychology*, *57*, 239–249. doi:10.1037//0022-3514.57.2.239

Gardner, W. L., Gabriel, S., & Hochschild, L. (2002). When you and I are "we", you are not threatening: The role of self-expansion in social comparison. *Journal of Personality and Social Psychology*, *82*, 239–251. doi:10.1037/0022-3514.82.2.239

Gibson, B., & Daniel, S. (2000). Sandbagging as a self-presentational strategy: Claiming to be less than you are. *Personality and Social Psychology Bulletin*, *26*(1), 56–70. doi:10.1177/0146167200261006

Gully, S. M., Joshi, A., Incalcaterra, K. A., & Beaubien, J. M. (2002). A meta-analysis of team-efficacy, potency, and performance: Interdependence and level of analysis as moderators of observed relationships. *Journal of Applied Psychology*, *87*(5), 819–832.

Heider, F. (1958). *The psychology of interpersonal relations*. Hoboken, NJ: Wiley.

Holt, N. L., & Dunn, J. (2006). Guidelines for delivering personal-disclosure mutual-sharing team building interventions. *The Sport Psychologist*, *20*, 348–367.

Holt-Lunstad, J., Clayton, C., & Uchino, B. (2001). Gender differences in cardiovascular reactivity to competitive stress: The impact of gender of competitor and competition outcome. *International Journal of Behavior Medicine*, *8*, 91–102.

Humphrey, S. E., Hollenbeck, J. R., Meyer, C. J., & Ilgen, D. R. (2007). Trait configurations in self-managed teams: A conceptual examination of the use of seeding for maximizing and minimizing trait variance in teams. *Journal of Applied Psychology*, *92*(3), 885–892.

Hunter, S. B. (2001). *Performance under pressure: The impact of challenge and threat states on information processing*. Unpublished doctoral dissertation, University of California, Santa Barbara.

Kelsey, R. M., & Guethlein, W. (1990). An evaluation of the ensemble averaged impedance cardiogram. *Psychophysiology*, *28*, 24–33. doi:10.1111/j.1469-8986.1990.tb02173.x

Kozlowski, S., & Ilgen, D. (2006). Enhancing the effectiveness of work groups and teams. *Psychological Science in the Public Interest*, *7*, 77–124. doi:10.1177/1368430205056466

Levine, J. M., & Moreland, R. L. (1998). Small groups. In D. T. Gilbert & S. T. Fiske (Eds.), *The handbook of social psychology* (pp. 415–449). Mahwah, NJ: Lawrence Erlbaum Associates, Inc.

Maccoby, E. E. (1990). Gender and relationships: A developmental account. *The American Psychologist, 45*, 513–520. doi:10.1037//0003-066X.45.4.513

Mendes, W. B., Blascovich, J., Lickel, B., & Hunter, D. (2002). Challenge and threat during social interaction with white and black men. *Personality and Social Psychology Bulletin, 28*, 939–952. doi:10.1177/01467202028007007

Mendes, W. B., Blascovich, J., Major, B., & Seery, M. D. (2001). Challenge and threat responses during downward and upward social comparisons. *European Journal of Social Psychology, 31*, 477–497. doi:10.1002/ejsp.80

Messé, L., Hertel, G., Kerr, N., Lount, R., & Park, E. (2002). Knowledge of partner's ability as a moderator of group motivation gains: An exploration of the Köhler discrepancy effect. *Journal of Personality and Social Psychology, 82*, 935–946. doi:10.1037/0022-3514.82.6.935

Miller, B. C. (2004). *Quick team-building activities for busy managers*. New York, NY: Amacom.

Mizruchi, M. (1991). Urgency, motivation and group performance: The effect of prior success on current success among professional basketball teams. *Social Psychology Quarterly, 56*, 181–189.

Mohammed, S., Ferzandi, L., & Hamilton, K. (2010). Metaphor no more: A 15-year review of the team mental model construct. *Journal of Management, 36*(4), 876–910.

Moskowitz, D., Suh, E., & Desaulniers, J. (1994). Situational influences on gender differences in agency and communion. *Journal of Personality and Social Psychology, 66*, 753–761. doi:10.1037/0022-3514.66.4.753

Mullen, B., Johnson, C., & Salas, E. (1991). Productivity loss in brainstorming groups: A meta-analytic integration. *Basic and Applied Social Psychology, 12*, 3–23. doi:10.1207/s15324834basp1201_1

Nisbett, R., & Wilson, T. (1977). Telling more than we can know: Verbal reports on mental processes. *Psychological Review, 84*, 231–259. doi:10.1037/0033-295X.84.3.231

O'Leary, M. B., Mortensen, M., & Woolley, A. W. (2011). Multiple team membership: A theoretical model of its effects on productivity and learning for individuals and teams. *Academy of Management Review, 36*(3), 461–478.

Platow, M. J., Durante, M., Williams, N., Garrett, M., Walshe, J., Cincotta, S., et al. (1999). The contribution of sport fan social identity to the production of prosocial behavior. *Group Dynamics: Theory, Research, and Practice, 3*, 161–169. doi:10.1037//1089-2699.3.2.161

Seery, M. D. (2011). Challenge or threat? Cardiovascular indexes of resilience and vulnerability to potential stress in humans. *Neuroscience and Biobehavioral Reviews, 35*, 1603–1610.

Seery, M. D., Blascovich, J., Weisbuch, M., & Vick, S. B. (2004). The relationship between self-esteem level, self-esteem stability, and cardiovascular reactions to performance feedback. *Journal of Personality and Social Psychology, 87*, 133–145. doi:10.1037/0022-3514.87.1.133

Seery, M. D. Weisbuch, M., Hetenyi, M., & Blascovich, J. (2010). Cardiovascular measures independently predict performance in a university course. *Psychophysiology, 47*, 535–539.

Sherwood, A., Allen, M. T., Fahrenburg, J., Kelsey, R. M., Lovallo, W. R., & van Dooren, L. J. P. (1990). Methodological guidelines for impedance cardiography. *Psychophysiology, 27*, 1–23. doi:10.1111/j.1469-8986.1990.tb02171.x

Sole, K., Marton, J., & Hornstein, H. A. (1975). Opinion similarity and helping: Three field experiments investigating the bases of promotive tension. *Journal of Experimental and Social Psychology, 11*, 1–13. doi:10.1016/S0022-1031(75)80004-7

Smith, E. R., Coats, S., & Watling, D. (1999). Overlapping mental representations of self, in-group, and partner: Further response-time evidence and a connectionist model. *Personality and Social Psychology Bulletin, 25*, 873–882. doi:10.1177/0146167299025007009

Snyder, C. R., Lassegard, M., & Ford, C. E. (1986). Distancing after group success and failure: Basking in reflected glory and cutting off reflected failure. *Journal of Personality and Social Psychology*, *51*, 382–388. doi:10.1037//0022-3514.51.2.382

Steiner, I. D. (1972). *Group process and productivity*. New York, NY: Academic Press.

Tabachnick, B. G., & Fidell, L. S. (1996). *Using multivariate statistics* (3rd ed.). New York, NY: HarperCollins.

Tajfel, H., & Turner, J. C. (1986). The social identity theory of intergroup behavior. In S. Worchel & W. Austin (Eds.), *Psychology of intergroup relations* (pp. 7–24). Chicago, IL: Nelson-Hall.

Tesser, A. (1988). Toward a self-evaluation maintenance model of social behavior. In L. Berkowitz (Ed.), *Advances in experimental social psychology* (Vol. 21, pp. 181–222). San Diego, CA: Academic Press.

Turner, J. (1985). Social categorization and the self-concept: A social cognitive theory of group behavior. In E. J. Lawler (Ed.), *Advances in group processes* (pp. 77–117). London, UK: Jai Press.

Turner, J., & Giles, H. (1981). The experimental social psychology of intergroup behavior. In J. Turner & H. Giles (Eds.), *Intergroup behavior* (pp. 66–101). Oxford, UK: Blackwell.

Van der Haar, S., Sigers, M., van den Bossche, P., & Jehn, K. (2011). *The influence of shared situation awareness and team learning processes on team effectiveness in emergency management*. Paper presented at the European Association of Work and Organizational Psychology small group meeting on Time and Change in Teams, Chenmitz University of Technology, Chenmitz, Germany.

Williams, K., & Karau, S. (1991). Social loafing and social compensation: The effects of expectations of co-worker performance. *Journal of Personality and Social Psychology*, *61*, 570–581. doi:10.1037/0022-3514.61.4.570

Yukelson, D. (1997). Principles of effective team building interventions in sport: A direct services approach at Penn State University. *Journal of Applied Sport Psychology*, *9*, 73–96. doi:10.1080/10413209708415385

Zarbatany, L., McDougall, P., & Hymel, S. (2000). Gender-differentiated experience in the peer culture: Links to intimacy in preadolescence. *Social Development*, *9*, 62–79.

EUROPEAN JOURNAL OF WORK AND
ORGANIZATIONAL PSYCHOLOGY
2012, 21 (5), 718–748

Introducing an intrateam longitudinal approach to the study of team process dynamics

Jia Li[1] and Robert A. Roe[2]

[1]Department of Social and Communication Psychology, Georg-Elias-Müller-Institute of Psychology, Georg-August-University of Göttingen, Germany

[2]Department of Organization and Strategy, School of Business and Economics, University of Maastricht, The Netherlands

In this article, we introduce an intrateam longitudinal approach to study the temporal dynamics of team processes and its relations to antecedent and consequence variables. We compare this approach with the conventional interteam longitudinal approach (e.g., repeated-measures [M]ANOVA, random coefficient modelling, latent growth modelling) and discuss the conceptual and methodological differences between the two approaches. Whereas the interteam approach follows a sample-to-cases order of inference and assumes random deviances of individual teams' change patterns from the sample-level pattern, the intrateam approach follows a cases-to-sample order of inference and allows for qualitative differences in individual teams' change patterns. In the intrateam approach, each team's change trajectory is directly measured and then used in the next-step multivariate analyses. We argue that the intrateam approach is more compatible with the current conceptualization of team processes as team members' interactions over time (Marks, Mathieu, & Zaccaro, 2001) and with the reasoning underlying the Input–Process–Output (IPO) framework. Next, we illustrate the intrateam approach and apply both approaches in an empirical longitudinal study of team conflict and team satisfaction ($N=42$). The results show the contrast between the two approaches and added value of the intrateam approach in the study of team process dynamics.

Keywords: Interteam longitudinal approach; Intrateam longitudinal approach; Team conflict; Team satisfaction.

Correspondence should be addressed to Jia Li, Department of Social and Communication Psychology, Georg-Elias-Müller-Institute of Psychology, Georg-August-University of Göttingen, Goßlerstraße 14, 37073 Göttingen, Germany. E-mail: jia.li@psych.uni-goettingen.de

Many studies on the effectiveness of work teams have postulated the existence of certain team processes, and have hypothesized causal links of these processes with antecedents and consequences (e.g., Ancona & Caldwell, 1992; Jehn, Northcraft, & Neale, 1999; Knight et al., 1999; Mohammed & Angell, 2004; Olson, Parayitam, & Bao, 2007; Pearsall, Ellis, & Evans, 2008; Pelled, Eisenhardt, & Xin, 1999; Shin & Zhou, 2007). Some studies further adopt the Input–Process–Output (IPO) framework (Hackman, 1987; McGrath, 1986) that considers team processes (e.g., communication, conflict) to mediate or moderate the relationships between so-called "team inputs" (e.g., team members' skills and personalities) and "team outcomes" (e.g., performance, satisfaction). For example, diversity in team members' functional background (i.e., the department or field a person works in such as product development or marketing) has been found to enhance project teams' innovation performance, because team members' extensive communication with their peers outside the teams brings in diverse information valuable for the innovation tasks (Ancona & Caldwell, 1992).

Although conceived as unfolding over time (McGrath, 1984), "team processes" had been long treated as static variables and measured at one moment in time. In recent years, researchers have begun to emphasize the temporal dynamic nature of team processes and to broadly define team processes as team members' internal and external interactions *over time*[1] (Ilgen, Hollenbeck, Johnson, & Jundt, 2005; Marks, Mathieu, & Zaccaro, 2001). Accordingly, repeated measurements and longitudinal analysis methods, such as repeated-measures (M)ANOVA, random coefficient modelling, and latent growth modelling have been recommended. Although these analysis methods have directed researchers' attention to patterns of change as the manifestation of team processes and have greatly advanced team process research, little attention has been given to the question how processes in different teams compare to each other—more specifically, whether all teams show similar change patterns or whether some teams show qualitatively different patterns. Furthermore, if teams indeed demonstrate differential change patterns over time, what are the antecedents and consequences of these differential change patterns? Answering this question is particularly important, because the central reasoning line in team process research, given the temporal dynamic nature of team processes, is that *interteam differences in antecedents lead to interteam differences in interaction patterns over time and interteam differences in interaction patterns over time further lead to interteam differences in consequences*. In this article, we argue

[1]As Marks and colleagues (2001, p. 357) conclude after a literature review of team processes, "the essence of the construct [of team processes] lies in team interaction" and "different forms of team processes describe the types of interactions that take place among team members during the course of goal accomplishment".

that teams can show qualitatively different change patterns,[2] and propose a methodology that enables team researchers to investigate between-teams differences in intrateam dynamics over time.

At the theoretical level, there are two prevailing models explaining how teams develop over time. One is the five-stage team development model proposed by Tuckman (1965) and modified by Tuckman and Jensen (1977). This model suggests that teams undergo a linear succession of stages over time, including the forming, storming, norming, performing, and adjourning stages. Each stage is characterized by the dominant team activities at the time. For example, at the forming stage, teams establish ground rules of work and shape the interpersonal relationships within the teams, while at the storming stage, teams brainstorm their tasks and may engender large disagreement on the tasks. Although the model generally applies to all teams, the duration of the five stages can differ across teams; hence, the unfolding of team processes associated with the stages can also differ across teams (e.g., Bonebright, 2010).

The other team development model is Gersick's (1988, 1989, 1991) punctuated equilibrium (PE) model that proposes a nonlinear development of teams over time and pertains to task-related activities in project teams. The model suggests that teams experience a sudden increase of work intensity at or around the middle point of the total project time. Empirical studies have shown that not all project teams complete the crucial transition at the midpoint and that teams that do, outperform those that do not (Chang, Bordia, & Duck, 2003; Gersick, 1989). Put differently, not only do project teams demonstrate divergent development patterns over time, but such differences also matter for their final performance. Altogether, the PE model provides a theoretical underpinning for a three-time-moment longitudinal design, in which team interactions are measured at the beginning, midpoint, and end of team projects (e.g., Jehn & Mannix, 2001). Furthermore although objective time moments may not necessarily coincide with cognitive, attitudinal, or behavioural shifts in teams (Poole & Holmes, 1995; van de Ven & Poole, 2005), they do serve as meaningful and convenient temporal intervals for researchers' observation (for more information, see Zaheer, Albert, & Zaheer, 1999). For example, if one team's transition occurs before the midpoint and another team's exactly at the midpoint, researchers are able to obtain differential development patterns of task conflict when measuring task conflict at the beginning, midpoint, and end in both teams.

---

[2]In the article, the terms "interaction patterns over time", "change patterns", "development patterns", "growth trajectories", and "temporal dynamics patterns" have the same meaning and are interchangeably used.

At the analytical level, the most often used methods include repeated-measures (M)ANOVA, random coefficient modelling (Bliese & Ployhart, 2002), and latent growth modelling (Chan, 1998; Vandenberg & Lance, 2000). Although differing in their capabilities of modelling complex data, these methods are similar in the assumption that the development pattern (or growth trajectory) identified at the sample level applies to each individual team[3] until the opposite evidence shows. They follow a top-down or "sample-to-cases" order of inference, first estimating the parameters of the generic change pattern at the sample level (e.g., intercept, slope) and next estimating and considering individual teams' change parameters as random deviations from the generic parameters. This order of inference carries the risk of ignoring qualitative differences in individual teams' development patterns that do not match the assumption of random variations. Failing to distinguish between different temporal patterns and collapsing individual teams' patterns into one overall pattern can lead to substantial misrepresentation of team process development at the sample level and at the level of individual teams. As these methods look at first the interteam differences in the estimated change parameters and then the intertemporal differences within each team, we refer to them as "interteam longitudinal approach".

In this article, we propose an alternative way to analyse longitudinal team data, which follows a bottom-up or "cases-to-sample" order of inference. Our approach does not seek to fit any particular mathematical function (linear or higher order) to the data or make any a priori assumption regarding the sample-level or individual teams' change parameters. It looks for similarities in individual teams' development patterns that are actually measured rather than being estimated, and gives more valid descriptions of the temporal dynamics of a team process. Since the approach looks at first each team's development pattern over time and then interteam differences in the intrateam dynamics, we refer to it as "intrateam longitudinal approach". The logic of the intrateam approach is similar to that of time series analyses in terms of the "cases-to-sample" order of inference, that is, to first examining each team's temporal dynamics and then to use such information estimate causality in the second step (e.g., Box, Jenkins, & Reinsel, 1994). However, the intrateam approach differs from conventional time series analyses in two ways. First, it takes into account the issue of temporal ordering and specific characteristics of changes, rather than using only such overall parameters as range or standard deviation to indicate each team's change over time. As Doboeck and colleagues (Deboeck, Montpetit,

[3]Here, we focus on studies in which teams are the unit of analysis. However, all the longitudinal methods and approaches discussed can be applied to studies in which persons and organizations are the unit of analysis.

Bergeman, & Boker, 2009) note, using the intrasubject standard deviation to indicate temporal dynamics neglects the ordering of observations over time and the notion of intra-subject variance (measured by standard deviation) is different from the notion of intrasubject variability (when the temporal ordering is to be considered). Second, the intrateam approach requires fewer measurement moments than conventional time series analyses.[4] The requirement of a large number of measurement moments restricts the use of time-series analyses to rare cases in which team interactions are observed or videotaped and shields away field survey studies (e.g., Chiocchio, 2007). The intrateam longitudinal approach, on the other hand, can be applied to as few as three measurement moments, and as many moments as what time series analyses require. In the next section, we discuss the characteristics of the interteam longitudinal approach and introduce the alternative intrateam longitudinal approach.

THE INTERTEAM LONGITUDINAL APPROACH

The interteam longitudinal approach builds upon the "uniformity of nature" assumption (Borsboom, Mellenbergh, & van Heerden, 2003) and considers all teams to be essentially the same in their attributes, behaviours, and (re)actions. Manifest in measurements, such uniformity implies that individual teams are either identical to or randomly variant from each other—not only in the level of an attribute, behaviour, or action at any time moment but also in the development of an attribute, behaviour, or (re)action over time. Particularly, in the study of team processes, each team is *assumed* to demonstrate the same interaction pattern as all the other teams. It suffices to identify the growth trajectory for a group of teams (e.g., sample), because the group-level trajectory informs individual teams' trajectories, with or without random deviations.

One major limitation in the using interteam approach in the study of team processes is that it may ignore interteam differences in intrateam dynamics that are not represented by the random variations from the group-level pattern. Qualitative differences, such as some teams showing a U-shape development pattern and others an elbow pattern with a steep decline followed by a stable phase, may remain unnoticed. We argue that acknowledging heterogeneous team development patterns is important for team research in that team research—especially that built upon the IPO model—applies such reasoning that *interteam differences in antecedent levels result in different team interaction patterns (over time) and different team interaction patterns further lead to different consequence levels*. As Hackman

[4]The "rule of thumb" suggests a minimum number of 20 measurement moments in order to generate reliable estimation.

(1987, p. 319) noted, "few social psychological studies have addressed the possibility that groups [or work teams] might perform better if members work together in ways that differ from typical interaction patterns. Argyris [1969] argues this is a serious failure of social psychology theory."

Another limitation of the interteam approach is that it makes difficult for researchers to establish meaningful associations between team processes and team inputs and outputs. The reason is that team processes is a by definition temporally integral concept *within each team* yet measured at one or multiple discrete time moments, whereas team inputs and outputs are often measured once. A common approach in repeated-measures (M)ANOVA is to divide a sample of teams by the median of an input or output variable (i.e., median split) and to compare the subsamples' means of a team process variable at one or more measurement moments (e.g., Jehn & Mannix, 2001). It then leads to a description of each subsample's development pattern (i.e., mean scores across multiple measurement moments) and implies that all teams in one subsample have the same development pattern of the team process variable. This analysis procedure, however, is inconsistent in its assumption on the heterogeneity of intrateam dynamics over time. Heterogeneity is accepted between the groups of teams but rejected within each group of teams at the same time. Random coefficient modelling and latent growth modelling establish associations between the intercept and slope of a team process variable and the level of an input and/or output variable at the sample level. The estimation of the sample-level change parameters and the causal relationships is based on individual teams' levels of the process variable measured at *discrete* moments in time, and does not treat the development of the process variable in each team as *one* holistic unit. Therefore, a discrepancy exists between the methods and the definition of team processes as a temporally integral concept (i.e., a within-team phenomenon unfolding over time) and hence between the methods and the central reasoning of the IPO framework.

Given these limitations, we propose an alternative analytical approach that acknowledges the possibility of teams' heterogeneous process dynamics *ex ante*, assesses the degree of heterogeneity, and uses this information to establish the causal links between team processes—as a temporally integral phenomenon within each team—and team input and/or output levels.

THE INTRATEAM LONGITUDINAL APPROACH

The intrateam longitudinal approach abstains from the uniformity-of-nature assumption. Instead, it acknowledges that teams can differ in the level of a particular attribute, behaviour, or team members' interaction at any moment in time as well as in the shape of a development pattern of an attribute, behaviour, or interaction over time. Some studies have shown that teams show development patterns in task progress (Chang et al., 2003; Gersick, 1989; Okhuysen & Waller, 2002), conflict (Jehn & Mannix, 2001), and trust (Raes, 2009) over time. In the intrateam approach, each team's development pattern of a team process variable is seen as meaningful in its own right, no matter whether it is to be compared with any other team's or a group of teams' development pattern(s). Some teams' development patterns may be found to be similar to each other and dissimilar to the others. The number of teams with a similar development pattern is not predetermined by any procedure (e.g., median-split on a team input or output variable). Teams either are all different, idiosyncratic in the development pattern of the process variable, or can be categorized into groups on the basis of the similarities in their development patterns. Unlike the interteam approach the intrateam approach regards each team's development pattern as a holistic unit, rather than a pattern estimated from a series of time-based data points.

In the analysis, the intrateam approach shares a similar logic and order of inference as other time series analyses. That is, it first depicts each team's temporal dynamics of a team process variable and then uses this information to estimate the causal relationships between the temporal dynamics and antecedent and consequence variables. The analysis consists of four steps. The first step is a preliminary step and entails developing a descriptive framework that allows the unequivocal identification of a potential development pattern. The framework provides an inventory of temporal development patterns and reminds researchers of the variety of individual teams' development patterns that can emerge empirically. Therefore, it avoids assuming a *default* linear or parabolic development pattern for each team and for a group of teams. In the second step, each team's development pattern of the process variable is charted and identified with the help of the inventory. This step shows which development patterns do or do not occur in a study, how frequently certain patterns occur, and which pattern surfaces at the sample level. In the third step, teams with similar development patterns are clustered into one group based on the inventory. This step results in a categorical variable that captures each team's temporal dynamics of the process variable. In the fourth step, this categorical variable is entered into a multivariate analysis that aims to establish between-team relationships of the temporal dynamics with antecedent and/or consequent variables. If researchers are interested in the antecedents of team process dynamics (e.g., the effect of team functional background diversity on task conflict change over time), multinomial logistic (or probit) regression is suitable in that it deals with categorical dependent variables and allows categorical and ratio independent variables. If the research interest pertains to the consequences of team process dynamics, linear regressions with dummy independent variables and (M)ANOVA can be applied in that they deal with categorical independent variables.

When developing the inventory, we formalize the description of temporal dynamics patterns by the mathematical language, using the concept of the *n*th order derivative in calculus. We use a function $f(t)$ to describe a team's development pattern of a team process variable over time ($t =$ time). The first order derivative of this function with respect to t indicates to what extent the raw score changes over time. The second order derivative indicates to what extent the first order derivative changes over time. The *n*th order derivative indicates to what extent the $n - 1$th order derivative changes over time. Altogether, the first to *n*th order derivatives across t moments[5] provide a complete and detailed picture of a team's temporal dynamics in the process variable. We do not propose to fit any particular mathematical function to the time-based data points of a single team or a group of teams and therefore not aim to estimate the parameters of such functions.

Next we elaborate the four steps of the intrateam approach for the three-time-moment longitudinal design. We choose the three-moment design, because it is a frequently used longitudinal design in team research[6] and particularly suited for studies with the PE model as theoretical foundation. We then present an empirical study to illustrate the intrateam approaches, and to contrast the results between the intrateam and interteam approach. In the last section of the article, we discuss the extension of intrateam approach to more than three time moments, the theoretical contribution of both intra- and interteam approaches to team research, and the limitation of the article.

Step 1: Developing an inventory of temporal dynamic patterns

The simplest longitudinal design consists of three time moments. A temporal dynamics pattern delineates a team's development pattern of a particular variable over time. It consists of three time moments (i.e., t_1, t_2, t_3) and two

[5]The letter t represents the total number of measurement moments in a study.

[6]This is supported by bibliographic analyses. For example, among the 20 articles with a longitudinal research design published in the *European Journal of Work and Organizational Psychology* since 1996, six use two measurement moments, whereas eight articles uses three moments, and only one used four moments. The other articles describe case studies or review longitudinal research. A search in the PsycLit database reveals 37 additional journal articles on longitudinal team research (longitudinal and team as title words); 14 of these studies have two measurement moments, eight have three moments, six have four moments, and four have more measurement moments (mostly for a dependent variable). Not all of these studies deal with work teams, and only some of them deal with team processes. These counts were collected on 24 October 2011. Although it seems that the two-moment design is the most popular to date, we consider that the two-moment design gives rather limited information on temporal dynamics and the three-moment design is the simplest longitudinal design to study the temporal dynamics of team processes.

consecutive time intervals between the moments (i.e., between t_1 and t_2, between t_2 and t_3). A temporal interval is the smallest temporal dynamics unit from which complex dynamics patterns with more moments are further constructed. To develop the inventory of temporal dynamics patterns, we define three change characteristics, that is, change direction, change rate, and change degree. *Change direction* captures the tendency of development, that is, whether the measured team interaction increases, decreases, or remains stable between two time moments. *Change rate* indicates how much the team interaction has changed over a time interval. For example, a five-Celsius-degree increase in temperature between 9:00 a.m. and 10:00 a.m. has a positive change rate of five degrees per hour; a five-degree decrease between 7:00 p.m. and 8:00 p.m. has a negative change rate of five degrees per hour. *Change degree* is the absolute difference in the level between two time moments. In the previous example, the five-degree increase between 9:00 a.m. and 10:00 a.m. and the five-degree decrease between 7:00 p.m. and 8:00 p.m. have the same change degree, that is, a five degree difference per hour.

Seventeen trajectories. When comparing the three change characteristics of the two adjacent time intervals, we can identify 17 dynamics patterns in total (see Figure 1). Pattern 1 is an increase-increase pattern with a larger change degree in the second interval than in the first one. Pattern 2 is an increase-increase pattern with an equal change degree in the second interval as in the first one (i.e., a straight upward line). Pattern 3 is an increase-increase pattern with a smaller change degree in the second interval than in the first one. Pattern 4 is an increase-stable pattern. Pattern 5 is a stable-increase pattern. Pattern 6 is a decrease-decrease pattern with a larger change degree in the second interval than in the first one. Pattern 7 is a decrease-decrease pattern with an equal change degree in the second interval as in the first one (i.e., a straight downward line). Pattern 8 is a decrease-decrease pattern with a smaller change degree in the second interval than in the first one. Pattern 9 is a decrease-stable pattern; Pattern 10 is a stable-decrease pattern. Pattern 11 is an increase-decrease pattern with a larger change degree in the second interval than in the first one. Pattern 12 is an increase-decrease pattern with an equal change degree in the second interval as in the first one. Pattern 13 is an increase-decrease pattern with a smaller change degree in the second interval than in the first one. Pattern 14 is a decrease-increase pattern with a larger change degree in the second interval than in the first one. Pattern 15 is a decrease-increase pattern with an equal change degree in the second interval as in the first one. Pattern 16 is a decrease-increase pattern with a smaller change degree in the second interval than in the first one. Pattern 17 is a horizontal straight line.

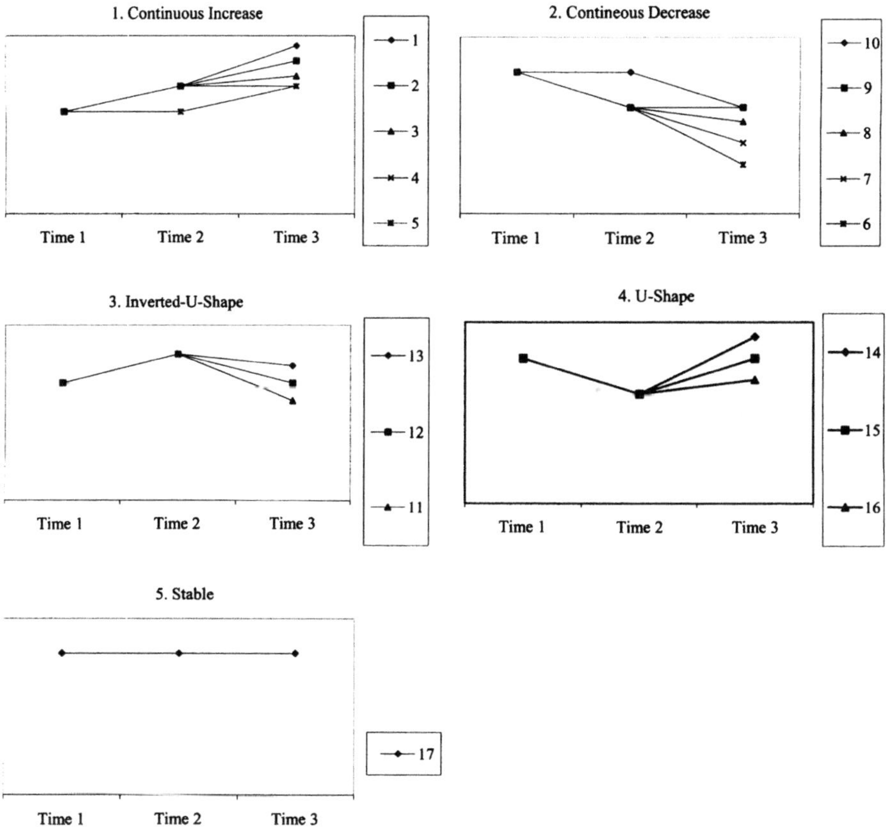

Figure 1. The 17 possible three-moment patterns categorized by change direction.

To facilitate the identification of temporal dynamics patterns in the descriptive framework, we consider each pattern a quadratic function $f(t) = at^2 + bt + c$, in which t is the time moment ($t = 0, 1, 2$) and $f(t)$ is the score of a variable, and use the concept of the *n*th order derivative to indicate change. The sign of the first order derivative function $f'(t) = 2at + b$ between *two time moments* (i.e., positive, negative, zero) indicates the change direction of a team's score between the two time moments to increase, decrease, or be constant. The contrast of the sign of the first order derivative function between *two time intervals* indicates the change direction of a three-moment dynamics pattern, that is, continuous increase, continuous decrease, inverted-U shape, U-shape, or being stable. The sign of the second order derivative function $f''(t) = 2a$ indicates the tendency of change rate. A positive $f''(t)$ from t_0 to t_2 indicates an increasing trend of the slope and convex curves such as the accelerated increase, U-shape, and decelerated decrease patterns. A negative $f''(t)$ from t_0 to t_2 indicates a decreasing trend of the slope and concave curves such as the accelerated decrease, inverted-U shape, and decelerated increase patterns. A zero $f''(t)$ from t_0 to t_2 indicates a constant change rate and include the linearly increasing, linearly decreasing, and stable patterns. We summarize the 17 temporal dynamic patterns described in mathematical language in Table 1.

Higher-level groupings. The 17 patterns are the most fine-grained categorization scheme of the three-moment temporal dynamics patterns and can be further grouped into three broader categorization schemes based on each of the three change characteristics. Based on *change direction*, the 17 patterns fall into five categories, that is, the increase patterns (Pattern 1, 2, 3, 4, 5), decrease patterns (Pattern 6, 7, 8, 9, 10), inverted-U-shape patterns (Pattern 11, 12, 13), U-shape patterns (Pattern 14, 15, 16), and a stable pattern (Pattern 17). We present the change-direction-based scheme in Figure 1.

Based on the *change rate* of the two adjacent time intervals, we obtain a categorization scheme of three categories, that is, convex curves (Pattern 1, 5, 8, 9, 14, 15, 16), concave patterns (Pattern 3, 4, 6, 10, 11, 12, 13), and straight lines (Pattern 2, 7, 17). Convex curves have a positive second order derivative function that indicates an upward tendency of change rate and consist of patterns that increase at an increasing rate, switch from decrease to increase, and decrease at a decreasing rate. In contrast, concave curves have a negative second order derivative function that indicates a downward tendency of change rate and consist of patterns that increase at an decreasing rate, switch from increase to decrease, and decrease at an increasing rate. Lastly, straight lines are the patterns with constant positive, negative, or zero rate of change. We present the change-rate-based scheme in Figure 2.

Finally, based on the *change degree* of the two adjacent time intervals, we obtain the third broader categorization scheme consisting of three categories. These categories are patterns with an accelerating change degree (Pattern 1, 5, 6, 10, 11, 14), patterns with a decelerating change degree (Pattern 3, 4, 8, 9, 12, 15), and patterns with a constant change degree (Pattern 2, 7, 12, 15, 17). The accelerating change degree indicates that the change degree in the second time interval is larger than in the first one, regardless of the change direction in each time interval. The decelerating change degree indicates that the change degree in the second interval is smaller than in the first one, regardless of the change direction in each interval. The constant change degree indicates that the change degree in the second interval is equal to that in the first one, regardless of the change direction in each interval. We present the change-degree-based scheme in Figure 3.

TABLE 1

The 17 temporal dynamic patterns in the mathematical language: $f(t) = at^2 + bt + c$, $(t = 0, 1, 2)$; $f'(t) = 2at + b$; $f''(t) = 2a$

Range of a	*Range of b*	*Range of c*	*Pattern*	*Change direction*	*Change rate*	*Change degree*
$a = 0$	$F'(t) = 0$	$c \neq 0$	17	horizontal	line	N.A.[a]
	$F'(t) > 0,\ t \in (0,2)$	N.A.	2	continuous increase	line	constant
	$F'(t) < 0,\ t \in (0,2)$	N.A.	7	continuous decrease	line	constant
$a > 0$	$F'(t) > 0,\ t \in (0,1)$ and $F'(t) > 0,\ t \in (1,2)$	N.A.	1, 5	continuous increase	convex pattern	accelerated
	$F'(t) < 0,\ t \in (0,1)$ and $F'(t) < 0,\ t \in (1,2)$	N.A.	8, 9	continuous decrease	convex pattern	decelerated
	$F'(t) < 0,\ t \in (0,1)$ and $F'(t) > 0,\ t \in (1,2)$	N.A.	14, 15	U shape	convex pattern	accelerated/constant
	$F'(t) < 0,\ t \in (0,1)$ and $F'(t) > 0,\ t \in (1,2)$	N.A.	16	U shape	convex pattern	decelerated
$a < 0$	$F'(t) > 0,\ t \in (0,1)$ and $F'(t) > 0,\ t \in (1,2)$	N.A.	3, 4	continuous increase	concave pattern	decelerated
	$F'(t) < 0,\ t \in (0,1)$ and $F'(t) < 0,\ t \in (1,2)$	N.A.	6, 10	continuous decrease	concave pattern	accelerated
	$F'(t) < 0,\ t \in (0,1)$ and $F'(t) > 0,\ t \in (1,2)$	N.A.	11, 12	inverted-U shape	concave pattern	accelerated/constant
	$F'(t) > 0,\ t \in (0,1)$ and $F'(t) < 0,\ t \in (1,2)$	N.A.	13	inverted-U shape	concave pattern	decelerated

[a]N.A. refers to "Not applicable".

Step 2: Depict temporal dynamics

We depict temporal dynamics patterns in terms of their shapes. We first calculate Z-scores of the measured variable across the three time moments *for each team*. These intrateam across-time Z-scores denote a team's

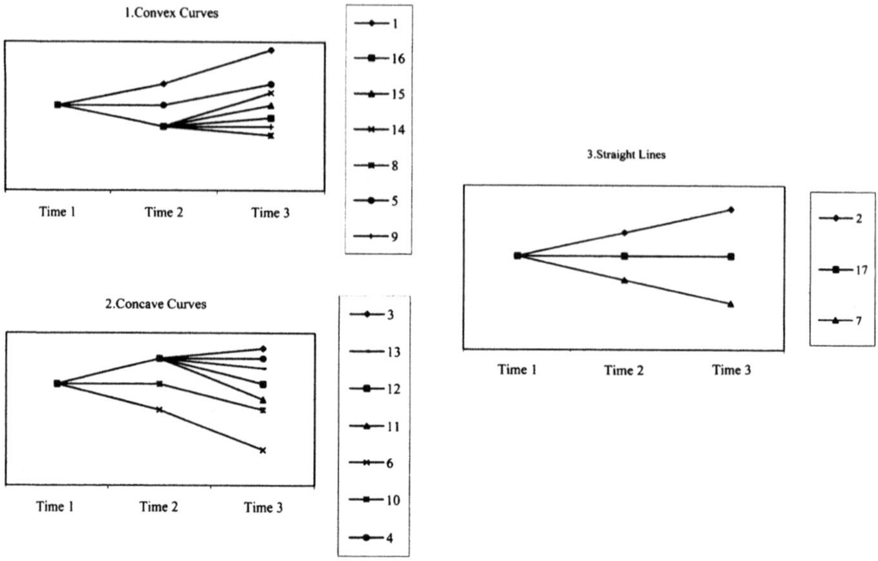

Figure 2. The 17 possible three-moment patterns categorized by change rate.

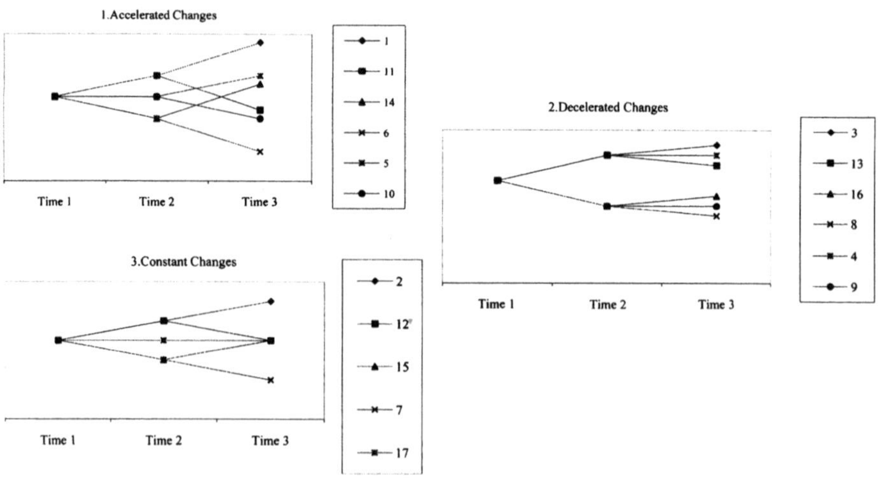

Figure 3. The 17 possible three-moment patterns categorized by change degree.

temporal dynamic pattern, regardless of the actual scores at respective moments. In other words, the temporal dynamics of a variable is considered as a concept independent from the level of the variable at any time moment. The inventory of the temporal dynamics patterns (i.e., the 17-pattern scheme and the three broader categorization schemes) is a helpful tool to describe the dynamics patterns found in this step: it allows researchers to identify which patterns do and do not occur empirically, and how frequently a pattern or pattern categorization occurs.

Step 3: Cluster individual teams by temporal dynamics

In the third step, individual teams are clustered into groups according to the similarity of their temporal dynamics patterns. When the sample size is small (e.g., $n < 30$), researchers can manually cluster teams into groups with the help of the inventory. When the sample size is large, researchers can perform hierarchical clustering analysis with the intrateam across-time Z-scores. We propose to use a within-cluster similarity algorithm as the clustering method and to choose cosine distance as the distance measure. The within-cluster similarity algorithm ensures that teams with the most similar structure in the Z-scores are clustered together first. Cosine distance, unlike Euclidean distance, allows the researchers to cluster teams by the shape of Z-scores over time, rather than by the level of Z-scores. It is noteworthy that hierarchical clustering analysis may not 100% correctly classify individual teams into the 17-pattern scheme, given a default .05 confidence level. Therefore, manual correction may be needed.

Furthermore, which categorization scheme to use, depends on the particular research question and sample size. First, the three broader categorization schemes denote three aspects of change that are of researchers' interest and make sense conceptually and theoretically. For example, if researchers are interested in understanding how teams' functional background diversity affects the *trend* of team task conflict change over time, the five-category change-direction-based scheme shall be used to measure the dependent variable. If the interest is to understand the effect on *how fast* team task conflict changes, the change-rate-based scheme is more suitable. In contrast, the 17-pattern categorization scheme reveals all the possible change patterns in a three-moment design but may not associate with a particular aspect of change. Second, although the 17-pattern scheme and the three higher level schemes encompass all the possible three-moment patterns, it does not necessarily mean that all the 17 patterns will be present in an empirical study or teams will be evenly distributed among all patterns or pattern categories found in a study. Since it is rather difficult to obtain large sample sizes in longitudinal team studies, we suggest that when the sample size is small in comparison with the number of emergent patterns,[7] the three higher-level categorization schemes can be used. In the end, the outcome of the manual clustering procedure or hierarchical clustering analysis is a categorical variable that captures each team's development of a process variable over time and is to be used as a dependent or independent variable in the multivariate analyses in the next step.

Step 4: Link temporal dynamics to antecedents and consequences

The fourth step is to enter the dynamics-based categorical variable into appropriate multivariate analysis techniques to examine its causal relationships with pertinent antecedent and consequence variables. When the temporal dynamics of a team process variable is the *dependent variable* and team inputs are the predictors, researchers can use such techniques as multiclass discriminant analysis, multinomial logistic regressions, and multinomial probit regressions that deal with categorical dependent variables. Multiclass discriminant analysis requires ratio variables as independent variables and assumes a normal distribution of independent variables. Multinomial logistic regression allows ratio and categorical independent variables and relaxes the normal distribution assumption, but it assumes the independence of the occurrence chance of each category in the dependent variable. Multinomial probit regression allows ratio and categorical independent variables and relaxes the assumptions of normality and independence of alternatives. When the temporal dynamics of a team process variable is the *independent variable* and team outputs are the outputs, researchers can use (M)ANOVA or linear regression with dummy variables, since both methods allow categorical independent variables but deal with only ratio dependent variables.

AN ILLUSTRATIVE EXAMPLE AND COMPARISON BETWEEN THE APPROACHES

We present an empirical study in which the effect of team conflict development on team satisfaction is examined. The aim of the study is to illustrate the application of the intrateam longitudinal approach and to compare and contrast results from the intra- and interteam longitudinal approach. We choose team conflict as the focal team process variable, since

---

[7]It is a rule of thumb that at least five observations (or data points) are needed in order to estimate one parameter. Therefore, the required sample size depends on how many parameters are to be estimated in specific models. When a single categorical variable is used to represent several dynamic patterns (e.g., in MANOVA), fewer teams are required than when each pattern (or each pattern category) is represented by a dichotomous dummy variable (e.g., in linear regressions with multiple dummy variables).

it is one of the most studied team processes in team literature (for an overview, see the recent meta-analyses by de Dreu & Weingart, 2003; de Wit, Greer, & Jehn, 2011). Team conflict has been defined as "the process emerging from perceived incompatibilities or differences among group members" (de Wit et al., 2011, p. 1). It consists of three forms, that is, task conflict, relationship conflict, and process conflict. Based on the team conflict literature, we are interested in finding an answer to the following questions: (1) What is the "typical" team conflict development pattern over time, if any? and (2) How does team conflict—defined as a temporally dynamic phenomenon—affect team satisfaction?

Using the PE model (Gersick, 1988, 1989, 1991) as the theoretical foundation for our study, we repeatedly measure team conflict at the beginning, midpoint, and end of team projects. We choose repeated-measures MANOVA as a representation of the interteam longitudinal approach, since it is the simplest one among the aforementioned interteam longitudinal methods and it is often used in team research. For the purpose of comparison, we take Jehn and Mannix's (2001) study as a prototype, using the same measures of team conflict and following the same analysis procedure of the interteam approach.

Sample, procedure, and measures

We collected data from business graduate students who followed a research methodology course in the business school of a large university in The Netherlands in 2008. A major course assignment (accounting for 30% of the grade) was to write research proposals in randomly composed teams of two or three persons. Forty-two teams completed all the questionnaires in the study, including 35 three-person teams and seven two-person teams.[8] In the 7-week course, we gathered the information of course participants' demographic features (e.g., gender, age, nationality) at the beginning of the first week and measured team conflict at the end of the first, fourth, and seventh week (i.e., t_1, t_2, t_3). Team satisfaction was measured at the end of the seventh week.

We measured task conflict (TC), relationship conflict (RC), and process conflict (PC) with the nine-item 5-point Likert scale used in Jehn and Mannix's (2001) study. The scale contains such items as "How

[8]We are aware of the debate among team researchers (Moreland, 2010; Williams, 2010) over whether dyads are groups or not. In this article, we follow Williams' (2010) argument and consider dyads as groups or teams for two major reasons. First, in our view, the phenomenon of our interest in the empirical study, that is, team conflict and team satisfaction does exist at dyad level and we have added team size as a control variable. Second, the generally accepted definition of groups or teams includes two-person groups or teams (e.g., Kozlowski & Bell, 2003).

frequently do you have disagreements within your team about the research proposal task you are working on?", "How much relationship tension is there in your research team?", and "How often are there disagreements about who should do what in your research team?" Team satisfaction (TS) was measured by the five-item team satisfaction scale developed by Behfar, *Peterson, Mannix,* and *Trochim* (2008). We adapted the original 9-point Likert scale to a 5-point Likert scale and asked team members to what degree they agreed with such statements as "I am satisfied with working in my research team", and "I would like to work with my team members on other team assignments in the future if given the opportunities to do so". The Cronbach's alphas for the team conflict scales at each time moment and for the team satisfaction scale range from .72 to .91, which justifies the aggregation of item scores to a composite score of the scale for each team; the average r_{wg} varies from .66 and .90 for the aforementioned scales, which justifies the aggregation of individual team members' scores to team-level scores.

Methods of analysis

Following the four steps of the *intrateam* approach, we first set up the descriptive framework to identify each team's temporal dynamics pattern for each conflict type, using the 17-pattern categorization scheme and the three higher order schemes. Second, we calculated the intrateam *Z*-scores for each conflict type and each team over the three time moments and graphed the resulting patterns. Third, we clustered the teams into groups according to the shape of their conflict development patterns (i.e., the shape of *Z*-scores). This allowed us to identify which of the 17 patterns in the scheme were present and how the 42 teams were distributed among the present patterns. Fourth, we entered the categorical variable of team conflict dynamics into ANOVA in order to examine whether and how team conflict—as a temporal dynamic phenomenon—affects team satisfaction.

Following the procedure of the *interteam* approach in Jehn and Mannix's (2001) study, we first divided the 42 teams into a high-satisfaction group ($n = 23$) and a low-satisfaction group ($n = 19$) by the median of team satisfaction (3.33 on the 5-point scale). Next, we performed repeated-measures MANOVA to test whether high- and low-satisfaction teams differed in the level of team task, relationship, and process conflict at the three time moments. For both approaches, we examined the correlations between team demographic diversity and team satisfaction as a preliminary check for potential control variables. None of the team diversity measures was related to team satisfaction. We also examined the influence of missing data at t_2 and t_3 and the initial team size on team satisfaction. We found that only team size was related to team satisfaction, $F(2,39) = 3.48$, $p = .041$, and added it as a covariate in the analyses.

Results

The intrateam approach. Following the intrateam approach, we found that out of the 17 possible patterns in the refined inventory, 12 patterns occur in the case of team task conflict, 12 patterns in the case of relationship conflict, and 13 patterns in the case of process conflict. The number of teams is not evenly distributed across the present patterns for the three conflict types. The accelerated increase pattern (Pattern 1) is the prevailing pattern, which shows a rise in team conflict in the first half of the project period and a stronger growth in the second half. This pattern was found in 10 teams (24%) for task conflict, 12 teams (29%) for relationship conflict, and 11 teams (26%) for process conflict. We present the distribution of teams across the shown conflict development patterns in Table 2.

Using the change-direction-based categorization scheme, we found that for task conflict, 21 teams have the continuous increase patterns; two teams the continuous decrease patterns; 11 teams demonstrate inverted-U-shape

TABLE 2
The distribution of the 42 project teams across the shown temporal dynamics patterns of task, relationship, and process conflict

	Conflict type		
Pattern	*Task conflict*	*Relationship conflict*	*Process conflict*
Pattern 1	10	12	11
Pattern 2	2	2	1
Pattern 3	6	2	4
Pattern 4	2	–	2
Pattern 5	1	4	4
Pattern 6	2	1	2
Pattern 7	–	3	–
Pattern 8	–	–	1
Pattern 9	–	–	–
Pattern 10	–	–	1
Pattern 11	5	1	3
Pattern 12	2	2	2
Pattern 13	4	4	3
Pattern 14	–	4	–
Pattern 15	1	1	2
Pattern 16	6	6	6
Pattern 17	1	–	–

patterns; seven teams demonstrate U-shape patterns. One team's task conflict remains stable over time. For relationship conflict, the numbers of teams in each of the five categories are 20, four, seven, 11, and zero. For process conflict, the distribution across the categories is 22, four, eight, eight, and zero. Using the change-rate-based categorization scheme, we found that for task conflict, 18 teams demonstrate the convex curves; 21 teams demonstrate the concave curves; three teams have the constant change rate (two positive and one negative). For relationship conflict, the distribution across the three categories is 27, 10, and five (two with a positive change rate and three with a negative change rate). For process conflict, the distribution is 24, 17, and one (with a positive change rate). Using the change-degree-based categorization scheme, we found that for task conflict, 18 teams have an accelerated change degree, 11 teams demonstrate a decelerated change degree, and 13 teams have a constant change degree. For relationship conflict, the distribution across the three categories is 22, five, and 15. For process conflict, the distribution is 21, 11, and 10.

The ANOVA shows the following results regarding the relationship between team conflict dynamics and team satisfaction. For *task conflict*, the overall *F*-statistics (controlled for team size) was not significant, indicating that, overall, teams with different task conflict development patterns did not differ in the level of team satisfaction at the end. A further analysis with the five-category change-direction-based scheme shows a slight effect, that is, overall the level of team satisfaction differed across teams with differential task conflict change directions, $F(4,36) = 2.56$, $p = .055$.[9] More specifically, results from pairwise comparison suggest that teams with the inverted-U shape ($M_{TS} = 3.57$) and continuous decrease patterns ($M_{TS} = 3.90$) have a significantly higher satisfaction level than teams with the U-shape ($M_{TS} = 2.96$) and continuous increase patterns ($M_{TS} = 2.90$), respectively.[10] It implies that as long as task conflict decreases, rather than increasing, in the second half of a project, regardless of its development pattern in the first half, a team will have a higher team satisfaction level at the end.

[9]In this article, we take .10 as the cut-off point for the significance level. We use this rather lenient standard, because the purpose of the article is to introduce the intrateam longitudinal approach and to make the first endeavour (to our knowledge) to compare whether the intra- and interteam longitudinal approaches produce differential empirical results.

[10]The mean difference between the inverted-U-shape group and the U-shape group is at the .018 significance level; that between the inverted-U-shape group and the continuous increase group is at the .04 level. The mean difference between the continuous decrease group and the U-shape group is at the .06 level; that between the continuous decrease group and the continuous increase group at the .064 level.

For *relationship conflict*, we also found a nonsignificant overall *F*-statistic across the shown 12 patterns, indicating no influence of relationship conflict dynamics on team satisfaction. However, with the five-category scheme, we found significantly different team satisfaction levels across the four emergent categories, $F(3,37) = 5.08$, $p = .005$. Results of pairwise comparison shows that teams with the inverted-U-shape ($M_{TS} = 3.51$), $t = 2.75$, $p = .009$, U-shape ($M_{TS} = 3.38$), $t = 2.50$, $p = .017$, and continuous decrease patterns ($M_{TS} = 3.86$), $t = 2.97$, $p = .005$, have a significantly higher team satisfaction level than teams with the continuous increase patterns ($M_{TS} = 2.76$). It appears that as long as relationship conflict decreases during a project, no matter whether it is in the first or second half of a project or throughout the entire project, the fact that interpersonal tension has declined in a team will enhance team satisfaction at the end.

For *process conflict*, results were similar to those for task and relationship conflict. The *F*-statistics showed no significant overall effect of process conflict development on team satisfaction, when the most fine-grained 17-pattern categorization scheme was used. However, using the five-category scheme, we found a significant difference in the level of team satisfaction across the four shown categories, $F(3,37) = 2.26$, $p = .097$. Results of

TABLE 3
ANOVA results for impact of team conflict dynamics over time on team satisfaction ($N = 42$)

Variable	*Team satisfaction*[a]
Task conflict	
Increase	3.01
Inverted-U shape	3.53
U shape	2.88
Decrease	3.98
Stable	2.20
F-statistics	2.56*
Relationship conflict	
Increase	2.76
Inverted-U shape	3.51
U shape	3.38
Decrease	3.86
F-statistics	5.08***
Process conflict	
Increase	3.07
Inverted-U shape	3.57
U shape	2.73
Decrease	3.58
F-statistics	2.26*

[a]Team size is controlled. *$p < .10$, ***$p < .01$.

pairwise comparison shows that teams with the inverted-U-shape ($M_{TS} = 3.57$), $t = 1.97$, $p = .056$, and continuous decrease patterns ($M_{TS} = 3.58$), $t = 2.07$, $p = .046$, are more satisfied than teams with the U-shape patterns ($M_{TS} = 2.73$). Thus, we can conclude that as long as process conflict declines after at the midpoint, a team will have a higher satisfaction level at the end. We summarize the results of the intrateam approach in Table 3.

The interteam approach. Following the procedure in Jehn and Mannix's (2001) study, we examined whether the sample mean of team conflict differed across the three time moments and whether high- and low-satisfaction teams, split by the median of team satisfaction (i.e., 3.33 on a 1–5 scale), differed in the conflict level across the three time moments. Repeated-measures MANOVA was performed for the analyses. For the first analysis, the sphericity assumption (assessed by the Mauchly's sphericity test) was violated for all the three types of conflict, $\chi^2_{TC(2)} = 13.99$, $p = .001$; $\chi^2_{RC(2)} = 23.14$, $p < .001$; $\chi^2_{PC(2)} = 28.07$, $p < .001$. Therefore, we used within-subjects contrasts to correct such violation. For task conflict, we found a linear increase over time, $F(1, 41) = 21.25$, $p < .001$, from 1.90 to 2.16 between t_1 and t_2 ($p < .001$) and from 2.16 to 2.39 between t_2 and t_3 ($p = .026$). For relationship conflict, we found a quadratic increase, $F(1, 41) = 8.74$, $p = .005$, in which the sample mean is stable between t_1 and t_2, but increased from 1.55 to 2.10 between t_2 and t_3 ($p < .001$). For process conflict, the increase was again linearly, $F(1, 41) = 22.05$, $p < .001$, from 1.60 to 1.78 between t_1 and t_2 ($p < .001$), and from 1.78 to 2.15 between t_2 and t_3 ($p = .002$). We present the results in Table 4.

For the second analysis, team satisfaction was included as a between-subjects factor. Results of the between-subjects effect show that high- and low-satisfaction teams differed in the level of each conflict type across the three time moments, $F_{TC}(1,39) = 12.67$, $p = .001$; $F_{RC}(1,39) = 21.31$,

TABLE 4
Results of repeated-measures ANOVA for team conflict over time ($N = 42$)

	Task conflict		*Relationship conflict*		*Process conflict*	
Effects	*F*	*df*	*F*	*df*	*F*	*df*
Between-subjects effect	818.59***	1	559.28***	1	506.39***	1
Within-subjects contrast						
Linear	21.25**	1	27.23**	1	22.05**	1
Quadratic	0.09	1	8.74**	1	2.10	1

**$p < .05$, ***$p < .01$.

$p < .001$; $F_{PC}(1,39) = 13.15$, $p = .001$. For task conflict, results of the within-subjects contrast shows that high-satisfaction teams follow an increase-stable pattern, $F(1,22) = 6.88$, $p = .016$, with an increase from 1.78 to 2.06 between t_1 and t_2 ($p < .001$) but stabilizing between t_2 and t_3. In contrast, low-satisfaction teams showed a quadratic increase pattern, $F(1,18) = 4.06$, $p = .059$, with an increase from 2.05 to 2.29 between t_1 and t_2 ($p = .045$) and a larger increase from 2.29 to 2.88 between t_2 and t_3 ($p < .001$). For relationship conflict, high-satisfaction teams showed a stable pattern from t_1 to t_3, and low-satisfaction teams showed a quadratic increase pattern, $F(1,18) = 14.93$, $p = .001$, with no significant difference between t_1 and t_2 but an increase from 1.68 to 2.77 between t_2 and t_3 ($p < .001$). As for process conflict, the results are somewhat similar to those for task conflict. That is, high-satisfaction teams' process conflict increased from 1.48 to 1.66 between t_1 and t_2 ($p = .016$) and stabilized between t_2 and t_3; low-satisfaction teams showed a quadratic increase, $F(1,18) = 8.00$, $p = .011$, with an increase from 1.74 to 1.93 between t_1 and t_2 ($p = .045$) and a larger increase from 1.93 to 2.74 between t_2 and t_3 ($p < .000$). We present the results in Table 5.

Comparison of results from the two approaches

We compared the results from the two approaches to see whether they lead to different answers to the two research questions, that is, what the typical team conflict development pattern over time is, and how team conflict development over time affects team satisfaction. For both questions, the

TABLE 5

Results of repeated-measures ANOVA for the differences of team conflict over time between high- and low-satisfaction teams

	Task conflict		*Relationship conflict*		*Process conflict*	
Effects	*F*	*df*	*F*	*df*	*F*	*df*
Between-subjects effect ($N = 42$)	12.21***	1	22.34***		13.89***	1
Within-subjects contrast in high-satisfaction teams ($n = 23$)						
Linear	2.90*	1	3.3*	1	2.79	1
Quadratic	6.88**	1	0.68	1	1.86	1
Within-subjects contrast in low-satisfaction teams ($n = 19$)						
Linear	29.17***	1	50.00***	1	31.60***	1
Quadratic	4.06*	1	14.93***	1	8.00**	1

[a]Team size is controlled. *$p < .10$, **$p < .05$, ***$p < .01$.

intrateam longitudinal approach and the interteam longitudinal approach provide rather different outlooks. Results from the *intrateam* approach reveal a great variety in teams' conflict development patterns over time and the absence of a common pattern at the (sub)sample level. The accelerated increase pattern is the dominant development pattern for all the three conflict types. Results from the *interteam* approach, on the other hand, suggest a linear increase for task and process conflict and an accelerated increase for relationship conflict. However, as found with the intrateam approach, *very few teams actually demonstrate the generic sample-level conflict development pattern found with the interteam approach.* Two teams (5%) showed a linear increase in task conflict over time; four teams (10%) showed the accelerated increase of relationship conflict; and only one team (2%) showed a linear growth of process conflict. Therefore, it may be "dangerous" to conclude that "task conflict in teams tends to increase linearly over time", while a small percentage of teams' task conflict actually develop in such a way. Even though the sample mean of team conflict level significantly differed across time moments and demonstrated a particular change pattern over time, it does not necessarily mean that all the teams in the sample followed the same development pattern as found at the sample level. In other words, using the interteam longitudinal approach to study intrateam dynamics (or change) over time carries the risk of serious ecological fallacy (i.e., to interpret indicate cases via aggregate data) that misleads researchers in their understanding the interteam differences in intrateam dynamics over time.

The two approaches also provide different results regarding the association between team conflict development and team satisfaction. Although the *intrateam approach* fails to show any overall effect across the conflict patterns identified with the 17-pattern scheme, we do find the effect of change direction in team task, relationship, and process conflict on team satisfaction using the five-category scheme based on change direction. Overall, the results show that change direction of task and process conflict in the *second* half of a project affects team satisfaction at the end and that change direction of relationship conflict throughout the entire project affects team satisfaction. These different results between the categorization schemes may be attributed to a rather small sample size. As discussed earlier (see Footnote 7), at least five teams are needed to estimate the effect of being in a particular cluster or not on team satisfaction. However, as seen in Table 2, the number of teams in some of the present patterns (according to the 17-pattern scheme) does not meet this criterion. In comparison, the results of the *interteam approach* suggest that high- and low-satisfaction teams' task, relationship, and process conflict differed only in the *second* half of a team project. They also show a significant between-subjects effect within the group of high-satisfaction teams and the group of low-satisfaction teams for each conflict type,[11] which casts serious doubts on the existence of *one* "generic" conflict development pattern for all the high- or low-satisfaction teams as shown in the interteam approach.

DISCUSSION

In the recent team literature, the concept of team processes has been explicitly conceptualized as team members' dynamic interactions over time (Hackman, 1987; Marks et al., 2001; McGrath, 1984) and evidenced as unfolding over time differently across teams (Arrow, 1997; Chang et al., 2003; Gersick, 1989; Jehn & Mannix, 2001; Raes, 2009). These conceptualizations and the available empirical evidence raise the question whether the logic of using a single growth pattern (even with random variations) to describe team process dynamics in all teams, as in the interteam approach, can satisfy the aim of team research to explain how team processes emerge in response to different team inputs and how they give rise to different team outputs that may subsequently form new inputs (Ilgen et al., 2005). In the past, interteam differences in intrateam process dynamics have been assessed with proxies of team tenure (e.g., Harrison, *Price, Gavin, & Florey*, 2002) and single moment measures (e.g., Jehn et al., 1999; Pelled et al., 1999), but these treatments do not grasp the temporal dynamic nature of team processes. Qualitative studies (e.g., Ericksen & Dyer, 2004; Gersick, 1989, 1991; Tuckman, 1965), on the other hand, although examining the interteam differences in team development over time, lack the power of statistical inferences to establish causal links between team development and team inputs and outputs. When interteam differences of intrateam dynamics are at the centre of investigation, the intrateam approach makes more sense theoretically, as it conceptualizes team processes in a truly dynamic way. It also offers a clear methodology to fit the notion of dynamic team processes in an otherwise differential design, and relates team processes to team inputs and outputs in a straightforward manner.

The logic of the intrateam approach is to define and develop a measure of "change over time" (or temporal dynamics) and then enter the variable of change into multivariate analysis techniques to establish causality. It follows the positivistic philosophy of social science and the

[11]In the group of high-satisfaction teams, between-subjects effect is significant for the three conflict types, $F_{TC}(1,22) = 664.48$, $p < .001$; $F_{RC}(1,22) = 495.87$, $p < .001$; $F_{PC}(1,22) = 410.21$, $p < .001$. So is in the group of low-satisfaction teams, $F_{TC}(1,18) = 431.53$, $p < .001$; $F_{RC}(1,18) = 384.95$, $p < .001$; $F_{PC}(1,18) = 288.35$, $p < .001$.

steps from defining a concept, operationalizing the concept, to modelling the nomological network of the concept. For example, in the study of team cohesion, the first step is to define the concept of team cohesion and then develop a measure that scales a team's cohesion level. Afterwards, empirical data are gathered, models tested, and conclusions drawn. In the same vein, if team processes are conceptualized as team members' internal and external interactions *over time*, the concept of a particular team process needs to be measured in a way that captures the temporal dynamics of each team's interaction. As Team A's cohesion can be quantified as 3 on a 1–5 scale, its conflict—defined as a team process and hence a temporally dynamic phenomenon—shall be assigned a "value" that indicates Team A's "process in the perceived team members' incompatibilities or differences" (de Wit et al., 2011, p. 1). In other words, a team's temporal dynamics of a process variable needs to be *measured* empirically, rather than being *estimated* from a group of teams' levels of the process variable across discrete time moments. Information of the temporal dynamics shall be entered into multivariate analysis techniques as an *input*, rather than being obtained as a modelling output. This is a major distinction in the analysis between the intrateam longitudinal approach and the interteam longitudinal approach.

To define and measure change over time, we use the mathematical concept of the *n*th order derivative and apply it to a measured team process. In calculus, the depiction of raw scores over time (i.e., the zero order derivative) shows the tendency of change; the first order derivative denotes the change of the score in relations to the change of time; the second order derivative indicates the change of the first order derivative in relations to the change of time, in other words, "the change of change of scores over time".

As a "proof-of-concept" study, the aim of the article has been to introduce the principles and procedure of the intrateam longitudinal approach and to compare results of the intrateam approach and interteam approach in an empirical study that contains only one team process variable, one team output variable, and three measurement moments. We see three directions to extend the intrateam approach and further use it to advance team research. First of all, the intrateam approach can be used to study a broad range of team process variables (see for example, the 10 categories of team processes, such as coordination and strategic planning, identified by Marks and colleagues, 2001) and their causal links with hypothesized antecedents and consequences. This practice can greatly enlarge the existing body of knowledge on team development and team interactions over time.

The second direction is to extend the approach to longitudinal designs of more than three time moments. There are two ways to do so. First, in a study with t measurement moments, researchers can estimate,[12] for each team, from the first order derivative function up to the $t-1$th order derivative function via the technique of generalized local linear approximation (GLLA; see Deboeck et al., 2009, for details). With the estimated nth ($1 \leq n \leq t-1$) order derivative function, researchers are able to calculate all the nth order derivatives of a team across the measurement moments. The nth order derivatives denote the $n-1$th "layer" of change in the variable scores over a time span and at particular time moments, in other words, how fast the $n-1$th order derivative changes over time and at particular moments. For example, the first order derivative indicates the change of raw scores; the second order derivate indicates change of the first order derivate or, the change of change of raw scores. In the next step, the obtained values of all teams' nth order derivatives are entered into regressions or other multivariate analysis techniques. Although it is technically feasible to estimate the first to $t-1$th order derivative functions and obtain the values of all nth order derivatives over time and at particular moments, it is admittedly difficult to interpret the theoretical meanings of the nth order derivative once n is larger than three. Consider the case of third order derivative, what does the change of change of change in, for example, the raw scores of team conflict mean? How about the case of 11th order derivative? Does it make theoretical or conceptual sense to study the 10th "latent layer" of change in the raw scores of team conflict?

The second, more simple, way is to collapse the information from more than three time moments into three time moments. *On the basis of theoretical reasons*, researchers can evenly or unevenly divide the actual time moments into three brackets and aggregate the level of a team's process variable within each bracket. For example, in the case of nine measurement moments, researchers can, for each team, aggregate the levels within the first, middle, and last three moments, or aggregate the levels across the first two, middle five, and last two moments. Or when a study contains a number of measurement moments (but still less than 20 moments), researchers can choose the levels of a few time moments *around* the beginning, midpoint, or end as proxy delineation of a team's temporal dynamics and treat the following analyses as in the three-moment design.

The final direction for developing the intrateam approach is to pursue "temporalism" (Roe, 2008, 2009), that is, to empirically examine the relationships of the temporal dynamics of multiple team inputs, processes, and outputs. This practice implies that not only team processes, but also

[12]We use the term "estimation" for abstracting information of within-team changes over time from the data of each team's temporal dynamics. It differs from estimating the sample-level temporal dynamics from the discrete data points of individual teams across measurement moments as in the interteam approach.

team inputs and team outputs, are conceptualized and analysed as temporally dynamic phenomena. Studying such causal relationships requires even greater interteam variances, not less, in the temporal dynamics and supports the usage of the intrateam approach and its emphasis on descriptive validity. The statistical counterargument of losing robustness in the intrateam approach can be eventually answered by increasing the number of teams in a study or by replicating studies.

This article has several limitations. First, we have not taken measurement errors into account and treated measured scores as reflecting the true scores. We acknowledge that future research should try to assess measurement errors in a way that addresses the divergent requirements of within-team and between-team measurement. Considering the debate on which measurement criteria to apply in other psychology fields, we suggest that the assessment of within-team measurement errors can be done in a similar ways to the within-person dynamic factor analysis (Hamaker, Dolan, & Molenaar, 2005; Molenaar & Nesselroade, 2009). Second, the empirical study is limited in sample size and hence in its power to differentiate the dynamic patterns of team conflict and to establish associations between team conflict dynamics patterns and team satisfaction. Third, the use of project teams of graduate students limits the generalizability of the empirical conclusions to other types of project teams. Likewise, the 2-month research interval limits the generalizability of the conclusions to time intervals of other lengths. Fourth, in the empirical study, we did not use the change-rate-based or change-degree-based categorization scheme and therefore did not provide a comprehensive picture regarding the impact of team conflict dynamics on team satisfaction.

Despite these limitations, the intrateam approach adds to the team literature in a number of ways. First, it offers a conceptual approach and an analysis method team research, which acknowledge the temporal dynamic nature of team processes. As such, it bridge the gap between current theoretical conceptions of team processes (Ilgen et al., 2005; Marks et al., 2001) and prevailing research practice. Second, it offers a conceptual and methodological apparatus to study heterogeneity in team process dynamics, a subject that has been given little attention in the existing team literature until now. A priori specification of possible change trajectories and assessment of which of trajectories occur and under which conditions provides a novel way to study teams, which can lead hitherto unknown observations and thereby stimulate new theoretical developments. It resonates with Hackman's (1987) reminder that teams acting in a nontypical manner may perform better than other teams. Third, the intrateam approach has a great potential for further development. With principles easy to grasp conceptually, we expect team researchers to find challenges in resolving measurement issues, developing designs with more time points, elaborating techniques to analyse within-team covariations between trajectories, and so on. Fourth, the intrateam approach offers a tool that allows team researchers to engage more in studying the temporal dynamics of team interactions. This research practice will generate new data, findings, and knowledge that sharpen our understanding of how teams function over time and what makes them effective and ultimately have repercussions for managerial practice in organizations.

In our view, the intrateam approach and the interteam approach, with their divergent assumptions and orders of inference, serve different theoretical inquiries. Which approach to use in a particular study depends on the purpose and guiding theoretical perspective of the study. The intrateam approach, with its heterogeneity assumption and bottom-up, cases-to-sample order of inference, portrays the temporal dynamics pattern of *each team*, and uses the information of teams' heterogeneous temporal dynamics patterns to establish causal links with other variables. It regards "change over time" as a temporally -integral concept and associates teams' differential temporal dynamics patterns with differential antecedent or consequence levels. Therefore, it answers such questions as *what factors lead teams to demonstrate differential interaction patterns over time and how teams' differential development patterns of a particular interaction over time affect team outputs*. On the other hand, the interteam approach, with its homogeneity assumption and top-down, sample-to-cases order of inference, fits a particular function to the data of *all teams* in a sample and differentiates individual teams' temporal dynamics patterns as far as needed. It first estimates the sample-level change pattern from individual teams' levels of a process variable across discrete time moments and then treats individual teams' change patterns as random variations from the sample-level pattern. By doing so, the interteam approach is more appropriate for forecasting the sample mean of a process variable in the next team functioning episode, rather than examining the causes and impacts of the temporal dynamics of the team process variable. For example, after finding that a group of continuously functioning teams shows a linear development of task conflict over time, researchers can predict the sample mean of team task conflict in the next episode. They may also examine how proposed antecedents and consequences relate to the change of the sample's mean task conflict level over time. However, it cannot provide such conclusion that teams' (or particularly *a* team's) task conflict tends to develop linearly over time or further examine how the development of teams' (or a team's) task conflict over time relates to proposed antecedents and consequences.

The comparison and contrast between the intrateam and interteam approach touches upon a broader theoretical issue, that is, how to design studies that allow the identification and analysis of temporally dynamic phenomena in general. Many researchers before us have pointed out that one cannot use differential data to make inferences about phenomena occurring over time. Particularly instructive is the work by van de Ven and Poole (2005) and van de Ven (2007) who distinguish between dynamic process-based models and static variances-based models in organizational research, and by Roe (2008, 2009) who contrasts differential and temporal approaches in conceptualization and analysis. Similar ideas in team research have been long propagated by McGrath and colleagues (McGrath, 1984; McGrath & Tschan, 2004). From this perspective, we see the intrateam approach as a tool that may bring team research forward.

REFERENCES

Ancona, D. G., & Caldwell, D. F. (1992). Demography and design: Predictors of new product team performance. *Organization Science*, *3*, 321–341.

Arrow, H. (1997). Stability, bistability, and instability in small group influence patterns. *Journal of Personality and Social Psychology*, *72*, 75–85.

Behfar, K. J., Peterson, R. S., Mannix, E. A., & Trochim, W. M. K. (2008). The critical role of conflict resolution in teams: A close look at the links between conflict type, conflict management strategies, and team outcomes. *Journal of Applied Psychology*, *93*, 170–188.

Bliese, P. D., & Ployhart, R. E. (2002). Growth modeling using random coefficient models: Model building, testing, and illustration. *Organizational Research Methods*, *5*, 362–387.

Bonebright, D. A. (2010). 40 years of storming: A historical review of Tuckman's model of small group development. *Human Resource Development International*, *13*, 111–120.

Borsboom, D., Mellenbergh, G. J., & van Heerden, J. (2003). The theoretical status of latent variables. *Psychological Review*, *110*, 203–219.

Box, G. E. P., Jenkins, G. M., & Reinsel, G. C. (1994). *Time series analysis: Forecasting and control*. Englewood Cliffs, NJ: Prentice Hall.

Chan, D. (1998). The conceptualization and analysis of change over time: An integrative approach incorporating longitudinal mean and covariance structures analysis (LMACS) and multiple indicator latent growth modeling (MLGM). *Organizational Research Methods*, *1*, 421–485.

Chang, A., Bordia, P., & Duck, J. (2003). Punctuated equilibrium and linear progression: Toward a new understanding of group development. *Academy of Management Journal*, *46*, 106–117.

Chiocchio, F. (2007). Project team performance: A study of electronic task and coordination. *Project Management Journal*, *38*, 97–109.

Deboeck, P. R., Montpetit, M. A., Bergeman, C. S., & Boker, S. M. (2009). Using derivative estimates to describe intraindividual variability at multiple time scales. *Psychological Methods*, *14*, 367–386.

De Dreu, C. K. W., & Weingart, L. R. (2003). Task versus relationship conflict, team performance, and team member satisfaction: A meta-analysis. *Journal of Applied Psychology*, *88*, 741–749.

De Wit, F. C., Greer, L. L., & Jehn, K. A. (2011). The paradox of intragroup conflict: A meta-analysis. *Journal of Applied Psychology*, *97*, 360–390.

Ericksen, J., & Dyer, L. (2004). Right from the start: Exploring the effects of early team events on subsequent project team development and performance. *Administrative Science Quarterly*, *49*, 438–471.

Gersick, C. J. G. (1988). Time and transition in work teams: Toward a new model of group development. *Academy of Management Journal*, *31*, 9–41.

Gersick, C. J. G. (1989). Marking time: Predicable transitions in task groups. *Academy of Management Journal, 32*, 274–309.

Gersick, C. J. G. (1991). Revolutionary change theories: A multilevel exploration of the punctuated equilibrium paradigm. *Academy of Management Review, 16*, 10–36.

Hackman, J. R. (1987). The design of work teams. In J. W. Lorsch (Eds.), *Handbook of organizational behavior* (pp. 315–342). Englewood Cliffs, NJ: Prentice Hall.

Hamaker, E. L., Dolan, C. V., & Molenaar, P. M. (2005). Statistical modeling of the individual: Rationale and application of multivariate stationary time series analysis. *Multivariate Behavioral Research, 40*, 207–233.

Harrison, D. A., Price, K. H., Gavin, J. H., & Florey, A. T. (2002). Time, teams, and task performance: Changing effects of surface-level and deep-level diversity on group functioning. *Academy of Management Journal, 45*, 1029–1045.

Ilgen, D. R., Hollenbeck, J. R., Johnson, M., & Jundt, D. (2005). Teams in organizations: From Input-Process-Output models to IMOI models. *Annual Review of Psychology, 56*, 517–543.

Jehn, K. A., & Bendersky, C. (2003). Intragroup conflict in organizations: A contingency perspective on the conflict-outcome relationship. *Research in Organizational Behavior, 25*, 187–242.

Jehn, K. A., & Mannix, E. A. (2001). The dynamic nature of conflict: A longitudinal study of intragroup conflict and group performance. *Academy of Management Journal, 44*, 238–251.

Jehn, K. A., Northcraft, G. B., & Neale, M. A. (1999). Why differences make a difference: A field study of diversity, conflict, and performance in workgroups. *Administrative Science Quarterly, 44*, 741–763.

Knight, D., Pearce, C. L., Smith, K. G., Olian, J. D., Sims, H. P., Smith, K. A., & Flood, P. (1999). Top management team diversity, group process, and strategic consensus. *Strategic Management Journal, 20*, 445–465.

Kozlowski, S. W., & Bell, B. S. (2003). Work groups and teams in organizations. In W. C. Borman, D. R. Ilgen, & R. J. Klimoski (Eds.), *Handbook of psychology: Vol. 12. Industrial and organizational psychology* (pp. 333–375). New York, NY: Wiley.

Marks, M. A., Mathieu, J. E., & Zaccaro, S. J. (2001). A temporally based framework and taxonomy of team processes. *Academy of Management Review, 26*, 356–376.

McGrath, J. E. (1984). *Groups: Interaction and performance*. Englewood Cliffs, NJ: Prentice Hall.

McGrath, J. E. (1986). Studying groups at work: Ten critical needs for theory and practice. In P. Goodman, & Associates (Eds.), *Designing effective work groups* (pp. 362–391). San Francisco, CA: Jossey-Bass, Inc.

McGrath, J. E., & Tschan, F. (2004). *Temporal matters in social psychology: Examining the role of time in the lives of groups and individuals*. Washington, DC: American Psychological Association.

Mohammed, S., & Angell, L. C. (2004). Surface- and deep-level diversity in workgroups: Examining the moderating effects of team orientation and team process on relationship conflict. *Journal of Organizational Behavior, 25*, 1015–1039.

Molenaar, P. M., & Nesselroade, J. R. (2009). The recoverability of P-technique factor analysis. *Multivariate Behavioral Research, 44*, 130–141.

Moreland, R. L. (2010). Are dyads really groups? *Small Group Research, 41*, 268–274.

Okhuysen, G. A., & Waller, M. J. (2002). Focusing on midpoint transitions: An analysis of boundary conditions. *Academy of Management Journal, 45*, 1056–1065.

Olson, B. J., Parayitam, S., & Bao, Y. (2007). Strategic decision making: The effects of cognitive diversity, conflict, and trust on decision outcomes. *Journal of Management, 33*, 196–222.

Pearsall, M. J., Ellis, A. J., & Evans, J. M. (2008). Unlocking the effects of gender faultlines on team creativity: Is activation the key? *Journal of Applied Psychology, 93*, 225–234.

Pelled, L. H., Eisenhardt, K. M., & Xin, K. R. (1999). Exploring the black box: An analysis of work group diversity, conflict, and performance. *Administrative Science Quarterly, 44*, 1–28.

Poole, M., & Holmes, M. E. (1995). Decision development in computer-assisted group decision making. *Human Communication Research, 22*, 90–127.

Raes, A. M. L. (2009). *Top management team impact on organizations: Determinants from inside and outside the boardroom.* Unpublished doctoral dissertation, Maastricht University, The Netherlands.

Roe, R. (2009). Perspectives on time and the chronometric study of what happens in organizations. In R. A. Roe, M. J. Waller, & S. R. Clegg (Eds.), *Time in organizational research* (pp. 291–313). Abingdon, UK: Routledge.

Roe, R. A. (2008).Time in applied psychology: The study of "what happens" rather than what "what is". *The European Psychologist, 13*, 37–52.

Shin, S. J., & Zhou, J. (2007). When is educational specialization heterogeneity related to creativity in research and development teams? Transformational leadership as a moderator. *Journal of Applied Psychology, 92*, 1709–1721.

Tuckman, B. W. (1965). Developmental sequences in small groups. *Psychological Bulletin, 63*, 384–399.

Tuckman, B. W., & Jensen, M. A. (1977). Stages of small-group development revisited. *Group and Organization Studies, 2*, 419–427.

Vandenberg, R. J., & Lance, C. E. (2000). A review and synthesis of the measurement invariance literature: Suggestions, practices, and recommendations for organizational research. *Organizational Research Methods, 3*, 4–69.

Van de Ven, A. H. (2007). *Engaged scholarship: A guide for organizational and social research.* New York, NY: Oxford University Press.

Van de Ven, A. H., & Poole, M. S. (2005). Alternative approach for studying organizational change. *Organization Studies, 26*, 1377–1404.

Williams, K. D. (2010). Dyads can be groups (and often are). *Small Group Research, 41*, 268–274.

Zaheer, S., Albert, S., & Zaheer, A. (1999). Time scales and organizational theory. *Academy of Management Review, 24*, 725–741.

EUROPEAN JOURNAL OF WORK AND
ORGANIZATIONAL PSYCHOLOGY
2012, 21 (5), 749–777

Setting the tone: Early interaction patterns in swift-starting teams as a predictor of effectiveness

Fred R. H. Zijlstra[1], Mary J. Waller[2], and Sybil I. Phillips[3]

[1]Department of Work and Social Psychology, Maastricht University, Maastricht, The Netherlands

[2]Schulich School of Business, York University, Toronto, Canada

[3]Institute of Aviation, University of Illinois at Urbana-Champaign, Champaign, IL, USA

Many organizations rely on the functioning of teams. In this study we focus on swift-starting teams—that is, ad hoc teams formed for immediate task performance, such as emergency or rescue teams or aviation crews, with highly trained members who have generally not previously worked together as a team. Previous research suggests that teams develop task performance capability over time, but that stable patterns of interaction in teams emerge very quickly. We suggest that these interaction patterns help swift starting teams engage in immediate task performance. In particular, we hypothesize that effective teams will exhibit more interaction patterns, but fewer unique patterns, than less effective teams. We describe an observational study of 18 swift-starting aviation crews. Our results identify the early emergence of specific interaction patterns and indicate significant differences between the patterns of effective and ineffective crews. The effective teams in our sample exhibited patterns that were more stable in duration, more stable in complexity, and more reciprocal as compared to those of less effective teams. We close with implications for work on team interaction, and suggestions for future research and team trainers.

Keywords: Team interaction; Behavioral patterns; Team effectiveness; Aviation crews; Swift-starting teams.

Correspondence should be addressed to Fred R. H. Zijlstra, Department of Work and Social Psychology, PO Box 616, Maastricht University, Maastricht 6200 MD, The Netherlands. E-mail: fred.zijlstra@maastrichtuniversity.nl

We thank Alex De Voogt, Robert van Doorn, Rachel Katterl and Fletcher Chauncy for their help in data coding.

Teams have become very important to organizations in recent decades. It has been well documented that organizations try to adapt to unpredictable, fast-paced environments by forming team-based structures (Barua, Lee, & Whinston, 1995; Bennis, 1965; Huber, 2004; Mohrman, Cohen, & Mohrman, 1995). While teams provide the means to decentralize decision-making power (Richardson, Vandenberg, Blum, & Roman, 2002), enhance cross-functional cooperation (Pinto, Pinto, & Prescott, 1993), and create knowledge in organizations (Argote, 1999), they also provide organizations with leverage through their flexible deployment. As demand shifts or critical unexpected events emerge, teams can be quickly formed and deployed to match organizational or societal needs.

In order to deal with unexpected events and emergencies, organizations often deploy teams that have specifically been created for these situations. These temporary teams are referred to as action teams and consist of highly skilled specialists that cooperate in events that require improvisation in unpredictable circumstances (Hollenbeck, Beersma, & Schouten, 2012; Sundstrom, De Meuse, & Futrell, 1990). These teams must begin task performance activities as quickly as possible, and their members must interact to perform complex, coordinated work (McKinney, Barker, Davis, & Smith, 2005). For example, ad hoc teams in healthcare organizations form rapidly in order to immediately address complex problems and emergencies (Marsch et al., 2005). Similarly, news organizations rely on teams of journalists to form and begin immediate coverage of unexpected events around the world (Archibold, 2003), later disbanding to follow different emerging events elsewhere. Flight crews in airlines are constantly formed and disbanded by rostering systems designed to meet a tangled array of logistical demands and events, and crew members are expected to effectively fly together immediately after meeting each other (Ginnett, 1987).

In many action teams, membership is based on who happens to be on shift or assigned to duty at the time and place of team formation. As a result, teams with low levels of familiarity are quickly formed to address critical, time-pressured situations with no time to explore personal similarities and differences, or to settle into familiar roles and go through the team development processes as described in the classic group literature (e.g., Lacoursiere, 1980; Tuckman, 1965; Tuckman & Jensen, 1977). However, previous research also suggests that the initial moments of team development prior to work activities are extremely important to subsequent team outcomes (Eriksen & Dyer, 2004). In this period, teams normally develop and build the trust that helps communication patterns involved in exchanging and sharing information, which are crucial for team performance (Uitdewilligen, Waller, & Zijlstra, 2010).

Since these swift-starting teams have little time together before engaging in cooperative task performance, understanding more about their initial patterns of interaction may provide insight into their subsequent effectiveness. As Gersick and Hackman note, whether teams create their patterns of interaction routines or import them from members' previous experiences, "both processes result in routines getting established very early in the life of the group, and established very quickly with little or no time specifically devoted to hammering them out" (1990, p. 78). Furthermore, early team interaction patterns tend to be extremely persistent, affecting team processes after initial team formation (Feldman, 1984; Ginnett, 1987), but little research exists regarding the relationship between such patterns and overall team effectiveness in new teams that engage in immediate task performance. Accordingly, we focus here on identifying stable patterns in the early interactions of new swift-starting teams, and on the relationship between these patterns and subsequent team effectiveness.

In the following section, drawing on previous work concerning team development processes and the emergence of patterns and routines in teams, we develop specific hypotheses linked to this focus. We describe a study of newly formed flight crews in their initial stage of activity, and analyse how their early interaction patterns develop over time. By doing so, we hope to extend knowledge concerning both team interaction and team effectiveness by comparing initial interaction patterns between more and less effective crews. We close with implications for future research and for trainers of teams that must make a swift start.

SWIFT-STARTING TEAMS

Action teams consist of "highly skilled specialist teams cooperating in brief performance events that require improvisation in unpredictable circumstances" (Hollenbeck et al., 2012; Ziegert, Klein, & Xiao, 2001)—circumstances such as crisis management situations in the civilian domain (Schraagen, Huis in 't Veld, & de Koning, 2010). A subcategory of action teams are swift-starting teams, which are newly formed, ad hoc teams composed of highly trained individuals who must engage in the immediate interdependent performance of complex tasks (McKinney et al., 2005). In general, swift-starting teams involve (1) members who are competent and familiar with their complex work environments, (2) teams working quickly under situations of very evident time pressure, (3) stable roles but ad hoc team membership, and (4) complex, interdependent tasks that rely on team members' interactions during the performance and coordinated execution of well-trained skills.

Although it is possible that members of swift-starting teams may be acquainted and may have worked together on past teams, swift-starting teams generally have ad hoc, fleeting, or even fluid memberships (Klein, Ziegert, Knight, & Xiao, 2006) with stable roles. For example, upon realization of a crisis situation, the Port of Rotterdam brings together top-level personnel from various organizational functions (e.g., fire brigade captain, police captain, medical adviser) to form a crisis management team (Uitdewilligen & Waller, 2011); in this swift-starting team configuration, the roles in each crisis management team remain stable, but the individuals occupying the roles change depending on which individuals happen to be on shift at that particular time. As James and Wooten (2010) note, whether the individuals occupying roles remain the same or not, teams with stable role configurations can leverage this stability by developing a set of role-based routines during training simulations. Indeed, some extremely novel and complex crisis situations may require teams with stable roles but with memberships that are fluid and shifting to allow a higher level of response and adaptation (James & Wooten, 2010). For example, Klein et al. (2006) describe "extreme action teams" that change their memberships in a fluid manner while performing extremely complex tasks, essentially letting the demands of the tasks and non-routine events drive what members the team needs at what times. However, even within these very adaptive teams, a core complement of stable roles exists in the teams across time, although individual team members and some peripheral roles circulate in and out of the team depending on the situation. Importantly, a substantial literature concerning teams in aviation (e.g., Wiener, Kanki, & Helmreich, 1994), medicine (e.g., Tschan et al., 2006), nuclear power plants (e.g., Waller, Gupta, & Giambatista, 2004), and other high-reliability contexts suggests that even given the stability of role- and expertise-based routines, teams with highly trained, role-occupying members may still exhibit a wide range of behaviors and interactions during task performance, leading to different levels of team effectiveness.

In addition to the presence of stable roles in swift-starting teams, the process of team formation sets these teams apart from other organizational teams. Following Owens, Mannix, and Neale's (1998) assumptions about teams in organizations, we assume the environment of swift-starting teams to be task- and performance-driven; thus, we assume the formation of teams to be motivated chiefly by organizational needs and situational demands, rather than by the social needs of individuals in search of a team. Indeed, swift-starting teams form due to the happenstance propinquity of trained individuals (e.g., nurses and doctors who happen to be on shift during an emergency), by organizational rostering methods (e.g., airline pilots who happen to be assigned to the same flight), or by a combination of the two. Thus, for swift-starting teams, the process of formation does not necessarily entail an initial perception of team attractiveness or an active choice by individuals to join the team. Instead, the formation of swift-starting teams entails the initial coming together, physically or virtually, of individuals who have been identified (or who self-identify) as team members. In contrast to this formation activity, the full development of swift-starting teams via the socio-emotional interaction described by many existing models of group and team development is not likely to occur due to the immediate and intense task focus and short duration of the team itself. Yet, the initial interaction between team members may have a pronounced effect on subsequent communication and interaction (Gersick & Hackman, 1990), and thus the effectiveness of swift-starting teams. Although a person holding a particular role may be expected to take the initiative in a situation, variance emanating from unique individual and team differences still exists, and influences if, when, and how it may be done.

SWIFT-STARTING TEAM INTERACTION PATTERNS

Marks and colleagues explicated a model of the rhythmic nature of team processes (Marks, Matthieu, & Zaccaro, 2001) depicting cycles or performance episodes within which teams repeatedly cycle between periods of actions (such as coordination and monitoring) and periods of transition (such as retrospective analysis or goal specification). This and other temporal team models (e.g., Kozlowski, Gully, Nason, & Smith, 1999) imply that patterns of team activity unfold over time and can vary dramatically, as different teams may structure their actions within a given episode in discrepant ways. One such type of pattern is an interaction pattern. Interaction patterns in teams are defined as recurrent sets of different types of verbalization, typically for the purpose of collective action and coordination (Zellmer-Bruhn, Waller, & Ancona, 2004). The models described above, combined with evidence that interaction patterns early in a team's time together may solidify or routinize how team members communicate and work together (e.g., Eriksen & Dyer, 2004), lead us to ask: What types of early interaction patterns in swift-starting teams are associated with team effectiveness?

One possible answer to this question can be found in recent work on group and team development. Much of the existing literature on group and team development suggests that a certain amount of team longevity is required for a team to mature and approach its maximum level of effectiveness. This literature on group development generally rests on stage or life-cycle models (Lacoursiere, 1980; McGrew, Bilotta, & Denney, 1999; Tuckman, 1965; Tuckman & Jensen, 1977; Wheelan, 1994), and suggests that groups pass through a sequential set of phases over time. Group effectiveness is seen as dependent in large part on the eventual entry into a task- or productivity-oriented stage "marked by energetic collective work focused on reaching group goals" (Arrow, Poole, Henry, Wheelan, & Moreland, 2004, p. 83). Other work offers alternatives to a sequential stage view of group development (Bradford, Gibb, & Benne, 1964; Bales, 1950;

Gersick, 1988, 1989). A recent departure from stage-based models is work that adopts the perspective of activity cycles—periods of time shorter than the entire lifecycle of the group—and the phases of activity within each cycle (cf. Ancona & Chong, 1996; Ancona & Waller, 2007). For example, Marks et al. (2001) proposed a model of team process that entails the episodic simultaneous and sequential performance of goal-oriented action by teams over time. Similarly, Wheelan and Williams' (2003) field study of interaction patterns in ongoing work groups during a group meeting entailed the mapping of interaction patterns and cycles, and categorizing groups based on these pattern characteristics. The authors were able to link specific pattern types to the frequency of work statements, dependency statements, and levels of development across groups.

Whether teams develop over time in a series of sequential phases or during episodic or cyclical action periods, we suggest here that most swift-starting teams conclude their "brief performance events" (Ziegert et al., 2001) and disband before having the time to reach the productive stages, established equilibriums, or advanced activity cycles depicted in many models of group development; additionally, the pressing focus on the task at hand, combined with the high level of familiarity of team members with the task environment in swift-starting teams, likely precludes much of the socio-emotional interaction used in previous work to define stages of team development. However, the interaction patterns that first emerge in a swift-starting team may exert considerable influence on team coordination and effectiveness even though the team quickly disbands. Therefore, considering the very short, task-focused tenure of swift-starting teams, and following Wheelan and Williams (2003) and Ginnett (1987), we focus here on identifying characteristics of the early patterns of interaction most likely to persist and influence swift-starting team coordination and effectiveness. For this we focus on the first 15 to 20 minutes of team interaction.

In line with Zellmer-Bruhn et al.'s (2004) work on team routines, we focused primarily on interaction patterns in teams, and distinguished verbalizations for the purpose of collective action and coordination (commands, questions), and verbalizations that are related to team development (laughter, anger). Whether as an attempt to alleviate social uncertainty and anxiety (Hackman & Morris, 1975) or due simply to practice in other contexts, individuals tend to form patterns of interaction quickly when they work in teams (Potter, Cooke, & Balthazard, 2000). Moreover, the interaction patterns that emerge early in a team's life tend to be extremely persistent (Feldman, 1984). For example, Gersick (1988) noted in her in-depth field study that in one team, interactions lasting less than one minute during the first moments of the team's formation "launched interaction patterns that lasted through the first half of the team's 12-week calendar" and effectively limited any task progress during that time (Gersick & Hackman, 1990, p. 77). In their study of project teams, Eriksen and Dyer (2004) found that a well-planned and thorough mobilization and launch effectively provided successful teams with a persistent "script" for future meetings and interactions.

While both Gersick's and Eriksen and Dyer's results concern teams that were not swift-starting, other work provides congruent evidence for swift-starting teams; Ginnett (1987), for example, found that captains' behaviors during the first moments of flight crew interactions effectively set the tone for crew interactions over the first and any subsequent flights. In general, and as Feldman observes, the "first behavior pattern that emerges in a group often sets group expectations" (Feldman, 1984, p. 52). Some scholars suggest that if patterns of interaction become entrenched, they may inhibit the adaptation of teams later to unexpected crisis situations (Gersick & Hackman, 1990); however, as noted by Zellmer-Bruhn and colleagues (2004), stable patterns of interaction in teams may improve efficiency by reducing uncertainty and saving time by eliminating the need to deliberate over who should say what or ask whom each time a situation is encountered. For example, when a command is issued, it is likely that a response will follow; likewise a "question" will generally be followed by an "answer". These are two examples of simple interaction patterns that facilitate the coordination of a team's activities. However, a co-pilot who seemingly randomly vacillates between offering lengthy suggestions for some tasks and remaining silent during other similar tasks may increase uncertainty and reduce the efficiency of both pilots, especially when compared to an aviation crew in which the co-pilot engages in more stable, predictable task communication. As a consequence, one could argue that when comparing the overall predictability of communication—that is, the amount of communication that falls into any pattern—we might see less patterned communication in less effective teams. In other words, the portion of communication that falls into no pattern at all is higher in less effective teams. Given the paramount needs in swift-starting teams to save time and begin immediate and efficient task execution, we hypothesize:

> *Hypothesis 1:* Early in their interaction, effective swift-starting teams engage in more patterned communication than do ineffective swift-starting teams.

While the hypothesis above pertains to the overall frequency of patterned interaction, it does not specify how many unique patterns might occur in that interaction. A pattern of interaction can be any sequence of behavioral categories that occurs more than could be expected on a random basis. For example, the sequence of asking a question and providing an answer is a pattern that is more likely to happen in this order than the reverse order. The different combinations of behaviors are likely to occur several times, and thus are seen as patterns of behavior. Unique patterns differ from each other; a pattern with a behavioral sequence "question–question–command" is different from the pattern "command–question–command". They are both unique patterns. Furthermore, a team might exhibit two unique patterns of interaction, but engage in each pattern five times; a different team may exhibit five unique patterns of interaction, but only engage in each pattern twice. Both teams would exhibit the same amount of patterned interaction (i.e., 10 occurrences), but the second team would spend significantly more time switching from one pattern to another, all else being equal, which could be detrimental to the efficiency of team coordination. Supporting this reasoning, Kanki and colleagues (Kanki, Folk, & Irwin, 1991; Kanki & Foushee, 1989; Kanki, Lozito, & Foushee, 1989) found that higher performing teams created a constrained set of unique interaction patterns, while lower performing teams created a wide range of complex interaction patterns that involved more switching among actors and combined numerous smaller patterns.

Kanki and colleagues interpreted the low number of unique interaction patterns in the higher performing teams as the adoption of a straightforward, standard form of communicating, and the complexity and heterogeneity of lower performing teams' patterns as the relative absence of such a straightforward, standard form. Although this previous work focuses chiefly on the range of patterns across teams, we suggest here that a similar difference occurs within teams—namely, that effective teams exhibit fewer unique interaction patterns of less complexity than do less effective teams. Accordingly, we hypothesize:

> *Hypothesis 2:* Early in their interaction, effective swift-starting teams develop significantly fewer unique patterns of interaction than do ineffective swift-starting teams.

In addition to the creation of patterns of interaction that facilitate team coordination processes, the timing of interaction patterns may also influence the effectiveness of swift-starting teams. For example, in her study of airline flight crews, Waller (1999) found that higher performing crews typically followed the occurrence of non-routine events with interactions concerning task prioritization and resource allocation, and did so more quickly than did lower performing crews. Consistent with Kanki and colleagues (see above), Stachowski, Kaplan, and Waller (2009) also found that higher performing teams had significantly fewer patterns, less complex patterns, and shorter patterns than did lower performing teams. Given our assumptions here that swift-starting teams are embedded in task-focused environments and are compelled to engage in immediate task execution, it seems reasonable to expect the initial patterns of interaction in such teams to revolve around task execution as well. Based on the existing results described above, it can be argued that effectiveness in communication is related to the frequency, length, and complexity of patterns. Therefore, we focus here on extending this existing work and suggest that higher performing teams exhibit fewer fluctuations among their interaction patterns, thus enabling even higher levels of predictability and rapid coordination. We therefore expect that interaction patterns of high performing teams will be more stable as expressed in less variation in duration (length) of the communication pattern, and fewer fluctuations in the levels of communications (complexity). We used changes in standard deviations as indicators of stability: A smaller standard deviation means more stability. Thus, we hypothesize:

> *Hypothesis 3:* Early in their interaction, effective swift-starting teams exhibit initial patterns of interaction that vary significantly less in duration than those of ineffective swift-starting teams.

> *Hypothesis 4:* Early in their interaction, effective swift-starting teams exhibit initial patterns of interaction that vary significantly less in complexity than those of ineffective swift-starting teams.

Finally, the work of Meyerson, Weick, and Kramer (1996) suggests that effective temporary teams establish patterns indicating "swift trust" very early in their interactions, and that team members trust each other immediately due to their categorical judgements of other team members based on positive stereotypes. The professional context (i.e., medicine, aviation, etc.) within which swift-starting teams operate, as well as members' highly trained status, may create a preliminary sense of trust through the expectation that professional norms and standards will be followed by all team members. Importantly, Jarvenpaa and Leidner (1999) found in their study of virtual temporary teams that the pattern of action initiation by team members followed by responses from other team members was linked to higher levels of trust in teams. Other research focusing on swift-starting teams suggests that higher performing teams exhibit more reciprocal interaction patterns than do other teams (Kanki, Palmer & Veinott, 1991). A reciprocal interaction pattern is a pattern in which the parties of an interaction participate in a balanced, two-way exchange. Given the relationship between trust and team effectiveness (Costa, Roe, & Taillieu, 2001; Edmondson, 1999; Korsgaard, Schweiger, & Sapienza, 1995), we hypothesize:

> *Hypothesis 5:* Early in their interaction, effective swift-starting teams exhibit more reciprocal patterns of interaction than do ineffective swift-starting teams.

To summarize, although previous research on project teams, virtual teams, and swift-starting teams suggests important effects of initial development activity and interaction patterns that emerge early in teams, we know little about how development and interaction patterns influence the effectiveness of swift-starting teams. For our study of such development, we have chosen to focus on newly formed aviation flight crews as they train in a flight simulator. Members of flight crews working for commercial airlines are often scheduled to work together as strangers, only becoming acquainted on their first meeting on the flight deck or in the flight preparation room. Many flight crews are composed of two pilots and may be considered to be dyads or teams. We are aware that the status of dyads as teams has been debated in recent literature (Moreland, 2010; Williams, 2010), with some in favor of and some opposed to the classification of dyads as teams. Here, while acknowledging that some aspects of team behavior and dynamics (for example, network emergence) cannot be ascertained through the study of dyads, we follow Williams' perspective on teams, relying on the definition of team as "a distinguishable set of two or more people who interact, dynamically, interdependently, and adaptively toward a common goal/objective/mission, who have each been assigned specific roles or functions to perform, and who have a limited life-span of membership" (Salas, Dickenson, Converse, & Tannenbaum, 1992, p. 4; see also Hackman, 1993). All aspects of this definition apply to a flight crew, and thus from this perspective, dyads are the smallest form of teams.

A flight crew consists of a captain and a first officer, which indicates the hierarchy within this team. The role of captain refers to the responsibilities for the entire crew (including cabin crew) and passengers with respect to safety. However, while flying the airplane, the roles are generally geared towards operating the aircraft, and each of the two pilots performs the role of pilot flying (PF) and pilot not flying (PNF) in either the inbound or outbound leg of the flight. This division of roles refers to the specific tasks the pilots have during the flight (i.e. navigation, communication with air traffic control, aircraft handling, monitoring and balancing fuel, and so on). In every instance pilots must communicate and consult with each other before taking any action, as they both must be aware of and agree with the steps taken in the various procedures. This requires interacting with each other in order to establish and maintain a shared mental model of the situation. Typically pilots are assigned flights according to an individual rostering system, and they must begin working immediately as a team, without knowing each other from previous flights. Very often they meet for the first time during pre-flight preparation.

A theoretical (and practical) reason for this choice of sample could be that since there is very little information available to address our topic, it may be good to begin empirical inquiry with situations that are relatively unambiguous and not very complex as far as the interactions are concerned. For these reasons, we will describe a study of 18 newly formed aviation flight crews, and present results based on detailed analyses of the crews' interactions during their initial pre-flight activities.

METHOD

We investigated early interaction patterns of swift-starting teams by collecting data from newly formed flight crews during their first interactions together (i.e., the flight preparation phase—lasting approximately 15–20 minutes) in flight simulator training sessions conducted as part of a semester-long aviation course. Each crew consisted of two licensed pilots who were undergoing their initial training as members of multi-pilot aviation flight crews; none of the pilots in our sample had prior experience flying as a crew member with another pilot. All participants were FAA-licensed pilots enrolled in a crew resource management (CRM) course as part of an aeronautics programme at a large Midwestern university in the United States. For our data collection we relied on procedures and methods of data collection that have been used in previous studies of team dynamics with pilot teams (Foushee, 1984; Ginnett, 1990; Kanki, 1996; Kanki & Foushee, 1989). In addition we used a pattern recognition algorithm to identify and characterize interaction patterns in team process data that was previously used by Stachowski et al. (2009). This procedure will be outlined in more detail below.

We collected data from 18 crews as they prepared to "fly" their first leg of flight together as a crew in a stationary flight simulator. Each simulator flight was videotaped. The simulator included all instrumentation and manual controls found in a light twin-engine aircraft such as a Beechcraft Duchess or Piper Seminole. Pilots were randomly assigned to the role of PF (left seat) or PNF (right seat). The hierarchical role elements referring to the roles of captain and co-pilot were not emphasized in these sessions as there were no passengers or other crew members.

The leg of simulated flight followed a scripted scenario that included origination, destination, route, air traffic control information, weather information, and any non-routine events (e.g., engine malfunctions, systems failures, or weather-related events) that were scripted to occur. Scenarios were developed by the flight instructors teaching the course, in accordance with Federal Aviation Administration guidelines. Pilots were aware that their crew performance in the simulator comprised 25% of their course grade and impacted the flight instructors' overall assessments of their flying skills; thus, the context was both realistic and consequential for participants' professional flight certifications. All pilots in the class volunteered to participate in the study. One of two flight instructors observed each leg of flight flown by each crew. Both flight instructors had extensive licensure and experience in aviation training, and both had worked as commercial pilots. During each flight simulation, the flight instructor sat behind the two pilots and played the role of ground operations and air traffic control personnel during the simulation, using information scripted for that flight. After each videotaped simulator flight, the instructor rated crew effectiveness using the LINE/LOS behavioral marker checklist (Helmreich, Merritt, & Wilhelm, 1998), which is widely cited in the aviation literature and is the basis of many airlines' crew effectiveness evaluations (Flin & Martin, 2001). The checklist is used to evaluate non-technical team coordination behaviors of crews as they fly actual or simulated flights. It consists of behavioral anchors that instructors use to indicate whether or not specific behaviors have occurred (similar to Behaviorally Anchored Rating Scales—BARS). For example, the dimension "Situational Awareness and Decision Making" includes the following behavioral anchors: Workload and task distribution is clearly communicated and acknowledged by crew members. Adequate time is provided for completion of tasks, e.g., establish well in advance who is flying the leg; establish responsibility for non-routine types of communications. As an additional example, the dimension "Automation Management" includes the behavioral anchor: Crew members verbalize and acknowledge entries and changes to automated systems parameters.

The LINE/LOS checklist requires instructors to rate crew effectiveness for each phase of the flight (i.e., preflight, take-off, cruise, and approach and landing), indicating whether performance is "poor" (significantly below expectations), or meets "minimum expectations" (is less than desired for effective crew operations), or is "standard" (as should normally occur in flight operations), to "outstanding" (truly noteworthy and effective). After the flight, instructors made an assessment of overall crew effectiveness based on their assessments per phase of flight. We used instructors' evaluations of overall crew effectiveness as our measure of crew effectiveness. Crews with assessments of "standard" and "outstanding" were considered to be effective crews (high performers). Of the crews in our study, 11 were assessed to be "low performers" (i.e., rated as "poor" or "minimum expectations") and seven were assessed to be "high performers". Based on these effectiveness ratings, crews were assigned an effectiveness score of 1 (low) or 2 (high) for our analyses.

Each flight simulation was recorded on videotape, and two coders were trained to observe and code the pilots' behavior from video recordings. The two coders independently coded each incidence of a variety of crew member behaviors. The categories of behavior were drawn from previous research on crew communication and coordination behaviors (Kanki & Foushee, 1989; Kanki et al., 1991) and from previous research on team development (Sarker

& Sahay, 2003; Tuckman & Jensen, 1977). These behavior categories encapsulate the majority of behaviors pilots use in their work (Flin & Martin, 2001), and the crew behaviors that were coded included those behaviors that are associated with crew communication and coordination (commands, observations, suggestions, enquiries, and answers) and those behaviors associated by previous research with initial team development (disagreeing, laughing, anger, apologies, and non-work communication). The various behaviors that were coded by the raters, their definitions and examples are presented in Table 1.

Following Waller (1999), the entire preflight period was divided in intervals of 10 s, and each type of behavior was coded as present (1) or absent (0) for every 10 s interval for each crew. "Preflight" was defined as all activity from the moment the pilots arrived on the simulator flight deck until they received takeoff clearance. The average duration of this segment of flight for the crews we observed was 17 minutes. The title of the pilot engaging in a behavior (PF or PNF) was also recorded, as was the sequential number of the 10 s interval. Both coders were extensively trained and achieved an inter-coder reliability of 0.82 (Cohen's kappa), indicating a high level of agreement as to the occurrence of the specific behaviors.

TABLE 1
Descriptions and examples of behavioral coding

Verbalization type	*Description*	*Example*
Command	Specific request or demand for action	"Go ahead and input the frequencies"
Observation	Recognizing or noting a fact or occurrence	"We have good weather today"
Suggestion	Recommendation for action	"Maybe we should call the tower for that"
Inquiry	Request for information	"What is that supposed to be?"
Answer	Supplying information for an inquiry	"It should be set to 4100"
Disagreeing	Response not in agreement with a previous statement	"No, actually that should be 4200"
Laughing	Laughter or clearly humorous remark	"Ha ha!"
Anger	Comment beyond mere disagreement, or a ridiculing remark	"No, I told you that's wrong!"
Apologies	Remark expressing sorrow or regret for prior action	"Sorry about that"
Non-work	Social non-task communication	"Did you have a good weekend?"

ANALYSES

The coded data were used to identify patterns in the interactions of the crews. In order to identify patterns of interactions, we used the software algorithm Theme (Noldus Software). This software has been used for a number of years by researchers in animal behavior, psycho-pharmacology, child development and child psychology, sports performance, and also in team research (Ballard, Tschan, & Waller, 2008; Stachowski et al., 2009) to detect non-obvious temporal patterns of behavior.

Patterns of interaction and behavior can be extremely difficult to detect with the naked eye, especially when other behaviors interrupt the temporal sequence of the behaviors forming a pattern. Such patterns may also be extremely difficult, if not impossible, to detect with procedures such as time series analysis or Markov chains (Magnusson, 2000). In general, the Theme algorithm identifies patterns in sequential data by using three steps. First, the algorithm identifies simple temporal patterns—or "T-patterns"—of two behaviors that occur in time-coded sequential data significantly more often than by chance (see Figure 1). For instance, the sequence: "Question (A)—Answer (B)" is a T-pattern, consisting of two behaviors. A T-pattern is "essentially a combination of events in which the events occur in the same order with the real-time differences between consecutive pattern components remaining relatively invariant (i.e., the time difference between A and B will be $x+/-\ y$) with respect to an expectation assuming, as a null hypothesis, that each component is independently and randomly distributed over time" (Borrie et al., 2002, p. 846). As explained by Magnusson, "if A is an earlier and B a later component of the same recurring T-pattern, then after an occurrence of A at t, there is an interval $[t+\text{d}1,\ t+\text{d}2]$ $(\text{d}2 \geq \text{d}1 \geq 0)$ that tends to contain at least one occurrence of B more often than would be expected by chance" (2000, p. 94). In sum, the algorithm detects whether there are sequences of behavior that occur more frequently than would be expected by chance.

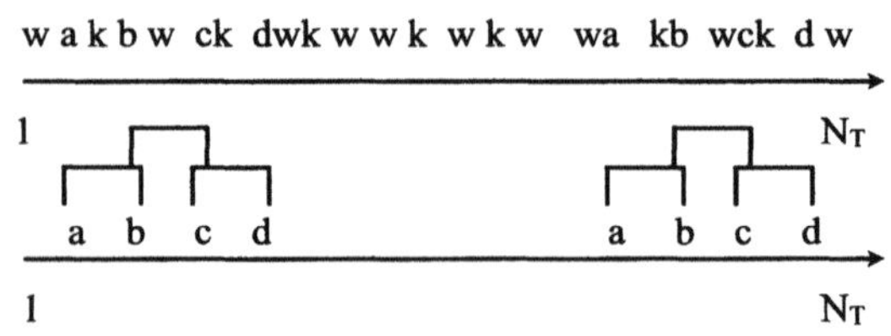

Figure 1. Representation of recurrent T-patterns of behavior (characters represents a behavior on a time line). The characters w, a, k, etc. on the top line represent various types of behaviors; the second line shows the recurrent behavior patterns that are hidden in the top line. In fact this figure shows two related T-patterns (a,b and c,d), and this is repeated some time later.

Second, after simple two-behavior T-patterns are identified, the algorithm cycles through the data, building more complex hierarchical patterns of relationships among T-patterns. This so-called "bottom-up" approach of pattern detection identifies simple patterns first and then detects larger patterns as a combination of the simpler ones. Finally, the algorithm eliminates patterns that are less complete versions of other patterns. For example, as explained by Borrie and colleagues: "a pattern Q = (ABCDE) may be partially detected as, for example, (ACDE) or (BDE) or (ABCE); since elements of Q are missing, these three patterns constitute less complete descriptions of the underlying patterning. A newly detected pattern Q_x is thus considered equally or less complete than an already detected pattern Q_y if Q_x and Q_y occur equally often and all events in Q_x also occur in Q_y. In this case, Q_x is eliminated" (2002, p. 847)

The algorithm allows the user to select frequency and probability requirements for the patterns detected. In our analyses, we chose to include only those patterns that occurred at least three times during the pre-flight activities for our crews. This criterion of three times was chosen because it implied that the pattern would, on average, occur at least once every five minutes with an average of 17 minutes for the observed periods. Furthermore, we required a 95% probability that patterns occurred above and beyond chance.

Using the algorithm, we determined the number of times patterns of verbalizations occurred (H1), the number of unique patterns generated (H2), the length of patterns (H3), the number of levels in pattern hierarchies (H4), and the number of unique mono-actor patterns and their occurrences (H5) for each team. Following Magnusson (2000) and Stachowski et al. (2009), we used the number of levels in the hierarchies of patterns to represent pattern complexity (see Figure 2), and we used the number of unique mono-actor patterns (i.e., patterns of interaction that involve only one person) and the frequency of their occurrences as an inverse measure of the reciprocity or balanced nature of interactions. We chose to use the number of mono-actor patterns and the incidence of these patterns rather than the number of multi-actor patterns because multi-actor patterns, while involving both pilots, could mask the fact that a pattern might be dominated by the behavior of one pilot; for example, a recurrent pattern involving one verbalization by Pilot B and four verbalizations by Pilot A would be categorized as a multi-actor pattern, but would mask the domination of the pattern by Pilot A. Conversely, the number of mono-actor patterns represents more clearly the evidence of one-sided, non-reciprocal interactions in teams. A mono-actor pattern would be identified if, for example, the same pilot made an inquiry and subsequently answered his or her own inquiry (assuming this pattern met our frequency and probability requirements); if the pilot engaged in this pattern numerous times, the frequency of the pattern's occurrence would also be high.

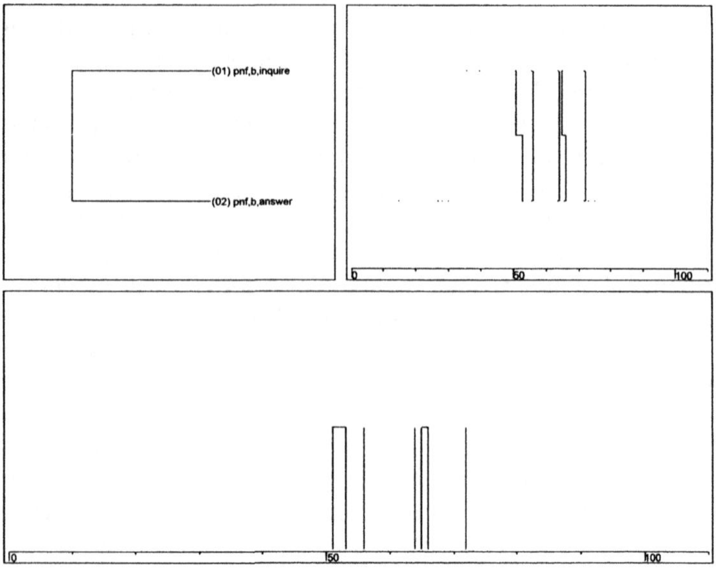

(a)

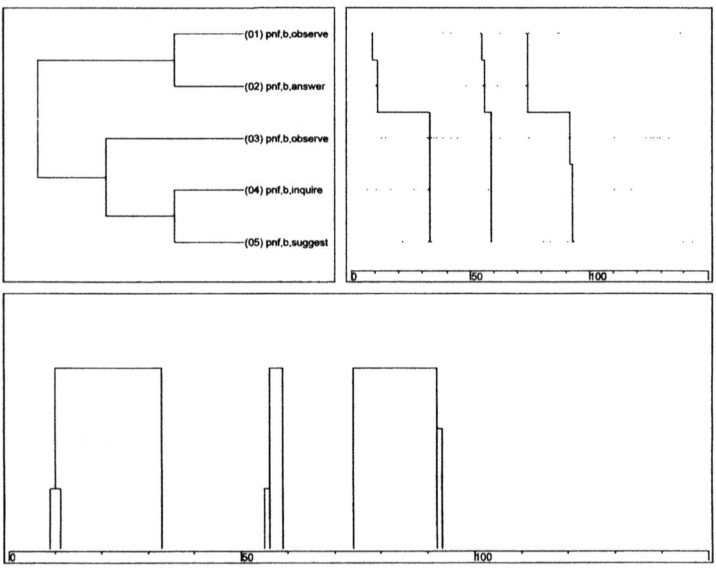

(b)

Figure 2. (a) This represents an example of a "simple pattern" because it involves a pattern with only two behaviors. 01: PNF = pilot not flying has an inquiry; 02: PNF gives an answer. In this example the person answers his own question. (b) This represents a complex pattern due to the multiple levels of T-patterns.

We used *t*-tests to determine differences in the frequencies of verbalizations and in interaction pattern characteristics between effective and ineffective crews.

RESULTS

The analysis of interaction patterns using the algorithm revealed that crew interaction did indeed fall into discernible temporal patterns (T-patterns) that occurred significantly more frequently than by chance. This satisfied our analysis parameters and allowed testing of Hypotheses 1 through 5.

Table 2 depicts the descriptive statistics (including means and standard deviations) and Table 3 depicts the correlations for the study variables. Table 3 shows that the number of unique patterns is highly associated with the number of mono-actor patterns ($r = .79$). This makes sense since mono (one actor) patterns tend to be unusual in a team training setting. Furthermore, Table 3 suggests that the *number* of mono patterns is highly correlated with the number of mono pattern *occurrences* ($r = .99$), such that they are (almost) identical. This also makes sense, certainly in a relatively small sample where the effect of one team member persisting in this behavior is noticeable. However, given this high correlation we will only include *number* of mono patterns in the analysis.

TABLE 2
Psychometric properties of the major study variables

Parameter	*Minimum*	*Maximum*	*M*	*SD*
Command	.00	8.00	2.94	2.07
Observation	12.00	39.00	23.11	8.41
Suggestion	1.00	20.00	5.11	4.76
Inquiry	3.00	30.00	13.22	7.46
Answer	4.00	58.00	18.22	12.56
Disagree	.00	9.00	1.28	2.11
Laugh	.00	31.00	11.94	9.41
Anger	.00	2.00	.17	.51
Sorry	.00	2.00	.56	.78
Social	.00	6.00	1.06	1.66
No. patterns	0	16	6.83	5.40
No. mono patterns	0	5	1.33	1.41
No. mono pattern occurrences	0	25	5.72	6.70
Length	0	2.69	1.79	1.01
Levels	0	1.69	.95	.65
Effectiveness (1 = low)	1	2	1.39	.50

$n = 18$ teams.

TABLE 3
First order correlations between study variables

Parameters	*1*	*2*	*3*	*4*	*5*	*6*	*7*	*8*	*9*	*10*	*11*	*12*	*13*	*14*	*15*	*16*
1. Command	–															
2. Observe	.10	–														
3. Suggestion	.05	.32	–													
4. Inquiry	.14	.59**	.47	–												
5. Answer	.17	.57*	.74**	.69**	–											
6. Disagree	.13	.34	−.19	.19	.16	–										
7. Laugh	.35	.29	.21	.18	.09	−.04	–									
8. Anger	.01	.12	−.22	−.26	−.15	.39	.11	–								
9. Apologies	.17	.45	.38	.63**	.47	.29	.56*	−.10	–							
10. Social	−.03	−.07	−.21	−.35	−.19	−.07	.38	.26	.11	–						
11. No. unique patterns	−.04	.53*	.46	.78**	.69**	.29	.37	−.03	.69**	.04	–					
12. No. mono patterns	.11	.48*	.17	.56*	.44	.70**	.25	.24	.46	−.06	.79**	–				
13. No. mono occurrences	.07	.45	.05	.50*	.39	.76**	.18	.27	.43	−.00	.74**	.99**	–			
14. Length	−.10	.39	.24	.47	.46	.20	.26	.10	.36	−.05	.65*	.53*	.48*	–		
15. Levels	−.10	.40	.24	.50*	.46	.19	.22	.07	.36	−.03	.68**	.57*	.52*	.79**	–	
16. Effective	.14	−.07	.18	−.06	.19	−.28	−.26	−.27	−.28	−.24	−.39	−.53*	−.51*	−.35	−.40	–

Correlations are based on $n = 18$ teams. ** Correlation is significant at the 0.01 level (two-tailed). * Correlation is significant at the 0.05 level (two-tailed)

First, we determined whether effective and less effective crews differed with respect to the frequency of coded behaviors. Therefore, we compared the averages for each coded behavior (command, suggestion, etc.) between effective and less effective crews. However, we found no significant difference ($p < .10$) between these types of crews regarding the number of times they engaged in any of the coded verbalizations. Additionally, we examined the difference in frequency between task-focused interactions and development-focused interactions of the crews. Development-focused interactions are expressions that relate to developing a team climate, such as laughing, expressions of anger, social or non-work-related remarks (cf. Bales, 1950). We used a paired t-test to compare the averages of the crew communication and coordination verbalizations (i.e., totals of command, observation, suggestion, and inquiry) to the frequencies of the team development verbalizations (i.e., totals of laugh, anger, sorry, social) previously coded. Our crews engaged in significantly more crew communication and coordination verbalizations, $M = 62.61$; $SD = 28.29$, as opposed to team development verbalizations, $M = 15.00$; $SD = 10.87$, $t(17) = 7.28$; $p < .001$; $d = 3.53$, supporting their identification as task-focused swift-starting teams.

Our next step was to test our hypotheses. Using t-tests, we compared the total number of pattern occurrences, total number of unique patterns, stability of pattern length, the stability of the number of hierarchical levels in patterns, and number of mono-actor patterns between the higher and lower effectiveness crews. The results of our t-tests are depicted in Table 4. We formulated specific expectations concerning the direction of the differences between groups, and will therefore test one-tailed. The results show that our first and second hypotheses—that effective teams would engage in more patterned interaction (H1) and have fewer unique patterns (H2) than less

TABLE 4
Comparison of pattern characteristics between low-effective and high-effective crews

	M		*SD*				
Parameters	*Low*	*High*	*Low*	*High*	*t(16)*	*p*	*Cohen's d*
No. pattern occurrences (H1)	40.27	24.14	26.60	27.83	1.23	.118	0.62
No. unique patterns (H2)	8.45	4.29	5.39	4.68	1.68	.056	0.84
Stability in duration of patterns (H3)	0.39	−0.01	0.28	0.49	2.25	.019	1.13
Stability in levels in patterns (H4)	0.37	−0.01	0.25	0.49	2.22	.018	1.11
No. unique mono-actor patterns (H5)	1.91	0.43	1.44	0.79	2.47	.012	1.24

p is based on one-tailed testing. Multiple comparisons require a correction for α inflation. Accepting a chance level of $p = 0.10$, this would require a $p \leq .02$ (Bonferroni correction) for a statistically significant result.

effective teams—were not supported ($p = .12$ and $p = .06$, respectively). However, the results do indicate that the effective crews in our sample displayed patterns of interaction that had less variation in length (H3, $p < .02$) and in complexity (H4, $p < .02$) than those of less effective crews.

Concerning our final hypothesis (H5), we used the number of unique mono-actor patterns to indicate the balanced nature of the interaction between the pilots. Our analysis depicted in Table 4 suggests that interaction patterns of less effective crews are characterized by significantly more unique mono-actor patterns ($p < .02$) as compared to effective crews.

In order to test the discriminant power of the six pattern characteristics listed in Table 4, we used the discriminant function analysis procedure in SPSS. The model was significant at $p = 0.08$, Wilks' $\lambda = 0.43$, $\chi^2 = 11.11$, and indicated that 88.9% of the crews were correctly classified as effective or less effective by the behavior pattern characteristics. These results suggest that, for our sample, less effective and more effective swift-starting teams exhibit significantly different interaction patterns immediately after beginning their work.

ADDITIONAL EXPLORATORY ANALYSIS

One of the most striking results in our analysis was the hypothesized difference in the number of mono-actor patterns between the effective and less effective crews. The less effective crews displayed a total of 75 mono-actor patterns, while the effective crews displayed a total of 11 such patterns. We suspected that the pilots flying (PFs) were engaging in directive leadership by monopolizing communication in the less effective crews. However, a closer look at our data revealed that in less effective crews, the pilots not flying (PNFs) were responsible for 58 of the 75 mono-actor pattern occurrences. Of these 58 mono-actor pattern occurrences, 25 were an inquiry/answer pattern and 20 were an observation/answer pattern. Thus, our suspicion of authoritarian PFs was incorrect. If anything, the PFs were silent while the PNFs made inquiries or observations, waited for a response, and then proceeded to provide their own answers. We explore possible causes of these patterns of interaction, and other issues, below.

DISCUSSION

Our study focused on developing more understanding about the early patterns of interaction exhibited by swift-starting teams. Specifically, we focused our efforts on identifying the nature of initial interaction patterns in new swift-starting teams, and on examining the relationship between those patterns and overall team effectiveness. Our preliminary analyses showed that crews in our study displayed significantly more task-oriented behaviors than development-oriented behaviors, providing support for our claim that our crews are indeed "swift-starting" teams.

Furthermore, our analyses provided results in several areas. First, we found that the frequencies of various types of coded behaviors during early interactions (H1) did not differ significantly between effective and ineffective teams. Our second hypothesis was also not supported, yet effective crews did seem to have fewer unique patterns, as can be seen in Table 4. The lack of statistically significant support may be due to the somewhat constrained time period for which we observed the crews and the routinized nature of the work. Nevertheless, we found significant differences between effective and ineffective crews' interaction patterns: Effective teams in our sample exhibited patterns that were more stable in duration (H3), more stable in complexity (H4), and more reciprocal (H5) as compared to those of less effective teams.

These findings indicate that effective and ineffective teams did not so much differ with respect to their activity levels (number of counted behaviors), but instead that effective teams displayed qualitatively different interaction patterns as compared to ineffective teams. Early in their interaction, effective teams established patterns of communication that were more stable and balanced. A balanced pattern implies that both crew members are involved in the interaction, indicating more reciprocity in the interaction. This is a prerequisite for exchanging information in order to establish and maintain a shared understanding of the task and situation (Uitdewilligen et al., 2010). By engaging in more mono-actor patterns, the ineffective crews most likely missed opportunities for sharing information, cooperatively making decisions, and developing shared understanding of actions and plans. Our findings clearly suggest that even from its inception, an effective team's interactions are substantially different from those of other teams. Other researchers have also found relationships between interaction patterns and team effectiveness (Jehn & Mannix, 2001; Waller, 1999; Waller et al., 2004). As previously mentioned, Kanki et al. (1989) found that high-performing flight crews exhibited similar interaction patterns across crews, while low-performing crews displayed a wide, heterogeneous assortment of patterns across crews. We found similar results while focusing on the characteristics of interaction patterns over time within crews.

Furthermore, we found that the PNFs in ineffective crews engaged in significantly more mono-actor patterns than did other pilots, often posing and answering their own questions or commenting on their own observations. This lack of interaction—whether caused by inattentive, overburdened PFs or overbearing PNFs—was associated with a low level of crew interaction and imbalanced communication between pilots in the ineffective crews. This result supports the conclusions of several studies in communication regarding the positive effects of turn-taking and balanced communication in groups (cf. Paulus, 2000). Similarly, research on mental model development suggests that reciprocal, balanced communication among team members results in more information sharing and mental model accuracy (cf. Rasker, Post, & Schraagen, 2000; Uitdewilligen et al., 2010). This result can also be interpreted as if the natural division of roles in the cockpit between PF and PNF is not the most likely explanation for the mono-actor patterns. If such would be the case, than one would expect that the PF would be responsible for the majority of the mono-actor patterns, as the PF can be expected to have the lead and therefore should initiate most of the interactions. As noted previously, the difference in hierarchy between "captain" and "first officer" is not emphasized in the specific context of this flight simulator training and therefore does not lend itself to a sufficient explanation for these results. Altogether, the results indeed seem to be attributable to interaction styles that develop early in the interaction between members of the crew. These seemingly subtle differences may play a large role in setting the stage for subsequent interaction and effectiveness.

The newly formed crews in our sample established patterns of interaction very early in their work. This suggests that new crews are subject to the same motivation to quickly establish routines, norms, and interaction patterns as are other teams in less technical, non-aviation contexts (see Gersick & Hackman, 1990). Given the requirement of experienced pilots in commercial aviation to form new crews continuously, the emergence of norms and patterns of interactions in experienced crews may occur even more rapidly than in our novice crews. As the longevity of patterns in teams likely acts to solidify their persistence, more research comparing interaction pattern emergence in novice and expert teams is needed in order to ascertain differences associated with expertise level.

Based on our results, it seems possible that in swift-starting teams, the characteristics of interaction patterns serve as a rapid enactment of characteristics considered in previous literature as hallmarks of mature teams that have developed over time. For example, previous literature suggests that as teams mature, they are more likely to engage in open, balanced communication (see Chang, Bordia, & Duck, 2003), to have responsive and activated members, and to increase in task coordination and efficiency (Wheelan & Williams, 2003). In swift-starting teams, these characteristics may be quickly enacted through initial interaction patterns rather than through the socio-emotional communication often used to indicate levels of team development. For example, teams with low mono-actor pattern frequency and occurrence enacted higher levels of reciprocity than other teams. Similarly, swift-starting teams with short, simple patterns enacted responsiveness and efficiency in their interactions, and teams with a high number of pattern occurrences enacted coordination as they worked together. Thus, the characteristics of efficient and mature teams suggested by previous work may be applicable to swift-starting teams, but may need to be measured by the analysis of interaction patterns rather than by the examination of socio-emotional interactions.

With this study, we have extended previous research by digging deeper to identify subtle differences in team interaction in a routine (as opposed to non-routine or crisis) context. In particular, we replicate and extend the work of Waller et al. (2004), who studied nuclear power crews during routine and non-routine situations, and who also found no significant differences in behavior frequency between high- and average-performing crews during the routine situations. These authors did, however, find that the same crews differed significantly in both adaptive behavior and effectiveness during crisis situations. By specifically examining the critical first moments of team interaction in a new team, we help explain the subsequent bifurcation in behavior and effectiveness during crisis situations that Waller and colleagues (2004) found. It could be that those teams displaying the subtle qualitative differences we saw in the first moments of routine task performance are able later to engage in the adaptive behavior displayed by the high-performing teams in their study. By examining the variation of length and complexity among patterns within teams, we tap into the stability, predictability, and even rhythm of their interaction patterns, as we also do by examining the reciprocity of their patterns.

Additionally, by using the pattern recognition algorithm to analyze our data, we were able to identify such recurrent patterns of interaction embedded within sequential strings of behavioral data. This approach differs from techniques such as Markov chains primarily in that irrelevant behaviors (noise) occurring between the behaviors included in a pattern must not be removed or discounted a priori before the pattern can be detected (see Kerepesi et al., 2005; Stachowski et al., 2009).

Overall, the results of our study demonstrate that for newly formed swift-starting teams, the first few moments of interaction are consequential for overall team effectiveness. The interaction patterns that are established early are significantly related to effectiveness and, most likely, to the climate in the team. In particular, whether the team manages to establish a climate that is perceived as psychologically safe is important for communication and interaction (Edmondson, 1999); the more "psychologically safe" people perceive the climate in the team to be, the better and more open the communication. Given the time scarcity allowed by a swift-starting context for teams to build interpersonal relationships, this may be particularly important in contexts such as aviation and medicine, which are also hierarchical status relations (i.e., captain–first officer; physician–nurse) that may hamper communication (Lingard, Reznick, Espin, Regehr, & DeVito, 2002). Training that underscores the importance of early interaction and communication for all hierarchical levels, such as those recommended in many permutations of

Crew Resource Management training programs (Helmreich et al., 1998) would seem to be particularly important for swift-starting teams.

PRACTICAL IMPLICATIONS

The findings of this study are relevant for team training, as they demonstrate the importance of a team's first moments of interaction together. The reciprocity of interactions and the avoidance of mono-action patterns are elements that trainers could take into account when training and assessing team performance. Additionally, managers should be aware of the important subsequent influences those early interactions may have. They should monitor the interactions of new teams carefully, watching for teams that seem to have episodes of interaction that obviously vary wildly in terms of length, complexity, or reciprocity. In particular, mono-actor patterns may be easier than the other nuances to identify with real-time observation.

Apart from training consequences, there may also be consequences of this work for research. Although the early interaction patterns we have studied were in a particular context, these patterns, and the methods used for their coding and analysis, can easily be transferred to other contexts, and the important variables in our study ("reciprocity in patterns", number of "unique patterns", "mono-actor patterns", and so on) are in fact "context-free" elements for the study of team interaction. These methods may facilitate the accessibility of studying other behavioral team processes and interaction patterns in various settings, including a laboratory setting.

STUDY LIMITATIONS

There are inevitable limitations associated with this study. The limited number of teams participating in it reduces the statistical power of our analyses. However, this is not automatically a problem (cf. Stachowksi et al., 2009), as it also marks the robustness of the effects we report. On the other hand, there is little empirical work detailing the initial interactions of swift-starting teams composed of highly skilled members, and we strive to offer a view of such interactions here. Further, as Peterson, Smith, and Martorana asked in their defence of small-sample studies: "Is it better to take some risk in publishing small-sample studies that could inspire theory development and large-scale quantitative studies but that also open the field to the possible need for correction through meta-analysis, or is it better to face the risk of having virtually no research at all published on an important topic?" (2006, p. 6). Future studies should examine such causality, along with possible antecedents of the verbalizations and patterns as we observed, with a larger sample of swift-starting teams across multiple contexts. Additionally, although our instructors have many years of experience (and the requisite licensure) in training new aviators, and are therefore expert raters of crew effectiveness, we also minimized the subjectivity in ratings by using the LINE/LOS behavioral marker checklist for their assessment; future research should employ more than one expert rater to determine the effectiveness of crews, and should calculate and report inter-rater agreement. We employed a binary division of high/low effective teams based on the LINE/LOS checklist. Using a coarse-grained effectiveness scale could mask the fact that real differences in crew effectiveness were actually quite small; alternatively, our binary measure might mask the fact that instructors were very lenient in their assessment of effectiveness. It should be noted that the crews were only at the beginning of their crew training and that instructors assumed that substantial improvement would be made later, and marked accordingly in order not to discourage students, as instructors and teachers sometimes do. Nevertheless, the differences in effectiveness were real differences, and we have no reason to believe that the flight instructors' assessments of effectiveness were asymmetrically biased among the crews.

In sum, swift-starting teams are critical "first responders" in organizations facing unexpected, complex issues. The ability of individuals to come together and immediately coordinate their efforts successfully can provide organizations with the ability to remain as flexible and responsive as possible in dynamic, complex environments. Based on analyses using a software-based technique to identify patterns of interaction, our results suggest that the patterns emerging from the first moments of interaction in these teams may indeed be the harbingers of team success or failure. Future research should examine the antecedents and malleability of early patterns in these important and consequential teams, as understanding and correcting such patterns early may help them avoid the creation or importation of ineffective patterns in their future behavioral repertoires.

REFERENCES

Ancona, D. G., & Chong, C. T. (1996). Entrainment: Pace, cycle, and rhythm in organizational behavior. In B. Staw & T. Cummings (Eds.), *Research in organizational behavior* (Vol. 18, pp. 251–284). Greenwich, CT: JAI Press.

Ancona, D. G., & Waller, M. J. (2007). The dance of entrainment: Temporally navigating across multiple pacers. In B. Rubin (Ed.), *Research in the sociology of work* (Vol. 17, pp. 115–146). Oxford, UK: Elsevier.

Archibold, R. C. (2003, March 22). A nation at war: The new organizations; Papers debate use of teams to react quickly to terror. *New York Times*.

Argote, L. (1999). *Organizational learning: Creating, retaining, and transferring knowledge*. Norwell, MA: Kluwer.

Arrow, H., Poole, M. S., Henry, K. B., Wheelan, S., & Moreland, R. (2004). Time, change, and development: The temporal perspective on groups. *Small Group Research*, *35*, 73–105.

Bales, R. F. (1950). *Interaction process analysis: A method for the study of small groups*. Chicago, IL: University of Chicago Press.

Ballard, D. I., Tschan, F., & Waller, M. J. (2008). All in the timing: Considering time at multiple stages of group research. *Small Group Research, 39*, 328–351.

Barua, A., Lee, C.-H. S., & Whinston, A. B. (1995). Incentives and computing systems for teambased organizations. *Organization Science, 6*, 487–504.

Bennis, W. G. (1965). Beyond bureaucracy. *Trans Actions, 2*, 31–35.

Borrie, A., Jonsson, G. K., & Magnusson, M. S. (2002). Temporal pattern analysis and its applicability in sport: An explanation and exemplar data. *Journal of Sports Sciences, 20*, 845–852.

Bradford, L. P., Gibb, J. R., & Benne, K. D. (1964). *T-group theory and laboratory method.* New York, NY: Wiley.

Chang, A., Bordia, P., & Duck, J. (2003). Punctuated equilibrium and linear progression: Toward a new understanding of group development. *Academy of Management Journal, 46*, 106–117.

Costa, A. C., Roe, R. A., & Taillieu, T. (2001). Trust within teams: The relation with performance effectiveness. *European Journal of Work and Organizational Psychology, 10*, 225–244.

Edmondson, A. (1999). Psychological safety and learning behavior in work teams. *Administrative Science Quarterly, 44*, 350–383.

Eriksen, J., & Dyer, L. (2004). Right from the start: Exploring the effects of early team events on subsequent project team development and performance. *Administrative Science Quarterly, 49*, 438–471.

Feldman, D. C. (1984). The development and enforcement of group norms. *Academy of Management Review, 9*, 47–53.

Flin, R., & Martin, L. (2001). Behavioral markers for crew resource management: A review of current practice. *International Journal of Aviation Psychology, 11*, 95–118.

Foushee, H. C. (1984). Dyads and triads at 35,000 feet: Factors affecting group process and aircrew performance. *American Psychologist, 39*, 886–893.

Gersick, C. J. G. (1988). Time and transition in work teams: Toward a new model of group development. *Academy of Management Journal, 31*, 9–41.

Gersick, C. J. G. (1989). Marking time: Predictable transitions in task groups. *Academy of Management Journal, 32*, 274–309.

Gersick, C. J. G., & Hackman, J. R. (1990). Habitual routines in task-performing groups. *Organizational Behavior and Human Decision Processes, 47*, 65–97.

Ginnett, R. C. (1987). The formation process of airline crews. In R. S. Jensen (Ed.), *Proceedings, Fourth International Symposium on Aviation Psychology* (pp. 399–405). Columbus, OH: Ohio State University Press.

Ginnett, R. C. (1990). Airline cockpit crews. In J. R. Hackman (Ed.), *Groups that work and those that don't*. San Francisco, CA: Jossey-Bass.

Hackman, J. R. (1993). Teams, leaders, and organizations: New directions for crew-oriented flight training. In E. Wiener, B. Kanki, & R. Helmreich (Eds.), *Cockpit resource management* (pp. 47–70). San Diego, CA: Academic Press.

Hackman, J. R., & Morris, C. G. (1975). Group tasks, group interaction process, and group performance effectiveness: A review and proposed integration. In L. Berkowitz (Ed.), *Advances in experimental social psychology* (Vol. 8). New York, NY: Academic Press.

Helmreich, R. L., Merritt, A. C., & Wilhelm, J. A. (1998). The evolution of Crew Resource Management training in commercial aviation. *International Journal of Aviation Psychology, 9*, 19–32.

Hollenbeck, J. R., Beersma, B., & Schouten, M. E., (2012). Beyond team types and taxonomies: A dimensional scaling conceptualization for team description. *Academy of Management Review, 37*, 82–106.

Huber, G. P. (2004). *The necessary nature of future firms: Attributes of survivors in a changing world.* Thousand Oaks, CA: Sage.

James, E. H., & Wooten, L. P. (2010). *Leading under pressure*. New York, NY: Routledge.
Jarvenpaa, S. L., & Leidner, D. E. (1999). Communication and trust in global virtual teams. *Organization Science, 6*, 791–815.
Jehn, K. A., & Mannix, E. A. (2001). The dynamic nature of conflict: A longitudinal study of intragroup conflict and group performance. *Academy of Management Journal, 44*, 238–251.
Kanki, B. G. (1996). Stress and aircrew performance: A team-level perspective. In J. E. Driskell & E. Salas (Eds.), *Stress and human performance* (pp. 127–162). Mahwah, NJ: Lawrence Erlbaum Associates.
Kanki, B. G., Folk, V. G., & Irwin, C. M. (1991). Communication variations and aircrew performance. *International Journal of Aviation Psychology, 1*, 149–162.
Kanki, B. G., & Foushee, H. C. (1989). Communication as group process media of aircrew performance. *Aviation, Space, & Environmental Medicine, 60*, 402–410.
Kanki B. G., Lozito S., & Foushee H. C. (1989). Communication indices of crew coordination. *Aviation, Space, and Environmental Medicine, 60*, 56–60.
Kanki, B. G., Palmer, M. T., & Veinott. E. S. (1991). Communication variations related to leader personality. *Proceedings, 6th International Symposium on Aviation Psychology* (pp. 253–259). Columbus, OH: Ohio State University.
Kerepesi, A., Jonsson, G. K., Miklósi, A., Topál, J., Csányi, V., & Magnusson, M. S. (2005). Detection of temporal patterns in dog–human interaction. *Behavioural Processes, 70*, 69–79.
Klein, K. J., Ziegert, J. C., Knight, A. P., & Xiao, Y. (2006). Dynamic delegation: Shared, hierarchical, and deindividualized leadership in extreme action teams. *Administrative Science Quarterly, 51*, 590–621.
Korsgaard, M. A., Schweiger, D. M., & Sapienza, H. J. (1995). Building commitment, attachment, and trust in strategic decision-making teams: The role of procedural justice. *Academy of Management Journal, 38*, 60–84.
Kozlowski, S. W. J., Gully, S. M., Nason, E. R., & Smith, E. M. (1999). Developing adaptive teams: A theory of compilation and performance across levels and time. In D. R. Ilgen & E. D. Pulakos (Eds.), *The changing nature of work performance: Implications for staffing, personnel actions, and development* (pp. 240–292). San Francisco: Jossey-Bass.
Lacoursiere, R. (1980). *The life cycle of groups: Group developmental stage theory*. New York, NY: Human Sciences Press.
Lingard, L., Reznick, R., Espin, S., Regehr, G., & DeVito, I. (2002). Team communication in the operating room: Talk patterns, sites of tension, and implications for novices. *Academic Medicine, 77*, 232–237.
Magnusson, M. S. (2000). Discovering hidden time patterns in behavior: T-patterns and their detection. *Behavior Research Methods, Instruments, & Computers, 32*, 93–110.
Marks, M. A., Mathieu, J. E., & Zaccaro, S. J. (2001). A temporally based framework and taxonomy of team processes. *Academy of Management Review, 26*, 356–376.
Marsch, S. C. U., Tschan, F., Semmer, N., Spychiger, M., Breuer, M., & Hunziker, P. R. (2005). Performance of first responders in simulated cardiac arrests. *Critical Care Medicine, 33*, 963–967.
McGrew, J. F., Bilotta, J. G., & Deeney, J. M. (1999). Software team formation and decay: Extending the standard model for small groups. *Small Group Research, 30*, 209–234.
McKinney, E. H., Barker, J. R., Davis, K. J., & Smith, D. (2005). How swift starting action teams get off the ground. *Management Communications Quarterly, 19*, 198–237.
Meyerson, D., Weick, K. E., & Kramer, R. M. (1996). Swift trust and temporary groups. In R. Kramer & T. Tyler (Eds.), *Trust in organizations: Frontiers of theory and research* (pp. 166–195). Thousand Oaks, CA: Sage.
Mohrman, S. A., Cohen, S. G., & Mohrman, A. M., Jr. (1995). Designing team-based organizations. San Francisco, CA: Jossey-Bass.
Moreland, R. L., (2010). Are dyads really groups? *Small Group Research, 41*, 251–267.

Owens, D. A., Mannix, E. A., & Neale, M. A. (1998). Strategic formation of groups: Issues in task-performance and team member selection. In M. A. Neale, E. A. Mannix, & D. H. Gruenfeld (Eds.), *Research on managing groups and teams* (pp. 149–166). Stamford, CT: JAI Press.

Paulus, P. (2000). Groups, teams, and creativity: The creative potential of idea-generating groups. *Applied Psychology*, *49*, 237–262.

Peterson, R. S., Smith, D. B., & Martorana, P. V. (2006). Choosing between a rock and a hard place when data are scarce and questions important: Reply to Hollenbeck, DeRue & Mannor (2006). *Journal of Applied Psychology*, *91*, 6–8.

Pinto, M. B., Pinto, J. K., & Prescott, J. E. (1993). Antecedents and consequences of project team cross-functional cooperation. *Management Science*, *39*, 1281–1297.

Potter, R. E., Cooke, R. A., & Balthazard, P. A. (2000). Virtual team interaction: Assessment, consequences, and management. *Team Performance Management*, *6*, 131–137.

Rasker, P. C., Post, W. M., & Schraagen, J. M. C. (2000). Effects of two types of intra-team feedback on developing a shared mental model in command & control teams. *Ergonomics*, *43*, 1167–1189.

Richardson, H. A., Vandenberg, R. J., Blum, T. C., & Roman, P. M. (2002). Does decentralization make a difference for the organization? An examination of the boundary conditions circumscribing decentralized decision-making and organizational financial performance. *Journal of Management*, *28*, 217–244.

Salas, E., Dickenson, T. L., Converse, S. A., & Tannenbaum, S. I. (1992). Towards an understanding of team performance and training, In R.W. Swezey & E. Salas (Eds.), *Teams: Their training and performance* (pp. 3–29). Norwood, NJ: Ablex.

Sarker, S., & Sahay, S. (2003). Understanding virtual team development: An interpretive study. *Journal of the AIS*, *4*, 1–38.

Schraagen, J. M., Huis in 't Veld, M., & de Koning, L. (2010). Information sharing during crisis management in hierarchical vs network teams. *Journal of Contingencies and Crisis Management*, *18*, 117–127.

Stachowski, A. A., Kaplan, S. A., & Waller, M. J. (2009). The benefits of flexible team interaction during crises. *Journal of Applied Psychology*, *94*, 1536–1543.

Sundstrom, E., De Meuse, K. P., & Futrell, D. (1990). Work teams: Applications and effectiveness. *American Psychologist*, *45*, 120–133.

Tschan, F., Semmer, N. K., Gautschi, D., Hunziker, P., Spychiger, M., & Marsch, S. C. U. (2006). Leading to recovery: Group performance and coordinative activities in medical emergency driven groups. *Human Performance*, *19*, 277–304.

Tuckman, B. W. (1965). Developmental sequence in small groups. *Psychological Bulletin*, *63*, 384–399.

Tuckman, B. W., & Jensen, M. A. C. (1977). Stages of small group development revisited. *Group and Organizational Studies*, *2*, 419–427.

Uitdewilligen, S., & Waller, M. J. (2011). Adaptation in multiteam systems: The role of temporal semistructures. In S. J. Zaccaro, M. A. Marks, & L. DeChurch, (Eds.), *Multiteam systems: An organizational form for dynamic and complex environments*. London, UK: Taylor & Francis.

Uitdewilligen, S., Waller, M. J., & Zijlstra, F. R. H., (2010). Team cognition and adaptability in dynamic settings: A review of pertinent work. In G. P. Hodgkinson & J. K. Ford (Eds.), *International review of industrial and organizational psychology* (Vol. 25, pp. 293–353). Chichester, UK: Wiley.

Waller, M. J. (1999). The timing of adaptive group responses to non-routine events. *Academy of Management Journal*, *42*, 127–137.

Waller, M. J., Gupta, N., & Giambatista, R. C. (2004). Effects of adaptive behaviors and shared mental models on control crew performance. *Management Science*, *50*, 1534–1544.

Wheelan, S. (1994). Group processes: A developmental perspective. Boston: Allyn & Bacon.

Wheelan, S., & Williams, T. (2003). Mapping dynamic interaction patterns in work groups. *Small Group Research, 34*, 443–467.

Wiener, E. L., Kanki, B. G., & Helmreich, R. L. (1994). *Cockpit resource management*. New York: Academic Press.

Williams, K. D. (2010). Dyads can be groups (and often are). *Small Group Research, 41*, 268–274.

Zellmer-Bruhn, M., Waller, M. J., & Ancona, D. (2004). The effect of temporal entrainment on the ability of teams to change their routines. In S. Blount (Ed.), *Research on managing groups and teams* (pp. 135–158). Oxford, UK: Elsevier.

Ziegert, J., Klein, K., & Xiao, Y. (2001). Team leadership: A review and extension of existing theory through a qualitative study of shock trauma teams. In J. L. Pearce & R. L. Tung (Eds.), *Proceedings, Academy of Management Meeting* (pp. 135–140). Washington, DC: Academy of Management.

EUROPEAN JOURNAL OF WORK AND
ORGANIZATIONAL PSYCHOLOGY
2012, 21 (5), 778–802

Chaotic dynamics and team effectiveness: Evidence from professional basketball

Pedro J. Ramos-Villagrasa[1], José Navarro[2], and Antonio L. García-Izquierdo[1]

[1]Department of Psychology, University of Oviedo, Oviedo, Spain

[2]Department of Social Psychology, University of Barcelona, Barcelona, Spain

Considering teams as complex adaptive systems (CAS) this study deals with changes in team effectiveness over time in a specific context: professional basketball. The sample comprised 23 basketball teams whose outcomes were analysed over a 12-year period according to two objective measures. The results reveal that all the teams showed chaotic dynamics, one of the key characteristics of CAS. A relationship was also found between teams showing low-dimensional chaotic dynamics and better outcomes, supporting the idea of healthy variability in organizational behaviour. The stability of the squad was likewise found to influence team outcomes, although it was not associated with the chaotic dynamics in team effectiveness. It is concluded that studying teams as CAS enables fluctuations in team effectiveness to be explained, and that the techniques derived from nonlinear dynamical systems, developed specifically for the study of CAS, are useful for this purpose.

Keywords: Basketball; Complex adaptive systems; Nonlinear dynamical systems theory; Team effectiveness; Team stability.

Correspondence should be addressed to Pedro José Ramos Villagrasa, Facultad de Psicología, cabina n°5, Plaza Feijóo s/n, 33003 Oviedo, Spain. Email: ramospedro@uniovi.es

Financial support to PJR-V (grant: UNOV-09-BECDOC-S) given by the University of Oviedo and Banco Santander is acknowledged. JN wishes to acknowledge the support given by the Spanish Ministry of Science and Innovation (PSI2009-07076 project). The contribution of ALG-I is partially supported by project DER 2010-21686-C02-01, Spanish Ministry of Science and Innovation. The authors would like to thank the Action Editor, Bertolt Meyer (University of Zurich), and two anonymous reviewers who provided thoughtful comments on drafts of this article. A previous version of this article was presented at the VII Ibero-American Congress of Psychology in Oviedo, Spain (July 2010) and the EAWOP Small Group Meeting Time and Change in Teams in Chemnitz, Germany (February 2011).

This article focuses on the temporal dynamics of team effectiveness in a specific context: professional basketball teams. The premise is that seemingly random patterns of team effectiveness over time could actually reveal discernible trends. As such the study is of interest not only for team psychology research, which has emphasized the need to consider teams as complex systems (e.g., Arrow, McGrath, & Berdahl, 2000), but also for the applied perspective, since it provides information about the possibility of predicting and intervening in team effectiveness.

TEAM EFFECTIVENESS AND TEAMS AS COMPLEX ADAPTIVE SYSTEMS

Teams can be defined as a set of two or more people with specific roles who interact dynamically, interdependently, and adaptively towards a common objective (Salas, Dickinson, Converse, & Tannenbaum, 1992). In this study the focus is on effectiveness, the core of team research as it reflects the results of a team's actions (Kozlowski & Bell, 2003).

Surprisingly there is no consensus regarding the definition of team effectiveness. Although Campbell, McCloy, Oppler, and Sager (1993) clarified many years ago that performance refers to behaviour itself while effectiveness is an outcome of performance, team effectiveness is nowadays considered alternatively as behaviour (i.e., performance) and in terms of outcomes (Mathieu, Maynard, Rapp, & Gilson, 2008). Here, we follow the proposal of Salas, Rosen, Burke, and Goodwin (2009), who have defined team effectiveness as an evaluation of the results of performance in accordance with certain standards.

The explanation and prediction of effectiveness is a key question in the field of team research. As noted by Ilgen, Hollenbeck, Johnson, and Jundt (2005), and more recently by Mathieu et al. (2008), various models based on the input-process-output (I-P-O) framework of McGrath (1964) have been developed in an attempt to explain team effectiveness. However, these models have been criticized for ignoring the dynamic nature and temporal evolution of teams (Ilgen et al., 2005; Mathieu et al., 2008; McGrath, Arrow, & Berdahl, 2000). Consideration of the temporal aspect may therefore provide new insights and enable researchers to ask questions that can only be answered with a dynamic approach (Ancona, Goodman, Lawrence, & Tushman, 2001; Arrow, Poole, Henry, Wheelan, & Moreland, 2004). For example, Mitchell and James (2001) show that a causal relationship between two variables can be affected by time in five different ways, with the number of such possibilities growing as more variables are added. Research that takes account of time is also useful for practitioners as it allows phenomena to be monitored from the moment they begin. By identifying critical changes in trajectories the practitioner may then be able to prevent unfavourable turns in them, thereby avoiding negative consequences (Roe, 2008).

Current explanatory models of team effectiveness have begun to include time and consider teams as complex, adaptive and dynamical systems (e.g., Arrow et al., 2000; Ilgen et al., 2005; Mathieu et al., 2008). A complex adaptive system (CAS) can be defined as a set of independent agents that act in parallel, develop models of how things function in their setting, and, most importantly, refine these models through learning and adaptation (Gell-Mann, 1994). According to McGrath et al. (2000) and Arrow et al. (2004), conceptualizing teams as CAS implies that teams interact with other systems, some smaller (i.e., the members of the team), some of the same size (i.e., other teams) and others larger (i.e., the organizations in which the teams find themselves and their context). These authors also argue that team research has shown a number of serious limitations, such as considering teams as simple systems characterized by unidirectional cause–effect relationships, failing to take into account the context in which teams operate, and studying them as static entities that do not change over time and which are comprised of generic individuals who can be exchanged without consequence (McGrath et al., 2000). One way of overcoming these limitations would be to consider teams as CAS.

In addition, Ilgen et al. (2005) point out that empirical research about teams is more problem driven than theory driven (i.e., the changing demands of the applied setting have constrained empirical research, with few studies being conducted on the development and testing of theories). One example is the construct of CAS itself: Many authors talk about teams as CAS, but very little research has actually sought to demonstrate this.

According to McGrath (1991) the way to study teams as CAS is through nonlinear dynamical systems (NDS) theory, which is specifically designed for this purpose (Lewin, 1993). NDS theory considers CAS as a development of open systems that show an evolution over time, one in which their components interact in a nonlinear and dynamical way (Guastello & Liebovitch, 2009). From the perspective of NDS theory the characteristics of CAS are interdependence, interaction, uncertainty, and chaos (Nowak & Vallacher, 1998). Interdependence occurs when team members need not only to cooperate to achieve shared goals (Cummings & Blumberg, 1987) but also to take into account how external factors influence the team (Kozlowski & Bell, 2003). Interaction is intrinsically related to interdependence, because teams need to be related to their context in order to perform their task in a mixed-motive situation, as suggested by studies about cooperation and competition (Stewart & Nandkeolyar, 2007). Uncertainty refers to the lack of surety about the results of team effectiveness due to within-team dynamics and context interdependence. Last but not least, chaos refers to a type of temporal dynamics that

EUROPEAN JOURNAL OF WORK AND
ORGANIZATIONAL PSYCHOLOGY
2012, 21 (5), 749–777

Setting the tone: Early interaction patterns in swift-starting teams as a predictor of effectiveness

Fred R. H. Zijlstra[1], Mary J. Waller[2], and Sybil I. Phillips[3]

[1]Department of Work and Social Psychology, Maastricht University, Maastricht, The Netherlands

[2]Schulich School of Business, York University, Toronto, Canada

[3]Institute of Aviation, University of Illinois at Urbana-Champaign, Champaign, IL, USA

Many organizations rely on the functioning of teams. In this study we focus on swift-starting teams—that is, ad hoc teams formed for immediate task performance, such as emergency or rescue teams or aviation crews, with highly trained members who have generally not previously worked together as a team. Previous research suggests that teams develop task performance capability over time, but that stable patterns of interaction in teams emerge very quickly. We suggest that these interaction patterns help swift starting teams engage in immediate task performance. In particular, we hypothesize that effective teams will exhibit more interaction patterns, but fewer unique patterns, than less effective teams. We describe an observational study of 18 swift-starting aviation crews. Our results identify the early emergence of specific interaction patterns and indicate significant differences between the patterns of effective and ineffective crews. The effective teams in our sample exhibited patterns that were more stable in duration, more stable in complexity, and more reciprocal as compared to those of less effective teams. We close with implications for work on team interaction, and suggestions for future research and team trainers.

Keywords: Team interaction; Behavioral patterns; Team effectiveness; Aviation crews; Swift-starting teams.

Correspondence should be addressed to Fred R. H. Zijlstra, Department of Work and Social Psychology, PO Box 616, Maastricht University, Maastricht 6200 MD, The Netherlands. E-mail: fred.zijlstra@maastrichtuniversity.nl

We thank Alex De Voogt, Robert van Doorn, Rachel Katterl and Fletcher Chauncy for their help in data coding.

that low-dimensional chaos can fluctuate a lot, but the rules which determine these fluctuations are discernible and predictions can be made, at least in the short term. By contrast, in high-dimensional chaotic series many values are possible, the fluctuations are greater, and sudden changes occur very often, which makes any kind of prediction quite difficult.

Although near-linear patterns can be studied using the techniques developed under the assumptions of the generalized linear model (such as ARIMA models), the study of nonlinear patterns requires specific techniques that are rarely used in psychology (e.g., visual recurrence analysis, phase space maps, etc.; Guastello & Liebovitch, 2009). This is especially true for the analysis of chaotic patterns, where chaos and randomness could be confounded when using linear models (Heath, 2000). However, NDS techniques are able to determine whether a time series is deterministic or not. If it is deterministic, one can then identify the kind of deterministic pattern (linear, low-dimensional chaos or high-dimensional chaos) and, therefore, the most suitable method for analysing the data (Ramos-Villagrasa & García-Izquierdo, 2011).

Given that teams are now widely considered as CAS, and taking into account the growing research that shows how NDS theory can be applied to team dynamics (e.g., Gorman, Amazeen, & Cooke, 2010; Pincus, Fox, Perez, Turner, & McGeehan, 2008; Wheelan & Williams, 2003), our goal here is to analyse patterns of team effectiveness across time and to determine whether or not they are chaotic. Specifically, we seek to provide empirical evidence that can help to clarify whether it is indeed appropriate to conceptualize teams as CAS. Furthermore, we would like to contribute knowledge about the effects of time on teams, this being a question that remains largely unexplored to date (Conroy, Kaye, & Schantz, 2008). If, as expected, teams are CAS and their effectiveness shows chaotic patterns, it will then be necessary to conduct more in-depth research into their dynamics (e.g., monitoring, predicting, optimizing) so as to obtain new insights and, consequently, to propose ways of intervening in teams (Roe, 2008).

THE PRESENT STUDY

The aim of this study was to analyse team effectiveness over time. Specifically, we sought to determine if there were chaotic patterns in the behaviour of a sample of Spanish professional basketball teams and, also, if there was some kind of dynamical pattern associated with the achievement of better team outcomes.

Team research in sport settings offers certain advantages to researchers. Following Browne and Mahoney (1984) and Loy, McPherson, and Kenyon (1978) these advantages are: (1) research is conducted mainly in the natural context; (2) the rules, organizational systems, and hierarchy of sport enable a better analysis and control of variables; (3) the activity usually develops under zero-sum circumstances, enabling the analysis of cooperation, competition, and conflict between teams; and (4) objective measures of effectiveness are available, thereby allowing a longitudinal approach.

The sport studied here, basketball, is described by Barnes and Morgeson (2007) as follows: "At any given time, only 5 members are actively participating in the competition, though other team members may be substituted in at any time .... Each team has the opportunity to attempt to both score points (i.e., accumulate points for their team by having the player put the ball through a hoop) and prevent the other team from scoring points" (p. 266). In line with Landis (2001), García-Izquierdo, Ramos-Villagrasa, and Navarro (in press), and Wolfe et al. (2005), we consider basketball as an organizational setting. Sports teams are a part of organizations (Carron & Brawley, 2008) in which the same processes and behaviours occur as in the case of conventional work organizations (Dirks, 2000). Additionally, professional players are employees of their sports clubs and have job duties that are set out in law (in Spain, Law on Sport 10/1990, art. 46).

Like other sports teams, basketball teams have been considered as CAS (Davids, Araújo, & Shuttleworth, 2005; García-Izquierdo et al., in press). As regards the previously mentioned characteristics of CAS, i.e., interdependence, uncertainty, interaction, and chaos (Nowak & Vallacher, 1998), at least three are present in the basketball setting: high task interdependence (Landis, 2001), high interaction, and uncertainty, as a consequence of the interaction between team members and their context (Wall, Cordery, & Clegg, 2002). In other words, basketball teams are *task interdependent* because they cannot play a match without there being *interaction* between players and the context (i.e., the other team, the spectators, and so on), and *uncertainty* is high because in every match the composition of each team changes several times and the final outcome also depends on the rival team's performance; the circumstances may also change from one match to another.

Regarding *chaos*, García-Izquierdo et al. (in press) have shown that more than 80% of professional basketball players reveal chaotic dynamics in their individual outcomes, but to the best of our knowledge no one has yet studied the effectiveness dynamics of basketball teams. Indeed, very little research has been conducted into the chaotic nature of team effectiveness, although the empirical evidence suggests that team sports such as indoor football and water polo do show typical chaotic dynamics (e.g., Davids, Vilar, Travassos & Araújo, 2010; Passos et al., 2011). Given the conceptualization of CAS and the empirical evidence derived from other sports, it therefore seems reasonable to expect that basketball teams will show chaotic patterns in their outcomes. Thus, our first hypothesis is:

Hypothesis 1: The patterns of team effectiveness in professional basketball teams will be mostly chaotic in nature, as opposed to other types of patterns.

Additionally, and inspired by the work of Bak (1991), we are interested in identifying which chaotic pattern (i.e., low dimensional or high dimensional) is the most frequent. The empirical evidence suggests that low-dimensional chaos (i.e., deterministic and predictable to some degree) is more frequent than high-dimensional chaos (i.e., deterministic but unpredictable and near to random) in organizational settings. For instance, Cheng and van de Ven (1996) studied the innovation processes in a biomedical context by analysing three time series: decisions made by innovation teams, the results obtained by these teams, and the number of contextual events relevant to the innovation processes. Their results revealed low-dimensional chaos in decisions and results, but a random pattern in contextual events. For their part Navarro and Arrieta (2010) used a diary method to examine the work motivation of 48 workers, and found that 42 of them (87.5%) showed a low-dimensional pattern. Finally, Richards (1990) studied the dynamics of three different decision-making processes, one in an experimental context and two in the real context. Both the real-context series had low-dimensional chaotic patterns.

Given their preponderance in organizational settings we would also expect to find patterns of low-dimensional chaos in the present study of basketball teams. As such, our second hypothesis is:

Hypothesis 2: The chaotic patterns found in the team effectiveness of professional basketball teams will be mostly of the low-dimensional kind.

In the context of professional sports it is common practice to change some squad members each season in order to improve team results and introduce innovations in playing style (Montanari, Silvestre, & Gallo, 2008). The empirical evidence suggests that squad changes do improve team effectiveness provided a certain degree of stability is guaranteed (e.g., Arrow & McGrath, 1995; Berman, Down, & Hill, 2002; Montanari et al., 2008), i.e., a core group of players is retained from one season to another. These changes may influence the dynamics of team outcomes, and one might postulate that team stability would generate fewer fluctuations in outcomes (i.e., they will tend to display linear or low-dimensional chaotic patterns, but not high-dimensional or random ones). As such, the third hypothesis is subdivided into two:

Hypothesis 3a: The stability of the squad will be positively associated with team effectiveness.

Hypothesis 3b: Teams with more stability in their squads will tend to show more predictable patterns of team effectiveness (linear or low-dimensional chaos).

A final aim of the study is to understand the relevance of chaotic dynamics for team effectiveness. Research in the field of psychophysiology has demonstrated that low-dimensional chaotic patterns are associated with healthy outcomes, whereas linear patterns and the absence of any pattern as well (i.e., random dynamic) are linked to malfunctions (e.g., Freeman, 1991; Goldberger, 1991; Kaplan et al., 1991). This phenomenon, termed *healthy variability* by Ceja and Navarro (2011), has also been reported in the context of organizational psychology, where low-dimensional chaos has been shown to be associated with better results in work motivation (Arrieta, Navarro, & Vicente, 2008), flow experiences (Ceja & Navarro, 2011), and teams (Guastello, 2010). The work of Guastello (2010), for instance, shows that the more effective emergency response teams exhibit indicators of low-dimensional chaotic patterns.

Generalizing these results to the team sports context, one would expect to find healthy variability in our study. Basketball teams that respond flexibly and creatively to the uncertainty of their environment, changing their behaviour to adapt continuously and to evolve with the environment, should achieve better outcomes. One of the reasons for this is that the wide variety of behaviours displayed by CAS makes them capable of adapting to changing and unpredictable environments. Applied to the present study, the healthy variability phenomenon would mean that a team showing low-dimensional chaotic patterns would obtain better outcomes (e.g., better results, reaching play-offs, etc.) than would teams with other patterns. Thus, our final hypothesis is as follows:

Hypothesis 4: Teams with low-dimensional chaotic patterns in their effectiveness tend to obtain better results at the end of the competition than do those teams with other patterns.

METHOD

Participants

The study sample comprised teams from the Spanish Premier Basketball League (known as the ACB), in which 18 teams participate each year. As in other European competitions the teams with the worst end-of-season results are relegated to a lower league (Wolfe et al., 2005). In this regard, a prerequisite for inclusion in the sample was that a team had played for at least three consecutive seasons in the league during the 12-year observation period (1996–2008), thus ensuring a sufficient number of recordings for a time-series analysis from the perspective of NDS theory (Heath, 2000). Twenty-three of the twenty-nine possible teams (79.31%) that made up the sample pool fulfilled this condition and were entered into the analyses, with the remainder being excluded. The data were gathered between January and June 2009 from the league's official website.

Measures

Two effectiveness measures were used by robust time series based on team outcomes recorded during every match by trained observers. Team statistics and the results of each match were published on the league's official website, from where the research team gathered these data. In accordance with the classification of Guzzo and Dickson (1996), the two measures used referred to group-produced outputs.

The first measure was a composite criterion established by the league and which includes various positive and negative results that a team achieves in every match. This criterion captures the behavioural outcomes of the team (shots, rebounds, turnovers, etc.), is referred to as Statistics ("S") and is calculated via the following formula:

$$S = (a + b + c + d + e + f) - (w + x + y + z)$$

where a is the number of points per game, b is the number of rebounds obtained per game, c is the number of assists per game, d is the number of steals per game, e is the number of personal fouls committed by the other team per game, f is the number of blocked shots per game, w is the number of missed shots per game, x is the number of turnovers per game, y is the number of rebounds failed per game, and z is the number of personal fouls committed per game.

The second measure of team effectiveness was the position of each team in the league at the end of each day's play ("Ranking"). This position varies according to the number of matches won by the team, and in the event that two teams have won the same number of matches, the ranking is decided by the number of points scored and conceded during the season. The best rankings are represented by the lowest values (i.e., 1 for first, 2 for second, and so on).

We also measured the teams' end-of-season results by the number of play-offs ("Play-offs") for the title of champion in which they were involved during the observation period (12 years). The play-offs are the final phase of the competition, and only eight teams qualify for this each season. Being able to reach a play-off position at the end of the league is seen as a sign of success by all teams.

Finally, team stability was measured by the mean proportion of players in the squad who remained from one season to another. This piece of data was also recorded for teams that were relegated and later returned to the Premier League.

All these measures are objective, thereby avoiding the problems associated with perceptual measures (Humphrey, Morgeson, & Mannor, 2010). Moreover, the use of robust time series (i.e., with hundreds of records) reduces the likelihood of committing Type I and Type II errors when establishing relationships between variables in research involving time (see McGrath, Arrow, Gruenfeld, Hollingshead, & O'Connor, 1993).

Procedure and analysis

The first step involved conducting a descriptive analysis of the time series (Statistics and Ranking) for the participating teams. Then, in order to test Hypotheses 1 and 2, the patterns were analysed by means of three complementary techniques which have been developed within the framework of NDS theory: maximal Lyapunov exponent, recurrence plot, and surrogate data. As stated earlier, techniques derived from NDS theory are used because they enable us not only to identify patterns that other techniques do not (i.e., linear and near-to-linear ones), but also to differentiate between chaotic and random patterns, a critical distinction in contexts involving dynamic systems such as teams. All the analyses were performed using specific software: Chaos Data Analyzer (Sprott & Rowlands, 1995) for the maximal Lyapunov exponent, Visual Recurrence Analysis 4.8 (Kononov, 2005) for the recurrence plots, and TISEAN 3.0 (Hegger, Kantz, & Schreiber, 2007) for surrogate data. Given that these techniques have not been widely used in research on teams, they are briefly described next. A more detailed review can be found in Heath (2000).

Lyapunov exponents indicate the rate of divergence of two initially close trajectories in phase space. Phase space is a geometric representation in which the values adopted by the variable over time are the coordinates of an m-dimensional space (where m is the number of variables necessary to describe the behaviour of a system, also called the embedding dimension). If the rate of divergence is greater than zero then the series is regarded as chaotic, whereas a value of zero or less indicates that the series is linear. If all we are interested in knowing is the time series pattern then we only need to calculate the maximal Lyapunov exponent, since a single positive exponent is sufficient for a series to be considered as chaotic (Heath, 2000). However, it is advisable to use this measure in combination with other statistics because the maximal Lyapunov exponent is not adequate for distinguishing between random and chaotic cases.

The recurrence plot can be used as a complement to the results derived from Lyapunov exponents. A recurrence plot is a graph that calculates the proximity of points on a two-dimensional graph containing all the possible trajectories of the time series, distinguishing between deterministic series (both linear and chaotic) and nondeterministic series (i.e., random; Heath, 2000). Its main limitation is that the identification of the pattern represented by the recurrence plot always depends on the interpretations made by the researcher. This is especially problematic when it comes to differentiating between random and high-dimensional chaotic patterns. However, one way of resolving any discrepancies between the maximal Lyapunov exponent and the recurrence plot is to use surrogate data.

Surrogate data are used to rule out the possibility that the time series pattern is due to chance, in other words, the possibility that although the values of the series are distributed in this way it is equally likely that they could have been distributed in any other way. The logic behind the surrogate data procedure is simple: Random series are generated from the original series and a rank-order test is then performed in order to rule out the possibility that the original series is also random (Theiler, Eubank, Longtin, Galdrikian, & Farmer, 1992). If previous analyses (Lyapunov exponents and recurrence plot) have identified a given series as random but the surrogate data rule out this possibility, then the series in question is considered to show high-dimensional chaos. If all the analyses (Lyapunov exponents, recurrence plot, and surrogate data) produce congruent results (e.g., they all indicate chaotic behaviour), the series is considered to show low-dimensional chaos.

In order to test Hypothesis 3a, we analysed the correlations between the stability of each team and its effectiveness. The association between variables was established by means of Spearman correlations, which do not require the assumption of normality to be fulfilled. Lastly, ANOVA was used to test Hypotheses 3b and 4.

RESULTS

Table 1 shows information regarding the teams that made up the sample, along with the results of the descriptive analysis of the time series used in the present study. It can be seen that the squad size ranged between 11 and 15, and squad stability between 28.85% and 58.69%. The number of play-offs contested by the teams varied between 0 and 12. As regards the size of the time series these ranged between 102 and 408 points, which is sufficient for the analyses performed (Heath, 2000). As expected, teams with better mean statistics have longer time series (more years in the Premier League), whereas those with poorer statistics tend to get relegated and have shorter time series. The mean value for the Statistics measure ranged between 71.27 and 92.05. As regards the Ranking, this is an ordinal variable and it was therefore

TABLE 1
Squad, team results, and descriptive statistics of the time series

Team	Size of the squad	Mean stability of the squad	Number of play-offs	Time series size	Statistics				Ranking			
					M	*SD*	*Min.*	*Max.*	*Mdn*	*Mode*	*Min.*	*Max.*
A	13	44.65%	2	204	78.73	19.81	35	135	14	18	1	18
B	14	56.34%	12	408	90.94	19.58	39	151	3	1	1	15
C	15	34.87%	1	136	76.93	18.14	23	117	12	14	1	18
D	13	34.44%	0	238	74.67	19.53	23	140	13	11	4	18
E	12	33.36%	0	238	77.14	19.38	29	128	13	16	4	18
F	13	28.85%	0	170	72.67	19.83	17	133	16	14/17	3	18
G	13	58.69%	10	408	85.57	20.22	25	143	7	4	1	18
H	12	38.38%	3	340	76.49	19.98	10	128	11	6	1	18
I	11	29.30%	0	102	71.27	21.99	17	122	17	17	6	18
J	13	40.74%	4	408	82.16	20.07	17	154	11	13	2	18
K	13	44.83%	6	408	79.15	19.37	16	135	8	5	1	17
L	14	35.23%	0	306	78.27	18.69	33	149	14	14	2	18
M	14	48.22%	8	408	88.42	18.98	42	156	8	4	1	18
N	13	29.12%	1	170	73.71	20.38	33	123	14	18	4	18
O	14	37.10%	1	136	80.49	18.56	29	129	13	13/18	1	18
P	12	42.00%	2	306	80.66	18.95	20	132	11	11	2	18
Q	12	32.13%	0	102	73.98	17.78	32	125	16	17	10	18
R	14	49.41%	9	408	89.14	18.95	33	151	2	1	1	15
S	14	40.87%	12	408	79.28	17.85	17	124	10	12	1	18
T	14	38.26%	2	408	92.05	20.79	13	167	4	4	1	18
U	13	45.60%	11	408	83.50	20.33	31	146	7	7	1	18
V	14	46.06%	11	408	85.16	19.75	28	139	6	5	1	18
W	12	37.80%	1	408	77.90	19.39	24	138	13	16	1	18

$N = 23$. The names of the teams have been replaced by a letter to avoid their identification.

analysed using the median (whose values ranged between 2 and 17) and the mode (values between 1 and 18). It is also worth noting that all the teams occupied the first and eighteenth league positions at one time or another.

The next step involved identifying the pattern of each time series. Table 2 shows the results broken down by effectiveness measure (Statistics and Ranking), and Figure 2 provides examples of results derived from each technique for each pattern (linear, low-dimensional chaos, high-dimensional chaos, and random). It can be seen that all the teams show chaotic patterns in their effectiveness, thus confirming the first study hypothesis. Because neither linear nor random patterns were found in the sample, Figure 2 also includes, for illustrative purposes, a mathematical example of each of these dynamics. As regards the second hypothesis, it was expected that chaotic patterns would be low-dimensional for both measures (Statistics and Ranking), but the results show that this was only the case with respect to Statistics, specifically in 65.22% of cases. Therefore, the second hypothesis is only partially supported.

Hypothesis 3a was tested by obtaining the correlations between the mean squad stability and team effectiveness. As can be seen in Table 3, the Spearman correlations reveal a strong association between team stability and Statistics, $r_s = .83, p \leq .01$, Ranking, $r_s = -.81, p \leq .01$, and the number of play-offs contested, $r_s = .88$, $p \leq .01$. These results therefore support Hypothesis 3_a.

TABLE 2
Patterns of team effectiveness

	Statistics	*Ranking*
Step 1. Maximal Lyapunov exponent		
Linear patterns	0 (0.00%)	0 (0.00%)
Chaotic patterns	23 (100.00%)	23 (100.00%)
Step 2. Recurrence plot		
Linear patterns	0 (0.00%)	0 (0.00%)
Low-dimensional chaotic patterns	15 (65.22%)	7 (30.43%)
High-dimensional chaotic patterns or random patterns	8 (34.78%)	16 (69.57%)
Step 3. Surrogate data (final results)		
Linear patterns	0 (0.00%)	0 (0.00%)
Low-dimensional chaotic patterns	15 (65.22%)	7 (30.43%)
High-dimensional chaotic patterns	8 (34.78%)	16 (69.57%)
Random patterns	0 (0.00%)	0 (0.00%)

$N = 23$.

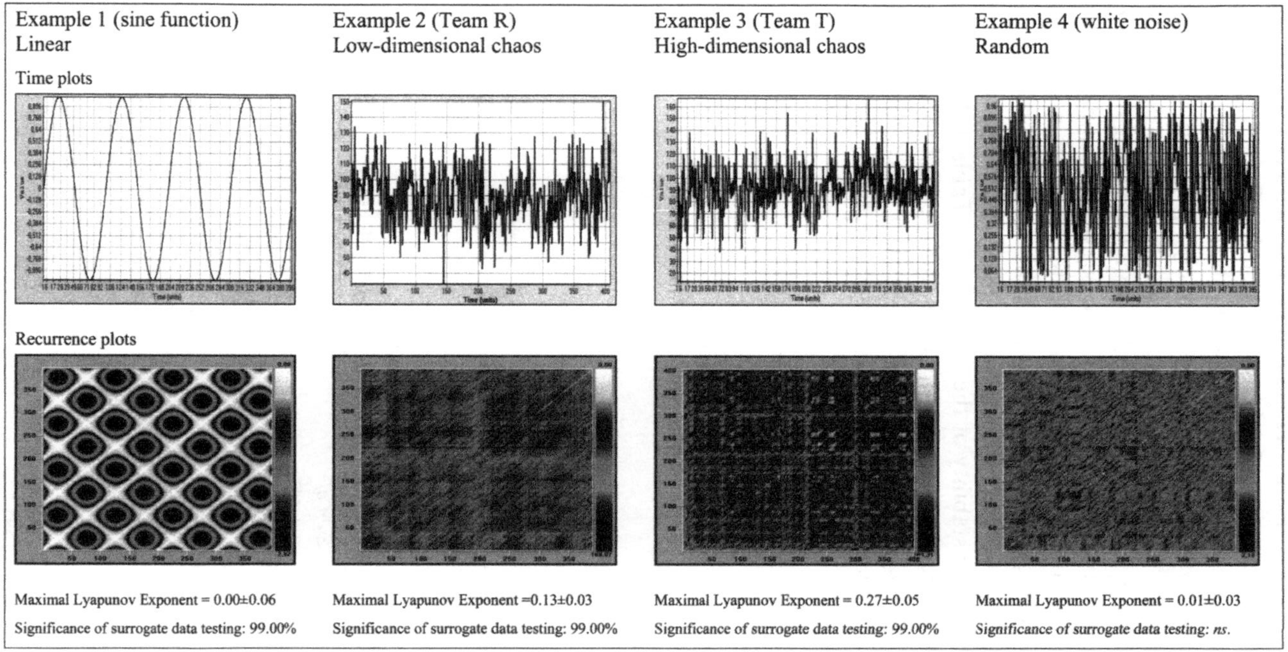

Figure 2. Sample cases of linear, low-dimensional chaos, high-dimensional chaos, and random patterns. Examples of low-dimensional chaos and high-dimensional chaos belong to the sample; the two remaining series were generated ad hoc.

With respect to Hypothesis 3b, we tested for the presence of a relationship between team stability and the patterns found in team effectiveness. As our sample is small, Durbin-Watson, Kolmogorov-Smirnov, and Levene's tests were first applied to analyse independence, normality, and homoscedasticity, respectively, prior to performing the ANOVA. The results showed that homoscedasticity was not supported in the case of Ranking. Welch's test was therefore used instead of the F-test in the analyses regarding Ranking. As all the cases were identified as chaotic by the surrogate data analysis, the differences were examined by considering the type of chaos, i.e., distinguishing between time series according to whether they showed low- or high-dimensional chaos. We then compared team effectiveness with the stability of the series, but as Table 4 shows there were no significant differences between the teams with respect to either Statistics, $F = 0.62$, $p \leq .44$, or Ranking, Welch = 1.64, $p \leq .22$. Given that squad stability was not related to patterns in team effectiveness, Hypothesis 3b was not supported.

TABLE 3
Spearman correlations

	1	*2*	*3*	*4*
1. Statistics	1			
2. Ranking	−.87**	1		
3. Number of play-offs	.76**	−.84**	1	
4. Team stability	.83**	−.81**	.88**	1

$N = 23$. **$p \leq .01$, one-tailed.

TABLE 4
ANOVA between team effectiveness patterns and team stability

	Sum of squares	*Degrees of freedom*	*F*	*Sig. F*
Statistics				
Intergroups	45.81	1	0.62	.44
Intragroups	1552.72	21		
Total	1598.53	22		
			Welch	
Ranking				
Intergroups	106.92	1	1.64	.22
Intragroups	1491.60	21		
Total	1598.52	22		

$N = 23$.

The final study hypothesis was related to the phenomenon of healthy variability. This was tested by using ANOVA to analyse the association between the observed patterns and the number of play-offs contested. As before, we tested for independence, normality, and homoscedasticity, and as the same results were obtained Welch's test was again used for Ranking. The ANOVA results are shown in Table 5, where it can be seen that the relationship was significant in the case of Statistics, $F = 5.68$, $p \leq .03$. Additionally, and as illustrated in Figure 3, teams with low-dimensional chaotic patterns were involved in more play-offs ($M = 5.67$) than were teams with high-dimensional chaotic patterns ($M = 1.38$). Therefore, the fourth hypothesis is partially confirmed.

DISCUSSION AND CONCLUSIONS

This article reports the analysis of two objective measures of team effectiveness in 23 professional basketball teams over a period of 12 seasons (12 years). The aim was to identify any chaotic patterns characteristic of CAS, and to determine whether any pattern was associated with better team outcomes. As already noted, teams have been considered as CAS by various authors, but few studies to date have provided empirical evidence that teams show a defining characteristic of CAS (e.g., Gorman et al., 2010; Pincus et al., 2008; Wheelan & Williams, 2003) and, to the best of our knowledge, there is no research of this kind in relation to professional basketball. The main findings of this study were as follows: (1) all the teams showed a deterministic pattern; (2) this deterministic pattern was chaotic; (3) the pattern was not related to team stability; and (4) teams with low-dimensional

TABLE 5
ANOVA between team effectiveness patterns and number of play-offs contested

	Sum of squares	*Degrees of freedom*	*F*	*Sig. F*
Statistics				
Intergroups	96.10	1	5.68*	.03
Intragroups	355.20	21		
Total	451.30	22		
			Welch	
Ranking				
Intergroups	0.65	1	0.03	.86
Intragroups	450.65	21		
Total	451.30	22		

$N = 23$. $^{*}p \leq .05$.

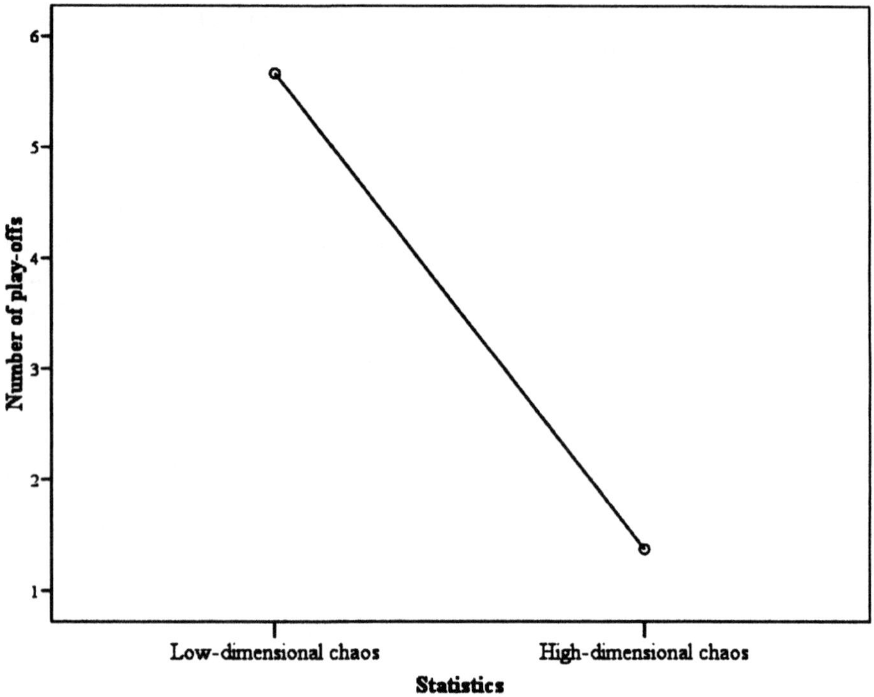

Figure 3. Mean differences between low-dimensional chaotic patterns and high-dimensional chaotic patterns with respect to the number of play-offs contested.

chaotic patterns achieved better results at the end of the season. Let us consider each of these findings in more detail.

Pattern identification is basic to NDS theory because it reveals any noteworthy consistency in the phenomenon under study (in this case, team effectiveness). Consequently, it shows that prediction is possible despite apparent irregularity (see time plots in Figure 2). This occurs because CAS tend to display changes that result from intrinsic dynamics, although external variables may also produce changes in them (Guastello & Liebovich, 2009; Nowak & Vallacher, 1998). As Nowak and Vallacher (1998, p. 33) state, "the causal effects of external variables are difficult to describe without taking into account the system's internally generated sources of change. In attempting to model and predict change, then, it is necessary to consider the interaction of both external and internal forces." Our data are consistent with this assertion: When team effectiveness is measured by Ranking, characterized by high external influence (the results of all matches are taken into account), it is less predictable than when measured by the Statistics measure, which depends solely on the effectiveness of the team and its rival.

The predictive capacity of a given team depends on whether its effectiveness is characterized by low- or high-dimensional chaos. This aspect must clearly be taken into account in professional practice, in which decisions are frequently based on the most recent results, even though this would only be valid if the team shows a linear or near-linear pattern. In our view it would be advisable, when making decisions, to begin by identifying and analysing the pattern so as to determine the type of fluctuations shown by the team in the past, before considering this information alongside current results.

The study also examined the stability of teams. The literature suggests that squad changes can lead to better results provided a certain degree of stability is ensured, although research into effectiveness patterns over time is scarce. On the basis of the present results it can be concluded that stability is related to team effectiveness (i.e., greater stability leads to greater effectiveness), although surprisingly the patterns found in team effectiveness are not attributable to team stability (i.e., greater stability is not related to more predictable patterns). One possible explanation for this result, which was unexpected, is provided by findings in other team contexts (e.g., Gorman et al., 2010; Guastello, Bock, Caldwell, & Bond, 2005; Weick & Gilfillan, 1971). For example, Guastello et al. (2005) found that team coordination (see Weick & Gilfillan, 1971) persisted after changing up to two members of a four-person group; the original study by Weick and Gilfillan (1971) showed that effectiveness patterns persisted in a group after everyone had sequentially changed. More recently, Gorman et al. (2010) analysed the dynamics in intact versus mixed teams across time, reporting that mixed teams (i.e., teams with changes to their members) were more stable but also more adaptive. In the sports context, Montanari et al. (2008) found that team stability had a positive impact on effectiveness up to a critical point, after which it might be detrimental. Our results are consistent with this literature. Indeed, a possible explanation for our results is that patterns are intrinsic to the team and its collective, dynamic and changing nature (McGrath et al., 2000), regardless of team stability (Guastello et al., 2005; Weick & Gilfillan, 1971). Obviously, these results and their corresponding explanation, founded on NDS theory and its proposal regarding intrinsic dynamics, must be tested with further research. Nonetheless, the findings have both theoretical and practical relevance. Specifically, we suggest that introducing a few squad changes, even when a team's evolution over time is unknown (i.e., in the case of high-dimensional chaotic patterns) could increase effectiveness by making the team more adaptive.

Another noteworthy finding was that teams with low-dimensional chaotic patterns in Statistics had better results at the end of the season. In addition to providing further evidence of healthy variability (Ceja & Navarro, 2011), this raises the question as to which variables predict the type of pattern that a team will show. This aspect should be addressed in future research as it would enable the formation of more effective teams. The variables proposed as being predictive of team effectiveness by dynamic models, such as those based on the IMOI framework (Ilgen et al., 2005; Mathieu et al., 2008), would be a good starting point for research into this question. These models conceptualize teams as CAS whose outputs influence the organizational system, contextual contingencies, and environmental dynamics and complexity, which, in turn, influence the inputs, thereby generating a cyclical and reciprocal process (Kozlowski & Ilgen, 2006).

A further finding of note is that no association was found between the pattern of the Ranking measure and teams that were involved in more play-offs. This could be due to the fact that whereas the Statistics measure depends mainly on the team and its most immediate context (the opposing team), a team's ranking is also influenced by the behaviour of other teams, which would explain the increased presence of high-dimensional chaotic patterns (i.e., a higher number of variables is necessary to explain Ranking dynamics).

Given these findings, we suggest that coaches need to acknowledge the inherent instability in teams, avoiding attempts to control the team and trying, by contrast, to manage uncertainty. In other words, they should embrace the instability that is inherent in teams and use it to their benefit. As stated by Zimmerman, Lindberg, and Plsek (2001), this implies: managing teams through flexible criteria that can be modified according to the situation; encouraging a variety of opinions so as to foster innovation and adaptation; creating the right conditions for facing challenges; establishing guidelines that are not so specific that they cannot be altered; taking into account informal relationships; and promoting cooperation and competition at the same time. The research by Bourbousson, Poizat, Saury, and Seve (2011) is an example of how this kind of management can be applied to the sports context. According to these authors, shared knowledge of the team promotes effectiveness, but this shared knowledge changes during the course of a match. Consequently, coaches must teach team members to use the opportunities for coordination as they appear in a match, thereby updating the shared knowledge of the team.

Finally, the study has demonstrated the appropriateness of the chosen statistical methods and techniques for studying teams as CAS, this being an aspect which other authors had previously recommended (Mack, Huddleson, Dutler, & Mintah, 2000; Mathieu et al., 2008; McGrath, 1997). The advantage of these techniques is that they focus on whether the series are deterministic or not, but without presupposing a given data structure. Thus, they can be used as a form of screening, after which the appropriate analytical technique (linear or nonlinear) can be applied (Ramos-Villagrasa & García-Izquierdo, 2011).

Limitations and recommendations for future research

The present study does have certain limitations. First, although conducting the research in the context of professional basketball makes it easier to replicate, caution should be exercised when extrapolating the results. For example, it may be that the particular features of basketball, such as the relationships between team components and the need for high-level effectiveness in a competitive setting, lead to the emergence of chaotic patterns. Another example is the low stability of the squad compared with other organizational settings. In longitudinal sports research, a team's name remains the same yet its composition may change drastically (Montanari et al., 2008). This turnover does not mean that sports teams cannot be studied, but it is an aspect that must be considered in the future. Further research should therefore aim to determine the degree to which the present results can be generalized to other similar teams and contexts. Other teams to which these results might generalize must share at least the three characteristics that we stated earlier: interdependence between team members, uncertainty about the future, and a close interaction between the team and its immediate context.

A second limitation of the study is the possible effect of range restriction due to the uniqueness of the sample. The study has focused on the highest level of competition in Spain, where both teams and players are more homogeneous than at lower levels due to the entry requirements and the standard of results and resources required in order to participate, etc. This circumstance could have influenced the results. It would therefore be advisable to conduct similar studies at other competitive levels that are characterized by greater diversity.

A third limitation concerns the measures used in the study. The use of archival data has both critics and supporters. Critics such as Campbell et al. (1993) argue that objective measures are influenced by context and that they are related to results rather than to behaviour. Conversely, authors such as Landis (2001) and Stewart and Nandkeolyar (2007) consider that such measures show consistency and objectivity. In our view, both objective and subjective measures are useful, and which kind is used will depend on the purpose of the study (Muckler & Seven, 1992). In this regard, we believe that our measures of effectiveness are consistent with our objectives.

Last, the number of teams studied here is too low to rule out any effect of methodological artefacts (e.g., low statistical power in correlations) on the results, and hence more research is needed to provide additional support. Furthermore, the techniques used do not test if the time series are affected by seasonality, i.e., periodic fluctuations derived from context (e.g., the beginning or the end of the league). Further research about the potential presence and influence of seasonality in relation to basketball time series is therefore required. Nonetheless, we believe that our research is valuable as an important step towards understanding how professional basketball teams might be conceptualized as CAS.

Continuing with recommendations for future research, there is a need to determine which variables predict the patterns of team effectiveness. To this end the potential of the NDS framework should be explored in greater depth so as to develop predictive short-term models that explain a high proportion of variance with a few variables (Mathews et al., 1999). An especially interesting example of these applications is the work of Keil and Cortina (2001), who performed a meta-analysis about the temporal consistency of cognitive ability and its relationship to performance at the individual level, showing that the methodology based on NDS theory provides a new and promising perspective.

In terms of predictive capacity, and as already stated, one can distinguish what is known as low-dimensional chaos, which can be described with a few variables and in which short-term predictions are possible. One avenue for further research would therefore be to use dynamical and nonlinear models of prediction to investigate which variables are key when it comes to explaining the greater amount of variance. In this regard it would also be interesting to analyse how team effectiveness emerges out of the individual effectiveness of team members, as Arrow et al. (2004) and García-Izquierdo et al. (in press) have suggested. One could tentatively assume that teams will tend to show more complex patterns than would their members, due to the interaction and interdependence of the latter, and this would generate emergent processes (e.g., cohesion or shared mental models) and results that act as feedback. As such, team effectiveness would appear as showing new properties that cannot be reduced to individuals, but which nonetheless remains predictable, at least in most cases.

CONCLUSION

The present study continues a line of research conducted over the last two decades which has shown that in order to understand group behaviour it is necessary to consider teams as complex, adaptive, and dynamical systems. This article brings the question to the professional sports context, where effects of time have been largely unexplored. Having provided new empirical evidence in support of the conceptualization of teams as CAS, the next step is to determine precisely how this can be used to improve team effectiveness. Our study has four key findings: First, team effectiveness fluctuates considerably; second, it is possible to find discernible trends in team effectiveness; third, these trends are not related to stability of the squad; and last, a low-dimensional chaotic pattern is related to better team results.

Further research using the longitudinal, dynamical, and nonlinear approach of the NDS framework will add greater depth to these findings, increasing our knowledge about team effectiveness and about teams themselves.

REFERENCES

Ancona, D. G., Goodman, P. S., Lawrence, B., & Tushman, M. L. (2001). Time: A new research lens. *Academy of Management Review, 26*, 645–683.

Arrieta, C., Navarro, J., & Vicente, S. (2008). Factores asociados a la emergencia de patrones diferenciales de la motivación en el trabajo [Variables related to the emergence of differential patterns in work motivation]. *Psicothema, 20*, 745–752.

Arrow, H., & McGrath, J. E. (1995). Membership dynamics in groups at work: A theoretical framework. In B. M. Staw & L. L. Cummings (Eds.), *Research in organizational behavior* (Vol. 17, pp. 373–411). Greenwich, CT: JAI Press.

Arrow, H., McGrath, J. E., & Berdahl, J. L. (2000). *Small groups as complex systems: Formation, coordination, development, and adaptation*. Thousand Oaks, CA: Sage.

Arrow, H., Poole, M. S., Henry, K. B., Wheelan, S., & Moreland, R. (2004). Time, change, and development: the temporal perspective on groups. *Small Group Research, 35*, 73–105.

Bak, P. (1991). *How nature works: The science of self-organised criticality*. New York, NY: Copernicus Press.

Barnes, C. M., & Morgeson, F. P. (2007). Typical performance, maximal performance and performance variability: Expanding our understanding of how organisations value performance. *Human Performance, 20*, 259–274.

Berman, S., Down, J., & Hill, C. (2002). Tacit knowledge as a source of competitive advantage in the National Basketball Association. *Academy of Management Journal, 45*, 13–31.

Bourbousson, G., Poizat, J., Saury, J., & Seve, C. (2011). Description of dynamic shared knowledge: An exploratory study during a competitive team sports interaction. *Ergonomics, 54*, 120–138.

Browne, M. A., & Mahoney, M. J. (1984). Sport psychology. *Annual Review of Psychology, 35*, 605–625.

Campbell, J. P., McCloy, R. A., Oppler, S. H., & Sager, C. E. (1993). A theory of performance. In N. Schmitt & W. C. Borman (Eds.), *Personnel selection in organisations* (pp. 35–70). San Francisco, CA: Jossey-Bass.

Carron, A. V., & Brawley, L. R. (2008). Group dynamics in sport and physical activity. In T. S. Horn (Ed.), *Advances in sport psychology* (pp. 213–237). Champaign, IL: Human Kinetics.

Ceja, L., & Navarro, J. (2011). Dynamic patterns of flow in the workplace: Characterizing within-individual variability using a complexity science approach. *Journal of Organizational Behavior, 32*, 627–651.

Chatfield, C. (1996). *The analysis of time series: an introduction*. New York, NY: Chapman & Hall.

Cheng, Y. T., & van de Ven, A. H. (1996). Learning the innovation journey: Order out of chaos? *Organization Science, 7*, 593–614.

Conroy, D. E., Kaye, M. P., & Schantz, L. H. (2008). Quantitative research methodology. In T. S. Horn (Ed.), *Advances in sport psychology* (pp. 15–30). Champaign, IL: Human Kinetics.

Cummings, T., & Blumberg, M. (1987). Advanced manufacturing technology and work design. In T. Wall, C. Clegg & N. Kemp (Eds.), *The human side of advanced manufacturing technology* (pp. 37–60). Chichester, UK Wiley.

Davids, K., Araújo, D., & Shuttleworth, R. (2005). Applications of dynamical systems theory to football. In T. Reilly, J. Cabri, & D. Araújo (Eds.), *Science and football* (Vol. V, pp. 537–550). London, UK: Routledge.

Davids, K., Vilar, L., Travassos, B., & Aráujo, D. (2010). Ball and goal location as constraints on decision making in team sports. *Journal of Science and Medicine in Sport, 13S*, e89. doi:10.1016/j.jsams.2010.10.650

Dirks, K. T. (2000). Trust in leadership and team performance: Evidence from NCAA basketball. *Journal of Applied Psychology, 85*, 1004–1012.

Freeman, W. J. (1991). The physiology of perception. *The Scientific American, 264*, 78–85.

García-Izquierdo, A. L., Ramos-Villagrasa, P. J., & Navarro, J. (in press). Dynamic criteria: A longitudinal analysis of professional basketball players' outcomes. *Spanish Journal of Psychology*.

Gell-Mann, M. (1994). *The quark and the jaguar*. New York, NY: Freeman.

Goldberger, A. L. (1991). Is the normal heartbeat chaotic or homeostatic? *News in Physiological Sciences, 6*, 87–91.

Gorman, J. C., Amazeen, P. G., & Cooke, N. J. (2010). Team coordination dynamics. *Nonlinear Dynamics, Psychology, and Life Sciences, 14*, 265–289.

Guastello, S. J. (2010). Nonlinear dynamics of team performance and adaptability in emergency response. *Human Factors, 52*, 162–172.

Guastello, S. J., Bock, B., Caldwell, P., & Bond, R. W., Jr. (2005). Origins of group coordination: Nonlinear dynamics and the role of verbalization. *Nonlinear Dynamics, Psychology, and Life Sciences, 9*, 175–208.

Guastello, S. J., & Liebovitch, M. (2009). Introduction to nonlinear dynamics and complexity. In S. J. Guastello, M. Koopmans, & D. Pincus (Eds.), *Chaos and complexity in psychology: The theory of nonlinear dynamical systems* (pp. 1–40). New York, NY: Cambridge University Press.

Guzzo, R. A., & Dickson, M. W. (1996). Teams in organizations: Recent research on performance and effectiveness. *Annual Review of Psychology, 47*, 307–338.

Heath, R. A. (2000). *Nonlinear dynamics: Techniques and applications in psychology*. Mahwah, NJ: Lawrence Erlbaum Associates, Inc.

Hegger, R., Kantz, H., & Schreiber, T. (2007). TISEAN: Nonlinear time series analysis 3.0 [Computer software]. Retrieved 1 March 2007 from http://www.mpipks-dresden.mpg.de/~tisean/Tisean_3.0.1/index.html

Humphrey, S. E., Morgeson, F. P., & Mannor, M. J. (2010). Developing a theory of the strategic core of teams: A role composition model of team performance. *Journal of Applied Psychology, 94*, 48–61.

Ilgen, D. R., Hollenbeck, J. R., Johnson, M., & Jundt, D. (2005). Teams in organizations: From Input-Process-Output models to IMOI models. *Annual Review of Psychology, 56*, 517–543.

Kaplan, D. T., Furman, M. I., Pincus, S. M., Ryan, S. M., Lipsitz, L. A., & Golderberger, A. L. (1991). Aging and the complexity of cardiovascular dynamics. *Biophysical Journal, 59*, 945–949.

Kauffman, S. A. (1993). *The origins of order: Self-organization and selection in evolution*. New York, NY: Oxford University Press.

Keil, C. T., & Cortina, J. M. (2001). Degradation of validity over time: A test and extension of Ackerman's model. *Psychological Bulletin, 127*, 673–697.

Kononov, E. (2005). Visual recurrence analysis 4.8 [Computer software]. Retrieved 24 October 2006 from http://pweb.netcom.com/~eugenek/

Kozlowski, S. W., & Ilgen, D. R. (2006). Enhancing the effectiveness of work groups and teams. *Psychological Science in the Public Interest, 7*, 77–124.

Kozlowski, S. W. J., & Bell, B. S. (2003). Work groups and teams in organizations. In W. C. Borman, D. R. Ilgen, & R. J. Klimoski (Eds.), *Handbook of psychology Vol. 12. Industrial and organizational psychology* (pp. 333–375). Hoboken, NJ: Wiley.

Landis, R. S. (2001). A note on the stability of team performance. *Journal of Applied Psychology, 86*, 446–450.

Lewin, R. (1993). *Complexity: Life at the edge of chaos*. London, UK: Phoenix.

Lorenz, E. N. (1993). *The essence of chaos*. Washington, WA: University of Washington Press.

Loy, J. W., McPherson, B. D., & Kenyon, G. S. (1978). *Sport and social systems*. Reading, MA: Addison-Wesley.

Mack, M. G., Huddleston, S., Dutler, K. E., & Mintah, J. K. (2000). Chaos theory: A new science for sport behavior? *Athletic Insight: The Online Journal of Sport Psychology, 2*, 8–16.

Mathews, K. M., White, M. C., & Long, R. G. (1999). Why study the complexity sciences in the social sciences? *Human Relations, 52*, 439–462.

Mathieu, J. E., Maynard, M. T., Rapp, T., & Gilson, L. (2008). Team effectiveness 1997–2007: A review of recent advancements and a glimpse into the future. *Journal of Management, 34*, 410–476.

McGrath, J. E. (1964). *Social psychology: A brief introduction*. New York, NY: Holt, Rinehart & Winston.

McGrath, J. E. (1991). Time, interaction and performance (TIP): A theory of groups. *Small Group Research, 22*, 147–174.

McGrath, J. E. (1997). Small group research, that once and future field: An interpretation of the past with an eye to the future. *Group Dynamics: Theory, Research, and Practice, 1*, 7–27.

McGrath, J. E., Arrow, H., & Berdahl, J. L. (2000). The study of groups: Past, present, and future. *Personality and Social Psychology Review, 4*, 95–105.

McGrath, J. E., Arrow, H., Gruenfeld, D. H., Hollingshead, A. B., & O'Connor, K. M. (1993). Groups, tasks, and technology: The effects of experience and change. *Small Group Research, 24*, 406–420.

Mitchell, T. R., & James, L. R. (2001). Building better theory: Time and the specification of when thing happen. *Academy of Management Review, 26*, 530–547.

Montanari, F., Silvestre, G., & Gallo, E. (2008). Team performance between change and stability: The case of the Italian "Serie A". *Journal of Sport Management, 22*, 701–716.

Muckler, F. A., & Seven, S. A. (1992). Selecting performance measures: "Objective" versus "subjective" measurement. *Human Factors, 34*(4), 441–455.

Navarro, J., & Arrieta, C. (2010). Chaos in human behavior: The case of work motivation. *Spanish Journal of Psychology, 13*, 244–256.

Nowak, A., & Vallacher, R. R. (1998). *Dynamical social psychology*. New York, NY: Guilford Press.

Passos, P., Davids, K., Araújo, D., Paz, N., Minguéns, J., & Mendes, J. (2011). Networks as a novel tool for studying team ball sports as complex social systems. *Journal of Science and Medicine in Sport, 14*, 170–176.

Pincus, D., Fox, K. M., Perez, K. A., Turner, J. S., & McGeehan, A. R. (2008). Nonlinear dynamics of individual and interpersonal conflict in an experimental group. *Small Group Research, 39*, 150–178.

Ramos-Villagrasa, P. J., & García-Izquierdo, A. L. (2011). Técnicas de análisis de patrones caóticos en Psicología [Techniques for analysing chaotic patterns: A review of empirical studies in psychology]. *Anales de Psicología, 27*, 239–248.

Richards, D. (1990). Is strategic decision making chaotic? *Behavioral Science, 35*, 219–232.

Roe, R. A. (2008). Time in applied psychology: The study of "what happens" rather than "what is". *The European Psychologist, 13*, 37–52.

Salas, E., Dickinson, T. L., Converse, S. A., & Tannenbaum, S. L. (1992). Toward an understanding of team performance and training. In R. W. Swezey & E. Salas (Eds.), *Teams: Their training and performance* (pp. 3–29). Norwood, NJ: Ablex.

Salas, E., Rosen, M. A., Burke, C. S., & Goodwin, G. F. (2009). The wisdom of collectives in organizations: An update of the teamwork competencies. In E. Salas, G. F. Goodwin, & C. S. Burke (Eds.), *Team effectiveness in complex organizations: Cross-disciplinary perspectives and approaches* (pp. 39–79). New York, NY: Psychology Press.

Sprott, J. C., & Rowlands, G. (1995). *Chaos data analyzer: The professional version. PC user's manual.* New York, NY: American Institute of Physics.

Stewart, G. L, & Nandkeolyar, A. K. (2007). Exploring how constraints created by other people influence intraindividual variation in objective performance measures. *Journal of Applied Psychology, 92*(4), 1149–1158.

Theiler, J., Eubank, S., Longtin, A., Galdrikian, B., & Farmer, J. D. (1992). Testing for nonlinearity in time series: The method of surrogate data. *Physica D, 58*, 77–94.

Wall, T. D., Cordery, J. L., & Clegg, C. W. (2002). Empowerment, performance and operational uncertainty: A theoretical integration. *Applied Psychology: An International Review, 51*, 146–169.

Weick, K., & Gilfillan, D. (1971). Fate of arbitrary traditions in a laboratory microculture. *Journal of Personality and Social Psychology, 17*, 179–191.

Wheelan, S. A., & Williams, T. (2003). Mapping dynamic interaction patterns in work groups. *Small Group Research, 34*, 443–467.

Wolfe, R., Weick, K., Usher, J., Terborg, J., Poppo, L., Murrell, A., et al. (2005). Sport and organizational studies: Exploring synergy. *Journal of Management Inquiry, 14*, 182–210.

Zimmerman, B., Lindberg, C., & Plsek, P. (2001). *Edgeware: Insights from complexity sciences for health care leaders.* Irving, TX: VHA, Inc. Retrieved from http://www.plexusinstitute.org/edgeware/archive/think

Aims and scope

The mission of the ***European Journal of Work and Organizational Psychology*** is to promote and support the development of Work and Organizational Psychology by publishing high-quality scientific articles that improve our understanding of phenomena occurring in work and organizational settings. The journal publishes empirical, theoretical, methodological, and review articles that are relevant to real-world situations.

The journal has a world-wide authorship, readership and editorial board. Submissions from all around the world are invited.

The journal primarily publishes freely submitted contributions, but will occasionally also publish a themed issue, although all contributions are submitted to rigorous peer review. Papers and themed issues are published on a wide range of topics covered by the umbrella of work, organizational, industrial and occupational psychology.

Submission of manuscripts

Manuscripts are invited for submission. New manuscripts should be submitted through our ScholarOne Manuscripts online submission site at: **http://mc.manuscriptcentral.com/pewo**.

Submitted papers are subject to a double blind academic peer review process. Please ensure your submitted files include a blinded copy with all identifying information removed.

Your covering e-mail/letter must include full contact details (including e-mail), the title of the journal to which you are submitting, and the title of your article.

All manuscripts should be submitted in American Psychological Association (APA) format following the latest edition of *Publication Manual of the APA* (currently 6th edition).

Full instructions for authors are available on the journal website at: **www.psypress.com/ejwop** The *European Journal of Work and Organizational Psychology* offers an open access option for authors called Taylor & Francis Open Select. For more information, see: http://journalauthors.tandf.co.uk/preparation/OpenAccess.asp#link2

Abstracting services

This Journal is covered by the following indexing/abstracting services: Current Contents/Social & Behavioral Sciences, Ergonomics Abstracts, European Reference Index for the Humanities (ERIH), PsycINFO, PubsHub, SCOPUS, Social Sciences Citation Index, Social Scisearch, Social Services Abstracts, Sociological Abstracts.

Copyright

Back issues

Taylor & Francis retains a 3-year back issue stock of journals. Older volumes are held by our official stockists: Periodicals Service Company, 11 Main Street, Germantown, NY 12526, USA to whom all orders and enquiries should be addressed. Tel: +1 518 537 4700; Fax: +1 518 537 5899; E-mail: psc@periodicals.com.

Free article access

As corresponding author, you will receive free access to your article on Taylor & Francis Online. You will be given access to the *My authored works* section of Taylor & Francis Online, which shows you all your published articles. You can easily view, read, and download your published articles from there. In addition, if someone has cited your article, you will be able to see this information. We are committed to promoting and increasing the visibility of your article and have provided this guidance <http://journalauthors.tandf.co.uk/beyondpublication/promotearticle.asp> on how you can help.

Reprints and journal copies

Corresponding authors can receive a complimentary copy of the issue containing their article. Reprints can be purchased through Rightslink® when proofs are received. If you have any queries about reprints, please contact the Taylor & Francis Author Services team at reprints@tandf.co.uk. To order extra copies of the issue containing your article, please contact our Customer Services team at Adhoc@tandf.co.uk

Disclaimer

Typeset by KGL, UK. Printed by Hobbs the Printers Ltd., www.hobbs.uk.com. This publication has been produced with paper manufactured to strict environmental standards and with pulp derived from sustainable forests.

For Product Safety Concerns and Information please contact our EU representative GPSR@taylorandfrancis.com Taylor & Francis Verlag GmbH, Kaufingerstraße 24, 80331 München, Germany

Batch number: 10725802

Printed by Printforce, the Netherlands